SEX, MARRIAGE, AND FAMILY
IN JOHN CALVIN'S GENEVA

RELIGION, MARRIAGE, AND FAMILY

Series Editors

Don S. Browning
John Witte, Jr.

SEX, MARRIAGE, AND FAMILY IN JOHN CALVIN'S GENEVA

• VOLUME 1 •

Courtship, Engagement, and Marriage

John Witte, Jr., *&* Robert M. Kingdon

WILLIAM B. EERDMANS PUBLISHING COMPANY
GRAND RAPIDS, MICHIGAN / CAMBRIDGE, U.K.

Wm. B. Eerdmans Publishing Co.

255 Jefferson Ave. S.E., Grand Rapids, Michigan 49503 /
P.O. Box 163, Cambridge CB3 9PU U.K.

Printed in the United States of America

10 09 08 07 06 05   7 6 5 4 3 2 1

ISBN-10: 0-8028-4803-6
ISBN-10: 978-0-8028-4803-1

www.eerdmans.com

Contents

5. Honor Thy Father (and Thy Mother)   164

Parental Consent to Engagement and Marriage

6. Capacity to Contract Marriage   202

The Impediments of Infancy and Mental Inability

The Impediment of Infancy or Impuberty   203

The Impediment of Mental Inability   209

Summary and Conclusions   212

Contents

10. Do Not Be Unequally Yoked with Unbelievers   354

The Theology and Law of Interreligious Marriage

Theological Teachings   356

Consistory Cases   361

Summary and Conclusions   364

Contents

Series Preface

The Religion, Marriage, and Family series has a complex history. It is also the product of some synergism. The books in the first phase evolved from a research project located at the University of Chicago and supported by a generous grant from the Division of Religion of the Lilly Endowment. The books in this new phase of the series will come from more recent research projects located in the Center for the Study of Law and Religion in the School of Law of Emory University.

This second phase of the series will include books from two of this Center's projects, both supported by generous grants from The Pew Charitable Trusts and Emory University. The first project was called Sex, Marriage, and Family in the Religions of the Book and began with an Emory University faculty seminar in 2001. The second project was called The Child in Law, Religion, and Society and also was initiated by a semester-long Emory faculty seminar that met during the autumn of 2003.

Although the first phase of the Religion, Marriage, and Family series primarily examined Christian perspectives on the family, it also included books on theological views of children. In this second phase, family in the broad sense is still in the picture but an even greater emphasis on children will be evident. The Chicago projects and the Emory projects have enjoyed a profitable synergistic relationship. Legal historian John Witte, director of the two Emory projects, worked with practical theologian Don Browning on the Chicago initiatives. Later, Browning worked with Witte on the research at Emory. Historian Martin Marty joined Witte and Browning to lead the 2003 seminar on childhood.

Some of the coming books in the Religion, Marriage, and Family series will be written or edited by Emory faculty members who participated in the two seminars of 2001 and 2003. But authors in this new phase also will come from other universities and academic settings. They will be scholars, however, who have been in conversation with the Emory projects.

This series intends to go beyond the sentimentality, political manipulation, and ungrounded assertions that characterize so much of the contemporary debate over marriage, family, and children. In all cases, they will be books probing the depth of resources in Christianity and the other Abrahamic religions for understanding, renewing, and in some respects redefining current views of marriage, family, and children. The series will continue its investigation of parenthood and children, work and family, responsible fatherhood and motherhood, and equality in the family. It will study the responsibility of the major professions such as law, medicine, and education in promoting and protecting sound families and healthy children. It will analyze the respective roles of church, market, state, legislature, and court in supporting marriages, families, children, and parents.

The editors of this series hope to develop a thoughtful and accessible new literature for colleges, seminaries, churches, religious institutions, and probing laypersons. In this post-9/11 era, we are all learning that issues pertaining to families, marriage, and children are not just idiosyncratic preoccupations of the United States; they have become worldwide concerns as modernization, globalization, changing values, emerging poverty, changing gender roles, and colliding religious traditions are disrupting families and challenging us to think anew about what it means to be husbands, wives, parents, and children.

In *Sex, Marriage, and Family in John Calvin's Geneva,* legal scholar John Witte and historian Robert Kingdon tell a story that is almost totally unknown, even to conscientious members of the Reformed tradition, let alone the general public. Based on many fresh translations of largely unknown documents, this book gives us the story of Calvin's voluminous writings on sex, marriage, and family. It is also a story of his profound influence on the sex, marriage, and family laws of the flagship city of the Reformed wing of the Protestant Reformation — Geneva, Switzerland.

But the story does not end in Geneva. The ecclesial and legal precedents of Geneva influenced societies wherever Calvinists lived, built their churches, ordered their lives, and shaped their surrounding societies. Hence, the legal and ecclesial writings of Calvin on sex, marriage, and family influenced Scotland and England, Northern Ireland and many parts of the United States, and even Asian countries such as South Korea where Presbyterian missionaries made such a strong witness. Hence, what Calvin wrote on these subjects in Geneva helped shape the familial, religious, and civil life of many parts of the modern world.

A new angle of vision on Calvin's theology emerges on the pages of *Sex, Marriage, and Family in John Calvin's Geneva.* Calvin was interested in good order on these subjects, but he also could be very humane. The concept of covenant was central to his understanding of marriage, but he could also use powerful arguments drawn from the natural law tradition. He believed that church and state should cooperate on these matters. He understood that the state had a right to be interested in the contractual and utilitarian aspects of marriage. Witte and Kingdon have assembled and written a remarkable book that will deeply inform our understanding of marriage and greatly enrich our appreciation of Calvin.

DON S. BROWNING *and*
JOHN WITTE, JR.

Foreword

Sex, Marriage, and Family in John Calvin's Geneva is a lucid and profound contribution to family studies, Calvin studies, and a wide range of issues pertaining to the relation of religion and the law. This book merits a careful reading and analysis by all of these fields of study. It is likely to stimulate a grand constructive dialogue about how sex, courtship, engagement, and marriage should be ordered in modern societies.

Organization of the Book

Two important features of this book must be noted. First, Robert Kingdon and John Witte have provided many translations of little known writings by Calvin, many of which were provided by Kingdon's former students. The second impressive feature is its clear organization and highly readable prose. Much of the commentary was done by Witte, who as a lawyer and legal historian brings remarkable talents to the analysis of John Calvin, the lawyer and theologian. It is one lawyer reading and interpreting another lawyer. This accounts for much of the power and perceptiveness of this book.

The book begins with a discussion of pre-Reformation Geneva and how its family law was organized around Roman Catholic canon law. After a clear summary of that tradition, an initial review of the differences between canon law and the Geneva Marriage Ordinance of 1546 is set forth (with careful attention to the relevant prior Ordinances of 1541 and 1543). The outline of the content of the 1546 Ordinance then neatly provides the map for the rest of the book. Each successive chapter goes deeper into the simple, yet finally very complex, reforms of the 1546 Ordinance on courtship (Chapter 3); consent (Chapter 4); parental consent (Chapter 5); the impediments of infancy and mental inability, polygamy and precontracts, fitness (virginity, contagion, sexual incapacity) and incest (Chapters 6-9); interreligious marriage (Chapter 10); economics (Chapter 11); duration of engagement (Chapter 12); and the banns and the wedding (Chapter 13). The reader gets an architectonic overview of the entire book and its basic argument in Chapters 1 and 2 and has the pleasure of going deeper into surprisingly complex theological and legal reasoning on these same issues at later points in the book. In short, the book organizes the underlying arguments that run through a massive amount of diverse genres (theology, letters, cases, legal judgments, commentaries, and sermons) in a simple and convincing narration with a high degree of coherence. Hence, it can be read, not as a handbook (although it can serve as a handbook), but as a coherent scholarly study with clear arguments throughout. This, I think, is a remarkable accomplishment, especially in view of the complexity of the material covered.

Starting with Canon Law Rather than Luther

In the early chapters, I sometimes wondered why I was not reading more about Luther. Witte and Kingdon start with canon law because that indeed had been the law for pre-Reformation Geneva. Then they compare canon law to the 1546 Ordinance. But I think they are doing the right thing. Luther and others in his circle get worked into the text throughout as the authors move into the different topics and issues. But setting forth the simple comparative framework between Roman Catholic canon law and the various elaborations of the 1546 Ordinance shows how the Geneva ordinances were both similar to and different from canon law on marriage and family and gives the book a coherence that would have been lost had Luther been introduced as a full-blown third party from the very beginning.

A Spark of Romance and Other Learnings

Although I have been a student of marriage and family for over a decade, there are several things I learned in reading this text.

First, I learned that for Calvin, Beza, and their followers, engagement to be married was nearly as serious a contract and covenant as marriage itself. On the other hand, courtship received a new emphasis and emerged as a differentiated step in the process of moving toward marriage. Courtship, I learned, was important because not only did Calvin emphasize the value of mutual consent, as did canon law, but he also believed that mutual attraction was crucial for marriage. A spark of romance for Calvin was essential for a good marriage, and courtship was the time to determine whether it was there. But engagement entailed a simple but real promise to marry and most of the impediments that applied to marriage applied to engagement in Calvin's Geneva, although the dissolution of marriage (divorce and annulment) were indeed more complicated. I found this interesting and relevant to the dating and courting situation in the U.S. today.

Second, I had been aware that natural law played a larger and more visible role in Calvin than in Luther, but this book really brings home that point. In fact, as I will show later, this insight opens up a whole range of important possibilities for relating law and religion in the contemporary situation. We need not turn only to Roman Catholicism and Thomas Aquinas for a natural law model that can be applied to marriage and family. We also can turn to Calvin. This is something that many scholars know, but now we have in this book a detailed guide through the maze of Reformed theological thinking that shows in much more detail how a form of natural law thinking concretely functioned in that context.

Third, I learned that Calvin's thinking on sex, marriage, and family was multidimensional. It functioned at several different levels. The theological level *framed* the other dimensions of his thinking, but it did not determine these other dimensions in all respects. I discern a narrative level (built around the drama of divine command and, later in his thought, the concept of covenant); a justice level built around love of neighbor and what this implies for marital contracts; a natural law level; a utilitarian dimension that shows the efficiency of marriage; and an analysis of social context, e.g., the disarray of contemporary marriage and family mores in Geneva. In Calvin's thought, divine command and covenant do not swamp the entire field of relevant judgments pertaining to sex, marriage, and family. Calvin was aware that pagans do sometimes make the same judgments, at a broad minimum level, that Christians make. This is because they have access to some of the same levels of thinking as Christians do. This capacity to see similarities and differences with other points of view makes Calvin a candidate for guiding contemporary dialogue on the relation of religion, law, and other secular disciplines on matters pertaining to sex, marriage, and family. One especially sees all of these dimensions of thinking in Calvin's analysis of the issues of polygamy (Chapter 7) and incest (Chapter 9). The presence of all of these levels gives Calvin grounds for criticizing biblical figures such as Abraham, Isaac, Jacob, and others for their sins of polygamy and incest. The natural-law level of his analysis as to why these behaviors are sins gives him the analytic power to make these judgments. Calvin was not a Biblicist.

Fourth, because of his multidimensional thinking, marriage becomes central for Calvin, not simply because it is commanded by God but because it integrates several dimensions of human life into a working whole that is good for both individuals and society. I believe that the integrative power of marriage is the central message needed today to rehabilitate this institution in both society and church. The authors' reading of Calvin makes him a significant resource for developing this message.

Fifth, in addition to the way the theological ideas of divine command and covenant framed his thought, Calvin could enter at lower levels of his thinking into both utilitarian and out-and-out economic styles of analysis. His understanding of the economic aspects of rape, broken engagements (he called them "theft"), various marriage-relevant contracts, and dowry would have made it possible for him to dialogue with leading scholars on marriage and family in the Chicago school of economics. Because Calvin had both a natural law and economic level of analysis, his thinking provides a resource for understanding the bio-economic dimension of marriage that is almost completely absent in contemporary Protestant discussions, with the exception, I believe, of the bio-economic dimensions of "critical familism," the constructive direction of the Chicago Religion, Culture, and Family Project.

Role of Law in Guiding Moral Aspirations

Calvin saw law, both ecclesial and secular, as a source of judgment and correction but also as a guide for our moral aspirations. It is this third use of the law that so desperately needs to be understood and rehabilitated today. The book brings this use of the law out very clearly at several points. In the contemporary situation, law scholars tend to reject this view of law. But they contradict themselves when they urge passing laws that clearly are intended to change behaviors and form new images of the moral good. Calvin is a resource for clarifying the norm-setting functions of the law and can help to reclaim this view in contemporary discussions about the purposes of the law.

Calvin's Flexibility

Although Witte and Kingdon point out that the cooperation between Consistory and Small Council demonstrated just how serious the Geneva Reformers were about sex and marriage matters, they also show the humane and flexible features of both Calvin and the bodies he influenced. Most of the Consistory cases ended in reprimands or reconciliations. Even the civil punishments of the

Small Council were frequently chastisements such as bread and water in the local jail. These were more like saying "eat your porridge" (but with a dash of public shaming) than severe penalties, although these also happened.

More specifically, because Calvin had a complex model guiding his thinking, this book demonstrates how his mind could change, as it did on the issue of clandestine marriage, especially if children were involved.

The Complexity of Calvin's Natural Law Argument

Much of Calvin's natural law argument relied on assumptions about the centrality of kin altruism, i.e., the investment of natural parents in their children, and the need to reinforce these natural inclinations as much as possible. Kin altruism functioned as a principle that applied to parents and their offspring as well as a metaphor that applied to both the husband-wife relation (who are not kin) and the relation of God to humankind. The one-flesh passages of the Old and New Testaments and the interpretation of Eve coming from Adam's rib both function to say that the husband-wife relationship channels the obligations of kinship onto the marital bond. The wife is *similar* to kin — "bone of my bone." A father is to love his children as "his own blood" and children are to honor their father and mother "as those from whom they have their lives" (Doc. 7-2, pp. 241-42). Kin altruism and love of God are not contradictory, but two ways of loving God and being faithful. (Calvin is brilliant in showing the consistency of various aspects of law and gospel.) When husband and wife become "one flesh," the natural inclinations and obligations of kin altruism apply to the marital dyad. All of this is in the order of creation. Notice also Calvin's use of the inclinations of kin altruism as a similitude referring to Christ's relation to his church and his spiritual relation to the saved (Doc. 7-2, p. 241); the saved become spiritually "one flesh" with Christ. To see how a natural law argument becomes a theological metaphor is quite instructive.

Calvin's Double Language

I have been saying for some time in my writings that the power of the Roman Catholic tradition on sex, marriage, and family is that it provides a double language that is simultaneously confessional and philosophical. This double language is useful for both the confessional life of the church and the public debate between church and world. Thomas Aquinas has been a major resource for this double language.

This book elevates Calvin as another major candidate providing this double language. This double language may be more visible in these working documents on sex and marriage than it is in his formal and more systematic theological writings. Nonetheless, it is a major resource, sorely needed by contemporary Protestants, for both the retrieval of their tradition as well as for the purposes of public deliberation and influence.

Calvin on Covenant

The concluding chapter on the emerging centrality of the concept of covenant in Calvin's later thought is very instructive. But Witte and Kingdon may have accomplished here more than they realize. Because this discussion comes at the end of the book where they have already shown the multidimensional thinking that runs throughout Calvin's writings, covenant now becomes something more than what most people associate with the term. Covenant not only stands for *mutual promise* and *loyalty* between humans, husband and wife, individuals and institutions, and God and humans. Covenant emerges as a highly integrative concept; it integrates the narrative, justice, natural-law, and economic-utilitarian levels of Calvin's thought to a working whole, and it does this by also relating these dimensions to various institutional and religious manifestations of social life — church, state, family, and God. I often have been unsatisfied with how some theologians use covenant in narrow ways that stand solely for fidelity and commitment. Yes, covenant does contain these meanings. But the power of covenant commitment is also found in the way it faithfully integrates and reinforces the multidimensional levels and goods of life that are brought together in marriage and family. I think this book shows that the idea of covenant for Calvin did not impede moral thinking but opened it up and helped integrate its various dimensions into a larger view of life.

Refining Calvin on Natural Law

Witte and Kingdon demonstrate forcefully the clear role of natural law thinking in Calvin. Yet, for constructive purposes, Calvin probably can be improved on the topics of natural law. This would need to be done if he were to have the contemporary impact that Calvin's multidimensional model of moral and theological thinking actually deserves. His natural law theory is still somewhat static, still somewhat teleological in the medieval sense of the term, and often functions to conflate the doctrine of creation (which I read as God's intentions for both nature and spirit) with natural inclination and logic. So, there is reconstructive work to be done on Calvin by those who would actually use him, but there are also resources that can be employed to this end. The new breed of natural law thinking to be found in Stephen Pope, Lisa Cahill, Jean Porter, and Mary Midgley are sources for improving Calvin's more static thinking at this level of his moral theology. Calvin's larger framework, however, is for my money quite usable.

Saying More about the Geneva Experiment

Witte in his commentary mentions that there were reactions to the Consistory-Small Council partnership that developed in the mid-1550s in Geneva. But he says little about this reaction. Maybe this will come out in the later volumes that Witte projects on Calvin, marriage, and Geneva. But this reaction is relevant to our evaluation of just how the Geneva model can inform the vastly more complicated and pluralistic society of today — a society toward which Geneva was perhaps moving, even in Calvin's time. Clearly, Calvin did not have all the answers. And he made more than a few mistakes. But reading this book convinced me that we cannot move forward into the future unless we build more directly on one of the most influential Protestant thinkers on the relation of theology to the secular law of sex, marriage, and family.

Don S. Browning
Divinity School,
University of Chicago

Preface and Acknowledgments

This book is partly a history of ideas, partly a history of institutions. It started when John Witte, Jr., who has worked on the history of marriage, set out to write a volume on original Calvinist views of that subject, documented with legal and theological sources translated into English. This was to be an expansion of the chapter, "Marriage as Covenant in the Calvinist Tradition," in his volume, *From Sacrament to Contract: Marriage, Religion, and Law in the Western Tradition* (1997). The project grew considerably when Witte recruited as a co-author Robert M. Kingdon, who for years has researched institutions created in Geneva as a result of the Calvinist Reformation. Kingdon had already produced a number of studies on point, notably his *Adultery and Divorce in Calvin's Geneva* (1995), which presented nine sensational divorce cases from the Genevan archives, including the *cause célèbre* divorce of John Calvin's brother Antoine. Kingdon and his collaborators agreed to help in several ways, most importantly in mining for relevant cases and documents in the huge archive they had gathered for a critical edition of the 21-volume *Registers of the Consistory of Geneva in the Time of Calvin*. The scope of the project grew considerably when Kingdon and Witte began to study these Consistory materials closely and began to see all manner of new connections between these newly discovered documents and the many formal and informal writings on sex, marriage, and family by John Calvin and his allies. This volume and its sequels contain a detailed analysis and report of what we have discovered.

We have incurred a number of debts in the preparation of this volume. We owe a very special word of thanks to M. Wallace McDonald for lending so liberally of his exquisite research skills and linguistic expertise. Wallace spent a great deal of time over the past few years combing through the Genevan Consistory and Council materials to track down case records and other valuable documents to be used in this volume and its sequels. He also prepared fresh translations of virtually all of the Consistory cases, many of the statutes, and a good number of Calvin's sermons, letters, and commentaries that we have used here. Wallace's enviable command of sixteenth-century French and his refined paleographic skills have contributed immeasurably to this project. We are enormously grateful to him for all that he has done for us.

We owe a special word of thanks as well to other members of the team working with Robert Kingdon on the *Consistory Registers* project. Foremost among them, we recognize Dr. Thomas A. Lambert, who has given invaluable counsel on the subtleties of Genevan religious and legal life and on the nuances of sixteenth-century French texts. Tom was also kind enough to read through the entire manuscript of this volume, and to make numerous corrections and edifying suggestions. We also thank Isabella M. Watt who is responsible for the large majority of rough transcriptions from the Consistory Registers that we have used, as well as being co-editor with Tom Lambert on all published editions of these registers. And we give warm thanks to Fr. John Patrick Donnelly, S.J., Professor of History at Marquette University, and a former student of Robert Kingdon, who was kind enough to supply us with crisp translations of several difficult passages from Theodore Beza that we have used in this volume.

Several other scholars contributed significantly to this project. We are particularly grateful to our friends and colleagues Professors Don S. Browning, E. Brooks Holifield, and Timothy P. Jackson, each of whom read through this entire manuscript and gave us the benefit of their sage and acute counsel. We also thank Professors Frank S. Alexander, Anita Bernstein, Michael J. Broyde, Elsie A. McKee, James W. Fowler, M. Patrick Graham, R. H. Helmholz, Mark D. Jordan, Martin E. Marty, Jeannine Olson, Steven Ozment, L. Philip Reynolds, Max L. Stackhouse, and Steven M. Tipton who offered valuable advice and bibliographical leads on particular issues.

We express our deep gratitude to several Emory colleagues who worked on this volume and its sequels. Special recognition is owed to Janice Wiggins for her masterful work in preparing this manuscript, and to Amy Wheeler and Anita Mann for masterminding the administration of this project and several other book projects related to it. We also thank several research assistants who worked with John Witte. Foremost among them are two graduates of the Law and Religion Center at Emory University. One is M. Christian Green, a J.D./ M.T.S. graduate from Emory, and a recent Ph.D. graduate from the University of Chicago, now teaching at Harvard Divinity School. While at Emory, Christy assembled a huge collection of primary and secondary sources on the Calvinist Reformation on which we have consistently drawn with profit. A second is

Jimmy Rock, a J.D./M.T.S. graduate from Emory, now serving in a distinguished federal judicial clerkship. Jimmy combed through the 59 volumes of Calvin's Opera to collect a treasure trove of relevant texts on sex, marriage, and family life. We would also like to express our gratitude to Will Haines and Kelly Parker of the Emory Law Library for their unstintingly helpful library services.

The preparation of this volume and its sequels was made possible by a generous grant from the Lilly Endowment to John Witte. John would like to express his sincere appreciation to Dr. Craig Dykstra, Vice-President of the Endowment, and his colleagues for their very generous support of this volume and a series of related writings on law, religion, and the Protestant tradition. He would also like to thank Professor Don S. Browning of the University of Chicago Divinity School for generously recommending Witte's book projects to the Lilly Endowment, and for his sage and stalwart advice throughout.

Finally, we wish to thank Jon Pott and his colleagues at Wm. B. Eerdmans Publishing Co. for taking on this volume and for their generous permission to reprint various Eerdmans imprints herein. We also wish to thank the authors, editors, and publishers for their permission to reprint herein excerpts from the texts.

JOHN WITTE, JR.
ROBERT M. KINGDON

Abbreviations

A.E.G.	Archives d'Etat de Genève
Aquinas, Comm. Sent.	Thomas Aquinas, *Scriptum super Libros Sententiarum Petri Lombardiensis*, in *Opera Omnia Sancti Thomae Aquinatis Doctoris Angelici* (Rome, 1882-), vol. 7.2
Aquinas, SCG	Thomas Aquinas, *Summa contra Gentiles*, trans. V. J. Bourke (Notre Dame, IN, 1975)
Aquinas, ST	Thomas Aquinas, *The Summa Theologica*, English trans. by English Dominican Fathers (London, 1912-1936)
Balke	Willem Balke, *Calvin and the Anabaptist Radicals*, trans. W. J. Heynen (Grand Rapids, 1981)
Benedict	Philip Benedict, *Christ's Churches Purely Reformed: A Social History of Calvinism* (New Haven/London, 2002)
Beza, TRD	Theodore Beza, *De repudiis et divortiis* (Geneva, 1569), reprinted in id., *Tractationum Theologicarum*, 2d ed. (Geneva, 1582), 2:50ff.
Bohatec, CR	Josef Bohatec, *Calvin und das Recht* (Graz, 1934)
Bohatec, CSK	Josef Bohatec, *Calvins Lehre von Staat und Kirche mit besonderer Berücksichtigung des Organismusgedankens*, repr. ed. (Aalen, 1961)
Bonnet	*Letters of John Calvin*, ed. Jules Bonnet, trans. D. Constable and M. R. Gilchrist, repr. ed. (New York, 1972)
Bouwsma	William J. Bouwsma, *John Calvin: A Sixteenth Century Portrait* (New York/Oxford, 1988)
Brundage	James A. Brundage, *Law, Sex, and Christian Society in Medieval Europe* (Chicago, 1987),
Coing	Helmut Coing, *Handbuch der Quellen und Literatur der*

	neueren europäischen Privatrechtsgeschichte (Munich, 1973-1977), vols. 1-2/2
CO	*Ioannis Calvini opera quae supersunt omnia*, ed. G. Baum, et al., 59 vols. (Brunswick, 1863-1900) (Corpus Reformatorum Series, vols. 29-87)
Cottret	Bernard Cottret, *Calvin: A Biography*, trans. M. Wallace McDonald (Grand Rapids, 2000),
Hotman	François Hotman, *De jure connubiorum: hoc est, De sponsalibus et matrimoniis rite contrahendis ac dissoluendis, seu repudiis tam veterum Romanorum quam hominum nostri seculi* (Frankfurt an Oder, 1592; Leipzig, 1618), with appendix to 1618 edition of Hotman's *De Spuriis et Legitimatione*
Institutes (1536)	*Ioannis Calvini Institutio Religionis Christianae* (Basel, 1536), CO 1:1, translated as John Calvin, *Institution of the Christian Religion*, trans. Ford Lewis Battles (Atlanta, 1975)
Institutes (1559)	*Ioannis Calvini Institutio Religionis Christianae* (Basel, 1536), CO 2:1, translated as *Institutes of the Christian Religion*, ed. John T. McNeill, trans. Ford Lewis Battles (Philadelphia, 1960)
Joyce	George Hayward Joyce, *Christian Marriage: An Historical Doctrinal Study*, 2d. enl. ed. (London, 1948)
Kingdon, AD	Robert M. Kingdon, *Adultery and Divorce in Calvin's Geneva* (Cambridge, MA/London, 1995)
Köhler	Walter Köhler, *Zürcher Ehegericht und Genfer Konsistorium*, 2 vols. (Leipzig, 1942)
Lambert	Thomas A. Lambert, "Preaching, Praying, and Policing in Sixteenth-Century Geneva" (Ph.D. Diss. Wisconsin, 1998)
Naef	Henri Naef, *Les Origines de la Réforme a Genève*, 2 vols. (Geneva, 1968)
Naphy, Calvin	William G. Naphy, *Calvin and the Consolidation of the Genevan Reformation* (Louisville, KY, 2003)
Naphy, Sex Crimes	William G. Naphy, *Sex Crimes from Renaissance to Enlightenment* (Stroud, Gloucestershire/Charleston, S.C., 2002)
NTC	*Calvin's New Testament Commentaries* (William B. Eerdmans Publishing Co. edition)
Orme	Nicholas Orme, *Medieval Children* (New Haven/London, 2001)
OS	*Joannis Calvini opera selecta*, ed. Peter Barth, Wilhelm Niesel, and Dora Scheuner, 5 vols. (Munich, 1926-52)
OTC	*Calvin's Old Testament Commentaries* (William B. Eerdmans Publishing Co. edition)
RCP	*Registres de la compagnie des pasteurs de Genève au temps de Calvin*, ed. Jean-Francois Bergier and Robert M. Kingdon, 2 vols. (Geneva, 1964)

RCP (Hughes trans.) Ibid., translated as *The Register of the Company of Pastors of Geneva in the Time of Calvin,* trans. Philip E. Hughes (Grand Rapids, 1966)

R. Consist. *Registers of the Consistory of Geneva in the Time of Calvin: Vol. 1: 1542-1544,* gen. ed. Robert M. Kingdon, trans. M. Wallace McDonald (Grand Rapids, 2000); *Registres du Consistoire de Genève au Temps de Calvin: Vol. 2: 1545-1546,* Robert M. Kingdon gen. ed. (Geneva, 2001); ibid., *Vol. 3: 1547-1548,* gen. ed. Robert M. Kingdon (Geneva, 2004); vols. 4-21 (unpublished; transcription available in the Meeter Center, Calvin College and Seminary, Grand Rapids, Michigan)

R. Conseil *Les Registres du Conseil de Genève,* ed. Emile Rivoire and Victor van Berchem, 13 vols. (Geneva, 1900-1940)

Sanchez Thomas Sanchez, *De sancto Matrimonii sacramenti disputationum* [1610] (Venice, 1712)

SD *Les sources du droit du canton de Genève,* ed. Emile Rivoire and Victor van Berchem, 4 vols. (Aarau, 1927-1935)

Searle and Stevenson Mark Searle and Kenneth W. Stevenson, *Documents of the Marriage Liturgy* (Collegeville, MN, 1992)

Seeger Cornelia Seeger, *Nullité de mariage divorce et séparation de corps a Genève, au temps de Calvin: Fondements doctrinaux, loi et jurisprudence* (Lausanne, 1989)

Lombard, Sent. *Petrus Lombardus, Libri IV sententiarum* [1150], 2d rev. ed. (Florence, 1916)

Selderhuis H. J. Selderhuis, *Marriage and Divorce in the Thought of Martin Bucer,* trans. John Vriend and Lyle D. Bierma (Kirksville, MO, 1996)

Spierling Karen E. Spierling, *Infant Baptism in Reformation Geneva: The Shaping of a Community, 1536-1564* (Aldershot, England and Burlington, VT, 2005)

Supp. Calv. *Supplementa Calviniana: Sermons inédits,* ed. Erwin Mülhaupt, et al. (Neukirchen-Vluyn, 1936-)

Vuilleumier Henri Vuilleumier, *Histoire de L'Eglise Réformée du pays de Vaud sous le Régime Bernois,* 2 vols. (Lausanne, 1927)

Weigand Rudolf Weigand, *Die Bedingte Eheschliessung im kanonischen Recht,* 2 vols. (Munich, 1963)

Witte, FSC John Witte, Jr., *From Sacrament to Contract: Marriage, Religion, and Law in the Western Tradition* (Louisville, KY, 1997)

Witte, LP John Witte, Jr., *Law and Protestantism: The Legal Teachings of the Lutheran Reformation* (Cambridge/New York, 2002)

Introduction

John Calvin (1509-1564), the Protestant reformer of Geneva, transformed the Western theology and law of sex, marriage, and family life. Building on a generation of Protestant reforms, Calvin constructed a comprehensive new theology and jurisprudence that made marital formation and dissolution, children's nurture and welfare, family cohesion and support, and sexual sin and crime essential concerns for both church and state. Working with other jurists and theologians, Calvin drew the Consistory and Council of Geneva into a creative new alliance to govern domestic and sexual affairs. Together, these authorities outlawed monasticism and mandatory clerical celibacy, and encouraged marriage for all fit adults. They set clear guidelines for courtship and engagement. They mandated parental consent, peer witness, church consecration, and state registration for valid marriage. They radically reconfigured weddings and wedding feasts. They reformed marital property and inheritance, marital consent and impediments. They created new rights and duties for wives within the bedroom and for children within the household. They streamlined the grounds and procedures for annulment. They introduced fault-based divorce for both husbands and wives on grounds of adultery and desertion. They encouraged the remarriage of divorcées and widow(er)s. They punished rape, fornication, prostitution, sodomy, and other sexual felonies with startling new severity. They put firm new restrictions on dancing, sumptuousness, ribaldry, and obscenity. They put new stock in catechesis and education, and created new schools, curricula, and teaching aids. They provided new sanctuary to illegitimate, abandoned, and abused children. They created new protections for abused wives and impoverished widows. Many of these reforms of sixteenth-century Geneva were imitated and elaborated in Calvinist communities on both sides of the Atlantic, and a good number of these reforms have found their way into our modern civil law and common law traditions.

What made this Calvinist reformation of sex, marriage, and family life so resolute and resilient was that it was a top-to-bottom reformulation of ideas and institutions, theology and law, learning and living. Calvin set out his legal reforms in scores of new statutes and *consilia* that were applied and adapted in hundreds of cases that came before the Genevan authorities. He set out his theological reforms in hundreds of sermons, commentaries, and systematic writings that were then echoed and commented upon by a whole army of Reformed preachers and theologians in succeeding decades. He set out his pastoral advice in thousands of letters and pamphlets that ultimately gave rise to a whole industry of Protestant household manuals. And Calvin did not work and write alone. He had brilliant allies in Theodore Beza, Germain Colladon, Guillaume Farel, François Hotman, Pierre Viret, and others, often forgotten today, each of whom was indispensable to the success of the reformation.

This volume and its sequels seek to bring to light these rich Calvinist theological and legal teachings and practices respecting sex, marriage, and family life. Our particular earnest is to show the extraordinary interdependence of these theological and legal resources and to demonstrate how they concretely informed the daily lives of Genevan citizens and institutions. Our further interest is to demonstrate that the Calvinist reformation of this intimate private sphere was remarkably thorough, touching everything from conception and abortion to death and inheritance. The reformers' new theological and legal system of sex, marriage, and family life was ultimately every bit as sweeping and sophisticated as the medieval sacramental theology and canon law it set out to replace. Accordingly, it stands today as one of the enduring models of marriage and family life in the Protestant world and well beyond.

We analyze this reformation in three interlocking volumes that are roughly divided according to stages in the family cycle. This first volume takes the reader from courtship and engagement to the wedding day. The second volume crosses the threshold with the newly wed couple and studies the law, theology, and actual experience of the new Christian family in Geneva as well as the nurture and education of children. The third volume takes up the theological and legal implications of marital and family discord and abuse, adultery and desertion, spousal sickness, death and inheritance, and the remarriage of widows and widowers.

What follows in this Introduction and in the first two chapters is an overview of the whole reformation of sex, marriage, and family life in Calvin's Geneva, and a close sifting of its main sources, personalities, and institutions. Chapter 3 brings us to the more particular story of this volume, beginning with

Calvin's views of courtship and matchmaking. Chapters 4 and 5 address the intricate issues of individual and parental consent in making engagement and marriage contracts. Chapters 6-9 explore the tangled jungle of impediments to engagement and marriage whose presence could lead to annulment — infancy, mental inability, polygamy, lack of virginity, sexual incapacity, contagion, age disparities, and incest. Chapter 10 addresses the delicate issue of interreligious courtship and marriage. Chapter 11 works through the complex laws of marital property. Chapter 12 deals with premarital sex, cohabitation, and desertion. Chapter 13 follows the couple on their wedding day, and the surprising liturgy and celebration that awaited them. We have provided summaries and conclusions at the end of each chapter. In a concluding Chapter 14, we have sketched the outlines of Calvin's first synthesis of these sundry topics of reform, using the biblical doctrine of covenant. We shall return to Calvin's synthetic exercise in sequel volumes as well, when we have a fuller range of materials before us.

The Sources of Reform

John Calvin and his associates disseminated their ideas through several media. They often used the medium of print, and in fact helped build an entire printing industry in the city of Geneva, making it one of the three most significant centers in the day for the printing of material in French. They also used the medium of correspondence, preparing a great variety of letters and formal opinions to elaborate their ideas for individuals, usually prominent theologians or political leaders who were in a position to influence policy. They used the medium of oral speech as well, delivering sermons and lectures to explain their ideas to the general public. They even arranged, through the city Council, for town criers to announce some of their views orally in public proclamations.

Oral, written, and visual media alike helped to communicate the many new rules and procedures created to govern sex, marriage, and family life. Important new ordinances and statutes were printed in pamphlets and city act books, and sometimes read aloud by town criers and posted in prominent quarters of the city. The decisions of the Consistory and Council were not only pronounced from the bench but also inscribed by notaries in bulky registers. Punishments for serious sins and crimes were often public events — involving admonitions and confessions, confessions and shaming, and, in more serious cases, whippings, banishments, or executions.

In preparing this volume and its sequels, we have sought to analyze and illustrate all these media. The sources that tell the story of the reformation of sex, marriage, and family life in Calvin's Geneva fall into seven general categories: (1) systematic writings; (2) sermons, lectures, and commentaries on the Bible;

(3) letters and *consilia;* (4) catechisms and teaching materials; (5) polemical writings; (6) statutes; and (7) Consistory cases. We first describe these sources and their relevance to our topic, and then explain how we have used them in the preparation of this volume and its sequels.

(1) Systematic Writings

Calvin's reformation of sex, marriage, and family life might well be much better known and understood today if he had devoted a long chapter or two to the topic in his *Institutes of the Christian Religion.*[1] Even the casual student of Calvin will know of this remarkable work of systematic theology. The first edition of the *Institutes* was impressive enough — written when Calvin was still in his early twenties and a new Protestant convert. He published it in 1536, just before coming to Geneva for the first time. The *Institutes* grew in length, depth, and complexity in four succeeding editions, culminating in that of 1559. This last edition was a brilliant work of more than 1500 tightly written pages divided into four books. It became for many the Protestant analogue, if not answer, to Thomas Aquinas's *Summa Theologica* published three centuries before. In this masterwork, Calvin gave many of the great doctrines of the Christian tradition full and fresh examination.

The *Institutes* would have been the natural place for Calvin to systematize his new theology of sex, marriage, and family life, and perhaps to summarize some of his new laws as well. But Calvin did nothing of the kind. He included in the first 1536 edition of the *Institutes* a few pages of familiar Protestant critiques of the prevailing Catholic sacramental theology and canon law on marriage and family life. Calvin repeated these passages in every succeeding edition of the *Institutes* without changing a word.

The *Institutes,* particularly the later editions, do include a few valuable discussions of discrete themes pertinent to our project. Noteworthy are Calvin's interpretations of the moral law, particularly as revealed in the fifth commandment ("Honor thy father and mother") and the seventh and tenth commandments (on adultery and coveting one's neighbor's wife). Also valuable is Calvin's discussion of the power and relationship of church and state and his differentiation of the church offices of pastor, elder, deacon, and teacher. These distinctions helped to shape the institutional framework and focus of his marital reforms and the city's new programs of catechesis, education, and social welfare. Further, the 1559 *Institutes* are the source of Calvin's most authoritative discussions of infant baptism.

---

1. See CO 1-2 for the editions of 1536, 1539, 1543, 1550, and 1559.

Calvin's *Institutes* are not the only systematic writings to consult. Shortly after Calvin's death in 1564, his protégé and successor Theodore Beza prepared a systematic treatise on annulment and divorce as well as a looser volume on polygamy and related issues. These two tracts, first published in 1568 and 1569 and often reprinted together, elaborated many of the technical rules of marriage, annulment, and divorce that Calvin had only adumbrated.[2] Another valuable synthesis of Reformed teachings on marriage, divorce, illegitimacy, and inheritance came from the pen of François Hotman, a friend and follower of both Calvin and Beza.[3]

(2) Sermons, Lectures, and Commentaries

A particularly rich source of teachings for our project is the ample collection of Calvin's sermons, lectures, and commentaries on the Bible. Calvin began his career in Geneva as a public lecturer, hired to explain to Genevans the meaning of the religious changes that their government had just adopted. He soon became a preacher in church services as well. In fact the sermons that he and others delivered soon became the most distinctive feature of Genevan church services, displacing the sacrament of the Eucharist that had previously been the centerpiece of worship. Records of the period always speak of a Catholic service as a "mass" and a Protestant service as a "sermon."

Among the preachers at the beginning of the Genevan Reformation, Guillaume Farel was the most inflammatory, capable of preaching a sermon that would provoke a riot. Pierre Viret was the most eloquent, delivering sermons that would grip people's imaginations, even move them to tears. John Calvin was the clearest and most authoritative homilist of Geneva. He developed a style of speaking that was easy for people of all backgrounds to follow. His sentences were usually concise. In fact one modern scholar has given Calvin credit for inventing the modern French sentence.[4] Calvin was also authoritative

---

2. Beza, TRD; also *Tractatio de Polygamia, et divortiis: in qua et Ochini apostatae pro polygamia . . . refutantur* (Geneva, 1568), reprinted in *Tractationum Theologicarum*, 2d ed. (Geneva, 1582), 2:1.

3. François Hotman, *De gradibus cognationis et affinitas libri duo* (Paris, 1547; Strasbourg, 1556); also *De castis incestisque nuptiis disputatio: In qua de sponsalibus et matrimonio ex iure civili, pontificio, et orientali differitur* (Louvain, 1594); *De jure connubiorum: hoc est, De sponsalibus et matrimoniis rite contrahendis ac dissoluendis, seu repudiis tam veterum Romanorum quam hominum nostri seculi* (Frankfurt an Oder, 1592; Leipzig, 1618); *De Spuriis et Legitimatione*, appended to Hotman, *De jure connubiorum*.

4. Francis M. Higman, *The Style of John Calvin in His French Polemical Treatises* (Oxford, 1967).

in his delivery, able to persuade his listeners not only that the Bible really is the Word of God but that he, Calvin, understood its meaning better than any of his contemporaries; in listening to him, many felt, they could gain truths that were accessible in no other way. Calvin drew larger crowds than any other preacher in town. In fact he drew a large audience from outside of the city. Religious refugees often came to Geneva in preference to other communities because they wanted to hear Calvin.

We do not know much about the content of Calvin's sermons in his early years of preaching. We know a great deal about it after 1549. Beginning in that year, public secretaries took down everything Calvin said in a kind of shorthand and then transcribed these notes into fair copies for deposit with the board of deacons assigned to care for poor refugees from France. The secretaries were chosen from among these refugees and were paid for their services with funds raised by the deacons. Some of these manuscript copies still survive, and a few have never been published.[5]

Even the extant scraps of Calvin's earliest sermons, however, suggest a consistent approach with his later preaching. The subject of Calvin's sermons was almost always biblical exposition. He favored the expository method, furthermore, of *lectio continua*. That meant that he would choose one book of the Bible and follow it chapter-by-chapter and verse-by-verse, first reading the verses in question, then adding his explanations, sometimes of key Greek or Hebrew words in the original text, and then finally advancing his comments. He often chose a New Testament book for exposition in Sunday morning sermons and a set of Psalms for Sunday afternoons. He then selected a book of the Old Testament for preaching on weekdays. He preached on the New Testament and the Psalms every week and on another part of the Old Testament every other week, from three to five days that week. He interrupted this routine for church festivals: during Easter week and at Christmas and Pentecost, he preached on Bible passages appropriate to those occasions. He preached always in French. Typically he delivered his Sunday sermons in the cathedral church of Saint-Pierre, whereas his weekday homilies were given in other Geneva churches.

In addition to his vernacular sermons, Calvin gave lectures in Latin in alternate weeks. These followed the same pattern of biblical exposition and the same method of *lectio continua* but were intended for a more highly educated

---

5. See the collection in CO 23-58 and OS. See discussion in Lambert; Robert M. Kingdon, "Stone Lecture: The Genevan Revolution in Public Worship," *Princeton Seminary Bulletin* 20 (1999): 264; T. H. L. Parker, *Calvin's Preaching* (Louisville, 1982), which includes a chronological chart of sermons on pp. 150-52. A convenient summary of what is published and what is still in manuscript is provided in W. de Greef, *The Writings of John Calvin: An Introductory Guide*, trans. Lyle D. Bierma (Grand Rapids, 1993).

audience. They were often lengthy, a number of them bristling with lengthy recitals and rejoinders of traditional interpretations. He collected and published many of these lectures as commentaries. Calvin also wrote additional biblical commentaries that were not delivered orally, at least in their entirety, in this lecture format. These tended to be somewhat pithier, though they did not lack for erudition.

In looking for Calvin's views of sex, marriage, and family life in his sermons, lectures, and commentaries, we cannot simply scan his writings topically. We must rather look for biblical passages that addressed these topics. Only when the Scripture text scheduled for the day's sermon, or for commentary, dealt with marriage and family-related issues would Calvin speak on them.

These topics did obviously emerge in the course of his biblical exposition. Calvin treated some key passages, in fact — those in Genesis 1–2, and 16, Deuteronomy 5 and 21–25, 1 Corinthians 5–7, and Ephesians 5–6 — both in early commentaries and in some of his mature sermons. These are particularly important pairings of sources to gauge the evolution of his thought.

Calvin left several key biblical passages on sex, marriage, and family life unexplored. He never preached or commented, as far as we know, on the Book of Judges, with its rather graphic stories (e.g., Samson and Delilah, Jephthah's daughter, the Levite's concubine). Though he did preach on 2 Samuel's account of the sexual exploits of King David and his family, Calvin did not address the Books of Kings[6] and Chronicles. These books hold several relevant passages, not least the lengthy discussion of King Solomon's polygamy. Calvin left no sermons or commentaries on Proverbs, with its many injunctions concerning sexual ethics, as well as the relationship between husbands and wives and parents and children. He did not touch the Song of Solomon with its lush, sometimes torrid, description of female beauty and sexuality. His lectures on Ezekiel broke off at his death at 20:44, leaving unexplored some of the later passages on covenant marriage and divorce as well as on death and inheritance. And Calvin ignored the Apocrypha, which includes many relevant passages.

It is noteworthy that even when Calvin did address biblical passages, he did not always mine them fully. Sometimes, Calvin read volumes of insight into a single verse, as he did with the seventh commandment, "Thou shalt not commit adultery." Sometimes, however, he touched only lightly on important issues of sex, marriage, and family. A good example is his superficial treatment of the several troubling biblical texts on illegitimacy of children, topics to which his friend and follower François Hotman returned with greater depth and acuity.

---

6. Calvin apparently began to preach on 1 Kings near the end of his life, but the sermons have not survived. De Greef, *The Writings of John Calvin*, pp. 112-13.

(3) Consilia and Pastoral Letters

Calvin was a prolific correspondent, whose letters hold a cache of valuable information and insight on sex, marriage, and family life. Ten of the 59 volumes of his collected works, comprising 4,271 entries, are devoted to his correspondence. Hundreds of letters are included in other collections.[7] New letters still surface in private libraries and archives. Calvin corresponded with all manner of persons throughout Europe — political and religious figures, nobles and aristocrats, friends and family members, enemies and detractors, fellow ministers and reformers, parishioners and strangers who wrote to him for counsel. Calvin's letters often provided a fundamental lifeline between Geneva and the many widely scattered co-religionists in the Calvinist world. They also laid down some of the fundamental lines of disagreement between Calvin and his opponents.

Calvin's most frequent correspondents were fellow reformers Pierre Viret and Guillaume Farel, to whom he sent nearly 800 letters.[8] Some of these were lengthy and candid documents. A few included remarkable testimonies about his emotions during his own courtship, his eventual marriage to Idelette de Bure, and her illness and death nine years later as well as the death of their son.

Some of the letters to Viret and Farel, as well as hundreds of others, include nuggets of information on Calvin's evolving views on issues of marital formation, maintenance, and dissolution; parental rights, roles, and responsibilities; child care, custody, and control; sexual crime, sin, and deviation; and much else. These letters are sometimes especially helpful in providing personal context or commentary on important themes in Calvin's formal theological and legal writings on sex, marriage, and family life.

Particularly poignant sources for our project are Calvin's lengthy exchanges with women, often French noblewomen, who sought his advice.[9] Most of these women were new converts to the Reformed cause, who were being

---

7. See CO 10/2:20; A.-L. Herminjard, ed., *Correspondence des Réformateurs dans les pays de langue française,* 9 vols. (Geneva, 1866-1897); Jules Bonnet, *Lettres de Calvin,* 2 vols. (Paris, 1854), translated as *Letters of John Calvin,* trans. D. Constable and M. R. Gilchrist, repr. ed., 4 vols. (New York, 1973); Jean Calvin, *Lettres à Monsieur et Madame de Falais,* ed. Françoise Bonali-Fiquet (Geneva, 1991); Rodolphe Peter and Jean Rott, eds., *Les lettres de Calvin de la collection Sarrau, publiés avec une notice sur Claude et Isaac Sarrau* (Paris, 1972).

8. Jean-Daniel Benoît, "Calvin the Letter Writer," in *Studies in Reformation Theology,* ed. William J. Courtney (Grand Rapids, 1966), p. 67 (referencing 390 letters to Viret and 301 to Farel).

9. See a list of these letters in Charmarie J. Blaisdell, "Calvin's and Loyola's Letters to Women: Politics and Spiritual Counsel in the Sixteenth Century," in *Calviniana: Ideas and Influence of John Calvin,* ed. Robert V. Schnucker (Ann Arbor, MI, 1988), pp. 235, 248-50.

abused and persecuted by their husbands or by local authorities for abandoning the Catholic faith. Many of their letters to Calvin were anguished entreaties for both pastoral and legal advice, including queries about whether they could leave their husbands and move to Geneva. Calvin had put firm laws on the books about interreligious marriage, separation, and divorce. These letters forced him to think hard about how to apply these laws with full equity.

Calvin wrote comparably tender pastoral letters to many friends about their engagements and weddings, the birth, baptism, and education of their children, their domestic trials and troubles, the illness, infirmity, and death of loved ones, and more. These letters often show a very gentle and generous side to Calvin that is harder to see in his stern laws, Consistorial rebukes, and his biblical exposition.

Like other theologians and jurists of the day, Calvin also wrote several formal opinions *(consilia)* in response to specific questions on incest, divorce, and other comparable issues.[10] These questions were evidently put to him by fellow reformers, sometimes ministers in distant cities. Most of Calvin's *consilia* on marriage briefly restated the problem and then worked out a judgment or recommendation, usually combining light biblical exposition with simple casuistry. These *consilia*, which circulated widely as open letters in the Reformed world and beyond, built some key bridges between Calvin's theological and legal writings.

Calvin was not the only reformer to write *consilia*. Theodore Beza wrote a large volume of them after his arrival in Geneva in 1548 and was even more prolific after he succeeded Calvin in 1564. More important still were the opinions of fellow reformer and jurist Germain Colladon, who wrote hundreds of memoranda advising the Genevan authorities on legal matters, including notably the procedures and punishments to be used for those suspected or convicted of adultery and other sexual felonies.

(4) Polemical Writings

Calvin's views on sex, marriage, and family were sharpened in part by the views of his opponents. Calvin was a brilliant polemicist. He could not always match Luther's rhetoric or Erasmus's elegance, but Calvin was second to none in pressing a relentlessly logical case to gainsay his opponents. Calvin's verbal pillorying of others could be severe, even judged by the rhetorical standards of his day. Some readers will know of Calvin's vitriolic attacks on Michael Servetus,

---

10. Guido Kisch, *Consilia: Eine Bibliographie der juristischen Konsilensammlungen* (Basel, 1970). Calvin's *consilia* which have survived are collected in CO 10/1:153-266, with translations in *Calvin's Ecclesiastical Advice.*

Sebastian Castellio, and Jérôme Bolsec on issues related to the Trinity, heresy, and predestination.

Ample vitriol flows as well in Calvin's polemical writings on sex, marriage, and family. These he directed at three main groups. Calvin's most formidable opponent was the Catholic Church with its detailed sacramental theology and canon law of marriage that governed Genevan life until 1536. In his 1536 *Institutes*, Calvin joined the loud Protestant chorus denouncing the Catholic Church's commendation of celibacy, toleration of secret marriages, celebration of marriage as a sacrament, swollen roll of impediments to marriage, prohibition of divorce, and counsel against remarriage. Calvin elaborated these criticisms in several later letters, sermons, and biblical commentaries as well as in his tracts against various Catholic reform measures, notably the 1548 Augsburg Interim and the decrees of the Council of Trent from 1545 to 1563. Both Pierre Viret and Theodore Beza joined in some of these polemical battles against Trent's reforms, particularly the sweeping 1563 decree Tametsi which reformed and systematized the Catholic theology and canon law of marriage, and declared anathema on many Protestant teachings. For all their dispute with the Catholic Church, however, Calvin, Beza, and their fellow reformers accepted a number of discrete canon law rules on marriage and family life, tolerated interreligious marriage with Catholics, and often recognized the marriages of new immigrants to Geneva who had been married under Catholic auspices.

Calvin's second main adversaries were the so-called "Libertines" whom he denounced in a blistering 1545 tract and in later correspondence.[11] This group, led by the "heretic" Quintin Thieffrey, promoted, in Calvin's view, an unduly permissive sexual ethic. They deprecated the seriousness of fornication and adultery and allowed for much easier separation and divorce than Calvin thought biblically warranted. In his later writings, Calvin sometimes also used "libertine" to label other Genevans who were too permissive in their sexual and marital habits or too contemptuous of the attempts of Calvin and his colleagues to bring about reform.

The third major opponents were Anabaptists, against whom Calvin inveighed sharply in a 1544 tract and in several later letters, pamphlets, and passages in his *Institutes*, commentaries, and sermons.[12] Particularly relevant for our project are Calvin's lengthy denunciations of Anabaptist views of adult baptism and their corresponding understanding of children. Also pertinent are his criticisms of their views of church-state relations and of the nature of ecclesiastical power. Calvin said surprisingly little, however, about various Anabap-

---

11. CO 7:145-278, with translation and discussion in John Calvin, *Treatise Against the Anabaptists and Against the Libertines*, trans. and ed. Benjamin W. Farley (Grand Rapids, 1982).

12. CO 7:45-142, translated in ibid., and discussed with many other writings in Balke.

tist experiments with polygamy, though he denounced polygamy itself rather loudly. And he was not averse to marriages between Reformed and Anabaptist partners; indeed his own wife, Idelette de Bure, was of Anabaptist stock.

(5) Catechetical and Educational Writings

From the start of his reform movement, Calvin pressed for the proper catechesis and education of children. He repeated this insistence in sundry statutes. Calvin prepared two different catechisms in 1537 and 1542.[13] These were used not only to teach children the basics of the Christian faith, but also to test the spiritual adherence and coherence of all members of the household. These documents provide good samples of the instructional materials that parents and teachers used to transmit the Reformed faith to the next generation and to shape children. They also contain useful summary statements on the meaning of marriage, parenthood, and adultery.

For advanced students, Calvin recommended study of his *Institutes,* which he called, no doubt with tongue-in-cheek, a "simple" and "elementary" form of teaching proper Christian doctrine.[14] The *Institutes* would become a staple of the curriculum of the Genevan Academy that was formed in 1559 under Theodore Beza's rectorship.[15] Several of Calvin's other biblical commentaries and learned tracts became staples of the curriculum, too. So did several texts by Beza, including his lengthy commentaries on the many relevant passages on sex and marriage in 1 Corinthians, his catechism and confession book, and his tracts on annulment and divorce, polygamy, and the power of the church.[16]

(6) Statutes

The Genevan reformation of sex, marriage, and family life was not only theological; it was also legal. Indeed, on many topics, Calvin set out his legal views first, in statutes and other legal instruments. He then gradually laid out his theological rationale, often making modest legal refinements in light of the same. This was a fairly typical pattern of reform in other Protestant cities of the day in France, Switzerland, and Germany. Statutes reflecting Protestant mar-

---

13. CO 22:33-114. See further sources referenced in Jeffrey R. Watt, "Calvinism, Childhood, and Education," *Sixteenth Century Journal* 33 (2002): 439.

14. Institutes (1536), Pr. 1.

15. CO 10/1:65-90.

16. These are collected in Beza, *Tractationum Theologicarum.*

riage and family teachings were often on the local books within a few years after acceptance of the Reformation, and then gradually revised as local beliefs and practices were refined and routinized.[17]

Geneva followed this general Reformation pattern. On May 21, 1536, two months before Calvin arrived in Geneva, the authorities issued a statute renouncing the Catholic Church and its canon law in favor of the "Holy Evangelical Law and Word of God."[18] Over the next decades, the city authorities issued hundreds of new statutes to reform and govern public and private life, many of them regarding issues of sex, marriage, and family life. These statutes ranged from short "proclamations" *(cries)* or "declarations" *(serment)* of a few lines, to longer "orders" *(ordres)*, "articles," and "regulations" *(reglements)*, to full "edicts" *(edits)* and "ordinances" *(ordonnances)* that could run for several dozen pages.[19]

The process of creating new statutes for Reformed Geneva began in earnest in 1541, with the return of John Calvin after being banished from the city in 1538. Among the first new laws were the 1541 Ecclesiastical Ordinances, the 1542 Edict of the Lieutenant, and the 1543 Ordinances on Offices and Officers.[20] Together, these three documents functioned as something of a city constitution that defined the structure, power, and relationships of church and state in Geneva.[21] The 1541 Ecclesiastical Ordinances also included a number of discrete rules about marriage, weddings, education, and catechesis. The 1541 Ecclesiastical Ordinances were Calvin's own creation. The other two documents were products of committees on which Calvin sat. Calvin, however, was the most highly qualified lawyer on these committees, and his input was thus essential.

In 1545 and again in 1546, Calvin drafted and presented to the city government a Marriage Ordinance.[22] This Ordinance included detailed rules not only about engagements and marriage, but also about weddings, marital property, household relations, spousal care and responsibilities, impotence, abuse, adultery, desertion, separation, and divorce. Though the Genevan authorities did not formally adopt the Marriage Ordinance at the time, our research reveals that many of its provisions did in fact guide the Consistory and Council in the

---

17. Witte, LP, pp. 177-256.

18. SD, vol. 2, item 701.

19. Many of the statutes are collected in SD, vols. 2 and 3 (which include more than 350 statutes on point from 1536 to 1564). Most of these statutes in SD, and a good number of others, are scattered throughout the respective registers of the Council, the Consistory, and the Company of Pastors. Several ordinances that Calvin drafted or helped to draft are in CO 10/1.

20. These are excerpted in Docs. 2-1 and 2-2 in Chapter 2.

21. Robert M. Kingdon, "Calvin et la constitution Genevoise," in *Actualité de la Réforme* (Geneva, 1986), p. 209; also his "Calvinus Legislator: The 1543 'Constitution' of the City-State of Geneva," in *Calvinus Servus Christi*, ed. Wilhelm H. Neuser (Budapest, 1988), p. 225.

22. This is reproduced in Chapter 1, Doc. 1-2.

succeeding years. The Ordinance was binding customary law even before it was formally promulgated as a statute. Calvin ran into considerable local political opposition beginning at about the time he was pressing for passage of his Ordinance, opposition led by the so-called "Children of Geneva." Only after the suppression of this group in 1555 did Calvin feel free to proceed. In 1561, he drafted and secured adoption of a revised version of the Ecclesiastical Ordinances, which now included a full set of laws on marriage drawn mostly from the 1545/6 Marriage Ordinance.[23]

Another essential text for our subject is the Marriage Liturgy that Calvin prepared in 1542, expanded in 1545, and amplified with a series of discrete rules and regulations passed by the Council.[24] This liturgy was mandated for use immediately, not only in Geneva but in surrounding towns and rural churches as well.

Several statutes governed the baptism and care of children by parents and godparents. Included was a 1546 Ordinance on the naming of children that caused perennial controversy and occasional rioting in Geneva because of its prohibition of many popular names that were rooted in traditional Catholic devotion to saints.[25] Several other statutes, beginning already in 1536, governed formal education and schooling, culminating in the 1559 charter of the Genevan Academy.

Another long series of statutes governed public and private sexual morality — adultery, fornication, prostitution, public bathing, dressing, dancing, parties, dissolute songs, sumptuousness, and much more. These early statutes were brought together in sweeping ordinances of 1560 and 1566, both of which Calvin and Beza had a strong hand in shaping.[26]

Calvin and his colleagues also drafted laws to govern the economic arrangements of marriage and family life — betrothal gifts, dower, dowry, trusts, wills, legacies, inheritance, probate, and related issues of marital and family property. Most of these topics were part of a comprehensive code of civil law and civil procedure that Calvin was planning to draft for Geneva. Only small fragments of this code were ever drafted — or at least have survived.[27] Few new individual rules were issued between the 1540s and 1560s — though a number of surviving marriage contracts and last wills and testaments (including Calvin's) from this period provide some evidence of the law in action. In 1568, however, the authorities issued a comprehensive new edict on civil law, with

23. CO 10/1:93-124.

24. The 1545 Marriage Liturgy is reproduced in Chapter 13, Doc. 13-2.

25. CO 10/1:49-50.

26. SD, vol. 3, items 992, 1065.

27. What survives is included in CO 10/1:125-46, with a sample included in Chapter 11, Doc. 11-6. See further Bohatec, CR.

lengthy articles on marital contracts, inheritance, and probate.[28] A commission headed by Calvin's fellow reformer, Germain Colladon, drafted this edict.

These statutes were essential parts of the reformation of sex, marriage, and family life in Calvin's Geneva. Not only did they help to preserve and to normalize a number of the reformers' cardinal theological teachings. They were themselves useful teaching documents — literal expressions of Calvin's emphasis on the "educational use of the law."[29] Most importantly, they taught the faithful how to live by the Bible's sundry teachings on sex, marriage, and family: how and whom to court, betroth, and marry; how to structure a Christian marriage and household; what to teach one's children, catechumens, and students; whether to separate, divorce, or remarry; how to devise and divide one's property on death; and the like. The statutes helped to make concrete what the sermons had made cogent.

(7) Consistory Cases

The Consistory was an equally essential vehicle for the communication and enforcement of proper Christian discipline respecting sex, marriage, and family life. The Geneva Consistory was a new institution, created by Calvin's Ecclesiastical Ordinances of 1541. It was designed to control the behavior of the entire population, to see to it that all Genevans not only accepted the new Reformed teachings set out in sermons and statutes, but lived them in their daily lives. At the height of its power after 1555, the Consistory acted at once as a hearings court, as a compulsory counseling service, and as an educational institution. It penetrated life in almost all of its aspects in sixteenth-century Geneva. Some six or seven percent of the city's population, by our estimate, came before the Consistory each year as plaintiffs, defendants, or witnesses. Some of the Consistory's work was remarkably officious — intruding on the intimacies of bed and board with unusual alacrity. Some of its work was also remarkably solicitous — catering to the needs of the innocent, needy, and abused with unusual efficiency.

The registers of the Genevan Consistory's deliberations, with only a few gaps, are voluminous for the period when John Calvin was active — 21 thick volumes in total, many of which have, until recently, lain largely unbroken and unread. The Consistory records are unique windows through which to view the reformation of sex, marriage, and family life in Calvin's Geneva. Well over half of all the hundreds of cases heard by the Consistory each year concerned sexual

---

28. SD, vol. 3, item 1081, with a sample included in Chapter 11, Doc. 11-13.

29. John Witte, Jr., and Thomas C. Arthur, "The Three Uses of the Law: A Protestant Source of Criminal Punishment?" *Journal of Law and Religion* 10 (1994): 433.

and family issues: 182 of the 309 cases heard by the Consistory in 1546, 253 out of the 390 cases heard in 1552, 323 out of the 566 cases heard in 1557 involved these issues.[30] Adultery and fornication, disputed engagements and weddings, and family quarrels were by far the most common cases. But intricate and delicate issues concerning incest, polygamy, rape, sodomy, buggery, prostitution, voyeurism, public bathing, abortion, child neglect, child abuse, baptismal disputes, education disputes, spousal abuse, mistreatment of maids, family poverty, embezzlement of family property, sickness, divorce, marital property disputes, inheritance, and others all crowded onto the Consistory's docket as well. Some of these cases were very complex; a few required intense evidentiary investigation and legal disputation that went on for years.

What makes the Consistory record particularly valuable for our project is that John Calvin sat as a judge on the Consistory. He rarely missed the weekly meetings of the Consistory, and he sometimes dominated its proceedings, particularly in complex cases that required advanced legal training. The Consistory provided Calvin with a laboratory to test and refine many of the theological ideas in his *Institutes*, commentaries, sermons, and statutes. It was one thing for Calvin to insist that marriages should be publicly celebrated with parental consent. It was quite another to decide whether a secretly married couple with a brand new child should be separated and their child thereby illegitimated and become a public ward. It was one thing to thunder loudly from the pulpit that adulterers of all sorts should be stoned. It was quite another to decide whether an engaged couple caught in heavy foreplay in their own bedroom should be sent to the gallows. It was one thing to declare anathema on interreligious marriages. It was quite another thing to deal with the hundreds of desperate new immigrants who poured into Geneva with spouses of various confessions on their arms. It was one thing for Calvin to say that married couples must live together at all costs, save in cases of adultery or desertion. It was quite another to insist on such reconciliation when a battered wife, already bent and lame from her husband's repeated savageries, stood before him with newly blackened eyes.

It was on the Consistory bench that Calvin was forced to integrate theory and practice, theology and law, principle and precept, rule and equity. Some of these Consistory cases forced him to rethink and refine his prior theological positions on sex, marriage, and family. Other cases sent him scurrying back to his Bible and his books in search of new edification. Still other cases drew him back to the rules and procedures of the Roman civil law and Roman Catholic canon law. This Consistory experience certainly made some parts of Calvin's reformation messier, more volatile, more difficult to follow or appreciate at points. But it also made his reformation more realistic, rigorous, and resilient.

30. See Chapter 2, Tables 1-3.

In the end, the Consistory work ensured that Calvin's new teachings on sex, marriage, and family were both principled and pragmatic, not only formed through new biblical exegesis but also reformed through practical experience.

Calvin's Allies

As the foregoing recitation of sources has already intimated, Calvin was by no means the only, nor even the first, reformer of sex, marriage, and family life in Geneva. The Reformation of Geneva began before his first arrival in 1536, went on without him from 1538 to 1541 when he was kicked out of the city temporarily, and went on after his death in 1564. Even when Calvin was at the height of his power in the 1550s, he depended heavily on theological and legal allies both to teach the new ideas and to implement the new institutions. This was true in many arenas of reform in Geneva, not least those of sexual and family life.

Two key allies for Calvin in his early years were the preachers, Guillaume Farel and Pierre Viret. Farel had started the Reformation in Geneva and had originally recommended Calvin's appointment in 1536. After the Genevan authorities threw him and Calvin out in 1538, Farel became leader of the Reformed Church in nearby Neuchâtel. He never again worked for Geneva, though he visited occasionally, and periodically put questions on marriage and family for Calvin and his colleagues to resolve. Farel remained a steady confidant and counselor throughout much of Calvin's adult life, though their friendship was heavily strained, if not broken, by Calvin's protests over Farel's late-life marriage to a young woman in 1558.[31] Pierre Viret had been one of the early preachers of the Reformation in Geneva, but he left late in 1536 for nearby Lausanne, and spent much of his career there, directing the Reformed Church of the Pays de Vaud. When he was expelled from that position by the Bernese in 1558, he returned briefly to Geneva. But he soon moved on to France and spent the rest of his career in Reformed parts of France and the neighboring enclave of Béarn. Both Farel and Viret kept in close touch with Calvin and other Genevans, and their advice was sometimes useful in working out their theological and legal positions. Viret was also an immensely popular teacher and writer of polemical pamphlets. His skills as preacher and writer no doubt helped to popularize Calvinist views on many topics widely beyond Geneva.[32]

Calvin was joined in Geneva by two French refugees, Theodore Beza and Germain Colladon, in making and enforcing many of the city's new institu-

---

31. *Guillaume Farel: Biographie nouvelle par un groupe d'historiens* (Paris, 1930).

32. Jean Barnaud, *Pierre Viret: Sa vie et son oeuvre (1511-1571)* (St. Amans, 1911; repr. ed., Nieuwkoop, 1973).

tional and legal adjustments on sex, marriage, and family life. Calvin, Beza, and Colladon all studied law at universities in central France, specifically Orléans and Bourges, and had received degrees in law. They had all studied at roughly the same time, between 1527 and 1539. Calvin and Beza had earned the *license* degree (roughly equivalent to an M.A.) in law at the University of Orléans. Colladon held, in addition to the *license*, the degree of *juris doctor utriusque* (doctor of both laws, that is, of civil and canon law) at the University of Bourges. After earning these degrees, he had taught law at the same university from 1531 to 1542, and then resigned to enter practice in Bourges both as a lawyer and a legal consultant. Calvin and Beza had never gone into practice as lawyers, but had instead changed careers and become religious leaders.

The legal training these men had received at French universities was primarily in Roman law, the law of the Roman Empire as codified in *The Theodosian Code* (438) and the *Corpus Iuris Civilis* (529-533), the body of civil law.[33] These two collections consisted of hundreds of early pronouncements and comments by Roman lawyers on a wide variety of legal matters, arranged by topic, and collected at the command of several Roman emperors, most prominently Theodosius II and Justinian. Law students of the day studied two of the books of the *Corpus Iuris Civilis,* the *Digest* and the *Institutes,* with great intensity and committed large parts of them to memory. Advanced students like Colladon further studied the many medieval commentaries on the Roman law texts, which by the sixteenth century were being drawn together in impressive syntheses and compilations.

Another body of law that Calvin, Beza, and Colladon had studied, although not so intensively, was the law of the Roman Catholic Church. This was codified after 1586 as the *Corpus Iuris Canonici,* the body of canon law. It consisted of declarations, cases, and opinions of experts on all manner of public and private law questions, including numerous issues of sex, marriage, family, education, catechesis, inheritance, and related subjects. The anchor text of the body of medieval canon law was the *Decretum* of Gratian of ca. 1140, with four later books of papal and conciliar legislation. The sections of these volumes devoted to marriage alone occupied nearly 300 pages.[34] These five books of canon law supported a whole medieval industry of glosses and commentaries that were also part of the regular diet of the sixteenth-century law student, particularly doctoral students.

33. *Corpus Iuris Civilis,* ed. and trans. Paul Krüger and Theodore Mommsen, 2d exp. ed., Okko Berends (Heidelberg, 1997); *The Theodosian Code and Novels and the Sirmondian Constitutions,* trans. Clyde Pharr (Princeton, 1952).

34. *Corpus Iuris Canonici,* ed. Emil Friedberg, repr. ed., 2 vols. (Graz, 1959). An English translation of the marriage and family portions of this collection is being prepared by John T. Noonan, Augustine Thompson, and Charles J. Reid.

Calvin, Beza, and Colladon had also studied the Bible, and they were inclined to give the force of law to rules contained within it, especially in the Old Testament, most obviously the Ten Commandments. Calvin and Beza, of course, had studied the Bible with even greater intensity than Colladon, given their careers as religious leaders. Colladon had also studied closely the customary laws of his native province, the province of Berry, in which the University of Bourges was located.

We can find traces of all four of these sources of law — civil, canonical, biblical, and customary — in the laws these men helped to create for Geneva. Native Genevans, of course, had their own ideas of how they should be governed and by what principles of equity and justice they should be guided. And we find Genevan courts often making judgments on what they believed fairness and tradition demanded, without pointing to any specific written laws to justify their decisions. This habit would persist in Calvin's day. But as laws were written down to provide more secure guidance to members of the ruling councils and courts, principles from classical forms of law were used more and more to give greater precision and authority to the laws of Geneva.

Of these classical forms of law, the Bible was regarded as the most authoritative in Reformation Geneva. Of the three legally-trained reformers, Calvin was the most industrious and inventive exegete of the Bible. He drew ingenious legal lessons from the Mosaic law and the Gospels, from the admonitions of the Prophets and the injunctions of St. Paul. But Calvin was the first to admit that the Bible was not detailed and comprehensive enough to cover the many types of legal cases that he encountered. Roman civil law and its medieval commentary were next in prestige, and were in fact widely used by Geneva's experts, most strikingly by Colladon, in fleshing out the body of Genevan law. The canon law of the Roman Catholic Church, though not highly regarded because of its connections to the papacy, nonetheless provided many discrete rules. The customary law of Berry, one would think, would have little role in Geneva, which was located in an entirely different area with its own legal traditions. Yet some types of problems were not covered by any of the other available bodies of law, so Colladon, since he knew it so well, used the custom of Berry as well.[35] Both Calvin and Beza often pointed to canon, civil, and customary laws as indicia of a natural law that antedated and anticipated the fuller revelation of biblical law.

The legal reconstruction of sex, marriage, and family life born of the

---

35. See illustrative sources in Gabriel L'Abbé de Montveron, *Les coutumes générales des pays du duché de Berry* (Bourges, 1579; rev. ed., Paris, 1607); Jean Mauduit, *Nouveau commentaire sur la coutume des pays et duché de Berry, avec les notes de Charles DuMoulin* (Paris, 1624). See further Coing 2/1:277-78.

Genevan Reformation began already in the 1540s under Calvin's leadership. It reached its apex in the 1550s and 1560s when Beza and Colladon arrived in Geneva and joined the city's leadership. Beza arrived in 1548, as a refugee from France, and immediately arranged to be married in public to a wife he had married secretly in France while still holding religious offices. He then moved to nearby Lausanne, and from 1549 to 1558 served as a teacher in its Academy. In 1558, he returned to Geneva, and became rector the following year of a new Academy, created at Calvin's suggestion, to prepare young men for the Christian ministry. He also became one of the pastors of the Genevan Church. Following Calvin's death in 1564, the other ministers elected Beza to be the moderator of their Company, as Calvin's successor. They reelected him to this position every year until 1580, when he finally resigned for reasons of health.

Beza did not try to teach law in either Lausanne or Geneva. Indeed in Geneva he tried to find others to teach that discipline. But he soon joined both Calvin and Colladon in offering advice both political and legal to the city government. His political advice may have been the more important. He made direct contact with the political and military leaders of the French Protestant movement and often traveled to other countries to meet them. The fact that he was himself a nobleman, albeit from a minor provincial family, may have made it easier for him than for others in Geneva, to handle these negotiations. In 1561 and 1562, for example, he spent much of his time in France negotiating with the military leaders of French Protestantism up to and during the first French war of religion. Even after returning definitively to Geneva, Beza kept in touch with these magnates, and continued to negotiate with them throughout his long life. In later years, these negotiations were most often made on behalf of Geneva.

The opinions Beza supplied to the Geneva government, however, sometimes touched upon legal problems, including those dealing with marriage and the family. Probably the most famous and influential of those opinions were those on polygamy and divorce which he brought together into two books which he had published in several editions, often together, beginning in 1568, including even a translation into Dutch. They became standard reference works on those subjects. The treatise on annulment and divorce, in particular, contained a number of important reflections in general on the laws governing marriage, including sharp criticisms of traditional Catholic laws requiring celibacy of the clergy or those prohibiting marriage between distant relatives.[36]

Colladon arrived in Geneva in 1550 as one of the more prominent in a substantial number of Protestants taking refuge from persecution in their native

---

36. Kingdon, AD, pp. 166-75; Robert Kingdon, "Introduction" to Théodore de Bèze, *Du Droit des Magistrats* (Geneva, 1970), p. viii; Alain Dufour, *Théodore de Bèze,* published as volume 42 of the *Histoire littéraire de la France* (Paris, 2002), pp. 315-470 + i-xiii.

France. He immediately set up practice as a lawyer and before long became as successful as he had been in Bourges. He also immediately made his expertise available to the city councils, and before long was producing opinions both oral and written on both political and legal matters. He was even soon negotiating for Geneva with foreign powers in the area. Calvin had been providing political and legal assistance to the Genevan government since 1541. With Colladon's arrival much of this responsibility could be transferred from Calvin to him. Colladon also assumed a significant volume of legal work previously handled by less qualified local lawyers.

Hundreds of memoranda drafted by Colladon in the Geneva State Archives provide testimony of all that he did both for the government and for his private clients. Many are found in the dossiers of criminal trials. If the examiners in a criminal case became frustrated by the evasions of a person suspected of a crime, they would often ask Colladon for an opinion as to whether they could use torture. And following the conviction of a criminal, they would often ask Colladon for an opinion on what penalty to apply, particularly if the crime seemed serious enough to deserve death. In general Colladon was very severe in his judgments, often recommending both torture and death sentences. But he would also try to be fair, marshalling with care all the evidence he felt justified his recommendation, and citing all the law, drawn chiefly from the Bible and the Roman civil codes, that he felt justified severity. Some of these cases involved marital problems, particularly accusations of adultery and occasionally of sodomy. The case law of how to handle problems of this sort owes a good deal to Colladon.[37]

The climax of Colladon's contributions to Geneva came in 1568, when he headed a commission that drafted an Edict on Offices containing a new set of constitutional laws, coupled with a set of Civil Edicts codifying laws. They replaced and expanded the laws that Calvin had helped draft in 1542 and 1543. They remained in effect until the republican government of Geneva collapsed in 1792, as a by-product of the French Revolution.

There were, to be sure, others who contributed to the positions we have come to label Calvinist, but none as directly as Colladon and Beza. It is worth mentioning a brilliant legal scholar named François Hotman. He came from a family of lawyers, and had acquired legal training like Calvin, Colladon, and Beza in Bourges and Orléans, earning his *license* in 1540, just one year after Beza. He then began teaching law in Paris. He converted to Calvinism at about the same time as Beza, sought refuge with him in Switzerland, and briefly taught in Lausanne, but on a relatively elementary level. He was devoted to Calvin and a close friend of Beza. Although he taught law in Geneva briefly for

---

37. Erich-Hans Kaden, *Le jurisconsulte Germain Colladon* (Geneva, 1974).

short periods, he never found the long-term position there he deserved. He spent most of his career teaching law at a variety of universities in France and Germany. He won a European-wide reputation as a legal scholar and a fiery polemicist on behalf of the Calvinist cause. While it is unclear how much his advice may have helped shape the Calvinist reformation of sex, marriage, and the family, it is clear that his learned tracts on marriage, annulment, and divorce helped make Calvinist legal learning on these subjects part of the European *ius commune*.[38]

These men remained completely devoted to Calvin. That is most striking in the cases of Beza and Hotman, who regarded Calvin as a kind of spiritual father. But it is also true of Colladon, Farel, and Viret. They all defended Calvin with ferocity against opponents both within the city and without. Colladon and Beza in their work within Geneva insisted they were simply applying and working out principles they had learned from Calvin. To the degree these men were right, we can identify all of their work as belonging to a single tradition, a tradition that can fairly be labeled as Calvinist.

How We Arranged the Material

We have arranged this volume and its sequels with several general methodological goals in mind. First, as indicated, the volumes and chapters roughly follow stages in the family lifecycle. Second, we have made use of all seven types of sources that Calvin and his allies left us. This will give readers a real sense of the complexity and continuity of Calvin's own thought in different contexts, and of the inevitable casuistry and occasional contradictions that sometimes attended their application. Third, we have paid close attention to chronology. Calvin's theological and legal views on a number of issues grew over time, and we have thus taken special note of the dates of texts, and the contexts in which they were written. On some issues, Calvin's views remained unchanged, undeveloped, or unclear, and in these areas, we have looked especially to Beza's tracts in the late 1560s to round out the story. Fourth, we have included in each chapter both our own analysis and a selection of primary texts. Our analysis comprises roughly the first half of each chapter. There we offer a crisp analysis of the doctrine under discussion in the chapter — courtship, interreligious marriage, the wed-

---

38. Donald R. Kelley, *François Hotman: A Revolutionary's Ordeal* (Princeton, 1973). Hotman is better known today for his leadership in the Huguenot struggle against French religious oppression. See Robert M. Kingdon, *Geneva and the Coming of the Wars of Religion in France, 1555-1563* (Geneva, 1956); John W. Sap, *Paving the Way for Revolution: Calvinism and the Struggle for a Democratic Constitutional State* (Amsterdam, 2001), pp. 11-128.

ding, and the like — and analyze all the pertinent sources we could find (at least in Calvin's writings). Thereafter, we provide a critical English edition of the most important and illustrative of the primary texts — writings by Calvin, Beza, or others, relevant statutes, illustrative cases, and more.

Many of the primary sources that we are presenting here are either unknown, out of print, or haphazardly scattered in sundry collections of widely varying quality and vintage. We have sought to provide accurate and readable translations of each of them. We are grateful for permission to select excerpts from the excellent modern translations of Calvin's 1536 and 1559 *Institutes*, several of his translated sermons and *consilia*, two of his catechisms, and a few of his Bible commentaries. We have also provided adaptations of some of the excellent, but older, translations of Calvin's biblical commentaries published by William B. Eerdmans Publishing Company and the old collection of Calvin's letters translated by Jules Bonnet. On these latter texts, we have checked the translations against the original sources, and modernized the spelling, punctuation, and paragraph breaks throughout. We have expunged the pedantic linguistic ornamentation and sentence structures that the translators sometimes added. We have restored Calvin's salty language that they sometimes toned down in the translation. And here and there as noted, we have had to retranslate some of the passages, particularly those with technical legal terms that required a more careful rendering.

We have prepared new translations of a large number of materials that, to our knowledge, have not been translated into modern English before. These include new translations of several of Calvin's lectures on Genesis and sermons on Deuteronomy as well as several of Calvin's letters not included in the Bonnet collection. They also include virtually all the legal materials that are included herein — Genevan statutes and Consistory records, as well as opinions and commentaries on legal topics by both Calvin and Beza.

While we are quite confident that we have presented the most pertinent statutes, we make no pretense to have studied all the relevant legal cases in the Genevan Consistory Registers. This would take far more than the several years that we have already devoted to this project. What we have done instead is to focus especially on three sample years, 1546, 1552, and 1557. These are watershed years in the evolution of the Genevan Reformation, as we shall see in Chapter 2. The year 1546 saw the initial circulation of Calvin's Marriage Ordinance; the Consistory began to draw on its provisions with alacrity, even as anticlericalism began to increase. The year 1552 was one of change and controversy in Geneva, occasioned both by the massive influx of new immigrants as well as by the growing challenges to the authority of Calvin and his allies. And 1557 was a year when Calvin and the Consistory were at the height of their power: having just won a major battle with the "Children of Geneva," they were comfortably at work fine-tuning the Reformation. For these three sample years, we have read, counted, and analyzed all the relevant cases, and have selected the more illustrative and interesting case records to include in our sample documents. We have included a good number of cases from beyond these three sample years as well, but these latter selections must perforce be viewed as more anecdotal.

Other Pertinent Literature

An excellent place to begin further reading on the general movement of which this subject is a part is a recent book by Philip Benedict, *Christ's Churches Purely Reformed: A Social History of Calvinism* (2002).[39] It sets the entire Reformed movement in a broad context, considering the entire period from 1500 to 1800 and all parts of Europe affected by Calvinism, both east and west, paying close attention to developments in both thought and practice. For the medieval tradition against which the Reformers were reacting, particularly the canon law of marriage and family life, the classic studies by James Brundage, R. H. Helmholz, G. H. Joyce, and John Noonan have not been superseded.[40]

There is a large bibliography on Calvin himself. Emile Doumergue's seven-volume *Jean Calvin: les hommes et les choses de son temps* (1927) remains the largest and most complete of these biographies, albeit a relentlessly hagiographic one.[41] There is similarly a large bibliography of work on Geneva during this period. Amédée Roget's seven-volume *Histoire du peuple de Genève depuis la réforme jusqu'à l'Escalade* (1870-1883) is still the fullest and most judicious narrative history.[42] E. William Monter's *Calvin's Geneva* (1967) provides a useful and authoritative, if brief, overview in English.[43] For a close analysis of the beginnings of the Reformation in Geneva, the best study is the two-volume work by Henri Naef, *Les origines de la Réforme à Genève* (1936, 1968).[44] For a

---

39. (New Haven/London, 2002).

40. Brundage; Joyce; R. H. Helmholz, *Marriage Litigation in Medieval England* (Cambridge, 1974) and *The Spirit of the Classical Canon Law* (Athens, GA, 1996); John T. Noonan, Jr., *Power to Dissolve: Lawyers and Marriages in the Courts of the Roman Curia* (Cambridge, MA, 1972) and *Canons and Canonists in Context* (Goldbach, 1997). See also the recent volume, Charles J. Reid, Jr., *Power Over the Body, Equality in the Family: Domestic Relations in Medieval Canon Law* (Grand Rapids, 2005).

41. (Lausanne, 1899; Neuilly-sur-Seine, 1927). See also more recently Bouwsma and Cottret.

42. (Geneva, 1870-1883).

43. (New York, 1967).

44. (Geneva, 1936, 1968).

close analysis of the immediately following period, between 1541 and 1555, in which Calvin's power was consolidated, see William G. Naphy, *Calvin and the Consolidation of the Genevan Reformation* (1994).[45]

There are many books on Calvin's thought on various subjects. On his religious ideas, one of the best compact surveys is by François Wendel, *Calvin, Sources and Development of His Religious Thought* (1963)[46] as well as the recent work of Richard A. Muller, *The Unaccommodated Calvin.*[47] On Calvin's legal ideas, the best studies remain those by Josef Bohatec, in particular his *Calvin und das Recht* (1934)[48] and *Calvins Lehre von Staat und Kirche mit besonderer Berücksichtigung des Organismusgedankens* (1937).[49] Calvin's views on natural law have attracted several recent studies, most notably those of Susan Schreiner.[50] On Calvin's economic and social thought, the fullest studies are those by André Biéler, *La pensée économique et sociale de Calvin* (1959)[51] and, most to the point for this study, *L'homme et la femme dans la morale calviniste: la doctrine réformée sur l'amour, le mariage, le célibat, le divorce, l'adultère et la prostitution considérée dans son cadre historique* (1963).[52] Biéler's books are basically anthologies of extended quotations from Calvin on these subjects, arranged topically with running commentary, but without much analysis or attempt to place them in a larger context either intellectually or institutionally. A good deal of additional recent work explores Calvin's view of women. Most of it focuses on his attitude toward the role of women in the church. Some of it, however, particularly the work of John L. Thompson and Jane Dempsey Douglas, considers, in part, his perspective on the role of women in marriage.[53]

As we have already observed, Calvin used several media to spread his ideas. He arranged for the publication of dozens of books, he wrote thousands of letters and memoranda, and hundreds of sermons, lectures, and commentaries. Much of this material is gathered in a 59-volume edition, the *Ioannis Calvini Opera quae supersunt omnia* (1863-1900).[54] Some of this material is now being re-edited in a new series begun in 1997 titled *Ioannis Calvini Opera om-*

45. (Manchester, 1994; repr. ed., Lousiville, 2003).

46. Trans. Philip Mairet (New York, 1963).

47. (Oxford/New York, 2000).

48. (Graz, 1934; repr. Aalen, 1991).

49. (Graz, 1937; repr. Aalen, 1961).

50. Susan Schreiner, *The Theatre of His Glory: Nature and the Natural Order in the Thought of John Calvin* (Durham, NC, 1991).

51. (Geneva, 1959).

52. (Geneva, 1963).

53. See, e.g., John Lee Thompson, *John Calvin and the Daughters of Sarah: Women in Regular and Exceptional Roles in the Exegesis of Calvin, His Predecessors, and His Contemporaries* (Geneva, 1992); Jane Dempsey Douglas, *Women, Freedom & Calvin* (Philadelphia, 1985).

54. CO.

nia, published by the Librairie Droz in Geneva. Additional material, from hitherto unpublished sermons, is being published in the *Supplementa Calviniana: sermons inédits,* though a number of key texts for our subject remain unpublished, including Calvin's Sermons on 1 Corinthians 1–9.[55] On Calvin's skills as an author, the many works of Francis Higman and Jean-François Gilmont are excellent, and they are summed up masterfully in Gilmont's recent *Jean Calvin et le livre imprimé.*[56] On Calvin's performance as a preacher, see T. H. L. Parker's tidy and concise *Calvin's Preaching.*[57] On his biblical hermeneutics, see Barbara Pitkin's recent study, *What Pure Eyes Could See: Calvin's Doctrine of Faith in Its Exegetical Context.*[58]

The fullest study of the Geneva Consistory remains that of Walter Köhler, in his two-volume *Zürcher Ehegericht und Genfer Konsistorium* (1932, 1942).[59] It sets the Consistory in a wide context of disciplinary institutions created all over southern Germany and Switzerland during the early Reformation. Its material on Geneva, however, is not based on direct archival research but rather on a selection of excerpts from the Geneva Consistory Registers gathered by Frédéric-Auguste Cramer in 1853.

There is a good deal of more recent work, however, based on intensive research in the Geneva Archives. This includes the useful summary in English of the Consistory's organization and activities, as well as additional material of relevance to this book, in Robert M. Kingdon's *Adultery and Divorce in Calvin's Geneva* (1995).[60] It also includes, on the question of divorce, Cornelia Seeger's masterful *Nullité de mariage, divorce et séparation de corps à Genève au temps de Calvin* (1989), which is informed as well by a thorough knowledge of Swiss law both at that time and in the present.[61] Yet another important study of the Consistory in its earliest years, based on intensive research in Genevan records, is Thomas A. Lambert, "Preaching, Praying, and Policing the Reform in Sixteenth-Century Geneva" (Ph.D. dissertation, University of Wisconsin-Madison, 1998).[62] It concentrates particularly on ways in which the Reforma-

---

55. Suppl Calv. (Neukirchen, 1936-).

56. (Geneva, 1997).

57. (1947; reissued Louisville, 1992).

58. (New York/Oxford, 1999). See also Barbara Pitkin, "'The Heritage of the Lord': Children in the Theology of John Calvin," in *The Child in Christian Thought,* ed. Marcia Bunge (Grand Rapids, 2001), p. 160.

59. Köhler.

60. (Cambridge, Mass., 1995). See also the articles on the Consistory and related subjects in E. William Monter, *Enforcing Morality in Early Modern Europe* (London, 1987).

61. (Lausanne, 1989).

62. Available in microform from UMI Dissertation Services in Ann Arbor, Michigan, as no. 9819828.

tion transformed Catholic practices in worship. Another recent valuable dissertation is Karen E. Spierling's study, *Infant Baptism in Reformation Geneva: The Shaping of a Community, 1536-1564,* which presents a number of interesting cases on baptismal disputes, illegitimacy, child support, and godparenting.[63]

This survey presents only a selective overview of a field of wide and active research. But it should provide some historiographical setting for this book as well as indicating paths for further study. The notes that follow in succeeding chapters provide further direction to the secondary literature. However, it must be noted that our principal preoccupation in this volume and its sequels is with the primary sources that tell the story of the reformation of sex, marriage, and family life in John Calvin's Geneva.

---

63. (Aldershot, England, and Burlington, VT, 2005).

CHAPTER 1

Making and Breaking Intimate Bonds

An Overview of the Reformation of Engagement, Annulment, and Marriage in Geneva

On the eve of the Reformation, Geneva subscribed to the Catholic theology of marriage that was taught throughout Western Christendom. It also submitted to the Catholic canon law of marriage that was enforced by a hierarchy of church courts headquartered in Rome. Many of the Catholic Church's theological teachings were rooted in ancient biblical and patristic sources. Many of its canon laws were grounded in apostolic church constitutions and in Christianized Roman law from the fifth and sixth centuries. This ancient pedigree not only contributed to the enduring authority of this theology and law of sex, marriage, and family life in the Catholic tradition. It also ensured that much of this traditional theology and law survived the Protestant Reformation, albeit cast into a bold new ensemble and applied by a strikingly new set of institutions of church and state.

This chapter surveys the major changes to the traditional theology and law of marriage introduced by the Reformation in Geneva. The next chapter analyzes the new institutional framework used by Calvin and his allies to implement their legal and theological teachings.

The Tradition[1]

Theology

Marriage had been a central concern of the Christian Church from the very beginning. The earliest Church Fathers and apostolic canons taught that the institution of marriage was created and ordered by God. Already in Paradise, God brought the first man and the first woman together and commanded them to "be fruitful and multiply" (Gen. 1:28). God created them as social creatures, naturally inclined and attracted to each other. God gave them the physical capacity to join together and to beget children. God commanded them to love, help, and nurture each other and to inculcate in each other and in their children the love of God, neighbor, and self. "Therefore a man leaves his father and mother and cleaves to his wife, and the two become one flesh," Genesis 2:24 concludes. These duties and qualities of marriage continued after the fall into sin. After the fall, however, marriage also became a remedy for lust, a balm to incontinence. Rather than allowing sinful persons to burn with lust, God provided the remedy of marriage, in order for parties to direct their natural drives and passions to the service and love of the spouse, the child, and the broader community.

While these patristic teachings on marriage were subject to endless variation and amendment in the first millennium, they were first fully systematized during the Papal Revolution of ca. 1075-1300. This was the era when the Catholic clergy, led by Pope Gregory VII (1073-1085), threw off their royal and civil rulers and established the Roman Catholic Church as an autonomous legal and political institution within Western Christendom.[2] In this revolutionary context, the Church developed a detailed systematic theology and canon law of marriage. From the twelfth century forward, the Church's doctrine of marriage was categorized, systematized, and refined, notably in the works of Hugh of St. Victor, Peter Lombard, and Thomas Aquinas, and the scores of thick glosses and commentaries on their texts published in subsequent centuries.[3] From the twelfth century forward, the Church's canon law of marriage was also systematized, first in Gratian's *Decretum* (ca. 1140), then in a welter of later legal commentaries and new papal and conciliar laws that eventually would form the *Corpus Iuris Canonici*.[4]

---

1. This section is adapted from Witte, LP, pp. 202-14.

2. See Harold J. Berman, *Law and Revolution: The Formation of the Western Legal Tradition* (Cambridge, MA, 1983).

3. See esp. Hugh of St. Victor, *On the Sacraments of the Christian Faith*, part II, trans. R. Deferrari (Cambridge, MA, 1951); Lombard, Sent., bk. 4, dist. 26-42; Aquinas, Comm. Sent. IV, dist. 26ff. revised in Aquinas, ST, pt. III Supp., qq. 41-68 [hereafter ST III Supp.]; Aquinas, SCG, bk. III, pt. II, ch. 122-26.

4. See detailed sources in 1:1011ff. and analysis in Brundage, pp. 176-550; Joyce, passim.

Medieval theologians and canonists treated marriage in a threefold manner: (1) as a created, natural association, subject to the laws of nature; (2) as a consensual contract, subject to the general laws of contract; and (3) as a sacrament of faith, subject to the spiritual laws of the Church.

First, marriage was regarded as a created natural association, which served both as "a duty for the sound and a remedy for the sick."[5] As a created, natural institution, marriage was subject to the law of nature, communicated in reason and conscience, and often confirmed in the Bible. This natural law, medieval writers taught, communicated God's will that fit persons marry when they reach the age of puberty, that they conceive children and nurture and educate them, that they remain naturally bonded to their blood and kin, serving them in times of need, frailty, and old age. It prescribed heterosexual, life-long unions between a couple, featuring mutual support and faithfulness. It required love for one's spouse and children.[6] It proscribed bigamy, incest, bestiality, buggery, polygamy, sodomy, and other unnatural relations.

Many medieval writers, however — following St. Paul's teachings in 1 Corinthians 7 — subordinated the duty of propagation to that of celibate contemplation, the natural drive for sexual union to the spiritual drive for beatitude.[7] For, as Peter Lombard put it: "The first institution [of marriage in Paradise] was commanded, the second permitted . . . to the human race for the purpose of preventing fornication. But this permission, because it does not select better things, is a remedy not a reward; if anyone rejects it, he will deserve judgment of death. An act which is allowed by permission, however, is voluntary, not necessary."[8] After the fall into sin, marriage remained a duty, but only for those tempted by sexual sin. For those not so tempted, marriage was an inferior option. It was better and more virtuous to pursue the spiritual life of celibacy and contemplation than the temporal life of marriage and family. For marriage was regarded as an institution of the natural sphere, not the supernatural sphere. Though ordained by God and good, it served primarily for the protection of the human community, not for the perfection of the individual. Participation in it merely kept a person free from sin and vice. It did not contribute directly to his or her virtue. The celibate, contemplative life, by contrast, was a calling of

---

5. Lombard, Sent., bk. 4, dist. 26.2; Aquinas, ST, II-II, qq. 151-56; III, q. 41, pt. 1; Hugh of St. Victor, *Sacraments*, 325-29.

6. See John T. Noonan, "Marital Affection in the Canonists," *Studia Gratiana* 12 (1967): 489; Jean Leclercq, *Monks on Marriage: A Twelfth Century View* (New York, 1982), pp. 12-39, 72-81; Alan MacFarlane, *Marriage and Love in England, 1300-1840* (Oxford, 1986), pp. 124ff., 321ff.

7. Lombard, Sent., dist. 26.3-4; Aquinas, ST III Supp., q. 41, art. 2. See further sources and texts in Joseph Friesen, *Geschichte des kanonischen Eherechts bis zum Verfall der Glossenliteratur*, 2d. ed., repr. ed. (Aalen, 1963), pp. 25ff.

8. Lombard, Sent., dist. 26.3.

the supernatural sphere. Participation in it increased a person's virtue and aided the pursuit of beatitude.[9] To this pursuit, Thomas Aquinas put it, "marriage is a very great obstacle," for it forces the person to dwell on the carnal and natural rather than the spiritual and supernatural aspects of life.[10]

Second, marriage was a contractual relation subject to general rules of contract. Marriage depended on the mutual consent of the parties to be legitimate and binding. "What makes a marriage is not the consent to cohabitation nor the carnal copula," Peter Lombard wrote; "it is the consent to conjugal society that does."[11] The form and function of this conjugal society, and the requirements for entrance into it, were set by the laws of nature. But the choice of whether to enter this society lay with the parties. "Marriage, therefore," said Peter Lombard, "is the marital union between persons legitimate according to the [natural] law, who persevere in a single sharing of life."[12]

As a contract, marriage was subject to the general moral principles of contract that prevailed at medieval canon law and civil law.[13] One such principle was freedom of contract, and this applied equally to marriage contracts.[14] Marriage contracts entered into by force, fear, or fraud, or through inducement of parents, masters, or feudal or manorial lords were thus not binding.[15] A second general principle of contract was that consensual agreements, entered into with or without formalities, were legally binding. Absent proof of mistake or frustration, or some condition that would render the contract unjust, either party could petition a court to enforce its terms. This general principle also applied to marriage contracts. Both husband and wife had an equal right to sue in court for enforcement even of a naked promise of marriage, for discharge of an essential and licit condition to marriage, or for vindication of their conjugal rights to the body of their spouse.[16]

Third, marriage was also raised by Christ to the dignity of a sacrament and thus subject to the Church's spiritual laws.[17] Unlike the other six sacraments,

---

9. Christopher N. L. Brooke, *The Medieval Idea of Marriage* (Oxford/New York, 1991), pp. 61-92.

10. Aquinas, ST III Supp., q. 41, art. 2.

11. Lombard, Sent., bk. 4, dist. 28.4. For earlier views, see Brundage, pp. 235-42, 260-78.

12. Lombard, Sent., bk. 4, dist. 27.2.

13. See Harold J. Berman, *Faith and Order: The Reconciliation of Law and Religion* (Atlanta, 1993), pp. 190-96.

14. John T. Noonan, *Canons and Canonists in Context* (Goldbach, 1997), pp. 173-98.

15. See Charles J. Reid, "The Canonistic Contribution to the Western Rights Tradition," *Boston College Law Review* 33 (1991): 37, 73-80.

16. See Weigand; Reid, "The Canonistic Contribution," pp. 80-91.

17. Jaroslav Pelikan, *Reformation of Church and Dogma 1300-1700* (Chicago, 1984), pp. 51ff.; Brundage, pp. 430ff.

however, marriage required no formalities and no clerical or lay instruction, witness, or participation. The two parties were themselves "ministers of the sacrament." Their consciences instructed them in the taking of the sacrament, and their own testimony was considered sufficient evidence to validate their marriages in a case of dispute. Although the Fourth Lateran Council of 1215 and later canon laws strongly encouraged the couple to seek the consent of their parents, to publish their banns for marriage in the church, to solemnize their union with the blessing of the priest, to invite witnesses to the wedding, and to comply with the marital customs of their domicile, none of these steps was an absolute requirement.

Like the other six sacraments, marriage was conceived to be an instrument of sanctification that, when contracted between Christians, caused and conferred grace upon those who put no obstacle in its way. Marriage sanctified the Christian couple by allowing them to comply with God's law for marriage, and by reminding them that Christ the bridegroom took the Church as his bride and accorded it his highest love and devotion, even to death. It sanctified the Christian community by enlarging the Church and by educating its children as people of God. The natural marital functions of propagation and education were thus given spiritual significance when performed by Christians within the extended Church.

When performed as a Christian sacrament, marriage transformed the relationship of a husband and wife, much like baptism transformed the character of the baptized. In baptism, the seemingly simple ritual act of sprinkling water on the forehead spiritually transformed the baptized party — canceling the original sin of Adam, promising the baptized party divine aid and protection in life, and welcoming the baptized believer into the sanctuary of the Church, into the spiritual care of the parents and godparents, and into the community and communion of the congregation. Similarly in marriage, the simple ritual act of a Christian man and woman coming together consensually in marriage spiritually transformed their relationship — removing the sin of sexual intercourse, promising divine help in fulfilling their marital and parental duties, and welcoming them into the hierarchy of institutions that constituted the Church universal.[18]

The simple exchange of present promises between Christian parties rendered this union sacramental, and triggered God's sanctifying grace. Neither consecration of the marriage through a church wedding nor consummation of the marriage through sexual intercourse were critical in the sacramental process. Even a secretly contracted, unconsummated marriage between a man and a woman capable of entering conjugal society in accordance with natural law

18. Theodore Mackin, *What Is Marriage?* (New York, 1982), pp. 20-22, 31-33, 332-33.

could be an instrument of sacramental grace. It was the mutual exchange of wills, the genuine union of mind to be married, that triggered the conferral of sacramental grace. The fruits of that sacramental grace pervaded the institution from that time forward.[19]

Once this channel of sacramental grace was properly opened, it could no longer be closed. A marriage properly contracted between Christians, in accordance with the laws of nature, was thus an indissoluble union, a permanently open channel of grace. Thomas Aquinas captured this in a critical passage on the indissolubility of marriage:

> [S]ince the sacraments effect what they figure, it is to be believed that grace is conferred through this sacrament on the spouses, whereby they might belong to the union of Christ and the Church. And this is very necessary to them so that as they concern themselves with carnal and earthly matters, they do not become detached from Christ and the Church. Now since the union of husband and wife designates the union of Christ and the Church, the figure must correspond with that which it signifies. Now the union of Christ and the Church is a union of one to another, and it is to last in perpetuity. For there is only one Church, . . . and Christ will never be separated from his Church. As he himself says in the last chapter of Matthew, "Behold I am with you even unto the end of the world. . . ." It follows necessarily then that a marriage, in so far as it is a sacrament of the Church, must be one holding to another indivisibly.[20]

Canon Law

The medieval Church built a complex and comprehensive law of marriage upon this theological foundation. This was called the canon law of marriage. Medieval canon lawyers, or canonists, distinguished between two types of contracts: contracts of engagement and contracts of marriage, or betrothals and espousals as they were historically called. An engagement contract or betrothal was a promise to be married in the future — "I, John, *promise to take you,* Mary, to be my wife." A marriage contract or espousal was a promise to marry here and now — "I, John, *now take you,* Mary, to be my lawfully wedded wife."

Neither contract required much formality to be valid and enforceable at medieval canon law. Parties were required simply to exchange these formulaic words — or, if they were mute, deaf, or incapable of *de facto* exchange, some

---

19. Aquinas, ST, II-II, q. 100, art. 2; X.4.1.14.
20. Aquinas, SCG, IV.78.

symbolic equivalent thereof. Parties could add much more to either contract. They could attach conditions. We shall marry "so long as my parents agree"; "only after you have completed your apprenticeship"; "when you have secured a job"; "after you have completed your military service"; "provided the wedding takes place within six months"; "so long as we live in my hometown"; and the like. The medieval Church also urged the parties to seek their parents' consent, to secure the testimony of witnesses, to publish banns of their pending nuptials, and to swear their marital vows in a wedding ritual before a priest. But none of this was mandatory. A private voluntary exchange of promises between a fit man and fit woman of the age of consent was a valid and enforceable marriage at medieval canon law.

Not all parties were free and fit to make such marital promises, however, and not all marital promises had to be, or could be, enforced. Certain relationships or experiences could disqualify the parties from engagement and marriage — altogether or at least with each other. Certain actions or conditions discovered after the exchange of promises could, and sometimes had to, lead to the dissolution of these promises.

These disqualifying and disabling factors were called impediments. Impediments provided the two parties, and sometimes third parties as well, with grounds to seek annulment of the engagement or marriage contract. An annulment was an order by a church court or a qualified religious official that declared the engagement or marital contract to be null and void and the relationship between the parties dissolved. A declaration of annulment meant that the engagement or marriage never formally existed at law; it was never a legally binding union, however contrary to fact that might appear. In cases involving serious impediments, even fully consummated long-standing marriages that had yielded children could be annulled.

The late medieval canon law recognized a variety of impediments to the engagement contract. While canonists differed widely in emphasis, and in nomenclature, most cited fourteen such impediments to engagement:

1. infancy — where one or both parties were below the age of consent at the time they exchanged promises;
2. precontract/polygamy — where either party was already betrothed or married to another;
3. incest — which prevented a party from marrying a relative by blood or marriage;
4. disease or deformity — the contracting or discovery of a physical or mental disease or deformity that would endanger the other or preclude intercourse;

33

5. physical desertion by either party for more than two years (in some formulations, three years);

6. failure of a condition that went to the essence of the marriage;

7. expiration of the agreed-upon period of engagement;

8. cruelty or dissent — where either party exhibited excessive hatred, cruelty, or abuse of the other;

9. bodily fornication — either engaged party's voluntary sexual contact with a third party;

10. special affinity — where, after engagement, either party had sexual intercourse with a relative of the other; this was a special and more serious case of bodily fornication;

11. spiritual fornication — one party's abandonment of the faith, particularly his or her conviction for heresy, apostasy, or infidelity;

12. entry of the man into the clergy;

13. entry of either party into a religious order; and

14. mutual consent of the parties to dissolve their engagement.

During the period of engagement the man and the woman, separately or together, had standing in a church court to press a case for annulment at any time. Third parties had standing as well — particularly parents, guardians, or relatives of the parties. A final invitation for any person to allege an impediment came during the formal wedding service (if there was one), where the priest invited the congregation: "If any man or woman knows of any . . . impediment standing in the way of this marriage, let them say so now, before we proceed any further."[21] Other late medieval marriage rituals concluded with the still familiar words, "or let him forever hold his peace."

Not all these cases of annulment of engagements required litigation. In cases six and seven, the expiration of a set engagement time or the breach of an essential condition automatically dissolved the engagement. Similarly, in cases twelve and thirteen involving religious vows and orders, the engagement was automatically dissolved. The final case of dissolution by mutual consent generally required church involvement only when the engagement had been made public.

A public or private future promise to marry, followed by sexual intercourse, was viewed as a consummated marriage at canon law, and was considered valid, even though the act of premarital sex was punishable as fornication. Intercourse after engagement raised the presumption that the parties had implicitly consented to be married and to consummate their marriage. A woman

21. This from a popular marriage service used in Geneva, "Ritual from the Abbey of Barbeau," in Searle and Stevenson, pp. 156-62, at 158.

could escape the marriage if she could demonstrate that her fiancé had raped her.

The canon law also recognized two types of impediments to fully consummated marriages: (1) prohibitive impediments, which rendered the contracting of marriage voidable, but whose violation did not necessarily render the marriage void, unless one party insisted; and (2) absolute (or diriment) impediments, which proscribed the contracting of marriage and rendered the putative marriage void regardless of what the parties wished.

The canonists captured the common prohibitive impediments in a little Latin rhyme that they used to teach the canon law to their students:

> Incestus, raptus, sponsatae mors uxoris
> Susceptus propriae sobolis, mors presbyteralis
> Vel si poeniteat solemniter, aut monialem
> Accipiat, prohibent haec coniugium sociandum.[22]

Seven prohibitive impediments were defined thus:

1. *Incestus* prevented a party from marrying a blood relative within the prohibited degrees of blood or affinity relationship, though some of the extra-biblical incest impediments were sometimes dispensable.
2. *Raptus* prevented marriage by a man who had raped or violently abducted his would-be spouse or her relative, and this became known after the nuptials.
3. *Sponsatae mors uxoris* precluded remarriage to a man who had killed his prior wife.
4. *Susceptus propriae sobolis* prevented remarriage to a person who had fraudulently or in bad faith become a godparent of his prior step-child in order to prevent his wife's remarriage in the event of his death.
5. *Mors presbyteralis* prohibited marriage to a party who had killed an ordained priest or monastic.
6. *Si poeniteat solemniter* precluded marriage to a party who had been assigned public and solemn penance for a mortal sin.
7. *Aut monialem accipiat* was an impediment that precluded marriage to a former nun or monk.

Discovery of any of these conditions after the couple had already been married gave the innocent spouse standing in a church court to press a case for

---

22. Hostiensis, *Summa Aurea,* quoted by James D. Scanlan, "Husband and Wife: Pre-Reformation Canon Law on Marriages of the Officials' Courts," in *An Introduction to Scottish Legal History* (Edinburgh, 1958), pp. 69ff.

annulment. An annulment suit based on one of these impediments was relatively easy to win if it was brought shortly after the marriage by a spouse who knew nothing of this impediment beforehand. It was harder, though not impossible, to win if a party had entered the marriage with full knowledge of this impediment and then had a change of heart, or learned of the impediment after the marriage but delayed long in suing for annulment on that basis.

The absolute (diriment) impediments were outlined by the canonists in a second Latin jingle:

> Error, conditio, votum, cognatio, crimen
> Cultus disparitas, vis, ordo, ligamen, honestas,
> Dissensus, et affinis, si forte coire nequitis,
> Haec facienda vetant connubia, facta retractant.[23]

These absolute impediments fell into four clusters. One set of impediments sought to preserve the freedom of consent of both parties. Lack of consent by either party *(dissensus)* voided the marriage. Thus proof of extreme duress, fear, compulsion, or fraud *(vis)* — by a parent, putative spouse, or third parties — impinged on consent and could invalidate a marriage contract, particularly if the action was brought soon after the union. A mistake *(error)* about the identity of the other party, and in some cases of the virginity of the woman prior to marriage, was also a ground for annulment.

A second set of absolute impediments defined which parties were free to give their consent. Parties who had, prior to the putative marriage, made religious vows of celibacy *(votum)* or of chastity in one of the religious orders of the Church *(ordo)* were eternally bound to God and thus could not bind themselves to another in marriage. Their marriage was thus automatically void. Christians could not contract marriage with infidels, Jews, or pagans *(cultus disparitas)*, since the sacrament of baptism was a prerequisite for marriage. Such marriages could not symbolize the union of Christ with his faithful Church, and they were automatically annulled on discovery. Moreover, if a party departed from the faith after consummation and remained incorrigible, a church court could declare the marriage void, particularly if the couple had children who would be forced to choose between their parents' faiths. Persons related up to the fourth degree either to a common ancestor or to a couple (whether or not married) who had engaged in sexual relations were prohibited from marrying. These were the impediments of consanguinity and affinity set out in Leviticus. They were grouped under the general topic of *cognatio:* parents could not marry their adopted children or grandchildren, nor the spouses

23. Ibid.

of their adopted children. One who baptized or confirmed a party or who became a godparent could not marry him or her; for these persons were considered to be the "spiritual fathers or mothers" of the party who received the sacrament. One could not marry the relative up to the fourth degree of a now-deceased fiancé *(iustitia publicae honestae)*. And a once adulterous spouse could not, upon becoming free to remarry, enter into marriage with his or her former paramour — particularly if he or she contributed in any way to the former spouse's death *(crimen)*.

A third set of absolute impediments protected the ultimate sanctity and sanctifying function of the sacrament of marriage. Conditions attached to marriage promises that were illegal or repugnant to the sacrament or harmful to the offspring automatically rendered the marriage contract void. Thus a promise with the condition "that we abstain for a season" was valid. But a condition "that we engage in contraception," "that we abort our offspring" or "that we permit each other sexual liberty with others" nullified the marriage contract. Such conditions vitiated the spiritual purpose of marriage — to unite together in love and to raise children in the service of God. Likewise, permanent impotence, insanity, or bewitchment of either party were generally grounds for nullification, provided that such a condition was latent before marriage, and unknown to the parties.

A fourth set of absolute impediments *(ligamen)* annulled all bigamous and polygamous relations, as contrary to biblical command, even if the parties had children. Annulment for such an impediment required proof of one's spouse's prior marriage contract, which was not dissolved by the former spouse's death or by a formal annulment.

Both the innocent spouse and his or her parents or other third parties had the right to sue for annulment in a church court on grounds of an absolute impediment. The court's order of annulment broke the putative marriage and (under some interpretations) illegitimated any children born of the same. It left the man and woman free to remarry, but also sometimes saddled them with serious charges of sin and crime. The church court judge, or a higher religious official, had power to dispense these impediments in individual cases and allow the marriage to continue. But the spouses themselves had no corresponding right to ignore the impediment and continue the marriage. For the parties to live in violation of an absolute impediment was a crime, a type of strict liability status offense. It was no defense to this crime that the parties had entered this status innocently or that the victim had consented to its continuation.

Absolute divorce, with a subsequent right to remarry, was not permitted in canon law. The marital bond, once properly formed, remained indissoluble — at least until the death of one of the parties. Divorce, in the terms of canon law, meant only separation. Both husband and wife were given standing in church courts to sue for such a separation. During the case, a church court could order a husband to pay his wife temporary alimony to sustain her, particularly if she had moved out of the marital home out of fear of or under pressure from her husband. If a church court found adequate grounds for divorce — on evidence of adultery, desertion, or cruelty — it would order the estranged parties to live separately, and sometimes make further orders respecting custody and support of the children. A separated spouse, though freed from the physical bond of marriage, was not freed from the spiritual bond. A subsequent marriage contracted before the death of one's estranged spouse was an act of bigamy — a prima facie case of mortal sin at canon law and a capital crime at civil law. Even remarriage of widows and widowers was frowned upon; many medieval canonists regarded it as a form of serial polygamy or "digamy."

The Reformation

Critique of Tradition

On May 21, 1536, the Genevan authorities renounced this traditional canon law in favor of "the Holy Evangelical Law and Word of God."[24] Two months later, John Calvin arrived in Geneva, armed with a copy of his new *Institutes of the Christian Religion* in which he, too, renounced the traditional theology and canon law of marriage (**Doc. 1-1**).

Calvin's 1536 *Institutes* repeated, with only modest embellishment, the by-then familiar Protestant attack on the prevailing Catholic theology of marriage.[25] Like the Lutheran reformers before him, Calvin grounded his initial attack in the theory of the two kingdoms.

> [T]here is a twofold government in man. One aspect is spiritual, whereby the conscience is instructed in piety and in reverencing God; the second is political, whereby man is educated for the duties of humanity and civil life that must be maintained among men. These are usually called the "spiritual" and the "temporal" kingdoms (not improper terms) by which is meant that the former sort of regime pertains to the life of the soul, while the latter has to do with the concerns of the present life — not only with food and clothing but with laying down laws whereby a man may live his life among

24. SD, vol. 2, item 701. Only a decade before, the city council had unequivocally confirmed its support for the church's jurisdiction over marriage. Statute of December 20, 1528, in SD, vol. 2, item 621; see also ibid., item 571 (a November 13, 1521, confirmation of ecclesiastical jurisdiction by Charles II, Duke of Savoy). Köhler, 2:514-15, 541-55; Seeger, pp. 22-29, 188-89, 200.

25. Witte, FSC, pp. 42-193.

other men honorably and temperately. For the former resides in the mind within, while the latter regulates only outward behavior.[26]

Marriage, family, and sexuality are matters of the earthly kingdom alone, Calvin believed. Marriage is "a good and holy ordinance of God just like farming, building, cobbling, and barbering." Marriage serves to procreate children, to remedy incontinence, and to promote "love between husband and wife." Its morals and mores are subject to the laws of God that are written on the "tablet" of conscience, rewritten in the pages of Scripture, and distilled in the Ten Commandments. Marriage, however, is not a sacrament of the heavenly kingdom. Though it symbolizes the bond between Christ and his Church, Yahweh and his chosen people, marriage confirms no divine promise and confers no sanctifying grace, as do true sacraments. Though it is a righteous mode of Christian living in the earthly kingdom, it has no bearing on one's salvation or eternal standing.

Moreover, celibacy is not an obligation of the earthly kingdom. The celibate life is a "special gift of God," commended only to those "rare persons" who are continent by nature. "[I]t is the hypocrisy of demons to command celibacy," and "giddy levity" to exalt the celibate state over the marital estate, Calvin charged. For the Church to command celibacy is to "contend against God" and to spurn his gracious "remedy" for lust. For the Church to subordinate marriage to celibacy is to commit the spiritual "arrogance" of supplanting God's ordinance with a human tradition. Two decades before, such teachings would have been revolutionary. By the late 1530s, they had become familiar refrains in the Protestant litany.

In his 1536 *Institutes*, Calvin also took up, with more originality, the Protestant attack on the Catholic canon law of marriage. He issued a lengthy and bitter broadside against the arguments from Scripture, tradition, and the sacraments that the Church had adduced to support its ecclesiastical jurisdiction. "[T]he power to frame laws was both unknown to the apostles, and many times denied the ministers of the church by God's Word," he insisted. "[I]t is not a church which, passing the bounds of God's Word, wantons and disports itself to frame new laws and dream up new things" for spiritual life. The Bible alone is a sufficient guide for a person's Christian walk and a church's corporate life. For the Church to impose new laws upon its own members is to obstruct the simple law and liberty of the Gospel. For the Catholic Church to impose its own laws upon civil society is to obscure its essential pastoral, prophetic, and pedagogical callings. To be sure, said Calvin (quoting St. Paul), "all things

26. Institutes (1536), 6.13; see also 6.14, 6.35; David Vandrunen, "The Context of Natural Law: John Calvin's Doctrine of the Two Kingdoms," *Journal of Church and State* 46 (2004): 503.

[must] be done decently and in order." Certain rules and structures "are necessary for internal discipline [and] the maintenance of peace, honesty, and good order in the assembly of Christians." But the Church has no authority to impose laws "upon consciences in those matters in which they have been freed by Christ" — in the so-called "adiaphora," the external and discretionary things of life that do not conduce to salvation. Marriage and family life are among these adiaphora. Laws governing such matters lie within the province of the state, not the Church.[27]

Particularly the Church's sacramental theology of marriage, Calvin argued, has led all Christendom down a "long legal trail of errors, lies, frauds, and misdeeds." Calvin singled out for special critique the familiar targets of earlier Protestant attacks — the Church's "usurpation" of marital jurisdiction from secular judges, its condoning of secret marriages of minors without parental consent, its restrictions on the seasons for engagement, its long roll of marital impediments beyond "the law of nations and of Moses," its easy dispensations from marital rules for the propertied and the powerful, its prohibitions against divorce and remarriage. "[P]apal tyranny" and "iniquitous laws," he wrote, have "so confused matrimonial cases . . . that it is necessary to review the controversies that often ensue therefrom in light of the Word of God" and "to make certain new ordinances by which [marriage] may be governed."

1546 Marriage Ordinance

Within a decade, Calvin saw to it that "certain new ordinances" on marriage were in place in Geneva. Building on provisions in several statutes in the later 1530s and 1540s — including the 1541 Ecclesiastical Ordinances which included several relevant passages on sexual morality, marriage, and children[28] — Calvin prepared a detailed Marriage Ordinance in 1545. This draft was slightly amended the following year, and circulated widely thereafter in Geneva and in surrounding polities (Doc. 1-2). Though not formally enacted until 1561, despite Calvin's repeated efforts, this 1546 draft Marriage Ordinance from the start governed most questions of engagement, annulment, and marriage in Geneva.[29] Many of

27. This critique is included not only in Doc. 1-1, but also scattered throughout Institutes (1536), 6.14-32. See further early sources in John Witte, Jr., "Moderate Religious Liberty in the Theology of John Calvin," *Calvin Theological Journal* 31 (1996): 359.

28. Excerpted in the next chapter, Doc. 2-1.

29. On October 13, 1545, the Council commissioned Calvin to prepare a draft marriage ordinance, which he produced on his own (R. Conseil 40:259). On November 5, the Council sent Calvin a syndic and councilor to confer about the draft (R. Conseil 40:283). On November 10, Calvin presented to the Council a draft marriage ordinance, though it is not clear whether he

its provisions were enforced to the letter by both the Consistory and Council of Geneva in the later 1540s and 1550s.

The 1546 Ordinance provides us with a convenient overview of most of the reforms that Calvin introduced into the law of marital formation, maintenance, and dissolution.[30] Like the medieval canonists, Calvin started with the principle of freedom of marital contract. Marriage depended in its essence on the mutual consent of both the man and the woman; absent proof of free consent by both parties there was no marriage. Calvin defended this principle repeatedly in his later commentaries and sermons. "While all contracts ought to be voluntary, freedom ought to prevail especially in marriage, so that no one may pledge his faith against his will."[31] "God considers that compulsory and forced marriages never come to a good end. . . . [I]f the husband and the wife are not in mutual agreement and do not love each other, this is a profanation of marriage, and not a marriage at all, properly speaking. For the will is the principal bond."[32] When a woman wishes to marry, she must thus not "be thrust into it reluctantly or compelled to marry against her will, but left to her own free choice."[33] "When a man is going to marry and he takes a wife, let him take her of his own free will, knowing that where there is not a true and pure love, there is nothing but disorder, and one can expect no grace from God."[34] Dozens of such sentiments, scattered throughout Calvin's writings, attest to this principle of freedom of marital contract.

Also like the medieval canonists, Calvin distinguished between contracts of engagement and contracts of marriage — or engagements and espousals as he called them, following the tradition. Engagements were future promises to

---

made any changes to his first draft after his conference with the syndic and councilor (R. Conseil 40:286). On November 13, the Council appointed thirteen representatives to review and revise the draft (R. Conseil 40:291). They made several small changes to the ordinance, and recommended in early 1546 that the Council approve it. The Council did not approve it formally, leaving both the November 10, 1545, draft and revised 1546 draft to circulate among ministers and magistrates of Geneva and beyond in slightly varying copies (CO 10/1:33n). On November 11, 1549, another committee, again led by Calvin, was convened to study existing marriage law and to recommend improvements to the Marriage Ordinance (R. Conseil 44:261v). Calvin presented his report on November 25, but complained on January 20, February 17, and February 24, 1550, that still no official position had been taken on the ordinance (R. Conseil 44:273v, 306v, 324v, 329v). On May 1, 1551, Calvin again complained to the Council that the lack of clear guidelines led to much confusion over questions of marriage (CO 10/1:33n; *Registres du Consistoire de Genève au Temps de Calvin*, ed. Robert M. Kingdon et al. [Geneva, 2001], 2:81, n. 260).

30. See further discussion in Chapter 2.

31. Comm. Josh. 15:14.

32. Serm. Deut. 25:5-12.

33. Comm. Gen. 24:57.

34. Serm. Deut. 25:5-12.

be married. Marriages were present promises to be married. But, unlike the medieval canonists, Calvin removed the need for the parties to use specific formulaic words: any clear indication of an intent to marry would do. He softened the distinction and shortened the duration between engagements and espousals. And he insisted that these contracts be public as well as private in nature.

Because the consent of the couple was the essence of the engagement contract, Calvin took pains to secure it in the 1546 Ordinance. Engagement promises had to made "simply," "unconditionally," and "honorably in the fear of God." Such engagements were to be initiated by "a sober proposal" from the man, accepted by the woman, and witnessed by at least two persons of "good reputation." Engagements made in secret, qualified with onerous conditions, or procured by coercion were automatically annulled — and the couple themselves, and any accomplices in their wrongdoing, could face punishment. Engagements procured through trickery or "surprise," or made frivolously, as when merely touching glasses when drinking together, could be annulled on petition by either party. Engagement promises extracted by or from children below the age of consent were presumptively invalid, though children could confirm them upon reaching majority. Engagements involving a newcomer to the city were not valid until the parties produced proof of the newcomer's integrity of character and eligibility for marriage. Absent such proof, the couple had to wait a year before they could marry.[35]

The consent of the couple's parents, or their guardians, was also vital to the validity of the engagement. The consent of fathers was the more critical; maternal consent was required only when fathers were absent, and would be respected only if (male) relatives would concur in her views. In the absence of both parents, guardians would give their consent, again with priority for the male voice. Minor children — men under twenty, women under eighteen years of age — who became engaged without such parental consent could have their engagements unilaterally annulled by either set of parents or guardians. Adult or emancipated children could proceed without their parents' consent, though "it would be more fitting for them to let themselves always be governed by the advice of their fathers."

The Ordinance made clear that parental consent was a supplement to, not a substitute for, the consent of the couple themselves. Parents could not, on pain of imprisonment, coerce their children into unwanted engagements or marriages, or withhold their consent or payment of dowry until the child chose a favorite partner. They could not force youngsters into marriage before they were mature enough to consent to and participate safely in the institution. Minor children, "always preserving modesty and respect," could refuse to follow

35. SD, vol. 2, item 732.

their parents' insistence on an unwanted partner or a premature engagement. Other children, confronting a negligent or excessively strict father, could have him compelled to give a dowry in support of their marriage.

The consent of the broader state and church community also played a part in the engagements. Betrothed couples were to register with a local civil magistrate, who would post notices of their pending nuptials and furnish the couple with signed banns. Couples were then to request the local pastor to announce their banns from the pulpit on three successive Sundays. Such widespread notice was an open invitation for fellow parishioners and citizens alike to approve of the match or to voice their objections. Any objections to the engagement could be raised at this point. But all such objections had to be voiced privately to the Consistory, and only by citizens or by persons of good reputation. Such precautions helped to avoid the prospect of "blame or injury," particularly "to some respectable girl." Those who objected in an untimely or improper manner could be sued for defamation by the couple or their parents. A final call for objections to the marriage came during the wedding liturgy.

While the Consistory had wide discretion to review these objections, the strong presumption was that engagement contracts, once properly made, could not be broken. Objections that raised formal impediments, however, required closer scrutiny, and sometimes could result in orders of annulment, or at least delay of the wedding.

Of the fourteen formal impediments to engagement recognized at canon law, the Ordinance listed only five: (1) infancy; (2) precontract/polygamy; (3) incest; (4) contagious disease or physical deformity; and (5) physical desertion by either party. The Ordinance listed as an impediment to either engagement or marriage: (6) discovery of the lack of presumed virginity. Though the Ordinance was silent on the question, in practice, Calvin and the Consistory also raised to the level of an impediment to engagement: (7) lack of consent by either the man or woman; (8) lack of parental consent to a minor's marriage; (9) bodily fornication with another by either party; and (10) failure of a condition that went to the essence of marriage.

In practice, Calvin and the Consistory differed sharply on whether great differences in age, or in religious confession, between the two parties, were impediments that could be used to dissolve engagements involuntarily. Calvin pressed for annulment on these two grounds in several cases, especially those involving disparity of age, but the Consistory sometimes resisted him.

The Ordinance did not list, and the Consistory did not readily recognize, the seven other impediments to engagement recognized at canon law — expiration of time; cruelty or dissent towards a fiancé(e); special affinity; spiritual fornication; a man's entry into the clergy; either party's vow of chastity; or dissolution by mutual consent of the engaged couple.

43

The removal of this last canon law impediment, dissolution of the engagement by mutual consent of the couple, was particularly surprising. The medieval canonists had introduced this impediment not to encourage transient troth but to give parties a final chance to walk away from the budding union if their relationship did not work out. Calvin and his colleagues provided no such escape: they forced into marriage many couples who had earlier been properly engaged but had become alienated in their affections. This drove home a perennial lesson of the law of Calvin's Geneva — that engagement contracts, like marital contracts, were "sacred contracts" that could not be entered or dissolved easily.[36]

Theodore Beza summed up this sentiment, and the prevailing law of engagements and their annulment neatly in 1569:

[T]rue and valid engagements cannot be dissolved any more than consummated marriages, since God's command also applies here: "What God has joined together, let man not put asunder." They cannot be broken by mutual consent of both parties, far less by the will of either party as once was tolerated by the Romans, and even by Moses because of the stubbornness of the Jews.

Certain things that are called "engagements," however, are not binding, because they are invalid and void. These are of two sorts. Some bonds can never be valid — those that are incestuous because of a blood relationship or affinity [between the parties] that prohibits marriage, those initiated with the husband or wife of another, with a eunuch, or with someone laboring under some incurable disease that in fact removes all hope of consummating the marriage. Other bonds, though initially invalid, nevertheless may be confirmed afterwards — those contracted between the sexually immature, those contracted without the authority of parents (or of those in place of parents), or those contracted by deception of the parties, or only for a future time, or with a condition added, or by force or fear. Finally, some [bonds] are initially valid but later are dissolved not so much by men as by God himself — when the [future] husband or wife commits adultery, when an unfaithful [future] spouse deserts a faithful one, when a woman betrothed as a virgin was not one, or when [one party betrays] madness or some other permanent and incurable disease that in fact removes all hope of carrying out the marriage, or when a contagious and incurable disease interferes with an engagement.[37]

A Genevan couple, once properly betrothed, had little time to waste and little room to celebrate. Neither their publicly announced engagement nor the

36. Serm. Deut. 22:25-30.
37. Beza, TRD, p. 204.

procurement of banns was sufficient to constitute a marriage. A formal church wedding had to follow — within six weeks of engagement. If the couple procrastinated in their wedding plans, the Consistory would reprimand them: if they persisted, they would be "sent before the Council so that they may be compelled to celebrate it."

If the prospective groom disappeared without cause, the woman was bound to her engagement for a year. If the prospective bride disappeared, the man could break off the engagement immediately — unless there was evidence that she had been kidnapped or involuntarily detained. Cohabitation and consummation, in the brief period prior to the wedding, were strictly forbidden to the parties, on pain of imprisonment. Pregnant brides-to-be, though spared prison, were required to do public confession for their sexual misconduct prior to the wedding, and to wear a veil signifying their sin on the day of the wedding.

Weddings were to be "modest affairs," "maintaining the decorum and gravity befitting Christians," and featuring a mutual swearing of oaths by the couple, as well as by their witnesses, followed by the blessing and sermon of the pastor. Weddings were held on Sundays during the sermon or on weekdays when the congregation gathered for a sermon or lecture on the Bible. Weddings could not be held on the same Sunday for which the eucharist was scheduled lest "the honor of the sacrament" be impugned. This was a marked departure from prevailing Catholic and other Protestant traditions which saw eucharistic celebration as a vital part of the consecration of the marriage.

A marriage, once properly contracted, consecrated, and celebrated, was presumed permanent. The married couple was expected to maintain a common home. Both parties could be called to account for privately separating — particularly if there was suspicion of adultery, harlotry, concubinage, or sodomy. Couples who "wrangled and disputed with each other" were to be admonished by the Consistory to "live in peace and unity" — with severe cases of discord reported to the congregation for popular reproof or to the Council for criminal punishment. Husbands were forbidden to "ill treat," "beat," or "torment" their wives, and were subject to severe criminal sanctions if they persisted. These sanctions became increasingly severe in later years as the Consistory and Council sought to clamp down on domestic abuse. The Ordinance made no provision, even in extreme cases, for the traditional halfway remedy of separation (without divorce). An ethic of perpetual reconciliation of husband and wife coursed through the Ordinance, with ministers, magistrates, and members of the broader community all called to foster this end.

The presumption of permanent marriage was not incontestable, however. In instances of serious marital impediments or individual fault, a party could sue for annulment or divorce. The Ordinance rendered the process of marital dissolution as open and communal as it had rendered the process of marital formation. Calvin was as eager to safeguard against the prior canon law practice of private dissolutions as against the traditional canon law toleration of secret marriages.

No new grounds for annulment of fully consummated marriages were recognized in Calvin's Geneva. The Genevan authorities allowed parties to sue for annulment of marriage on six of the nine impediments to engagement: (1) infancy; (2) precontract/polygamy; (3) incest; (4) contagious disease or physical deformity; (5) lack of consent by either party; and (6) discovery of the lack of presumed virginity.

Either party, or a third party, could sue for annulment on discovery of a condition of infancy or bigamy. Thereafter, the minor was free to marry on reaching majority, but the knowing bigamist was subject to severe sanction. Either party, or a third party, could also sue on discovery of a blood or familial relationship between them that rendered their marriage incestuous. Upon annulment both were left to remarry. A husband could sue if he discovered that his wife lacked presumed virginity, was incurably diseased, or refused to correct a "defect of her body" that prevented intercourse — again, leaving both parties free to remarry. A wife could sue on grounds of the impotence or incurable disease of her husband — leaving her free to remarry, but him "forbidden to defraud any woman again." In all such cases, the parties were expected to prepare a register of their individual and collective properties and, with appropriate judicial supervision, reach an "amicable" parting of property and person.

Lack of parental consent was no longer recognized as an impediment to marriage, and the Consistory worked hard to prevent parents from interfering with the couple after the wedding day. But the Consistory did not prevent parents from disinheriting and disowning their children who had married against their will or without their consent.

The 1546 Ordinance recognized none of the sundry other canon law impediments to fully consummated marriage. In practice, particularly in the early years of the Reformation, the Genevan Consistory repeatedly spurned attempts to introduce impediments based on traditional concerns about the sacramentality of marriage, spiritual incest, and the need to protect clerics, and their vows of celibacy and chastity.

Annulment was only one form of marital dissolution. Following Protestant conventions, Calvin and his colleagues introduced absolute divorce on proof of adultery or desertion, and a subsequent right for at least the innocent party of divorce to remarry. A judgment of divorce required proof in open court that a marriage, though properly contracted, was now broken by reason of the adultery or desertion of one of the parties.

In cases of adultery, husband and wife were accorded an equal right to sue — a deliberate innovation to "ancient [i.e., Roman law] practice," which the

Ordinance grounded in St. Paul's teaching that husband and wife have a "mutual and reciprocal obligation" "with respect to cohabitation of the bed." Only an entirely innocent plaintiff could bring such a divorce suit; any evidence of mutual fault, fraud, or collusion in the adultery was fatal to the case. Failure to bring suit in a timely manner was taken as a sign of forgiveness, and cut off the suit for divorce. After bringing suit, the plaintiff was urged to reconcile with the wayward spouse — and doubtless told that such reconciliation would likely exonerate the latter from criminal punishment. But the plaintiff could insist on the divorce, and in such instance, the case would be referred to the Council for adjudication. The innocent party was free to remarry thereafter. The adulterer faced criminal punishment — imprisonment in the usual case, banishment or execution by drowning in an egregious case.

Parties could also sue for divorce on grounds of desertion. These divorce cases were procedurally more complicated and substantively less egalitarian in their treatment of husband and wife. In cases where the husband left home for a legitimate reason (such as for business or military service), but inexplicably did not return and could not be found, the wife had to wait ten years before he could be presumed dead and she permitted to remarry. In cases where the husband left "through debauchery or some evil feeling," the wife was to find him and to request his return. If she could not find him, she would have to wait one year before proceeding further. If she did find him and he refused to return — or the year of waiting had expired — she was to request three biweekly announcements of his desertion, both by the minister in the church and by the lieutenant of the city council. If he still failed to respond, she was to summon two or three of his relatives or close friends to try to find him and urge his return. If that proved futile, she could appear before the Consistory to state her case, and with their approval, petition the magistrate for an order of divorce. The return of the husband anytime before such an order would end the proceedings. The husband would be admonished for his desertion. The wife would be compelled to welcome him back to bed and board. If the husband repeated his desertion, he faced prison. If he deserted habitually, the wife could sue for divorce ex parte, with no further notification requirements.

A husband who brought suit for his wife's desertion followed the same procedures, but with three simplifications. First, cases of intentional desertion and legitimate departure by the wife were treated alike. Second, the husband had no obligation to wait for one year (let alone ten) if he could not locate his wife; the public announcements of her departure and petition for divorce could commence immediately. Third, even if a wife returned, her husband could reject her if he had "suspicion . . . that she has mismanaged her body." The Consistory would urge their reconciliation, but if he insisted, they would investigate her conduct while away. If they found no evidence of misconduct, he would be compelled to accept her. If they reached "a very strong presumption" that she committed adultery or kept "bad and suspect company" and did not maintain "the proper behavior of a respectable woman," the Ordinance reads, "let the husband's request be heard and he be granted what reason justifies."

1-1 Calvin's Attack on the Catholic Theology and Canon Law on Marriage (1536)[38]

The last [false sacrament] is marriage. All men admit that it was instituted by God [Gen. 2:21-24; Matt. 19:4ff.]; but no man had ever seen it administered as a sacrament until the time of Gregory [VII]. And what sober man would ever have thought it such? Marriage is a good and holy ordinance of God; and farming, building, cobbling, and barbering are lawful ordinances of God, and yet are not sacraments. For it is required that a sacrament be not only a work of God but an outward ceremony appointed by God to confirm a promise. Even children will discern that there is no such thing in matrimony.

But it is, they say, "the sign of a sacred thing, that is, of the spiritual joining of Christ with the church." If by the word "sign" they understand a symbol set before us by God to raise up the assurance of our faith, they are wandering far from the mark; if they simply understand "sign" as what is adduced by way of comparison, I will show how keenly they reason. Paul says, "As star differs from star in brilliance, so will be the resurrection of the dead." [1 Cor. 15:41-42] There you have one sacrament. Christ says, "The Kingdom of Heaven is like a grain of mustard seed." [Matt. 13:31] Here you have another. Again, "The Kingdom of Heaven is like leaven." [Matt. 13:33] Behold a third. Isaiah says, "Behold, the Lord will feed his flock like a shepherd." [Isa. 40:10-11] Behold a fourth. In another place, "The Lord shall go forth as a giant." [Isa. 42:13]. Here you have a fifth. Finally, what end or measure will there be? There is nothing that by this reasoning will not be a sacrament. There will be as many sacraments as there are parables and similitudes in Scripture. In fact, theft will be a sacrament, inasmuch as it is written, "The Day of the Lord is like a thief." [1 Thess. 5:2] Who can bear these Sophists when they prate so ignorantly? I admit that whenever we see a vine, it is a very good thing to recall what Christ said: "I am the vine, you are the branches" [John 15:5]; "My Father is the vinedresser." [John 15:1] Whenever we meet a shepherd with his flock, it is good that this also come to mind: "I am the good shepherd" [John 10:14]; "My sheep hear the voice." [John 10:27] But anyone who would classify such similitudes with the sacraments ought to be sent to a mental hospital.

But they press us with Paul's words, by which they say the term "sacrament"

---

38. Institutes (1536), in CO 1:192-95, using translation in *Institution of the Christian Religion,* trans. Ford Lewis Battles (Atlanta, 1969), pp. 236-40. The biblical citations are included in the translation, not the original. Paragraph numbers and notes in the translation have been omitted.

is applied to marriage: "He who loves his wife loves himself. For no man ever hated his own flesh, but nourishes and cherishes it, as Christ does the church, because we are members of his body, of his flesh, and of his bones. 'For this reason a man shall leave his father and mother and be joined to his wife, and the two shall become as one flesh.' This is a great sacrament. But I say, in Christ and the Church." [Eph. 5:28-31]. Yet so to handle the Scriptures is to mix earth with heaven. Paul, to show to married men with what singular love they ought to embrace their wives, sets forth Christ to them as prototype. For as he poured out his godly compassion upon the church, which he had espoused to himself, thus he wishes every man to feel toward his own wife. Then the words follow: "He who loves his wife loves himself . . . as Christ loved the church." [Eph. 5:28] Now to teach how Christ loved the church as himself, nay, how he made himself one with his bride the church, Paul applies to Christ what Moses relates that Adam said of himself. For when Eve (who he knew was formed from his rib) was brought into his sight, he said, "She is bone of my bones, and flesh of my flesh." [Gen. 2:23] Paul testifies that all this was spiritually fulfilled in Christ and in us, when he says that we are members of his body, of his flesh, and of his bones, and thus one flesh with him. Finally, he adds this summation: "This is a great mystery." And that nobody may be deceived by an ambiguity, he explains that he is not speaking of carnal union of man and woman, but of the spiritual marriage of Christ and the church. Truly, indeed, this is a great mystery, that Christ allowed a rib to be removed from himself to form us; that is, when he was strong, he willed to be weak, in order that we might be strengthened by his strength; so that we ourselves should now not only live, but he should live in us [Gal. 2:20].

The term "sacrament" has deceived them. But was it right that the whole church should suffer the punishment of their ignorance? Paul has said "mystery." The translator could have left this word, as one not unfamiliar to Latin ears, or rendered it as "secret." He preferred to use the word "sacrament" [Eph. 5:32], but in the same sense that the word "mystery" had been used in Greek by Paul. Let them now go, and clamorously rail against skill in languages, through ignorance of which they have so long been most shamefully deceived in a matter easy and obvious to anyone. But why do they press so hard for this word "sacrament" in this one place, but overlook it at other times? For in the first letter to Timothy [I Tim. 3:9], and in this same letter to the Ephesians itself [Eph. 1:9; 3:3, 9], the translator of the Vulgate has used it consistently for "mystery."

Still, [let] this slip be pardoned them; liars at least ought to have good memories. But, having graced marriage with the title of sacrament, to call it afterward uncleanness and pollution and carnal filth — what giddy levity is this? How absurd it is to bar priests from this sacrament! If they say they do not debar them from the sacrament, but from the lust of copulation, they will not give me the slip. For they teach that copulation itself is a part of the sacrament, and that it alone is the figure of the union which we have with Christ, in conformity to nature; for man and woman are made one flesh only by carnal copulation. However, some of them have found two sacraments here: one of God and the soul, in the bridegroom and bride; the other, of Christ and the church, in the husband and wife. However, copulation is still a sacrament, from which it is unlawful to bar any Christian. Unless, perhaps, the sacraments of Christians are so out of accord that they cannot stand together. There is also another absurdity in their grand offices. They affirm that in the sacrament the grace of the Holy Spirit is conferred; they teach copulation to be a sacrament; and they deny that the Holy Spirit is ever present in copulation. Not to have mocked the church simply in one thing, what a long train of errors, lies, frauds, and misdeeds have they attached to this one error? Thus, you may say that they sought nothing but a den of abominations when they made a sacrament out of marriage. For when they once obtained this, they took over the hearing of matrimonial cases; as it was a spiritual matter it was not to be handled by secular judges. Then they passed laws by which they strengthened their tyranny, laws in part openly impious toward God, in part most unfair toward men. Such are these: That marriages between minors contracted without parental consent should remain firm and valid. That marriages between kinsfolk even to the seventh degree are not lawful, and if contracted, must be dissolved. They forge the very degrees, against the laws of all nations and also against the ordinances of Moses: that a man who has put away an adulterous wife is not permitted to take another; that godparents may not be coupled in matrimony: that marriages may not be celebrated from Septuagesima to the octave of Easter, and in the three weeks before the nativity of John, and from Advent to Epiphany; and innumerable like regulations which would take too long to recount. At length, we must extricate ourselves from their mire, in which our discourse has already stuck longer than I should have liked. Still, I believe that I have accomplished something in that I have partly pulled the lion's skin from these asses.

1-2   Marriage Ordinance (1546)[39]

Which Persons May Not Marry without Permission

1. Regarding young people who have never been married, none, whether sons or daughters, who have a father still living shall have the power to contract a marriage without the permission of their father unless they have attained the

---

39. RCP 1:30-38. The 1561 draft adds a brief preamble, repeating most of the language that now appears in the 1541 *Ecclesiastical Ordinances:* "After the publication of the customary banns, let the marriage be celebrated and blessed in the church when the parties decide, either on

legal age, that is twenty years for a son and eighteen for a daughter.[40] And if after reaching this age they have asked their fathers or had them asked to marry them and their fathers have not attended to it,[41] in that case it shall be lawful for them to marry without their fathers' authority.[42]

2. Let the same apply to wards who are under the authority of guardians or trustees; nevertheless the mother or guardian may not arrange a marriage for the boy or girl they have in their charge without consulting one of the[43] relatives, if there are any.

3. If it happens that two young people have contracted marriage by their own action, through folly or recklessness, let them be punished and chastened and such a marriage be dissolved at the request of those who have charge of them.

4. If it is found that there has been some deception or that anyone, man or woman, has induced them to do this, let the punishment be three days on bread and water and to beg mercy before the court of those who are affected.

5. Let the witnesses who were involved in making such a marriage also be punished with prison for one day on bread and water.

6. Let no one make clandestine promises, conditionally or otherwise, between young people who have not yet been married, but let there be at least two witnesses; otherwise the whole [secret engagement] shall be void.

7. Where children marry without their father's or mother's permission at the age permitted above and it is established by the court that they have done this lawfully because of the negligence or excessive strictness of their fathers, let the fathers be required to grant them a dowry or provide them such a share or position as [they would have given] if they had consented to it.[44]

Sunday or working days, provided that this is at the beginning of the sermon. And as for refraining from this, it would be proper to refrain only on the day when communion is celebrated, in honor of the sacrament. Concerning differences in matrimonial cases, because this is not a spiritual matter but rather concerns politics, it will remain under the Council. Nevertheless we have decided to leave to the Consistory the duty of hearing the parties in order to report their opinion to the Council, which will base its judgment on this. And let proper ordinances be drafted to be followed henceforward." CO 10/1:105.

40. The 1545 draft has twenty-four for a son and twenty for a daughter.

41. The 1561 draft inserts ". . . and this has been established by the Consistory, after it has summoned the said fathers and exhorted them to do their duty. . . ."

42. Calvin had glossed the 1545 draft with: "However, if the father claims undue influence or prejudice, whatever promise there may be, one shall proceed no farther until it is known whence it comes."

43. The 1545 draft adds "closest and most important."

44. Calvin glossed the 1545 draft with "according to the laws of the city." The 1561 draft adds: "at the command and with the knowledge of the Small Council, after getting the opinions and statements of the relatives, and having regard for the circumstances and character of the persons and their goods."

8. Let no father compel his children to such a marriage as seems good to him except with their goodwill and consent, but let him or her who does not want to accept the partner his father wants to give be excused, always preserving modesty and respect, without the father imposing any punishment for such a refusal. The same shall be observed for those under guardianship.

9. Fathers or guardians shall not have marriages contracted for their children or wards until they have reached an age to confirm them. Nevertheless, if it happens that a child, having refused to marry according to the will of his father, thereafter chooses a marriage that is not so much to his profit and advantage, because of such rebellion or defiance the father shall not be required to give him anything during his [the father's] lifetime.

Those Persons Who May Marry without Permission

10. Men or women, who have already been married once, although they still have fathers living, nevertheless shall be at liberty to marry provided they are of the aforesaid age, that is twenty years for a son and eighteen for a daughter,[45] and that they have been emancipated, that is they have left their father's house and established a separate household: although it would be more fitting for them to let themselves always be governed by the advice of their fathers.

11. Let all promises of marriage be made honorably and in the fear of God and not in dissoluteness or through reckless frivolity, as by merely offering a glass to drink together without previously having agreed in sober discussion, and let those who do otherwise be punished. But at the request of one of the parties, who claims to have been taken by surprise, let the marriage be dissolved.

12. If anyone takes another to court, alleging a promise of marriage, unless there are two respectable witnesses of good repute, let an oath be administered to the defendant, and on his denying the charge let him be absolved.

For What Reasons a Promise May Be Withdrawn

[13.][46] Once it is established that a promise has been made between capable persons, the marriage shall not be dissolved except in [two] cases,[47] that is

---

45. These are the ages given in the 1545 draft, but Calvin's gloss had changed them to twenty-four and twenty.

46. Following statutory conventions of the day, the 1545 draft had numbered the first nine paragraphs then inexplicably stopped in mid-section. The 1546 draft numbered the first 12 paragraphs, and then stopped. Numbers 13 and following are inserted herein at the heads of succeeding paragraphs for easier reference.

47. Following the 1545 draft, the 1546 draft says "three" exceptions, but discusses only two in this section; the 1561 draft properly renders this "two exceptions." The 1545 draft had dis-

when it is found by sufficient proof that a girl who was taken for a virgin is not one, or if one of the parties has a contagious and incurable bodily disease.

[14.] Failure to pay a dowry or money or provide an outfit shall not prevent the marriage from coming into full effect, since these are only accessory.

Let Promises Be Made Simply[48]

[15.] Although in discussing or arranging a marriage it is lawful to add conditions or reserve someone's consent, nevertheless when it comes to making the promise let it be pure and simple, and let a statement made conditionally not be regarded as a promise of marriage.

On the Term for Completing the Marriage after the Promise Is Made

[16.] After the promise is made, let the marriage not be delayed for more than six weeks; otherwise let the parties be called to the Consistory to be admonished. If they do not obey, let them be remanded before the Council to be compelled to celebrate it.

[17.] If there is any opposition [to the marriage], let the minister send the opponent before the Consistory on the earliest day and admonish him to have the accused party cited. However, let no one be received in opposition who is not of this city or otherwise known or accompanied by someone who knows him, to prevent others from causing blame or injury to some respectable girl, or the opposite.[49]

[18.] If the opponent does not appear on the day he has been summoned, let the banns and the marriage proceed as if no impediment had arisen.

[19.] To avoid all the frauds that are committed in these matters, let no foreigner coming from a distant country be admitted to marriage unless he has good and certain testimony, either by letters or by respectable people, worthy of faith, that he has not been married elsewhere, and also of his good and respectable behavior; and let the same be observed with respect to girls and women.

---

cussed briefly a third exception in this paragraph as well — the case of a man who, after giving his engagement promise, left the city. The 1546 draft deals with deserted engagements at greater length in paragraphs 46-50 below.

48. Hereafter, the 1546 draft deviates from the order of the 1545 text, though it tracks most of its language.

49. Although the text is not clear, it probably means, "and also to prevent an unknown girl from causing injury to some respectable young man."

On Banns and Matters Depending on Them

[20.] Let the banns be published for three Sundays in the church before the wedding is held, the signature of the first syndic being obtained beforehand to attest that the parties are known; nevertheless the wedding may be held on the third publication. And if one of the parties is from another parish, let there also be an affidavit from that place.

[21.] During the engagement the parties shall not live together as man and wife until the marriage has been blessed in the church after the custom of Christians. If any are found who have done the contrary, let them be punished by prison for three days on bread and water and be called to the Consistory to be admonished for their fault.

On the Celebration of the Marriage

[22.] When it is time for the parties to be married, let them come modestly to the church without drummers or fiddlers, preserving the order and gravity proper to Christians, and do this before the end of the tolling of the bell, so that the blessing of the marriage may take place before the sermon. If they are negligent and come too late, let the marriage be postponed.

[23.] It is permissible to celebrate marriages every day, that is on working days at the sermon that seems best to the parties, on Sunday at the sermon at dawn or at three in the afternoon, except on the days when communion is celebrated, so that then there may be no distractions and everyone may be better disposed to receive the sacrament.

On the Cohabitation of the Husband with His Wife

[24.] Let the husband have his wife with him and let them live in one house, maintaining a common household. If it happens that one withdraws from the other to live apart, let them be summoned to be admonished and be compelled to return to each other.

On the Degrees of Consanguinity That Prevent Marriage

[25.] In a direct line, that is of father with daughter or mother with son or all other descendants in order, no marriage may be contracted, since this contravenes natural decency and is forbidden both by the law of God and by the civil law.

[26.] Likewise of uncle with [niece] or great-[niece],[50] of aunt with

---

50. The 1546 draft referred mistakenly to "nephew or great-nephew" (*neveu ou arrière-*

nephew or great-nephew and so on, because the uncle represents the father and the aunt is in the place of the mother.

[27.] Also between brother and sister, whether of [the same] father and mother or of one of these.

[28.] In the other degrees, although marriage is not forbidden either by the law of God or the Roman civil law, nevertheless to avoid scandal, because for a long time this has not been the custom, and from fear that the Word of God may be blasphemed by the ignorant, a cousin-german may not contract marriage with his cousin-german until, with the passing of time, it is otherwise decided by us. To the other degrees let there be no impediment.

On the Degrees of Affinity

[29.] Let no man take to wife the widow of his son, or of the son of his son, and let no woman take the husband of her daughter or of the daughter of her daughter, nor of those following traced down in a direct line.

[30.] Let no one take the daughter of his wife or the daughter descending from her, and so on.

[31.] A woman also may not take the son of her husband or the son of his son, and so on.

[32.] Likewise let no one take the widow of his nephew or of his great-nephew, and also let no woman take the husband of her niece or great-niece.

[33.] Let no one take the widow of his brother, and no woman may take the one who was her sister's husband.

[34.] The one who has committed adultery with the wife of another, when it has come to be known, may not take her in marriage because of the scandal and dangers this entails.

[Cruelty and Abuse]

[35.] If a husband does not live in peace with his wife, but they have conflicts and quarrels with each other, let them be summoned to the Consistory to be admonished to live in good concord and unity and each be remonstrated with for his faults according to the needs of the case.

[36.] If it is known that a husband mistreats his wife, beating and tormenting her, or that he threatens to do her an injury and is known to be a man of uncontrolled anger, let him be sent before the Council to be expressly forbidden to beat her, under pain of certain punishment.

---

neveu), rather than niece or grand-niece *(nièce ou arrière-nièce)*, as in paragraph 32 below. The 1561 draft corrects this.

For What Reasons a Marriage Should Be Declared Void [and Annulled]

[37.] If it happens that a woman complains that the one who has taken her in marriage is physically maimed and not able to have the company of a woman, and this is found true by confession or examination, let the marriage be declared void, the woman be declared free, and the man be forbidden to defraud any woman again.[51]

[38.] Likewise if the man complains of not being able to have the company of his wife because of some defect in her body and she does not want to allow it to be cured, after the truth of the fact is established let the marriage be declared void.

For What Reasons a Marriage May Be Dissolved [by Divorce]

[39.] If a husband accuses his wife of adultery and proves her to be such by sufficient testimony or evidence and asks to be separated by divorce, let it be granted, and by this action let him have power to marry [another] when it seems good to him, although one may exhort him to pardon his wife. But let no pressure be brought to compel him [to divorce or to reconcile] against his will.

[40.] Formerly the rights of the wife were not equal to those of the husband in cases of divorce. But, according to the testimony of the apostle, the obligation is mutual and reciprocal with respect to cohabitation of the bed and in this the wife is not more subject to the husband than the husband to the wife. Thus, if a man is convicted of adultery and the wife asks to be separated from him, let it also be granted to her, unless by strong admonitions they can be reconciled with each other. But they are not eligible to ask for divorce in cases where the wife fell into adultery through the evident fault of the husband or the husband through the fault of the wife, so that both are culpable, or if it is established that some fraud has been practiced to achieve a divorce.

[41.] If a man goes on a journey to deal in merchandise or otherwise without fraud or alienation from his wife, and he does not return for a long time and it is not known what has happened to him, so that by reasonable conjecture he is presumed dead, nevertheless let his wife not be permitted to remarry until after a term of ten years has passed since the day of his departure, unless there is certain testimony of his death: which being received, one may give her permission. This permission [to remarry] after ten years, however, extends only to the point that if one suspects either from reports or evi-

---

51. The 1545 draft adds: "Nevertheless, in order to avoid any collusion or deceitful conspiracy, let diligent inquiry be made into all the circumstances until the case is duly verified."

dence that the man is held prisoner or is hindered by some other obstacle, then let the wife remain in widowhood.

[42.] If a man through debauchery or some evil feeling goes away and abandons his place of residence, let his wife make diligent inquiry to learn where he has gone. Having learned where he is, let her come ask for official letters so she can summon him or otherwise compel him to do his duty, or at least notify him that he must return to his household under penalty of being proceeded against in his absence. If this is done and there is no way of compelling him to return, let one not fail to proceed as he was warned, that is, to proclaim him [a deserter] in the church for three Sundays, two weeks apart, so that the term is six weeks. Let the same be done three times in the Lieutenant's court, and let two or three of his closest friends, or relatives if he has them, be notified of this. If he does not appear, let his wife come to the next Consistory [meeting] to ask for a separation, and let it be granted to her, sending her before the Council [for them] to make a judicial decision about it. And let the one who has been so rebellious be banished forever. If he appears, let them be reconciled[52] in good accord and in the fear of God.

[43.] If any man makes a habit of thus abandoning his wife to wander about the country, the second time let him be punished by imprisonment [on] bread and water, and let him be commanded with strong threats not to do so any more. The third time let greater rigor be employed against him, and if there is no improvement, let one provide that the wife is no longer bound to such a man, who gives her neither faith nor companionship.

[44.] If a man, being debauched as aforesaid, has abandoned his wife without his wife having given him occasion or having been to blame, and this is duly established by the testimony of the neighbors and friends, and the wife comes to complain, asking for a remedy, let her be admonished to make diligent inquiry to find out what has become of him, and let his closest relatives and friends, if he has any, be summoned to get news from them. However, let the wife wait till the end of a year to see whether she cannot learn where he is, commending herself to God. At the end of the year, she may come to the Consistory, and if it is known that she needs to marry, after exhorting her let her be remanded to the Council to be asked on oath whether she knows where he has gone, and let the same be done to his closest relatives and friends. After this, proceed to the aforementioned proclamations to give the woman liberty to remarry. If the absent [husband] returns afterwards, let him be punished as one thinks reasonable.

[45.] If a wife departs from her husband and goes to another place and the husband comes to ask to be separated from her and set at liberty to remarry, let it

---

52. The 1545 draft inserts here, "with each other, commanding them to establish a common household."

be determined whether she is in a place from which she can be summoned or where she can at least be notified that she must appear to respond to her husband's request, and let the husband be aided with letters and other means to do this. If this is done, let one make such proclamations as were described above, having first summoned her closest relatives or friends to admonish them to make her return if they can. If she appears within the term and her husband refuses [to take her][53] because of the suspicion he has that she has mismanaged her body and because it is too scandalous a thing for a wife thus to abandon her husband, let one try to reunite them, exhorting the husband to pardon her fault. Nevertheless, if he persists in making an issue of this, let inquiry be made in the place where she was as to what people she associated with and how she behaved. If no certain evidence or proof is found to convict her of having breached marital faith, let the husband be compelled to be reconciled with her. If she is charged with a very strong presumption of having fornicated, as by having associated with bad and suspect company and not having maintained the proper behavior of a respectable woman, let the husband's request be heard and he be granted what reason justifies. If she does not appear during the term, let the same procedure be followed against her as against the husband in a similar situation.[54]

[Desertion of Fiancés or Fiancées]

[46.] If a man,[55] after having sworn faith [that is, become engaged] to a girl or woman, goes to another country, and the girl or woman comes to make a complaint about this, asking to be delivered from her promise because of the other's disloyalty, let inquiry be made whether he did this for an honorable reason and with the knowledge of his fiancée, or instead through debauchery and because he does not wish to complete the marriage. If it is found that he has no apparent reason [for his departure] and that he has done it from bad motives, let one inquire where he has gone, and if possible let him be notified that he must return by a certain day to carry out the duty he has promised.

[47.] If he does not appear, having been warned, let it be proclaimed for three Sundays in the church that he must appear, such that there is a gap of [two weeks][56] between two proclamations and thus that the whole term is six

53. The 1545 draft adds "to take her."

54. The 1545 draft adds this sentence: "If there are relatives or friends in the city who have aided in thus removing a woman from it, and this is clearly established, let them be summoned and advised to bring her back from the place so that the case may be investigated in her presence."

55. This paragraph and the four following were not included in the 1545 draft. They cover what the 1545 draft had called the "third exception" mentioned above in paragraph 13.

56. Following the 1561 draft that speaks of *"quinze jours,"* rather than the 1546 draft that says literally "always" *(toujours).*

weeks. If he does not appear within the term, let the girl or woman be declared free and the man banished for disloyalty. If he appears, let him be compelled to celebrate the marriage the first day it can be done. If it is not known where he has gone and the girl or woman, along with his closest friends, swear they do not know [his whereabouts], let the same proclamations be made as if he had been notified, with the object of freeing her [from the engagement].

[48.] If he had some good reason and also informed his fiancée, let the girl or woman wait for the space of a year before proceeding against him in his absence, and meanwhile let the girl herself and her friends make diligent efforts to induce him to return.[57] If after a year has passed he does not return, then let the proclamations be made in the manner described above.

[49.] Let the same course be observed against a girl or woman, except that the [prospective] husband[58] shall not be required to wait a year even if she departed with his knowledge and consent, unless he gave her permission to make a journey that requires such a long absence.

[50.] If a girl duly bound by a promise is fraudulently transported outside the territory [of Geneva] in order not to complete the marriage, let one inquire whether there is anyone in the city who has aided in this so he may be compelled to make her return, under whatever penalty may be decided: or if she has guardians or trustees, let them likewise be enjoined to make her come back if they can.

[Collusion in Divorce Cases]

[51.] If a man, after his wife has abandoned him, makes no complaint but remains silent, or a wife likewise abandoned by her husband dissimulates without saying a word about it, and this comes to be known, let the Consistory make them appear to find out how the case stands. This will prevent all scandals, since there may be collusion,[59] which is not to be tolerated, or even something much worse. And having found out the facts, let one deal with it according to the means available, so that there may be no voluntary divorces, that is at the pleasure of the parties without the authority of the law. And let married parties not be permitted to live apart from each other. Nevertheless, at the request of the husband let the wife be compelled to follow him if he wishes to change his habitation or is compelled to it by necessity, provided that he is not a

---

57. Rendering the phrase *"de l'induire à se retirer,"* which means literally "to induce him to withdraw," but the context makes it clear that *retirer* here means to withdraw from his public pursuit, and to "return" home.

58. An engaged man was often referred to literally as a "husband" *(mari)*.

59. Reading "collision" in the original as "collusion"; this was corrected in the 1561 draft.

debauched man who is leading her astray and into an unknown country, but that it is a reasonable country where he wants to make his residence in a decent place to live as a respectable man and keep a proper household.

[Jurisdiction Over Matrimonial Cases]

[52.] Let all matrimonial cases concerning personal relations, not property, be handled in the first instance in the Consistory, and there, if a friendly settlement can be reached, let it be made in the name of God. If it is necessary to pronounce a judicial sentence, let the parties be remanded to the Council with a statement of the decision of the Consistory, to give the definitive sentence about it.

CHAPTER 2

The New Alliance of Church and State

The Reformation Work of the
Genevan Council and Consistory

The most important institutions charged with implementing the 1546 Marriage Ordinance and other reformation measures on sex, marriage, and family in Calvin's Geneva were the Small Council and the Consistory. To understand how they operated, we need first to sketch how the entire government of Geneva was organized after the ejection of the prince-bishop and the creation of a Protestant regime. We shall then summarize the structure and procedures of the Small Council and the Consistory in Reformation Geneva, and profile the cases on sex, marriage, and family that they adjudicated.

Council and Consistory

The Protestant Reformation in Geneva began as a revolution in government, law, and religion.[1] A prince-bishop who had been sovereign in both the political and religious realms was forced to leave. So were most of the members of his entourage, including a number of canon lawyers who staffed the bishop's court — called the court of the *official* — that was responsible, among other things, for resolving problems involving marriage and family throughout the diocese. So was an officer called the *vidomne* who superintended the administration of

---

1. Robert M. Kingdon, "The Protestant Reformation as Revolution: The Case of Geneva," *Journal of the Historical Society* 1 (2001): 101; Robert M. Kingdon, "Was the Protestant Reformation a Revolution? The Case of Geneva," in *Transition and Revolution: Problems and Issues of European Renaissance and Reformation History*, ed. Robert M. Kingdon (Minneapolis, 1974), p. 53.

justice, arresting people and enforcing law between sundown and sunrise (during daylight hours this fell to officers of the commune), and arranging for punishment of those found guilty. The *vidomne* had actually been chosen by the government of the duke of Savoy, which worked in close collaboration with the bishop in maintaining order within and around Geneva.

The government that remained after the expulsion of the bishop's court and officials was a hierarchy of councils and the committees dependent on those councils. These councils had been given some powers by earlier bishops to govern the city internally, to maintain public order and control sexual and public morals and, from 1364 on, to judge criminal cases.[2] The most important summary of those earlier grants of power was a document called the *Franchises*, signed by Bishop Adhémar Fabri in 1387.[3] After 1536, the city councils had to fill the vacuum created by the expulsion of the bishop and his entourage, which they accomplished by realigning the power and procedures of some of the councils as well as creating the Consistory.

At the base of the hierarchy of councils in Reformation Geneva was the General Council. In theory, it consisted of all the adult male residents of the community over the age of twenty. In practice, only two privileged groups of residents, the citizens and the bourgeois, were active in this government. These were men who possessed substantial property and practiced honorable professions. They held special legal privileges that distinguished them from mere inhabitants. Citizens had to have been born in the city as members of bourgeois families. Bourgeois could gain that title by formal application, swearing an oath of allegiance to the city, and payment of a fee that varied considerably in size, no doubt reflecting the resources of the applicant. This payment of money could be waived if the applicant was in a position to make contributions to the operation of Genevan institutions, if, for example, he was expected to become a minister or a jurisconsult. The General Council met twice a year to elect officers of the government for the coming year and supervise the elections of the members of the smaller Councils. It also met on occasion to ratify particularly important laws, like the Reformation Ordinance of 1536, pledging the city to live according to evangelical law and abandon Catholic religious practices, and the Ecclesiastical Ordinances of 1541, creating a structure for the Reformed Church.

The Council of Two Hundred was a smaller body, created early in the sixteenth century in imitation of a similar body in Bern. Bern, which became Protestant before Geneva, adopting a Zwinglian variety of the new faith, had

2. See the numerous statutes on sexual morals passed by the Genevan Councils from 1481-1536 in SD, vol. 2, items 290, 294, 297, 300, 302, 345, 373, 398, 405, 420, 447, 485, 496, 510, 524, 562, 580.

3. SD, vol. 1, item 102.

been a crucial ally in the process by which Geneva came under the Reformed banner. Bern had sent Farel into Geneva, providing him with financial support, in the effort to chase out the bishop and make Geneva a Protestant city. And Bernese armies had conquered areas around Geneva, creating a buffer zone against Savoyard attempts to reconquer the city and restore the bishop and Catholicism. Even before these steps had been taken, the Genevans had decided to block Savoyard maneuvering and imitate Bern in creating this new Council that had proved useful to its ally. The Two Hundred met occasionally, at the call of the Small Council, to handle special cases. It was often asked to ratify laws adopted by the Small Council. It was also authorized to handle appeals from people convicted of crimes by the Small Council who felt that its sentence had been too harsh, thus providing a useful safety valve in a system accustomed to making very rapid and arbitrary judgments.

The Council of Sixty was an older institution, which had earlier been a Council of Fifty. It also met at the call of the Small Council, to handle special cases. Most of these cases involved relations with foreign governments, especially Bern, France, and Savoy. The members of the Council of Sixty were also members of the Council of Two Hundred.

The Small Council was the real executive of this government, and its responsibilities were defined in some detail in the 1543 Ordinances on Offices and Officers that Calvin helped draft (**Doc. 2-1**). The Small Council was made up of twenty-five citizens. Simple bourgeois could be members of the other councils, but they could not be members of this body. It met at least three times a week. Its presiding officers were four men called syndics, arranged in order of seniority in government service. They represented the government in announcements to the general public and often, but not invariably, in negotiations with foreign powers. They also supervised the criminal justice system, including the prosecution and punishment of sex crimes. One of the syndics also signed the banns of marriage of a newly engaged couple, which banns would be pronounced in the local church. New syndics were elected annually for a term of only one year from among members of the Small Council. The remaining members of the Small Council were normally reelected every year. Failure to reelect a man to this body could be a sign of disgrace and sometimes revealed a significant shift in local politics. Syndics were often elected again after a period of four years or more, but could not serve consecutive terms.

A number of officers and standing committees reported to the Small Council, whose members were also chosen in the annual elections. These officers and committees had responsibilities such as maintaining the city's accounts, managing the city's grain supply, arranging for the watch that guarded the city's walls, and handling legal cases in both civil and criminal arenas. One important such officer was the *lieutenant*, who assumed many of the powers traditionally exercised by the bishop's *vidomne*.[4] The court of the lieutenant rendered summary justice, with no written record and no right of appeal, for small civil cases involving sums of five florins or less. Larger civil cases were resolved in formal trials with lawyers, written records, and the right of appeal to a special court of appeals appointed annually by the Small Council. Minor criminal infractions were handled directly in the streets by the lieutenant or officers of the Small Council. Many of these infractions we would not consider criminal, such as being outside after nine at night without a candle, or failing to attend a sermon. In these cases the officers would order people to pay a small fine on the spot, of which the officers took a cut, based on a variety of edicts issued over the years by the Council. In cases of more important criminal offenses or when an individual had repeatedly committed minor infractions, there would be formal legal proceedings supervised by the lieutenant in consultation with the Small Council. The lieutenant would oversee the gathering of evidence and would conduct interrogations with members of the Council present. The lieutenant, however, would play no role in rendering a verdict or imposing a sentence in these criminal cases. That was left to the syndics, the city's chief executives, in consultation with a quorum of the Small Council.

Two of the committees that reported to the Small Council were semi-religious in character. One was the board of procurators for the General Hospital. It was responsible for supervising the administration of charity throughout the city, primarily by maintaining a hospital, an all-purpose institution housing orphans, cripples, and others so handicapped they needed assistance, and also providing weekly rations of bread to selected poor families and widows. The city created this body before Calvin's arrival in the city, but he gave it his blessing in the 1541 Ecclesiastical Ordinances, and called its members "deacons." He felt they were like the deacons described in the New Testament who took the place of the apostles in serving the faithful at tables.[5]

The other semi-religious committee to work with the Small Council was the Consistory. Calvin created this institution in his 1541 Ecclesiastical Ordinances (**Doc. 2-2**). It was intended to secure Christian "discipline," to see to it that everyone in Geneva not only accepted true Christian belief but tried to live in a truly Christian manner. The Ecclesiastical Ordinances set high moral standards for the religious officials who served on the Consistory. It also required systematic catechesis and education of children under the supervision of the

4. His role was redefined in the Edict of the Lieutenant (Nov. 11, 1542), SD, vol. 2, item 803, that Calvin helped to draft.

5. Jeannine Olson, *Calvin and Social Welfare: Deacons and the* Bourse Française (Selingsgrove, PA, 1989); Elsie Anne McKee, *John Calvin on the Diaconate and Liturgical Almsgiving* (Geneva, 1984).

company of pastors. Calvin had demanded the creation of the Consistory and had made it clear that he would not have returned to the city in 1541 without the creation of an institution of this character.

The Consistory was made up of about two dozen men. Its presiding officer was one of the four syndics of the year. Its members sat on two benches. On one sat all the ordained pastors of the city and occasionally those from the villages attached to it, headed by Calvin as their moderator. On the other bench sat twelve lay commissioners, called "elders" by Calvin, who were elected for this duty in the February elections every year. Both deacons and elders were elected, as were members of most of the other standing committees, from slates prepared by the outgoing Small Council. For these two particular bodies, however, the ministers were supposed to be consulted in preparing the slates. The elders represented the three governing Councils: two from the Small Council and ten from the Council of Two Hundred, with four of those ten also members of the Council of Sixty. The Consistory also had two additional officers: a secretary, always a registered notary, who took minutes of each of its meetings, and an *officier* or summoner, who faced the often difficult task of bringing before the Consistory people it wanted to question. The elders, the secretary, and the summoner received small sums of money for attending meetings of the Consistory. The Consistory met once a week, on Thursdays, in sessions that often stretched out for several hours.

Cases came before the Consistory in a variety of ways. Sometimes an individual took the initiative. A man might report that his wife was cheating on him, and ask for a divorce with permission to remarry. A woman might report that her husband was beating her so badly that she feared for her life, and ask for a separation. More often cases began on the initiative of a government official who was generally not identified in the Consistory record. Occasionally they came from a minister or an elder, from the Consistory or officials of another city, or from one of the *dizainiers* or neighborhood wardens, each responsible for keeping track of his neighborhood and recruiting people from within it to take turns in guarding the city walls. Residents from the villages dependent on Geneva would often appear in groups with the castellan who had been placed in charge of their village by the city government.

Each person brought before the Consistory was identified, informed of the reason he or she had been summoned, asked to reply, and then questioned by members of the Consistory under the direction of the syndic. Individuals were not allowed to bring a lawyer or adviser, but had to handle questions entirely on their own. Sometimes they submitted affidavits, petitions, contracts, certificates, or other documents for the Consistory's review. The Consistory often questioned the parties about these documents, and summoned witnesses to validate their authenticity. The Consistory also had wide subpoena power to compel witnesses to appear. The Consistory would then reach a decision. The most common decision, especially in the early years of the Reformation, was simply to administer a scolding, an "admonition" or a "remonstrance," typically administered by a minister, and often Calvin himself. Although Calvin did not preside over these meetings, and had no formal position setting him apart from other Consistory members, the others tended to defer to him, to acknowledge his superior knowledge of both religion and the law.

In cases involving several people, the Consistory often tried to effect a reconciliation, to resolve a dispute within a family, among neighbors, in a business establishment. In these cases it acted more as a compulsory counseling or mediating service than as a court. In hearing a divorce petition, for example, the Consistory usually tried to bring a couple back together again rather than immediately granting the petition. Ceremonies of reconciliation were often staged before the Consistory, although if the problem had achieved general notoriety, a public ceremony of reconciliation might be held in a parish church, accompanying a regular service of worship. The Consistory could also order individuals to perform a "public reparation." People so sentenced had to appear at a main Sunday sermon, get down on their knees, confess the errors of their ways, and beg for forgiveness. This punishment was initially used to punish women convicted of adultery who were visibly pregnant and for that reason could not be sent to jail. Later it came to be applied most frequently to people who, while living in a Catholic area, had renounced their faith in order to avoid punishment.[6]

If the Consistory found someone guilty of particularly offensive behavior or particularly stubborn in resisting correction, it could ban the accused sinner from communion in the next one of the four communion services offered to the entire population every year. The ban from communion was a far more serious punishment then than it is now. People saw it as preventing them from receiving a sacrament that was a sign of God's grace and formerly, in Catholic times, a necessity for salvation. It was also a social humiliation that could interrupt normal social routines and business. Banned sinners could not act as godparents, an important honor, or marry, or be assured of poor relief and access to the hospital.[7]

If individuals made no attempt to rehabilitate themselves and be readmitted to communion, the 1541 Ecclesiastical Ordinances empowered the Consistory to have them "separated from the church and denounced to the Council." This was, in effect, the power of excommunication, though it was rarely called

6. Lambert, pp. 264ff.

7. Lambert, pp. 255-63; Christian Grosse, "Les rituels de la cène: une anthropologie historique de culte eucharistique réformé à Genève (XVI-XVII siècles)" (Diss., Geneva, 2001), pp. 47ff.

such in the 1540s and even more rarely used. The use of the term, let alone the practice, of excommunication by the Geneva Consistory was particularly controversial. It reminded too many Genevans of the previous Catholic authorities who had often used excommunication in a variety of ways that were sometimes not even religious — to enforce the payment of debts, for example. Most early Protestant regimes, including those created by Lutherans, Zwinglians, and Anglicans, refused to give their churches a general power of excommunication, only a power of the ban from communion. In Geneva a group of local leaders called "the Children of Geneva" strenuously resisted the idea that the church should reserve to itself the power to excommunicate. They insisted they should at least be able to appeal over the heads of the Consistory to the Small Council to revise or lift a sentence of excommunication. In a number of celebrated cases, Calvin and the other ministers flatly refused to permit an appeal from a Consistory decision. As ministers they would simply not offer communion to an excommunicated sinner. Tension over this issue became more and more intense until it provoked riots in 1555. Those sympathetic to Calvin and the other ministers ultimately prevailed. Others involved in the riots were brutally punished, all of them removed from political offices, several of them put to death, many more banished from the city or sentenced to death in abstentia.

A crucial new weapon won in this political battle was the Consistory's unequivocal power to enforce its spiritual discipline by using either the ban (temporary preclusion from communion) or excommunication (exclusion from the church altogether, which often also entailed banishment from the city as well). An important statute of 1560 confirmed the victory by urging the use of admonition and simple bans in routine cases, and the use of excommunication in serious cases.[8] The ban became a regular tool of discipline thereafter, but excommunication remained rare. Between 1560 and 1564 the Consistory banned nearly forty persons for every one it excommunicated.[9]

The Consistory had no further spiritual powers — and no formal legal power. If it decided that a case needed further investigation and further punishment, it had to refer it to the Small Council. In this respect, the Consistory often acted as a kind of preliminary hearings court, something like a Grand Jury in Anglo-Saxon practice, not like a court with formal judicial authority. We often find that on the Monday following a Thursday Consistory session, there would be on the Small Council's docket a number of cases referred from the Consistory. On occasion the Small Council dismissed a charge as frivolous. More often, however, it would proceed with its usual methods of investigating a case. If the case seemed minor, it might be handled immediately by the Council. If it

8. SD, vol. 3, item 986.
9. Grosse, pp. 47ff.

seemed serious, the lieutenant might take the accused into custody and place him or her in a municipal prison. This prison had earlier been the palace of the prince-bishop, but now it had been adapted for different purposes. It contained a number of holding cells for people awaiting trial. It also contained a large torture chamber. It did not house any long-term prisoners. Imprisonment for long periods of time was simply not a punishment used in sixteenth-century Geneva. Even people sentenced to life in prison as the result of a criminal trial were usually released within a few months, often paroled to the custody of relatives. Most prison sentences lasted for only a few days.

Following an arrest, the lieutenant and his assistants, called *auditeurs,* arranged for a series of cross examinations of the accused. They drew up a fairly long list of related charges, which the accused had to answer before a panel usually drawn from the Small Council. There would often be several "repetitions" in which the same questions were put to the accused again, sometimes in the presence of a different panel of Council members. This is the legal method called the inquisitorial process. It was commonly used all over Europe at this time.[10] It contrasts with the adversarial process used by courts in the Anglo-American legal tradition, which relies on a formal debate in court between the accused, represented by a lawyer, and the community, represented by a prosecutor. But we should not dismiss the inquisitorial process as an antique barbarism. These people really believed that truth was more likely to emerge if experts questioned someone accused of a crime again and again, from several points of view, involving several different groups of listeners, without the distraction of professional lawyers trying to score points off each other.

If the accused turned out to be stubborn and if the charges were really serious, the authorities were then allowed to administer torture when asking questions. Before that happened, however, a jurisconsult like Germain Colladon was called in to examine the dossier and to decide whether there was probable cause to believe that a crime had been committed and that the crime was serious enough to warrant such extreme methods. It was always preferable to have the accused confess the crime, for only a confession was regarded as really sure evidence that a crime had been committed. A confession extracted under torture, furthermore, could be retracted if the accused subsequently claimed it had been a false confession.

In complicated cases, the Small Council often referred issues back to the Consistory for further fact-finding, investigation of witnesses, or advice on novel questions that were not addressed at all or clearly enough in the statutes.

---

10. John H. Langbein, *Torture and the Law of Proof: Europe and England in the Ancien Régime* (Chicago, 1977); and *Prosecuting Crime in the Renaissance: England, Germany, and France* (Cambridge, MA, 1974).

The Consistory then made recommendations of whether or how to proceed, which the Small Council took under advisement. If an issue was particularly complex or pressing, or if the Consistory decided that the Small Council had not proceeded properly, they would send a representative to the next Council meeting to put their recommendations or press their case. Calvin was the one often tapped to represent the Consistory's interest before the Council in these cases. On occasion, Calvin showed up at the Council's meetings on his own initiative, sometimes to press the Council to enact clearer rules to address an issue heard by the Consistory, sometimes to urge equity in a given case that the Consistory had removed to the Council.

Once a trial dossier had been completed, and the full slate of Consistorial recommendations collected, the Small Council rendered a final judgment. On some minor matters, the Council's judgment was to send the case back to the Consistory to impose spiritual sanctions alone. On most matters that had been referred to them, however, the Council imposed civil and/or criminal orders or sanctions as well. This could be an order for quarrelling couples to post their banns and get married within a designated period of time. Or it could be a declaration that an engagement or marriage was to be annulled because of a proved impediment, or a couple was to be divorced because of the desertion or adultery of one of the parties. Or it could involve the payment of damages, the restitution of property, or the specific performance of the terms of a contract.

When the case involved criminal conduct (as well), the Council wrote out the verdict of guilty and had it read in public by a town crier, or by a syndic if it were a capital case, perhaps before the city hall, perhaps in a town market, perhaps at an execution site. Verdicts in a number of different kinds of cases could be appealed to the Council of Two Hundred. No case could be appealed, however, to a court outside of Geneva. The Reformation had put a definitive halt to appeals to courts of the ducal government, to the emperor, or to papal courts in Rome. Criminal punishments could involve ceremonies of public shaming, monetary fines, mutilation, banishment, short terms in prison on "bread and water," and, to a degree we would find appalling, capital punishment by a town executioner hired by the city for the purpose. There were a number of rather gruesome ways in which capital punishment was administered. Traitors might be beheaded, thieves hanged, notorious adulteresses drowned, heretics or witches burned. Every city of the period maintained an execution ground, usually with several rotting corpses of executed criminals on display, to let visitors know that this community maintained law and order. Geneva's main execution ground was on the hill of Champel, a short distance from the city walls.

The Consistory was a remarkably intrusive institution. Six to seven percent of the entire adult population was called before it every year. The Consistory was also a remarkably effective institution. The combination of scoldings, public reparations, bans, excommunications, and referrals to the legal system seems to have worked. Visitors like John Knox remarked that while they had found true doctrine rightly preached in other communities, they had never before found Christian life so rightly lived as in Geneva. If people did not like this lifestyle or the Consistory's presence or pressure, they could always leave Geneva. That was actually fairly easy. The geographic area controlled by the Genevan government was not large — the city itself, and a fairly small number of villages that had belonged personally to the bishop or other ecclesiastical and civic authorities before the Reformation. It was much smaller than the pre-Reformation diocese of Geneva or the modern canton of Geneva. There remained villages within easy walking distance beyond Geneva's jurisdiction, controlled either by Protestant Bern or by Catholic France or Savoy.[11]

Patterns of Consistory Cases

The Consistory did not limit itself to sex, marriage, and family life. In its early years, it spent a good deal of time trying to root out surviving Catholic religious practices. In later years it spent some time in trying to root out sharp business practices and disrespect for the leaders of government and church. But a clear majority of the Consistory's cases involved sexual and marital issues.

The Consistory handled many cases of sexual deviation, which before the Reformation had been handled by city courts. Minor sexual deviations could be resolved by admonition or reparation, or referred to the Small Council for minor punishment. The normal punishment for premarital fornication, for example, was a prison sentence of three to six days on bread and water. Major sexual deviations such as adultery or prostitution normally came to the Small Council for a full investigation and trial. Cases of notorious and repeated adultery could be punished (after 1560) with death sentences. So could rape, especially of children, and bestiality or sodomy. These more serious sexual crimes, however, rarely passed before the Consistory. They almost always went directly to the Small Council for criminal prosecution.[12]

The Consistory also handled a good many cases involving marital formation, maintenance, and dissolution, cases which before the Reformation had been handled by the court of the bishop's *official*. Many of these cases were

11. For fuller description of how these institutions operated in one kind of marital case, see Kingdon, AD, chap. 1. Other books in English that describe aspects of this government are William Monter's *Calvin's Geneva* (New York, 1967); and his *Studies in Genevan Government (1536-1605)* (Geneva, 1964). See also Naphy, Calvin.

12. Naphy, Sex Crimes.

breach of promise cases, in which one party alleged and the other denied a promise of marriage. That would often require a hearing in which witnesses would be summoned, very often including the parents of the presumptive couple, to find out what had really happened. Some cases also involved pleas to dissolve an engagement or marriage. Before the Reformation a plea of that kind could lead to an annulment or to a permanent separation but never to a divorce in the modern sense. With the Reformation, divorce could and did occur, although fairly rarely, with a subsequent right to remarry, at least for the innocent party. Both the Consistory and the Small Council, however, tried first to reconcile the parties. A great deal of the Consistory's time, indeed, was involved in trying to secure reconciliations, between married couples, between parents and estranged children, among neighbors, among business partners.

In general, the Consistory and the Council tried to maintain a single style of domestic life for everyone in Geneva, usually the style of a family group consisting of a husband and wife, dependent children, and almost always young servants, living together in harmony in a single household. Sometimes it would be extended by adding adult relatives. Several alternative styles of life were actively discouraged. Most obviously, the lifestyle of celibacy, so highly valued for Catholic clerics and monastics, was repudiated. It was felt to be unnatural, even impossible for most people. Church leaders were expected to marry and raise families. Calvin himself had married while in Strasbourg. Soon after arriving in Geneva, he and his wife had a son. The son died within weeks, however, and the wife a few years later. Calvin spent most of his career as a widower, living in a household with his younger brother Antoine, managed by his brother's wife. When Antoine's first wife was suspected of sexual misbehavior, she was on the first charge pardoned, then on a later charge convicted, divorced from her husband and exiled. Antoine soon married a second wife, who then took over management of the household. Theodore Beza, Calvin's successor, had married even before he arrived in Geneva, but never had children. When his first wife died, he married again, this time to a widow with a daughter he helped support.[13] Laymen were similarly expected to marry and establish families. We find cases in which the Consistory would summon a single man, usually one who had gotten into trouble for fornication, and ask him why he wasn't married. Another style of life that was repudiated was promiscuity. Before the Reformation, promiscuity was regarded as inevitable, a necessary evil. Geneva, like most cities of the period, permitted prostitution. It regulated prostitution closely, requiring prostitutes to organize and elect one of their number as "queen" to represent them before the government. They had to live in a defined area of town, sometimes owned by the city, and to wear costumes that would distinguish

13. Kingdon, AD, pp. 71-97.

them from honorable housewives. They were told to stay away from teenage boys and limit solicitation in the public baths, where they found most of their clients, to certain days and hours. The work of regulating prostitution was handled by the city government. The prince-bishop and his staff wanted no part of this dirty business. Prostitution was regarded as a necessary service, especially for the visiting merchants who came to the large fairs twice a year for which the city had been famous in the fourteenth and fifteenth centuries. After the Reformation, prostitution was abolished. A few professional prostitutes were treated fairly gently, told to move on to another community, even offered small sums of money to cover their travel expenses. Married women who played the prostitute, however, were treated very harshly. After 1560, a number of them were put to death by drowning. Even women forgiven by their husbands could be treated harshly. This was a lifestyle Geneva wanted to eradicate completely.

We can get a good sense of the volume of cases on sex, marriage, and family life, and of the patterns of litigation in the Consistory by contrasting the full case records from our three sample years of 1546, 1552, and 1557. These three sample years, as we saw in the Introduction, were key moments in the Reformation in Geneva. 1546 was the year the Marriage Ordinance was first available to the Consistory, and they began implementing its provisions. 1552 was a year when the Consistory and Calvin's leadership of the Reformation altogether were being actively challenged, and Geneva was changing dramatically with the influx of French immigrants. 1557 was a year when Calvin and his allies were at the height of their power, having gained among other things the power of excommunication.

Tables 1-3 summarize the main categories of cases and their disposition by the Consistory in these three sample years. The classifications are largely self-evident, but a word about a few of these categories, and the boundaries between them, might be helpful. "Fornication and Adultery" was a very expansive sexual offense in Reformation Geneva. It involved voluntary sexual intercourse or other intimate contact between any persons who were unmarried to each other — whether single, engaged, or married to another. Even loose circumstantial evidence of sexual impropriety between couples could lead to charges of fornication, and thus the cases were quite numerous each year. "Other Sexual Immorality" was conduct that fell short of sexual or intimate touching or interaction, but might well be a means to that end — dancing, seduction, use of obscene words or pictures, frequenting ribald plays, dissolute gestures or conduct, provocative dressing and makeup, and the like. "Rape/Sexual Assault" was involuntary sexual contact, including forced sexual intercourse. Most such cases went directly to the Council for criminal prosecution, but occasionally the Consistory encountered these cases, particularly in instances of disputed engagements where the fiancée cried foul. "Spouse and Family Quarrels" were verbal disputes between husband and wife or between parents and children over all manner of minor issues. Where those disputes involved allegations of fornication, adultery, or sexual immorality, we put them in those categories, rather than in the category of quarrels. Where those disputes were over engagements or when they ripened into allegations of wife abuse or petitions for divorce, we again put them into those categories. "Disputed Engagements" often turned on whether parties had properly promised marriage, or had done so without parental consent or witnesses, or while drunk, or with stipulated conditions that were illegal. A few cases involved disputes about the publication of banns or about what to do when one party to the engagement deserted the other. Several cases also raised questions concerning what to do about parties who had been engaged or married elsewhere, and were now seeking marriage to another in Geneva; those cases were sometimes referred to the Council for prosecution for polygamy as well.

Several patterns will be evident as you look across these three annual case profiles. First, in each year, roughly 60 percent of the Consistory's entire case load was devoted to issues of sex, marriage, and family. But the volume of cases on these issues nearly doubled in a decade — from 182 cases in 1546 to 323 in 1557. This reflected, in part, the growing population of Geneva. But it also reflected the growing aggressiveness of the Consistory in governing Genevan life.

Second, the severity of spiritual punishments increased in later years. In 1546, by far the most common remedy was an admonition for the parties to do better, and a good number of cases ended even short of admonition.[14] Only in very serious cases, involving either adultery or fornication coupled with other offenses, were parties banned temporarily from communion. The ban was used only rarely in 1546 — only 5 times in the 182 cases on sex, marriage, and family. The ban became a much more frequent punishment in later years — used 36 times in 1552, 114 times in 1557, with proportionate decreases in the uses of admonition.

Third, the Consistory rarely ordered excommunication in the sex, marriage, and family cases of 1557, even though this was a hard-earned new weapon in their arsenal of spiritual sanctions. Only in 10 of the 323 cases in 1557 did the Consistory recommend to the Council that a party be banished from the city for a serious sexual offense. This might have had the effect of excommunication, but it was not so ordered by the Consistory itself. The Consistory seemed content to make much heavier use of the ban, which at least left a *locus*

---

14. In several instances, the case is declared "continued" or open, but the record reveals no further disposition. Some of this could be a function of a sloppy notary; in most instances, we need to assume that the parties resolved their dispute themselves, or had it resolved for them outside of the formal Consistory hearing.

Table 1. 1546 Cases on Sex, Marriage, and Family

Subject Matter	No. of Cases	Resolved by Admonition	Banned Comm'n	Removed to Council
Fornication/Adultery	94	29	4	47
Other Sexual Immorality	23	11		6
Rape/Sexual Assault	1	0		1
Disputed Engagements	20	5	1	15
Spouse/Family Quarrels	66	39		18
Abortion	1	0		1
Baptism Disputes	3	2		1
Child Mistreatment	5	3		1
Schooling Disputes	1	0		0
Disobeying Parents	1	1		
Wife Beating	1	1		0
Divorce	6	0		6
Totals	182	91	5	96
Total: All Cases in 1546	309			

Table 2. 1552 Cases on Sex, Marriage, and Family

Subject Matter	No. of Cases	Resolved by Admonition	Banned Comm'n	Removed to Council
Fornication/Adultery	94	22	19	55
Desertion	8	4	2	4
Other Sexual Immorality	37	26	2	6
Rape/Sexual Assault	2			1
Disputed Engagements	38	7	2	22
Interreligious Marriage	2		2	
Spouse/Family Quarrels	89	54	9	22
Abortion	0			
Baptism Disputes	2	2		
Child Mistreatment	1			
Schooling Disputes	1			
Disobeying Parents	0			
Wife Beating	3	3		
Divorce	15			9
Totals	253	118	36	119
Total: All Cases in 1552	390			

Table 3. 1557 Cases on Sex, Marriage, and Family

Subject Matter	No. of Cases	Resolved by Admonition	Banned Comm'n	Removed to Council	Excommunicated
Fornication/Adultery	97	22	46	60	5
Desertion	16	7	4	8	1
Other Sexual Immorality	43	16	15	14	2
Rape/Sexual Assault	1		1	1	
Disputed Engagements	43	15	4	26	1
Interreligious Marriage	6	3	2	3	
Spouse/Family Quarrels	83	48	28	23	
Abortion					
Baptism Disputes	7	3	3	3	
Child/Maid Mistreatment	9	6	2	2	
Schooling Disputes	3	2	1	1	
Disobeying Parents	3		3	2	
Wife Beating	19	9	5	7	1
Divorce	13	2		8	
Totals	323	133	114	158	10
Total: All Cases in 1557	566				

poenitentiae, a possibility for repentance and reconciliation. Indeed, in several cases, the 1557 Consistory heard cases from parties who had been banned for prior sexual offenses and now sought (and were almost always granted) re-communion.

Fourth, the Consistory resolved roughly half the cases in each of our three sample years with spiritual sanctions. The rest went to the Council for legal or criminal disposition. This might at first appear counterintuitive, especially since the Council passed increasingly stern criminal laws against adultery, fornication, sexual immorality, and spousal abuse in the 1550s. But, as noted, the Consistory in this same period also imposed increasingly stern spiritual sanctions, making heavier use of the ban and occasional banishment to drive home their earnest of stamping out sexual deviations and family discord. Parties who repented after being banned, or forced to do public reparations, often escaped criminal sanctions for their offense.

Fifth, while the absolute number of cases of adultery, fornication, sexual immorality, and family disputes remained relatively steady across our three sample years, the relative numbers of such cases dropped (in relation to the growing population of the city and the increasing numbers of Consistory cases). This was in part because the authorities' growing rebuke of such conduct was evidently beginning to have an effect. It was also because the Consistory was in more active pursuit of other cases of sex, marriage, and family — particularly wife abuse, which was subject to increasingly firm sanctions in later years, as well as divorce on grounds of desertion or adultery.

Summary and Conclusions

Just as some of the late medieval canon law of marriage and the family lived on in Reformation Geneva, so some of the city's late medieval government lived on, albeit in truncated and revised form. The prince-bishop of Geneva and his courts and officials were banished. But the four city councils that had, under the bishop's supervision, governed secular life and sexual morality continued to operate. After the Reformation, the councils' powers and responsibilities, particularly those of the Small Council and the four syndics, were increased, as they assumed the spiritual jurisdiction of the departed bishop. This included the bishop's former jurisdiction over marriage and family life. On these subjects, the councils issued a steady stream of new statutes throughout the Reformation era, statutes that Calvin and other ministers sometimes helped to draft.

The Small Council adjudicated cases that arose under these statutes on sex, marriage, and family life in cooperation with the Consistory. The Consistory, a new institution created by Calvin in the 1541 Ecclesiastical Ordinances, was a hybrid of spiritual and civil authority. It consisted of two benches, one of ministers including Calvin, the other of elders or magistrates, including a syndic who served as the Consistory's moderator. The Consistory held only spiritual power. It could order only confessions, admonitions, reparations, bans from communion, and excommunication. The Consistory had original jurisdiction over most issues of sex, marriage, and family, save serious sexual crimes that it generally sent directly to the Small Council for criminal prosecution. It investigated cases, collected evidence, interviewed witnesses, and sought to resolve disputes. If the cases could be resolved by spiritual sanctions, the cases ended in the Consistory, as roughly half of them did. If the cases required civil remedies like the award of damages, the restitution of property, or orders of specific performance, annulment, or divorce, the Consistory removed the case to the Council (or for simple civic remedies, to the lieutenant) for disposition, often making specific recommendations of legal action that the Council generally heeded. Cases were also removed to the Council if they involved contemptuous or contumacious witnesses, if they required criminal investigation under oath or using torture, or if the parties' conduct was serious enough to require criminal sanctions like fines, flogging, imprisonment, banishment, or execution.

Calvin eventually grounded this new alliance of church and state in the governance of marriage and family questions in his theory of "the uses of the law."[15] Like other Protestant reformers of the day, Calvin believed that the moral laws of God, and the laws of the church and state that elaborate them, provide no pathway to salvation. Salvation comes through faith and grace, not by works and the law, said Calvin. Nonetheless, from God's point of view, the law continues to be useful in this earthly life — to have "uses." God uses both its basic norms known to all persons, and its more refined norms known only to believers through the Bible to govern and guide humanity.

On the one hand, said Calvin, the law has a "civil use" of defining for all persons what is absolutely necessary to maintain a modicum of civil and domestic order. In this sense, God uses the law as "a halter to check the raging and otherwise limitlessly ranging lusts of the flesh." "Hindered by fright or shame, [sinners] dare neither execute what they have conceived in their minds, nor openly breathe forth the rage of their lust."[16] The moral law thus imposes upon them a "constrained and coerced righteousness," a "civil morality."[17] "[E]ven the pagans," therefore, have always recognized the natural duties of sexual restraint, heterosexual monogamy, marital fidelity, procreation of children, bondage to kin, and the like, which are essential to sexual morality and the survival of marriage and the family.[18]

On the other hand, the law when properly understood and applied by Christian authorities has a "spiritual use" of defining for believers what is aspirationally needed to attain a measure of holiness or sanctification. Even the most devout saints, Calvin wrote, still need the law "to learn more thoroughly . . . the Lord's will [and] to be aroused to obedience."[19] In this sense, the law teaches them not only the "civil righteousness" that is common to nonbelievers, but also the "spiritual righteousness" that is becoming of believers. The law not only coerces them against violence and violation, but also culti-

---

15. Calvin first developed his theory of the uses of the law already in his 1536 Institutes, chap. 1.33. His fullest elaboration came in his 1559 edition of the Institutes. There he distinguished a "civil use of the moral law" (that yielded civil morality through coercion), a "theological use" (condemning persons in their sin to repent), and an "educational use" (teaching those who have repented spiritual morality). See Institutes (1559), 2.7.6-13. The fullest exposition of the doctrine before 1559 came in his Sermons on Deuteronomy of the mid-1550s, where Calvin was interpreting the Jewish laws of marriage, divorce, polygamy, adultery, and the like. See, e.g., Serm. Deut. 5:18, 21; 21:15-17; 22:25-30; 24:1-4. Here, Calvin generally distinguished only the civil use and educational use (he called it "spiritual" use), touching lightly on the "theological use" only in Serm. Deut. 5:21. Our discussion here, therefore, distinguishes only the first two uses.

16. Institutes (1559), 2.7.10. See also Serm. Deut. 24:1-4.

17. Institutes (1559), 2.7.10; see also 4.20.3.

18. Institutes (1559), 2.8.6-10; Serm. Deut. 5:18, 21; 21:15-17.

19. Institutes (1559), 2.7.12.

vates in them charity and love. It not only punishes harmful acts of adultery and fornication, but also prohibits evil thoughts of passion and lust.[20] It not only instructs them by its letter but inspires them by its spirit.

The law thus gives rise to two tracks of marital norms — civil norms, which are common to all persons, and spiritual norms, which are distinctly Christian. This law, in turn, gives rise to two tracks of marital morality — a simple "morality of duty" demanded of all persons regardless of their faith, and a higher "morality of aspiration" demanded of believers in order to reflect their faith.[21]

This two-track system of marital morality corresponded roughly to the division of marital responsibility between church and state in Reformation Geneva. It was the church's responsibility to teach aspirational spiritual norms for marriage and family life. It was the state's responsibility to enforce mandatory civil norms. This division of responsibility fit rather neatly into the procedural divisions between the Consistory and the Small Council. In marriage and family cases, the Consistory would first call parties to their higher spiritual duties, backing their recommendations with (threats of) spiritual discipline. If such spiritual counsel failed, the parties were referred to the Small Council to compel them, using civil and criminal sanctions, to honor at least their basic civil duties for marriage.

20. Institutes (1559), 2.8.6.

21. The terms are from Lon L. Fuller, *The Morality of Law,* rev. ed. (New Haven, CT, 1964). Calvin spoke of "civil morality" versus "spiritual morality." See Institutes (1559), 2.7.10; 4.20.3; Serm. Deut. 21:15-17.

SELECTED DOCUMENTS

2-1   Ordinances on Offices and Officers (1543)[22]

[January 28, 1543: In the General Council assembled in the customary manner there were read the ordinances enacted on the election of all officers of the city, such as the lords syndics, Councilors, treasurer, secretary, *sautier,* members of the Chambre des Comptes, members of the courts of appeals and Consistory, *contreroleurs,* master of the mint, guard of the same, master of the artillery, captains, bannerets, *dizainiers,* watchmen, gatekeepers, and other officers, with a statement of their duties and by what rules and how they should proceed. Which ordinances having been heard, they were found good and reasonable, and that they should be observed.][23]

1. On the Election of the Lords Syndics

Each year, on the Tuesday before the next Sunday after Candlemas or the Feast of Purification, let the Council meet specifically to elect them. Before beginning let the first syndic then in office give them a strong remonstrance and exhortation to elect men of good conscience who hold the honor of God in respect, loving equity and righteousness and the common good of the city, of good behavior and good reputation. Then let prayer be offered to God. Then let each Councilor take an oath to choose those he thinks most proper and capable, in the form that follows:

We promise and swear before God, in the presence of the Council, to elect and name to the office of the syndicate those we think proper and fit both to maintain the honor of God and the Christian religion in this city and to lead and govern the people in good order and preserve the liberty of the city: and in electing them we shall consider the public good and not any personal feelings, either of spite or favor. Let God be our witness of this promise to judge us if we do the contrary.

After this let each in turn name four, all citizens, before the syndics, and let the secretaries be present to record those named.

The next Friday let the Council of Two Hundred meet. And after the exhortation and the prayer let the form of oath be recited and all take it by raising their hands. Then let eight of those named in the election by the Small Council be listed, those having the most votes. And then let eight be elected, either from

22. SD, vol. 2, item 807; printed in part in CO 10/1:127ff.
23. R. Conseil, 36:223.

80

the number of those listed or others if it seems proper, provided that they are citizens: so that the election in the Small Council shall be as it were a recommendation, without prejudicing the liberty of choice of the Two Hundred.

The next Sunday let the General Council be assembled and there let the election by the Two Hundred be reported to the people, so that from the eight who are presented the people may elect four, provided that they are agreeable to them; but also, if it seems good to them, they shall have liberty to refuse either the whole list or a part.

If it happens that among the number presented there are not found four to the taste of the people, that is by the loudest voice, let a new election be held for the number who have been refused, first in the Small Council, then in the Two Hundred, so that no one may be received who has not been approved by the people.

Let this rule be followed: to take two of them from the lower part of the city and two from the upper.

The election having been carried out and confirmed by the people, let the four elected come to the city hall to take the oath at the hands of the four former syndics, to be installed in office.

2. The Form of the Oath

We promise and swear to acquit ourselves faithfully of the duties of our office: first to maintain and defend as far as we are able the liberty and the rights of the city, to administer carefully what we have in our hands, to exercise good and true justice, rendering to each his due, supporting the good and punishing the evil, without malice or favoritism.

Moreover, we promise to do and carry out what is included in the duties of the Councilors. And let God be our witness to all this, to punish us if we do the contrary.

Concerning precedence, to decide who will be first or second, if those elected have already previously held the office, look to see who was first and let him precede the others, and so each following in order. If there are any who never have, let the one who was a member of the Council before the others be recognized, and let the place be assigned according to this precedence. By being in the Council we mean in the office of treasurer or secretary as well as Councilor. Let anyone who has completed his year not be elected until he has rested [been out of office] three years.

If it happens that a syndic passes from life to death while he is in office and four months of his term still remain let another be elected as soon as possible. Otherwise, that is when the time is shorter, the year shall be allowed to go by without substituting another.

3. On the Election of the Small Council

The next Monday let the four newly-elected syndics, along with those of the past year and the treasurer, assemble the Two Hundred, and after the exhortation and the prayer and the oath let the list from the past year be recited, and then let each name those [Councilors] he wishes to leave in office and those he wishes to remove. Nevertheless let the four former syndics remain without dispute, unless they have committed a fault worthy of punishment which is to be investigated.

If there is someone who is removed by majority vote let another not be put in his place immediately, but the next day let the Small Council that has been elected name others in double number, that is two for each [seat], before the Two Hundred, for it to accept those who seem good to it or to elect [others] by its own judgment, as was stated for the syndics.

If it happens that a Councilor dies, let no successor be substituted in his place until the next year, unless by plague or other disaster the number has been so much diminished that the Council is badly depleted.

The election having been carried out, let all come to take the oath before being seated, or to renew it if they have all taken it previously.

4. The Form [of the Oath]

We promise and swear to employ ourselves faithfully in doing what our office requires. And first to show care and diligence in conserving and providing for the welfare, honor, and needs of the city, and to come always and whenever necessary to give good and faithful counsel on what we are required to decide.

Also to inform those it concerns of everything we think will be for the benefit of the city. Also to keep secret everything that is said and determined in Council, if it is not a public matter and one that should be published. Also not to prejudice in any way the honor or welfare of the city through favor or friendship for anyone or any other mundane consideration whatever. Also not to solicit by intrigues or any other practices any officer of justice to act contrary to his duty, but on the contrary to obstruct and overthrow such enterprises as far as we can. Also not to take any present or bribe to favor anyone in what concerns our office, or in general anything anyone wishes to give us because of our station to make us deviate from the fidelity we owe to the city and from the justice we are required to render to everyone.

Also in all cases we are required to try to pronounce what seems right to us in law and equity, without favor or spite toward the parties. Above all to see that the Christian religion is observed purely and that God is served and honored in the city and its territory. Let God be our witness to all these promises to judge us if we violate them.

Concerning assigning places to each, let the four former syndics be the first, then the others, according to how long they have been Councilors or in a higher office. . . .

26. On the Office, Duties, and Powers of the Lords Syndics

Let all four be always resident in the city during the year of their syndicate, so that none leaves to sleep outside it, even for one night, without making it known to the others, and let none undertake a long journey of six or eight days absent without asking leave of the Council.

Every day let them meet together after dinner, that is at one o'clock, to consult about what must be done and give orders for everything, and also to decide how to put into execution whatever has been ordered and concluded by the Council.

On the regular days when the Council meets let them always be the first at the city hall, both to set a good example to the others and to deliberate together about what must be brought forward.

If anything arises that requires them to assemble the Council let them meet together to do this at whatever time is necessary.

In matters that require their presence in different places let them agree so to distribute themselves that each is where it is most expedient.

If some public disturbance arises, such as a fire or riots or some similar event, let the first syndic immediately come to the city hall and remain there to await the news that will be reported, in order to assemble the Council at once if necessary or otherwise proceed according to need. Let the three others hasten swiftly to the place where the danger is, and then having seen what it is let two depart, one in one direction and the other in another, to inspect the crossroads and the gates if needed. And let the third remain in the place of danger until it is alleviated.

27. On the Special Duties of the First [Syndic]

Every day that there is no Council meeting let him come at some time in the morning to the city hall, that is at the end of the sermon, to see whether any orders of the Council remain to be executed or to hear those who come there.

Let him receive the letters addressed to the Council, but let him not open them except in the presence of at least one of his colleagues or of two Councilors. Then if it is an urgent matter let him summon his other colleagues to communicate it to them promptly, or otherwise let him wait until they meet together. And in general let him assemble his colleagues in all matters that require prompt consultation.

On Council days, immediately after the time of the sermon, let him be at the city hall to write [the names of] those who request a hearing.

At the end [of the meeting] he shall give the replies to the hearings granted, and the same day let him put into execution what has been ordered, if it is something that can be carried out so soon.

He shall sign banns of marriage before they are proclaimed in the church, inquiring diligently whether the marriage can be carried out according to the ordinances.

He shall keep the seal in his hands and have charge of sealing documents.

He shall be president of the second or supreme court of appeals.

28. On the Duties of the Other Three

Let one preside over the Consistory, another over the Chambre des Comptes, and the third over the court of first appeals.

Also let one be assigned to visit the prisons once a week.

And let these duties be assigned at the beginning of the year by the decision of the Council.

29. What Some of Them May Do

Two may sign ordinary orders to pay charges approved by the Council.

Also open letters addressed to the Council, as stated above.

30. What One Alone May Do

When some complaint arises, each of the syndics shall have the power to send those involved to be interrogated and examined and to have them imprisoned if necessary.

Also for all insolence, dissolute behavior, drunkenness, and similar matters, each may have people put in prison, then report to the Council. But he shall not have power to release the prisoner before having made his report.

31. On Criminal Matters

If they capture a criminal, within twenty-four hours they must command the Lieutenant to have him answer the charges he is accused of.

After he is remanded to them by the Lieutenant, if it is a case where the facts are proved easily or they are already proved and there is no difficulty in the law, as with murder, theft, and similar things, let them do justice immediately, and at the longest let them not hold it over more than ten days.

If it is a matter in which the facts are difficult to prove or that requires consultation concerning the sentence let the Lieutenant be given sufficient time to fetch and produce his witnesses, depending on the place where they are: nevertheless let him not have more than a month at most to do this, even if the witnesses must be brought from somewhere else; if they are in the city or within two leagues of it let him have only two weeks.

If the criminal asks to be allowed to enter his justifications let the Council consider whether this is proper or not. If the Council decides that he should be so allowed let him be given a term of thirty days [to do so].

The proofs being known and the defense having been heard (in case it is admitted), let the syndics order that the prisoner be sentenced within twelve days at most, even if the matter requires consultation; otherwise let them do it on the first day possible.

The syndics shall be judges of all criminal cases, nevertheless being accompanied by the Council. And let each of the four in turn pronounce the sentences; but nevertheless if several sentences are delivered at one sitting let only one of them pronounce them. If one or several of them are absent let those who are the first ones seated in Council after them take their places, with their batons; nevertheless they shall not pronounce sentence.

32. On the Office, Tasks, Duties, and Procedures of the Council

Three days a week, that is, on Monday, Tuesday, and Friday, let them appear at the sound of the bell without being summoned. Moreover, when some extraordinary matter arises they must also appear at the time they are told by command of the syndics, either by day or night.

On regular days, from Easter to Michaelmas at seven o'clock, and from Michaelmas to Easter at eight, they shall enter the Council, and anyone who does not appear and participate shall lose one *gros* of his salary.

In matters of great importance that require the presence of the entire Council let the syndics send to summon the councilors on the oath they have taken to the city, but let this not be done except with discretion. Whoever, being summoned on his oath, does not appear shall be fined five florins, unless he has a legitimate excuse, to which he shall swear if he wishes it to be received. Moreover it [the summons] must have been delivered to him in person, or to his wife.

Let no one depart to go away entirely before the Council rises without asking leave.

Whoever leaves against the will of the Council, and on being recalled by the bailiff at the command of the first syndic, if he leaves against this prohibition, he shall be fined five florins and kept in prison three days.

The prayer having been offered, no one shall speak except in his turn, and if several speak let the first syndic impose silence. Silence having been imposed, if anyone does not cease he shall be fined five florins.

Let each keep his place, to avoid confusion.

Let no one put himself forward to propose anything himself, but let this be solely for the first syndic. And if anyone has something to propose let him inform the said syndic before the Council is seated; then let the syndic propose it with his own mouth. Nevertheless, if it seems good to him let him command the other to say more about it in order to make the Council better informed.

If it happens that anyone receives a message after the Council is seated that concerns the public welfare, having entered, let him inform the first syndic quietly.

If anyone has anything to propose in his own interest let him put it in writing, or otherwise let him wait until everything is dispatched that has been written down.

Let no one reveal what is done or discussed in secret in the Council, under penalty of being deposed, of being considered permanently incapable of holding office, and moreover, according to the seriousness of the case, of being punished by decision of the Council with either a fine, a formal penance, or corporal punishment. If it appears that he did it to impede the course of justice let him offer a formal penance. If it was to injure the public welfare let him suffer corporal punishment.

Let no one in Council swear or wish anyone to go to hell, under penalty of five sous, and if he persists after being corrected for it several times, of being deposed.

Let no one blaspheme God, under penalty of solemnly asking mercy and being put in prison, and if he does it several times, of being deposed and punished with a more rigorous penalty.

Let no one insult another, and let no one enter into contention or quarrels or use contumelious or indecent language, but let everyone in giving his opinion speak with modesty, without attacking others or speaking against their honor, under penalty of five sous; and if he is accustomed to do so and after several admonitions he does not correct himself, let him be deposed from the Council. If someone accuses another of a crime let him be required to prove it or otherwise to ask his pardon, and let him be deposed from the Council for the rest of the year: and let the one who is accused receive an affidavit of it.

Let these same rules be followed in the Council of Sixty and the Two Hundred and the General Council, to avoid confusion: and so that the whole may be better observed, let what has been laid down be read every year, both to the first Small Council that meets after its election and before the Two Hundred, and then let all swear to observe it.

Let nothing be brought forward in the Two Hundred before being discussed in the Small Council, or in the General Council before having been discussed both in the Small Council and in the Two Hundred.

33. For what Reasons Councilors Should Withdraw

Each in judging his own case must withdraw without being commanded, or if he does not do so let him be made to.

In what concerns his relations and not his own person, in civil cases let a father not be present when the case of his son is tried, nor a brother, nor an uncle; and on the other hand if anyone does not withdraw by his own motion let him be admonished by the Council.

In criminal cases let no one be present at the trial of his relative or kinsman, as far as his cousin-german inclusive.

Also in any case where it seems proper to the Council to exclude anyone, he must depart.

2-2 Ecclesiastical Ordinances (1541)[24]

In the Name of Almighty God, we the Syndics, the Small and Great Council, assembled with our people at the sound of the trumpet and the great bell, in accordance with our ancient customs, having considered that it is a thing worthy of commendation above all else that the doctrine of the holy Gospel of our Lord should be carefully preserved in its purity and the Christian Church properly maintained, that the young may be faithfully instructed for the future, and the hospital well administered for the succor of the poor, which cannot be done unless there is a certain rule and method of living by which each estate attends to the duty of its office: for this reason, it has seemed advisable that the spiritual government of the kind which our Lord demonstrated and instituted by his Word should be set out in good order so that it might be established and observed among us. And accordingly we have made it a fixed rule to observe and maintain in our city and territory the ecclesiastical polity which follows, since we see that it is taken from the Gospel of Jesus Christ.

---

24. CO 10:15-30 (dated September/October 1541). This slightly later edition from RCP is translated in RCP (Hughes trans.), pp. 35-52. Following the style of this volume, we have rendered "Seigneurie" as "Council."

Four Orders in the Church

[The ordinance provides a detailed description of the offices of pastors, teachers, elders, and deacons. We have excerpted provisions relevant to the standards and institutions governing sex, marriage, and family.]

Ministerial Discipline

In order to obviate all scandals of conduct it will be needful to have a form of discipline for ministers, as set out below, to which all are to submit themselves. This will help to ensure that the minister is treated with respect and the Word of God is not brought into dishonor and scorn by the bad reputation of ministers. Moreover, as discipline will be imposed on him who merits it, so also there will be need to suppress slanders and false reports that may unjustly be uttered against those who are innocent.

But first of all it must be noted that there are crimes which are altogether intolerable in a minister and faults which may be endured provided that a fraternal admonition is offered.

Vices which are intolerable in a pastor

> Heresy
> Schism
> Rebellion against ecclesiastical order
> Blasphemy which is open and deserving of civil punishment
> Simony and all corruption by bribes
> Intrigues for usurping another's position
> Leaving one's church without lawful permission and genuine vocation
> Treachery
> Perjury
> Fornication
> Larceny
> Drunkenness
> Assault punishable by the laws
> Usury
> Games forbidden by the laws and of a scandalous nature
> Dancing and similar dissoluteness
> Offenses bearing civil infamy
> Offenses which in another would merit separation from the Church

Vices which can be endured provided they are rebuked

Strange methods of treating Scripture which result in scandal
Curiosity in searching out vain questions
The advancing of some doctrine or manner of conduct not accepted in the
  Church
Negligence in studying and especially in reading the Holy Scriptures
Negligence in reproving vices related to flattery
Negligence in performing all the duties of one's office
Buffoonery
Deceitfulness
Defamation
Dissolute language
Rashness
Evil scheming
Avarice and niggardliness
Uncontrolled anger
Brawling and quarrelling
Dissoluteness unbecoming a minister, whether in clothing or in conduct
  or in any other way

With regard to offenses which ought under no circumstance to be tolerated, if they are civil offenses, that is to say, those which are punishable by the
laws, and any minister is guilty of them, the Council shall take the matter in
hand and, over and above the ordinary punishment customarily imposed on
others, shall punish him by deposing him from his office.

With regard to other offenses of which the first investigation belongs to
the ecclesiastical Consistory, the delegates *(commis)* or elders together with the
ministers shall attend to them. And if anyone is convicted of them they shall report to the Council, with their decision and judgment — but in such a way that
the final judgment shall always be with the Council.

With regard to lesser vices which should be corrected by simple admonition, the procedure shall be according to the order of necessity, in such a way
that in the last resort cases shall be brought before the church for judgment....

The Frequency, Place, and Time of Preaching

On Sundays, there shall be a sermon at daybreak in Saint-Pierre and Saint-
Gervais, and at the customary hour in Saint-Pierre, La Madelaine, and Saint-
Gervais.

At noon the catechism, that is to say, instruction of little children, shall be conducted in all three churches, namely Saint-Pierre, La Madelaine, and Saint-Gervais; and also three o'clock in all three parishes. . . .

On workdays, in addition to the two customary sermons, there shall be preaching in Saint-Pierre three times a week, namely, on Monday, Wednesday, and Friday, and the bells are to be rung for these sermons, one after the other, at an hour such that they can be finished before one is started elsewhere. If there should be an extraordinary service for the necessity of the times, the order of Sunday shall be observed. . . .

Establishment of a College

But since it is possible to profit from such teaching only if in the first place there is instruction in the languages and humanities, and since also there is need to raise up seed for the future so that the Church is not left desolate to our children, it will be necessary to build a college for the purpose of instructing them, with a view to preparing them both for the ministry and for the civil government.

First of all it will be necessary to allocate a place both for the giving of lessons and for the housing of children and others who wish to benefit, to have a learned and experienced man in charge both of the house and of the studies who himself can also teach, and to engage and hire him with the provision that under his charge he shall have teachers of both languages and of dialectic, if possible. Again, there will be need of young men for teaching the little children, which we wish and order to be done.

All such persons shall be subject to ecclesiastical discipline, like the ministers.

There is to be no other school in the city for little children, but the girls shall have their school separate, as has been the case hitherto.

None is to be accepted unless he has been approved by the ministers, after having first notified the Council, and then in turn he is to be presented to the Council with their recommendation, as a safeguard against abuses. Moreover, the examination should be conducted in the presence of two members from the Small Council. . . .

The Hospital

It will be necessary to take every care that the communal hospital is well maintained and that its amenities are available both for the sick and for the aged who are unable to work. The same applies to widows, orphaned children, and other poor persons. These, however, are to be placed in a wing of the building apart and separate from the others. . . .

Concerning Marriage

After the calling of the customary banns the espousals shall be performed when the parties request it, whether on Sundays or on workdays, provided that it be done only at the beginning of the public worship. On a day when the supper is celebrated it will be desirable to abstain for honor of the sacrament. . . .

Regarding disputes in matrimonial cases, since this is not a spiritual matter but mixed up with civil law, it shall remain a matter for the Council. Nevertheless we have advised that the duty of hearing the parties should be left to the Consistory, so that they may report their decision to the Council for it to pass judgment. Suitable ordinances are being drawn up which will be followed henceforth. . . .

The Order to Be Observed with Little Children

At noon on Sundays all citizens and inhabitants shall take or send their children to catechism, of which we have spoken above.

A particular form of instruction is to be composed for them and, besides the teaching which is to be given them, they are to be questioned about what has been said to see whether it has been well understood and remembered.

When a child has been sufficiently instructed to pass on from the catechism, he shall solemnly recite the sum of what is contained in it, and he shall do this as a profession of his Christianity in the presence of the church.

Before this has been done, no child is to be admitted as a communicant to the supper, and parents are to cautioned not to bring them before the time, for it is very perilous both for their children and for their fathers to present them without good and sufficient instruction, which is the purpose of prescribing this order.

That there may be no misbehavior, it is ordered that when the children go to school they shall assemble there before twelve o'clock and that the instructors shall keep them in good order in each parish.

Furthermore, their fathers are to send them or see that they are taken; and so that there may be a minimum of confusion the distinction between the parishes is, so far as possible, to be observed in this connection, as has been said above concerning the sacraments.

Those who contravene this order shall be called before the Company of elders or delegates *(commis)*. And if they are unwilling to comply with good counsel the matter shall be reported to the Council.

For the purpose of observing who are performing their duty and who not, the above mentioned delegates *(commis)* shall keep a watchful eye.

The Order to Be Maintained in the Case of Adults for Preserving Discipline in the Church

. . . The delegates *(commis)* shall assemble once a week together with the ministers, namely on Thursdays, to see whether there is any disorder in the church and to consult together concerning remedies where necessary.

Since they have no authority or jurisdiction to coerce, we have decided to give them one of our officers for the purpose of summoning those to whom they wish to give some admonishment.

If through contempt anyone should refuse to appear, it is their duty to inform the Council so that remedial steps may be taken.

The Persons Whom the Elders or Delegates (Commis) Ought to Admonish and How They Ought to Proceed

If anyone speaks critically against the received doctrine, he shall be summoned for the purpose of reasoning with him. If he is amenable he shall be dismissed without scandal or disgrace. But if he is stubborn he shall be admonished for a number of times, until it becomes apparent that there is need for greater severity, and then he shall be forbidden the communion of the supper and denounced to the magistrate.

If anyone is negligent to come to church in such a way that a serious contempt of the communion of Christians is apparent or if anyone shows himself to be scornful of ecclesiastical order, he shall be admonished, and if he responds with obedience he shall be amicably dismissed. But if he persists, going from bad to worse, after he has been admonished three times, he shall be separated from the church and denounced to the Council.

As for correcting such faults as may be in the life of each person, one must proceed according to the order which our Lord has commanded.

This requires that secret vices should be rebuked in secret and that no one should take his neighbor before the church to accuse him of some fault which is neither notorious nor scandalous, except after finding him rebellious.

Furthermore, those who mock at the specific admonitions of their neighbor shall be admonished afresh by the church, and if they are willing neither to see reason nor to acknowledge their fault once they have been convicted of it, they shall be made to abstain from the [Lord's] supper until such time as they return to a better disposition.

As for those notorious and public vices which the church cannot condone, if they are faults which deserve admonishment only, it shall be the duty of the elders or delegates *(commis)* to summon those who have offended, to remonstrate with them amicably to the end that they may mend their ways, and if amendment is apparent to trouble them no further. If they persist in their evil ways they shall be admonished anew. But if at length they fail to profit they shall be denounced as despisers of God and be made to abstain from the [Lord's] supper until such time as a change becomes apparent in their lives.

As for those crimes which deserve not only verbal rebuke but correction, with punishment, if anyone should fall into them he shall, in accordance with the requirements of the case, be commanded to abstain for a period from the supper in order that he may humble himself before God and come to a better acknowledgement of his fault.

If through contumacy or rebelliousness such a person attempts to intrude himself contrary to the prohibition, it shall be the duty of the minister to send him away, seeing that it is not lawful for him to receive communion.

Nevertheless, all this is to be moderated so that no severity should have the effect of overwhelming the offender, but rather that the disciplines imposed should act as medicines to bring sinners back to our Lord.

All this is to be done in such a way that the ministers have no civil jurisdiction and wield only the spiritual sword of the Word of God, as St. Paul commands them, and that there is no derogation by this Consistory from the authority of the Council or the magistracy; but the civil power shall continue in its entirety. And in cases where there is need to administer some punishment or to restrain the parties, the ministers together with the Consistory having heard the parties and administered such reprimands and admonishments as are desirable, shall report the whole matter to the Council, which thereupon shall take steps to set things in order and pass judgment according to the requirements of the case.

This system shall apply not only to the city but also to the villages under the jurisdiction of the Council.

CHAPTER 3

Looking for Love in All the Right Places[1]

Calvin on Courtship and Matchmaking

Calvin addressed in detail why a couple might wish to choose marriage — for mutual love, comfort, and support, for mutual protection from sexual sin and temptation, and for the mutual procreation and nurture of children.[2] These were great gifts that God provided through the institution of marriage. No fit adults should spurn such gifts unless they were certain of their calling to live alone and could do so without sin.[3]

Calvin also addressed in detail what was forbidden to couples who chose to court with an eye to marriage. No sexy dressing. No fancy jewelry. No make-up. No immodesty. No exhibitionism. No dissolute plays, songs, or poems. No ribald letters or jokes. No excess in food. No drinking in taverns. No dancing. No bathing together. No unsupervised trips. No overnight stays. No seduction. And, certainly, no premarital sex. All these were forms and forums of fornication and lust that Calvin condemned and that the Consistory punished with increasing alacrity, as we shall see.

But these strictures only limited what one could properly do while courting. They did not address the questions of *how or whom* to court. These were

---

1. A variation on the popular song by Johnny Lee, "Looking for Love in All the Wrong Places."

2. See Chapter 14, and Witte, FSC, pp. 94-108.

3. Calvin denounced the traditional requirement of clerical celibacy repeatedly, and urged voluntary celibacy only for those with the rare gift of continence. See, e.g., *De Scandalis* (1550), CO 8:1-84, translated as *On Scandals*, trans. J. W. Fraser (Grand Rapids, 1978), pp. 102-5; Institutes (1559), 4.13.15-17; Comm. Harm. Law Lev. 21:7-9, 13-15; Serm. Deut. 5:18; Lect. Jer. 16:1-4; Comm. and Lect. 1 Cor. 7:1-2, 7-9, 25-28.

important and separate questions. *How* to court raised one set of issues — how to pick a mate, what qualities to look for, what overtures to make, what matchmaker to use if any, and similar issues. These were largely issues of prudence and ethics. The medieval tradition had addressed them mostly in household manuals, sometimes in confessional handbooks as well. Calvin addressed them in a series of pastoral and private letters. We shall analyze those materials in this chapter.

Whom to court raised a separate set of issues — what parties were eligible for courtship and eventual marriage, and, in turn, what conditions, experiences, or relationships past or present disqualified them from courtship and marriage. These were largely issues of law and theology. The medieval tradition had addressed them in sundry canon law texts and cases and in copious writings of moral theology and philosophy. Calvin addressed them in his biblical commentaries and sermons as well as in various *consilia*, statutes, and Consistory opinions. We shall analyze those materials in the next several chapters.

Theological Reflections on Courtship

While the Bible said a great deal about the sins of fornication, it said little about the ethics of courtship. Calvin, too, was cryptic in his reflections on this topic. The Bible did include a few relevant stories, and Calvin drew a few prudential lessons from several of these.[4]

One such biblical story was the account of the indiscriminate courtship of evil men in Noah's generation on the eve of the Flood (Gen. 6:1-4): "The sons of men saw that the daughters of men were fair and took to wife such of them as they chose" (**Doc. 3-1**). It was certainly good for men to have choices among women, and freedom of choice, Calvin insisted. But the problem was that these ancient men "did not choose those possessed of the necessary endowments" for marriage, but chose indiscriminately. The modern message of this passage is that "temperance is to be used in contracting holy marriage." "Marriage is a thing too sacred to allow that men should be induced to it by the lust of their eyes." "Elegance of form" may certainly have a place in the calculus of marriage.

---

4. See below, Docs. 3-1 and 3-2; Comm. Gen. 12:11, 39:6. Calvin left no commentary or sermon on the Book of Judges, with its rather graphic descriptions of Samson's courtship of his wife, and then his later trysts with a harlot and with Delilah (Judges 14:1–16:17). On David's adulterous courtship of Bathsheba, see Serm. 2 Sam. 11:1-5a. On the stories of seduction (and exhibitionism) involving Abimelech and Sarah, Abimelech and Rebekah, Shechem and Dinah, Judah and Tamar, Joseph and Potiphar's wife, and Amnon and Tamar, see Comm. Gen. 20:1-18; 26:5-11; 34:1-4; 38:1-30; 39:7-18; Serm. 2 Sam. 13:1-14. None of these documents, however, deals with the questions of courtship addressed in this chapter.

But we "profane the covenant of marriage" when "our appetite becomes brutal, when we are so ravished with the charms of beauty, that those things which are chief are not taken into account."[5]

Calvin continued in this vein in commenting on the Bible's account of Jacob's choice of Rachel over her elder sister Leah (**Doc. 3-2**). There was nothing wrong with Jacob's choosing Rachel because she was more beautiful. "Only excess is to be guarded against" for that leads to a "stifling of reason." A man who "chooses a wife because of the elegance of her form will not necessarily sin, provided reason always maintains the ascendancy." And reason teaches that a woman's "excellence of disposition" is the most important criterion in deciding whether to marry her.

These and other texts make clear that Calvin recognized and even celebrated the importance of the sexual human body — though nothing on the order of the Renaissance artists and playwrights of his day.[6] He extolled "beauty," "comeliness," "handsomeness," "health," "elegance of form," and similar attributes many times — mostly in women, occasionally in men. He viewed attractive physiques as special creations and gifts from God.[7] The body was "a temple of the Lord," St. Paul had written.[8] Some temples were more handsomely appointed than others. Some were more beautiful on the inside than on the outside.

Physical beauty was thus properly part of the natural calculus of courtship and marriage, Calvin believed. It was "not wrong for women to look at men."[9] Nor was it "wrong for men to regard beauty in their choice of wives."[10] For natural attraction helped to induce that "secret kind of affection [that] produces mutual love."[11] It was thus essential to Calvin that couples spend some time together before considering marriage so that their "natural disposition" towards each other "could be ascertained."[12] If there was no natural and mutual attraction, there was no use for a couple to go forward toward marriage. Accordingly, Calvin opposed the late medieval tradition of arranged or child marriages,

5. See also Comm. Gen. 39:6; Comm. 1 Thess. 4:1-5.

6. André Biéler, *L'homme et la femme dans la morale Calviniste* (Geneva, 1963), pp. 81ff.

7. But beauty could pose its own distinctive challenges. As Calvin put it in describing handsome Joseph, whom Potiphar's wife sought to seduce: "Those who excel in beauty are exposed to many dangers, for it is very difficult for others to restrain themselves from lustful desires." Comm. Gen. 38:7-18.

8. Comm. 1 Cor. 6:15-20. See also Comm. Gen. 39:6 (on Joseph's "elegance of form"); Comm. Harm. Law Exod. 2:1-10 (re: the physical "beauty" of Moses). Calvin left no commentaries or sermons on Proverbs or the Song of Solomon (or Song of Songs), which are filled with (sometimes sultry) passages on the physical beauty of women.

9. Comm. Gen. 39:6.

10. Comm. Gen. 6:2.

11. Comm. Gen. 29:18.

12. See below Docs. 3-9, 3-12, 3-15, 3-19.

sight unseen[13] — though he sometimes forgot this counsel when it came to his own marriage, as we shall see in a moment.

As with all such natural gifts of God, however, physical beauty had to be used moderately and modestly in courtship. Courting couples need not hide their physical beauty from each other. But they should not flaunt it either, lest others be tempted to sin. They need not avert their eyes from their partner's elegant form. But they should not dwell on it either, lest they be driven to lust.[14] They need not ignore physical attractiveness in deciding on a mate. But they should not make raw attraction their principal criterion of courtship or marriage.

Even generously considered, this was rather plain and vague instruction for a single man or woman looking to Calvin for advice on courtship. Calvin was quite clear on whether and how to assess a partner's anatomy. But, for the rest, Calvin left only platitudes. He urged parties to use "temperance" and "reason," not "levity" and "lust," in making their choice. He urged them to look for the "necessary qualities" and the "excellence of disposition" in their mate. And he urged them to take full account of "those things that are chief." But what precise virtues and attributes he intended by this talk of "necessary qualities," "proper dispositions," and "things that are chief," Calvin did not say.

Calvin's Own Courtship

Calvin did elaborate on the preferred attributes of a mate in corresponding about his own courtship and marriage.[15] Calvin had been content to remain a bachelor throughout his teens and twenties. There is no indication that he had seriously courted anyone before 1539, the year he turned thirty. In a *consilium* from this early period, addressed to the lustful dangers of clerical celibacy, he confessed that those dangers did not affect him: "I have never married, and I do not know whether I ever will. If I do, it will be in order to be freer from many daily troubles and thus freer for the Lord. Lack of sexual continence would not be the reason I would point to for marrying. No one can charge me with that."[16]

But during Calvin's sojourn in Strasbourg from 1538 to 1541, the charis-

---

13. See Brundage, pp. 494ff.; Orme, pp. 328ff.

14. Comm. Gen. 12:11, 20:3, 34:1, 38:2, 39:3-6; Serm. 2 Sam. 11:1-5a.

15. See generally Doumergue, *Jean Calvin*, 7 vols. (Lausanne, 1899; Neuilly-sur-Seine, 1927), 2:454-78; William J. Peterson, "John Calvin's Search for the Right Wife," *Christian History* 5 (4) (1986): 12-15.

16. CO 10:226-29. Calvin wrote similarly of his choice not to remarry after the death of his wife in 1549: "It is now eighteen months since the death of my wife, a woman of matchless type, and ever since I have again been practicing celibacy, and not unwillingly." CO 8:1-84, using translation in Calvin, *On Scandals*, p. 102.

matic Martin Bucer pressed the young reformer to marry. At minimum, marriage would free Calvin from the daily efforts of running his busy new parsonage. But Bucer stressed even more the bounties and beauties of marital love. Indeed, he made love the *sine qua non* of marriage and its absence a ground for divorce.[17] This was not just book lore. Bucer, a former Dominican friar, was now happily married. He was leading a sweeping reform of marriage in Strasbourg and in several other cities in Germany, Switzerland, and Scandinavia. After Calvin arrived, Bucer focused on reforming Calvin's domestic life, too. Within a few months of Calvin's arrival, Bucer (or a colleague) found Calvin a woman to consider for marriage.

A "completely worn out" Calvin inserted a few lines about the possible marriage in a long letter to Farel reporting on various matters of church and state (**Doc. 3-3**). Even these few lines reflected Calvin's considerable ambivalence about getting married. "Would that only a single opportunity were allowed me," he wrote quietly to Farel, "to confide" in you and to "have your advice." The bride to be was not yet in town, and there is no evidence that Calvin had even met her. But she was to arrive in Strasbourg just after Easter, and we "hope that the marriage shall come to pass." If it did, Calvin wanted Farel or indeed anyone else from Geneva to marry them, perhaps reflecting his discomfort with the matchmaking pressures of Bucer and company. Calvin would try to delay the wedding if Farel could make the trip.

Nothing came of this wedding, and nothing survives as to why. Within three months, however, Farel had found another woman for Calvin to consider. Farel apparently had asked Calvin what he was looking for in a mate. Calvin blurted out the requisite qualifications bluntly (**Doc. 3-4**). "I am not one of those insane kind of lovers who, once smitten by the first sight of a fine figure, cherishes even the faults of his lover. The only beauty that seduces me is of one who is chaste, not too fastidious, modest, thrifty, patient, and hopefully she will be attentive to my health." If Farel's preferred woman measured up, he should seize the moment immediately for Calvin, lest another suitor interfere. If not, Farel should let her go.

With such a prosaic overture, Calvin could not have been too surprised that Farel's woman disappeared. In early February, 1540, however, a more suitable woman appeared — indeed, two of them. Calvin wrote again to Farel, now with a good deal more enthusiasm (**Doc. 3-5**). "I am so much at my ease, as to have the audacity to think of taking a wife," he wrote. A wealthy young woman had been proposed to him, holding out a sizeable dowry. But Calvin was put off both by her wealth and by her inability to speak French. When the woman's brother and sister-in-law began to press him, Calvin sent his brother Antoine to

17. See Selderhuis, passim; Witte, LP, pp. 214-32.

contact another woman, who was more modest in wealth, and came "mightily commended." Calvin had such high hopes for this second woman that, even before meeting her, he was already planning the wedding for the following month. He again wanted to have Farel preside and his Genevan friends attend. But then, catching himself, Calvin admitted that he would "look very foolish" if this new courtship "falls through."

This new courtship did fall through, and Calvin was doubtless ashamed. He was mightily inconvenienced, too, for the breakdown of that second courtship only encouraged the family of the first wealthy young lady to renew their pursuit of Calvin. An "exceedingly annoyed" Calvin complained of their pressure in a letter to Farel of March 29, 1540 (**Doc. 3-6**). The woman's relatives were "overwhelming" him "with kindness," making it difficult for Calvin to be "unpleasant" in rejecting them. But he thought it was "crazy" to marry such an unusually rich woman who did not even speak his native French. Calvin was "desperate" to escape these marvelous but misguided suitors. Escape he eventually did, but this only left him both ashamed and alone. By June, 1540, he was ready to give up on getting married. "I have still not found a wife, and I doubt that I'll look for one anymore," he wrote glumly to Farel.[18]

To everyone's great surprise, Calvin was married two months later to Idelette de Bure, an Anabaptist widow with two children of her own. Idelette certainly met Calvin's stated criteria of piety, modesty, frugality, and the like. But she was also savvy, sociable, respectable, and "actually pretty," Farel noted with some surprise.[19] Calvin's first biographer Theodore Beza reports that Idelette and "Calvin lived in marriage about nine years in perfect chastity."[20] This has led some to speculate that they had a sexless spiritual marriage, as was occasionally practiced by earnest Catholic couples of the day.[21] But the facts do not bear out such an austere picture, nor do they square with Calvin's repeated advice that married couples should enjoy each other sexually. Calvin reports that he and Idelette had a "very happy honeymoon" that was unhappily cut short by the plague.[22] Quarantined from Idelette, Calvin wrote in anguish that "my wife is in my thoughts day and night."[23] The couple had at least three children, maybe

---

18. Letter to Farel (June 21, 1540), CO 11:50-54.

19. Farel's Letter to Calvin (Sept. 6, 1540), CO 11:78-81. See also Cottret, pp. 141-42; Balke, pp. 133-38; N. Weiss, "Un portrait de la femme de Calvin," *Bulletin de la Société de l'Histoire du Protestantisme française* 56 (1907): 222.

20. CO 21:37.

21. See Dyan Elliott, *Spiritual Marriage: Sexual Abstinence in Medieval Wedlock* (Princeton, 1993); Agnès Walch, *La spiritualité conjugale dans le catholicisme français, XVIe-XXe siècle* (Paris, 2002).

22. Letter to Farel (September, 1540), CO 11:83-86.

23. Letter to Farel (March, 1541), CO 11:174-79.

four. To their great grief, these children were all stillborn or died in their cribs.[24] Idelette's premature death in 1549 devastated Calvin, as we shall see.

Calvin the Matchmaker

It had long been a common practice in the Christian West for people to seek the help of clergy to find a spouse for themselves or their children. Clergy knew better than most who might be eligible for marriage within their communities — emancipated children, confirmed catechumens, graduated students, spurned fiancé(e)s, new immigrants, among others. Clergy knew better than most how to counsel and cajole the recalcitrant, reluctant, or remiss to consider the proper overtures of a suitor. And clergy knew better than most the leaders of surrounding churches and towns who could watch for eligible mates. In the later Middle Ages, good priests, with discretion and connections, presided over a veritable cottage industry of matchmaking.[25]

This custom of clerical matchmaking continued during the Reformation, as we already have seen in Bucer's and Farel's efforts to find Calvin a wife. Calvin took up this matchmaking role as well, and he left a good number of letters reflecting his efforts. Most of his matchmaking efforts — though not all[26] — were privately pursued on behalf of well-connected friends and patrons, particularly fellow ministers. On occasion, the Consistory deputized him to look into courtships that had gone awry.

Calvin the matchmaker sought for his suitors many of the same qualities that he had sought in his own bride — piety and modesty foremost among them.[27] Social, economic, and educational compatibility sometimes entered his calculus as well.[28] Beauty and love were again not lost on him. Sharp differences

---

24. Letter to Viret (July, 1542), CO 11:419-20; Letters to Farel (May 30, 1544; August 21, 1547), CO 11:719, 12:580; Letter to M. de Falais (April, 1546), CO 12:322; Bouwsma, pp. 23, 242n. In his *Respondio ad Balduini convicia* (CO 9:561-80), one of several attacks on the jurist Franciscus Baudouin, who had betrayed him, Calvin wrote: "Wishing to clear himself of the charge of a want of natural affection brought against him, Baudouin tweaks me for my lack of offspring. God had given me a son. But God had taken away my little boy." This suggests that Calvin had one son and two or three daughters.

25. Orme, pp. 199ff.

26. See, e.g., Letter to Duchess of Ferrara (May 10, 1563), CO 20:15-18 (requesting help in finding a husband for the daughter of the Duchess's former servant). Earlier, Calvin had also helped to send a governess to the Duchess's household. Letter to Duchess of Ferrara (August 6, 1554), CO 15:205-7. See further F. Whitfield Barton, *Calvin and the Duchess* (Louisville, 1989).

27. See below Docs. 3-4, 3-5, 3-8, 3-19; Letter to Farel (July 1, 1558), CO 17:227-28.

28. See below Docs. 3-4, 3-5, 3-6, 3-9, 3-13, 3-18, 3-19; Letter to Farel (July 1, 1558), CO 17:227-28.

in age and religion, as we shall see in Chapter 8, would be fatal to the couple's courtship if Calvin had his way — though neither his suitors nor the Consistory followed Calvin's judgment in all such cases.

Calvin took pains to seek the consent of both the parents and the couple in making the match. He suspended his overtures if the parents or guardians objected. Calvin did sometimes retort with anger when parents or other matchmakers sought to push their children onto him against his better judgment, or if the suitors themselves interfered in his efforts or resisted his counsel. He found himself more than once in a race to land a coveted bride for one of his suitors, or to escape the pursuits of women whom he thought unsuitable for his suitor. In such cases, Calvin was not above urging parties to make conditional betrothal promises to shut out the competition. Early in his career, he even volunteered to ask women and their parents if they would consider marriage to one of his suitors, sight unseen. But he insisted that any such marriage promise be conditional on the parties meeting first so that "their natural disposition" towards each other "could be ascertained." "True love," as he put it, "requires previous acquaintance."[29]

The best illustration of Calvin's matchmaking efforts was his rather feverish, self-appointed campaign to find a wife for his close friend Pierre Viret. It was 1546, the year that Calvin was putting the finishing touches on his Marriage Ordinance and had marriage reform much on his mind. Viret was the leading pastor in the nearby city of Lausanne.[30] He was a familiar and trusted visitor in Geneva and a skilled diplomat on whose services Calvin would later come to rely heavily.[31] He was comparable in age, education, and reformist ambition to Calvin. Viret became one of Calvin's closest confidants. Calvin exchanged at least 390 letters with him, more than with anyone else.[32]

In one of these exchanges, Calvin learned that Viret's first wife, Elizabeth,

---

29. See Doc. 3-12 below; Letter to Nicholas Colladon (ca. May 12, 1550), CO 13:562-63 (listing date as May 3, 1550); Bonnet, Letter 261 (listing date as May 12, 1550).

30. See analysis of his sundry attacks on Catholic views of holy communion in Christopher Elwood, *The Body Broken: The Calvinist Doctrine of the Eucharist and the Symbolization of Power in Sixteenth-Century France* (New York/Oxford, 1999).

31. George Bavaud, *Le réformateur Pierre Viret (1511-1571): Sa théologie* (Geneva, 1986); Jean Barnaud, *Pierre Viret: Sa vie et son oeuvre (1511-1571)* (Nieuwkoop, 1973); Robert Dean Linder, *The Political Ideas of Pierre Viret* (Geneva, 1964).

32. Robert D. Linder, "Brothers in Christ: Pierre Viret and John Calvin as Soul-Mates and Co-laborers in the Work of the Reformation," in *Calvin Studies Society Papers 1995, 1997*, ed. David Foxgrover (Grand Rapids, 1998), pp. 135-68, at 137ff.; also his "John Calvin, Pierre Viret, and the State," in *Calvin and the State*, ed. Peter De Klerk (Grand Rapids, 1993), pp. 171-86; Jean-Daniel Benoît, "Calvin the Letter Writer," in *Studies in Reformation Theology*, ed. William J. Courtney (Grand Rapids, 1966), pp. 67-109. By comparison, Calvin exchanged but 301 letters with his coworker Guillaume Farel.

had died in February, 1546, leaving Viret devastated and lonely.[33] Calvin sought to console him and urged him several times to come to Geneva to be comforted by Calvin and Idelette as well as his many other friends there.[34] Viret came for eight days, accompanied by Farel, but he remained despondent.[35] Calvin then took it upon himself to find Viret a new bride to ease his loneliness. On May 11, 1546, he wrote a brief note to his aristocratic patron, M. de Falais, to help him find a bride for Viret.[36] Calvin searched in vain in Geneva and beyond. Finding no one, he wrote again to de Falais on July 4, now at greater length (**Doc. 3-7**). While Calvin had found "many [potential] wives," he could not find "a single one with whom [he] should feel at all satisfied" to recommend to Viret. He asked the well-connected de Falais to be on the lookout for a more "suitable party."

Nine days later, Calvin wrote triumphantly to Viret that he had found an eminently suitable woman for him to consider (**Doc. 3-8**). "The more we inquire, the more numerous and the better are the testimonies with which the young lady is honored." She was very pretty and modest, too, which did not hurt the cause. Calvin urged Viret to prepare himself quickly to meet with the woman. For others in Geneva were proposing a different woman for him, one Mademoiselle Rameau, who was of higher social status but less desirable, in Calvin's view. We must "seize the moment quickly lest we be obstructed," Calvin whispered conspiratorially. Indeed, "it would tend to promote the matter if I, with your permission, should ask her" if she might be interested in a marriage proposal from you.

Two days later, Calvin was back at his letter desk, reporting to Viret at length on a conversation at a dinner party, which included influential members of the Genevan Council (**Doc. 3-9**). The virtues of the two women had been hotly debated, and Calvin's own matchmaking efforts questioned. Mademoiselle Rameau had been the obvious favorite of the dinner party. Calvin's choice was viewed as too poor and lowly in station for so distinguished and beloved a minister as Viret. This only doubled Calvin's resolve to be sure that Viret chose the right woman. He again asked Viret to let him make a proposal to his choice

---

33. Linder, "Brothers in Christ," pp. 151-52; Letter of Viret to Nicholas de Wattville (March 8, 1546), CO 12:306-9.

34. Letters to Viret (Feb. 22 and March 8, 15?, 26, 1546), CO 12:296, 305-6, 318-19, 323.

35. Letter to M. de Falais (April 16, 1546), CO 12:330-33.

36. CO 12:344-45. M. de Falais was Jacques de Bourgogne, Seigneur de Falais, who, with his wife Yolande de Brederode, Madame de Falais, were influential and generous patrons of the Reformation, with whom Calvin corresponded regularly. See discussion and a critical edition of fifty-three letters in Françoise Bonali-Fiquet, ed., *Lettres à Monsieur et Madame de Falais/Jean Calvin* (Geneva, 1991). Calvin dedicated to M. de Falais his 1546 Commentary on 1 Corinthians, CO 12:258-60.

of woman before Viret came to Geneva and fell victim to the matchmaking wiles of others. While there may be some "danger" in this course of action, Calvin admitted, it would "not be ridiculous" — particularly if the couple made only a conditional betrothal promise, pending their mutual satisfaction upon meeting. With such a betrothal already negotiated before your arrival, Calvin predicted, the champions of Mademoiselle Rameau "will not dare to press you." For they would then be acting as accessories to the crime of bigamy.

When Viret did not respond quickly enough, Calvin wrote to him yet again: "Only say the word, and the thing is settled. I would never have been in such haste had I not been stimulated by so many remarkable testimonies" about the woman (**Doc. 3-10**). Viret agreed to the strategy. Calvin went to work immediately to secure the conditional consent of the woman and her father. That proved impossible, Calvin reported with great indignation to Viret two weeks later (**Doc. 3-11**). The woman's father objected to having his only daughter move from Geneva to Lausanne to be with Viret, a condition that other matchmakers had falsely assured him would not be necessary. The father resisted Calvin's entreaties, and Calvin gave up the pursuit. By the end of his letter, he was urging Viret to consider an "admirably pleasant" widow in her stead.

Perhaps chastened by this experience, Calvin was now more cautious in pressing Viret to commit to this new woman without meeting her — a caution he showed in later matchmaking efforts as well.[37] But he remained bent on finding Viret someone better than Mademoiselle Rameau. Viret reported that another woman had been recommended to him, and he sought Calvin's counsel on what to do.[38] M. de Falais also found a widow for Viret to consider.[39] Calvin wrote to M. de Falais again (**Doc. 3-12**). He relayed Viret's thanks for his recommendation, but indicated that Viret could not commit to the woman without meeting her. Calvin respected Viret's caution, though he could not resist complaining a bit about the consequent delay in Viret's courtship.

The following month, Calvin wrote yet again to de Falais, saying that he did not know where matters stood with the widow but that he wanted to avoid any further intermeddling (**Doc. 3-13**). Calvin was even more circumspect in this letter. De Falais had evidently complained that the widow whom he had recommended for Viret was not getting serious enough consideration. De Falais must have taken his earlier matchmaking commission from Calvin as an

37. See below Doc. 3-13; Letter to Viret (Sept. 1, 1548), Bonnet Appendix Letter 6.

38. Letters of Viret to Calvin (Sept. 29, October 19, 1546), CO 12:386-88, 398; Calvin's Letter to Viret (October 19, 1546), CO 12:399. See also Barnaud, *Pierre Viret*, pp. 315-18.

39. It is not clear whether this is the same woman whom Viret mentioned in his letters of September 29 and October 19 or someone new.

exclusive license to find just the right woman for Viret.[40] So who was Calvin, of all people, to be suggesting other women to Viret before de Falais had even finished his search? And what was Viret doing in considering another woman without first considering de Falais's recommendation? This perceived affront — made worse by de Falais's recent illness and the death of his sister[41] — required some delicate diplomacy. Calvin tendered a lengthy apology and rehearsed his and Viret's actions in some detail to prove that neither was guilty of "feigned civility" or "double-dealing." Perhaps just to be sure that there were no hard feelings, Calvin wrote a letter to Madame de Falais four days later, assuring her that his "love and reverence" for her husband was as strong as ever.[42]

Neither Calvin's nor de Falais's matchmaking services ultimately proved necessary. Viret found his own wife, Sébastianne de la Harpe, and married her in late November, 1546, in Lausanne. Calvin participated in the wedding service, and later sent Viret a handsome sum of money, at least in part as a wedding gift.[43]

Calvin found himself apologizing to M. de Falais again the following year, this time over a veritable soap opera of events involving the young Reformed minister, Valeran Poulain. Poulain had apparently told de Falais that Calvin had been unhappy with de Falais's earlier rebuke of him. De Falais must have asked Calvin what this was all about. In a penitent return letter, Calvin denied making any such complaint, cast doubt on Poulain's credibility, and apologized profusely to de Falais, signing the letter "your servant and humble brother forever."[44]

Calvin then wrote an excoriating letter to Poulain (**Doc. 3-14**). He rebuked him both for his rumor-mongering, and for spurning Calvin's earlier matchmaking advice. Calvin had warned Poulain not to pursue a young woman because of her "censurable" qualities. Poulain had evidently heeded this advice and had promised greater caution in his courtship. But, in no time, Poulain had proposed marriage to another woman. And worse, the woman was now complaining that Poulain had tricked her into entering an unconditional betrothal contract. Poulain had assured her that he had already received the consent of

---

40. Calvin had said in his letter of July 4, 1546, to M. de Falais (Doc. 3-7): "I have not thought fit to inquire of anyone else than you, since no one has the prudence that is required."

41. Letter to Madame de Falais (Oct. 19, 1546), CO 12:401-2; Letters to M. de Falais (Oct. 19, 24, Nov. 20, 1546), CO 12:401-2, 407-8, 423-24.

42. Letter to Madame de Falais (Nov. 20, 1546), CO 12:424-25.

43. Barnaud, *Pierre Viret*, p. 318; CO 12:433-34. Calvin sent Viret sixteen crowns, though it is not clear from the letter whether this was Calvin's own gift, or a combination of gifts from others. See further "Testament de Viret (12 avril 1561)," *Bulletin historique de littéraire de la Société de l'histoire du protestantisme française* 16 (1867): 317.

44. Letter to de Falais (March 15, 1547), CO 12:487-88.

her guardian, and there was thus no need for her to condition her consent to their betrothal on receipt of her guardian's consent. Now the young woman was stuck with an unconditional contract with a duplicitous fiancé whom she neither loved nor wanted.

The guardian in question was none other than M. de Falais. The new woman in question was his relative, Mademoiselle Wilergy (or more fully, Isabelle de Haméricourt, dame de Willercies). An angry de Falais reported that he had given no such consent to Poulain to marry Wilergy.[45] Calvin and company now had the difficult task of trying to dissolve the couple's unconditional betrothal contract. Calvin wrote to Oswald Myconius, a trusted minister in Basel, where the case was being heard, and urged him not to let the slippery Poulain deceive the presiding court in Basel, nor mischaracterize Calvin's own position on the case (**Doc. 3-15**). The same day, Calvin reported to de Falais on these efforts (**Doc. 3-16**). He further reported with dismay that Poulain was now saying that it had been Wilergy's idea to get married and that, she, contrary to convention, had proposed marriage to him, even while Poulain was courting another woman. An exasperated Calvin had clearly had enough of this pastoral playboy.

No doubt happily for Calvin and de Falais, the Basel court dissolved the betrothal contract of Poulain and Wilergy. Calvin reported the matter some three weeks later (**Doc. 3-17**). He also reported, with some glee, that a despondent Poulain was listless, sleeps little, and "glories in his shame." Maybe through this experience, Calvin said, "God will give him better sense." Despite these youthful indiscretions, Poulain later married the sister of the distinguished English reformer Bishop John Hooper, and moved far away to serve a Reformed church near London and later a Reformed church in Frankfurt.[46]

Finally rid of Poulain, de Falais set about to find Wilergy a proper husband. By August, he had a proposal from a Savoyard aristocrat, and he sought Calvin's advice. Contrary to the lavish courtesy of his earlier letters to de Falais, Calvin was curt and dismissive (**Doc. 3-18**). "I certainly would never consent" to such a proposal, he wrote. "You have been rash in entertaining" it. The man's family is poor. His health is poor. He is "decent enough" but weak and prone to evil counsel. And Savoy aristocrats are just too different from us to be trusted. Calvin had a better man in mind.

A month later, Calvin wrote to recommend this better man, albeit in another testy letter to de Falais (**Doc. 3-19**). His preferred suitor was the son of one

---

45. *Lettres à Monsieur et Madame de Falais*, pp. 141-42n.

46. Letter to Bullinger (Jan. 21, 1549), CO 13:164-66; Letters to Church in Frankfurt (March, 1556), CO 16:53-56; Letters to Valeran Poulain (March 3 and June 24, 1556), CO 16:62-65, 201-3.

of Calvin's childhood friends in France. He had, admittedly, sown his share of wild oats. But Calvin ascertained that he was free from syphilis and was now a mature, gregarious, and loving soul, whom Calvin recommended heartily. A year later, Wilergy and a young man from Paris became engaged, with Calvin again involved in her contractual negotiations.[47] It is not clear whether this was the same young man whom Calvin had recommended. But Calvin seemed happy with the match, and he attended the wedding with de Falais.[48]

After getting embroiled in these two protracted debacles, it is perhaps no surprise that Calvin curtailed his matchmaking activities considerably. He continued to be solicitous for suitors until the last year of his life.[49] But Calvin now acted with far greater restraint, showing none of his earlier officiousness, competitiveness, and even brinkmanship. Indeed, he seemed to be mostly content to defer to the matchmaking efforts of others, not least to his friend Pierre Viret who was considerably better at the craft than Calvin. Calvin had many more pressing questions to address — notably the requests of many parties who were trying to get out of engagements and marriages, not into them.

Summary and Conclusions

In Calvin's Geneva, marriage was expected of all fit parties who reached the age of consent. Only those rare parties who had received God's gift of continence could forgo the gift of marriage. Mandatory celibacy for clergy was outlawed. Traditional prohibitions on remarriage of divorcees and widow(er)s were removed. A strong pro-marriage ethic and culture was the new norm of Reformation Geneva.

One key to a strong marriage, Calvin insisted, was picking the right mate — a person of ample piety, modesty, and virtue especially, of comparable social, economic, and educational status as well. A mate's physical beauty could play a part in the calculus of marriage, but spiritual beauty was the more salient issue. Another key to a strong marriage was taking the time to get to know one's

---

47. Letter to M. de Falais (July 17, 1548), *Lettres à Monsieur et Madame De Falais*, pp. 198-200, excerpted in Doc. 11-4 below where we have analyzed it for its treatment of marital property issues.

48. Letter to M. de Falais (July 17, 1548). Calvin's letter, which is missing from CO, does not mention the name of either the man or the woman in question. It indicates that the man had property connections in Paris and that the woman is de Falais's relative. Bonnet, Letter 225, indicates that the woman is Wilergy. Françoise Bonali-Fiquet suggests that the couple might be Antoine Popillon, a French noble, and Isabeau de Merne, another relative of de Falais. *Lettres à Monsieur et Madame de Falais*, p. 198n.

49. See, e.g., Letter to Duchess of Ferrara (May 10, 1563), CO 20:15-18.

mate before proceeding with engagement and marriage. Calvin had no patience with the tradition of arranged marriages sight unseen, or with rushed secret marriages driven by lust. He knew the power and possibility of "love at first sight"; indeed, he seems to have experienced it himself in his courtship of Idelette de Bure. But he insisted that parties take the time to get to know each other before taking the fateful step into marriage. "True marital love," he insisted repeatedly, "requires previous acquaintance."

Matchmakers could be helpful in locating the right mate and facilitating the match. Calvin and his colleagues played this role a number of times, particularly for fellow ministers and other leaders. But matchmakers could only do so much, as Calvin learned the hard way. The matchmaker's advice and opinion could not substitute for that of the courting couple, nor could it interfere in a parent's wishes for the child. The matchmaker could, however, play a valuable pastoral role, both in facilitating new relationships between parties who might not otherwise meet, and in guiding parties to relationships that seemed most conducive to their happiness.

3-1   Commentary on Genesis 6:2 (1554)[50]

Moses does not condemn men for regarding beauty in their choice of wives, but only lust. For marriage is a thing too sacred to allow that men should be induced to it by the lust of the eyes. For this union is inseparable, comprising all the parts of life. The woman, as we saw, was created to be the man's helper. Therefore our appetite becomes brutal, when we are so ravished with the charms of beauty that those things which are chief are not taken into account.

Moses more clearly describes the violent impetuosity of their lust, when he says, that they took wives of all that they chose. By this, he indicates that the sons of God did not make their choice from those possessed of necessary endowments. Instead, they wandered without discrimination, rushing in whatever direction their lust took them. Thus we are taught in these words that temperance is to be used in holy marriage, and that its profanation is no light crime before God. For it is not fornication which is here condemned in the sons of the saints, but too great an indulgence of license in choosing wives for themselves.

3-2   Commentary on Genesis 29:18 (1554)[51]

[I]t is not altogether wrong that Jacob was more inclined to love Rachel than Leah, . . . since Rachel excelled her altogether in elegance of form. For we see how naturally a secret kind of affection produces mutual love. Only excess is to be guarded against, doubly so because it is difficult to restrain affections of this kind, so that they do not result in the stifling of reason.

So, a man who is induced to choose a wife because of the elegance of her form will not necessarily sin, provided reason always maintains the ascendancy, and holds the wantonness of passion under control. . . . For it is a very culpable lack of self-control when any man chooses a wife only for her beauty. Her excellence of disposition ought to be deemed the most important.

50. CO 23:111-12 (OTC adapted).
51. CO 23:402-3 (OTC adapted).

3-3 Letter to Farel (February 28, 1539)[52]

I am completely worn out. . . . Would that only a single opportunity were allowed me to confide to you all my hopes and fears, and in turn to hear your mind and have your help, whereby we might be better prepared. An excellent opportunity will occur for you to come here, if, as we hope, the marriage comes to pass. We look for the bride to be here a little after Easter. But if you will assure me that you will come, the marriage ceremony could be delayed until your arrival. We have time enough beforehand to let you know the day. First of all, then, I request of you, as an act of friendship, that you would come. Secondly, that you assure me that you will come. For it is altogether indispensable that someone from there be here to solemnize and ask a blessing upon the marriage. I would rather have you than anyone else.

3-4 Letter to Farel (May 19, 1539)[53]

Concerning the marriage, I shall now speak more clearly. . . . I do not know whether anyone mentioned the person about whom I wrote before. But always keep in mind what I am looking for in [a wife]. For I am not one of those insane kind of lovers who, once smitten by the first sight of a fine figure, cherishes even the faults of his lover. The only beauty that seduces me is of one who is chaste, not too fastidious, modest, thrifty, patient, and hopefully she will be attentive to my health. If you think well of [her in light of this], set out immediately in case someone else get there before you. But if you think otherwise, we may let that pass.

3-5 Letter to Farel (Feb. 6, 1540)[54]

I am so much at my ease as to have the audacity to think of taking a wife. A certain young girl of noble rank has been proposed to me, and with a fortune above my condition. Two considerations deterred me from that connection — because she did not understand our language, and because I feared she might be too mindful of her family and education. Her brother, a very devout person, urged the connection, and on no other account than that, blinded by his affection to me, he neglected his own interests. His wife also, with a similar partial-

---

52. Bonnet, Letter 30 (adapted).
53. CO 10/2:347-48.
54. CO 11:12; Bonnet, Letter 44 (adapted).

ity, contended, as he did, so that I would have been prevailed upon to submit with a good grace, unless the Lord had otherwise appointed. When, thereupon, I replied that I could not engage myself unless the woman would agree to learn our language, she requested time for deliberation.

I then, without further delay, sent my brother, with a certain respectable man, to escort another woman here who is reputed to bring a large enough dowry, but no money at all. Indeed, she is mightily commended by those who are acquainted with her. If it comes to pass, as we may certainly hope will be the case, the marriage ceremony will not be delayed beyond the tenth of March. I wish you might then be present, that you may bless our marriage. As, however, I have troubled you so much more than I ought during the past year, I dare not insist upon it. If, however, any one of our brethren should have a mind to visit us, I would prefer that it were at that time, when he could take your place; although, nevertheless, I make myself look very foolish if it shall so happen that my hope again fall through. But as I trust the Lord will be present to help me, I express myself as though I spoke of a certainty. . . .

3-6   Letter to Farel (ca. March 29, 1540)[55]

I have already waited so long for your letter that I really doubt whether I should wait any longer. My anxious wish to hear from you has kept alive my expectation, and shall even now sustain my hope for a few more days. . . . The marriage [proposal to the second woman] is in a state of abeyance, and this annoys me exceedingly. The relatives of that young lady of high rank are so urgent that I take her to myself. I could not think of ever doing this, unless the Lord has altogether demented me. But it is unpleasant to refuse, especially in the case of such persons who overwhelm me altogether with their kindness. Most earnestly do I desire to be delivered out of this difficulty. We hope, however, that this will be the case very shortly, and that during the next four or five days another engagement will turn away my mind from the subject and will occupy all my attention.

3-7   Letter to M. de Falais (July 4, 1546)[56]

I have taken it upon me, Monsieur, to make a request of you. You know that our brother Viret is about to marry. I am as anxious about it as he is. We have plenty

---

55. CO 12:30-31 (dated April 4, 1540); Bonnet, Letter 45 (dated March 29, 1540).
56. CO 12:354-55; Bonnet, Letter 168 (adapted).

of [prospective] wives here, as well as at Lausanne and at Orbe. But yet there has not to date appeared a single one with whom I should feel at all satisfied. While we have this matter in hand, permit me to ask you earnestly that, if you have noticed anyone in your area who appears to you likely to suit him, could you please let me know of it. I have not thought fit to inquire of anyone else than you, since no one has the prudence that is required. You may reply to me that you are at least acquainted with someone in your neighborhood. I shall not venture to breathe a word about it, before having your opinion of her. You can tell me that in one word, for I shall take your silence as a judgment that she is not acceptable. . . . I am well aware that, for your part, knowing of how much consequence the marriage of such a man is for the Church of God, you would not spare yourself any pains therein. Indeed, I would not hinder your acting directly for him, supposing that a suitable party can be found there; but in regard to asking advice, I have taken for granted that you will allow me that liberty.

3-8   Letter to Viret (July 13, 1546)[57]

Think of what you are going to do, and then write to me again what you have decided. The more we inquire, the more numerous and the better are the testimonies with which the young lady is honored. Accordingly, I am now seeking to discover the mind of her father. As soon as we have reached any certainty, I will let you know. Meanwhile, do make yourself ready.

This match does not please Perrin, because he wishes to force upon you the daughter of Rameau. That makes me the more solicitous about seizing the moment quickly lest we be obstructed by having to make excuses. Today, as far as I gather, he will enter upon the subject with me, for Corne has invited us both to dinner. I shall gain time by making a civil excuse.

It would tend to promote the matter if I, with your permission, should ask her. I have seen her twice. She is very modest, with an exceedingly becoming countenance and person. Of her manners, all speak so highly that Jean Parvi recently told me that he had been captivated by her.

3-9   Letter to Viret (July 15, 1546)[58]

As I had predicted, three days ago, towards the end of supper, mention was made of your [pending] marriage. But then Domaine d'Arlod, whose help I

57. CO 12:359; Bonnet, Letter 169 (adapted).
58. CO 12:360-61; Bonnet, Letter 170 (adapted).

had sought, interrupted the conversation, and said that the matter was concluded. On hearing this, our friend instantly sprung up from the table, and, in his usual way, gave reins to his indignation. "Will he then marry that girl of low connections?" he said, his whole body shaking. "Could there not be found for him in the city someone from a better family? I regard as vile and infamous whoever started or aided this business. Of a brother and sister I am thus unwillingly compelled to speak."

I said in reply: "I could not have started it, because the young lady was unknown to me. I acknowledge that I was a promoter of it, and, indeed, the principal one. But that the matter is finally settled, as Dominic has asserted, is not true. Moreover, I have gone so far into it that to retreat now would be dishonorable. In that there is nothing for me to be ashamed of." His fury was thus turned into laughter. But he again began to grow hot, because you had concealed the matter from him. He was especially inflamed with a foolish jealousy, because Corne confessed that you and he, while riding, had talked over the thing together. "Is it even so?" he proceeded to say to Corne. "Was it for this I attended him along with you, that he might in the most insulting manner shut out from his counsels the most attached friend he has in the world? I would cheerfully prefer him to myself."

I objected that he had drawn the wrong conclusion, since you had not disclosed your mind even to Farel. He was, therefore, again pacified, though he talked of the daughter of Rameau, whom he extolled in an extraordinary manner. I nodded assent to all these praises, but remained firm regarding the other party.

Consider, now, whether it be expedient for you to come into the city already engaged. For there will be a hateful apologizing, if they proceed to force her [Mademoiselle Rameau] upon you. I know how dangerous it may be to give a promise before the natural disposition of the girl has been ascertained. I am full of anxiety, nor can I easily clear a way for myself. I think, however, that this course would not be ridiculous. Suppose you consent to my asking the young lady in your name, on condition that before the betrothal takes place, you are to meet her. That will give at least a certain enough promise that they will not dare to press you.

Write in return, therefore, by the earliest possible messenger, what your views are. At the same time, my advice is that you should not delay long but come on an early day. Of the lady, I hear nothing that is not highly pleasing. In her father and mother, also, there is nothing blamable. I am even more certain when I see that our opponents have nothing to carp at beyond this, that it was impossible for them to frighten us from our purpose. There are some things about the daughter of Rameau which I fear; nevertheless, as it is your own affair, you will be free to choose.

3-10 Letter to Viret (July, 1546)[59]

Only say the word, and the matter is settled. I would never have been in such haste had I not been stimulated by so many remarkable testimonies. But nothing gave me a greater impulse than the desire to be freed from those embarrassments of which you are aware.

3-11 Letter to Viret (July 25, 1546)[60]

[A]fter reading your letter, I waited on the father and daughter so that I might be absolutely certain of success. As soon as reference was made to a change of residence, however, the father took exception to it on the ground that something different had been promised him. I said that no promise to that effect had been made with our knowledge; and, moreover, that I had carefully instructed Pierre d'Orsières not to cajole them by such promises. I pointed out how absurd it would be if we were to leave our churches to follow wherever our wives called us; that a marriage consummated under such a condition would be an unhappy and unholy alliance, that would not pass without punishment falling on both you and the girl; finally, that you would never be prevailed upon to afford the first example of so disgraceful a practice, and, therefore, that it was in vain to make the request. I added that Lausanne was not so far from [Geneva] as to prevent his daughter from being with him as often as might be necessary. I also added that it would, likewise, be better to celebrate his absent daughter daily, than to see and hear her constantly weeping and bewailing the cruelties of her husband, as was the case with so many as he said.

He requested time for deliberation. At the end of three days, he replied that he was unwilling to send his only daughter from home. I felt greatly indignant at being so deluded by the folly of those in whom I trusted. I restrained myself, however, and dissembled my anger. But I do not need to offer any lengthier excuse to you, as I am free from all blame.

We may accordingly turn to some other quarter. Christoph spoke to me of a certain widow, who, he asserts, pleases him admirably. If such is the case, I am at rest, and [will] leave it [to you]. But if not, speak your mind.

---

59. CO 12:362; Bonnet, Letter 171 (adapted).
60. CO 12:363-64; Bonnet, Letter 172 (adapted).

3-12 Letter to M. de Falais (October 4, 1546)[61]

[Viret] has replied to me, thanking you very humbly for the kind affection you have shown him. He would desire above all things to have communication with the party, fearing that if there were no mutual understanding, they might not associate so well in the future. Besides, while these troubles last, it appeared to him that the journey could not be well undertaken, and I am much of the same opinion. There might thereby be some danger of a long protraction of the affair. This is by no means your intention, which I find very reasonable. As for the rest, there is no sort of impediment arising from health.

I find it annoying that a matter, uncertain at any rate, should be suspended for so long. But I do not find fault with his request, considering the reasons that he has related to me. It is necessary that the wife he shall take be informed beforehand of some domestic charges that he is obliged to bear. Besides, love requires previous acquaintance, and domestic affairs never go well without a private mutual understanding, and a settlement of the conditions required on both sides. The mischief lies in waiting for that length of time. Besides, I do not see any great object to be gained by it. I pray God that, in any event, he would well order it. . . .

3-13 Letter to M. de Falais (November 16, 1546)[62]

As concerns the marriage [of Viret], for which I requested your assistance, I implore you, Sir, to believe what I shall tell you. For I shall recount the pure truth without any dissimulation whatsoever. What induced me to write you was that a party had been proposed here who was in no way suitable for him. But because of the forwardness of some of those who have meddled in the affair, we had very great difficulty in getting the proposal set aside.

And so, to break the blow, it was my earnest desire to find someone else. For there would have been less envy and jealousy had he taken someone from far away. We have already had ample experience with the murmuring that some people make when we do not follow their lead.

I assure you, however, that he has not been making indirect application elsewhere. . . . As you know, your first letter loitered long upon the way. Before we had any news from you, I took the occasion to write to you again, and that at his instance, although I did not then comprehend very clearly why.[63] In the

---

61. CO 12:392-94; Bonnet, Letter 175 (adapted).

62. Bonnet, Letter 178 (adapted).

63. It is unclear whether Calvin is referring here to his letters of May 11 (CO 12:344-45) and

meantime I have learned that he had a proposition from another quarter. Nevertheless, after receiving news from you [about another woman], I communicated with him, and the result was such as I have just told you, without feigned civility or double-dealing.

Since then, I have understood that the proposal about a widow was still under consideration, although to this hour I do not know where it stands. And so far was I from meddling that, given the other proposals that were under consideration, I have not felt inclined to bring forward the name of a widow whom I know in this town. She is as well endowed as I could have wished for myself if God had so far afflicted me as to have deprived me of my helpmate, and that there was a necessity for my marrying again. I have no doubt whatsoever that it would prove an admirable match for him. But I have refrained all the more from active friendly interference. It was sufficient for me to commit him to God, and to let the stream find its own course.

3-14   Letter to Valeran Poulain (March, 1547)[64]

I only received your letter today, which was later than was proper. . . . I am constrained to think that you acted neither with prudence nor propriety in soliciting the girl in marriage. But I am still more displeased seeing she complains that you tricked her by means of numerous baseless accusations and indirect arts. . . .

I mentioned in an earlier letter, regarding the younger lady to whom you aspired, what I thought was wrong with her. In seeking after this [new] one, you seem to have forgotten what you wrote to the other on your departure. Even if nothing else had stood in the way, you should have absolutely abstained from the mention of marriage until she had reached her destination. But if what she herself testifies is true, the betrothal was brought about through the influence of the worst inducements.

Accordingly I shall not believe that the marriage is, as you say, from the Lord, until you prove that what she says is untrue, namely that you had beforehand filled her with numerous lies. She strongly asserts that she gave you no credence and that you two formed no engagement, for she always expressly stipulated to be allowed to do everything in accordance with the advice of Monsieur de Falais. She says, however, that you affirmed that his will was quite well known to you, that the only difficulty would be with his wife, as she still regarded with admiration the

---

July 4 (Doc. 3-7), or to his letter of July 4 and a subsequent letter that we have not found. The latter reading is more plausible.

64. CO 12:503-4; Bonnet, Letter 189 (adapted).

signs of nobility. These were not the signs of God, but you prohibit me from believing them. I can do nothing less, however, than hear both sides.

When I reflect on the whole circumstance, certain particulars appear with which, I confess, I am displeased. You remind me that illustrious men are sometimes guilty of grave offenses. It is on other grounds, however, that I love and reverence M. de Falais than on account of the mock greatness in which most of the nobility pride themselves exclusively. Further, I have, as yet, heard nothing from him but reasonable complaints. Moreover, I have looked more to the matter itself than to the persons. I wish that you had never involved yourself in those troubles; but since it has happened, it remains for me to desire to see you relieved from them in a short space, which I trust is now accomplished.

3-15   Letter to Oswald Myconius (May, 1547)[65]

I was very surprised when I heard that the suit which Valeran [Poulain] advanced against the noble young lady Wilergy was still pending there. . . . So far as I know from suitable witnesses, the matter is not so complex that it could not be handled quickly. I feel pity for Valeran, a person from whom previously I had hoped good things. . . . Still, we were all fooled by him, because now just like a man drinking a derisive toast to shameful prostitution he has disgraced the young lady along with himself. She was completely unworthy of such slanders. What did he gain, except being mocked like some cynic?

I don't say this so that you can warn the man, since I have no doubt that you already tried every remedy, and I have little hope that admonition will have any effect on such an impudent temperament. To be sure, I desire his return to his original state of mind. But I have experienced in one letter that it is like [telling] a story to a deaf dog if somebody gives him sound advice.

I admonished him gently and with great modesty. He wrote back as if he had been hurt by me in a way surpassing barbarity. In this he mounted an intemperate attack of a badly adjusted mind, which I easily forgave. In so far as I hear, he did not hesitate to boast before your illustrious senate that my letter supported his case. This is evil action not to be ignored. Still, having blabbered about everything, I do not see how he stonewalled the judges. He brought forth witnesses. He recently wrote to Farel that the matter had been carried out before God without human testimony. He wrapped his case up in a big mixture of nonsense. Why so, except to dull the eyes of the judges. They are, indeed, too patient who allow themselves to be tricked this way.

---

65. Letter to Myconius (May 1, 1547), CO 12:514-15, translated by Fr. John Patrick Donnelly, S.J.

But as I understand it, your job is to uphold with your vote the young lady whom you see as so wrongly abused and to take care at the same time that the insolence of that shameless fellow be cut short. Since I am privately involved in refuting the calumny by which he has branded me I beg of you that you be willing to show the judges and senate that what he boasts about in my letter is a complete lie. I do not want myself to be seen as so empty headed that I appear the patron of such an evil and illiberal cause. I have received repeated insulting letters full of wild charges from him about this matter. He has but one letter from me in which his action is gently condemned. So he is acting shamefully in seeking a protective mantle under my name.

3-16   Letter to M. de Falais (May 1, 1547)[66]

I wrote to Myconius, as you will see by the copy I shall send you. I was of the opinion that this would be better, because the judges will better comprehend my meaning from his mouth, and it will have more weight. If I were to write them directly, I would make myself too much a party in the case, and could not press the suit so strongly. I believe that our brother, Master Pierre Viret, will do the same in regard to Sir Bernard Mayer, on account of what I have told him.

Should there be any [further] need for it, he [Poulain] condemns himself of disloyalty in his letters to me. For, after he asked me in the month of January to intercede for him in regard to the marriage of Merne, he told me that Wilergy was in love with him many months before — so much so, as to propose marriage, rather than wait to be asked. How is that to be reconciled, unless he wanted to have both of them? He must be cut short in this whole troublesome nonsense, seeing that it is quite unworthy of a hearing. I have no doubt that the judges will very soon put an end to that.

3-17   Letter to M. de Falais (May 26, 1547)[67]

[Regarding the dissolution order] I advise that you only tell the young lady [Wilergy] of the general nature of the objection, without mentioning anything that may have happened to him [Poulain]. For that would only get repeated afterwards. I would just let her know that, "he sleeps little and is somewhat listless, which appears to be a bit dangerous. But consider whether you would be patient if God were to visit such a trial upon you." That, in my view, would be

---

66. CO 12:516; Bonnet, Letter 189 (adapted).
67. CO 12:529-30; Bonnet, Letter 195 (adapted).

enough. Since you can see how well disposed she is, you will do what you think is right about this. We have some news about the judgment. He is complaining about the judges, and glories in his shame. May God give him better sense.

3-18   Letter to M. de Falais (August 16, 1547)[68]

Regarding the [proposed] marriage, for my part, I would never consent to it. You will see that I am replying to you very confidentially. The family is very poor indeed. The nobility of Savoy are very different from those of our country. The man himself is decent enough. But he's not self-assured enough to resist evil counsels. He is also subject to illnesses because of weak blood. . . . You have been rash in entertaining his proposal [to marry Wilergy]. Forgive me if I am being too forward. If it were up to me, I would instead pick the other man whom I know.

3-19   Letter to M. de Falais (September 10, 1547)[69]

Regarding the party you inquired about, I fear that you think I am randomly building marriages in the air. But why? I think I have a good foundation in reason and confidence. Eight months ago, the son of M. de Montmor, with whom I grew up, told me that he would desire more than anything to settle here. He continues to be of that mind as he has written me more than once. He is a young man, some thirty-four years old, good-natured, very gentle and docile. He has drunk deep of youthful follies earlier in life. But, now that God has given him self-knowledge, I believe he will be quite to your liking. I have inquired diligently of Nicholas Loser, and Nicholas Picot, his son-in-law, to see if he has any hint of the disease [syphilis] that young men can get from their dissolute life. They have spoken to him, and have replied that he has none. My desire is now beginning to build an expectation. Should he come [to Geneva], as I expect, I will send him to you at once. You can then consider whether he would be suitable.

68. CO 12:574-78; Bonnet, Letter 203 (adapted).
69. CO 12:586-87; Bonnet, Letter 206 (adapted).

CHAPTER 4

Love Thyself as Thy Neighbor

Individual Consent to Engagement and Marriage

In Calvin's Geneva, as much as today, marriage was a contract between a fit man and a fit woman of the age of consent. It was, of course, much *more* than a contract: it was a spiritual, social, natural, and economic relationship that could involve many other parties besides the couple. But marriage was never *less* than a contract. It could not be created unless both the man and the woman consented voluntarily to this union.

Calvin and his colleagues took pains to ensure the free and full consent of both parties. The 1546 Marriage Ordinance required that engagement and marriage promises be made "simply" and "honorably," without "trick" or "surprise." The Consistory annulled engagement and marriage contracts procured by physical force or threat of force, or through fraud, deception, or seduction. They also annulled frivolous and drunken promises. The Consistory respected conditions to engagement contracts that went to the essence of marriage — such as conditioning one's own consent on the consent of one's parents. But they had no patience with other conditions about ancillary matters — such as conditioning one's consent on the other's delivery of marital property. Such conditional engagement contracts were enforced regardless of whether the ancillary condition had been breached — and regardless of whether this breach now put the couple at such odds that they both wanted out. The mutual consent of the parties was essential to form the engagement contract; but, once properly formed, the engagement contract could not be dissolved even by mutual consent.

Mutual Consent and the Impediment of Compulsion

Theological Reflections

Like the medieval canonists, Calvin treated marriage as a "sacred contract" that depends in its essence on mutual consent.[1] Calvin repeated this teaching many times. "While all contracts ought to be voluntary, freedom ought to prevail especially in marriage, so that no one may pledge his faith against his will."[2] When a woman wishes to marry, she must not "be thrust into it reluctantly or compelled to marry against her will, but left to her own free choice."[3] When a man "is going to marry and he takes a wife, let him take her of his own free will, knowing that where there is not a true and pure love, there is nothing but disorder, and one can expect no grace from God."[4]

The doctrine of mutual consent was so commonplace and uncontroversial in his day that Calvin offered little sustained theological analysis of it. On occasion, he did pause to show how to square this doctrine with other biblical commands. In his 1555 Sermons on Deuteronomy 25, for example, Calvin asked whether the doctrine of mutual consent should be read into God's command that a man must marry the widow of his deceased brother (**Doc. 4-1**).[5] This command of "Levirate marriage," as it was called, had been a central preoccupation of Protestants since Henry VIII's struggle with the papacy to annul his marriage with Catherine of Aragon, widow of his late brother Arthur. What if the surviving brother did not want to marry the widow, or the widow did not want to marry him? Did the couple have to marry against their will? What if the brother was already married; was he now required to be a polygamist?

No, no, said Calvin. "It was impossible for God to contradict himself" in writing his law.[6] So, God certainly would not want a brother to become a polygamist to fulfill his duty to his dead brother, for that would run directly counter to God's mandates for monogamy.[7] God also would not want a man to marry against his will. God anticipated this very possibility by providing in Deuteronomy 25:7-10 for a process to deal with cases when "the man does not wish to take his brother's wife." The spurned widow can plead her case before the authorities. If the authorities cannot persuade the man to marry her, the woman

1. Serm. Deut. 22:25-30.
2. Comm. Josh. 15:14.
3. Comm. Gen. 24:57.
4. Serm. Deut. 25:5-12.
5. See detailed discussion of this duty of "Levirate marriage" in Chapter 9 on incest impediments.
6. Comm. Harm. Gosp. Matt. 22:24.
7. See Chapter 7 on polygamy.

may ceremonially (and ruefully) reject him, leaving them both free from any further obligation to marry. "Our Lord did not want to condemn men irrevocably to take women," Calvin argued. "Although there was good reason [to compel marriage] here, God considered that compulsory and forced marriages never come to a good end. . . . [I]f the husband and the wife are not in mutual agreement and do not love each other, this is a profanation of marriage, and not a marriage at all, properly speaking. For the [mutual] will is the principal bond."

Calvin did not address here the corollary question of what to do if the widow did not want to marry her brother-in-law. But in several of his other Old Testament commentaries and sermons, Calvin insisted on protecting the consent of the woman as much as the man during courtship and marriage.[8] Indeed, even when a father arranged the marriage of his daughter to a particularly prized husband, Calvin argued that "according to common law the agreement implied the daughter's consent and was only to take effect if it was obtained."[9] Given that understanding, Calvin would likely have insisted that the widow had to consent to a Levirate marriage before it could be considered valid.

Calvin showed less obvious concern for consent when interpreting the biblical passages on rape and its aftermath (**Docs. 4-2 and 4-3**). Calvin regarded rape to be a heinous crime, "a kind of murder."[10] When a man raped another man's wife or fiancée, the Mosaic law called for his immediate execution. Calvin concurred in this view, as did the Genevan authorities in serious cases.[11] When a man raped a single woman, however, particularly a minor under her father's care, the Mosaic law commanded that "he shall give the marriage present for her, and make her his wife. If her father utterly refuses to give her to him, he shall pay money equivalent to the marriage present for virgins" (Exod. 22:16-17). There was no stated concern in this text for mutual consent.

Glossing Exodus 22 and a parallel passage in Deuteronomy 22, Calvin argued that, if the father of the woman victim consented, the parties should be compelled to marry and the man deprived of any right to divorce her thereafter. Calvin had no difficulty with compelling the man to marry, for this was more merciful than coercive. After all, the rapist had exercised his free will in choosing to rape the woman. Properly, he should be executed for his offense. But that would only compound the harm to the young woman who could now be left

8. Comm. Gen. 29:18-27; Comm. Harm. Law Exod. 21:7-11; Lev. 19:29; Comm. Josh. 5:14. See discussion of these texts in the next chapter on parental consent.

9. Comm. Josh. 5:14; see a fuller excerpt of this passage in Chap. 5, Doc. 5-4.

10. Serm. Deut. 22:25-30; Comm. Deut. 22:23; Serm. 2 Sam. 13:1-14; Comm. Gen. 34:1-31.

11. Serm. Deut. 22:25-30. See capital cases of rape recounted in Naphy, Sex Crimes, pp. 80ff.; E. William Monter, "Crime and Punishment in Calvin's Geneva, 1562," *Archiv für Reformationsgeschichte* 64 (1973): 281.

ravaged, stigmatized, and without ongoing support if her father dismissed her. So, the rapist had to marry his victim, to pay the full marriage price, and to live peaceably with his wife thereafter — and consider himself lucky to have escaped with his life.

The harder question was why compel the rape victim to marry her assailant? The woman had already been compelled to have sex. What if she did not wish to marry her rapist, regardless of the projected high social costs to her? Indeed, how could the modern church and state of Geneva even consider compelling a woman to marry her rapist, particularly since they had made a woman's consent so essential to the validity of marriage?

Calvin did not answer these questions. He may well have again assumed the operation of "the common law" that a marriage is not valid unless the woman fully consents thereto. He may also have assumed that requiring the victim's father to consent would provide an adequate safeguard. To be sure, Calvin knew that the Bible was full of examples of callous fathers who sold their daughters into slavery, prostitution, and arranged marriages.[12] But, surely in this kind of tragic case, a father would judge sympathetically whether his daughter should marry her rapist, or at least he would heed her pleas if she wanted out. Moreover, even a callous father had the economic incentive not to consent to her marriage. For the Mosaic law still allowed him to collect the full marriage price from his daughter's assailant, leaving him to collect a second marriage price from a later husband should there be one. But Calvin said none of this. Instead, his argument for compelling marriage in these cases was public morality — lest rape victims "should become prostitutes and the land defiled by prostitution." This was neither responsive to the gravity of the issue nor consistent with his solicitude for women's consent in other cases.

Outside of this difficult context of how to minimize the tragic fallout of rape, Calvin stood foursquare against engagements and marriages entered by force or threat of force. He addressed this issue directly in an undated *consilium* (**Doc. 4-4**). The case sent to him for his advice involved a young woman named Margueritte. Her mother had tricked and forced her into marrying a young man named Jean. Jean's brother, aunt, and servant were apparently part of the conspiracy as well. Margueritte was trapped into going through with the wedding. But she was distraught throughout the ceremony and maintained consistently thereafter that she was not married. At least two witnesses testified that the woman did not say her wedding vows but was silent throughout the ceremony. The notary who recorded the marriage contract testified that the mar-

---

12. Comm. Gen. 29:18-27; Comm. Harm. Law Exod. 21:7-11; Lev. 19:29. But cf. Serm. 1 Sam. 18:22-30; Serm. 2 Sam. 3:14-16 (where Calvin does not criticize fathers for offering their daughters as prizes for valor).

riage "was not of God" because Margueritte had not consented to it. Calvin concluded that because "the girl was forced into it, no foundation for marriage exists." A properly constituted court should examine Margueritte and her mother closely. If their testimony holds true, the court should annul the marriage, and leave the young woman free to marry another. Calvin said elsewhere that in such cases the coercing parent (and the minister, too, if he was party to the conspiracy) should be severely punished.

Theodore Beza wrote similarly in his 1569 *Tract on Annulment and Divorce*. If an engagement or marriage promise was induced by force or threat of force it was not binding unless the promise was later fully and freely confirmed before the authorities (**Doc. 4-5**). Beza offered two caveats, however. First, to deter parties from staging claims of coercion to escape unwanted engagements, judges should "warn plaintiffs gravely to examine over and over" what their "inner attitude" had been when making their promise, lest they "sin against conscience" in now seeking to annul it on grounds of coercion. Second, even if the promise had been coerced, subsequent consensual sex between the parties should defeat their claim of annulment by reason of coercion. For Beza, the couple's consent to sex cured any prior coercion in making the engagement promise.

Consistory Cases

The Genevan Consistory heard a number of cases of disputed and coerced consent. To resolve simple disputes, the Consistory generally asked the parties and their witnesses to recount their words exactly and relate the facts copiously. If the Consistory found an honest and reasonable difference of opinion, and one of the parties still refused to consent, they would annul their engagement, but not their marriage. Where one of the parties alleged that they were physically threatened or coerced into marriage, or they were seduced, tricked, blackmailed, or fraudulently induced into giving their consent, the Consistory annulled their engagement or their marriage, and often punished the coercing party quite severely. This was in conformity with the express provision of the 1546 Marriage Ordinance that promises formed by fraud, trick, or surprise were void.

It must be noted, however, that rather few annulment cases turned on physical or psychological coercion alone. As we shall see repeatedly in this volume, allegations of coercion were often intermixed with other defects of contract formation — drunkenness, infancy, abuse of parental authority, attempts to cover premarital pregnancy, exploitation of the other party's mental inability, breach of valid conditions to engagement, or exploitation by masters of their maidservants, by guardians of their wards, and by servants of their elderly or infirm mistresses. In many of these cases, the authorities treated coercion as an aggravating factor, not the stated ground for the annulment order.

The 1545 case of Pierre Jaqueno and Claude Conte featured a typical simple dispute over consent (**Doc. 4-6**). Pierre had proposed marriage to a widow named Claude in the company of her mother and others, and had given her an engagement gift. Claude had returned the gift immediately and declined his proposal. When Pierre persisted in his overture, Claude threatened to kick him in the stomach and stormed out of the room. Claude's mother said to Pierre: "Take charge of her; she is leaving my side now." Pierre took this to mean that Claude's mother consented to the engagement. So he persisted in his overture, to the point of requesting the Consistory to order Claude to marry him.

The Consistory summoned Claude and inquired closely about what she had said and intended. She remained adamant about her refusal to marry Pierre and insisted that she had never once consented to the marriage. The Consistory wanted to know if she was now pregnant by Pierre. This would have cast doubt on her claim to persistent refusal of his advances, perhaps even subjected her to an order for a shotgun wedding. Claude denied her pregnancy as well, and insisted that she had been chaste since her husband had died three years earlier. The Consistory was not so sure. They sent the case to the Council, with a warning to Claude that she should "protect the fruit of her womb" rather than seek an abortion. The Council, too, suspected her to be pregnant but found no basis for an engagement contract and thus released her.

In a 1546 case, the Consistory summoned Marco Ducloz and a young woman named Paula to answer charges that they had become publicly engaged and had toasted their engagement before several witnesses (**Doc. 4-7**). Both Marco and Paula admitted that they were drinking together with friends. Marco, however, denied making any marriage promises, despite testimony to the contrary. Paula testified only that the company had toasted them in the name of marriage "if it could be done." But she had not consented to any marriage, and her parents were not there to consent to it. With no witness testifying to Paula's statement of consent, the Consistory declared the engagement void. They admonished the parties to be more careful about making such dangerous promises in public.

A woman named Jehanne learned about these dangers the hard way (**Doc. 4-8**). At a party, she and a man named Nicolas had exchanged clear and unconditional promises to marriage and toasted their engagement in the presence of at least eight witnesses. Included in the company was Jehanne's uncle who had promised to send the couple an ample dowry. According to the witnesses, Jehanne had afterward requested that no one tell her brother about the engagement lest he be angry with her. When later testifying to the Consistory, however, Jehanne insisted that she never had any intent to marry Nicolas, and indeed that was part of the reason she asked that her brother not be told. She further claimed to have been "swindled" — in part because her alleged fiancé lied about the number of children he would be bringing into the marriage, in part because her uncle would not now tender the promised dowry. This latter claim, however, stood in some tension with her claim that she had no intent to marry: how could she feel "swindled" about not getting her dowry if she had no intent to enter the marriage that would have triggered the dowry payment?

The Consistory took this evidence under advisement. They initially held that "the marriage should not go into effect." Instead, they asked Jehanne to summon her uncle to testify. Given his promise to pay Jehanne's dowry, this uncle might well have been her guardian. Had he dissented, the Consistory could have recommended annulment regardless of whether Jehanne had consented to the engagement. The Consistory might well have been hoping to resolve the case this way. The uncle, however, could not appear to testify. Both Jehanne and Nicolas now said they wanted out of the engagement, and began to change their stories to press their case for release. The Consistory lost patience with them. They charged both parties with perjury and sent them to the Council with a recommendation of marriage. The Council ordered them to marry, despite Jehanne's continued strong protests.

Note how seriously the Consistory took the statements of the parties in forming the engagement contract. The central question for the Consistory was whether each party freely and fully consented to the engagement. The testimonial evidence showed that they had. For the Consistory that was the end of the matter. Nicolas's misrepresentation of the number of his children, Jehanne's uncle's subsequent failure to deliver dowry property, and the party's growing antagonism and perjury were all subordinate issues. None of this changed the validity of the engagement contract. The parties would have to marry unless they could find another impediment to plead for an annulment.

The Consistory would look beyond a party's stated words of consent, however, in cases of fraud, deception, or blackmail. In a 1552 case, for example, Anne de Beaumont challenged her engagement to Jaques Charvier on this ground (**Doc. 4-9**). Jaques had facilitated Anne's release from a prison in Vienne, apparently using his connections with his father who was a warden there.[13] As a condition for helping her, however, Jaques had asked Anne to move with him to Geneva and marry him. Desperate to be released, Anne had consented. The couple had moved to Geneva. Jaques now wanted to marry. Anne did not. Jaques then petitioned the Consistory to order the marriage. He produced a witness who testified that, even after her arrival in Geneva, Anne

---

13. As reported by Seeger, p. 369.

had told Calvin and others of her eagerness to marry "if the church of this city consented."

Anne countered that the church of the city should not consent to her marriage. She testified that, when Jaques proposed, she was "greatly troubled and disturbed in spirit." Rather than "take pity on her ignorance" and ill plight, "he persuaded her to her dishonor." Her engagement promise was insincere, "frivolous," and coerced, and she should not be held to it. Her parents did not consent to the marriage either, Anne added for good measure. Consistent with what Beza would later recommend, the Consistory urged Anne to search her "awakened conscience" as to whether she could go forward with the wedding. She held firm to her conviction that she had no desire to marry Jaques. The Consistory thus sent the case to the Council. The Council ruled that Anne had been coerced into making a promise, but asked her to document her parents' dissent as well. When their dissent was tendered, the Council ordered her engagement annulled. In the end, it was not clear whether it was the coercion of Anne or the dissent of her parents that drove the Council's decision for annulment.

In the 1559 case of Louise Fornier and Jean Tru, mere coercion proved enough to trigger an annulment (**Doc. 4-10**). Louise wanted to move from her Catholic home town to Geneva in order to join the Protestant cause. She was not being persecuted, but feared that it was only a matter of time before Protestants like her would face prosecution from the Catholic authorities. She was apparently too poor to afford to travel on her own. So, she asked Jean, a younger man, to take her to Geneva. Jean agreed, but on condition that she would marry him upon their arrival in Geneva. She accepted the condition, provided that the Genevan authorities concurred that "God was not offended because she was older than he."

When the couple arrived in Geneva, the Consistory summoned them to inquire about their wedding plans. Louise now said she had never had any desire to get married. She had made only an insincere promise to ensure her escape from a Catholic territory and to receive passage to Geneva that she could otherwise not afford. At the Consistory's request, she took an oath swearing that she "had neither intended nor desired to marry him," and requested that she be "freed from the said promise she gave, it having been made by compulsion and force." The Consistory recommended an annulment which the Council granted four days later.

The coercion at work in this case was rather attenuated. Louise said she feared persecution, but this was not imminent. The only real coercion in question was the limitations of her poverty. Though Jean was certainly exploiting her need, this case actually betrays more fraud by Louise than coercion by Jean.

Perhaps it was Jean's youth more than his coercion that moved the Consistory. The record makes clear that Louise was considerably older than Jean. Disparity of age between prospective couples was a tender subject in Geneva in 1559 when this case was brought. In the late 1550s, as we shall see, Calvin and his Consistory colleagues annulled several engagements on the ground of disparity of age alone. And Calvin had just risked his life-long friendship with fellow reformer Guillaume Farel in protesting Farel's decision to marry a woman less than half his age.[14] While the record does not say so, disparity of age might well have been a major factor in the Consistory's decision.

This is not to say that the Consistory failed to appreciate that (the threat of) poverty could be a powerful instrument of coercion. In a 1559 case, for example, the Consistory annulled the engagement of a young woman on just that ground.[15] The woman's mother had threatened to disinherit her and withhold her dowry if she did not marry a man named Jean Vernette whom the mother liked. Threatened by poverty born of disinheritance, the woman grudgingly agreed to the match though she maintained throughout that she had "no love" for Jean. The mother proceeded apace, and publicly toasted her future son-in-law on her daughter's behalf. The young woman now pled with the Consistory to annul the union, arguing that she "never had any courage or desire" to marry Jean, and what her mother had contracted on her behalf "was done by coercion." The Consistory agreed, and sent the case to the Council with a recommendation of annulment.

Though the record of the Council's final disposition of the case does not survive, this should have been an easy case for annulment. Not only was the daughter's consent not fully voluntary, but also the mother's threat of disinheritance represented the kind of coercion that the 1546 Marriage Ordinance outlawed: "Let no father compel his children to such a marriage as seems good to him except with their goodwill and consent, but let him or her who does not want to accept the partner his father wants to give be excused, always preserving modesty and respect, without the father imposing any punishment for such a refusal. The same shall be observed for those under guardianship."[16] Here, the young woman stated her reservation about the match with "modesty and respect," but her guardian mother still threatened the "punishment" of penury for her refusal to marry her choice of son-in-law. This violated the plain meaning of the Ordinance.

In several cases, the coercion came in the form of seduction. A man promises to marry a woman if she consents to have sex with him. She obliges. They have sex. He then leaves her, denying any interest in marriage. She is now stig-

---

14. See below Docs. 8-21 to 8-23.

15. The case of Jean Vernette and a girl from Brescia, as reported in Seeger, pp. 368-69. We have not been able to find the record of the case.

16. Doc. 1-2, item 8.

matized, sometimes pregnant too, and gets prosecuted for fornication. Her defense is that she was seduced on the false or fleeting promise of marriage. The question for the Consistory was whether to hold both parties to their marriage promises — particularly if either party wanted out, or if the seduction escalated into sexual assault or full-scale rape.

In a 1547 case of seduction, the Consistory held both parties to their promises (**Doc. 4-11**). The Consistory summoned an unmarried maid named Aima Portier to explain her pregnancy. She testified that her master's brother, Roland, had promised to marry her and they had then had sexual intercourse. The Consistory admonished Aima for her fornication, and sent her to the Council for punishment. But their real interest was to find Roland to compel him to marry her if it proved true that they were engaged. Roland was not to be found. He had evidently moved to Bernese-controlled lands. The Consistory sent the case to the Council who ordered that Roland be "properly punished" for his fornication and compelled to marry Aima if he returned.

Where the seduction was part of a more serious crime, however, the authorities seemed more bent on punishing the criminals than compelling them to marry. The 1557 case of Jaquema Quay and Claude Genod is a good case in point (**Doc. 4-12**). Claude had promised to marry Jaquema and had given her an engagement gift. The couple had then had sexual relations rather freely thereafter. Jaquema was now six months pregnant. The Consistory banned the couple from communion, and sent them to the Council, who ordered them imprisoned for their fornication. Claude apparently continued to visit the heavily pregnant Jaquema, and also left support money for her at the home where she was staying. On further investigation, the Consistory discovered that at least two other pregnant women were staying at the same home. Their boyfriends, too, continued to come by and to leave support money for them. The Consistory must have now suspected that the house was, in fact, a brothel, and that the money Claude was tendering was not for Jaquema's support, but for sexual services rendered. The Consistory sent the case immediately to the Council, who came down hard. They ordered Jaquema and the operators and other occupants of the home permanently banished, on pain of whipping if they returned. Claude was temporarily banished as well, though he was later permitted to return, suggesting that he had no obligation to marry Jaquema.

Sometimes the seduction escalated into (attempted) rape, and the authorities had to face some of the questions that Calvin had left unresolved in his exegesis of the Mosaic law on point. A 1547 case, for example, raised questions of assault, attempted rape, and coerced consent (**Doc. 4-13**). The case began innocently enough. A father named Jaques Gerod was called in to ask why his daughter Jeanne had suddenly left her position as maid to Pierre Durand. On investigation, the father discovered to his dismay that Pierre had been molesting Jeanne, and had attempted to rape her. Jeanne had discovered that several other maids who had served Pierre earlier had faced the same fate. She had thus left immediately. On hearing this, the Consistory called three other maids of Durand who related comparable experiences. They described Pierre's predatory pattern. He would pursue them with promises of marriage if they consented to his sexual advances. (Pierre's wife had been away for at least a year, making these promises of marriage believable.) These promises escalated into threats of rape if they refused him. All three maids, like Jeanne, had resisted Pierre's advances and left his employ before he could rape them.

When the Consistory confronted him, Pierre denied all impropriety, and suggested that this testimony was just a defamation campaign orchestrated by a local rival. He volunteered to be beheaded if he was guilty as charged. That evidently gave the Consistory enough pause to spare him from charges of attempted rape, forced seduction to marriage, and consequent solicitation of polygamy. They did, however, send him to the Council for his sexual assault and battery of Jeanne. That earned him twelve days in prison.

The 1552 case of Guillaume Darnex and Philippa involved full-scale rape coupled with a marriage promise (**Doc. 4-14**). Both Guillaume and Philippa had been servants in the same household. Guillaume raped Philippa several times. All along he promised to marry her and then gave her a small engagement gift, which she apparently kept. Their fellow servants had seen them together several times, though no one had witnessed any instance of rape or of consensual sex.

Philippa was later brought up on charges of fornication, perhaps because she had become pregnant. She testified twice under oath about Guillaume's repeated attacks on her and swore that she had not had sex with any other man. She also apparently insisted that she did not wish to marry Guillaume, despite his promises of marriage and her receipt of an engagement gift. The Consistory called in their master to see whether he knew anything or objected to his servants' conduct, but his testimony was inconclusive. Philippa's parents were also apparently not available. Guillaume denied any wrongdoing, and insisted that he did not wish to marry Philippa, despite the Consistory's best effort to persuade him. They sent the case to the Council for final disposition.

The Council now faced precisely the question that Calvin had left unresolved — how to interpret the Mosaic law requiring a rapist to marry his victim if her father did not object. Unfortunately, no record of the Council's final decision is at hand. But we have found no evidence that the couple was ever married.

The authorities came down hard in a 1557 case of rape of a young maid named Michee Morard (**Doc. 4-15**). Michee's master Hudry Rojod had raped her, and she was now pregnant. He gave her some fine clothing and a good deal of money — whether for her support or her silence is not clear. He also promised to find her a husband since he himself was already married. Rojod sought to arrange her marriage to an eligible man, but that match evidently did not occur. In an attempt to cover up the affair, Rojod's wife urged Michee to abort the child or to bring it to her on birth to be killed. A neighbor, who knew of the affair, urged Michee to carry the child to term and seek charitable support for its upbringing.

When this whole scandalous affair came to their attention, the Consistory moved swiftly. They questioned Rojod's wife closely. Though she denied any wrongdoing, they banned her from communion and sent her to the Council who imprisoned her. They banned both Michee and the neighbor woman from communion as well, evidently for failing to notify the authorities of this scandal. Michee was briefly imprisoned as well, for reasons not explained in the record. But the authorities saved their harshest punishment for Rojod, particularly when they learned he had earlier done the same thing to another maid. He was imprisoned for twelve days, heavily fined, and ordered to pay for the costs of Michee's child birth and convalescence, and further ordered to pay for the child's maintenance as well as continued support for Michee thereafter.

Frivolous, Drunken, and Mistaken Promises

The 1546 Marriage Ordinance called for the annulment of engagement promises made frivolously or while the parties were drunk:

> 11. Let all promises of marriage be made honorably and in the fear of God and not in dissoluteness or through reckless frivolity, as by merely offering a glass to drink together without previously having agreed in sober discussion, and let those who do otherwise be punished.[17]

Only a few such cases came before the Consistory for adjudication. In a 1546 case, for example, the Consistory summoned two young servants of Girard Perlet on suspicion of fornication (**Doc. 4-16**). The servants defended themselves by arguing they had exchanged marriage promises before their fellow servants, making their sex licit. The Consistory saw through the ruse. They pressed the parties, who betrayed that they had no real idea what marriage entailed and had not sought the approval of their guardians to marry. The Consistory de-

---

17. Doc. 1-2, item 8. On its face, this provision might well be read to outlaw not drunken promises, but frivolous toasts in the name of marriage. In Genevan practice, however, frivolous promises and drunken promises were distinguished, and both were viewed as independent grounds for annulling an engagement. Technically, a drunken promise could be viewed as a special kind of frivolous promise, but that was not how the impediments were interpreted.

clared their promises "frivolous" and sent the parties to the Council. The Council dissolved the purported marriage and sent the servants home with their guardians.

In a 1547 case, the authorities used the impediment of drunkenness to annul the engagement of Pierre Bron and a young maiden named Berte (**Doc. 4-17**). Pierre and Berte had been having sex rather freely both before and after their purported engagement, and Berte was pregnant at the time of the case. At a party one evening, when Pierre was "quite drunk," Berte's mistress had prompted Pierre to toast Berte on their engagement before witnesses. On hearing this development, Berte's father marched into the Consistory angrily charging Pierre with harming his daughter. The Consistory summoned a number of witnesses. They made quite clear that Berte was hardly innocent. Not only had she slept with Pierre and others, but in fact she may well have been already engaged to another man. That raised the stakes considerably, for Berte could now be charged not only with fornication but also with polygamy, a serious crime. The impediment of drunkenness saved her from the charge of polygamy. The Consistory determined that her engagement to Pierre was "void" because he had been drunk on the evening of his purported engagement promise to her. The Consistory determined further that Pierre was the father of Berte's child to be. On their recommendation, the Council imprisoned and fined him for fornication and ordered him to pay for Berte's birth expenses and subsequent maintenance.

Berte seems to have escaped with no punishment at all. Perhaps she was too advanced in her pregnancy to suffer the risk of prison. But normally (after 1546), the Council would order imprisonment of pregnant women, even if this sentence was suspended until after the birth. Berte was also not compelled to marry Pierre. Often when an eligible couple's illicit sex led to pregnancy, the Consistory would order a "shotgun wedding." Even if their verbal consent to marriage was impeded by Pierre's drunkenness, their mutual consent to have sex would normally have been enough to create a marriage promise. But in this case, Berte was not eligible for marriage. The Council determined that her first engagement remained valid. She would have to return to her fiancé, now armed with child support payments from Pierre.

Both in his writings and in his 1546 Marriage Ordinance, Calvin was silent on many of the traditional impediments of error or mistake. The medieval canon law had recognized a number of such impediments. These enabled parties to plead for an annulment on discovery that they had inadvertently married the wrong person (think of Jacob and Leah) or that the other party was of lower status or economic means, or had a decidedly different quality or character than was expected.

Calvin did say, in passing, that Jacob could have, and should have, dissolved his marriage to Leah.[18] But he did not translate this into a formal legal impediment of error of person. Calvin also recognized that engagements or marriages could be dissolved because of other kinds of errors — about the woman's virginity, or about either party's physical or mental health, sexual capacity, or prior marital history. But Calvin treated these as impediments of capacity and quality, not impediments of error, as we shall see in Chapters 7 and 9.

Writing in 1569, Theodore Beza took up various traditional impediments of error, and largely supported the medieval canon law on point (**Doc. 4-18**). Marrying the wrong person, or marrying a person who turned out to be enslaved rather than free, did create an impediment of error that could annul an engagement or marriage, Beza agreed with the canonists. For such errors intruded on the essence of a person's consent. But marrying a person who proved to be poorer in wealth, or to have a less desirable quality or character than expected, did not trigger an impediment. These errors did not go to the essence of the marriage but were only incidental. This, too, was in full accord with the tradition.

It was important, however, Beza warned, to ensure that plaintiffs in these cases were entirely innocent and had been tricked into entering the engagement or marriage on these mistaken terms. It was also important to ensure that only the innocent party could bring the action for annulment. The "trickster" could have no standing to sue for annulment in these cases. Furthermore, contracts entered mistakenly should be viewed as only voidable, not void, Beza maintained. The innocent party would have to file for an annulment to have them declared void. And, if the parties were already married, rather than just engaged, prudence strongly commended the innocent party to continue with the marriage if he or she could do so in good conscience.

Conditional Promises

Another prominent issue at medieval canon law concerned conditional consent to engagement and marriage.[19] What was the status of a promise when a party said: I shall marry you "if my parents agree"; "after you have secured a job"; "provided you quit your military service"; "so long as the wedding takes place within six months"; "if we can live in my hometown"; "provided you pay me certain property"; "after my father dies"; "if God preserves me"; "so long as we have no children"; "if you can touch the sky"; "whenever a woman becomes pope"; "if you can drink the sea empty"; "provided you kill my rival" or any

18. Comm. Gen. 29:27–30:3.
19. See Weigand, vol. 1; Bartholomew T. Timlin, *Conditional Matrimonial Consent: An Historical Synopsis and Commentary* (Washington, DC, 1934).

number of other such conditions. Did those promises automatically lapse if the condition was not met, or would the parties have to litigate? What if the conditions in question were impossible, silly, or downright illegal?

By the eve of the Reformation, the canonists had gathered a complex jurisprudence around these questions.[20] They herded conditional promises into a whole complex of categories. Three kinds of conditions were the most important and common at medieval canon law. "Honest possible" conditions ("if my parents consent"; "so long as you move to Geneva by September 1"; "provided you buy me a horse and carriage before the wedding") were valid, and engagement or marriage promises would be voided on their breach. "Dishonest possible" conditions that vitiated an essential dimension of marriage ("so long as we have no children"; "provided I may maintain a concubine"; "so long as you remain unbaptized") were invalid, and automatically voided the promises. All other conditions were generally disregarded and the promises enforced as if the condition had not been made. These included "dishonest possible" conditions that did not go to the essence of the marriage ("so long as you kill my rival") as well as conditions that were naturally or legally impossible ("if you empty the sea"; "when a woman becomes pope").[21]

Calvin and his Consistory colleagues continued much of the traditional law of conditions — though they simplified it considerably and explicitly outlawed the use of property conditions. The 1546 Marriage Ordinance had three provisions on conditional promises. Item 6 recognized that engagement promises could be made "conditionally or otherwise."[22] Item 14 made quite clear that property conditions would not be enforced: "Failure to pay a dowry or money or provide an outfit shall not prevent the marriage from coming into full effect, since these are only accessory."[23] Item 15 was more ambiguous:

> Although in discussing or arranging a marriage it is lawful to add conditions or reserve someone's consent, nevertheless when it comes to making the promise let it be pure and simple, and let a statement made conditionally not be regarded as a promise of marriage.[24]

Read together with items 6 and 14, item 15 seems to say that engagement contracts (those made "in discussing or arranging a marriage") could have non-property conditions attached, but marriage contracts had to be unconditional.

---

20. Good early modern summaries are provided in Sanchez, bk. 5, disp. 1-19; Henry Swinburne, *A Treatise of Spousals, or Matrimonial Contracts* (London, 1686), pp. 109ff.

21. R. H. Helmholz, *Marriage Litigation in Medieval England* (Cambridge, 1974), pp. 50ff.

22. See above Doc. 1-2.

23. Doc. 1-2.

24. Doc. 1-2.

This was, in fact, how the Consistory read the 1546 Marriage Ordinance. Parties could seek annulment of engagement contracts only, not marriage contracts, on grounds of breach of condition. And, if the conditions involved property or dowry payments, the Consistory disregarded them and enforced the engagement contracts without hesitation.

Michel Pesson and George Marin found this out in a case that came before the Consistory just after the 1546 Marriage Ordinance had been issued (**Doc. 4-19**). The couple had been properly engaged some two years before. George's father had consented, and Michel had given her an engagement ring. The Consistory wanted to know why they had not married. They both claimed that their engagement contract was conditioned upon George's delivery of certain property to Michel, which she had not yet been able to obtain. The Consistory would hear none of it. They sent the parties to the Council who ordered them to marry immediately. As we shall see in Chapter 11 on the economics of marriage, this remained the Consistory's unwavering posture on property conditions throughout Calvin's tenure.

While neither Calvin nor Beza explained his distaste for property conditions, this was, in part, a natural extension of their argument against the validity of coerced promises. Coercion, whether physical or psychological, kept parties from making their promises with free and full consent. Among the types of coercion that Calvin and Beza recognized was the coercion born of poverty, including threats of disinheritance or exploitation of someone's poverty. There was sometimes only a blurry line between cases of coerced consent and consent conditioned on property transactions. "I shall disinherit you unless you marry this man" was not so much different from "I shall marry you provided your guardian pays us your inheritance." There was also not much difference between the coercive promise: "I shall pay for your transport to Geneva provided you marry me on arrival" and the conditional promise: "I shall marry you so long as you pay for my transport to Geneva." The economic incentives and disincentives in these cases were comparable. They impeded a party's ability to give free and full consent. To be sure, not all such property conditions were inherently coercive. But enough were that this may have been one of the factors that motivated Calvin and his colleagues to outlaw them.

Another motivation was suggested by the language of item 14 of the 1546 Marriage Ordinance, namely, that issues of property were only "accessory" or "ancillary" to the essence of marriage. Calvin and his colleagues wanted to separate marriage contracts and marital property contracts more firmly than had become customary. The medieval canonists, too, separated these contracts. For a marriage to be valid at medieval canon law, a marriage contract, an oral or written agreement by the couple to marry, was essential. A marital property contract, an agreement to exchange property in anticipation or in consideration of marriage, was not essential. But allowing marriage contracts to include property conditions blurred this separation. It made the validity of a marriage turn in part on the delivery of marital property. The medieval canonists had elaborate philosophical arguments about the matter and form of contracts to keep marriage and property issues technically separate. For Calvin and Beza, this was all too casuistic and confusing. They thought it simpler to bar property conditions in engagement and marriage contracts, and that remained the law in Geneva during their lifetimes.

There were other conditions and reservations to engagement, however, that did go to the essence of marriage. These Calvin and his colleagues allowed and enforced. A good example was the 1547 conditional engagement contract signed by a former Genevan named Helias who was now living in a nearby town of Neuchâtel (**Doc. 4-20**). No doubt instructed by counsel, Helias's fiancée had conditioned her engagement to him on proof that he was "not bound by any other marriage bond." This condition did go to the essence of marriage, namely, whether Helias was in fact free to contract a new marriage. Calvin and other members of the Company of Pastors respected this condition, and certified to their Neuchâtel colleagues that Helias was not married or engaged and thus free to marry.

Contrast that with the condition that new immigrants to Geneva frequently asked the Consistory to enforce: "I shall marry you, provided you move to Geneva with me." This was the issue in a 1554 case of Jean Philippe and Anne Renaud (**Doc. 4-21**). The conditional promise in this case was the converse of the coercive promise in the case of Louise and Jean that we saw above (**Doc. 4-10**): "I shall move to Geneva with you provided you marry me." The Consistory distinguished these two cases. As we saw, they annulled the contract of Louise and Jean on grounds of coerced consent. But they upheld the contract of Jean and Anne on grounds that the condition concerned a matter ancillary to the essence of marriage. Where a married couple would live after their wedding was hardly relevant to the core question whether they were fit, competent, and eligible to consent to marriage. Jean and Anne had consented, and they would have to proceed with their marriage, even if they ultimately lived elsewhere.

It was quite common for parties to accept an engagement proposal conditioned on the approval of their parents or guardians. This added layer of consent marked the cases of Paula and Marco (**Doc. 4-7**), Jehanne and Nicolas (**Doc. 4-8**), and Guillaume and Philippa (**Doc. 4-14**). The Consistory usually respected these conditional engagements, and annulled them when parental consent was not forthcoming.[25] For parental consent, like individual consent, did go to the essence of the marriage, particularly if the party stipulating the condi-

---

25. See other examples in Seeger, pp. 311-14.

tion was a minor. Indeed in such cases, as we shall see in the next chapter, parental consent was as essential to the validity of the marriage as the consent of the couple.

Thus in a 1552 case, for example, Pierre Sautier proposed to Rolanda in the presence of witnesses and gave her a sou (**Doc. 4-22**). She accepted his proposal, conditional upon her parents' consent to the marriage. When her parents did not consent, Rolanda returned the ring to Pierre, who promptly became engaged to another woman. When he was accused of bigamy, Pierre defended himself by saying that the first engagement contract was automatically voided by the breach of the condition of parental consent. The authorities agreed, although they would have doubtless preferred that Pierre ask them for their judgment about this, rather than make it on his own.

Similarly in a 1556 case, a young woman named Guyonne conditioned her consent to Hugo Cant's proposal on the consent of her parents (**Doc. 4-23**). The parents dissented, and Guyonne petitioned the Consistory to annul her engagement. Although her parents were Catholics, and Guyonne gave only hearsay testimony of their dissent, the Consistory respected this breach of condition, and declared the engagement contract "void and fraudulent."[26]

It was one thing for fiancé(e)s to condition their consent on the consent of their parents. The Consistory enforced these conditions readily, without much second guessing of the parents who dissented. It was quite another thing, however, for the parents to give their consent conditionally. The Consistory would respect the parents' stipulated conditions only if those conditions, too, went to the essence of the marriage.

One condition imposed by parents (or guardians) that the Consistory did respect was the requirement that a fiancé(e) confirm an engagement contract executed on his or her behalf. Parents and matchmakers did sometimes make conditional engagement contracts, pending confirmation by the man or woman to be married.[27] These conditions were respected. Likewise, parents sometimes did enter engagement contracts on behalf of their minor children who had not yet reached the age of consent. These contracts, too, were conditioned on the child confirming them upon reaching the age of consent.[28] Such conditions, too, were respected. Indeed, the Consistory often looked hard to ensure that children, upon reaching maturity, had the opportunity to consent without pressure from parents or guardians; if they dissented, the engagement contract was annulled.

---

26. It was not entirely clear from the record, however, whether it was the lack of parental consent or the danger of interreligious marriage that motivated the Consistory. There was nothing to indicate why the contract was called "fraudulent."

27. See Chapter 3 on courtship.

28. See Chapter 6 on capacity to contract marriage.

The Consistory had less patience with more trivial parentally-imposed conditions. The 1547 case of Louis Bourgeoise and Mademoiselle Levrat is a good example (**Doc. 4-24**). Some nine months before, Louis had become properly engaged to Levrat. He had given her two engagement rings and had sought the consent of her parents. Levrat's mother gave her consent first, her father later. Levrat's parents, however, imposed a condition. Out of consideration for the feelings of their older daughter who was not yet married, they asked the couple to keep their engagement secret and their marriage postponed until the older daughter was herself married. Louis and Levrat had apparently agreed to this. But now, several months later, they were eager to get married — so eager in fact that they began fornicating together. They announced their wedding plans. Levrat's father objected, claiming this was a breach of a condition that they had all agreed to. The Consistory tried to persuade father Levrat to consent to the marriage. He continued to insist that this was in breach of an express condition. The Consistory had heard enough. They sent the couple to the Council recommending that they be ordered to marry.

Summary and Conclusions

One of the hallmarks of the medieval canon law was to make marriage a bilateral contract whose validity depended on the mutual consent of the parties. Even if a matchmaker facilitated the union, or a parent encouraged it, the new relationship was not a marriage unless and until both the man and the woman freely and fully consented. Contracts entered into by force, fear, or fraud, through trick, surprise, or mistake, by blackmail, extortion, or seduction, or while one or both of the parties were drunk or impaired, were all presumptively invalid at canon law. If one of the parties pled this impediment of non-consent after the engagement, or shortly after the wedding, the relationship would be annulled. If both parties pled that they had mutually consented to end their relationship, their engagement would also be annulled.

Calvin, Beza, and the Genevan Consistory retained much of this tradition, but rejected the traditional right of the parties to dissolve their engagements by mutual consent. Calvin grounded the doctrine of mutual consent in several Old Testament passages, and denounced both Old Testament patriarchs and modern-day parents who coerced their children into unwanted relationships. Calvin was particularly zealous to protect the consent of women to engagements and marriage, though he dealt with this issue rather clumsily in interpreting various biblical passages on rape. Outside of this tragic context, however, Calvin stood foursquare against enforcing any engagement or marriage contracts where the free will of either party was impeded. As he said repeatedly:

"[I]f the husband and the wife are not in mutual agreement and do not love each other, this is a profanation of marriage, and not a marriage at all, properly speaking. For the [mutual] will is the principal bond."

The Consistory and Council thus annulled engagement or marriage contracts where they found no full or free consent on both sides. They annulled contracts where one of the parties was physically threatened or psychologically coerced into marriage, where one or both of them was drunk or made frivolous or insincere promises, where one party was seduced, tricked, blackmailed, or fraudulently induced into giving consent, or where one party was exploiting the poverty or need of the other. In all these cases, the Consistory looked very hard at the evidence, and if they were satisfied that the parties had not mutually consented, they recommended annulment which the Council ordered.

Where the parties gave their mutual consent to engagement but then later changed their minds, however, the Consistory held them to their promises. Even if the parties were now fundamentally at odds and both wanted out of their engagement, Calvin and the Consistory often ordered them to marry in accordance with their engagement promises. For an engagement contract, once made, could not be broken unless the parties could prove another impediment. If it had been properly formed, the engagement contract could not be dissolved even by mutual consent. This underscored Calvin's repeated counsel that we reviewed in Chapter 3: that parties must meet, become well acquainted, and deliberate carefully with each other and their parents and peers before they became engaged. To be sure, it was easier to get out of an engagement than a marriage, for the roll of engagement impediments was considerably longer than the roll of marital impediments. But it was even easier to get out of a courtship. Either party could simply leave, or the parties could mutually agree to sever their relationship. All this was a notable departure from the medieval tradition, which had allowed parties to dissolve engagement contracts by mutual consent. What was a two-stage process in the medieval tradition now became a three-stage process in Reformation Geneva — courtship, engagement, and marriage.

Calvin and his colleagues also departed somewhat from the medieval law of conditional engagement or marriage contracts. In Calvin's Geneva, parties could seek to annul only their engagements, and not their marriages, on grounds of breach of condition. Further, the breached conditions that would warrant annulment had to go to the essence of the marriage, and not involve ancillary matters. The Consistory honored engagement contracts conditioned on the approval of the man's parents or on the woman's ability to prove that prior marriage was properly dissolved. Breach of those conditions would dissolve the engagement contracts, for they involved essential questions of whether the parties had and could consent to the engagement. The Consistory did not, however, honor engagement contracts conditioned on the man's delivery of a promised engagement gift or the wife's willingness to move to his hometown. Those matters were ancillary to the fundamental question of whether the parties had mutually consented to get married. Even if both parties now wanted out of the engagement because of the breach of these ancillary promises, the Consistory and Council ordered them to marry.

SELECTED DOCUMENTS

4-1 Sermon on Deuteronomy 25:5-12 (1556)[29]

These obligations [of Levirate marriage] must have some limit. . . . If a woman was required to take husbands until all those of a lineage had refused her, what would come of it? But it speaks here of the closest relationship, that is those [brothers] who live together so as to be known. For if a woman were obligated [to remarry], without knowing to whom, and were required to take someone whom she had never seen, this servitude would clearly be too cruel. There would be no fitness in it. And thus Our Lord wished this law to have certain limits. . . .

But if none of her relatives wants to receive her, "let the woman go to the elders of the town," and let the discharge of her duty be evident, so that she may provide [for] herself if God so decides. Let her go to the court and have the nearest relative summoned, that is, the one for whom it is lawful to take her, and let the judges try to induce him to do so. Our Lord did not want to condemn men irrevocably to take women. Although there was good reason here, God considered that compulsory and forced marriages never come to a good end. It is true that God might state and command a precise directive — that the man who is the nearest relative must marry the wife of someone who dies without heirs. God could state this. Why does he still permit the man to refuse with ignominy? It is because if the husband and the wife are not in mutual agreement and do not love each other, this is a profanation of marriage, and not a marriage at all, properly speaking.

For the will is the principal bond; the man must recognize that the woman is like his own body, is half of his own person. "This is the bone of my bone," said Adam, being inspired by God. And this gives a common rule to all men; it is not a question merely of Eve, but of what should be retained and observed until the end. Because then this mutual agreement is required for marriage, we note that Our Lord did not wish strictly to require relatives to marry women who were widows and without children, but he granted us a certain respite. And from this we must conclude, when a man is going to marry and he takes a wife, let him take her of his own free will, knowing that where there is not a true and pure love, there is nothing but disorder, and one can expect no grace from God. The outcome will always be evil when the parties do not endeavor to love each other in the name of God so that they live with a quiet conscience. . . .

Now it says here, "Let the judges exhort the man, if they see that he persists

29. CO 28:223-34.

140

in his opinion: let the woman pull the shoe from his foot, spit at him" in contempt, "and ask that God do the same to all those who do not wish to maintain a lineage in Israel." Now here we must note again that God wishes the judges to speak to the man to urge him as far as they can. If he still does not wish to consent, let them be content with the punishment that is given to him. From this we see that magistrates and officers of justice should abstain from force and violence in what they cannot simply command.

4-2 Commentary on the Harmony of the Law Exodus 22:16-17 (1563)[30]

"If a man seduces a virgin who is not betrothed, and lies with her, he shall give the marriage present for her, and make her wife. If her father utterly refuses to give her to him, he shall pay money equivalent to the marriage present for virgins." . . . Although God here remits the criminal penalty, fornication displeases Him. . . . But here he has consideration only for young women, lest, having been deceived and lost their virginity, they should become prostitutes and the land defiled by prostitution. The remedy is that a man who has corrupted a young woman should be compelled to marry her and also to give her a dowry from his own property. Otherwise, he might afterward cast her off and she would go away from her bed [both despoiled and] penniless. But, if the marriage does not please her father, the penalty imposed on her seducer is that he should assign her a dowry.

4-3 Sermon on Deuteronomy 22:25-30 (1556)[31]

[W]e see how God wishes marriages to be loyally maintained. And there is good reason for this, or otherwise the whole order of nature must be overthrown. For there is nothing that should be more strictly preserved and maintained among men. Other contracts should indeed be observed in good faith, but this contract, since it surpasses them in sanctity, should receive greater reverence. And so it is not without cause that God ordains that anyone who encounters a young girl who has already been promised [that is, already under an engagement contract] and who violates her, that he should die without reprieve. . . .

[N]ote that here he compares a man who has raped a girl to a brigand, who having encountered his neighbor murders him. He does not compare him

---

30. CO 24:652 (OTC adapted).
31. CO 28:54-59.

to someone who beats another. Now therefore this comparison shows clearly that the act in question is very dreadful and is not tolerable. For if the lives of men are precious to God, so is chastity and the faith that is promised in marriage; for a woman should be a companion for her husband in life and death.

And when this is falsified, what more remains among men? And so, to make the crime appear more serious, God says it is a form of brigandage when a man, having encountered a girl, takes away her honor, that is by force. This crime is unpardonable. . . .

God, however, has not always punished transgressions as he might — punished, I say, in the Law he gave for the regulation of Israel. For he tolerated many things because of the hardness of that people, as Our Lord Jesus showed them, in speaking of the divorces that were carried out against reason and equity. For it says here, "If a man finds a girl, and without his forcing her she lets herself be seduced, let him be set free if he gives money for the marriage of the girl and then takes her to wife, and he shall not have the common liberty of ever being able to leave her." Now it is true that this was a sort of punishment for a man who had fornicated; but that it was of such rigor as the case deserved, certainly not.

What shall we say, then? That God wished to permit fornication, or that he left the reins loose, or that he wished to declare that the sin was entirely pardoned? None of these. . . . For although God does not punish with extreme rigor a man who has fornicated with a young girl, this is not because fornication is to be pardoned in any way. If it is not punished before men, God still reserves his own rights. . . .

Thus in the fornication Moses speaks of here, since it involves injury and dishonor to a man because his daughter would be sent back, the one who has seduced her must provide her marriage portion. For otherwise, she will not thereafter be able to find a partner elsewhere. Thus he must take her as a wife if her father wishes it. Moreover, if, after a time he sent her away, she would again be left unprovided for. Therefore he must retain her. Let him be deprived of the common right [of divorce], so that he may never abandon her. This, I say, is a provision God has made because of the losses to one of the parties.

4-4 Calvin's *Consilium* on Coerced Consent of Children (n.d.)[32]

Dear Sir and Brothers: Insofar as you have found it desirable to request our counsel and advice concerning the marriage vows between M. Jean Focard and Margueritte Heberarde — that is, whether their vows are valid — we, having assembled in the name of God, are in accord to offer the following.

32. CO 10/1:238-39, translated in *Calvin's Ecclesiastical Advice*, pp. 129-31.

Having reviewed the acts and proceedings that we extracted from your registrar, concerning what Margueritte said, her mother and sister tell us, quite flatly, that the girl was deceived and that they forced her into it. Her aunt — the widow of M. Pierre Focard — as well as his brother-in-law and servant, have also sworn that they knew of this all along.

Furthermore, there are three witnesses, of whom one, an Alexis Myot, solemnly swears that he was present when their vows were exchanged. A second, Simon Gaillard, says that when it came time for Margueritte to make her vows, he never heard her say the first word. The third, M. Pierre Nemauso, the royal notary, says that when it was Margueritte's turn to make her vows, he could tell by her countenance that what she was saying brought her no pleasure, and because he turned his back while she was crying, he heard her say none of the words one is accustomed to hearing. He also swears that, since that day, whenever he addresses her by her married name, she always replies that this is not her name, as he well knows. Moreover, he has sworn under oath that he did not want to record this marriage, which he witnessed, since he knew that it was not of God, insofar as Margueritte had not consented to it.

Hence we note that although a ceremony for the exchanging of marriage vows occurred, not a single witness swears that the girl said anything by way of consent. The second witness says that he is uncertain that she said anything. The third — whose testimony we can most trust, since he is a notary public and accountable for recording marriages — swears he saw no signs of agreement.

Now, inasmuch as the girl cannot be expected to settle this matter, it remains to know who can. The notary public's testimony is amply sufficient. The aunt, the brother-in-law, and Pierre Havart's sister also constitute a valid witness. Above all, there is the mother's confession that she forced her daughter into it. Hence we conclude that the girl was forced into it; consequently, no foundation for marriage exists. Furthermore, M. Jean Focard himself affirms that he has not had an opportunity to speak to Margueritte for some time and that he has never understood what she actually said at their wedding. Therefore, given the present facts, we cannot rule that a marriage occurred. Rather, since the act took place contrary to order and reason, we judge it to be null.

Nevertheless, since this is a delicate matter and could cause a great deal of conflict between the parties, and, in order to forestall any unfortunate repercussions as well as to prevent future rumors and reproach, we are of the opinion that M. Focard should summon the mother and the girl before the common court and there have the marriage annulled. The two should solemnly swear and confirm what they have attested to be true. In any event, in our definitive judgment, their marriage vows are null, and each party is free to marry someone else.

4-5 Theodore Beza on Coerced Marriage Promises (1569)[33]

Promises to marry made through force or fear which fall upon a man of firm character . . . are thought to carry no weight unless another later free consent validates them. Even though this sort of promise is not without some appearance of consent, especially if an oath is attached, here the pledge seems to be carried out to our detriment. Still because wise men rightly judge, especially as regards this contract, that free consent is required so that the person who makes the promise can be forced to see it through. Such promises are held as void if [the person involved] shall have made a good case regarding force and this sort of fear. The person who made the pledge should be gravely warned to examine over and over what was his inner attitude when he did this, lest he sin against his conscience. But what I said a short time ago also must be observed, namely that when sexual intercourse followed or even an attempt at it which the woman did not resist, a later appeal to force or fear is worthless.

4-6 Case of Pierre Jaqueno and Claude Conte (1545)[34]

(Oct. 8, 1545). Le Corbet said it is true that he is engaged to a maidservant. Let them be made to come Thursday.

(Oct. 22, 1545). Again appeared Pierre Jaqueno, called Corbet, who had already been here last Thursday. He said he became engaged to a serving woman and that it is true that he gave her three sous in the name of marriage. The woman gave him back the three sous, and many respectable people told him he had taken a heedless woman. Also that she does not want him, saying she would give him a foot in his belly. He said she got up from beside her mother, and the mother said to him, "Take charge of her, she is leaving my side now."

Claude, his fiancée, daughter of Nouri [Mauris] Conte, was called. She does not want to confess having been engaged to him, saying it is true that she went to him to get a bucket of water. Corbet put three sous in her apron, and she does not think it was in marriage. She says she left him and restored the three sous.

Decided: that concerning marriage, that they be remanded before the Council for promise. For Monday before the Council.

(Oct. 22, 1545). Corbet was summoned to learn in what house he asked for her one evening. He said it was at the house of a young weaver living at the Tour de Boël. Claude was admonished because she denies being pregnant. She was admonished to protect the fruit of her womb, still denying being pregnant.

---

33. Beza, TRD, 2:82-83 (translated by John P. Donnelly, S.J.)
34. R. Consist. II, 1v, 4v, 5 (using existing published translation).

[The Consistory recommended to the Council that "the marriage may be declared of no validity, and inform them that it seems that the girl is pregnant, and it would be good for the mother of the girl to answer about this." The Council declared the marriage void on October 26, Claude Conte still claiming that she was not pregnant and that her husband had been dead for three years.]

4-7   Case of Marco Ducloz and Paula (1547)[35]

(April 21, 1547). Marco Ducloz of Peissy was asked about certain promises he made with certain girls. He answered that it is true that there was a gathering in a tavern where there was one named Paula. They drank together, but not in the name of marriage.

Paula was asked whether she is married. She answered no, and it is quite true that someone next to them [said?] they drank in the name of marriage if it could be done, and she has a father and mother who were not there.

Guillaume was asked whether he did not drink with Antoine, daughter of Henri Jaillod, in the name of marriage. He answered no, and that if they drank together it was for company.

Antoine, daughter of Henri Jaillod, answered it is true that between day and night [at dusk] they were at their house and they gave him drink in the name of marriage, saying, "Drink, master." He denied it. Marcoz was called again to confront him with Guillaume's denying that she ever drank in their company. He said yes.

Decided: that they be sharply admonished not to abuse such promises in this way any more, also for their lies spoken here, and declare the marriage void, and that it would be a bad example and result.

4-8   Case of Nicolas Adduard and Jehanne Pyto (1546)[36]

(April 8, 1546). Nicolas Adduard of Les Essertets and Jehanne, widow of the late Jean Pyto of Neydens, were admonished and asked why they are here. He responded that he swore faith to and drank in the name of marriage with her. She denied it, and said she was swindled. Asked whether there were any people present at the promise, the [alleged] husband said there were eight people, among which company was an uncle of hers who promised him six score florins and all of their household goods and cattle. She excused herself, producing an excusatory petition.

35. R. Consist. III, 58.
36. R. Consist. II, 48v, 50v.

Decided: that the marriage should not go into effect and that the woman should have the two she would most like to have speak about it come, that is her uncle, and with him also two of those who were at the promise. She answered that she cannot bring him because he does not dare to cross the bridge because of certain debts. Here on Thursday.

(April 15, 1546). Two witnesses produced by Nicolas Adduard of Les Essertets: Michel Gillard of Germany and Nicolas Marchant of Les Essertets [appeared]. Claude, widow of Petet of Neydens, was called, and was asked whether she knows anything against these witnesses and whether they are relatives of Nicolas Adduard. She said they are respectable people; she does not know about [whether they are] relatives. Gillard answered that he was present in the company when the parties drank together in marriage, and it was stated that she would give him six score florins and more and a cow. Asked whether there was any reservation made, he said no, except that she begged that no one yet disturb her brother about it, because he would be angry.

Asked the reason why he does not complete the marriage begun, he [Nicolas Adduard] answered that it is not his fault. Asked whether he would take her, he said he does not want her because he would get no money. He said it depends on the decision of the Council. She does not want to accept marriage. They were admonished because Nicolas told her that he had only three children, and he has four. Also she promised him six score florins p.p. [petit poids] and can give him nothing. They are both found to have lied and cheated.

Decided: that they be remanded before the Council, declaring to them that there is a marriage and about the lies on one side and the other, and praying our Lords to give consideration to having edicts [published] concerning marriages.

[The following Monday, when called before the Council, Jehanne still opposed the marriage, but Nicolas wanted the marriage. On April 19, the Council finally decided that the marriage should be recognized and celebrated.]

4-9   Case of Jaques Charvier and Anne de Beaumont (1552)[37]

(March 24, 1552). Jaques Charvier, carpenter of Vienne, presented a petition against Anne de Beaumont, formerly a nun of the abbey of Cîteaux in Dauphiné. In this he stated that he delivered her from the prisons of Vienne, and he was a son of Jollye, and then promised her marriage, as it is more fully stated in the petition.

Decided: that for Thursday they both be summoned. She lives in the Pellisserie in the house of Manissie.

37. R. Consist. VII, 12, 14, 17.

(March 31, 1552). Jaques Charvier and Anne de Beaumont [appeared]. The petition by the aforesaid was read. He alleged she promised him marriage, being and having been delivered from the prison of Vienne. She said it was true that on compulsion, wanting to leave the prison, she made such a frivolous promise, and that afterwards she was told both by some of her friends and on behalf of her father and mother not to marry. When she made such a promise it was when she was greatly troubled and disturbed in spirit, and may one take pity on her ignorance, and he persuaded her to her dishonor. He answered whether the things contained in the petition are not true. She was admonished separately to consider with an awakened conscience such a promise that was thus [made] for her and to take her from the prison; she still said she [was] badly informed.

Decided: that Monsieur Budé and his two journeymen be summoned for Thursday to hear what they may know before we may rightly decide regarding the promise and his wanting to take her by force, and because she has said that she has a letter of credence. Let us see it if she has it now, or on Thursday present the letter sent by her mother. That it is proven that her mother is trying to make her peace with her father, and that she not marry. Note: go to Master Raymond [Chauvet, minister] for the witnesses.

(April 7, 1552). Master Jean Budé, witness to the marriage of those named above, testified that when Anne arrived in this city she addressed him as a client, because she had come from the prisons of Vienne and he is one of the procurators of the poor. She told him that she had promised the aforesaid [Charvier] last Thursday on condition that the church of this city consented, and many other statements, such as having seen her in the presence of Monsieur Calvin. Confirmed such a promise.

[The case was evidently remanded to the Council. On April 19, the Council ordered that the engagement could be annulled because it was formed through coercion. But they also ordered Anne to produce documentation of her parents' dissent to the marriage. When Anne produced that the next week, her engagement was annulled.]

4-10 Case of Louise Fornier and Jean Tru (1559)[38]

(Aug. 3, 1559). Louise Fornier, daughter of Pierre Fornier, widow of Amied Revet, and Jean Tru of Dauphiné appeared. She stated that, being in her country and desiring to come here for the Gospel, she urged and asked Jean to bring her here, but Jean did not want to do anything unless she promised to marry him.

---

38. R. Consist. XV, 145v-146.

Because of her desire to leave the papacy, she told him that she promised him her faith in marriage, provided that God was not offended because she was older than he, and that she would follow the advice of respectable people when she was here. And it is true that he wanted to give her a coin [*teston*] in corroboration of the promise, but she did not want to receive it. Jean confessed it, and he wants to have her for his wife. She said she does not wish it, unless it is so decided, because of his poverty and youth.

Decided: to remand them before the Council for Monday to have the young lady purge herself before them by oath that she neither intended nor desired to marry him, but what she did in the matter, it was from desire to have herself brought and conducted here. And having taken such an oath, let her be freed from the said promise she gave, it having been made by compulsion and force.

[The Council ordered the annulment on August 7.]

4-11 Case of Roland Vuarrier and Aima (1547)[39]

(Nov. 17, 1547). Aima, daughter of Guillame Portier, [François] Vuarrier's maid, [appeared and] confessed being pregnant by Roland Vuarrier, brother of her master. He promised her marriage, and she intends to have no other husband.

Decided: that she be admonished to try to get her [purported] husband to come here Thursday to learn the truth, whether they are married.

(Nov. 24, 1547).[40] Aima, maid of the secretary Vuarrier, was also remanded before the Council. She confessed to being pregnant by Roland Vuarrier of Neydens, brother of her master, saying he swore faith to her as a wife. The decision is that she be remanded before the Council to be given such punishment as seems [good] to them.

(Nov. 24, 1547). Vuarrier's maid has been remanded to return to the Consistory and get her fiancé, by whom she is pregnant, to come here. She answered that he said that he is a subject of Bern. She confessed having fornicated since the month of May, and having afterwards received communion.

Decided: that she be admonished and remanded before the Council.

[The Council ordered that Roland Vuarrier be "properly punished" for his fornication when he reappeared.]

---

39. R. Consist. III, 148, 178, 181.

40. This passage, although it precedes the one above in the Consistory register, actually follows it in date. Its contents are repeated below in more detail. This is another case of a different scribe giving the same information as was given by Jean Porral, the regular scribe, on a different page.

4-12   Case of Jaquema Quay and Claude Genod (1557)[41]

(Aug. 12, 1557). Jaquema, sister of André Quay, was summoned because she is six months pregnant. She said that Claude, servant of Joly Claude, is her lover, and said that she began to fornicate at Joly Claude's house. She said he gave her a bouquet and a veil in the name of marriage.

Decided: that the fornicator be remanded here for Thursday with Joly Claude and the harlot and her sister. Communion forbidden to Jaquema. Henriette, wife of André Quay, remanded to Thursday.

(Aug. 19, 1557). Jaquema, sister of André Quay, was charged with having fornicated with Claude Genod of Habère, carpenter. She answered and confessed that he had her company at Darbey's at night and also at her brother's and at Joly Claude's, named Claude Abram.

Decided: that Jaquema be remanded before the Council and that Abram be required to present Claude Genod, who is absent and who lived in his house, where his property is, between now and Monday. Also to command Henriette, wife of Quay, to present Jaquema on Thursday. Abram and his wife were forbidden to release to Claude any of his property that is in their house. After this Jaquema said that Claude promised her marriage. [Prohibition of] communion was continued for her.

[On August 30 the Council condemned Jaquema Quay and Claude Genod to six days in prison on bread and water. On September 7, following their release, they were also fined 10 florins apiece.]

(Dec. 2, 1557). Claude Genod, carpenter, stated that he fornicated with the woman for whom he was punished ten full months ago, and has not fornicated with her since; therefore the child she carries is not his. On this Henriette, wife of Pierre de Monthouz, gilder, was summoned. She said that the woman who is pregnant by Genod lives at their house, and he often came there to find her in their house, at least five or six times within a short time. When he had entered there she went to get wine for him and for her husband, who was in the house with the pregnant woman. She also said that Jean Songey of Lancy comes to find another woman they are housing with them.

De Monthouz was called, and said they are housing the woman pregnant by Claude Genod, and it was at the solicitation and entreaty of Genod, who said to him, "Do her good." And another girl also lives there who begged them to shelter her until she found a master, who he said he has heard was pregnant by Jean du Songey of Lancy, who has sometimes come to visit her and whom he has lent ten florins. He said also that Genod came with him at least four or five times [to visit] his harlot, and he gave him money (to the

41. R. Consist. XII, 85v, 89v, 124-124v.

one speaking) three or four times, three or four sous, for him to give to the pregnant girl.

Louise, daughter of Claude du Villard of Moisin, was summoned. She said she has been in this city about eight months, and she has lived with Michel Le Cousturier and Jean Billard. Also she has lived with de Monthouz fully seven weeks. Nevertheless denied having ever spoken to Jean Songey, by whom she has had a child, except one Sunday. Also de Monthouz and his wife said that Songey came to their house one Sunday.

The aforesaid and above-named were confronted with Genod. It is evident that Genod, against the commands of God and of our Lords, has often gone to visit his whore at de Monthouz's house, [and therefore] deserves punishment; for which reason it was decided to send the whole bunch before the Council and beg them to purge their city of them. The pregnant girl is named Jaquema.

[On December 6 the Council banished Pierre de Monthouz, Henriette his wife, and Jaquema Quay in perpetuity, giving them seven days to leave the city on pain of being whipped. Claude Genod was ordered to leave within three days and not return for a month. The next day Pierre de Monthouz appealed his sentence. The Council maintained its decision, but said it would decide later whether to reconsider, "according to how he behaves outside (the city)."]

4-13   Case of Jeanne Gerod and Pierre Durand (1547)[42]

(March 17, 1547). Jaques Gerod was asked to tell the reason why his daughter [Jeanne] left the Drooler's[43] house where she served, regarding which the rumor is that Drooler wanted to rape her. He said he does not know; nevertheless that his daughter at present has gone to Lancy, and he will have her speak to the syndic today.

(March 31, 1547). The daughter of Jaques Gerod was asked about the articles presented concerning the violence her master the Drooler wanted to do her. She confessed as above. Asked whether she knew the other maid [struck: said yes, she has . . .] who lived there before her, she answered she has seen her and has heard that Durand had also solicited her like herself.

Pierre Durand, called the Drooler, was asked whether he knew the daughter of Jaques Gerod. He answered that it may be one of the daughters of Jaques Gerod who was called by his wife to help her and after that served a little in his house. Asked whether he did not take her and want to use her for his pleasure, he denied it. He was admonished according to the articles. He excused himself

---

42. R. Consist. III, 35, 44, 45, 48, 52.
43. Pierre Durand was called the Bavou or Baveu ("drooler" or "slobberer").

steadfastly and submitted to have his head cut off if it was proven. The girl was summoned to confront him and repeat the articles. The girl still held to her testimony without wavering. He still denied it, and said that it is Claude Magnin who did this because of a lawsuit.

Jaques Gerod, the father, was asked to tell how he learned things. He said it is true that after he knew and heard the stories that were going around he exhorted his daughter to tell the truth about it, and then she confessed to him the things as above. He was also feeling himself greatly to blame that he had commanded his daughter to be violated in this way.

The wife of the Drooler was asked whether the girl had not complained to her. She denied it. The girl told her as above. Denied having been in Onex for fully a year; her husband said three.

Decided: that they be remanded to another time, and meanwhile information will be obtained from Monsieur Antoine Favre's maid for greater corroboration before remanding them before the Council. They were admonished for not going to the sermons.

(April 5, 1547). Pernon, maid of Antoine Favre, of Pernin, was asked whether she knew a maid who had lived at the Drooler's. She said it is true that one was named Antoine from the town of Pernin, who complained to her, asking her to find her a master, since her master solicited her and strongly pursued her dishonor, with other vile words. And she thinks she went away because of this and at present lives near Rive, at the house of a widow who wears a black hood.

(April 7, 1547). Antoine, daughter of the late Bernard Sublet of Neydens, was admonished as to whether she lived at the Drooler's. She answered yes, from hay-making until harvest, about six weeks. Asked in what way she served him, she answered not in everything. Asked whether he did not want to take her by force; after it was repeated several times, she did not want to confess, and denied it, and was steadfast. In the end, she confessed that Drooler often incited her to her dishonor, and he promised her never to fail her and to marry her, and because of this she went away, and he did everything he could to force her, and she resisted. Asked how many times, three? Yes, several times. She also said that she several times complained of it to her mistress, the wife of the Drooler, and [the wife had said] that he did it in sport, and it was his habit. Asked where the maid who served before her was from, she said she was from Onex and named Mermetta. She also said that he told her that he was accustomed to behave so with all the other maids.

Decided: that he be remanded before the Council with depositions, and to purge their city of such infamous behavior.

[On April 18 the Council found Durand guilty of having molested Jeanne Gerod and ordered his imprisonment. On April 22 he was released to go to the wedding of his son Jean on condition of promising to return to prison within five days. He was finally released on May 6, having spent twelve days in prison.]

4-14   Case of Guillaume Darnex and Philippa (1552)[44]

(Oct. 13, 1552). Philippa, maid of Jean Chenu, was admonished that it has come to notice that she has fornicated with the servant of the secretary Mugnier. She denied it, confessing that he indeed forced her to have his company several times, saying that he would take her to [be his] wife. And one time he wanted to give her a coin, and once they were found by the servants. She also said that she never had the company of any [other] man.

Decided: that for Thursday Darnex be summoned here, and let her return here.

(October 20, 1552). Guillaume Darnex, servant of Mugnier, was admonished that it has come to notice that he persuaded a girl named Philippa, a maid at Chenu's, and solicited her to fornicate. He denied it, saying it is true that he wanted her as a wife; the rest of what she confessed Thursday he denied. He was further admonished about a great insolence he committed on the lake last harvest near the franchises with his master's maid. Answered that it was in fun.

Decided: that for Thursday Chenu and his wife should come here, and all their servants.

(Oct. 27, 1552). Georges, wife of Jean Chenu, was asked to tell the truth about what she said to someone on the Consistory, that the servant named Darnex, servant of Mugnier, [was] with their maid in their barn. She said that the servants said that they had found them about seven o'clock at night about a month ago.

Decided: that for Thursday they should all come here, or otherwise the Council will be informed.

(November 3, 1552). Jaques Vallet and Jean Champit, servants of Jean Chenu, witnesses against the maid and the servant of Mugnier, were asked to tell the truth about how they saw Mugnier's servant named Darnex. The older testified that they found them together several times in the barn [benenge]; they also saw them elsewhere. Nevertheless they did not see them do anything wrong. Another servant named Jean, who presently lives at Louis Gardet's, also saw them there. He saw them there almost every night.

Decided: that she be summoned separately to make her repeat her confession that she previously confessed on Thursday, October 13. She said as she had already said.

44. R. Consist. VII, 87, 89, 92, 93.

Decided: that the consequences are bad, and let them be remanded before the Council because of the confession of the maid. They were confronted with each other. Darnex said that he does not presently want to marry, and she maintained to him as she said before. Remanded.

4-15 Case of Michee Morard and Hudry Rojod (1557)[45]

(March 25, 1557). Michee, daughter of Claude Morard of Aire, was summoned to learn whose child she bears. She said it belongs to Hudry Rojod, and this is because he had her company in a winepress in the vineyards of Monsieur De Troches in Collogny. She said it was because he made fine pledges to her, that is, to clothe her and see that she was married. And afterwards he offered her a husband named Antoine Janin, claiming that he Rojod was married.

Decided that she be remanded to Thursday. She said besides this that Jehanne, wife of Hudry Rojod, urged her to put the child she carried to death, or if she did not want to do it, she should bring her the child and she would kill it herself. Pernette, widow of Bernard Roget, prevented this by strong admonitions, saying it would be better for her to support it all her life from charity, and this she stated to be true.

(April 8, 1557). Hudry Rojod of Aire was remanded here to confess the truth of having fornicated with Michee, daughter of Claude Morard of the same place. When questioned, he said and answered that it is true that she served him for five weeks, from mid-August until Michaelmas [September 29]. Michee was called and answered that what Rojod said is true, and being thus in his service she said that Rojod deflowered her in the place where he kept his vine-shoots. There he had her company by compulsion, and afterwards wherever she was, he had her company, so that the child she bears and with which she is pregnant belongs to Hudry, and this she affirmed to be true. On this she was remanded to Tuesday to verify that Rojod slept with her.

Jehanne, wife of Hudry Rojod named above, was called to learn the truth about whether she told Michee to have the child she bore and then to kill it. She answered it is true that she told her to preserve the child, and nothing else. Then Pernon, widow of Bernard Langrin, and Françoise, daughter of Pierre Baud of Langin, were called to learn from them whether they knew Michee. They answered they knew her, and they saw her when she lived at Rojod's, and she said she was pregnant by him. They saw and heard also that Jehanne, wife of Rojod, said to Michee that she was an old bag [*gambasse*] and a whore. But this

---

45. R. Consist. XII, 19v, 26, 29v-30.

was after Michee had told Jehanne that the child belonged to her husband. They know nothing more.

Rojod was recalled to confess the truth about this. He answered that he never had the company of Michee, and as for the support alleged by Michee, he denied having given or sent her anything, except that when he dismissed her he paid her at the rate of a sou per day. To this Michee replied and said that he bought her the bodice of blue cloth she was wearing and sent or brought her himself a quart of wheat and ten sous in a place named Auvenay which is under the king [of France]. She was remanded as above to prove her statements on Tuesday and if she can do better (?) as soon as possible. Note that she said that he gave her eighteen sous in this bodice [that is, the bodice is worth eighteen sous] and four sous, and he owed her much more, because she served him five weeks. The decision is that he be remanded to Tuesday, and as for Jehanne, wife of Hudry Rojod, and Pernon, widow of Bernard Langrin, they are forbidden communion.

(April 13, 1557). Pierre Lyon, living in Cologny, François de Brollier, Coline, wife of Boniface Conte, Jehanne Rapine, and Jeannette, widow of Louis Janin of Cologny, were summoned to testify to the truth against Hudry Rojod. Asked about his behavior, they answered, after having taken an oath, that Lyon has heard from several people that Rojod had a servant who was pregnant by Rojod, and he also heard from the servant that the child with which she was pregnant belonged to Rojod. De Brollier said he had indeed seen the chambermaid and heard and learned from her that she was pregnant by Rojod; heard moreover that Rojod had already had another who was pregnant by him before the present one. Coline said that Rojod took a chambermaid she had away from her and took her with him, and when Nicoline found the chambermaid she interrogated her about her behavior and then as above, and just then (?) Rojod arrived, who threatened the chambermaid and wanted to strike her with a billhook he was carrying. Then the chambermaid answered and cried aloud, "I am pregnant by you," and afterwards she saw that the chambermaid took the child to him. He heard moreover that afterwards he had the company of another chambermaid named Michee, who is said to be pregnant by Rojod. The others said they had indeed heard that the last-mentioned chambermaid was pregnant by Rojod.

Rojod was called and urged to tell the truth. He answered that this is not so. On this he was confronted with the same witnesses, who maintained to him that it is true. On this Rojod was recalled to learn whether he has not been in Mornex since last Friday. Answered no, and that last Friday he was in Marlioz at the de la Mars', to whom he had carried a letter. Because of this it was decided that communion be forbidden him, and as for the rest, since he denies the whole thing against the word of and after confrontation with the witnesses, which could not well be done without full awareness, let him be remanded before the Council to draw the truth from him more fully and to be punished for it.

And may it please our said Lords to grant Michee letters of subpoena to make the woman of Mornex come here to whom Rojod sent her to be supported. Afterwards Rojod was spoken to, to learn better (?) what [penalty] he wanted to submit to if it was found in truth that he was in Mornex. Answered that he did not want to submit to anything, and he had said previously that he would submit to whatever pleased the Council. Afterwards communion was forbidden to Michee.

[On April 19 the Council ordered Rojod and Michee Morard imprisoned. On the 23rd it condemned Rojod to twelve days on bread and water, a fine of twenty-five florins, to pay the expenses of the birth and the woman's convalescence, and to take and raise the child. He was allowed to defer his imprisonment for two weeks so he could tend his vines, pledging to reappear under a bond of fifty florins. On May 3 Rojod again appeared, claiming Michee was a "common whore" and the child was not his, since she had not given birth at the right time. She was required to affirm under oath that it was his child, after which he was ordered to "receive, nurse, and feed it at his own expense," and further, for her expenses he was to provide a further three florins besides the five already ordered, of which she had received two.]

4-16   Case of Girard Perlet's Two Servants (1546)[46]

(Dec. 9, 1546). Girard Perlet . . . was admonished about a fornication committed at his house.

(Dec. 16, 1546). The servant of Girard Perlet was asked whether she is married. She answered yes, and that the youngest of the servants gave her a drink in marriage. He confessed it, but that he does not know what this means. The boy asked whether he has a father or mother. He said only his mother, who is a widow. And likewise the girl, who is called "Great-Aunt" [*tante haute*]. The other servants were admonished for having made such a compact.

Decided: that they be remanded before the Council with the mothers of the servant and the maid, and declare that the promise of marriage was frivolous, and to admonish the mothers to keep watch over their children. Also the other servants were remanded.

[On December 23, 1546, the Council ordered that the "frivolous promise of marriage made between them" be pronounced void and they be admonished.]

46. R. Consist. II, 96v, 98v.

4-17 Case of Pierre Bron and Berte (1547)[47]

(Aug. 4, 1547). Pierre Bron, boatman, and a girl from Promenthoux [named Berte were called]. The father of the girl stated that he is angry because Bron did his daughter harm and gave her a drink in the name of marriage in the town of Promenthoux at the house of the master of the girl. Bron excused himself, saying it will not be proven that he made the promise. He confessed having had the company of the girl. She spoke and named her witnesses, who are [names omitted from record]. Also he wants to prove that she is a whore.

The decision: that considering that they want to prove things on both sides, that for Thursday they bring the witnesses on both sides.

(Aug. 11, 1547). Jean de Bart, boatman, was asked about the behavior of a maid in Promenthoux to whom Pierre Bron has become engaged. Testified it is true that one night, being lodged in Promenthoux, the girl slept in one room with a man who at present serves at Verna's and is named Claude Rava, and they wanted to break the door in on them.

Guillame Chambet, boatman, testified it is true that one night they got up and wanted to see and learn about the behavior of the girl. They saw as is testified above, and about the aforesaid man. Asked whether he knows anything else, he answered no, except that he has heard that she also swore faith to a haberdasher.

Mauris Savuard, boatman, asked as above, testified that it is said that she is not too well behaved. He testified as above, having been in the company when they found Claude Rava shut up with her. Asked about the time when this was done, he answered that it seems to him it was during Lent or about six months ago.

Pierre Bolen, boatman, as a witness, was named on behalf of Berte of Promenthoux to testify about the above. He answered that he does not know about it, except that being in a wine cellar, they called him to drink with them; that Bron had already drunk quite a bit. The mistress of the girl told Bron to give her drink in the name of marriage, which he did. He has also [heard] that she had already sworn faith to a haberdasher, and someone else was killed for the love of her.

Clauda Barge, hostess of Promenthoux, testified that on St. George's Day [April 23] Bron asked Berte to give him new wine to drink, and then it came and the two of them, Bron and the maid, drank in the name of marriage. She knows nothing else and does not know whether he was drunk. Nevertheless afterwards he went to load the boat. She has indeed heard that the woman was engaged to a haberdasher, but that they had separated. She also confessed that Claude la Rava was shut up as testified above.

47. R. Consist. III, 112, 116, 117.

Berte was asked whether she wants any other witnesses summoned. She said yes, one more who has not come. Asked whether she was not engaged to a haberdasher, she answered that the promise was not valid, and they separated publicly.

Pierre Bron was asked to tell the truth about whether he did not swear faith to the girl. He said on his faith that he did not make such a promise, and possibly he was drunk. He confessed he had her company, and if she lays the child on him he will take it.

Decided: as for the promise, by witnesses it appears to be void because it is said that he was drunk, along with its being proven that she had sworn faith to the haberdasher. Nevertheless let them be remanded before the Council for the fornication, and both of them before the Council with the decision of the Consistory.

[On August 18 the Council declared the marriage void and ordered Bron imprisoned for fornication. He was released on August 23, and fined five florins. He was further required to maintain the child, to pay the mother's birth expenses, and to give her "five sous for a pair of shoes, according to the edicts."]

4-18 Theodore Beza on the Impediments of Error (1569)[48]

Here the scholastics skillfully set up four kinds of errors. One was about the person, for instance when Leah was substituted for Rachel [Gen. 29:16-28]. A second kind deals with a lower status, for instance if the woman you believed was free is found to be a slave. The third kind [concerns] wealth: when the person said to be rich is poor. The fourth kind concerns quality: for instance when the woman is stubborn and they said she is compliant.

Then they also distinguish between those things which in the marital union function as either matter or form from those which are accidents in the same thing. They call the persons themselves matter, but the form is the obligation itself of matrimony. Other things they classify as accidents. Lastly, they concluded that an error about the person vitiates the obligation itself of the conjugal union so that such marriages are not validated. But an error about a lower status is opposed to its form since in matrimony one person hands over to the other the use of his or her body. But men or women slaves cannot do this since they do not have a body in their own power; hence as often as this happens there are no promises to marry or even consummated marriages if the injured party now demands that the marital union be rescinded, especially if the lord [of the slave] does not agree to manumission. Regarding an error based on

48. Beza, TRD, 2:83-87 (translated by John P. Donnelly, S.J.)

wealth or quality: since these can be present or absent with the marriage being saved, they want the promises to marry to be validated since in the thing itself there will have been the proper consent.

Although it seems to me that these arrangements in general have been set up properly, still I have something to say here. In the error about a person, even if there does not seem to have been any consent, and therefore the promises to marry are invalidated, still I think they are doing the right thing who, following the example of Jacob in this matter, do not use the highest law, if there will be subsequent sexual union. But what if, in a word, the delusion of a bad conscience comes into play, I think the male or female spouse should not be strongly urged to forgo any of his or her rights. But if one willingly does this, I think the guilty party deserves to be punished severely. But does the substitution of a false name involve an error about a person and also necessarily invalidate promises to marry? Surely not in the least if it will have concerned the body. . . .

[A]s regards error about a [person's] condition or status, for instance if she was a female slave rather than a free born woman, I would think that, since that sort of slavery has by a gift of God been abolished among us, there is nothing on this question we have to belabor any more.

As to what they call errors over wealth, for instance if the person they said was rich was a pauper: even if I confess that promises to marry pronounced as applying immediately are not voided, neither because of an unpaid dowry nor because of other things of the sort that do not pertain to the very substance or form of the promises (that is, the consent), still I say it is fair that such trickery be punished by both an ecclesiastical and civil penalty and the person deceived has the right to [legal] action against the deceivers. But if the promises to marry applied only to the future [that is, were engagements] and were made with conditions, it seems that the person who made the promises is not obligated in the forum of conscience unless the conditions are fulfilled.

4-19   Case of Michel Pesson and George Marin (1546)[49]

(Nov. 11, 1546). Pesson, the fifer, and George, his fiancée, were admonished as to why they [do not] pursue their marriage. Pesson answered that it is about two years since he promised marriage to her, and because she has not obtained for him what she promised him he does not want to marry her. Asked whether [these] conditions were laid down, he said yes.

Decided: that it is clear enough that the marriage should go into effect,

49. R. Consist. II, 90.

considering that he confessed having contracted the marriage and that her father consented to it and was present; also he gave her a ring in marriage. Before the Council.

[On November 15, the Council ordered them to publish their banns and marry.]

4-20   Letter of Attestation to Neuchâtel (1547)[50]

To the faithful servants and pastors of Christ in the church at Neuchâtel, both in the city and in the country, our beloved brethren and colleagues: Because our brother Helias who dwells among you wrote that a woman had betrothed herself to him on condition that, before the marriage was solemnized, he should certify to you by proper testimonies that he was not bound by any other marriage bond, at his request we appointed two from our college to inquire into this matter. After investigation, they reported to us as follows: that six men and one woman of acknowledged repute declared with one voice that Helias was known to them in La Rochelle when he was a priest in the church first of St. Nicholas and afterwards of St. Bartholomew, that he lived honorably among men without any whisper of fornication, that he never publicly had a wife there, and that there was never any rumor of a private or secret marriage known to them. Accordingly, they hold him to be a man free from any marriage tie. We wished this to be testified to you lest we should fail in our duty to our brother.

4-21   Case of Jean Philippe and Anne Renaud (1554)[51]

(Dec. 6, 1554). Jean Philippe, Jaques Renaud, his wife, and their daughter Anne, all masons, were admonished that Philippe presented a petition, whose contents are that in the city of Paris they promised him the girl on condition of marrying her when they reached the place they were going, and he gave her a silver ring in marriage. They confessed it, but now they do not want to consent to it, and as for the ring, she returned it to him, and he did not want to marry her there. The girl [Anne] said that she consented to it against the will of her mother, which the mother also said. She was asked separately whether she is promised to another; she said no, and as for another ring, said she bought it, asking that she be freed from such a promise, because he has boasted of leaving her.

50. RCP (Hughes trans.), p. 64.
51. R. Consist. IX, 179.

Decided: that they be exhorted to accomplish the marriage; otherwise, if they do not wish to do it, let them be remanded before the Council, and no reason is known why such a marriage should be dissolved. The father said that he asks that he be given strict remonstrances, and that there would be no impediment according to God. Philippe was admonished separately that it has come to notice that he has maligned the [true] religion and the city. He denied it, and promised to be obedient to them.

4-22 Case of Pierre Sautier (1552)[52]

(June 9, 1552). Pierre Sautier, a laborer from Chézery but now living in this city, was remanded by Master Raymond [Chauvet] because it is proved that he has promised [marriage to] two girls. He denied having broken off anything [with the first woman from Chézery] because she had conditioned [that is, she could not accept his proposal] if her parents did not consent. Afterwards he left this woman from Chézery, and she returned a sou he had given her for earnest money. As for the other [woman], who was from Présilly, he also left her because the lord of the town to which she is subject wanted to compel him to go live in the place and pay him homage, which he did not want to do. For the promise to the first woman, Mollex, Jaquet, and Grandjean were present at his house; for the promise to the second, there was a maid of Peytrequin's who was in the presence of Peytrequin and his wife, and he told them he had sworn faith to the other woman and they had separated.

Decided: considering his confession, that we summon for Thursday the witnesses who were at the promise. He said there was also a carpenter named Pierre Bibet, a carpenter near the house of Master Amied Le Barbier, and Mollex, who has always been at all his promises, and Jaquet.

(June 16, 1552) Jaques Danton of Tagnigo, Jean Mollies of Beaumont, and Jean Bocquet of Peillonnex, laborer, witnesses against Pierre Sautier, were asked whether they know he is married. They said they were present when Sautier promised [marriage to] a girl named Rolanda, then a maid in Bon, who is from Chézery. It was at his house and about Christmas. They drank together, and he gave her a sou; nevertheless she made a reservation that she wanted to inform her parents. Mollies further said that about three weeks ago he was at Peytrequin's, and he [Sautier] also promised [marriage to] a maid named Georges, drank, and gave her a sou also. But afterwards he and she did not keep their promise, and he made her return the earnest money. Afterwards he promised [marriage to yet] another woman named Pernette who was a maid of Plonjon's,

52. R. Consist. VII, 46, 48.

for which banns are to be proclaimed. A laborer named Claudon, called Le Neyret, was present.

Decided: that he be remanded before the Council, asking them to get to the bottom of the case, since he has promised [marriage] to three wives [i.e., fiancées], and to have them called to learn the character of such separations, which are not to be tolerated. Also to learn who were present. Also Mollies was remanded, who was present at two promises. Also return them their banns. Note to compare [the records].

4-23 Case of Guyonne Copponay and Hugo Cant (1556)[53]

(August 6, 1556). Guyonne, daughter of Claude Copponay, and Hugo Cant who presented a petition concerning a promise of marriage [between the two of them]. The petition stated that she made a condition [of her promise to marriage] of having the advice of her parents and that they do not wish to consent to it. The aforesaid [Cant] said it is true, and denied the bulk of the petition.

Decided: that they return here for Thursday and bring her parents and that he bring Jean Bellot, their host, and the witnesses in her petition to settle it finally. She will bring them; apply to the basket-maker in the Mollard.

(Aug. 13, 1556). Jean Bellot, Claude de Noyer, Tivent Tornier, and Guyonne Copponay were admonished that it has come to notice that they came to a tavern [at Bellot's] against the ordinances and committed insolences there. They said he has leave for it from the Lieutenant, for the day-laborers. They were also admonished that it has come to notice that in Bellot's cellar a certain promise of marriage was made. Bellot said that it is true that he saw both them and others who drank in his cellar. They called the girl who passed by and made her drink with a carter from the house of the host of the Bear. [The facts are] as [they are stated] in the contents of the petition on her behalf, except that she consented and was quite content, and she was admonished to ask her parents.

Decided: that de Noyer who . . . proposed making such a marriage should also be remanded before the Council to be punished. And as for the marriage, it is void and fraudulent. Since the fiancé is from the papacy and she from St. Julien, let everyone proceed as they wish concerning them and their quarter. Also Bellot is to be admonished for selling [wine] as in a tavern.

[On August 17 the Council decided to examine the parties more fully, particularly whether Guyonne had stipulated that she must get the approval of her relatives. The record says nothing further about this examination.]

53. R. Consist. XI, 48, 49, 50.

4-24   Case of Louis Bourgeoise and Mademoiselle Levrat (1547)[54]

(July 14, 1547). Jean Levrat and Louis Bourgeoise and the son of Levrat [appeared]. M. Calvin stated that on proclaiming the banns Levrat opposed them. To this Bourgeoise answered that Levrat promised him one of his daughters about nine months ago and now refuses her to him. To this he answered that it is true that at the instigation of his wife he confirmed the promise. It was on the condition, which he had agreed to, that the other [daughter], who is the older, was [already then] married. Again [Levrat said that] she would never marry him, with villainous words spoken to the girl.

Decided: that for the present an attempt be made to get Levrat to consent to the marriage, and if he does not want to consent that on Thursday the girl and his wife be made to come here. He still answered that the promise was conditional and that they gave him a reason not to carry out marriage. All to Thursday.

(July 21, 1547). Monsieur Levrat and Master Jean [that is, Louis] Bourgeoise were remanded to return here to understand better their wishes in carrying out the aforesaid promise of marriage. Levrat said it is true that half a year ago Bourgeoise proposed and spoke of marriage without his knowledge, and that then his wife granted it to him under the condition that because the girl is the younger it should be held secret and delayed until the older [daughter] was married.

The engaged daughter of Levrat was asked to state how the promise of marriage was given. She answered it is true that once at her father's house, near the hearth and in the presence of her father, he promised her marriage and gave her two small gold rings which have been presented here, and under condition of keeping the matter secret until her sister was also engaged. Asked whether the aforesaid ever had her company, she denied it, though she truly desires it if it pleases her father and mother. Asked whether it was not then stated and determined how long a time they should wait to announce the promise, she said that nothing was ever said about the time.

Bourgeoise was made to come to confront him with her, of having had each other's company. He confessed that it is true, as witnesses one of her brothers and the chambermaid [could confirm], that for six nights she slept with him. She denied it.

The mother of the aforesaid girl was admonished that they cannot deny that there was a promise of marriage. She answered like her husband that they would do what they had promised each other on conditions.

Decided: that we try to bring them to agree here in our presence to carry

54. R. Consist. III, 104, 107, 108.

out the marriage, considering that it is an accomplished thing. Otherwise let them be remanded before the Council, declaring that the marriage should go into effect.

CHAPTER 5

Honor Thy Father (and Thy Mother)

Parental Consent to Engagement and Marriage

In Calvin's Geneva, the consent of the couple was indispensable to the validity of both their engagement and their marriage. Without consent, both were void. This had been a commonplace of medieval canon law. Calvin and his colleagues retained this tradition with only minor refinements.

The consent of parents (or guardians) was equally indispensable to the validity of a minor child's engagement and marriage. The consent of the father was sufficient; the consent of the mother counted only if the father was absent and other relatives concurred. In the absence of both parents, guardians would give their consent, again with priority for the male voice. Parental consent had been a common teaching in the early church, but it was not the required practice of late medieval canon law. Calvin and his colleagues made parental consent a new priority.

Secret engagements, those contracted by minors without parental consent, were presumptively void in Calvin's Geneva. Either fiancé, either set of parents, or even a third party could have these engagements annulled and the children punished. Secret marriages, however, were presumptively valid. Neither the couple nor their parents could have their marriages annulled just because they had been contracted without parental consent. Calvin came to this position on secret marriages only reluctantly in later life, aware that he was now closer to traditional Catholic teachings than to the teachings of some other Protestants.

As with several other topics on sex, marriage, and family, Calvin first set out his legal views on parental consent in some detail in the 1546 Marriage Ordinance. Over the next fifteen years, he gradually laid out his theological rationale, and made modest legal refinements that Beza helped to systematize. From the start, the Geneva Consistory followed Calvin's Ordinance to the letter, help-ing to make parental consent a vital part of the Genevan Reformation.

The 1546 Marriage Ordinance and Its Interpretation

Calvin devoted no less than eight of the first ten articles of his 1546 Marriage Ordinance to the doctrine of parental consent:

1. Regarding young people who have never been married, none, whether sons or daughters, who have a father still living shall have the power to con-tract a marriage without the permission of their father unless they have at-tained the legal age, that is twenty years for a son and eighteen for a daugh-ter. And if after reaching the said age they have asked their fathers or had them asked to marry them and their fathers have not attended to it, in that case it shall be lawful for them to marry without their father's authority.

2. Let the same apply to wards who are under the authority of guard-ians or trustees; nevertheless the mother or guardian may not arrange a marriage for the boy or girl they have in charge without consulting one of the relatives, if there are any.

3. If it happens that two young people have contracted marriage by their own action, through folly or recklessness, let them be punished and chastened and such a marriage be dissolved at the request of those who have charge of them. . . .

6. Let no one make clandestine promises, conditionally or otherwise, between young people who have not yet been married, but let there be at least two witnesses; otherwise the whole [secret engagement] shall be void.

7. Where children marry without their father's or mother's permission at the age permitted above and it is established by the court that they have done this lawfully because of the negligence or excessive strictness of their fa-thers, let the fathers be required to grant them a dowry or provide them such a share or position as [they would have given] if they had consented to it.

8. Let no father compel his children to such a marriage as seems good to him except with their goodwill and consent, but let him or her who does not want to accept the partner his father wants to give be excused, always preserving modesty and respect, without the father imposing any punish-ment for such a refusal. The same shall be observed for those under guard-ianship.

9. Fathers or guardians shall not have marriages contracted for their children or wards until they have reached an age to confirm them. Never-theless, if it happens that a child, having refused to marry according to the

will of his father, thereafter chooses a marriage that is not so much to his profit and advantage, because of such rebellion or defiance the father shall not be required to give him anything during his [the father's] lifetime.

10. Men or women, who have already been married once, although they still have fathers living, nevertheless shall be at liberty to marry provided they are of the aforesaid age, that is twenty years for a son and eighteen for a daughter, and that they have been emancipated, that is they have left their father's house and established a separate household: although it would be more fitting for them to let themselves always be governed by the advice of their fathers.[1]

In his 1545 draft of the Marriage Ordinance, Calvin seemed so eager to maximize the rights of parental consent that he set the age of majority unusually high: Boys had to be twenty-four, girls twenty before they could marry without seeking their parents' consent. The 1546 Marriage Ordinance lowered the ages of majority to twenty and eighteen for boys and girls respectively (items 1, 10). This was closer to the Protestant norm but still a bit high, and the 1546 draft still advised that even fully emancipated children "always be governed by the advice of their fathers" (item 10).

The consent of the father was the most critical. The consent of the mother controlled only when the father was absent and no other relatives were present. If other relatives were at hand, the mother's views had to concur with theirs. In his 1545 draft, Calvin had said that, in the absence of the father, the mother needed to have the concurrence only of the "closest and most important" relatives. He dropped this qualification in the 1546 version. Now it read that the mother's consent would count only if and until she had "consulted one of the relatives, if there are any" (item 2) — evidently without regard for their "closeness" or "importance" to the family. In the absence of both parents, guardians would consent, again with priority for the male voice.

Calvin took pains to make clear that this parental consent was only a supplement to, not a substitute for, the consent of the couple themselves. Parents could not coerce their children into unwanted engagements, or withhold their consent or payment of dowry until the child chose a partner whom they favored. Parents could not force youngsters into marriage before they were mature enough. Minor children, "preserving modesty and respect," could refuse to follow their parents' insistence on an unwanted fiancé(e) or a premature engagement (item 8). Other children, confronting a "negligent or excessively strict" father, could have him compelled to give a dowry in support of a marriage they contracted in spite of him (item 7).

1. Doc. 1-2.

The main goal of these provisions was to stamp out traditional "clandestine promises" *(promesse clandestine)* (item 6) — that is, engagements and marriages contracted without parental consent.[2] The Ordinance made clear that secret *engagement* promises were "void" *(nulles)*. This did not necessarily prevent a secretly-engaged couple from going forward with their plans if they received their parents' consent after the fact. But, absent this parental consent, if anyone challenged this engagement because it had been secretly contracted, the engagement would be annulled.

The Ordinance was not so clear about the legal status of secret *marriage* promises — especially if they had been celebrated, consummated, and yielded children. The crucial statutory language was in item 3: "If it happens that *two young people have contracted marriage by their own action, through folly or recklessness,* let them be punished and chastened and such a marriage be *dissolved at the request of those who have charge of them.*" It was clear that children who entered such secret marriages would be punished. What was not clear was whether their marriage would be annulled if challenged by their parents.

A plain reading of item 3 suggests that parents could seek annulment of their children's secretly "contracted marriage." On this reading, while secret engagements were automatically "void" (per item 6), secret marriages were voidable. They would be voided only if and when the children's parents or others "who have charge of them" brought an action of annulment (per item 3).

But this reading does not pick up the studied ambiguity in the language of item 3. First, the opening phrase "two young people" might well have meant only youngsters who were not only below the age of majority but also below the age of consent. Read as such, item 3 was only a statement of the familiar medieval impediment of infancy: that infants and youth cannot enter marriage contracts, and when they do, their parents or guardians need to have those prom-

---

2. In Calvin's Geneva, the phrase "clandestine marriage" generally meant marriages contracted without parental consent (and occasionally also without two witnesses). According to some recent studies, "clandestine marriage" had a second meaning: marriages between parties who married despite an absolute impediment (such as incest or precontract) that they knew but kept secret. Some case studies in France and Germany suggest that the second type of secret marriage was heavily litigated in late medieval church courts. See Klaus M. Linder, *Courtship and the Courts: Marriage and Law in Southern Germany, 1350-1550* (Th.D. diss., Harvard, 1988), esp. pp. 126ff.; Beatrice Gottlieb, "The Meaning of Clandestine Marriage," in Robert Wheaton and Tamara K. Hareven, eds., *Family and Sexuality in French History* (Philadelphia, 1980), p. 53; Reinhard Lettmann, *Die Diskussion über die klandestinen Ehen und die Einführung einer zur Gültigkeit verpflichtenden Eheschliessung auf dem Konzil von Trent* (Münster, 1967). It was the first type of secret marriage that Calvin and his colleagues had in mind and that the Consistory adjudicated. The Consistory did occasionally encounter and punish parties who tried to keep their known impediments secret, but they did not apply the term "secret marriage" to these instances.

ises dissolved. This was, in fact, how item 3 came in part to be read by the Genevan Consistory.[3]

Second, the phrase "having contracted marriage" *(ayant contracté mariage)* could mean either (1) "contracted to get married in the future"; or (2) "had already entered a marriage contract." If the phrase meant that the children had "contracted to get married in the future," then item 3 would mean simply that parents had standing to bring an action to annul their child's secret engagement promise. These standing rights of the parents were not specified elsewhere in the statute. It made good sense to stipulate them, particularly since in 1546 the Consistory had no other rules of civil procedure.[4] Even if the phrase "contracted marriage" meant that the children "had already entered a marriage contract," the matter was still not entirely closed. For final validity of the marriage turned on whether the couple had celebrated their marriage in a proper marriage ceremony in the church, not whether they had entered a marriage contract.[5]

Third, the two subsequent phrases of item 3 were also ambiguous. The phrase, "by their own action" *(de leur propre mouvement)*, was separated by a comma from the next phrase, "through folly or recklessness" *(par follie ou legierté)*. These two phrases could be read separately. This reading would allow parents to seek annulment of the pending marriage either because (1) it was contracted secretly by the couple ("by their own action"); or (2) it proved to be "foolish" or "reckless." Alternatively, the two phrases could be read interdependently — with the second phrase understood as a qualification of the first. This reading would allow parents to attack a secret marriage only if it could be shown that the marriage itself was not only secretly contracted ("by their own action") but also was foolish or recklessly entered. This was not so easy a standard to meet. Children who married secretly sometimes did so not with recklessness but with elaborate plans to circumvent their parents. And many times their marriages, while not necessarily well advised, were hardly "foolish," especially if they were motivated by a desire to get away from overbearing, abusive, or bickering parents.

All this close exegesis might seem like silly legal hairsplitting. But Calvin, the lawyer, may well have intended the language of the Ordinance to be a bit open-textured. For the legal status of parental consent and secret marriages was a divisive question at the time he was drafting the Ordinance. The first genera-

---

3. See Chapter 6 below.

4. What survives of Calvin's efforts to draft a code of civil procedure is in CO 10/1:132-39, analyzed in detail in Bohatec, CR, pp. 209-79. Nothing in the fragmentary draft, however, addresses issues of standing in domestic litigation.

5. See discussion in Chapter 13 below on the legal requirement of wedding ceremonies.

tion of Protestant reformers had required parental consent in an effort to counter the late medieval Catholic practice of tolerating secret engagements and marriages. All the leading Protestant reformers allowed parents to annul their children's secret *engagements.* The question that divided Protestants sharply was whether parents could annul their children's secret *marriages,* too. Some reformers allowed parents to annul their children's secret marriages under any circumstances. Some allowed the same, unless the wife was pregnant or already had children. Some favored continuation of the secret marriage. Some insisted on it. The new Protestant laws of the day reflected these disparate views. This issue became even more divisive in the 1540s and 1550s, when Catholics began accusing Protestants of frivolously dissolving marriages and foolishly catering to the tyranny of parents.[6]

Calvin's 1546 Marriage Ordinance did not clearly answer the question whether parents could seek annulment of their children's secret marriages. Three years later, Calvin seemed inclined to allow such annulments. The occasion was Calvin's commentary on the *Adultero-German Interim* (1548), a proposed ecumenical concordat issued by Emperor Charles V. The Interim insisted that even secret marriages were indissoluble because they were sacramental.[7] Calvin stood this argument on its head: If a marriage was indissoluble because it was sacramental, should its sacramental status not turn on whether the couple had entered it properly, including their procurement of parental consent:

> Of marriages rashly contracted by young persons, let me just say this: It is as easy to deny a word as it is for our moderators to assert one. Who revealed to them that such marriages should be binding? . . . The dignity of the sacrament, they say, is to be preferred to a parent's right. [But] the more dignity there is in marriage, the more modesty and religion should attend those who enter it.[8]

---

6. See Witte, FSC, pp. 57-61, 80-84, 95, 112-16, 142-43; Hartwig Dieterich, *Die Protestantische Eherecht in Deutschland bis zur Mitte des 17. Jahrhunderts* (Munich, 1970), pp. 123-27; Joyce, pp. 116-24, 416.

7. Art. XXI.10 of the *Adultero-German Interim* reads: "Since the father's power justly yields to a union between the parties, you should not listen to those who now insist that contracted engagements or marriages are dissolved and nullified if there is no consent of the parents. In this, we do not derogate from the obedience that children owe to their parents. But we do not wish parents to abuse their power by impeding or dissolving marriages. But, since we think it is good for children not to contract [marriage] without the advice and consent of parents, the preachers should carefully instruct them in their duty." Translated in John Calvin, *Tracts and Treatises in Defense of the Reformed Faith,* trans. Henry Beveridge (Grand Rapids, 1958), 3:220.

8. John Calvin, *Vera Christianae Pacificationis et Ecclesiae Reformandae Ratio* (1549), CO 7:593-674, at p. 640.

A decade later, Calvin seemed inclined to regard secret marriages as ill-advised, but not subject to annulment by parents or anyone else. "All good men properly disapprove of clandestine marriages which offer an opportunity and even, in fact, an open door to many disgraceful acts," he wrote in a 1557 *consilium*.[9] But even a secretly contracted marriage precluded a second engagement or marriage — regardless of whether the parents or guardians of the doubly-contracted child now consented to the second match.

By 1560, Calvin had settled the matter in his mind. Secret marriages, once contracted, celebrated, and consummated, could not be annulled absent proof of some other impediment. Neither a dissenting parent nor a distraught husband or wife could seek annulment of the marriage on grounds that it was secretly contracted. Indeed, if the marriage was unhappy, it was just what the secretly married couple deserved. As Calvin put it in a *consilium* of 1560:

> When an adolescent has married without his parents' knowledge, he should recognize that he is paying a just penalty for his heedless behavior if his wife is unresponsive to him. He did not offer God and his parents the obedience he owed them, and he should not be surprised if he gets his just reward in the form of his wife's defiance.[10]

This moved Calvin close to the actual position of most medieval canonists: secret marriages were formally prohibited, but when they occurred it was best to let them stand and to punish the delinquent parties. The medieval canonists used sacramental logic: even secret marriages could not be dissolved because they were sacramental. Calvin used prudential logic: Even secret marriages could not be dissolved because that catered to parental tyranny, left despoiled virgins vulnerable to spinsterhood, and consigned any children of the union to the bane of bastardy.

Theological and Prudential Reflections

While Calvin dithered on the issue of whether parents could annul secret marriages, he was decisively in favor of the doctrine of parental consent. In his 1546 Commentary on 1 Corinthians 7, Calvin argued that parental consent to mar-

---

9. CO 10/1:242-44, using translation in *Calvin's Ecclesiastical Advice*, p. 135.

10. *Consilium* (Sept. 1, 1560), CO 10/1:252-62, using translation in *Calvin's Ecclesiastical Advice*, pp. 147-48. Calvin continued: "Because it is not disagreement over religion which is tearing the marriage apart, he should fulfill his marital duty as long as he can live with his wife without danger. If greater force and necessity compel him to leave her, he should remain celibate until his wife recovers her senses or gives him cause to divorce her."

riage was a "sacred right" of parents and a "moral duty" of children (**Doc. 5-1**). It enabled parents to guide their children in this final fateful step toward adulthood, and it prevented children from choosing their mates imprudently or impetuously. Particularly when children were still young and vulnerable, it ensured that the marriage was formed by free, full, and mature consent on all sides.

Parental consent, Calvin insisted, does not license "parental tyranny" over children nor can it substitute for the consent of the child to the marriage. The "proper rule" of parental consent is that "children should allow themselves to be governed by their parents, and that they, on the other hand, do not drag their children by force to what is against their inclination, and that they have no other object in view, in the exercise of their authority, than the advantage of their children." If parents abused their authority, and coerced their children into unwanted engagements or marriages, therefore, such contracts should be annulled.[11]

The doctrine of parental consent to marriage "originated in the common laws of nature," Calvin argued in his same 1546 Commentary on 1 Corinthians. Calvin adverted to these natural law origins of the doctrine several more times in later writings. "Nature herself dictates that the authority of parents is necessary," he wrote in 1549. "This has always been observed by the law of nations and is approved by the testimony of Scripture."[12] In his 1554 Commentary on Genesis, he wrote: "[S]ince marriage forms a principal part of human life, it is right that, in contracting it, children should be subject to their parents, and should obey their counsel. This order [is what] nature prescribes and dictates."[13] And again: "[I]t is not lawful for the children of a family to contract marriage, except with the consent of parents. And, certainly, natural equity dictates that, in a matter of such importance, children should depend upon the will of the parents."[14]

Surprisingly, Calvin did not ground the doctrine of parental consent to marriage in the fifth commandment of the Decalogue: "Honor thy father and thy mother" (Exod. 20:12; Deut. 5:16) and the amplification of the commandment by St. Paul (Eph. 6:1-2; Col. 3:20).[15] Other Protestant reformers had made

---

11. See Calvin's *consilium* above in Doc. 4-4, where he recommended annulment of a marriage that a young woman had entered through the coercion and trickery of her mother.

12. CO 7:639-40.

13. Comm. Gen. 21:20. In his Institutes (1536), 5.71, repeated in his Institutes (1559), 4.19.37, Calvin condemned Catholic canon law for allowing that "marriages between minors contracted without parental consent should remain firm and valid," which he considered contrary to "the laws of all nations and also against the ordinances of Moses."

14. Comm. Gen. 24:1-3.

15. This is treated as the fourth commandment in Catholic and Lutheran traditions. On various traditions of numbering and dividing the Ten Commandments, see Bo Ivar Reicke, *Die*

the fifth commandment a critical source of the right of both fathers and mothers to give their consent to marriage, and the correlative duty of their children to seek the consent of both parents. This was part and product of their elaborate efforts to ground a whole new Protestant legal system in the Ten Commandments. Calvin did not take this step, at least with respect to the doctrine of parental consent. He might well have been constrained by his insistence in the 1546 Marriage Ordinance that it was the father's, not the mother's, consent that was essential. It would have been hard for him to press the father's superior authority on the strength of a commandment to "Honor thy father *and thy mother.*"

This is not to say that Calvin had a narrow view of the fifth commandment or a restricted view of a parent's authority or a child's obedience. In his numerous pages of commentaries, sermons, and catechism entries on the fifth commandment, he regularly described parents, especially fathers, as God's vice-gerents on earth, in whose title and office God has invested a measure of his being and power, making them "something divine."[16] He called upon children to render to their parents forms of "reverence, obedience, and gratefulness" comparable to what they rendered to God — at least up to the point of violating the Bible and their conscience.[17]

Calvin gave many examples of the proper obedience that children should render to their parents in conformity with the Decalogue. Included was the duty of children to seek their father's consent to make "a binding oath," and the duty of the father, in turn, not to withhold or condition his consent capriciously (**Doc. 5-2**). Calvin concluded that, "if a daughter, while living with her father, has vowed anything without his knowledge, it is of no force." This was the closest Calvin came to tying the doctrine of parental consent to marriage to the fifth commandment.[18]

To ground his doctrine of parental consent, Calvin pointed favorably to examples in the Bible of early patriarchs participating in the marriages of their children. For Calvin these were examples, and sometimes counterexamples, of the natural law in operation.[19] He saw in the biblical story of Abraham's pursuit

---

Zehn Worte in Geschichte und Gegenwart (Tübingen, 1973); Paul Grimley Kuntz, *The Ten Commandments in History* (Grand Rapids, 2004).

16. Institutes (1559), 2.8.35.

17. Institutes (1559), 2.8.36-38. This caveat, of obeying up to the point of violating God's law, does not appear in the Institutes (1536), 1.17 nor in Calvin's 1555 Sermons on Deut. 5:16. It might well signal part of Calvin's emerging theory of resistance to tyrannical authority — whether parental, political, or ecclesiastical. See Bohatec, CSK, pp. 652ff.

18. See Comm. Harm. Law Exod. 20:12; Serm. Deut. 5:15; Comm. and Serm. Eph. 6:1-4.

19. Comm. Gen. 21:20 (Hagar and Ishmael); Comm. Gen. 24:1-67 (Abraham and Isaac; Rebekah and mother); Comm. Gen. 34:12 (Shechem and Jacob re: Dinah); Comm. Harm. Law Exod. 21:7-11.

of a wife for Isaac (Gen. 24:1-67) a particularly good lesson of how and why the natural law of parental consent should operate (**Doc. 5-3**). Abraham sought to ensure that his son Isaac, who had come of age, would marry a woman who was both spiritually and physically compatible with him. He sent his servant out to find just the right woman, armed with a clear recitation of the terms of the proposed marriage contract. The servant found a suitable woman in Rebekah. He sought the consent of Rebekah's father, uncle, and mother. He then put down a handsome bride price signified by rings and bracelets. All of this was done, Calvin noted, with full consideration of the consent of Isaac and Rebekah. The servant made sure that Isaac and Rebekah met together to ensure their compatibility before the contract was sealed. Particularly notable for Calvin was that Rebekah's father Bethuel "did not exercise tyranny over his daughter, so as to thrust her out reluctantly, or to compel her to marry against her will, but left her to her own free choice."

The solicitude shown by Abraham and Bethuel for their children's consent to marriage stood in marked contrast with Caleb's crass indifference to his daughter Achsah (**Doc. 5-4**). Caleb was one of the spies whom Moses had sent into the newly promised land of Israel. He was one of the two who had stood up against the majority of the people who had despaired about their ability to conquer Jericho and who wanted to return to Egypt (Num. 13:6, 30; 14:6). While God condemned the people of Israel for their unbelief, God spared Caleb: "because he has a different spirit and has followed me fully, I will bring him into the land in which he went, and his descendents shall possess it" (Num. 14:24). After the conquest of Jericho, Joshua rewarded Caleb with an ample plot of land. But the land was still occupied (Josh. 14:6; 21:12). Caleb wanted his soldiers to claim the land and to kill its pagan leader. Whoever killed the leader, Caleb promised, could marry his daughter Achsah. Othniel killed the leader, and was given Achsah to marry (Josh. 15:16-17).

Despite Caleb's noble place in Israelite history, Calvin condemned him for holding his daughter out as a prize of war, without ever consulting her. "How could Caleb presume to bargain concerning his daughter until he knew her wishes?" Calvin wrote incredulously. It was no excuse that Othniel was a valiant warrior. That did not necessarily make him the right husband for Achsah. It also did not matter that Achsah ultimately accepted him as her husband or indeed that Caleb later obliged her by giving the couple a choice plot of land (Josh. 15:18-19). Caleb must have just forgotten to ask Achsah her wishes while "in the heat of battle," Calvin concluded. But we have to assume that "according to the common law the agreement implied the daughter's consent and was only to take effect if it was obtained."

Calvin's condemnation of Caleb was of a piece with his condemnation of other fathers and guardians of the Bible who sold their children into slavery or prostitution, or put their daughters on the marriage market as prizes to be sold to the highest bidder.[20] Even with the power of parental consent, no father was allowed to do this to his daughter. It was the mutual consent both of the husband and the wife, and of the parents and their minor children, that makes the marriage. As he put it at the conclusion of his commentary on the Caleb story:

> Although it is the office of parents to settle their daughters in life, they are not permitted to exercise tyrannical power or to assign them to whatever husbands they think fit without consulting them. For while all contracts ought to be voluntary, freedom ought to prevail especially in marriage that no one may pledge his faith against his will.

Theodore Beza offered similar views on the doctrine of parental consent in 1569 (**Doc. 5-5**). Like Calvin, Beza hinted briefly that the doctrine of parental consent was rooted in the "divine law," perhaps even in the fifth commandment. But then, also like Calvin, Beza launched immediately into a lengthy recitation of the examples of ancient biblical patriarchs who practiced parental consent because of the "very natural equity" taught to them by "God as our creator." He went on to show how this doctrine was a commonplace among patristic and early medieval Christian theologians, moralists, and jurists, making the late medieval toleration of secret marriages all the more scandalous.

Beza made clear that both the minor children's consent and the parents' consent were essential to the validity of an engagement and marriage. The hard question was what to do when parents and children had conflicting views. First, if children had not consented, their views had to trump even if their parents disagreed. The engagement or marriage would be annulled on either child's petition. Second, if parents had not consented to the engagement, their views had to trump, even if the children wished to go forward. Third, if parents had not consented to the marriage, their views could trump only if and after they allowed the magistrates to try to mediate the conflict. And Beza hinted strongly that if the marriage was already consummated, it would not be wise or easy to countenance its annulment.

Consistory Cases

The Genevan Consistory heard a number of cases raising disputes over parental consent. The Consistory generally followed the letter of the 1546 Marriage Or-

---

20. Comm. Gen. 29:18-27; Comm. Harm. Law Exod. 21:7-11; Lev. 19:29. But cf. Serm. 1 Sam. 18:22-30; Serm. 2 Sam. 3:14-16 (where Calvin does not criticize fathers for offering their daughters as prizes for valor).

dinance. Secret engagements involving minor children were presumptively void, unless the parents would later consent. Secret marriages were presumptively valid, unless the children could demonstrate highly irregular circumstances. Parents who refused to give their consent were little questioned unless the Consistory suspected foul play. Guardians who refused consent were more closely questioned. Where the views of the fathers and mothers conflicted, the Consistory followed the father. Where the views of mothers and relatives conflicted, the mother prevailed. Parents or guardians who did consent to the engagement were responsible to see that the child was married properly and promptly. Such parents could neither leave the young couple to their own devices, nor seek to withdraw their consent once given.[21]

In most cases, if either party to the engagement was a minor, the Consistory would insist on knowing whether the father or guardian consented. In a 1552 case, for example, Louise Loup requested the Consistory to approve her marriage to Nicod des Planches, a minor (**Doc. 5-6**). The parties had been engaged before witnesses, and Nicod had given Louise an engagement gift. The Consistory wanted to know whether Nicod's father approved the match. When Nicod reported that his father would not consent, that was the end of the matter for the Consistory.

Similarly, in another 1552 case, the Consistory summoned to them two minor couples, Jenon Ramou and Humbert Gallatin as well as Françoise Tournier and Jean Berto (**Doc. 5-7**). The Consistory had learned that the couples had become secretly engaged during a party together, each couple apparently serving as witnesses to the other's engagement. When confronted, the couples said this was all done in jest, and they would not want to marry without the consent of the parents. The Consistory called in their parents. The parents of the two girls dissented because of the manner in which the couples had become engaged. The Consistory sent the case to the Council with a recommendation that the engagements be annulled and the two young men punished for seducing the women. They sent the young women home with a warning to exercise more care the next time.

It was not enough that only one of the parents of a minor couple consented. In a 1557 case, for example, Pierre Clerc asked the Consistory to approve the marriage of his minor daughter and Clement de Biffort, also a minor (**Doc. 5-8**). The parties had a notarized written engagement contract with what seemed to be mutually favorable terms. Father Pierre was eager to see his daughter get married and urged the Consistory's blessing. Clement, however, had not procured his father's consent. Even though Clement, too, wanted to marry, the Consistory refused to allow the marriage to go forward. Instead, they sent the case to

---

21. See analysis of several cases in Seeger, pp. 361-63.

the Council with a recommendation that the notary be punished for notarizing the contract without procuring the consent of one of the two fathers.

Once a father or guardian had consented to an engagement, he was obliged to see that the parties were properly and promptly married. A Genevan father named Nicolas found this out in 1552 (**Doc. 5-9**). About a year before, Nicolas had consented to the engagement of his daughter and her fiancé Jaques d'Orléans. Jaques had given the young woman some rings and some property as an engagement gift. The couple had then apparently moved away from Geneva and had put off their wedding. The woman had returned the gifts temporarily until Jaques and her brother could work out more suitable property arrangements. Father Nicolas had apparently not known of, or had at least not objected to, this delay, though the 1546 Marriage Ordinance required the couple to wed within six weeks of their engagement. Since Nicolas still wanted the wedding to go forward, the Consistory ordered him to try to persuade the couple to get on with their wedding plans. If that failed, the Consistory threatened to send them all to the Council to have them punished and the engagement annulled because of the untoward delay.[22]

Once a father or guardian consented to his minor child's engagement, he could not withdraw it.[23] A Genevan father named Nepveur learned this lesson in 1556 (**Doc. 5-10**). Nepveur had consented to the engagement of his daughter Jeanne to one Louis Blanchet. The parties had signed a written engagement contract, which specified the property payments that Louis was to make to Nepveur in consideration of the marriage. Shortly thereafter, Louis wanted to move to another town. Jeanne did not want to follow him. The parties agreed to dissolve their engagement by mutual consent. Louis had not delivered his promised payment to the Nepveurs, so father Nepveur decided to withdraw his consent to the engagement as well. Louis moved away. The Nepveurs then requested the Consistory for permission for Jeanne to marry another.

The Consistory denied their request. An unconditional engagement contract, they ruled, could not be broken either by the mutual consent of the couple or by the subsequent withdrawal of parental consent. Moreover, failure of a dowry payment was never a sufficient ground to annul an engagement. Jeanne was still bound by her engagement promise, unless she and her father could prove that Louis had actually deserted her — desertion being a separate ground for annulment as we shall see.

Similarly in another 1557 case, Jaques Gaudi had consented to his minor daughter Michee's engagement to Nicolas Millet (**Doc. 5-11**). Nicolas had prom-

---

22. See below Chapter 12 on delayed weddings.

23. The 1546 Marriage Ordinance, item 14 (Doc. 1-2) stipulated clearly that dowry or property disputes could not break engagements. See further Chapter 11.

ised to deliver an ample engagement gift to father Jaques, when Nicolas returned from a journey. Nicolas was delayed on his return, and then did not tender the full promised payment, causing Jaques to lose property he had intended to buy with the promised funds. An angry Jaques declared that he was withdrawing his consent to the engagement, and took his daughter Michee back into his own custody. The Consistory sought to reconcile the parties, explaining to them that his post hoc withdrawal of consent was ineffective. They also reprimanded Nicolas for his delinquency, and ordered him to make the full promised engagement gift. An enraged Jaques, however, said he would refuse the money if tendered because he now believed the young man to be dishonest and wanted him out of the family. After further attempts at reconciliation failed, the Consistory sent the matter to the Council for final disposition, recommending that "such marriage should not be broken and may not be dissolved, for this would open the door to many others."

The Consistory heard a few cases where fathers and mothers differed over whether to consent to their child's engagement. Each time the Consistory sided with the father.[24] Typical was the 1547 case of Etienne de Lonnay and a young girl named Maxima (**Doc. 5-12**). Maxima's mother had consented to the union and had signed an engagement contract that Etienne had prepared. When called before the Consistory, however, Maxima testified that she had not consented to the engagement. She reported further that her father, who was away at the time, also would not consent to the marriage. For the Consistory this was enough to trigger an instant annulment, even if the father was not available to testify. On the Consistory's recommendation, the Council annulled the engagement contract. They also imprisoned the mother both for perjury during trial and for consenting to the engagement, evidently in defiance of her husband's wishes for young Maxima.[25]

The Consistory also occasionally heard cases raising conflicts between mothers and other relatives regarding the engagement of a minor child. In a 1545 case, for example, Girard Reveillet asked the Consistory to approve his forthcoming marriage to a young woman (unnamed in the record) (**Doc. 5-13**). Girard testified that he had received the consent of his fiancée's uncle in the presence of several of her other relatives, and that they had all toasted to confirm the engagement. When questioned, the woman's aunt confirmed this. The young woman, however, testified that she had not consented or toasted to the marriage, and pled with the Consistory to protect her from this unwanted marriage. The Consistory ordered that she be given help in having her mother and

---

24. See other examples in Seeger, pp. 361ff.

25. See further below, Chapter 6, showing that this case turned also on the impediment of infancy.

brother come to Geneva to testify; her father was evidently not in the picture. The mother appeared the following week, and protested the engagement loudly. A local minister echoed her protest.

Confronted with this conflict between an uncle who consented and a mother who did not, the Consistory sent the case to the Council. The Council discovered that Girard was already engaged to someone else in a Catholic territory. Girard returned repeatedly to the Consistory with documents testifying that his first engagement was dissolved, and indeed that his first fiancée had married someone else. The Consistory did not believe him. They became doubly suspicious when they learned that his prior fiancée was a Catholic and that Girard had a reputation for making frivolous promises.[26] Though the record ends here, such a marriage could not have passed muster with both the young woman and her mother protesting the match.

What was left unclear in this case was what the Consistory would have done if both the young woman and her uncle wanted to go forward with the wedding, but the mother did not. The Consistory faced this question squarely in a 1561 case, and they sided with the mother (**Doc. 5-14**). Jean Casaux, a minor, had become engaged to Madeleine D'Agnon. Both Jean's brother and his guardian had consented to and helped facilitate the match. But none of the parties had consulted Jean's mother, who was a Catholic living in a Catholic territory. It turned out that Casaux's mother refused to consent to the engagement until Jean had reached twenty-five, even though she did not prohibit his move to Geneva (and presumably also his conversion to the Reformed faith). Though the case went down on different grounds, the mother's dissent seemed to have been enough for the Consistory to annul the engagement, despite Casaux's brother's consent and despite the fact that the mother was a Catholic living well outside Geneva's jurisdiction.

The Casaux case illustrates not only the superiority of a mother's voice to other relatives in consenting to her child's engagement, but also the duty of a father to state his consent or dissent clearly — a point Calvin had made in his exegesis of the Mosaic law (see **Doc. 5-3**). In this case, Madeleine's father, Monsieur D'Agnon, a minister no less, had failed to be clear. Casaux was a student in the Genevan Academy. He had been a regular visitor in the D'Agnon household and had made his interest in Madeleine clear to Monsieur D'Agnon. Casaux's guardian had spoken with D'Agnon about the engagement, as had D'Agnon's wife. Madeleine wore her engagement ring around the house for more than two weeks. Yet D'Agnon claimed to know nothing about the engagement, nor to have given his consent to the marriage. The Consistory did not believe him, and reprimanded him severely for his negligence.

26. On issues of precontract or polygamy, see Chapter 7.

In the absence of both fathers and mothers, the Consistory would turn to guardians to give their consent to a minor child's wedding. Unless the absent parent's last will and testament or a guardianship agreement stipulated otherwise, the views of paternal uncles and male siblings to the minor child were given priority. In their absence, paternal grandfathers, maternal uncles, and full sisters to the minor child were consulted. Paternal and maternal grandmothers, aunts, and more distant relatives were consulted only as a last resort. The guardian stood in the shoes of the absent parent and was generally free to consent to or dissent from a minor's engagement with little second guessing from the Consistory.[27]

The Consistory would inquire more closely, however, when a guardian neglected or abused his or her authority. An egregious example came in a 1546 case involving a young woman named Mademoiselle Fertz (**Doc. 5-15**). Fertz had just lost her parents to the plague. By their last will and testament, her parents had appointed Pierre Gravier as her guardian. Shortly thereafter, Gravier began sleeping with Fertz. Fertz herself then became infected with the plague. She went to the hospital. There she met another man, Pierre Dolen. They, too, began sleeping together. A few days later, Dolen and Fertz became engaged. They kept the matter secret, evidently not wishing to seek the consent of Gravier, Fertz's guardian and lover. But Dolen gave Fertz an engagement ring to wear. They also broke into Fertz's late parents' home and took some of the money and property they found there. They were imprisoned for their fornication and burglary, but thereafter continued to live together. They then sought to publish their banns of marriage.

The Consistory summoned Gravier to answer whether he consented to his ward Fertz's marriage. They learned more than they probably expected. Gravier admitted to his earlier affair with Fertz. He also testified that to his surprise (and no doubt his pique) Fertz had suddenly become engaged to Dolen. Gravier did not consent to the engagement, but also had done nothing either to care for Fertz or to safeguard the property she had inherited. For the Consistory, this nonfeasance was evidently more than enough to disqualify Gravier from his guardianship, for he faded from the story.[28]

The Consistory focused their attention on Fertz and Dolen. Because the couple had contracted and consummated a secret engagement, the Council, on the Consistory's recommendation, annulled their union and punished them se-

---

27. See examples in Seeger, pp. 363-65.

28. Gravier may well have faced criminal prosecution as well. Even consensual sex between a guardian and ward was a serious crime in Geneva. A 1566 statute that codified the prevailing law provided that a "guardian or trustee who has fornicated with his ward . . . will be proceeded against more severely, even to death if necessary, according to the severity and circumstances of their crimes, at the discretion of the judges." SD, vol. 3, item 1065.

verely for their flagrant fornication. Thereafter, they were left free to enter a new engagement contract — provided Fertz's closest relatives were found to give their consent, and provided further that the couple desist from future fornication and cohabitation until their wedding.

Summary and Conclusions

Parental consent to engagement and marriage was one of the staples of early Protestant theology and law. In the first generation of the Reformation, Luther, Bucer, Zwingli, and others had held up the doctrine of parental consent as their biblical answer to the late medieval toleration of secret engagements and marriages. Unless they had consented to their minor child's unions, parents could seek an annulment. For their part, unless they could prove parental abuse, children would be punished for entering such contracts secretly. For many reformers, the requirement of parental consent was a moral right and duty anchored in the fifth commandment: "Honor thy father and thy mother."

Calvin and his colleagues accepted much of the prevailing Protestant law of parental consent. They declared parental consent, like individual consent, to be indispensable to the validity of a minor's engagement. The Geneva Consistory inquired closely into the engagements of minors, and routinely dissolved them if their parents dissented. Not only the couple, but also a parent, guardian, witness, or notary to an engagement contract could be punished for failure to get the necessary consent from both sets of parents. Overbearing or officious parents or guardians would be punished for intruding on the consent of their children or wards. Once parents or guardians had given their consent to their minor children's engagement or marriage, they could not withdraw it. Only proof of another impediment would allow the parents to seek annulment of an engagement or marriage to which they had consented.

Calvin ultimately rejected the law of some Protestant communities that allowed parents to annul their children's secret marriages as well. Calvin had left this question unresolved in his 1546 Marriage Ordinance. Initially, he was attracted to conventional Protestant arguments that unless parents could annul their children's secret marriages, the doctrine of parental consent would be a mere form of words that guaranteed nothing. He was also, initially, unmoved by Catholic arguments that secret marriages could not be dissolved because they were sacramental. This, too, for Calvin was a mere form of words that proved nothing: If marriage was an indissoluble sacrament, why should its sacramental status not turn on whether it was properly formed by the couple and approved by their parents.

Calvin ultimately abandoned this early position and resolved that secret marriages once consummated could not be dissolved by anyone, including the couple and their parents. His concerns were in part prudential — about the dangers of parental tyranny and the costs of marital breakup to the couple and their children. His motivations were perhaps also pragmatic. After all, in a small city like Geneva, with its intensely active Consistory and its multi-step public marriage process, it would have been hard for a secretly engaged couple to sneak into marriage without discovery by parents or guardians. To be valid, their banns would have to be posted, their certificates publicly registered, their wedding publicly celebrated during a Sunday afternoon or weekday worship service. Throughout this time — and indeed until the very last step in the marriage liturgy when the pastor called "if anyone has reason to object to this marriage" — anyone could protest, not least the parents or guardians of the couple. This objection would have automatically halted the process, and put the couple before the Consistory. If they were minors, the Consistory would require them to prove that they had their parents' consent. If they did not have it, their engagement would be annulled. With all these safeguards in place, Calvin must have concluded that it was best to leave secretly married couples to lie in their marital beds undisturbed. At that point, it was as much the negligence of the parents and community as the delinquency of the children that the couple had been secretly married.

Calvin also accepted much of the prevailing Protestant theology of parental consent — but with two somewhat peculiar new accents. First, Calvin's concerns for daughters and mothers in the process of marital formation stood sharply juxtaposed. On the one hand, Calvin was surprisingly jealous to ensure that girls were as protected from tyrannical parents as boys in their decision to marry. This was biblically counterintuitive. Both the stories in Genesis and the laws of Moses were filled with examples showing that young women had little voice and few rights in the decision to get married, especially vis-à-vis their fathers. Yet, Calvin showed little patience with any of this. He repeatedly castigated biblical fathers who sold, coerced, or tricked their daughters into marriage. And he lifted up the one example of Bethuel and Rebekah as exemplary of what the natural law teaches about how a father was to care for his daughter's consent.

On the other hand, Calvin was surprisingly churlish about the role of the mother in consenting to her minor's engagement and marriage. Her views counted only if her husband was absent, and then only if they concurred with that of other relatives. Even hearsay testimony of a father's wishes was given priority to a mother's contrary written and oral statements before the Consistory. This strong accent on the father's voice was, of course, typical of the stories in Genesis and the laws of Moses, and of some of the New Testament household codes as well. But why should Calvin stick to the letter and spirit of the Bible on the place of a wife, but not on the place of a daughter? Calvin did not say.

This first peculiarity may well be related to a second, namely, Calvin's reliance on natural law, rather than the fifth commandment, for the doctrine of parental consent. This was not unprecedented. But both the early Church Fathers and other early Protestants had seen the doctrine of parental consent as part and product of the commandment: "Honor thy father and thy mother." Indeed, the rest of the commandment seemed to underscore the wisdom of such obedience for the future happiness of children: "so that your days may be long in the land that the Lord your God gives you."

For all his robust exegesis of the Decalogue as a source and summary of natural law on many other aspects of life, Calvin did not follow it on the issue of parental consent. Instead, he (and Beza) pointed vaguely and variously to natural law, the law of nations, common equity, and plain common sense to argue for the doctrine. It is hard to know what motivated Calvin in this choice of authority. Perhaps it came down to the simple fact that Calvin had written into his early law that it was the consent of the fathers, not the mothers, that counted, and he was sticking to it. It would have been hard to square this provision with the commandment to "[h]onor thy father and thy mother." But this was not Calvin's usual style. He was certainly firm and fierce in defending what he wrote, but he would sometimes change his mind, especially when the Bible charted a better way. On this issue, the Bible and the tradition did chart a more egalitarian way. Calvin did not follow it.

5-1 Commentary on 1 Corinthians 7:36-38 (1546)[29]

Paul now directs his discourse to parents who had children under their authority. For having heard the praises of celibacy, and having heard also of the inconveniences of marriage, they might be in doubt whether it was at all kind to involve their children in so many miseries, lest it should seem as if they were to blame for the troubles that might befall them. For the greater their attachment to their children, the more anxiously do they exercise fear and caution on their account. Paul, then, with the view of relieving them from this difficulty, teaches that it is their duty to consult their advantage, exactly as one would do for himself when at his own disposal. . . .

[F]athers ought to look carefully on all sides before giving up anxiety and intention as to giving away their daughters in marriage. For they often decline marriage, either from shame or from ignorance of themselves, even though they are no less wanton or prone to be led astray. Parents must here consider well what the interests of their daughters are, so that by their prudence they may correct their ignorance or unreasonable desire.

Now this passage serves to establish the authority of parents, which ought to be held sacred, as having its origin in the common laws of nature. Now if in other, less important, actions, no liberty is allowed to children without the authority of their parents, much less is it reasonable that they should have liberty given them in the contracting of marriage. And that has been carefully enacted by civil law, but more especially by the law of God.

Let us know, therefore, that in disposing of children in marriage, the authority of parents is of first-rate importance, provided they do not tyrannically abuse it, as even the civil laws prohibit. The Apostle, too, in requiring exemption from necessity, intimated that the deliberations of parents ought to be regulated with a view to the advantage of their children. Let us bear in mind, therefore, that this limitation is the proper rule: that children allow themselves to be governed by their parents, and that they, on the other hand, do not drag their children by force to what is against their inclination, and that they have no other object in view, in the exercise of their authority, than the advantage of their children.

29. CO 49:424-26 (NTC adapted).

5-2   Commentary on the Harmony of the Law
Numbers 30:2-5 (1563)[30]

[Moses] begins by repeating the basic law that every one should faithfully pay whatever he has vowed. While this is the general rule, he only refers to those who are their own masters. Women or girls, who are under the power of another, were not free to make vows without the consent of their fathers or husbands. . . . [I]f a daughter, while living with her father, has vowed anything without his knowledge, it is of no force. He lays down the same rule, when the father, hearing the vow, has disallowed it. But if the father has held his peace, it is declared that his silence is equivalent to consent. Hence we gather that all those with power do not do their duty unless they frankly and discreetly express their opposition whenever anything displeases them. Their silence is a kind of tacit approval [and] once approved of, it cannot be disallowed.

5-3   Commentary on Genesis 24:1-3, 57 (1554)[31]

Moses expressly describes Abraham as an old man, in order that we may learn that he had been admonished, by his very age, to seek a wife for his son. For old age itself, which, at most is not far distant from death, ought to induce us to order the affairs of our family, so that when we die, peace may be preserved among our posterity, the fear of the Lord may flourish, and rightly-constituted order may prevail. . . .

Abraham here fulfils the common duty of parents, in laboring for and being solicitous about the choice of a wife for his son. But he is even more forward-looking. Since God had separated him from the Canaanites by a sacred covenant, he justly fears that if Isaac joins himself in marriage to them, he will shake off the yoke of God. . . . [T]he disposition and even the virtue of Isaac were obvious. In addition to his riches, he had such endowments of mind and person that many would earnestly desire to marry him. His father, therefore, feared that, after his own death, the inhabitants of the land would captivate Isaac by their allurements. . . .

Now this example should be taken by us as a common rule, to show that it is not lawful for the children of a family to contract marriage, except with the

---

30. CO 24:572 (OTC adapted). It must be noted that Calvin adduced this passage as a gloss not on the fifth commandment, but on the third commandment, "Thou shalt not take the Lord thy God in vain."

31. CO 23:326-41 (OTC adapted).

consent of parents. Certainly natural equity dictates that, in a matter of such importance, children should depend upon the will of their parents. . . .

[After rehearsing the story of the servant's discovery of Rebekah, meeting her parents, requesting their consent, and giving them engagement gifts, Calvin writes of Rebekah's father, Bethuel:] Moses declares that he did not exercise tyranny over his daughter so as to thrust her out reluctantly, or to compel her to marry against her will, but left her to her own free choice. Truly, in this matter, the authority of parents ought to be sacred. But a middle course is to be pursued, so that the parties concerned may make their contract spontaneously, and with mutual consent. It is not right to understand that Rebekah in answering so explicitly, showed contempt for the paternal roof, or was too anxious in her desire for a husband. But since she saw that the affair was transacted by the authority of her father, and with the consent of her mother, she also herself acquiesced in it.

5-4   Commentary on Joshua 15:14 (1563)[32]

How could Caleb presume to bargain concerning his daughter until he knew her wishes? Although it is the office of parents to settle their daughters in life, they are not permitted to exercise tyrannical power over them or to assign them to whatever husbands they think fit without consulting them. For, while all contracts ought to be voluntary, freedom ought to prevail especially in marriage so that no one pledges faith against his will.

Caleb was probably influenced by the belief that his daughter would willingly give her consent, for she could not reject such honorable terms without immodesty. For her proposed husband was not a commoner, but one who was to exceed all others in military valor. It might well be that in the heat of battle, Caleb, without thinking, promised something over which he had no authority. It seems to me, however, that according to common law the agreement implied the daughter's consent and was only to take effect if it was obtained.

5-5   Theodore Beza on Parental Consent and
   Clandestine Marriages (1569)[33]

We now have to speak of clandestine promises to marry which are made without the consent of those who have power over those making the promises. Since

32. CO 25:528-29 (OTC adapted).
33. Beza, TRD, 2:76-82 (translated by John P. Donnelly, S.J.)

those promises are diametrically opposed to God's will and commandment and to natural equity itself, it seems that they cannot be reconciled with God as our creator. They are therefore void and (as they say) have no standing in law.

Let us first talk about divine law. Children owe honor to their parents. In my view, no one will deny that this [honor] should be measured by the power of the parents over their children. That children were counted among the goods or wealth of the father of their family is altogether clear in the very ancient story of Job: Satan attacked Job's children after he had been given power to destroy all of Job's possessions (Job 1:12, 18-19). Children were no more allowed to free themselves from the authority of others than were slaves, unless they had their parents' consent. That very reality proclaims that this was fair and honorable, since, according to God, children owed their being to their parents, and hence they were counted among their parents' goods on far better grounds than any slave or subject who was under their dominion or was bought at a price.

The Lord did not amend the law that parents were allowed, when pressed by need, to sell off their children as slaves, even though this is perhaps because of their number and the hard hearts of that people that [God] tolerated rather than approved this (Exod. 21:7). Still this argues for the supreme power which parents have always had over the bodies of their children. The same practice long flourished among the Romans. For example, fathers had the power of life and death over their sons. But if a question arises that is something more particular and looks specifically at the marriage of the children, what prevents there being an explicit law which clearly has been in use forever? Rebekah was sought after and received only from the hand of Bethuel (Gen. 24, 27, 28). Jacob took his wives from Laban, and so on.[34] Moses inculcates the same paternal authority in talking about who has raped a virgin and also about not having sons-in-laws and daughters-in-laws from pagan nations. The same [practice] is clear from the oath that Israelites took against Benjaminites. Samson too, although captivated by the love of a foreign woman, still requested his father's consent. Tamar tried this way to escape from the hands of her rapist brother (2 Sam. 13:11-15). Paul in speaking about virgins and hired women who needed protection clearly shows that he supported the right of fathers over their children.

Both the early Greek and Latin Fathers agree here with the Word of God to the point that not one can be found who disagrees. What else? The popes, too, judge the same — Evaristus, Leo I, Pelagius, Urban, Nicholas. The ancient councils also go so far that they condemn clandestine marriages (which are among the main subjects we are dealing with) and even subject to the sentence

---

34. The marginal notes here give a wealth of other scriptural and patristic citations, which are omitted.

of excommunication *ipso facto* (as they call it) those who know about, attend, or help [the formation of clandestine marriages].

The civil laws written on these matters by ancient lawyers and by the emperors are in such complete agreement that not even a widow under twenty-five years old, though she enjoys the freedom of emancipation, is exempted. [These laws] are too well known to be ignored, too clear to be obfuscated, too hallowed to be abolished by law.

What prevents us from declaring that such promises to marry are completely void and invalid once and for all? Yes, even if the promises to marry entered into without the parents' knowledge by widows who are now legally independent are not void, still they do not lack very just censure.

But what if such promises to marry are followed by an actual marriage? Certainly if the cause is examined why such promises are completely void (namely because those who do not possess that right cannot agree to hand over themselves) then the marriage itself is made to have far less validity, so that in it a more explicit and also fuller consent is needed. The arguments which assert the contrary need to be refuted. But we will postpone dealing with these until our treatment of divorce.

But on this subject some very important questions arise. Are children forced to agree necessarily with those in whose power they are? I reply that they are not forced since a free and fully voluntary consent is a first requirement for marriage. But still the respect owed to parents and to those who take the place of parents demands that [a minor child] should not disagree with them, except for a very serious reason. But in turn, it is only fair that parents treat their children with moderation and not force them into this or that marriage against their will.

But what if either the parents and children cannot come to a satisfactory agreement or the parents do not carry out their duty? Here all the more gentle solutions are to be tried. Severity of fathers in all aspects of their role should be shunned, and likewise fathers must be warned against abusing the power entrusted to them by God. But if no fair solution can be obtained on a different basis, then the magistrates may be approached whose duty it is partly to lay down laws as fair as possible on these matters and partly to offer themselves as mediators so that neither paternal authority is violated nor their children oppressed by unfair fathers who are unworthy of so sweet a name.

But should a person be judged to have agreed who does not disagree? For fairness seems to demand that parents or those who take the place of parents be seen as having consented unless they shall have explicitly disagreed since neither any force nor violent suspicion of fear falls upon them. But as regards the children and those who are under the power of others, even if the lawyers seem to think the same thing, I cannot come to the same conclusion. I think that this rather should be observed: since both paternal authority and the weakness of youth can easily impede full liberty of choice, the very expression of consent requires a situation above all suspicion. I also add that, even when the consent was explicit, still if sexual union will have been tenaciously denied, the matter seems worthy of being looked into carefully, so that no marriage partners be bound except by a clearly free and voluntary consent. But when sexual union has taken place, the allegation of a husband that he was under duress surely is in vain. It seems the same should be applied to the wife unless perchance she will have proved clearly that force was used against her and that she neither then nor later ever consented.

5-6   Case of Louise Loup and Nicod des Planches (1552)[35]

(Nov. 10, 1552). Louise, daughter of the late François Loup of Loisin by Ballaison, presented an affidavit that she was engaged to one named Nicod, son of Nicod des Planches of Gy by Foncenex.

Decided: that she make her witnesses come, and inform the castellan of St. Victor to remand des Planches for Thursday.

(Nov. 17, 1552). Louise, daughter of François Loup of Loisin, and Nicod des Planches of Gy were asked whether they are not promised to each other in marriage. He confessed it, but said that his father does not want to consent and he does not want to disobey him. He gave her a Geneva sou and drank in the name of marriage.

5-7   Case of Jenon Ramou, Françoise Tournier, Humbert Gallatin, and Jean Berto (1552)[36]

(March 24, 1552). Jenon, daughter of the late Pierre Ramou, and Françoise, daughter of Tibaud Tournier of Dardagny, Humbert Gallatin, and Jean Berto of Dardagny were admonished to state the reason why they were remanded here. They said they drank in the name of marriage with the aforesaid, but it was using a bowl of water six weeks ago today. They said they did not expect to be taken by surprise this way, and that if they wanted to marry they would not want to marry without the leave of their parents and friends.

Witnesses François Paquier, Tibaud Tournier, Pernette, wife of Jean Tournier, the wife of Pierre Ramou, and Jeannette, widow of Jean Bornand,

---

35. R. Consist. VII, 96, 98.
36. R. Consist. VII, 10.

were deposed. They testified that they were present when the aforesaid marriage was [contracted] and was drunk [that is, toasted]. [They] think it was done in jest, and as for the parents of the girls, they do not want to consent to such a promise made in this way.

Decided: that the two young men be remanded before the Council, and given remonstrances, also punish them for being seducers of girls as they were, and that such a marriage should not take effect. And as for the girls and witnesses, let them be wiser from now on, so as not to engage or be found in such a practice.

5-8   Case of Pierre Clerc, Clement de Biffort, and Fiancée (1557)[37]

(Feb. 25, 1557). Pierre Clerc of Bonne said that he has engaged his daughter to the son of Clement de Biffort, and he did this without the knowledge and consent of the father of the [prospective] husband de Biffort. The document contracting the marriage was recorded by de Chenelet. He asked to carry out the marriage. The [prospective] husband de Biffort said this is true, and asked that, notwithstanding that his father does not consent, the marriage be carried out, [since he] wished to stay and live in this city.

The decision of the Consistory is that this be remanded before the Council to remedy it on Monday, and that the notary de Chenelet should appear there, who registered such a contract contrary to his duty.

[The Council register of March 1 says that de Chenelet should be examined "after dinner," after which the case will be considered further. There is no record of any decision, however, and the case is not mentioned again.]

5-9   Case of Nicolas, Jaques d'Orléans, and His Fiancée (1552)[38]

(December 8, 1552). Jaques d'Orléans, Nicolas, bookseller, and his daughter [were] admonished that it has come to notice that there has been a promise of marriage between d'Orléans and the girl. The father [Nicolas] answered that about a year ago there was talk of the said marriage but it was not concluded. D'Orléans and his daughter were questioned separately. He said it is true that the girl received some rings and a serge apron, hoping that the matter would come to marriage, but afterwards it was returned because they put off the solemn swearing until he and Salomon her brother had agreed and rendered their accounts. She said the same.

37. R. Consist. XII, 8.
38. R. Consist. VII, 106.

Decided: to exhort the father to go there in good conscience to proceed and carry out [the marriage]. Answered that he did not decide on the matter during the time they had stipulated as their condition.

Further decision: that between now and Monday they be admonished whether they can decide according to their consciences, because there is no testimony; otherwise let them be remanded before the Council to put them on oath about the case, and if they swear to what they have said let them be set at liberty.

5-10   Case of Jeanne Nepveur and Louis Blanchet (1556-1557)[39]

(Aug. 6, 1556). Guillaume Nepveur, his wife, and their daughter Jeanne, Louis Blanchet and Olivier, brother-in-law of Blanchet, presented a petition for a declaration about a promise to his daughter. It is more fully explained very verbosely in the petition, aimed at having such a promise declared void. Blanchet said it is true that they wrote their promise down. But that by their mutual will they broke it, and this was done because they did not want to wait until he returned from Orléans in his own country. And, for his part, he was content, and moreover, the Nepveurs said they would not agree to it unless he brought the promised sum that he said he had with him. He said he does not intend to and does not have the money at hand.

Decided: that the father and mother be admonished that since they made such a promise, simply and without conditions, that they should not negotiate about any marriage for half a year, and they should return here to carry it out. Also admonished that they cannot break such bonds, and told that the contents of a torn paper that Monsieur De Saule saw previously declare to them that there is a marriage.

(Feb. 18, 1557). Concerning the case of Monsieur Dubois [read: Guillaume Nepveur] because of the alleged marriage of his daughter with Louis Blanchet. It was ordered and decided that Dubois [through] Master Delestra should write to Louis Blanchet who is in his own country, having withdrawn there after the promise, between now and Easter and advise him of the situation here and summon him by it [the letter] to come here to carry out such a marriage. And let this be done pleasantly, so that after getting an answer from him to such a letter one may proceed properly.

(April 1, 1557). Guillaume Nepveur, host of the Orléans Arms, stated that, following the command of the Consistory, he sent a letter to Louis Blanchet who was engaged to his daughter. In it he wrote that he was sending him news

39. R. Consist. XI, 47-47v, XII, 5, 24v-25, 96.

about the engagement between him and the daughter of Nepveur. To this letter he has had no answer. He asked, therefore, that his daughter be provided for, because she is getting old and Blanchet laughs at them. He produced to this effect Etienne Vyault, who carried the letter and who spoke to Blanchet. He was examined, and said that he gave him [Louis] the letter in person, to which he had no answer, saying he did not take much notice of him, and said that Blanchet feared it would come to notice that he had been in this city.

It was decided that the case be remanded to the Council to Monday, and that Olivier, brother of Blanchet, be remanded so that after he is heard one may proceed and provide for the girl in this manner: that is that Olivier must write to Louis, his brother, a letter to which he may send a short answer, and that between now and Pentecost he must appear in this city. Otherwise, if between now and Pentecost he does not come and appear in this city, he will be found remiss and contumacious, and the girl will thus be able to marry.

[On April 5 the Council ordered Olivier Le Villain, Blanchet's brother (or brother-in-law), to write to him as the Consistory had proposed, and he said he would. On July 12 Nepveur, appearing through his lawyer, requested that the divorce be pronounced as he had proposed before, but the Council decided more information was needed first.]

(Sept. 9, 1557). Concerning the request presented on behalf of Guillaume Nepveur and remanded here by our Lords, Olivier Le Villain and Charles de Vergier having been heard. Villain said that he wrote to Louis Blanchet, his brother-in-law, concerning the promise of marriage between him and the daughter of Nepveur, according to the order of our Lords. And he sent him a letter by Vergier, here present and so confessing, and he gave the letter to Blanchet, who took no notice of him and did not want to make or give him any answer.

Decided: since someone spoke in person to Blanchet and enjoined him to return to this city, appointing a term for his return on pain of being regarded as forsworn, and he did not come, but pretended to be ill in his own country; and, since then, the father of the girl, Guillaume Nepveur, wrote to him, on which Blanchet excused himself; and, since then, by an order of our Lords to Olivier to write to Blanchet, his brother-in-law, to come here to carry out the marriage [on pain] that he would be declared forsworn, remiss, and contumacious, and nevertheless he took no notice; that for these reasons he be held as such and that the girl be set free [from the engagement] and that a proclamation be made once in this city, since it concerns only an engagement entered into in Paris and not here.

5-11   Case of Nicolas Millet and Michee Gaudi (1557)[40]

(May 13, 1557). Nicolas Millet presented a petition aimed at giving him a decision concerning the promise of marriage between him and Michee, daughter of Jaques Gaudi of Vandoeuvres. Jaques, the father, and Michee, the daughter, were summoned to learn the truth of the matter. The father and daughter said that they do not wish to permit such a marriage to be carried out. It was decided to admonish Millet to go seek money in his own country to give it to Jaques Gaudi for the purpose of helping him to clear his lands. As for father Jaques and his daughter, let them be told that this marriage must still be completed within a month, and if they do not wish it to be carried out within this said term let them be remanded before the Council for Monday. Having been told this, he [Jaques] said that he did not want it carried out, because Millet has failed in his promise to give him money within a certain period, which expired before Millet's return, and because of his fault he lost three pieces of land. Note that in leaving the Consistory he said: "Cursed be the one who brought Millet to this country."

Petition Presented in Consistory by Nicolas Millet (July 27, 1557)

Magnificent and most honored Lords: Nicolas Millet humbly states that it is the case that following the decision previously made concerning the marriage between him and Michee, daughter of Jaques Gaudi, parish of Vandoeuvres, he pursued his case before the Lord Justices of first instance where Michee was living, and that it was ordered that the said petitioner be faithful to the orders issued by you concerning the marriage and its approval. For these reasons he very humbly pleads that it may please you to order and command your secretary to deliver and supply the said petitioner with the orders, acts, and procedures issued in the case of the marriage between him and Michee to assist him and for him to produce them when desirable, praying God for your prosperity.

(July 27, 1557). Concerning the petition given above, the petitioner having been heard, it was decided to direct the secretary of the Consistory, Pierre Alliod, to give and provide him a signed copy of what he asks and to produce it where it is proper according to law, so that through lack of it he may not suffer harm, and otherwise as is more fully contained in the petition.

(May 13, 1557). The petition of Nicolas Millet was heard, aimed at giving him a decision concerning the promise of marriage between him and Michee, daughter of Jaques Gaudi of Vandoeuvres, who refuses to carry out the marriage. Jaques Gaudi and Michee, his daughter, were summoned, who being

---

40. R. Consist. XII, 45-45v. The July 27, 1557, petition seems to be misdated by the notary.

questioned about this, said that they do not consent to the marriage. Especially Gaudi, the father, does not wish it carried out, because Millet has not performed the promise he made them to give them money to clear certain lands.

They having been heard, it was decided to tell and admonish Millet to go seek money in his own country, which he should bring and give to Gaudi to assist him in clearing his lands [of debt] according to his promise. [It was also decided] to command Gaudi and his daughter to complete the marriage within a month, and in case they do not wish to promise this, let them be remanded for Monday before the Council so that it may please them to compel them to do this. Having been told this, Jaques Gaudi answered and said that he did not wish it to be carried out, because Millet has failed in his promise to him to give him money within a certain term, already expired before Millet's return, as a result of which and through default of which he lost three pieces of land, which did him great injury.

Decided: considering his refusal, let him be sent as stated, and his daughter also, with the said petitioner, before the Council to deal with the matter.

[We found no Council record, but evidently the case was returned to the Consistory.]

(May 20, 1557). Concerning the instruction given to the Consistory by Our Lords to deliberate and advise once again concerning the claimed marriage between Nicolas Millet and Michee, daughter of Jaques Gaudi. Monsieur Colladon, minister, having been heard, said he himself had pronounced the promise of marriage between the said parties, and that if they deceived themselves by any promises they made each other this is not his fault. It seemed proper, after having again heard the said parties, to remand them to the Council with a statement that, despite the promises, such a marriage should not be dissolved, but should hold and be indissoluble: since if it were the case that it was dissoluble, this would be to open the door for many others. And such is the advice of the Consistory returned to the Council with the parties to decide about it.

5-12 Case of Etienne de Lonnay and Maxima (1547)[41]

(April 5, 1547). Etienne de Lonnay and Thevena, wife of Dommenget, and Maxima her daughter, were questioned to learn about the promise of marriage made between de Lonnay and the girl. He answered that it is true they arranged a marriage, and indeed there is a contract recorded by the younger Cuvat, and he gave her a coin in the name of marriage. The woman, the mother of the girl, on the contrary denied having said such words. The girl was asked, and said

41. R. Consist. III, 48.

that he tossed a teston on the table and gave her a silk neckcloth and also wanted to give her half-sleeves of filled serge. Admonished as to how old she is, she answered that at the end of the month of April she will be ten, and does not want to accept marriage. She also said that her father, who is in Lyon, sent to tell her not to marry without his consent. She also said that the aforesaid [de Lonnay] gave her a pair of knives, and she gave him another pair, and that it was her mother who gave her the drink.

Decided: that they be remanded before the Council and that the consistory cannot consent to such a marriage, because it sets a bad example. And ask them to summon the notary who recorded such a contract and the witnesses, also to find out who made the inventory, and to admonish them for it, considering also that girl is not of age.

[On April 12, 1547, the Council declared the marriage void and ordered the notary Cuvat imprisoned for three days for having drawn up the contract, and also forbade him to act as a notary for one year. The mother was imprisoned for three days, and the daughter was to return everything she had received from de Lonnay. On April 26 Cuvat asked the Council to reinstate him as a notary, saying he had not recorded the marriage contract, but merely a gift from the mother to the daughter. The Council granted his request.]

5-13 Case of Girard Reveillet and Fiancée (1545)[42]

(Oct. 29, 1545). Girard Reveillet, quarryman from Soral, living in St. Jean de Gonville, appeared. He said that a few days ago one named M. Martin Masson asked him whether he wanted his niece in marriage. He said yes, and many other words, and said it is true they drank with each other in marriage. The fiancée, maid of Pierre Veyron, said she did not drink in marriage, begging the Council to have consideration for her, since she is a poor girl. Jean [that is, Girard] said that certain relatives of the girl were present, and said it is true that he offered the cup and that the girl drank with him and then kissed him. The girl denied everything. Let the aunt of the girl be called.

(Nov. 5, 1545). The quarryman and his fiancée, a woman named Massonnes, Bastian her son, and the wife of Bastian, appeared. The quarryman was questioned according to last Thursday's remand. He said as he did before, asking the girl to keep her promise to him, the promise that was made at the house of Bastian [and of] his mother. Bastian confessed that it is true that the promise was made at their house and that they drank together.

Decided: that the girl be assisted to get her mother and brother to come

42. R. Consist. VII, 6, 8v, 11, 49v, 56, 58.

Thursday, because the witnesses have also testified that the girl reserved the consent of her mother and brother [that is, conditioned her consent on their consent].

(Nov. 12, 1545). Girard Reveillet, quarryman, and Veyron's maid were called according to the previous remand to investigate again their differences about the [the engagement] promise. And the mother of the girl appeared, who does not agree to the promise, saying that if her daughter made such a promise she will never appear before her again. And she was asked whether it is not true that they returned to take the great oath and to inform their relatives on one side and the other, and then her mother did not agree to it.

Decided: that they be remanded before the Council for Monday, declaring the promise void.

[There is no mention of this case in the Council minutes for November 16.]

(April 15, 1546). Jaques Bernard, minister of Peney, spoke against an engagement for marriage. Girard Reveillet, quarryman of Soral, by whom a release was presented registered by a notary in the present year, January 12, signed at Collonges in the house of notary Tissott, with many admonitions that he is accustomed to make agreements and that the promise mentioned in the release was not argued before the official and court, which is still the custom in the papistry. And that Girard later became engaged to someone else, that he was . . . [words missing], and he was told that he must have another more adequate release before proceeding to another marriage.

(May 6, 1546). Girard, quarryman of Soral, presented still another release entered by his fiancée on the back of the other already presented formerly and signed by the vicar of Frangy. Decided: that release is not sufficient.

(May 13, 1546). Girard, quarryman, brought another affidavit that his wife [i.e., his fiancée] whom he was engaged to is married, signed by the vicar of Frangy. Decided . . .

[The decision is not given, but on May 30, 1546, Girard Reveillet of Soral married Michée, daughter of Gonet Dufour, of Cartigny. They baptized their daughter Françoise on April 1, 1548. We do not know whether this was the same woman or, more likely, another who waited until Reveillet had been released from his promise and given permission to contract another marriage.]

5-14 Case of Jean Casaux and Madeleine D'Agnon (1561)[43]

(October 9, 1561). Jean Casaux appeared because he said that there have been certain words between him and Monsieur D'Agnon about the marriage of his

---

43. R. Consist. XVIII, 135v, 136v-138, 141-141v, 143.

daughter, and that he having his mother [living], he has been to her to get leave and arrange the marriage. She did not want to consent to the marriage, and she is a papist, but his brother, who is his guardian, consented to it. To this end, he produced a letter from his brother and an affidavit of a notary. The decision is that Casaux should bring witnesses next Thursday to verify the notary's signature and his brother's letter, and let Monsieur D'Agnon bring his daughter.

(October 16, 1561). Master Jean Casaux produced as witnesses Master Martial Neufville and Jean Brogneres to verify the signature on the affidavit and the letter produced by him last Thursday. They said under oath that they knew the said signature to be that on the letter from Hugues Casaux, brother of Jean, and they recognized his letter. They also know their mother, who is a papist. They said that Master Jean Casaux came to this city with his brother's consent and not his mother's. They also recognized the handwriting and signature of the affidavit, which was signed by Delenthillac, notary, and by Debazin and Genastet, witnesses. They said they knew the contents of the said letter, which should state that the brother of Jean consented to the marriage between Jean and the daughter of Monsieur D'Agnon, and also that he sent him a letter in which he wrote him that before making any marriage he should take counsel from those testifying and from Monsieur Nord and Monsieur Rigottier, which he did not do, as they are well assured.

Jean Casaux, when summoned and questioned about this, confessed that he did not speak to Monsieur Nord or Monsieur Rigottier or to the above-named witnesses, although his brother's letter advised him to. He said that he has been here [in Geneva] for seven months, and that he got leave from his mother to come here. Asked whence this marriage came and how it was arranged, he said that it was by means of a woman named Madeleine Du Trieur, living with Monsieur Pelissier's wife, who is from their country, because the girl had lived there with her. He said that she spoke of it to Monsieur D'Agnon, the girl's father, and also that his friend Jourdain Sauvin assisted in arranging this marriage. He said he had spoken to [the] girl in her father's presence, to whom he did not promise marriage. He confessed that he did give her a ring on the advice of Madeleine and of Monsieur Sauvin in the presence of Monsieur D'Agnon's wife, Madeleine, and Monsieur Sauvin. Asked whether the girl has not been in his room since Thursday, he answered that he cannot say anything about it, since Thursday; knows indeed that she has been there. Here he was admonished that he acted against his mother's will, who decided, as is seen in the said affidavit, that she does not want him to marry until he is 25.

The girl named Madeleine when questioned said that Casaux promised her marriage, giving her a gold ring, saying to her: "Behold what I give you in the name of marriage," saying nothing else, without drinking, and this was in the presence of Monsieur D'Agnon's wife, her stepmother, Master Jourdain

Sauvin, and the aforesaid Madeleine Du Trieur. She also said that it was her mother who spoke of it to her first, who said and asked whether she wanted to marry. She answered yes, if it pleased her father and her. Then she told her that her father indeed wanted it. She has been there for a week today, and her mother went there to sup with her. She also said that she has worn the ring on her finger for two weeks.

Here Monsieur D'Agnon, father of the girl named Madeleine, protested and declared that he never knew anything about it, at least about the promise, nor that the girl's or her mother's intention was such. Here it was decided to summon the wife of Monsieur D'Agnon, Madeleine Du Trieur, and Jourdain Sauvin. They appeared and were questioned separately.

First, the wife of Monsieur D'Agnon denied having been present when Casaux promised the girl marriage, and she did not consent that she take the ring. She did confess having asked whether she wanted him as her husband, because her father would indeed consent to it. She said that the girl did show her the ring.

Madeleine Du Trieur, when asked who gave her authority to undertake and arrange this marriage, answered that it was at the request of Monsieur Sauvin and of Casaux, and she spoke of it to Monsieur D'Agnon, who told her that for the moment he could not give an answer. Nevertheless, he thanked God that Casaux asked his daughter in marriage, and he must pray to God and communicate with his friends, so that for the moment he could not give her an answer. She confessed that she was in her room when Casaux gave the girl a ring. She said and confessed that she advised him to give her a ring, saying that there was no harm in it or bad intention. She said that she and Monsieur Sauvin were present and that the ring was given in the name of marriage. She said that she did not know that the girl's mother was there. She does not know that they drank in the name of marriage.

Jourdain Sauvin, when asked about this, said that he was present when Casaux gave a ring in the name of marriage to Monsieur D'Agnon's daughter, although he did not hear the words, because he spoke in her ear. He indeed said and confessed to him afterwards that it was so and that he would never have another wife than her. Said that the girl's mother, the wife of Monsieur D'Agnon, her father, was not there.

Jean Casaux was summoned and asked again whether the ring was not given by him in the name of marriage; he answered no, and that he never made this statement. Concerning this, he was accused of lies from the testimony of the said Sauvin, and after this he was ordered to leave.

The whole having been heard, it was decided to give Monsieur D'Agnon strict admonitions, with remonstrances that he should keep better watch in his household than he has, and that the marriage of his first daughter should have warned him to keep his eye on matters better than he has, so that another time he would keep better guard. Moreover, it was decided as below.

Meanwhile, Casaux was recalled and asked whether Monsieur D'Agnon gave him his daughter in marriage, as is seen in the letter that Casaux's brother wrote to Monsieur D'Agnon. He answered that Monsieur D'Agnon did not speak to him about it, nor he to him, but he did have someone speak to him about it. Nevertheless, he did see the letter in which this is stated before it was sealed. The misbehavior of Casaux appears in this very clearly. Moreover, it was decided because Casaux was advised by his brother by letter to take the counsel of Monsieur Rigottier, Monsieur Nord, and the two witnesses before making any marriage, and so far he has done nothing about it, it was decided to remand him to the Council for Monday, and the girl also, to declare this marriage, or beginning of one, void and that for such reasons it should be dissolved.

As for the rest, Monsieur D'Agnon's wife, Madeleine Du Trieur, and Jourdain Sauvin should also be sent there [to the Council] to be punished for having meddled in arranging such a clandestine marriage, and let the Council follow a single rule. Let Monsieur D'Agnon also be remanded there because this took place through his fault, because he should resist it strongly and keep watch on it, considering that he had been warned so that by his means a great scandal might result.

And if this marriage took place we would have to close the gates of the College, since Monsieur Sauvin has done likewise with Madeleine Du Trieur. Thus we pray the Council to take action in good time.

(October 23, 1561). Following the report made by Noble Claude de La Maisonneufve and Amied de Chasteauneuf, councilors of our Lords and members of the Consistory, that the Council has remanded the case of Monsieur D'Agnon, minister, because of the marriage of Madeleine, his purported daughter, with Jean Casaux, it was decided to summon him first to give him remonstrances about the matter according to the orders of Our Said Lords and about his faults to make him acknowledge them. This was done, and being questioned about the matter, he did not want to answer anything. Wherefore it was decided to read him the report the Consistory made to the Council. This was also done, and being asked what one should say about the fact that a young man, having been sent to this city to study, gets married, and also to the daughter of a minister, he answered truthfully that he did not know at all that the promise of marriage would be made. Here he was admonished that he cannot be excused in this, because his daughter wore the ring given to her by Casaux on her finger for two weeks. But again he protested never having observed anything, since he had inquired carefully about the matter. Concerning this he was told that we do not find this excuse sufficient, because it is difficult to believe that for two weeks he did not see the ring on his daughter's finger, or if he did not see it, he was very negligent, and this negligence should be strongly objected to and reproved. Concerning which he said that he would like to be far away so as not to offend anyone and would like to be banished. Finally, he being admonished that he could not excuse himself, he said that he is ready to do what is ordered against him. On which he was answered that he should condemn himself. Which he did, asking to be pardoned, and on this he departed according to the order given him, and meanwhile it was decided that he must acknowledge his fault more fully, and especially because he said that he would like to be far away from here in order not to offend anyone; also because he said that he would like to be banished. Because he meant that the Council had been very merciful to him in having sent him here, because in this we think that he wanted to tax the Consistory with having been very rough with him, especially because he said that the Council had treated him gently. Which he did, being recalled. Afterwards it was decided to tell him to withdraw, and meanwhile we shall proceed in the case of the marriage.

The wife of Monsieur D'Agnon, minister, his stepdaughter named Madeleine, Master Jean Casaux, and Madeleine Du Trieur were remanded here by the Council to sift the case of the claimed marriage between Casaux and Madeleine, daughter of Monsieur D'Agnon, which nevertheless today was declared void by Our Said Lords. They appeared, and were questioned about this and admonished that they have behaved very badly in having hidden the truth, even though they had taken an oath, at least some. The said Mme D'Agnon persisted in her statements and said that she was not present when Casaux gave the ring in the name of marriage to Madeleine. It is true that on the same day and immediately after having received it from him she came to find her, showing it to her and telling her that Casaux had given it to her in the name of marriage, which she quickly went on the same day and at the same moment to repeat to Monsieur D'Agnon, her husband, who was in his study. Then she said that Monsieur D'Agnon spoke to her about it first. The girl also confessed likewise that she told a lie when she said here that her stepmother had been present at the reception of the ring, and before the Council she said and confessed she was not.

Casaux, excusing himself, said that he did not act out of malice. Wherefore it was decided to tax him with frivolity and inconsistency and carelessness and not with malice. And moreover let the matter be remanded before the Council, who will be informed that we do not know what to do, because the witnesses have reversed themselves, except to undertake a criminal prosecution against them because of the perjury, and to state to them that Sauvin has shown himself rebellious in that he has not appeared, and concerning this may it please the Council to proceed as is proper.

5-15 Case of Pierre Dolen and Mademoiselle Fertz (1546)[44]

[This case concerns the marriage of Pierre Dolen and the daughter of the late Claude Fertz who died of the plague. Her father's will appointed Pierre Gravier to be her guardian. Fertz herself ended up in the plague hospital shortly thereafter. On August 30, 1546, the Council accused Pierre Dolen of becoming engaged to Fertz without her guardian's consent. On September 2, Fertz and Dolen were forbidden to associate with each other. The ministers then appeared before the Council, reporting that their liaison had begun when she was in the plague hospital, infected with the plague. Jean Chautemps, then in charge of the plague hospital, was ordered to "carefully protect the property of the girl." On September 3, he reported to the Council that he believed Dolen and Fertz had "entered the house of late Claude Fertz and there seized the money and deeds" they found there. The Council ordered them both imprisoned. Fertz and Dolen were still living together on October 22, when Dolen asked that their banns of marriage be signed. The Council in response ordered him imprisoned again. Dolen was freed on October 28 and remanded before the Consistory.]

(Oct. 28, 1546). Consistory decision concerning Pierre Dolen, who was remanded here to the Consistory by the Council to learn whether the marriage should go into effect. The syndic declared that neither he nor the girl was constrained by anyone who prevented the marriage, considering that the girl has no relatives. The decision is that the marriage was badly begun and that before proceeding further the parties should be called before the Council, and the matter will be considered.

(Nov. 4, 1546). Master Pierre Gravier and Pierre Dolen [were summoned]. Dolen was asked to explain the form of the engagement he made with the daughter of the late Master Claude Fertz. He said it is true that on coming to the plague hospital he found the girl sitting on a rock in front of the hospital, being very cold, and with many verbose exculpatory words. He also said that he became engaged to the girl, since she told him she had no relatives in this city except an uncle who is in Chambéry. Then he engaged himself to her and drank with her to marriage.

Gravier was asked what he wants to say about the promise. He answered it is true that the late Master Claude Fertz after the death of his wife complained that the girl was not obedient to him, and he asked him to take her in and watch over her. He also said that after the death of Fertz he went to the hospital to see the girl and offer her assistance. He was astonished when he saw rings on her fingers. Then Dolen came with insulting words, telling him, "You are nothing but a preacher." Huguet [Dolen's brother-in-law] did likewise. Gravier was

44. R. Consist. II, 86v, 88, 100v.

asked to say who was present at the insults. He cannot at present name them. He confessed that he has had the company of the girl.

Decided: that the Consistory declare to the Council that what has been done is void and a bad example. It is nothing but fornication. If it pleases the Council [for Dolen and Fertz] to start again and carry out a marriage in another form [it may be done] at their good pleasure. Let him be forbidden to live with her any more. Before the Council, as well as the girl.

[On November 8 the Council declared this "clandestine marriage" void and again ordered the imprisonment of Dolen and Fertz. On November 15, after six days in prison, Fertz was released and granted permission to marry Dolen. The next day the Council ordered that her closest relatives be summoned to consent to the marriage.]

CHAPTER 6

Capacity to Contract Marriage

The Impediments of Infancy
and Mental Inability

While marriage required mutual consent, not all men and women could give their consent, and not all their engagement or marriage promises could be enforced. Certain actions or conditions discovered after the exchange of promises could be grounds for dissolution of these promises. Certain relationships or experiences could disqualify the parties from engagement and marriage — altogether or at least with each other.

These disqualifying and disabling factors were called impediments, as we saw in Chapter 1. Calvin and his colleagues recognized a number of such impediments, though not nearly so many as the medieval canonists. The impediments that came to prevail in Reformation Geneva fell into three clusters.

First, Calvin and his colleagues recognized three impediments of *capacity to contract marriage:* (1) the impediment of infancy or impuberty, which precluded under-aged children from contracting marriage; (2) the impediment of mental inability, which precluded marriage to the insane or mentally impaired; and (3) the impediment of polygamy or precontract, which precluded an already engaged or married person from engaging or marrying another. These three impediments of capacity were serious business. They could be pled by anyone at any time. They could be used to annul both engagements and fully consummated marriages. And the impediment of precontract could lead to charges of polygamy, a serious crime if entered into intentionally. The impediments of infancy and mental inability will occupy us in this chapter. The impediment of precontract will occupy us in Chapter 7.

Second, the reformers recognized four impediments of *quality or fitness for marriage:* (1) the lack of presumed virginity; (2) the presence of a contagious disease; (3) the incidence of sexual incapacity or dysfunction; and, more controversially, (4) wide disparity of age between the man and the woman. These four impediments addressed the physical qualities of the parties to enter marriage, regardless of their legal capacities. They were serious business, too. At least the first three of these impediments of quality could be pled by the fit party to annul either an engagement or a newly contracted marriage. The fourth impediment could annul at least an engagement. These impediments of quality will occupy us in Chapter 8.

Third, the Reformers recognized a number of incest impediments, that is, blood or family ties between the two parties that rendered their engagement or marriage incestuous. Even if the parties were of proper age and mental ability to enter contracts, and even if they had the requisite physical qualities to enter marriage in general, their blood or familial ties prohibited them from marrying each other. Engagements or marriages contracted innocently in violation of these incest impediments were automatically dissolved. Those contracted knowingly could trigger severe criminal punishments. These impediments of incest will occupy us in Chapter 9.

Calvin and his colleagues did not recognize the traditional impediments prohibiting interreligious marriage. Marriage outside the faith was imprudent, even foolish, they argued, but it was not formally prohibited. Neither engagements nor marriages between parties of different faiths could be annulled on that ground alone. This teaching on interreligious marriage will occupy us in Chapter 10.

The 1546 Marriage Ordinance defined these clusters of impediments in widely varying detail. It briefly mentioned the impediments of capacity, though they attracted a good deal of commentary from both Calvin and Beza and raised a number of complex cases for the Consistory to adjudicate. It specified more clearly the impediments of quality, but these garnered less commentary from Calvin and more sporadic litigation in the Consistory. It set out the impediments of incest in copious detail, and these attracted a huge volume of commentary from Calvin and occupied the Consistory in several intriguing and intricate cases. The Marriage Ordinance did not touch on interreligious marriage at all, but this was sometimes the subject of intense litigation in the Consistory and Council.

The Impediment of Infancy or Impuberty

The 1546 Marriage Ordinance stipulated an age of *majority* — the minimum age children needed to reach before they could enter marriages without seeking their parents' consent.[1] The Ordinance did not, however, stipulate an age of

---

1. See Doc. 1-2, items 1, 10 stipulating eighteen for girls, twenty for boys.

consent — the minimum age children needed to be before they could enter marriages in the first place. Instead, the Ordinance declared that marriages contracted by "young people" were *void*.[2] It provided further that "child marriages" arranged by their parents or guardians were *voidable:* a child was free to consent to or dissent from such an arranged marriage upon reaching the age of consent. Calvin put it thus in the Ordinance:

> 3. If it happens that two young people have contracted marriage by their own action through folly or recklessness, let them be punished and chastened and let such a marriage be dissolved at the request of those who have charge of them. . . .

> 9. Fathers or guardians shall not have marriages contracted for their children or wards until they have reached an age to confirm them.[3]

This was the classic teaching of the medieval canon law. "Where there is no consent by both parties, there is no marriage," Gratian wrote in his Decretum of c. 1140. "Those who give boys to girls in their cradles achieve nothing unless each of the children consents when it comes to the age of discretion, even if the father and mother have arranged and willed the marriage."[4] Some noble and royal families of the day still arranged the marriages of their minor children for financial or diplomatic reasons. Think of young Prince Henry VIII of England and Catherine of Aragon who were engaged when Henry was only eleven. But medieval canon law mandated that such marriages could not go forward unless and until the children consented to them upon reaching the age of consent.[5]

Both Calvin and Beza thought this to be sound teaching. For Calvin, it was a mere "childish game" for two youngsters to make engagement or marriage promises (**Doc. 6-1**).[6] Such promises could not be considered binding contracts. For Calvin, it was also a "profanation" of marriage for parents or guardians to arrange marriages for their minor children. Such parents should be punished for abusing their authority.

A child needed to be both physically and morally mature enough to enter marriage, Calvin insisted. At minimum, the child needed to reach puberty be-

---

2. See also 1537 Ordinance in SD, vol. 2, item 732: "Young people not of age may not marry."

3. Doc. 1-2.

4. Corpus Iuris Canonici, ed. Emil Friedberg, repr. ed., 2 vols. (Graz, 1959), 1:1100. See further Sanchez, I, Disp. li.

5. Orme, pp. 334-37.

6. See also *R. Conseil*, 48:169-169v, which includes Calvin's opinion about the sexual culpability of boys at different stages of development. See further Naphy, Sex Crimes, pp. 108-9.

fore marriage was possible. For sexual intercourse was an inherent and essential part of marriage; thus no prepubescent child could be married. But equally important, the child needed to reach moral maturity before marriage was proper. Even if capable of sexual performance, the child might still lack the moral discernment to know what marriage involved. Such views led Calvin to resist setting a specific age of consent for marriage. Children mature at different paces and ages, he argued. It was thus best to make a case-by-case inquiry whether a child was mature enough rather than mandate a specific age of consent to apply in all cases.[7]

Writing in 1569, Beza focused not only on the child's physical and moral immaturity, but also on the child's mental incapacity to create a binding marriage contract (**Doc. 6-2**). Beza argued that consent was the essential ingredient of any binding marriage contract. A child simply lacked the intelligence necessary to form this requisite consent. Thus any agreements to marry made by two children alone were not binding contracts, for they lacked consent. Both the boy and the girl were free, upon reaching maturity, to pursue marriage with anyone, including with each other. It was a different matter, however, when parents made or approved the contracts on behalf of their children, or if an adult became engaged to a minor. Parents and other adults did have the requisite intelligence to form consent. Parents were thus bound to the promises they had made in consenting to or contracting arranged marriages for their child. They could not enter other marital contracts for that child without becoming accessories to the crime of polygamy. Adults were also bound by their engagement promises to minors. Once engaged to a minor, such an adult was not free to contract marriage with anyone else without courting charges of polygamy — and premarital adultery if the second relationship was consummated. Only if and when the engaged child reached the age of majority and rescinded the engagement contract could the parents and the adult party be freed from their promises.

Calvin had encountered the problems of child marriage early in his career. In a 1541 letter to Farel, written before his return to Geneva, Calvin described the travails of one of his former servants who had contracted a marriage in Geneva while he was still a boy (**Doc. 6-3**). Without his father's consent, the boy had become engaged to a young girl. When the couple came of age both the young man's father and the Genevan authorities ordered them to get married. The young man refused, saying that he had never intended to marry the girl and had been pressured into making the promise. When the authorities persisted, he fled the country. After his father died, the young man wanted to return home. But now his relatives were pressing him to marry. Calvin had ques-

---

7. R. Conseil 54:73 (1558); *Annales Calviniani* (September 1, 1558), CO 21:702.

tioned the young man himself at some length. He had found no guile in him but also no desire whatsoever to get married to this young woman. Calvin thought the engagement contract should be annulled. He urged Farel and others to see whether this could be done.

Consistory Cases

Perhaps informed by this early case, Calvin wrote both the impediment of infancy and the prohibition on parental pressure to marry into the 1546 Marriage Ordinance. In the next few years, the Geneva Consistory heard a number of cases involving disputes over child marriages, most of them arranged marriages. The Consistory usually ordered that the engagement contract be reconsidered when the child reached maturity. The Consistory sometimes sanctioned parents and other adult parties as well if they were found to be exploiting or pressuring their children.

In a 1548 case, for example, Claude Gringet asked the Consistory whether he might marry his fiancée. The young woman in question was, in the Consistory's judgment, a girl around twelve years old (**Doc. 6-4**). The girl's mother had consented to the engagement and was ready for the marriage to go forward. Without even questioning the girl, the Consistory declared that to proceed with such a marriage would be "against reason and equity." The engagement contract was "without value" to support a marriage now. Claude was ordered to wait "two or three years more" before asking the young woman whether she wished to consent to the marriage.

It made no difference to the Consistory that these arranged marriage contracts were elaborately written or accompanied by elaborate engagement gifts. For example, in a 1547 case, Etienne de Lonnay sought to enforce a notarized engagement contract with a ten-year-old girl, Maxima.[8] He testified that the girl's mother had consented to the union and that he had lavished various gifts on young Maxima in consideration of the engagement. The mother now denied giving her consent. Maxima testified that she had accepted the gifts but had never consented to the marriage. She reported further that her father, who was away at the time, also did not consent. This was enough, in the Consistory's judgment, to trigger an annulment. On their recommendation, the Council annulled the engagement contract and ordered Maxima to return all the gifts. They imprisoned the notary for drafting the contract. They also imprisoned the

---

8. The full record of this case is included as Doc. 5-12 above. In Chapter 5, we analyzed the case for how it resolved paternal versus maternal consent to marriage. Here, we analyze it for how it deals with the impediment of infancy.

mother for consenting to the engagement, evidently in defiance of her husband's wishes for young Maxima. And, because Maxima's father had not consented, the Council declared the engagement contract void rather than just voidable. Maxima would not have the opportunity to consent to or dissent from the marriage once she reached the age of majority.

The Consistory became doubly zealous in their protection of a child's right to dissent from an arranged marriage when they suspected foul play. In a 1547 case, for example, the Consistory learned that Pierre Mestrazat had, already two years before, become engaged to a girl of ten in another town (**Doc. 6-5**). Pierre had forced the girl's mother to give her consent to the engagement. Even worse, he was now threatening to take the child away to a Catholic territory. This was "scandalous," said the Consistory. They called upon the mother to testify. She confirmed that Pierre had not only threatened her but in fact had beaten her "villainously" in order to extract her consent. Yet, the mother said she was willing to accept Pierre as her "son" if he promised to live by the Word of God. The mother was not just being pious and charitable. Pierre had evidently signed a contract to pay the costs of the girl's apprenticeship and maintenance in exchange for her later hand in marriage. With no mention in the record of any father, it was likely that this was a single mother doing the best she could to support her child.

Pierre intimated that he would be happy to cancel the engagement contract — and, by implication, his contract to pay the girl's maintenance and support expenses as well. The Consistory would hear none of it. No doubt still scandalized by the evidence of Pierre's belligerence and his threat to take the girl to a Catholic home, the Consistory insisted on full performance of both the engagement contract and the maintenance contract. At the same time, they reserved the girl's right to rescind the engagement contract when she reached the age of consent, which they stipulated as fourteen in this case. The Consistory thereby made Pierre the victim of his own hard bargaining. Pierre had forced the mother into accepting what was, in effect, an installment contract to marry a virgin. The Consistory converted this into a mandatory child support contract with no guarantee of a bride in return. Indeed, we have found no record that Pierre and the girl were ever married upon her reaching the age of consent.

The Consistory ruled similarly in a 1546 case involving the purported marriage of two nine-year olds, Jean Dimier and Nicolarde du Pont (**Doc. 6-6**). This "marriage" was a guardianship arrangement gone utterly amiss. Nicolarde's parents needed to find a place for her to live. They had arranged with Jean's father, Claude, to become a guardian to Nicolarde and to take her into his home. Claude promised to raise her as if she were his own child. Nicolarde's parents gave him funds for Nicolarde's maintenance and support. So far, there was nothing unusual in this arrangement.

But then, inexplicably, the parents had their local minister marry young Nicolarde to young Jean, Claude's son. Even more inexplicably, the minister married the youngsters without reservation. It is hard to know what was motivating the parties to take this unusual step. There was no obvious legal advantage for the couple to be married at this early stage of life. Whatever testamentary advantages might have been gained by the marriage were so remote that this could not have been the motivation. Perhaps Nicolarde's parents thought that Claude's duties of guardianship would be more effectively delivered if his ward Nicolarde were his daughter-in-law rather than just a stranger. Perhaps Claude and his wife wanted to have a daughter, and this arrangement gave them the benefits of effectively adopting a daughter without having to pay for her support. The record does not clearly say.

The record does make clear, however, that Jean's parents thought that the couple was married. Young Nicolarde and Jean were made to sleep together, albeit with father Claude present. But when Nicolarde wet the bed "under him," Jean became "disgusted" with her. Claude and his wife beat her and wanted her out of the house.

A complaint about the minister from Nicolarde's home town brought this whole unusual arrangement to the Geneva Consistory's attention. The Consistory rebuked both sets of parents for their "monstrous" impropriety. They questioned the children closely. It was obvious that neither Nicolarde nor Jean really understood what marriage meant, nor considered themselves to be married. The Consistory thus asked the Council to remove Nicolarde from Claude's home and guardianship and to safeguard her assets. They also asked the Council to declare the marriage contract "void[able]" and to give the two children the right to confirm or deny the marriage when they reached maturity. Four years later, when the couple came of age, Nicolarde's father, no doubt still chastened by their earlier rebuke, asked the Council whether the couple could marry. Though Jean wanted to marry, Nicolarde dissented because of her earlier mistreatment by Jean's family. The Council thus dissolved the engagement contract and declared that the parties were free to court and marry others.

The Consistory maintained this position on arranged child marriages in later years. This can be seen in a 1557 case of Jacques Rosset and his fiancée (**Doc. 6-7**). The couple had become engaged when both were apparently minors. Jacques had apparently used ample gifts of liquor to induce the woman's family to consent. Since then, he had fraternized rather freely with their daughter, much to her family's chagrin. The couple had now reached the age of consent, and the issue was whether they should marry or could they break their engagement with impunity.

Upon learning of the couple's fraternizing, the Consistory ordered the young woman to remain in her parents' home while the case was pending.

The marriage could proceed only if both sets of parents would come to the Consistory to give their consent. Jacques' parents appeared the following week to protest the marriage — loudly. The Consistory thus removed the case to the Council, recommending annulment of the engagement, and a permanent prohibition against the parties seeing each other again. The Council ordered the engagement annulled and also imprisoned the couple for their evident fornication.

Had this been a simple case of two youngsters promising marriage, the Consistory could have enforced the letter of the 1546 Marriage Ordinance, namely, that such promises were automatically void. But, it was the consent of the girl's parents, even though fraudulently procured, that must have given the Consistory pause.

What was left uncertain in these and other cases was the precise age of consent in Geneva. Before the Reformation, sixteen was the presumptive age of consent for both boys and girls in Geneva.[9] In some of the early cases in Calvin's day, the Consistory allowed marriage to children as young as thirteen but barred it to children as old as seventeen. This variation was consistent with Calvin's argument that the age of consent should turn on the maturity, not the age, of the child. But this variation also invited perennial litigation in close cases, which swelled an already full Consistory docket.

In 1558, the Consistory therefore requested the Council to fix an age of consent by statute. Calvin, apparently on his own initiative, requested that the Council make the age of consent, at least for girls, turn on whether the party was a fully professed communicant member of the church — again underscoring his concern that maturity, in this case spiritual maturity, was the salient test.[10] No record of the Council's response to Calvin survives, but no statute was forthcoming in Calvin's lifetime. In 1576, however, the Council set the minimum age of consent at fourteen for girls, and eighteen for boys.[11]

The Impediment of Mental Inability

Beza had articulated an important argument for the impediment of infancy — that children lacked the intelligence to form the requisite consent to make a binding marriage contract. A similar argument supported a second impediment of incapacity, the impediment of "insanity," "madness," or "lunacy" as it was traditionally called — or more generically the impediment of mental in-

9. Seeger, pp. 332-34.
10. *Annales,* CO 21:702; Seeger, p. 335.
11. SD, vol. 3, item 1183.

ability. Like children, individuals who suffered from chronic mental inability lacked the intelligence to form the requisite consent to make a binding marriage contract. Thus, promises of engagement or marriage made by a mentally impaired person could not be considered binding.

Calvin said nothing directly about this impediment of mental inability, though he hinted at a position several times.[12] Prompted by Farel's late-life engagement, for example, Calvin asked the local Consistory of Neuchâtel whether Farel had "lost his mind" — suggesting that this might be a ground to annul Farel's engagement.[13] In his discussion of the propriety of elderly widows and widowers seeking remarriage, Calvin always assumed that these parties were free from "the chronic decrepitude of old age," which presumably could mean mental as well as physical "decrepitude." And he did allow for annulment of engagements contracted when the parties were drunk (that is, had their minds temporarily impaired). These passages suggest strongly that Calvin would regard mental inability as an impediment that could support the annulment of an engagement.

It is unlikely, however, that Calvin regarded mental inability as a ground to annul a fully consummated marriage. In a *consilium* on sexual incapacity Calvin recognized that a husband who became afflicted by a form of leprosy called elephantiasis might be driven to "a brutish form of stupor." His wife could separate from him for her own protection and that of their children, Calvin argued. But the marriage could not be dissolved by annulment or divorce. For a marriage was contracted for "better or worse," "in sickness and in health."[14] Moreover, in his 1546 Marriage Ordinance, Calvin provided remedies for wives who were abused by husbands who had "uncontrolled anger" — a common symptom of dementia, insanity, and other mental disease.[15] But the only remedies provided in such cases were Consistory admonitions to peace and reconciliation, backed by criminal punishment of the husband in extreme cases. The 1546 Ordinance did not even countenance separation in such cases, let alone annulment or divorce. With so robust an understanding of the presumed per-

---

12. Calvin did comment and preach at length on the several biblical passages describing lunatics and madmen. Following Scripture, he often described these mental abnormalities as evidence of devil possession. See, e.g., Comm. Harm. Law Deut. 28:28; Serm. 1 Sam. 16:14-23, 19:24; Comm. Harm. Gosp. Matt. 8:28-34; 20:29; Mark 5:1-20; Luke 8:2, 26-39; Comm. Acts 19:13-17. But Calvin saw nothing in these texts about the incapacities of such madmen to make agreements of any sort, let alone to make marriage contracts. Calvin also once described the bizarre suicide of a debauched man afflicted with the plague as evidence of devil possession. See Letter to Pierre Viret (November 15, 1546), CO 12:413-16.

13. See below Doc. 8-23.

14. See below Doc. 8-11.

15. 1546 Marriage Ordinance, items 35-36; above Doc. 1-2.

manence of marriage "in sickness and in health," it is hard to imagine Calvin condoning annulment of marriages on grounds of mental inability.

This, in fact, was the common understanding of the impediment of mental inability in Protestant circles of the day, and in at least some schools of medieval canon law.[16] Mental inability was an impediment to engagements, but not to marriages. In 1569 Theodore Beza summarized this prevailing law with attention to the exact timing of the onset of the mental condition (**Doc. 6-8**). Persons who were permanently insane, retarded, or otherwise mentally handicapped could never make engagement or marriage contracts. If they tried to enter them, those contracts had to be unilaterally dissolved. Persons who became mentally disabled by disease or accident after their engagement but before their wedding could not get married, and the healthy spouse could not be bound to the contract. After a time of waiting — in part to ensure that the mental inability was permanent, in part to ensure that the woman was not pregnant — the able party could seek annulment and be free to pursue marriage with another. Persons who were mentally disabled but had intervals of lucidity should not get engaged or married. But if both parties knowingly proceeded with the marriage despite this intermittent mental handicap, Beza hinted that neither party could later seek annulment of the marriage, even if the party became completely disabled after the wedding. Beza's younger colleague François Hotman took this latter position firmly, and also made clear that if a once lucid party became mentally disabled after the wedding, the marriage could not be annulled.[17]

The 1546 Marriage Ordinance was silent on this impediment, and we have found no cases (at least in our three sample years) where the Consistory annulled an engagement or marriage on the ground of mental inability alone. The absence of case law is not so surprising. Few parties would be eager to marry or have sex with the permanently insane unless they had prurient or base financial motives. Such cases would be dealt with by the criminal courts, not by the Consistory. Sex with the mentally disabled or incapacitated was rape; taking such an incapacitated person's property was theft. Moreover, without an explicit impediment law of mental inability on the books, parties who sought to escape unwanted engagements or marriages to someone who became mentally disabled would likely just desert them. Or they would likely find a recognized impediment to plead and then use the other party's mental inability as an aggravating condition to strengthen their argument.

---

16. See Hotman, caps. VI-VIII; Sanchez, I, Disp. lxx; Brundage, pp. 201, 288.
17. Hotman, cap. VII.

Summary and Conclusions

Calvin, Beza, and their colleagues drew a distinction between the age of majority and the age of consent. The age of *majority* was the minimum age children needed to reach before they could enter marriages on their own, without seeking their parents' consent. The 1546 Marriage Ordinance set this age at twenty for boys, eighteen for girls. The age of *consent* was the minimum age children needed to be before they could enter marriages in the first place. Both Calvin and Beza preferred to judge the age of consent on a case-by-case basis, for children reached the physical, sexual, and spiritual maturity needed for marriage at different paces and ages. The Genevan authorities went along with this for a time. But the lack of a clear age of consent spawned endless litigation, particularly since the Consistory in its early years had come down hard on parents who entered children into marriage at too young an age. The Council eventually set the age of consent at eighteen for boys, fourteen for girls.

Children under the age of consent could not marry. If they sought to marry, or if their parents entered engagement or marriage contracts for them, the Genevan authorities treated these contracts as "voidable." The contracts bound the child's parents as well as the other party if he or she were an adult. But the validity of the contract turned on whether the child accepted or rejected it on reaching the age of consent. If the matured child consented to this contract, the engagement was valid, and the marriage would go forward absent proof of another impediment. If the child dissented from the contract, however, all parties were freed from their promises and the engagement "voided."

The main reason that children could not enter engagement or marriage contracts was that they lacked the mental ability to give their consent. This same reason informed the impediment of mental inability. This impediment precluded parties who suffered from permanent and chronic mental inability from entering into engagement or marriage contracts. For those who had bouts of lucidity, the authorities allowed them to enter engagements and marriages, though they considered these contracts ill-advised. If the party's mental inability came on for the first time between engagement and marriage, the healthy party could seek to annul the engagement. If the mental inability came on after the wedding day, however, the parties were bound to the marriage. They had taken vows to remain together "in sickness and in health," and this was a trial of sickness that they would have to endure. If the mentally disabled party became violent or dangerous, the parties could separate from bed and board. But their marriage could not be broken on the ground of mental inability alone.

6-1   Calvin's *Consilium* on Marriage of Youngsters (n.d.)[18]

It has always been judged, and properly so, that marriage is not legitimate except between those who have reached puberty. When a boy marries, then, this is a childish game, and the sort of levity that deserves punishment.

First of all, it must be stated that those who are under the authority of their parents or guardians are not free or independent, especially in this matter. Even if the parents or guardians consent, or even if they are the principal instigators of the marriage — nonetheless, the contracts made before the proper age do not bind the children unless, after they reach puberty, they feel the same way, and voluntarily acknowledge that they consider their premature marriage valid.

If any parents betroth their children before they reach puberty, and pledge themselves and their possessions, they nevertheless cannot bind the children who are not yet ready for marriage. A contract of this sort is a profaning of marriage. If anyone has rashly put himself in a guilty position, let him bear the punishment he deserves. The terms of the marriage cannot be carried out, since the children, when they reach puberty, are free to retract whatever their parents wrongfully transacted on their behalf.

6-2   Theodore Beza on Marriage of Children (1569)[19]

But what if the promises to marry were performed with the consent of the parents or even by their command, but both parties or at least one has not reached puberty? I reply that these promises to marry have no force unless they are later reconfirmed by a new consent after puberty is reached or, with malice making up for age, sexual intercourse was delayed. There seems to be no consent if those, because of their age, are unable to understand what is involved. But because there is a middle period between infancy and puberty, as between two extremes, in which humans are not completely without intelligence but are not sufficiently intelligent, so too a certain middle ground like degrees of consenting can be posited between the consent of those who clearly understand what is being done by those who have power over them and the consent of those who are quite incapable of understanding these matters. It is from this that the distinction of those three states of man comes which Modestinus followed in not

---

18. CO 10:231-33, translated in *Calvin's Ecclesiastical Advice*, pp. 122-23.
19. Beza, TRD, 2:81-82 (translated by John P. Donnelly, S.J.).

wanting promises to marry to be made by those under seven. Emperor Leo also warned against this, and Alexander III responded. But whatever is the case, such promises to marry regardless of the time and words you use can only be about future time and cannot fully bind persons before puberty unless after reaching puberty they give another consent, either tacit or explicit. I confess that during the wait for puberty the post-puberty person cannot break off the promises made to a pre-puberty partner and has an affinity like one previously contracted until time itself will make clear what the future outcome of the matter will be. I also agree that the pre-pubescent person cannot dissent before the years of puberty but has to wait for puberty.

6-3   Letter to Guillaume Farel (1541)[20]

There has lately occurred a circumstance which I must not omit to mention. Maurice has an attendant, who was for some time servant to Louis and me in Basel. He is a decent, honest young man, trustworthy and modest. About five years ago, when he was still a boy, without the knowledge of his father, he promised to marry a young woman. His father, once he learned of the affair, had remonstrated with his son upon the subject. The youth told him that he had been imposed upon.

Though the case has not been fully investigated or well understood or weighed properly or maturely considered, your Consistory judges under Marcourt's direction have pronounced that the marriage ought to be held good. The young man, in order to avoid this connection, has left his country. He has now received news of the death of his father. His relatives have advised him to take the young woman as his wife. Mirabeau has advised him to the same effect.

I have examined him to the uttermost, and almost worn him out by my entreaties. Yet, he is so averse to it that I cannot prevail on myself to urge him any farther. He repeatedly acknowledges that the girl is an honest woman, but positively affirms that he never had any inclination to marry her. Because I wish him well, I would like it if this affair could be settled by a friendly agreement and mutual understanding between the parties. This will also be for the advantage of the girl herself.

I have written to Mirabeau about the business. On my account, however, I do not wish you to do anything except what you shall judge just and right in the circumstances. Nor would I do more myself if the case were referred to my decision.

20. Letter of May 12, 1541, CO 11:217-18 (n.d.), Bonnet, Letter 68 (adapted).

6-4   Case of Claude Gringet (1548)[21]

(Jan. 19, 1548). Claude Gringet, velvet-maker, stated he has promised himself to a girl who is present with her mother. In the beginning, the mother did not consent, but afterwards she was won over. The girl is less than twelve to thirteen years of age. He asked the opinion of the Consistory to know the way to proceed in this case.

Decided: the act is of no value and would have bad results. Considering that it clearly appears that the girl is less than twelve years of age, it is against reason and equity [to allow them to marry]. The marriage should not go into effect, and Claude deserves strong remonstrances declaring that he should refrain from such a promise and marriage for two to three years more.

6-5   Case of Pierre Mestrazat (1547)[22]

(Aug. 30, 1547). Pierre Mestrazat was admonished that it is said that he is engaged to a young girl from Thonon and wanted to use violence with indecent words. He confessed at great length having been engaged to the girl for about two years under condition she had accepted. He also confessed that the girl cannot be more than ten years old.

Decided: that the mother, the girl, and Pierre come here Thursday, so that a more definite conclusion can be reached about the affair. He asked to be remanded to a week from Thursday, because he has a case before the bailiff next Friday.

Decided: that considering that the matter is scandalous and could cause greater difficulties, the matter cannot remain so delayed, and is remanded to Thursday.

(Sept. 1, 1547). Pierre Mestrazat, his fiancée, and the mother of his fiancée were admonished to learn about their differences. He was admonished that the mother-in-law had complained that Pierre threatened to beat her and also said that he would carry the girl off and take her into the papistry. He answered and denied everything, except that it is true that he is engaged to her and has sent her to a master to learn and to be supported, being satisfied that if it is known that he does not have the girl he is content. The mother complained strongly, saying she had been struck villainously; nevertheless if the aforesaid [Pierre] wanted to keep good company and the Word of God she would take him as her son. Moreover, they are in good accord, and in the presence of respectable peo-

21. R. Consist. III, 199.
22. R. Consist. III, 124, 128.

ple who intervened yesterday they agreed, and are in good accord by their favor. Also the aforesaid [Pierre] asked for advice on the condition that was made: that is, when he promised [to marry] her, because the girl is under age, that if she does not want it at the age of fourteen the promise will be null; and meanwhile he wastes his time and pays her debts, which will cause him great loss.

Decided: concerning the contract, that although the reservation was not in it, the girl should not be obligated, not being of age; but as for the rest, let him concur so well with the mother-in-law that the marriage will go into effect.

6-6   Case of Jean Dimier and Nicolarde du Pont (1546)[23]

(June 3, 1546). Claude Dimier of Jussy, his wife, and his son and his wife both very young, appeared. The son, [the purported] husband, would not be more than nine years old and the girl not more than nine or ten. This is a monstrous thing, and it was fifteen months ago [that they were purportedly married].

Guillaume Grillon and Bartholomie Bransmerel [parents or guardians of the girl] were admonished for having made such a marriage. Bartholomie answered that it is true they made the marriage, on the condition that the girl receive all her support through the accounts of her guardian, and then the father of the boy promised them to treat her like his own child. The father and mother of the boy excused themselves that she has a bad character.

The son was taken aside and was asked whether he understands what marriage means. He said no. Asked whether he promised the girl anything, he said that if she wanted to be a good girl she would have a good time with them. Asked whether he sleeps with her, he said he slept [with her] to begin with and that she is indecent, so much so that he confessed that she wet the bed. Asked whether the minister, Master Henri [de La Mare], had anything to do with marrying them, he answered that if Henri had said the least word about refusing to marry them it would all have been stopped.

The girl was asked whether she understands what marriage means. She said no, and does not believe she is married, and does not want the husband. She also said that the boy's father and mother beat her. She denied having slept with her husband. She was confronted with him. She said she pissed under him, and then he no longer wanted to sleep with her. She also said that the boy's father has always slept with them.

Decided: that the Council be asked to arrange to remove the girl, by some good means, from the father and his son until three or four years from now, and then if the marriage should take effect let it be celebrated again. And let the

23. R. Consist. II, 63.

Council write to the town of Jussy, declaring publicly that the marriage should be void. Also let the property of the girl be managed so it is not wasted.

[On June 7, 1546, the Council ordered that, if four years later, the girl did not want to marry the boy their engagement contract should be annulled. On November 28, 1550, Guillaume Grillon, Nicolarde's father, presented the couple to the Council, saying they did not dare to contract a marriage without its consent. When questioned, Jean said he wanted to marry Nicolarde. Nicolarde, however, said she had been so badly treated by the Dimiers that she did not want to marry him. The Council declared the engagement contract void, and gave the parties permission to marry others.]

6-7   Case of Jacques Rosset and Madeleine Lechiere (1557)[24]

(March 11, 1557). Claude de La Couse, Louis Lechiere, Claude Lechiere, Raymond Pitard, and Madeleine, daughter of Antoine Lechiere, [were] summoned to learn from them what marriage was arranged for Madeleine. They said, [that is] Lechiere said, that Jaques Rosset, called Blackhead, came to their house to ask for Madeleine to be his wife. He was told that she was not of his rank, [but] he said that they should give him a drink, which was done, and they drank in the name of marriage.

De La Couse said that [Madeleine] Lechiere was in his house, that someone came to find her and to talk to her in his house, and that de La Couse went away with Lechiere. Lechiere said that he saw that de La Couse had two glasses in his hands and was drinking to Rosset and Madeleine. De La Couse confessed this.

Madeleine, when questioned, said and answered that Jaques [Rosset] came after her to this city, that at other times the two of them went to Jussy; other times she found him in Jussy, sometimes, he came to find her in this city. She affirmed having spoken to him twice in this city in the public street, and at the time when she was living at Thyven Laurens' he came to find her to speak to her once. She was asked again about the point that Jaques said to her, namely, that if it did not please his father for him to have her as a wife he would take her to the wars with him. This Madeleine did not contradict.

The decision is that in the first place the witnesses be left alone for the present, and when they are summoned to come to the Consistory, let them promise to return here. As for the marriage, the girl is forbidden to speak at all to Jaques her fiancé, and meanwhile she will be left in the custody of her parents, from fear that something may happen. Also let a letter be sent to Monsieur

24. R. Consist. XII, 13v, 17.

François Rosset, father of Jaques, in which he will be told to forbid the banns if such a marriage does not please him, and if it pleases him let him accept it, then proceed in the matter according to the needs of the case.

(March 18, 1557). François Rosset and Mathée his wife presented themselves to oppose the marriage between Jaques their son and Madeleine, daughter of Antoine Lechiere of Jussy, in the presence of Jaques and of Madeleine. They opposed it, saying that they did not consent at all. The decision is that this matter be referred to Our Lords and that the parties and the daughter's parents should appear before them, and let the daughter be forbidden and her parents commanded not to let her associate with Jaques. Remand before the Council to Monday. Letter to the castellan of Jussy.

[On March 22, 1557, the Council decided that the marriage should be held void, since his parents had not consented to it, and the two were ordered not to associate further. Also the castellan of Jussy was to have Rosset pay an appropriate fine. Moreover, because Rosset had been disobedient to his parents, he was kept in prison until March 25, when he was ordered released after being admonished and begging his father's pardon.]

6-8   Theodore Beza on Impediments of Mental Inability (1569)[25]

Reason also demands that, since a mad person does not give any consent, promises to marriage between people who are already mad are worthless and likewise when one person is of sound mind and the other mad. And this is true without exception as regards permanent madness. But in a person who has lucid intervals and then is well, this [invalidity] also applies if he has determined that he was mad when the engagement was contracted, unless the previously agreed upon promise has been confirmed by a new consent during a lucid interval.

But what if permanent madness will have overtaken engaged persons? The lawyers respond that the promises to marry are not invalidated; this dissolves already consummated marriages far less, except when the madness is completely beyond remedy. But Emperor Leo decreed the contrary both as regards engagements and marriages already entered into, but this exception was added: that a married man was to wait for his mad wife for three years, and a wife was to wait for her mad husband for five years. The canon lawyers are not sufficiently in agreement among themselves.

I am now discussing only engaged couples; on their breaking up I completely agree with Leo. Fairness and reason seem to be totally mocked when nei-

25. Beza, TRD, 2:90-91 (translated by John P. Donnelly, S.J.).

ther a holy blessing can be requested nor can the marriage be rightly and properly consummated, matters still integral as far as the union of bodies go, so that such promises to marry, from which they could never obtain a way out (as if God himself had set up this permanent impediment), are dissolved. Still, both so that it may be clearly be in accord with God's clear will and so that full consideration may be given to promise made, an appropriate space of time should be set up for trying out all remedies.

CHAPTER 7

The Two Shall Become One Flesh

The Impediment of Polygamy
or Precontract

Even if a party was of consenting age and of sound mind, he or she could be incapacitated by the presence of a previous contract of engagement or marriage that had not been dissolved. This was the impediment of precontract. This impediment precluded a party who was already engaged or married to one party from engaging or marrying another. If a party did enter this second contract, his or her first fiancé(e) or spouse could seek the annulment of this second contract. The doubly contracted party could also be brought up on criminal charges of polygamy, crimes which both Calvin and Beza denounced as serious violations of the letter and spirit of the Bible.

If parties contemplating new engagements or marriages were unsure whether a prior engagement or marriage contract was still binding, they were best advised to bring an action for annulment or divorce of this previous contract before proceeding with a new one. The Consistory often facilitated this extra step of caution by allowing weddings to be delayed until the parties produced proper documentation of their eligibility for marriage, or by writing to their counterparts in other cities for the same documentation.

Theological Writings on Polygamy

Although Calvin wrote little about the technicalities of precontract impediments, he did write at some length against polygamy. Polygamy was a pressing concern for Calvin — in part because some Anabaptists and Lutherans of the day were experimenting with polygamy,[1] in greater part because the Old Testament was filled with examples of polygamists, including such leading patriarchs as Abraham, Jacob, David, and Solomon.[2] How could Calvin insist that Christians follow these Old Testament patriarchs in so much else, yet denounce their polygamy so vehemently and denounce anyone who sought to emulate the patriarchs in their polygamous practice?

Calvin denounced polygamy because he believed that God had prescribed monogamy as part of the "order of creation."[3] God created one man and one woman in Paradise, and brought them together in holy matrimony. This first marriage of Adam and Eve set the norm and form for all future marriages, and it distinguished proper sexual relationships among humans from the random and multiple sexual associations of other animals. After recording the story of the creation and coupling of Adam and Eve, Moses wrote: "Therefore shall a man leave his father and his mother, and shall cleave unto his wife: and the two shall become one flesh" (Gen. 2:24). Christ repeated and confirmed these words (Matt. 19:5), as did St. Paul (Eph. 5:31).

In his 1554 Commentary and 1559 Sermon on Genesis 2:24, Calvin read the phrase the "two *shall* become one flesh" as an imperative (**Docs. 7-1 and 7-2**). In this phrase, God commanded marriage as the "most sacred" and "primal" institution. And, at least by implication, God also condemned polygamy as "contrary to the order and law of nature."[4] In his 1559 Sermon on Genesis as

---

1. See generally Witte, LP, pp. 224ff.; John Cairncross, *After Polygamy Was Made a Sin: The Social History of Christian Polygamy* (London, 1974); Paul Mikat, *Die Polygamiefrage in der frühen Neuzeit* (Düsseldorf, 1987); Hasting Eells, *The Attitude of Martin Bucer Toward the Bigamy of Philip of Hesse* (New Haven, 1924). In 1541, Calvin wrote: "It not only alarms me but is altogether overwhelming when we see new causes of offense daily arising, such as that sad affair of the double marriage." Letter to Farel (March, 1541), CO 11:174-80, at p. 180. In 1554, he wrote more specifically that Philip of Hesse's "double marriage" was "illegal." See Letter to Ministers of Zurich (November 13, 1554), CO 15:303-7, at p. 306.

2. See, e.g., the reports of polygamy by Abraham (Gen. 16; 25:1-5), Jacob (Gen. 29:15-30), Esau (Gen. 26:34; 28:9; 36:2), Gideon (Judg. 8:30), Elkanah (1 Sam. 1:2), David (1 Sam. 18:7-30; 25:38-43), Solomon (1 Kings 3:1; 11:3-8), and Rehoboam (2 Chron. 11:2).

3. Letter to Antonius Pignaeus (October, 1538), CO 10/2:255, 258; John L. Thompson, "Patriarchs, Polygamy, and Private Resistance: John Calvin and Others on Breaking God's Rules," *Sixteenth Century Journal* 35 (1) (1994): 3, 7-15.

4. Comm. Gen. 1:27. See also John Calvin, *Contra la Secte . . . Libertines* (1545), CO 7:145-268, at p. 214, condemning Libertine views of marriage and divorce: "It is as if it were in vain that Scripture says that 'the two shall become one flesh.' It does not say 'three' or 'four', but only 'two'. It adds that 'a man shall leave his father and mother and cleave unto his wife' (Gen. 2:24, Mark 10:7). Is it in vain that the Lord gave his laws forbidding the coveting of another man's wife (Ex. 20:14, 17)? Is it without purpose that He condemned adulterers and the lecherous? Did Paul speak in vain when he exhorts every man to be content with his wife (1 Cor. 7:2)?"

well as his 1555 Commentary on Matthew, Calvin underscored that through marriage the man and the woman become "one person," bound to serve and support each other presumptively for life (**Doc. 7-3**).[5] For a husband to seek another woman was an act of adultery; for him to marry her "perverted the whole order of nature."[6] No third party could be added to any marriage, for it was "the mutual union of *two* persons that was consecrated by the Lord," and symbolized in Yahweh's relationship with Israel and Christ's relationship with his Church.[7]

To obey this primal and primary command of marriage does not require persons to forsake their bonds and duties to others, Calvin argued in these two commentaries as well as in his 1548 Commentary on Ephesians 5:31 (**Doc. 7-4**). Children are commanded to "honor" their parents (Exod. 20:12). All persons are commanded to love God and to love their neighbors as themselves (Deut. 6:5; Lev. 19:2, 19; Matt. 22:37-40). These commandments continue to bind a person after marriage. The Bible says that a man shall "leave" his father and his mother and "cleave" to his wife. It does not say that he must abandon his parents, friends, and neighbors altogether. "The marriage bond does not set aside the other duties of mankind, nor are the commandments of God so inconsistent with each other, that a man cannot be a good and faithful husband without ceasing to be a dutiful son," a supportive sibling, or a loving neighbor. "It is altogether a question of degree," Calvin insisted. In a case of absolute conflict of duties, a person must put the duties to a spouse and children above all others, save the duties to God. But in the normal course, marriage should not be considered monopolistic nor used as an excuse to breach duties of love to families, friends, and neighbors.[8] Calvin put this matter of balancing one's domestic duties strongly in a 1559 Sermon on Genesis:

> When it says that "the man will leave his father and mother," this does not mean that marriage breaks the bond, which is also from God, that a father should love his children as his own blood; children also should honor their father and mother as those from whom they have their lives, for God does not contradict himself. There is harmony in all his works; we do not find variation or conflict in them. Therefore marriage must not break or abolish the obligation the father should have to his children and the connection of the children with their father and mother. And why then does it say that the man will leave his father and mother to be joined with his wife? This is meant by comparison, that is that previously he had to leave his father,

5. See also Lect. Mal. 2:15-16, excerpted in Doc. 7-8 below.
6. Comm. Ps. 45:8; see also Comm. Harm. Law Deut. 17:17; Serm. Deut. 21:10-15, 15-17.
7. See Comm. Eph. 5:31 excerpted in Doc. 7-4 below; Lect. Ezek. 16.
8. Comm. Harm. Law, Exod. 20:12; Comm. Harm. Gosp. Matt. 22:27-30.

mother, and wife, as when Our Lord Jesus Christ also says, "Whoever does not hate his father and mother, wife and children and everything he has for the sake of the Gospel is not worthy of being among my disciples." Now these are not incompatible things, for a man to love his wife, to honor his father and mother, and nevertheless for them all to serve God and have such zeal for maintaining his truth that they will not spare their own lives if need be. But this, as I have said, is meant by comparison, that is that there must be no excuse involving either wife or children, either father or mother, when it is a question of maintaining the doctrine of our salvation and making confession of our faith. If we consider everything that might happen and say, "I will put myself in danger of death, and then behold my poor wife who will be a widow, I will leave my children orphans, I must take pity on them. I also have a father and I would not wish to annoy him, I am bound and obligated to him by nature." When, I say, we have alleged all this, these are very frivolous excuses, for we must prefer the truth of God to all these human considerations. And thus if a man must defect from his father and mother, he has such a union with his wife that he must hold fast to that side. But these things are fully compatible, that is for a man to live peaceably with his wife, knowing that they are two in one flesh, and at the same time to show reverence to his father and mother, to assist them, to employ himself in all the services he can do them, to obey them and show himself subject to them: both these things can well be done.

Calvin brought his reflections on polygamy together in a forceful sermon on Deuteronomy 21:15-17, which he preached in Geneva in 1555 (**Doc. 7-5**). At creation, God could have created two or more wives for Adam. But he chose to create one. God could have created three or four types of humans to be the image of God. But he created two types: "male and female he created them."[9] In the law, God could have commanded his people to worship two or more gods, but he commanded them to worship one God.[10] In the Gospel, Christ could have founded two or more churches to represent him on earth, but he founded one Church.[11] Marriage, as an "order of creation" and a "symbol of God's relationship with his elect," involves two parties and two parties only. "[W]hoever surpasses this rule perverts everything, and it is as though he wished to nullify the very institution of God," Calvin concluded.

In this same sermon, and in several other passages, Calvin lamented that, while God commanded monogamy at creation, polygamy had become commonplace already soon after the Fall into sin. The first polygamist in the Bible

9. See also Doc. 7-2 and Comm. Gen. 1:27.
10. Serm. Deut. 21:10-14, Comm. Harm. Law Exod. 20:3-6.
11. Comm. Eph. 5:31; Serm. Eph. 5:31.

was Lamech, a descendent of the first murderer, Cain (**Doc. 7-6**). Calvin denounced Lamech, for he knowingly "perverted" the "sacred law of marriage" set by God that "two shall become one flesh." Whether driven by lust or by a lust for power, Lamech upset the "order of nature" itself in marrying a second wife.

Lamech's sin of polygamy became the custom of subsequent generations of God's people. Indeed, the sin of polygamy has persisted to this day among Muslims, the descendents of Ishmael, the bastard son of Abraham's polygamous relationship with Hagar.[12] Many of Israel's great patriarchs and kings after Abraham — Jacob, Gideon, David, Solomon, Rehoboam, and others — succumbed to the temptation of polygamy just like Abraham. The Bible's account of the chronic discord of their polygamous households should be proof enough, Calvin argued, that their polygamy was against human nature and God's command. Each polygamist became distracted by multiple demands on his time and energy and multiple divisions of his affections. His wives competed for his attention and approval. His parents became torn in their devotion to their daughters-in-law. His children vied for his property and power.[13] In King David's polygamous household, the sibling rivalry escalated to such an extent that the stepchildren of his multiple wives raped and murdered each other.[14]

Jacob's travails with his two wives, Rachel and Leah, was a sobering illustration of these evils of polygamy, Calvin argued in his 1554 Commentary on Genesis (**Doc. 7-7**). Jacob's uncle Laban had tricked him into marrying his elder daughter, Leah, instead of Rachel whom Jacob loved. Jacob had reluctantly married Leah. Later he married her sister Rachel as well. Both Laban and Jacob thereby "pervert[ed] all the laws of nature by casting two sisters into one marriage bed," and forced them to spend their "whole lives in mutual hostility." After his second marriage, Jacob did not accord Leah "adequate respect and kindness"; indeed, he "hated" her. Yet the Lord "opened her womb" so that she produced many sons for him. Jacob loved and doted on Rachel to the point of fault, but she produced no children. Leah thus lorded her fertility over Rachel. Incensed, Rachel gave Jacob her servant Bilhah as a concubine in the hopes of

---

12. Comm. and Lect. Gen. 16:15-16; Comm. Gen. 25:12-18; Comm. Ps. 45:8; Comm. 1 Tim. 3:2. In Lect. Dan. 11:37, Calvin declared: "For Mohammed allowed to men the brutal liberty of chastising their wives and thus he corrupted that conjugal love and fidelity that binds the husband to the wife. Unless every man is content with a single wife, there can be no love, because there can be no conjugal happiness whenever rivalry exists between the inferior wives. As, therefore, Mohammed allowed full scope to various lusts, by permitting a man to have a number of wives, this seems like an explanation of his being inattentive to the love of women."

13. Comm. Gen. 16:1-6; 22:19; 26:34-35; 28:6-9; 29:27–30:34; 31:33-42; Lect. Mal. 2:15-16.

14. Serm. 1 Sam. 1:6; Serm. 2 Sam. 13.

having at least a surrogate child. Jacob obliged her and produced two sons by Bilhah. Leah countered by giving Jacob her servant Zilpah as a second concubine, with whom Jacob sired yet another son. All the while, Jacob continued to sleep with Rachel, who finally conceived and had a son Joseph. This only escalated the feud between Rachel and Leah and their children and the children of their concubines.

For Calvin this entire scandalous affair proved that "there is no end of sinning, once the divine institution" and law of marriage are breached. Jacob's fateful first step of committing polygamy led him to commit all manner of subsequent sins — rampant incest, concubinage, adultery, lust, and then even more polygamy. Jacob's initial sin was perhaps excusable; he was after all tricked into marrying Leah. His subsequent sins, however, were an utter desecration of God's law. Calvin blamed Rachel as well, rebuking her for her "petulance," her blasphemy and lack of faith, her abuse of her servant Bilhah, and her complicity in Jacob's concubinage, adultery, and polygamy. Why did Genesis go on at such length about this whole scandalous affair, Calvin asked? His answer: to underscore the efficacy of God's command for monogamy and the quality of God's mercy for sinners.

Jacob could well have mitigated his sin by divorcing Leah, before marrying Rachel, Calvin argued here and in several later passages. For divorce was "a lighter crime" than polygamy in ancient Israel.[15] After all, God did allow Jewish men to divorce their wives (Deut. 24:1-4) — even if this was only a concession to their "hardness of heart" and perennial lust.[16] God's provision for divorce created a hierarchy of proper marital conduct. Marriage for life was best. Divorce and remarriage were tolerable. Polygamy, however, was never allowed, for it was a desecration of the primal form and norm of marriage.

Calvin repeated this argument of the superiority of divorce to polygamy several times.[17] His fullest formulation came in his late-life Lectures on Malachi (**Doc. 7-8**). Malachi 2:14 defined marriage as an enduring covenant between a husband and wife, symbolizing the enduring covenant between God and his people. Malachi 2:15-16 then added, rather opaquely:

> Because the Lord hath been a witness between thee and the wife of thy youth, against whom thou has dealt treacherously; yet she is thy companion, the wife of thy covenant. *And did not he make one? Yet he had the residue of the Spirit. And wherefore one? That he might seek a godly seed.*[18]

15. Lect. Mal. 2:14-16.
16. Comm. Harm. Gospel Matt. 19:5-6.
17. Comm. 1 Tim. 3:2; Comm. Titus 1:6; Comm. Harm. Gosp. Matt. 19:3-9.
18. KJV (emphasis added).

Calvin read this passage as a confirmation of monogamy and as a condemnation of polygamy. The point of this passage, said Calvin, is that God "breathed his spirit" of life into "one" woman, Eve. God had plenty of spirit left to breathe life into more women besides Eve. But God chose to give life to Eve only, who alone served to "complete" Adam, to be "his other half." And it was this union only that could produce "godly seed," that is, legitimate children.

Both divorce and polygamy were deviations from this primal command of life-long monogamy, Calvin recognized. But when compared, "polygamy is the worse and more detestable crime" — and this shows in how the children of each were to be treated according to God's law. Divorce for cause was allowed by Moses, and even recognized by Christ. Polygamy enjoyed no such license. Children of divorce remained legitimate heirs. Indeed, the Mosaic law protected their inheritance against unscrupulous fathers who might be tempted to favor the children of their second wives.[19] Children of polygamy, however, were illegitimate bastards who deserved nothing. Indeed, Mosaic law barred such bastards "from the assembly of the Lord . . . until the tenth generation." Later passages ordered that bastards be "cast out" of their homes — just like Abraham had cast Ishmael out into the wilderness.[20]

Having made so much of this distinction between divorce and polygamy, Calvin dismissed out of hand traditional Catholic arguments that the remarriage of divorcees was a form of serial polygamy, or "digamy." "I do not consider polygamy to be what the foolish Papists have made it," Calvin declared derisively. Polygamy is about marriage to two or more wives at once, as is practiced today among Muslims. It has nothing to do with remarriage to a second wife after the first marriage is dissolved by divorce or death. For Calvin, that was the end of the matter, and he left it to Theodore Beza to elaborate this argument against the concept of serial polygamy.[21]

19. See Comm. Harm. Law Deut. 21:15-17, where Calvin writes: "When, therefore, the husband grew tired of his first wife, and desired a second, he might be coaxed by her blandishments to take away from the children of his first marriage what naturally belonged to them. Hence, therefore, the necessity of the remedy whereby the father's power of altering the right of primogeniture is barred; for, although they might allege that they only gave what was their own, yet it was an act of ungodly arrogance to reject him whom God had deigned to honor. For he who arrogates such power to himself, or who assigns the birth-right to whom he will, almost arrogates to himself the ability to create."

20. Comm. Harm. Law Deut. 23:2; Serm. Deut. 23:1-3; Comm. Gen. 21:8-18; Comm. Gal. 4:21-31. See further John Witte, Jr., *Ishmael's Bane: Illegitimacy Reconsidered* (Cambridge/New York, 2006), chap. 1.

21. See Theodore Beza, *Tractatio de Polygamia, et divortiis: in qua et Ochini apostatae pro polygamia . . . refutantur* (Geneva, 1568), reprinted in *Tractationum Theologicarum*, 2d ed. (Geneva, 1582), 2:1-49, at pp. 7, 11-26, 37-49.

In his final writing on polygamy, his 1563 Commentary on the Harmony of the Law, Calvin combined these foregoing moral arguments with new utilitarian arguments (**Doc. 7-9**). In Deuteronomy 17:17, Mosaic law ordered a king not "to multiply wives for himself." In his earlier Commentary on 1 Timothy 3:2, Calvin had already linked this law of monogamy for the kings of ancient Israel to St. Paul's rule of monogamy for the bishops of the church (**Doc. 7-10**).[22] The point of these passages, Calvin argued, was not that polygamy was permitted to everyone except for kings and bishops. It was rather that kings and bishops were to set moral examples of monogamy for their sinful subjects who flouted God's laws against polygamy. Calvin followed this with his familiar moral arguments that monogamy was an order of creation and law of nature and must not be breached through the pagan practice of polygamy.

To avoid polygamy was not only the right thing to do, Calvin went on. It was also the expedient thing to do. After all, the more wives a man had, the more he would lust after further wives thus distracting him from his main vocation. The more wives a king had, the more taxes he would need to collect to keep his burgeoning household in "royal finery." The more wives a ruler had, the more his mind would be "ensnared" and "stifled" of all "manly good sense." He would be made "effeminate" and driven to "worship false gods" and to make bad judgments. Even the great kings of Israel David and Solomon fell prey to these temptations. They and their households and their people suffered miserably on account of this sin.[23]

This combination of arguments from morality and utility, though sometimes blatantly misogynist, became standard fare in later Calvinist briefs against polygamy. Polygamy was to be avoided because it was wrong and because it did not work. Even the great patriarchs of salvation history could not bring their polygamous households in order. So who are we modern-day Christians to experiment with such a dangerous institution?

Beza pressed this argument at length in his 1568 *Tract on Polygamy*. This tract was, in part, a refutation of the polygamous speculations of Bernard Ochino.[24] Ochino was a distinguished Italian scholar and preacher, and a former leader of the Franciscan order. He had converted to Protestantism in 1542 and had lived in Geneva for a time before moving to Strasbourg, Zurich, Basel,

---

22. See also Comm. Titus 1:6.

23. Though he refers here to the problems of Solomon's polygamy, Calvin left no commentary on 1 Kings 11:3-8 where Solomon's wives are reported to have led him to worship other gods. Calvin also left no commentary on Judges 8:30 and 2 Chronicles 11:2 reporting on the polygamy of Gideon and Rehoboam.

24. See Henry Martin Baird, *Theodore Beza: The Counsellor of the French Reformation, 1519-1605* (New York, 1899), pp. 275ff.; Tadataka Maruyama, *The Ecclesiology of Theodore Beza: The Reform of the True Church* (Geneva, 1978), pp. 70ff.

and Protestant centers in England. Calvin had recommended him warmly in a 1545 letter.[25] But, in a late-life title, *Thirty Dialogues* (1563), Ochino offered a series of Socratic musings about the cogency of various standard theological doctrines. Included was a dialogue "whether in some instances an individual man should make his own decision under the inspiration of Almighty God to marry a second wife."[26] Ochino's interlocutors went over many of the same biblical passages respecting polygamy that Calvin had analyzed. They left hanging the suggestion that because there was no clear biblical commandment against polygamy the decision about the propriety of polygamy might be better left to the judgment of an individual Christian conscience instructed by God.

This proved to be perilous speculation. When Ochino's volume reached Geneva, Beza immediately wrote a blistering attack; this brief formed part of his later *Tract on Polygamy*. Much of Beza's argument was an echo and distillation of Calvin's views about polygamy, and was drawn from the lectures on 1 Corinthians that Beza had just delivered in the Genevan Academy. It did not help Ochino's cause that his tract was translated into Latin by Sebastian Castellio, one of Calvin and Beza's bitter enemies.[27] Beza condemned Ochino as an "apostate" and "heretic," terms that Beza had already put to grim effect in his defense of the 1553 execution of Michael Servetus for heresy.[28] Beza's attack on Ochino's views on polygamy was a key piece of evidence used by the Zurich authorities to prosecute Ochino later that year. The Zurich authorities found Ochino guilty of heresy and banished the frail seventy-six year old and his four children in midwinter. He wandered through Germany and Poland in search of refuge, and died the following year in Moravia. Ochino's case stood as a sober but clear lesson that neither the practice nor the preaching of polygamy was welcome in the Reformed world.

Consistory Cases on Precontract

Polygamy was a serious crime not just in Zurich, but also in Geneva. Cases of open and intentional polygamy went directly to the Genevan criminal courts for prosecution and punishment. If convicted, polygamists were banished, sometimes after being whipped, imprisoned, and subjected to various shame

---

25. Letter to Oswald Myconius (August 15, 1545), CO 12:136-37.

26. *Bernardini Ochini Senensis Dialogi XXX* (Basel, 1563), pp. 186ff. See Roland Bainton, *Bernardino Ochino* (Florence, 1941); Benedetto Nicolini, *Il pensiero di Bernardino Ochino* (Naples, 1939).

27. Roland H. Bainton, *Concerning Heretics . . . An Anonymous Work Attributed to Sebastian Castellio* (New York, 1935).

28. See Theodore Beza, *De haereticis a civili Magistratu puenindis* (Geneva, 1554).

penalties. Repeat offenders, or those who compounded their polygamy with other felonies, faced execution.[29]

The cases that came before the Consistory generally raised the narrower question of precontract impediments. Did a party have a previous contract of engagement or marriage that required annulment of his or her second engagement or marriage contract? This question came up quite regularly. For Geneva was a haven for refugees and immigrants, and the prior marital histories of these new residents often required investigation before a new marriage could be authorized. The 1546 Marriage Ordinance provided for this specifically:

> [19.] To avoid all the frauds that are committed in these matters, let no foreigner coming from a distant country be admitted to marriage unless he has good and certain testimony, either by letters or by respectable people, worthy of faith, that he has not been married elsewhere, and also of his good and respectable behavior; and let the same be observed with respect to girls and women.[30]

The 1552 case of Blaise de la Croix and his fiancée Yolande was typical of the kind of inquiry that the Consistory undertook (**Doc. 7-11**). Blaise and Yolande had just moved to Geneva from a Catholic town in Provence. Before moving, they had already become engaged. They now wanted to get married in Geneva. The Consistory questioned them and their witnesses whether any precontract or other impediment stood in the way of marriage. Yolande, it turned out, was a former nun who had relinquished her vows. She had later met Blaise whom she found to be a good man. Both sets of parents had consented to their marriage. But, as a former nun, Yolande would not have been able to marry in a Catholic territory. That may well have prompted the couple's move to Geneva. Previous monasticism was no impediment to marriage in Geneva. Finding no other precontract or impediment, the Consistory approved the match.

Not all cases proved so easy. The Consistory came upon a good number of cases of precontract — either during routine background investigations of new residents, or from testimony by third parties or sometimes even self-incriminating testimony by the parties themselves. In escalating order of gravity, the Consistory heard cases when one party: (1) engaged a second party, while already being engaged to a first; (2) engaged a second party, while already married to a first; (3) married a second party, while already engaged to a first; and (4) married a second party, while already married to a first.

---

29. See Kingdon, AD, pp. 62, 129ff.; Naphy, Sex Crimes, pp. 48ff. See also Naphy, Calvin, p. 31.

30. Doc. 1-2. See a prototype of this provision in 1537 Ordinance in SD, vol. 2, item 732.

Engagement-Engagement

In simple cases of back-to-back engagements, the Consistory generally upheld the first engagement contract. If it was somehow imperfectly formed or subject to a legitimate condition that had been breached, however, the Consistory annulled the first engagement contract and upheld the second.[31]

A good example is the 1557 case of Philiberte Le Chapuis and her two fiancés, Antoine and Pierre (**Doc. 7-12**). Philiberte was first engaged to Antoine. Four months later, she became engaged to Pierre. A distraught Antoine appeared before the Consistory seeking to annul Philiberte's second engagement, and to have her compelled to marry him. Philiberte's defense was that she and Antoine had made their contract in secret and that Antoine had failed to make any marital gift. Moreover, she argued that her aunt, who was also her guardian, had not consented to this match, and indeed feared that Philiberte and Antoine were second cousins who could not marry in any event because of incest laws. Accordingly, her aunt had found Pierre as a substitute whom Philiberte was happy to marry.

There was enough contradiction in the testimonies of Philiberte and her aunt to give the Consistory some pause. They sent the two women and Philiberte's two purported fiancés to the Council to sort out the testimony. The Council eventually imprisoned Philiberte briefly, apparently for perjuring herself concerning the whereabouts of her parents. But the Council also dissolved her first engagement with Antoine since it was contracted secretly — without witnesses or parental consent. They ordered Philiberte to marry Pierre instead. It was the secrecy of her first engagement to Antoine that was fatal in the Council's judgment. The other two allegations in Philiberte's defense against Antoine would not have been sufficient. Failure of dowry was not a ground for annulment of engagements in Geneva.[32] And, as second cousins, the parties were too distantly related to make out an impediment of affinity under the new Genevan law.[33]

A 1552 case of Pierre Sautier involved allegations of three sequential engagements.[34] Pierre first became engaged to a woman in Chézery, and he gave her an engagement gift. She conditioned her consent on her parents' consent, however, and her parents would not approve the match. The woman returned

31. See examples in Seeger, pp. 348-52.

32. See Marriage Ordinance (1546), item 14, Doc. 1-2.

33. Given what her aunt testified, Philiberte and Antoine were at best second cousins. This did not trigger an impediment of affinity at Genevan law, though it would have at medieval canon law. See Chapter 9 on incest impediments.

34. The full case record is provided above in Doc. 4-22, where we have also analyzed the case as an illustration of conditional engagement contracts.

Pierre's gift, and Pierre assumed the engagement was over. He then moved to Présilly and became engaged to a second woman, and gave her an engagement gift. This engagement was apparently made with the condition that Pierre remain in Présilly under the rule of the local lord. Pierre did not want to remain in the town under that lord's authority, so he broke this engagement, too, although without retrieving his engagement gift. He became engaged to yet a third woman, also in Présilly, and then moved to Geneva. The Consistory regarded Pierre's conduct as altogether improper and sent him and his witnesses to the Council to "get to the bottom of the matter."

The Council's record for the case does not survive. It is likely that Pierre's second engagement promise would have been enforced, after he had been punished for his polygamous engagement with the third fiancée. Engagement contracts conditioned on parental consent could be annulled in the absence of such parental consent, as we saw in Chapters 4 and 5. Thus the first engagement to the woman from Chézery would have been broken. But engagement contracts conditioned on less material considerations — such as relocation to a new city or procurement of a job — could not be so easily broken. Unless the lord of Présilly who insisted that Pierre live in the town under his rule happened also to be the parent or guardian of Pierre's second fiancée, this condition would not have been considered material enough to justify an annulment. Pierre would thus have been bound to this second engagement contract. That made his third engagement contract a prima facie act of polygamy.

The Consistory came down even harder on parties who compounded their sequential engagements with other crimes. In a 1561 case, for example, Claude Plantain had become engaged to a woman named Jeanne who was a ward of Mauris and Françoise Gaillard (**Doc. 7-13**). The Gaillards, as guardians, had consented to this union. Claude, however, grew disenchanted with Jeanne. Without seeking annulment of his first engagement to Jeanne, Claude became engaged to Jeanne's older sister, also named Claude. This sister Claude was also a ward of the Gaillards, and they encouraged this engagement when Plantain rejected their younger ward Jeanne. This seemed to be incest piled upon polygamy, and the Consistory sent Plantain to the Council for close investigation. Plantain did not help his cause by disappearing for a year. When the authorities came upon him a year later, they came down hard. The Consistory summoned a battery of witnesses against him. Despite their conflicting testimony, the Consistory thought this case was sufficiently serious to send Plantain, his two purported fiancées and their guardians to the Council. Apparently all five parties involved, including the man named Claude who was a Genevan citizen, were banished from the city and ordered not to return on pain of whipping.[35]

---

35. This judgment of the Council is as reported by Naphy, Sex Crimes, p. 48. We have not

Marriage-Engagement

To engage a second party after being engaged to a first was bad enough. To engage a second party, while being *married* to a first was worse. The gravity of this offense could be seen in a 1542 case that came to the Consistory in Calvin's first year back in Geneva (**Doc. 7-14**). Four or five years before, Pierre Rapin had become properly engaged to Pernette Maystre. He had given her a piece of property as his engagement gift. The couple had been properly married, and now had a child. In the months before the case, the couple had become estranged. They no longer slept together, and Pierre was given to lengthening absences from home. This raised suspicions. Two months before the case was filed, Pierre became engaged to another woman named Françoise. They had sexual intercourse. Françoise testified, however, that "she did not consent to his company," which suggests that Pierre may have raped her. Moreover, she said, Pierre left her shortly thereafter "because she did not give him any money."

Calvin and Pierre Viret, on behalf of the Consistory, urged the Council to punish Rapin's offense. The Council's sentence was severe. Rapin was condemned to a public whipping and to "carrying a miter on his head," a form of shame punishment. He was then banished from the city and forced to abandon his property "under penalty of the gibbet." This was rather severe punishment, firmer than what would become standard punishment for simple polygamy in Calvin's day. But Pierre was guilty not only of polygamy but also of adultery with Françoise. Moreover, the authorities might well have suspected him of rape and fraud as well, though these charges were evidently not pursued. He was lucky to have escaped with his life.

During Calvin's tenure, the Genevan authorities continued to punish firmly parties found guilty of contracting new engagements while they were already married. A good example is the 1559 case of Charles Fournat.[36] Charles was a fervent new convert to the Reformed cause, who had recently moved to Geneva from the Catholic city of Rouen. Shortly after his arrival, he became engaged to Thomasse de Reancourt. The Consistory summoned them on charges of premarital fornication. During the investigation, the Consistory learned from several witnesses that Charles was already married and that his wife was alive and well in Rouen. When confronted with this evidence of his polygamy, Charles defended himself by saying that his wife had committed adultery four years before and had thereby not only "ruptured the oath of marriage" but also

---

been able to find this judgment in the Council record, and the Consistory record of the case differs somewhat from what Naphy reports.

36. As reported in Naphy, Sex Crimes, pp. 50-51.

"given him a serious illness," probably syphilis. His first marriage was over, Charles insisted, leaving him free to marry another.

Charles's marriage may have been over in fact, but not in law, the Consistory determined. Charles had not sought an annulment or divorce to his first wife, and he was thus still married. It made no difference that the Catholic authorities in Rouen would not hear a case of divorce. Charles should have brought an *ex parte* divorce action against his first adulterous wife after he moved to Geneva and before he became engaged to Thomasse. A private person had no power to dissolve a marriage; only a properly authorized tribunal could make this judgment. Charles was found guilty both of deserting his wife in Rouen and committing polygamy with Thomasse in Geneva. Notwithstanding his new fervency for the Reformation cause, which the authorities acknowledged, the Council sentenced him to the public humiliation of carrying a torch through the streets, and it then banished him from the city and ordered him not to return on pain of whipping.

Engagement-Marriage

For the Genevan authorities, an engagement was a serious contract much like a marriage contract. To have sex with a third party in breach of one's engagement was an act of adultery, as we shall see in Chapter 12. To marry a third party after engagement to another was an act of polygamy.

The seriousness with which the authorities took such cases of back-to-back engagement and marriage can be seen in a tangled and tawdry case that went on for more than a year in 1555 and 1556 (**Doc. 7-15**). The case began before the Council. Denis Potier testified that he had earlier proposed the marriage of his daughter Marthe to Amied Varo who was courting her. Amied had refused the marriage. Shortly thereafter Denis had approved Marthe's marriage to Andre Dumonet. After her wedding night, Marthe was found to be already pregnant; she gave birth to a healthy son within six months of the wedding. Her former lover Amied, not her husband Andre, turned out to be the father. Amied had revealed as much in several secret love letters he had sent to Marthe, which her husband Andre had discovered. When confronted with these letters, Amied pled guilty to charges of fornication, and the Council imprisoned and fined him.

These same love letters suggested to the Council that Amied and Marthe might well have been engaged to be married as well. Amied denied any such engagement, and testified that he was already engaged to another woman in Antwerp, and was in fact trying to annul that engagement. This testimony only compounded Amied's problem, for now the Council suspected both parties of polygamy — Marthe for marrying Andre after her engagement to Amied, Amied for engaging Marthe after his engagement to the woman in Antwerp. The Council sent the whole case to the Consistory for close investigation.

Before the Consistory, Marthe testified that Amied had indeed promised to marry her. That was why she had yielded to his sexual advances and had kept his secret love letters, despite the risk of being found out. She further testified that when Amied spurned her she "wanted to die." When she found out she was pregnant, she sought medical advice on how to abort the child. When her efforts at abortion failed, she quickly married Andre apparently under some pressure from her father.

Amied again insisted that he had made no such engagement promise to Marthe. He loved Marthe more than the Antwerp woman but could not and would not promise to marry her until he had broken off this prior engagement. He further testified that he had explained all this to Marthe's father Denis, but Denis would not hear him.

Denis at first denied Amied's whole story as a self-serving cover-up and angrily denounced Amied before the Consistory. The Consistory had little reason to trust Denis's credibility, however. They had just heard Marthe's testimony that Denis had apparently pressured her into marrying Andre quickly, and likely suspected that he was trying to cover up her fornication and find support for her illegitimate son. Moreover, the Consistory discovered that Denis had also just carried his new baby grandson to baptism, and had him registered as the son of Andre, Marthe's husband, in a further attempt to cover up the illegitimacy.[37] Andre, it turned out, had not consented to any of this, and indeed now wanted out of his marriage to Marthe altogether.

The case bounced back and forth between the Consistory and the Council for the next half year. The Council investigated Amied and Marthe under oath several times and imprisoned Amied for a time evidently because of his recalcitrance and perjury. It became quite clear to the authorities that Marthe had married Andre while believing that she was already engaged to Amied. The Consistory sent Calvin to the Council to impress on them the gravity of her offense. The Council ultimately fined her heavily, dissolved her marriage with Andre, and barred her from marriage to anyone else, consigning her to effective spinsterhood. The Consistory banned her from the Eucharist, admitting her only a half year later when she made another full confession. Calvin later sought the Council's permission to allow her to remarry after a further time of repentance.

It also became quite clear to the authorities that Amied did not believe

---

37. For a report on this case, and the implications of this false baptismal registration, see Spierling, pp. 169ff.

himself engaged to Marthe, because of his engagement to the Antwerp woman. This was apparently ample mitigation in their mind. The Council fined him, too, but barred him from marriage for only a year to "consider his conscience." They also determined that his engagement to the woman in Antwerp was no longer binding. The Consistory banned him from Communion as well, and re-admitted him several months later when he did full confession for his sins.

Most cases of engagement to one party followed by marriage to another were not nearly so complicated.[38] What this case illustrates is how seriously Calvin and his Consistory colleagues took this offense. Especially notable was their emphasis on the *intent* to commit polygamy, rather than the proof of polygamy. It was because Marthe *believed* she was already engaged to Amied when she married Andre that she was punished so severely for her polygamy. But the legality of both her contracts was suspect. Her engagement contract to Amied was never proved to exist, even if she intended or believed its existence. Her marriage contract to Andre was vulnerable to attack on two fronts: Marthe was not of fully sound mind when she entered that marriage contract, and her father had evidently coerced her into this marriage as part of the cover up. Such a marriage might well have been annulled if attacked directly on grounds of lack of consent by Marthe.

Moreover, Marthe's punishment of forced permanent spinsterhood was a rather harsh sentence. She was now forced to be a single mother of an illegitimate child. The child's father, Amied, was ready and willing to marry her and support the child, and after a year of forced bachelorhood would be able to do so. Perhaps it was this reality that prompted Calvin to go back to the Council to have Marthe's sentence of forced widowhood reduced.

Marriage-Marriage

One marriage contract followed by another was the purest case of polygamy, and the Consistory sent these cases swiftly to the Council with recommendations of stern punishment. Claude Du Noyer found this out in 1558 (**Doc. 7-16**). The Consistory summoned him to answer charges that he was married to two wives. He admitted the offense, saying he had earlier married a woman and had produced children who were now fully grown. Ten years earlier, apparently without dissolving the first marriage, he had married a second woman and had moved with her to Geneva. Though Claude had remained faithful to his second wife, he was routinely drunk and had not registered himself as a *habitant*. The Consistory had little sympathy for him. They banned

---

38. See other examples in Seeger, pp. 348-52.

him from Communion, and urged the Council to "purge" him from the city. The Council imprisoned Claude, and then banished him on pain of whipping if he returned. They must have also annulled his second marriage, though there is no such order in the record.

Not only the doubly married spouse, but also the second spouse could be punished for being an accessory to polygamy. This happened to Robert Cuysin in a 1552 case (**Doc. 7-17**). Six years before, Robert had married a woman (whose name is not revealed in the records). At the time, the woman had claimed she was a widow. Friends of her former husband had told Robert that the man had died. He had thus married the woman. After the marriage, however, Robert found out that his wife's former husband was still alive, but had remarried and was living in the town of Chalon.

The Consistory was suspicious of Robert's story. They summoned Mrs. Cuysin to testify. She admitted that she had married another man ten years before but he had deserted her, and she had then remarried with the approval of her former mother-in-law. After she had remarried Robert, however, her first husband had sought to have her marriage to Robert annulled by the court of the bishop in Lyon. She had refused the Lyon court's subpoena: apparently, her first husband had then received a proper *ex parte* dissolution of his first marriage to her, and later had married another woman. When pressed, Mrs. Cuysin admitted that she would be happy to return to her first husband if he wanted her back — hardly a vote of confidence about her marriage to Robert Cuysin.

This was all too much for the Consistory. They sent Mr. and Mrs. Cuysin to the Council, recommending that they be separated while the case was pending. On investigation, the Council annulled the Cuysins' six-year marriage because the woman had "remarried before her first [husband] remarried." Both Cuysins were then banished from Geneva — the woman for her polygamy, her second husband for being an accessory to the same offense. In the Council's judgment, Robert Cuysin should have inquired about the legality of his marriage once his wife's first husband was found to be alive. The Council must have determined that his failure to inquire was willful blindness to the offense, if not a deliberate cover up.

Summary and Conclusions

The foregoing cases illustrate the seriousness with which the Genevan authorities took the crime of polygamy and the impediment of precontract. Calvin and Beza had underscored the gravity of these cases. For them, polygamy violated the order of creation and the commandment of the law and the Gospel. At creation, God could have created two or more wives for Adam. But he chose to create one. God could have created three or four types of humans to be the image of God. But he created two types: "male and female he created them." In the law, God could have commanded his people to worship two or more gods, but he commanded them to worship one God. In the Gospel, Christ could have founded two or more churches to represent him on earth, but he founded one Church. Marriage, as an order of creation and a symbol of God's relationship with his elect, Calvin and Beza argued, involves two parties and two parties only.

To marry more than one wife was not only to mock God but to court "trouble."[39] Just look at the chaos of the polygamous households of Abraham, Jacob, and David. Just look at the diffusion of their energies and resources and the perennial strife of their children. If even the great patriarchs of salvation history could not make polygamy work, who are we to try? The point of the many biblical stories of polygamy, Calvin insisted, was not to illustrate an alternative form of marriage, but to show how dangerous it was to violate God's law for monogamy.

If a man could not contain himself, it was better for him to divorce his wife rather than to marry a second wife while his first marriage remained intact. After all, divorce was allowed by Moses, and even recognized by Christ. Polygamy enjoyed no such license. After all, children of divorce remained legitimate heirs, and their rights to inheritance were specially protected by the Mosaic law. Children of polygamy, however, were condemned as illegitimate bastards who deserved nothing. Indeed, Mosaic law barred such bastards "from the assembly of the Lord . . . until the tenth generation." The Gospel ordered that bastards be cast out, just like Abraham had cast Ishmael out into the wilderness. Permanent marriage to one wife was best. Divorce of the first wife and marriage of a second was tolerable. Marriage to two wives at the same time was anathema.

The Genevan authorities took this teaching to heart. They regarded back-to-back engagements and marriages of any combination as a prima facie case of polygamy. And if the second relationship was consummated, it was also a prima facie case of adultery. The cases that came before the authorities in Calvin's lifetime fell into an escalating order of gravity. When someone engaged a second party while already being engaged to a first, the Consistory and Council generally upheld the first engagement and administered spiritual sanctions. When someone engaged a second party, while already married to a first, or married a second party while already engaged to a first, the authorities generally upheld

---

39. Michael Broyde points out that the biblical Hebrew word for a co-wife in a polygamous relationship, *tzrah,* means literally "trouble." See Michael J. Broyde, ed., *Marriage and Family Life in the Jewish Tradition* (Lanham, MD, 2005).

the marriage and administered severe spiritual and criminal sanctions. When someone was found in a double marriage, not only was the second marriage annulled, but the second couple faced severe criminal punishment — flogging, banishment, and in serious cases of intentional polygamy, execution.

One reason that the Genevan law of precontract and polygamy was so complex and sweeping was that the reformers had rendered both engagement and marital contracts presumptively indissoluble, absent proof of an impediment. As Beza put it:

> [A]s long as the earlier promises to marry remain valid somebody can no more be engaged to two fiancé(e)s than one can be married to two wives since such a fiancée is under obligation to be his wife, even though she is not actually so. The Word of God declares clearly that the same punishment as for adultery is laid down against him who will have violated a woman pledged to a different man and also from what Adam said when a woman was given to him by God, even before their sexual union, that she was bone of his bone, and flesh of his flesh.[40]

Fiancé(e)s and spouses were both subject to the law of precontract and polygamy, thereby doubling the number of possible cases for the authorities to consider.

A second reason that the law was so sweeping was that Geneva had become an increasingly popular destination for Protestant immigrants from throughout Europe. Calvin was all for parties' desire to convert to the Reformation, to confess their sins, and to start their lives afresh. But a fresh start did not mean that newly arrived parties could "marry lightly."[41] Their prior engagements and marriages were binding, even if their spouses remained Catholics or had been hard and abusive. Only if and when these prior relationships had been properly dissolved could parties contract marriage anew.

---

40. Beza, TRD, 2:98-99 (translated by John P. Donnelly, S.J.)

41. This was a phrase that Calvin was said to have used; quoted in *Annales Calviniani*, CO 21:654-55.

7-1 Commentary on Genesis 2:24 (1554)[42]

[A]mong the offices pertaining to human society, this is the principal, and as it were the most sacred: that a man should cleave unto his wife. And he [Moses] amplifies this by saying that, in comparison, the husband ought to prefer his wife to his father. The father is to be left not because marriage severs sons from their fathers, or dispenses with other ties of nature; if this were the way, God would be acting contrary to himself. The piety of the son towards his father ought to be most earnestly cultivated and ought in itself to be deemed inviolable and sacred. But Moses speaks of marriage in this way to show that it is less lawful to desert one's wife than one's parents. Those who thus, for slight causes, rashly permit divorces violate, in one single particular, all the laws of nature, and reduce them to nothing. If we should make it a point of conscience not to separate a father from his son, it is a still greater wickedness to dissolve the bond that God has preferred to all others.

"They shall be one flesh." Although the ancient Latin interpreter has translated the passage "in one flesh," yet the Greek interpreters have expressed it more forcibly: "They two shall be into one flesh"; Christ cites this in Matthew 19:5. But though here no mention is made of two, yet there is no ambiguity in the sense; for Moses had not said that God has assigned many wives, but only one to one man; and in the general direction given, he had put the wife in the singular number. It remains, therefore, that the conjugal bond subsists between two persons only, whence it easily appears that nothing accords less with the divine institution than polygamy. . . . [P]olygamy is a corruption of legitimate marriage.

7-2 Sermon on Genesis 2:22-24 (1559)[43]

[W]e must observe this passage well when it says that God gave and assigned the woman to the man, for in this we are shown that God honored marriage by making himself its author. Therefore those who are married, knowing now that this estate was ordained by God, should proceed in all purity, for to pollute marriage and abuse it in any way whatever is a sacrilege. And when a husband

---

42. CO 23:50-51 (OTC adapted).

43. John Calvin, *Sermons sur la Genèse,* ed. Max Engammarre, 2 vols. (Neukirchen-Vluyn, 2000), 1:139-49.

and wife do not live in concord they are at war with God, as though they wished to dissolve this sacred bond, as will be treated below at more length. In short, we are admonished in this sentence to hold marriage in honor because it proceeded from God. And those who are in it should be exhorted by this means to remain in the fear of God, to live in peace and union together, and to preserve complete decency, because marriage must indeed differ from fornication and all dissolute behavior. Because it is not without cause that God gave this remedy to men and women, even after the fall of Adam and the corruption that befell the entire human race. So much for these words.

Now Moses adds that "Adam said: Behold by this act bone of my bone and flesh of my flesh; because the woman was taken out of the man, she shall be called woman of man." The word he uses means as it were *"hommasse,"* that is woman of man, as we have said.

Now one might doubt here how Adam knew that Eve had been created from his substance, since God had made him fall into a deep sleep. Therefore he was asleep, so that he did not feel that God took one of his ribs to make the woman out of it. And how is it now that he speaks of it as of something known to him? Now we set aside the gloss that some introduce that Adam had such subtlety and was so acute that he could conjecture this although the matter had not been manifested to him; but we see that God had stated it to him earlier. And in fact it would have been pointless for Eve to have been taken from Adam's body unless to the end that the husband and wife might be all the more united, knowing that they were as it were one flesh. We have already said above that God could have created Eve out of earth; he could even have created her from nothing if he had wished. And therefore why did he thus take her from the man's body? It was so that the unity that should be present in marriage might be more holy and might be preserved inviolable. For if there was no purpose of instruction, the thing in itself would have been useless; it would have achieved nothing for God thus to have taken the woman from the man's body. Therefore we conclude that Adam did not speak here out of his own imagination but that he had been taught by God.

And in fact we will never consider the works of God properly unless we are instructed by his word that conducts us, for it is from this that all our prudence and discretion derives. In short, when Adam speaks here, it is in conformity with what God had already shown him. And we must note this well, that after the example of our first father we should receive what God tells us without any contradiction and find it good and just. And this is what we must follow him in, not in his rebellion, which will be spoken of below. This then is the true perfection of men, to be taught by God and, accepting everything that we know is agreeable to him, to find it good and adhere to it, as Adam says: "Behold, by this act," according as God had said, "It is not good for the man to be alone, let us make him an helpmeet that may be proper for him." Now he adds, "Behold, therefore, by this act," recognizing the special blessing of God and that it was the true perfection and completion of his condition, because the rule of the whole world would not have profited him at all, nor the power he had to use all creatures, if he had not had a companion. Now God had stated this previously. Here Adam receives it and says "amen" and approves what God has decreed. This then is what we must do if we wish to enjoy properly the grace of God; we must recognize to what end he expends it on us and taste his bounty, wisdom, and justice in order to know how to profit from all the good things we enjoy.

"By this act, behold bone of my bone," he says; he knows that he could not have the other animals for companions, but that it was necessary for a woman to be given him who was of his own substance. Moreover, this applies to Our Lord Jesus Christ and to his church, as Saint Paul shows in the fifth chapter of Ephesians, for he cites this passage, not in a literal sense but by a similitude, as if he said that what was done in the man and the woman when God created them is today accomplished spiritually and in Jesus Christ and his church. For we must be joined with him in such a union, as if we were bone of his bone. It is true that Jesus Christ took on human flesh to be of Adam's seed, but as we have stated above, we have a double obligation to him: one is that he was made our brother when he was vested with our nature and took a human body, and the other is when he gives us life and nurture with his flesh as if we were drawn from it, according to the spirit that is, for this is not a question of ordinary life. When we are called bone of the bone of the Son of God and flesh of his flesh this is not as we crawl here on earth, but it is because we are vivified by him and by his virtues. Now this is not achieved simply because his flesh is joined with ours, but by a secret and incomprehensible link with his Holy Spirit. However this may be, marriage is an image and figure of the union there should be between Our Lord Jesus Christ and all the faithful. And as the woman was honored when God took her from the substance of the man so that he might recognize her as part of himself and of his own person, we also are raised to a high degree of honor in being of the substance of Our Lord Jesus Christ. And this is also why Saint Paul, in another passage, says that we are the completion of Our Lord Jesus Christ. And is he not perfect in himself? Must he borrow anything from another? It is not a question here of diminishing his dignity but of showing us the honor he does us, treating us as though he was only half of himself until he had gathered us all together and made us participants in all his possessions in order to bring us to the celestial life and the glory that was prepared for us in his name. This is what we must remember from this passage. . . .

Moreover, when it says that "the man will leave his father and mother," this does not mean that marriage breaks the bond, which is also from God, that a father should love his children as his own blood; children also should honor their father and mother as those from whom they have their lives, for God does not contradict himself. There is harmony in all his works; we do not find variation or conflict in them. Therefore marriage must not break or abolish the obligation the father should have to his children and the connection of the children with their father and mother. And why then does it say that the man will leave his father and mother to be joined with his wife? This is meant by comparison, that is that previously he had to leave his father, mother, and wife, as when Our Lord Jesus Christ also says, "Whoever does not hate his father and mother, wife and children and everything he has for the sake of the Gospel is not worthy of being among my disciples." Now these are not incompatible things, for a man to love his wife, to honor his father and mother, and nevertheless for them all to serve God and have such zeal for maintaining his truth that they will not spare their own lives if need be. But this, as I have said, is meant by comparison, that is that there must be no excuse involving either wife or children, either father or mother, when it is a question of maintaining the doctrine of our salvation and making confession of our faith. If we consider everything that might happen and say, "I will put myself in danger of death, and then behold my poor wife who will be a widow, I will leave my children orphans, I must take pity on them. I also have a father and I would not wish to annoy him, I am bound and obligated to him by nature." When, I say, we have alleged all this, these are very frivolous excuses, for we must prefer the truth of God to all these human considerations. And thus if a man must defect from his father and mother, he has such a union with his wife that he must hold fast to that side. But these things are fully compatible, that is for a man to live peaceably with his wife, knowing that they are two in one flesh, and at the same time to show reverence to his father and mother, to assist them, to employ himself in all the services he can do them, to obey them and show himself subject to them: both these things can well be done. And thus we note that God did not stir up discord between children and their fathers and mothers when he ordained the union of marriage, but he wished in short to declare that this is the closest and most sacred bond there is in the world when the husband is joined to his wife. . . .

And then this also applies to plurality of wives, for we see that in oriental countries this excess has been too common, and the Jews thought that this was permitted them by the example of the patriarchs, as when Abraham took Hagar. But this was because he fell off, not being satisfied that God would execute his promise. This was a severe fault in Abraham, although he was the father of all the faithful. When Jacob had four it was even worse, and this came about in part through mistakes, because he had been swindled in the person of Leah when he had been promised Rachel, and his wives themselves also compelled him to take others. This therefore was how marriage was violated. And thus we see that it is an uncertain thing to follow the example of this person or that without having proof from the Word of God. When the saints followed the rule that should be common to all, their example must serve us and be a goad to prod us into doing right. But when we wish to take what they did and say that we shall follow them in this or that regardless, this is out of bounds. And nevertheless Our Lord Jesus Christ says that it was not so from the beginning when he reproves divorces that are made at will and without legitimate occasion, and then plurality of wives. "Let us," he says, "look to the beginning," for what God said about marriage should be held as an infallible rule; it must retain its vigor to the end of the world. For where shall we take our rule, unless from the institution of God? Men then may change about easily; one may do this, another that, but we must consider what God commanded and it must hold: and let us do such honor to his word that it is inviolable for us, although men in their inconstancy and frivolity change from day to day. . . .

Now although Moses does not state that they were two in one flesh, nevertheless we must remember well what has already been stated, that is that God created one aide for Adam, and not two or three. Therefore it is against the nature of marriage for a man to take two or three wives. He must be content with one. And this is why Saint Paul also notably says that in this corruption we are in it is necessary for a man to have a wife and every woman a husband. When he speaks in this way he condemns the confusion by which marriage has been profaned. It was thus a species of adultery when men took several wives. And although it was done by holy patriarchs, as also later by David, the authority of God must remain infallible and the most holy people, even if they were angels, must be reproved for not conforming to this commandment, which we must hold by. This in short is how we should profit by this doctrine.

7-3   Commentary on the Harmony of the Gospel
Matthew 19:4-5 (1555)[44]

Christ assumes as an admitted principle, that at the beginning God joined the male to the female, so that the two made an entire person. . . . God, who created the human race, made them male and female, so that every man might be satisfied with his own wife, and might not desire more. For he insists on the number two. . . .

"And the two shall be one flesh." This expression condemns polygamy no less than it condemns unrestrained liberty in divorcing wives. For, if the mutual union of two persons was consecrated by the Lord, the mixture of three or four persons is unauthorized. But Christ, as I stated a little ago, applies it in a differ-

---

44. CO 45:528-29 (NTC adapted).

ent manner to his purpose; namely, to show that whoever divorces his wife tears himself in pieces, because such is the force of holy marriage, that the husband and wife become one person.

7-4 Commentary on Ephesians 5:31 (1548)[45]

Two subjects are shown together. The spiritual union between Christ and his church is so treated as to illustrate the common law of marriage, to which the quotation from Moses relates. He [Paul] immediately adds that the saying is fulfilled in Christ and the church. Every opportunity which presents itself for proclaiming our obligations to Christ is readily embraced, but he adapts his illustration of them to the present subject.

It is uncertain whether Moses introduces Adam, as using these words, or gives them as an inference drawn by himself from the creation of man. It is not of much consequence which of these views be taken, for, in either case, we must hold it to be an announcement of the will of God, enjoining the duties which men owe to their wives.

"He shall leave his father and mother." It was as if he had said: "Let him rather leave his father and mother than not cleave to his wife." The marriage bond does not set aside the other duties of mankind nor are the commandments of God so inconsistent with each other that a man cannot be a good and faithful husband without ceasing to be a dutiful son. It is altogether a question of degree. Moses draws the comparison in order to express more strongly the close and sacred union which subsists between husband and wife. A son is bound by an inviolable law of nature to perform his duties towards his father; and when the obligations of a husband towards his wife are declared to be stronger, their force is the better understood. He who resolves to be a good husband will not fail to perform his filial duties, but will regard marriage as more sacred than all other ties.

"And the two shall be one flesh." They shall be one man, or, to use a common phrase, they shall constitute one person. This certainly would not hold true with regard to any other kind of relationship. All depends on this, that the wife was formed of the flesh and bones of her husband. Such is the union between us and Christ, who in some sort makes us partakers of his substance. "We are bone of his bone, and flesh of his flesh" (Gen. 2:23) not because, like ourselves, he has a human nature, but because, by the power of his Spirit, he makes us a part of his body, so that from him we derive our life.

---

45. CO 51:771-84 (NTC adapted).

7-5   Sermon on Deuteronomy 21:15-17 (1555)[46]

It says, "If a man has two wives." What?! Does this conform to the order of marriage? It is just the opposite. Marriage cannot be more greatly violated than when a man takes two wives. It is written: "The two shall be one flesh." It does not say there "three, or four." Our Lord created a woman so she might be a companion for the man. And before he created her, he did not say it would be good for the man to have several helpmates. "I will make him a helpmate," he said, "to be with him." Now since God was content with one helpmate for one man, it is certain that whoever surpasses this rule perverts everything, and it is as though he wished to nullify the institution of God.

Who is the author of marriage? Did not God pronounce what should be inviolable, that is that the two will be one flesh, and that the man will have a single helpmate? If a man takes two wives, however, is this not manifestly to scorn God? This is quite certain. And this is why Our Lord, through his prophet, says that it is a more supportable thing for a man to put away his wife by giving her this dismissal [of divorce] that existed under the Law than to have two wives. Now those who violate in this, he brings back to the creation. "Behold," he says, "God who created man." And this is also where what Our Lord Jesus Christ said leads to, that it was not so from the beginning; for God created a man, that is the male, and the female. And the prophet Malachi mentions this, and adds that God had the residue of the Spirit abounding in him. Would he have been prevented from creating two wives for Adam if it had seemed good to him? Now God was content with one. It must therefore be concluded that someone who desires to have two wives perverts everything, and that he does not take care to preserve marriage as it was instituted by God. It is therefore fornication, and not marriage, when a man thus desires a second wife.

Now this was an ancient vice, and from this one can see and judge what safety there is in basing oneself on custom. For this was done at all times; it had always been done. Indeed, but this does not absolve us before God; for this polygamy, as it is called, that is to say, plurality of wives, would indeed have a specious appearance if one considered only what was customary and ancient. What of it? Here is the institution of God that went before, and it should be permanent until the end. Therefore we see that it is a most disorderly and infamous act if men are so permitted and given license to have a plurality of wives. And nevertheless it befell the patriarchs. And from this one may see that one will be entirely at fault if one wishes to found oneself on men, even the most holy who have ever been. Behold Abraham, who was the father of the faithful; he had several wives. True, but he did not escape being condemned. All the rest

---

46. CO 27:663-70.

of his life he was a mirror of angelic perfection, but in this he sinned. Therefore let us hold to the pure Word of God, and not pretend that anything is lawful to us except what is regulated according to it. This includes, I say, plurality of wives, about which it says here that if anyone has two wives, he acts against the order that God has established. Thus it is not the case that those who go so far afield are absolved if they are not punished according to human law: but we must always return to this, that God has as it were established regulations, recognizing what can be obtained from the infirmity of men. All the same, this does not prevent the existence of that perfection that is contained in the Word of God, to which we should aspire. And if we deviate even a little from it we are culpable before him. And it will do us no good to declare that men ask nothing of us, if it must come to an accounting before the celestial judge.

7-6   Commentary on Genesis 4:19 (1554)[47]

We have here the origin of polygamy in a perverse and degenerate race; and the first author of it [Lamech] was a cruel man, destitute of all humanity. Whether he had been impelled by an immoderate desire of augmenting his own family, as proud and ambitious men are wont to be, or by mere lust, it is of little consequence to determine. Either way he violated the sacred law of marriage, which had been delivered by God. For God had determined, that "they," "the two" should be one flesh, and that is the perpetual order of nature. Lamech, with brutal contempt of God, corrupts nature's laws. The Lord, therefore, willed that the corruption of lawful marriage should proceed from the house of Cain, and from the person of Lamech, in order that polygamists might be ashamed of the example.

7-7   Commentary on Genesis 29:27-31, 30:1-3 (1554)[48]

Laban has now become callous in his wickedness, for he extorts another seven years from his nephew [Jacob] to allow him to marry his other daughter [Rachel]. . . . Blinded by avarice, Laban sets his daughters together in such a way that they spend their whole lives in mutual hostility. He also perverts all the laws of nature by casting two sisters into one marriage bed, so that the one becomes the competitor of the other.

Since Moses sets these crimes before the Israelites at the very commence-

47. CO 23:99 (OTC adapted).
48. CO 23:403-9 (OTC adapted).

ment of their history, they should not be inflated by the sense of their nobility, or boast of their descent from holy fathers. For whatever his excellence, Jacob had only impure offspring. Contrary to nature, two sisters were brought together in one bed as if they were beasts. Then two concubines were afterwards added to the mix as well. We saw above that this license was too common among oriental nations. But men were not allowed, at their own pleasure, to subvert by a depraved custom the law of marriage divinely sanctioned from the beginning.

Laban is altogether without excuse. Although necessity may, to some extent, excuse the fault of Jacob, it cannot altogether absolve him. He could have dismissed Leah, because she was not his lawful wife. The mutual consent of the man and the woman constitutes marriage, and here the error makes it impossible. But Jacob reluctantly retains her as his wife, from whom he was released and free. He thus doubles his fault by polygamy, and trebles it by an incestuous marriage. Thus we see that the inordinate love of Rachel, which had once excited his mind, was inflamed to such a degree, that he possessed neither moderation nor judgment. . . .

Rachel is loved, not without wrong to her sister, to whom due honor is not given. The Lord, therefore, intervenes as her vindicator. By a suitable remedy, he turns the mind of Jacob into that direction, to which it had been most averse. When Moses asserts that Leah was hated, his meaning is that she was not loved so much as she ought to have been. For she was not intolerable to Jacob, neither did he pursue her with hatred. But Moses, by the use of this word, amplifies Jacob's fault, in not having discharged the duty of a husband, and in not having treated her who was his first wife with adequate kindness and honor. . . .

The tenderness of Jacob's affection [to Rachel] rendered him unwilling to offend his wife. Yet her unworthy conduct compelled him to do so, when he saw her petulantly exalt herself not only against her sister, who piously, humbly, and thankfully was enjoying the gifts of God, but even against God himself of whom it is said that the fruit of the womb is his reward (Ps. 127:3). On this account, therefore, Jacob is angry, because his wife ascribes nothing to the providence of God, and, by imagining that children are the offspring of chance, would deprive God of the care and government of mankind. Jacob had likely already been sorrowful on account of his wife's barrenness. He now, therefore, fears lest her folly should still farther provoke God's anger to inflict more severe strokes. This was a holy indignation by which Jacob maintained the honor due to God, while he corrected his wife, and taught her that it was not without sufficient cause that she had been barren. For when he affirms that the Lord had shut her womb, he obliquely intimates that she ought the more deeply to humble herself.

"Behold my maid Bilhah." Here the vanity of the female disposition appears. For Rachel is not induced to flee unto the Lord, but strives to gain a victory by illicit arts. Therefore she hurries Jacob into a third marriage. We infer from this that there is no end of sinning, once the divine institution is neglected. And, as I said, Jacob was not immediately brought back to a right state of mind by divine chastisements. To be sure, in this case, he acts at the instigation of his wife. But is his wife in the place of God, from whom alone the law of marriage proceeds? But to please his wife, or to yield to her importunity, he does not hesitate to depart from the command of God. . . . Rachel [also] acted sinfully, because she attempted, by an unlawful method, and in opposition to the will of God, to become a mother.

It is wonderful that God should have deigned to honor an adulterous relationship with offspring. He does sometimes thus strive to overcome by kindness the wickedness of men, and pursues the unworthy with his favor.

7-8 Lecture on Malachi 2:15-16 (1559)[49]

"Has he not made one?" That is: "Was not God content with one woman, when he instituted marriage?" . . . Here the Prophet takes the residue of the Spirit to mean overflowing power. For God could have given to one man two or three wives, for the Spirit did not fail him after forming one woman. Just as he breathed life into Eve, so also he might have created other women and imparted to them his Spirit. He might then have given to Adam two or four or ten women, for there was Spirit remaining in him. We now then understand what the Prophet means at the beginning of this verse. . . .

But someone may ask here why the Prophet says that God made one? This seems to refer to the man and not to the woman. To this I answer, that man with the woman is called one. This is what Moses says: "God created man, male and female he created them." After having said that man was created, he adds by way of explanation, that man, both male and female, was created. When he speaks of man [that is, humankind], the male makes one-half and the female the other half. When we speak of the whole human race, one half doubtless consists of men, and the other half of women. So also when we come to individuals, the husband is as it were the half of the man, and the wife is the other half. . . .

"The seed of God" is to be taken for what is legitimate; for what is excellent is often called "of God" in Hebrew, and also what is free from all vice and blemish. He sought then the seed of God, that is, he instituted marriage so that legitimate and pure offspring might be brought forth. Thus the Prophet indirectly shows that all children born of polygamy are bastards. They cannot be

49. CO 44:453-57 (OTC adapted).

deemed legitimate children; only those who are born according to God's institution for marriage are legitimate. Thus when a husband violates his pledged faith to his wife, and takes another, he subverts the ordinance of marriage, and he cannot be a legitimate father. . . .

If a comparison is made, Malachi says, it is a lighter crime to dismiss a wife than to marry many wives. We thereby learn how abominable polygamy is in the sight of God. I do not consider polygamy to be what the foolish Papists have made it. They call polygamists not those who have many wives at the same time but those who marry another when the former one is dead. This is gross ignorance. Polygamy, properly called, is when a person takes many wives, as it was commonly done in the East. Those nations, we know, have always been libidinous, and never observed the marriage vow. Their lasciviousness was so great that they were like brute beasts. Every one married several wives, and this abuse continues at this day among the Turks and the Persians and other nations.

Here, however, where God compares polygamy with divorce, he says that polygamy is the worse and more detestable crime. For the husband impurely connects himself with another woman, and then not only deals unfaithfully with his wife to whom he is bound, but also forcibly detains her. His crime is thus doubled. For if he replies and says that he keeps the wife to whom he is bound, he is still an adulterer as to the second wife. It is as if he blends holy with profane things. And, then, he adds cruelty by his adultery and lasciviousness, for he holds a miserable woman [his first wife] under his authority. She would prefer death to such a condition, for we know what power jealousy has over women. And when anyone introduces a harlot, how can a lawful wife bear such an indignity without being miserably tormented?

This is the reason the Prophet now says, "If thou hatest, dismiss." He is not granting indulgence to divorce, as we have said, but that he might by this circumstance not enhance the crime [of polygamy].

7-9 Commentary on the Harmony of the Law
Deuteronomy 17:17 (1563)[50]

Polygamy at that time had generally prevailed so that the very humblest of the people violated the marriage vow with impunity. Therefore it was necessary that the kings should be bound with closer restrictions, lest by their example they should give greater countenance to incontinency. And thus their ignorance is easily refuted who conclude that what was specially forbidden to the kings was permitted to private individuals, by which the law of chastity was imposed

50. CO 24:370-72 (OTC adapted).

upon the former, because without this remedy there would be no bounds to their lust. Besides, the people would have been subjected to great expense on their account, since such is the ambition of women, that they would all have desired to receive royal treatment, and would have even vied with each other in finery, as actually came to pass. David transgressed this law, and in some degree excusably on account of his repudiation by Michal. Still it appears that lust had more power over him than the continence prescribed by God. What follows is so connected by some as if it were the reason of the foregoing sentence, in this way, "that kings were not to multiply wives to themselves, lest their heart should turn away from what was right," as was the case with Solomon. For, by being too devoted to his wives, and deceived by the snares of women, he fell into idolatry. And assuredly it can scarcely fail to happen, that when many wives beset a man, they must render his mind effeminate and stifle in him all his manly good sense. I prefer taking the clause separately, that kings must beware lest the splendor of their dignity should affect the soundness of their judgment, for nothing is more difficult than for one in great power to continue disposed to temperance. Therefore God does not in vain enjoin that they should constantly persevere in their duty, and not lose their understanding.

7-10   Commmentary on 1 Timothy 3:2 (1548)[51]

The only true exposition [of the verse "the bishop must be above reproach, the husband of one wife"] is that of Chrysostom. He expressly condemns polygamy in a bishop, which at that time the Jews almost reckoned to be lawful. This corruption was borrowed by them in part from sinful imitation of the patriarchs, Abraham, Jacob, David, and others of the same class who were married to more than one wife at the same time. They thought that it was lawful for them also to do the same. It was borrowed in part from neighboring nations, for the inhabitants of the East never observed that conscientiousness and fidelity in marriage which was proper. However that might be, polygamy was exceedingly prevalent among them. Thus with great propriety does Paul enjoin that a bishop should be free from this stain. . . .

    Paul forbids polygamy in all who hold the office of a bishop, because it is a mark of an unchaste man, and of one who does not observe conjugal fidelity. It might be objected that what is sinful in all ought not to have been condemned or forbidden in bishops alone. The answer is easy. Just because it is expressly prohibited to bishops it does not therefore follow that it is freely allowed to others. Beyond all doubt, Paul condemned universally what was contrary to an

51. CO 52:281-82 (NTC adapted).

unrepealed law of God. For it is a settled enactment that "they shall be one flesh" (Gen. 2:24). But he might, to some extent, bear with something in others which in a bishop would have been excessively vile, and therefore not to be endured.

7-11 Case of Blaise de La Croix and Yolande (1552)[52]

(August 25, 1552). Blaise de La Croix stated that the Council has allowed them to stay and has remanded them here to learn whether he did not have leave to marry, and presented the witnesses below to show his honesty.

(August 30, 1552). Jeanne de Pestere and Salme de Provence testified that they are relatives of the aforesaid and do not know anything that is an impediment of marriage, and they know the parents consented to it and engaged her to him, because she was in religion, in a nunnery.

Decided: that she be exhorted separately. She said that long enough ago in the presence of her mother and brother he promised to marry her in this city, and her mother and brother intend to come here. She knew that he was a respectable man.

Decided: considering such testimony the Consistory decided that he may be free to proclaim the banns.

7-12 Case of Philiberte Le Chapuis et al. (1557)[53]

(May 20, 1557). Antoine, son of Jehan de Mante of Languedoc, and Philiberte, daughter of Guillaume Le Chapuis of Geneva [were called]. Antoine stated that, about four months ago, feeling true liking for each other, they had promised each other marriage. But now she has sworn and promised herself to another husband. Philiberte said it is true. But Antoine had given her nothing [as an engagement gift] and this had been done without anyone being present except the two of them, at the instigation of her aunt, a box-maker in Longemalle. She thus promised marriage to another from Petit Bornand named Pierre, whom she did not know otherwise.

Decided: that they must appear here Thursday and that her aunt, the box-maker, be summoned here.

(May 27, 1557). The box-maker of Longemalle was subpoenaed to testify concerning the marriage or promise of marriage of Antoine de Mante and

---

52. R. Consist. VII, 70, 71v.
53. R. Consist. XII, 48v, 52-52v, 60, 62.

Philiberte, daughter of the late Guillaume Le Chapuis. She said she did not know they were in any way promised to each other except as she heard it from the two of them after she had provided her with another husband. She also said that his [Antoine's] mother is her cousin-german, and for this reason she did not afterwards want to let her [Philiberte] marry [Antoine] de Mante. Besides, she had provided her with another husband [Pierre Du Suet] who is from Les Bornes and is a gilder now living in this city.

Decided: that the [promise of] marriage between [Pierre] the gilder and Philiberte should be suspended until it is otherwise decided about the promise made with de Mante, and that she should provide good evidence about her parents. The box-maker was afterwards recalled with Philiberte to learn the names of her father and her mother. She said he was named Guillaume Le Chapuis; as for her mother, she does not remember her name. [The later Council record says that she thought her mother was from Petit Bornand.]

Concerning this it was decided, since she [Philiberte] prevaricates and has contracted marriage twice, it was decided to remand them before the Council, she and the box-maker with the two [prospective] husbands. Also to remind the Council [to inquire] how once the box-maker said she was her aunt and nursed her and another time that she was of this city, and then changing her mind said that she does not know whether she is [of this city] and whether she was born here. Also how the box-maker said she did not know her mother otherwise and did not see her more than six times. Also that Philiberte said that her father died on the Arve Bridge, and she truly does not know her mother's name, and considering that to permit such a girl from who-knows-where to make such a scandal in this city [sentence incomplete]. Thus may it please the Council to attend to the matter after being informed more fully, and this on Monday.

[On May 31 the Council decided that Philiberte Le Chapuis should be imprisoned three days for her offense, and meanwhile the advice of the Consistory concerning the marriage promises would be taken.]

(June 3, 1557). Philiberte, daughter of the late Guillaume Le Chapuis, appeared according to the remand made by the Council to hear the admonitions she deserves to receive. Having been heard and strongly admonished, she was forbidden to associate with or frequent at all the second sworn husband, who is named Pierre and is a gilder.

(June 10, 1557). Concerning the Council's remand to the Consistory by our Lords of Philiberte, daughter of the late Guillaume Le Chapuis, concerning the two husbands promised by her, that is Antoine de Mante and Pierre the gilder. She having been heard on her refusal to take the first-named Antoine de Mante because he has no property, it was decided that the first marriage, since it was secret, is of no validity, and that the second should hold because the box-maker, her aunt or mistress, consented to it.

[On June 14 the Council decided, in conformity with the Consistory, that Philiberte's first engagement with Antoine was secret and therefore invalid, while the second, with Pierre, should go into effect.]

7-13   Case of Claude Plantain et al. (1561)[54]

(June 13, 1560). Leonard Moret, cabinetmaker, said that he heard from Mauris Gaillard and his wife that they said "Good luck to you,"[55] because they arranged a marriage in their house between Claude Plantain, boatman, and Claude, daughter of Jeanne Pommier of Bonneville, after having first made a promise to Jeanne, her younger sister. Mauris said this was true, and he was present and heard from Plantain that he had already been engaged to her younger [sister] Jeanne, and he himself went to find the mother, who brought with her the older Claude. He said that Jeanne first drank to marriage with Plantain, but he did not know whether this was [truly] to marriage. Claude Remondon and Claude Froniere said they heard it from the wife of Mauris Masson.

Decided: to remand Plantain to the Council for Monday for him to be required to have his promised wife and her sister, also promised, with their mother, come to learn what this is about; otherwise he will not be permitted to marry this one or any other, but will remain in suspension.

(June 26, 1561). Claude Plantain, son of the late George Plantain, was asked how long it is since he appeared here for having engaged himself to two sisters; he answered that it is about a year. Asked why he went away instead of appearing before the Council where he was sent, he said that he was forced to return to serve a master he had. Asked where his banns are, he said he had them and presented them, between him on the one part and Claude Pommier. The decision is to remand him to the Council to be punished for his rebelliousness and then come here on Thursday, and let witnesses be brought, namely Leonard Moret, living in the Rue Du Boule at the Oven, and those he shall name, and let the register be examined for the case, and meanwhile the marriage will be put off. Notice to the secretary of the Consistory.

(July 3, 1561). Claude Plantain remanded from Thursday because of his banns with Claude Pommier, his fiancée. He appeared, denying having promised marriage to Jeanne, sister of Claude, for which the witnesses named below were produced. First, Claude, the fiancée, said she had not otherwise heard that Plantain, her fiancé, had promised marriage to Jeanne, her sister. When urged to tell the truth, she said she had heard from someone that he had indeed wanted to

---

54. R. Consist. XVII, 94; XVIII, 70, 73v.
55. This is a formal salutation in dialect, used on special occasions.

have Jeanne [as his wife], but she did not wish it. Mauris Gaillard, mason, brother-in-law of the [prospective] bride, said that he had not heard from anyone that Plantain had been engaged to Jeanne, but certainly to Claude. Leonard Moret said that he heard from Mauris's wife that they had arranged a marriage between Plantain and Jeanne, his sister-in-law, and that they said, "Good luck to you." And thereupon there appeared Mauris, who told him that this was true. Mauris confessed it, then denied it. Asked whether he did not go to find the mother, he answered yes. Mauris's wife said this was true, and that she went to tell her husband that Claude Plantain wanted to drink in the name of marriage with Jeanne, her sister. Claude, daughter of Michel Fornier, wife of Claude Pictet, carpenter, testified that Mauris's wife told her to come to see whether Claude Plantain wanted to drink to marriage with her sister Jeanne. Claude Revaudon said he had heard it as a general rumor. Claude Espaulla said that Plantain came to find him to do him [Plantain] the honor at his engagement at Mauris Gaillard's, where he went with Cugnard and ten other people. And being there, instead of drinking in the name of marriage with Jeanne, he [Claude] said he did not wish to and rejected (?) her parents. They were irritated at this, and said he should at least take Claude, the older [sister], and that it was right that she be married before the other. For this reason he engaged himself to her, that is to Claude. Mauris, who had previously said that he knew nothing about the engagement of Claude, said that what Espaulla had testified was true.

The whole [case] being heard, since it was not proved by witnesses that he had drunk with [that is, become engaged to] Jeanne, but only with Claude, it was decided to remand him before the Council for Monday. He was enjoined to have appear there Jeanne the younger [sister], who they said was with her mother, named Marie, in Bonneville, for both of them to purge themselves by oath that no marriage was promised between them.

Afterwards, Plantain was asked who spoke to him about taking Claude in marriage. He answered that it was Claude Espaulla. Summoned, Espaulla answered that he knew nothing about it except that he himself asked for it. In this, Plantain is found wavering and contradictory. Afterwards, the mason was asked whether when he went to find the girl's mother to come there, whether this was not for the engagement of Jeanne. He did not want to answer.

The decision is to remand the whole matter to the Council with Plantain, his fiancée, her sister Jeanne, Mauris, mason, and his wife to proceed against them as they shall see in their prudence to be proper. They are enjoined to have Jeanne and her mother come on Monday. This being done, the [prospective] bride was asked whether she did not know that Claude had been engaged to her sister and whether the gathering they had was not for her said sister. She said no, but for her. This is inconsistent.

Decided: to inform the Council about it.

7-14   Case of Pierre Rapin (1542)[56]

(Thursday, March 2). Pernette, daughter of the late Jaquemoz Mastre, of Suaverny, versus Pierre Rapin, carpenter, formerly servant of Jacob in Versoix, where she was a maid. [He was charged] that he swore faith twice in the presence of her brothers, Mauris Mastre being present, and that it is public knowledge that this is so, and their mistress was present. And that he married another and that she had a child by him and that he gave her a piece of money in the name of marriage, which is a three-sous piece of Savoy which she has presented here, and that it was four or five years ago. And he married his wife in St. Gervase. And that she has lived in this city two years on the Charriere des Peyroliers and that she did not know when he published his banns. And that he was never in her room and that he last slept with her about a year ago during the fair of Saint Peter's and he has always said he truly wanted her. . . . The Consistory resolves that Pierre Rapin be summoned for Thursday at the customary time. And inform the Council on Monday.

(Thursday, March 16). The advice of the lords preachers Calvin, Viret.

[Two days later the Council declared that "Pierre Rapin . . . was condemned to public whipping, 'carrying a miter on his head,' and to banishment 'from the city, lands and *franchises* . . . under penalty of the gibbet' for having engaged himself to two women and having 'consummated marriage with both.'"]

7-15   Case of Marthe Piguier et al. (1555-1556)[57]

[This case opened before the Council on Oct. 15, 1555. Denis Potier, a bailiff, complained that he had offered his daughter, Marthe Piguier, as a wife to Amied Varo, but he had refused her. When she then married Andre Dumonet, she was already pregnant. Dumonet found secret letters she had received from Varo that revealed their earlier fornication. Varo admitted fornicating with Marthe. He said he had not promised to marry her, for he was already engaged to another woman in Antwerp, but was trying to annul that contract. The Council imprisoned him and then sent the case to Consistory for advice.]

(Oct. 17, 1555). Andre Dumonet was asked about the child his wife had recently had, who was baptized in his name, though he was absent. [The child was

---

56. R. Consist. I, 6-7 as translated in *Registers of the Consistory of Geneva at the Time of Calvin,* ed. Robert M. Kingdon et al., trans. M. Wallace McDonald (Grand Rapids, 2000), pp. 16-18.

57. R. Consist. X, 59v, 61-62, 80, 81, 85v, 88v; R. Consist. XI, 3-3v, 29, 50v, 91.

born] only six months after he was married. It was carried to baptism by the bailiff Potier, stepfather of the girl. He [Andre] answered that the child is not his, and he truly does not believe it. He had also said this to the bailiff who wanted to make him accept it [as his own child].

Decided: that for Thursday Amied Varo and the woman and the bailiff Potier [be summoned].

[On October 22 the Council ordered that Varo pay "the customary fine," evidently for his fornication, and appear before the Consistory for remonstrances.]

(Oct. 24, 1555). Amied Varo and the bailiff Potier were admonished because he [Varo] has been punished according to the edicts and remanded here by the Council for having committed fornication with Marthe, daughter of the wife of the bailiff Potier. He was asked to confess truthfully before the bailiff Potier whether there was any promise of marriage before Potier gave her to another [to marry]. He [Amied] said he had already said this to the Council, and he leaves it to the judgment of God: that about four months ago he went to the bailiff to beg mercy of him for his offense, and that there was never any promise [of marriage to Marthe]. The bailiff said he heard nothing about it until after the child was born and that he did him a wicked deed illegally and underhandedly, whether in marriage or otherwise. [Varo] may also have abused someone else, and he [Potier] asks that it be investigated; and as she will maintain to him.

(Oct. 24, 1555). Marthe Piguier was exhorted to tell the truth about the marriage [with Varo]. She said that, once when speaking to him, she said if he intended to marry and she pleased him she would take him willingly. To this he gave her no answer until another time, when he spoke to her about a girl from Flanders [Antwerp]. And then he pursued her to have her company, telling her he would never have another wife. Before having her company he told her she should not fear reproach for it if they were together. Then he promised [to marry] her; there was no other promise made in the presence of any person. To this [Varo] replied that he put off the oath by which he will take her, and that he never said it. He also said that he could not marry [Marthe] until he was free from his engagement to a woman in Flanders. Two letters were read written by him before she was married, and two [that were written] afterwards before the birth.

Decided: that Dumonet be called.

(Oct. 24, 1555). Andre Dumonet presented some letters he had recovered from her that she had in her purse. There were three in number, which she had torn up. But he had gathered the pieces which he copied, presenting the copies, which were also read.

Decided: that first they be made to acknowledge them, and that each point be asked about. [Amied] said that he wrote the letters as they are, after she was married [to Andre]. As he had [stated] before, there was never an absolute promise [of marriage to Marthe]. It is true that he had more love for her than for the other [woman] from Antwerp. He was asked to say whether he did not know that she was pregnant before she was married and that he advised her to marry and that he told her he would give her up. He was admonished concerning a point in one letter, that he said that the father of the woman in Antwerp was dead, and that it pleased God to have it occur two months before. He answered that it was her father who promised her to him in the absence of his daughter, and he understands that she indeed consented to it. He was admonished that despite the death [of the Antwerp woman's father] the marriage was not dissolved.

And regarding making the fruit disappear [having an abortion] she confessed having been to the doctor about it and having herself bled. He denied knowing anything about it except that she told him and wrote to him that she would like to die.

Decided: that in the first place, before proceeding further let the bailiff be summoned to be admonished for having presented the child for baptism, since he knew well it was not by Dumonet, and let him be remanded before the Council. Also let the baptismal register be corrected, since the Consistory has established that the child was not born in wedlock or to the one for whom it was presented.

Further decision: that Marthe be summoned to learn the truth about why she had herself bled [in an attempted abortion]. She said that it was the advice of the doctor, and she also took wintergreen and an enema; at the time she was not certain she was pregnant. She also said to Varo that she wanted to die and that he would have killed her. [He] denied having been told that if she had the means to kill herself she would do it; denied this point. They were confronted for him to maintain it to her, which he did, but that she did not think about the fruit [the child], and he remonstrated with her, saying that it was because of the torments she had from her father, mother, and husband.

Decided: that they both be remanded before the Council to be put under oath to tell the truth about all the points they have been asked about here, as well as about the marriage. And as for Dumonet, let him assemble the pieces of the letters he stuck together and give them to the syndic, and if it pleases them [the Council] let the parties be remanded here after such an oath.

[The Council examined Denis Potier on October 28. He maintained that he had refused to talk with Amied when the latter tried to see him about his daughter's child because he already suspected him. Also Andre, Marthe's husband, had refused to support the child. Potier confessed that he was at fault with regard to the baptism, however, but said he had done it to try to alleviate his daughter's dishonor. Moreover he was not certain at the time that the child was Amied's. Potier was required to kneel and beg for the mercy of God and of the Council. He was then released with remonstrances and remanded to the Consistory for further remonstrances and so the register of baptisms could be corrected.

The Council further decided that Amied and Marthe should be examined under oath concerning the marriage promise. Marthe was also to be examined under oath about whether she had tried to induce an abortion. The case was then referred back to the Consistory.]

(Dec. 22, 1555). Re: Amied Varo. The decision concerning the articles the Council have sent here to obtain the advice of the Consistory. Decided: that on Thursday Messieurs de Saule and Jean de La Maysonneuf make their report here for action to be taken on it.

(Jan. 2, 1556). Marthe, wife of Andre Dumonet, was asked that it be remembered that Amied Varo confessed both verbally and by his letters that were read here and before the Council asking that it be dealt with to discharge their consciences, and that he told her he would take her to Neuchâtel if Dumonet did not want her.

Decided: having heard the report of Monsieur de Saule assigned with Lord Jean de La Maysonneuf that it is not found that they were confronted to pursue this matter, which is sufficiently weighty. Let the Council be asked to proceed with greater diligence and energy and take it better in hand. Let Monsieur de Saule, who is acquainted with it, along with Monsieur Françoys Lullin, go before the Council, and they should answer each point with greater diligence.

[On January 6 Nicolas Des Gallards, Msr. de Saule, appeared before the Council on behalf of the Consistory, stating that Amied and Marthe contradicted themselves and the written evidence and therefore should be examined by the Council. Apparently they had not yet examined the defendants under oath as ordered previously. The Council decided to examine them in the presence of two ministers, who would then report to the Consistory.]

(Jan. 16, 1556). Andre Dumonet asks that he be dealt with according to the petitions he has presented, for Varo wants to depart, and it will be for a long time. He was answered that the Council has [the case] in hand, and that shortly they will have news of it.

(Jan. 30, 1556). Further decision against Amied Varo and Marthe Piguier: that the Council has again investigated and inquired about their persons.

Decided: let it please Master Calvin to go there to declare to the Council word-for-word that she is exceedingly guilty, and should answer for it as such.

[On February 3, 1556, Calvin appeared before the Council to urge action in this case. He stated that it appeared that Marthe had married despite being previously engaged to Amied, which should not be allowed to go unpunished. The Council ordered that both parties be examined in prison. On February 14

Amied petitioned to be released from prison, since the accusations against him were false. The Council promised to advance his case as rapidly as possible. On February 18 the Council referred the case to the *avocats,* or lawyers, the usual last step before imposing a sentence. On February 20, the *avocats* Guilletat and Chevalier having reported, the Council decided to question Amied and Marthe again in detail. They then sought the advice of the Consistory as to whether the evidence proves they were engaged.]

(Feb. 24, 1556). The decision is, concerning the Council's request for the advice of the Consistory concerning the alleged marriage between Amied Varo and Marthe Piguier, since it appears by the letters of Varo that they had discussed marriage with each other for a long time when Marthe married Dumonet, that at the least there is a very strong presumption of a conditional promise if he could extricate himself from the promise made to the merchant from Antwerp. Considering also that according to the answers of Varo there was no tie on the side of Antwerp that would prevent him from contracting marriage; having also heard and understood the answers given by Varo in which he often wavers and contradicts himself, denying what he had confessed and employing many frivolous subterfuges; also that by his letters he is convicted of bad faith and perjury; the decision of the Consistory is that Varo should not be considered free or capable of marrying, and even less Marthe, who according to her own statement is bound to Varo. Nevertheless, since matters are a little confused and were not clarified at the proper time and place, it seems that the gentlest course that can be followed is to forbid Varo to make any proposal of marriage for a year from now, so he may have leisure to think better in his conscience, and at the end of this term let him again be exhorted to repair the fault he has committed. And in case he persists in his denial, he will then have to purge himself by a solemn oath at the open gate according to custom. As for Marthe, let marriage be forbidden to her without an assigned term, but let her live in widowhood until it is decided otherwise. As for Dumonet, who has been defrauded, let him be permitted to repudiate Marthe, and also let him be notified that we cannot advise him to live with her. Nevertheless, if he should wish to retain her, let him not be prevented when the aforesaid term has been expired. And if he complains that it is too long, it will be within the discretion of the Council to shorten it at his request. As for the punishment that each of the two parties has merited, the Consistory does not deal with it, reserving it to the Council, but only advances its advice concerning the status of the marriage, as it was requested. Also it was decided to forbid Communion to both.

[On February 25 the Council decided to accept and abide by the opinion of the Consistory above. As further punishment, Amied and Marthe were required to beg mercy of God and justice on their knees and to pay ten gold écus apiece and their trial expenses. On February 27 they did so and were released.

On March 12 Andre Dumonet asked to be informed of what had been done in this case so he could know how to proceed. The Council ordered that he be given a copy of the decision. On April 3 Calvin appeared before the Council to explain that the term of forced widowhood assigned to Marthe Piguier could be shortened, as previously decided.]

(May 21, 1556). Marthe Piguier asks to be admitted to Communion, confessing having done wrong in having commerce with Amied Varo, and being pregnant was married to another, and previously promised and defrauded him.

Decided: that considering that she comes too late and does not make a complete confession, that it [the prohibition] be continued until the next [Communion].

(Aug. 13, 1556). Marthe Peguier asks, with a profession of repentance, that it might please us to admit her to Communion, and begged mercy of God.

The decision: that considering that it has already been a long time that it has been forbidden her, one may permit it to her, and she was freed [to take Communion].

(Dec. 24, 1556). Amied Varo came, asking to be received for Communion, which had been forbidden him. Asked about the cause of the prohibition, he said because of the fornication he committed with the daughter of bailiff Potier. He was admonished that there was also a promise of marriage he had abused.

The decision: that he be admonished to acknowledge his fault better and look into himself, then be admitted to Communion, remanding him to his judge.

7-16   Case of Claude Du Noyer (1558)[58]

(Jan. 20, 1558) Pierre Chopin said that Claude Du Noyer or Jehan du Noyer has married two wives, as he has heard from two witnesses, one named Du Boulle of Sionnet and another from the lands of the king [of France]. Claude Du Noyer of Thorens was called. He said he had been married ten years ago in Vandoeuvres, and previously he had been married in Thorens, from which he has grown children by his first wife. Moreover he has lived in this city for ten years and has not been registered as a *habitant,* and before he had this last wife he had married another, which is two [women], since he has been here. He further confessed that he was indeed reproached by Rollet Ficlet of Thorens for having married two [women], one in his own country and the other here, but he is not a man worthy of belief. He also confessed that he was drunk.

58. R. Consist. XII, 149.

Decided: to remand him for three reasons: the first because he has no letter of habitation, the second because he gets drunk, the third because he is reputed to have two wives; to purge the city, considering the reproach cast on him, as he confesses, at Chopin's. Communion is forbidden him. Remand to Monday before the Council.

[On January 24 the Council decided that Du Noyer should be imprisoned three days and then banished on pain of being whipped if he returned.]

7-17 Case of Robert Cuysin (1552)[59]

(March 31, 1552). Robert Cuysin of Noyon Le Roy, cobbler, was admonished as to whether he is married. He said yes, to a woman who told him after they had come to this city that she had news of another husband, who is presently in Chalon in Burgundy. He also has heard that he [the other husband] was remarried in the town of Chalon. And he said that it has been about six years since he married her, and before he married her he was told by certain companions of her first husband that he had died in Scotland.

Decided: that for Thursday she and he appear to be confronted, and that he bring her.

(April 7, 1552). Robert Cuysin, cobbler, and his wife were admonished concerning the last remand of Thursday to learn whether she does not have another husband. She said yes, and that he sent her a letter that he is in Mâcon and is married. She also said that he was never a good householder and that it is true that after she had remarried her first husband came to Lyon and had her taken before the official to make her leave him [her new husband], which she did not want.

Decided: that she be asked how long it is since her first husband left her. Said it is ten years, and seven years since she married this one here. She said that it was she who remarried before her first [husband] remarried. But it was badly carried out, and it was by his mother's consent, and if her first [husband] wanted her she would return to him willingly. He is named Antoine Cheneta.

Further decision: that they be remanded before the Council, and let her get and show diligence in obtaining an affidavit from her first husband, and forbid them each other's company until the truth of the whole matter is known.

[The Council eventually annulled this second marriage of the woman and Robert, because she remarried before her first husband had done so. Both she and Robert were banished, since they could "have found out that the first husband was alive."]

59. R. Consist. VII, 16, 18.

CHAPTER 8

Fitness for Marriage

The Impediments of Lack of Virginity, Contagion,
Sexual Incapacity, and Disparity in Age

The 1546 Marriage Ordinance listed three impediments of quality or fitness for marriage that could annul an engagement or newly contracted marriage: (1) the lack of presumed virginity; (2) the presence of a contagious disease; and (3) the incidence of sexual incapacity or dysfunction. Both Calvin and Beza offered ample theological reflections on all three impediments, but none of them was subject to much litigation. Calvin also pressed hard for the inclusion of a fourth impediment of quality — wide disparity of age between the prospective couple. Though this impediment was not included in the 1546 Marriage Ordinance, the Consistory annulled several engagements on this ground as well.

Lack or Betrayal of Presumed Virginity

The 1546 Marriage Ordinance allowed for the annulment of engagements and marriages "when it is found by sufficient proof that a girl who was taken for a virgin is not one."[1] The point of this impediment, Calvin insisted, was not so much to elevate virginity as to castigate duplicity. There was nothing wrong for a man to seek a virgin for a wife, though for Calvin virginity was hardly the most essential quality of a prospective spouse. But it was scandalous for a woman to hold herself out falsely as a virgin to her fiancé. It was even worse for the woman to lose her virginity to another man after contracting her en-

---

1. 1546 Marriage Ordinance, item 13, Doc. 1-2.

gagement — an offense Calvin found equally serious if committed by the engaged man.

Theological Reflections

The term "virgin" and its derivatives were biblical commonplaces, appearing some sixty-five times in the Bible. The Old Testament often used the term metaphorically — as in the Prophets' various denunciations of the "virgin of Israel" who had fallen from the law. Commenting on several of these passages, Calvin treated Israel's "virginity" not so much as its "unspoiled purity and delicacy," as its willingness to live under the law and the protection of Yahweh.[2] The metaphorical equivalent of "virginity" in the New Testament, Calvin argued, was for the Christian to live in purity of faith before God, waiting patiently for the return of Christ.[3]

The Bible also used the term "virgin" to designate a woman who had not "known" sexual intercourse and/or was living under the protection of her father (or guardian). Calvin regarded it as a father's duty to protect the virginity of his daughter, and the daughter's duty to stay at home under his protection. Commenting on the rape of Jacob's daughter Dinah as described in Genesis 34, Calvin wrote:

> Dinah is ravished, because, having left her father's house, she wandered about more freely than was proper. She ought to have remained quietly at home, as both the Apostle teaches and nature itself dictates. . . . [F]athers of families are taught to keep their daughters under strict discipline, if they desire to preserve them free from all dishonor. If a vain curiosity was so heavily punished in the daughter of holy Jacob, no less danger hangs over weak virgins in our day if they go too boldly and eagerly into public assemblies and excite youthful passions towards them.[4]

It was one thing for a negligent father or a careless virgin to risk rape. It was quite another if an engaged virgin, living properly under her father's protection until her wedding day, was raped. Calvin insisted, on the strength of Mosaic law, that the rapist must not only be prosecuted for rape, but also be re-

2. Comm. Jer. 14:7; 18:13; 31:4, 13, 21; Comm. Isa. 37:3; Lect. Amos 5:2.

3. Comm. 2 Cor. 11:2; Comm. Harm. Gosp. Matt. 25:1.

4. Comm. Gen. 34:1-31; see also Serm. 2 Sam. 13:2 noting that King David's daughter Tamar's virginity was "evidence of honesty in the house of David. . . . [S]he had been raised in such a way that there had been no occasion for her to be raped, and also that those who would have wanted to corrupt her did not have access to her."

quired to pay the father the full marriage price dower his daughter would have attracted as a virgin.[5] This forced payment, Calvin argued, was an appropriate penalty for the man's fornication and ample compensatory damages for despoiling the young woman.[6] And, if the rapist was in fact the woman's fiancé, he faced even sterner sanctions: he had to pay her full dower, to marry her if her father consented, and to waive his rights to pursue either annulment or divorce from her on any ground.[7]

Calvin took ample note of the Mosaic requirement in Leviticus 21 that a priest, particularly a high priest, was to "take a wife in her virginity" (**Doc. 8-1**).[8] But Calvin read this commandment in light of St. Paul's later instructions that ministers of the church were to lead honest and decent lives in order to earn the respect of their congregants. In Old Testament Israel, where virginity was more highly prized, priests had to marry virgins in order to earn this respect. In the New Testament church, however, where virginity carried less of a premium, marriage to a virgin was no longer a requirement. Indeed, Calvin himself married a widow, as did Viret and other Protestant ministers.

When a man engaged a presumed virgin and discovered, after the engagement or the wedding, that she was not a virgin, he could sue for annulment. The fiancée or her father may have lied about her virginity at the time of the engagement. Or she may have had sexual relations for the first time between the engagement and wedding day. In either case, a man had the right to plead the impediment of the lack of presumed virginity.

This impediment was grounded in the Mosaic law. The core biblical text was Deuteronomy 22:13-21 that set out the proper procedure for a husband to allege that his new wife lacked "the tokens of virginity." If the woman or her father could prove that this was a false accusation, the new husband was to be whipped, fined for his defamation, and deprived of his right to divorce her. If the charge proved true, the woman was to be stoned to death.

In his 1563 commentary on the Mosaic law, Calvin saw in this passage a sound and sensible procedure for negotiating a very tender and high-stakes issue for both parties and their families (**Doc. 8-2**). The procedure established by the Mosaic law protected the wife from her husband's false charges of duplicity or fornication, and from being divorced on trumped-up charges. If found innocent, the wife was assured of the permanent support of her husband, and her family was ensured of ample compensatory damages for the scandal visited on

---

5. Comm. Harm. Law. Exod. 22:16-17.

6. For further discussion, see Chapter 4, and Docs. 4-2 and 4-3.

7. Serm. Deuteronomy 22:25-30.

8. Lev. 21:7-9, 13-15. This prohibition recurs for Levites in Ezekiel 44:22, but Calvin's Lectures stop at Ezekiel 20:44.

them. A husband, in turn, was protected from the deception of his wife and from the duplicity of her father who would have extracted a higher marriage price for his virgin daughter.

In his 1556 Sermon on Deuteronomy, Calvin focused on a different kind of deception, that of premarital adultery (**Doc. 8-3**).[9] Premarital sex on the part of an engaged couple was serious enough, Calvin argued. It deserved criminal punishment, but it did not break the engagement. Premarital adultery, however — sex with a third party between the engagement and the wedding — was much worse, especially if the woman had been a virgin at the time of the engagement. This was a fundamental breach of faith with God and with one's future spouse. It not only broke the engagement; it was a capital crime.

Deuteronomy 22 focused on the wayward woman, and Calvin spent a good bit of time explaining why her crime of premarital adultery was so heinous. The woman desecrated her soul and body. She stole her future husband's exclusive rights to her, which he had purchased from her father. She heaped on her future husband the obligation to raise her illegitimate child. She deprived the couple's own later legitimate children of precious family resources. And, such a fundamental breach of faith so early in the relationship would inevitably lead to similar serious sins. Both her husband and the broader society would be better off if this adulterous fiancée were executed.

"The male fornicator should be punished equally," Calvin insisted. By his premarital adultery, he not only "stole the honor" of his bride-to-be and her family. But he "acted against a holy and sacred promise," in open defiance of God and society. Pagan and Christian societies alike punish men severely for breaking commercial contracts, forging documents, or defrauding strangers. Premarital adultery is much more serious. It deserves the same death penalty that God prescribes for the adulterous fiancée. Calvin did nothing to distinguish the various other passages in the Mosaic law that treated male adultery more leniently. For Calvin, this fundamental breach of faith by either party to the engagement deserved death.

Nonetheless, Calvin argued that these stern laws against premarital adultery should not be applied woodenly. Leviticus 20:23 already made this clear (**Doc. 8-4**). There, Mosaic law provided that if an engaged virgin is raped, her fiancé cannot accuse her under the procedures that Moses had laid down to charge her and her family that she lacked presumed virginity or to seek an annulment on this ground. It was the duplicity of the woman, not her lack of vir-

---

9. Calvin did not call this "adultery," but given the solemnity that he attached to engagement contracts, sex with a third party was closer to adultery than fornication. The Genevan statutes, including the major 1566 statute reforming the laws of fornication and adultery, did not single out for special treatment the third party sex of engaged parties. SD, vol. 3, item 1065.

ginity, that was at the heart of this impediment. In cases of third party rape of an engaged woman, Calvin preferred that couples carry on with their marital plans — though he acknowledged that loss of virginity (even if involuntarily) was an impediment that could break a engagement.[10] Calvin acknowledged full well that the rape of an "engaged virgin" was the "most painful thing of all" for the parties to endure — though he communicated this principally as a severe property loss for the man.[11] At minimum, the raped fiancée was not to be punished for fornication,[12] assuming she resisted mightily,[13] but her abductor should face capital punishment.[14] But more fully, Calvin hoped that her fiancé could see his way clear to marrying her, despite her loss of virginity. Indeed, true love for his fiancée should make him eager to comfort her for her loss rather than condemn her for her defect.

Joseph's conduct toward the Virgin Mary, as reported in Matthew, underscored this need for equity, Calvin argued (**Doc. 8-5**). Before the angel explained to him that Mary's conception of Jesus was "by the Holy Spirit," he evidently assumed that his pregnant fiancée had been unfaithful to him. That he was a "just man," said Calvin, meant that Joseph could not simply overlook Mary's presumed crime of premarital adultery. But he did not want to shame her, or to expose her to the possibility of execution. Joseph thus contemplated annulling the engagement quietly and moving away, as was his right.[15]

Citing these same biblical texts, Beza expounded on this right to sue for annulment for lack of presumed virginity (**Doc. 8-6**). Natural law teaches that

10. See 1546 Marriage Ordinance, item 13, Doc. 1-2. Cf. Comm. Harm. Law Lev. 19:20-22 (Calvin notes with approval that voluntary fornication by an engaged woman should be punished with scourging).

11. Comm. Harm. Law Deut. 28:30.

12. Comm. Harm. Law Deut. 22:22-27; cf. also Harm. Law Lev. 19:20-22.

13. Serm. Deut. 22:25-30: "Our Lord declares here that girls should live in such honesty that if they have an unfortunate encounter, if they meet some debaucher who wishes to seduce them, they must not have more regard for their lives than for their honor, and they should rather let their throats be cut than their bodies be violated, to live under such blame."

14. Serm. Deut. 22:25-30.

15. While Joseph's conduct was equitable, Calvin contrasts it to the overwhelming graciousness of Yahweh in his treatment of wayward Israel, who fell into idolatry just as a young espoused woman falls into adultery. In Lectures on Hosea 2:19-20, Calvin writes: "The Prophet here again makes known the manner in which God would receive into favor his people. As though the people had not violated the marriage vow, God promises to be to them like a bridegroom, who marries a virgin, young and pure." It is as if God says to them: "I will engage thee unto me for ever; yea, I will engage thee unto me in righteousness, and in judgment, and in loving kindness, and in mercies. And I will even engage thee unto me in faithfulness" — despite Israel's lack of faithfulness. Calvin found particularly poignant, and prescriptive, the notion that God "espouses to himself a people infamous through many disgraceful acts; and having abolished their sins, he contracts as it were a new marriage and joins them again to himself."

a man cannot be forced to accept less than what he bargained for, Beza argued. Both Roman law and biblical law have applied this general principle to the specific issues of lack of virginity. Modern Genevan law, said Beza, has properly done the same. The lack of presumed virginity is a material breach of the engagement or marital contract. A man must have the right to terminate the contract with impunity if he wishes, or to renegotiate its terms as a condition for going forward. This right becomes doubly important if the fiancée's premarital adultery results in pregnancy. It "seems shameful and intolerable in a Christian church for a pregnant woman to be married to somebody else" than the father of the child to be, said Beza. In Geneva, principal responsibility for an illegitimate child lay with the father and his family. And the Consistory was not above imposing shotgun weddings. A man had the right to marry his fiancée who was pregnant with her lover's child. But he had the equal right to spurn her and annul the engagement, leaving the woman to seek financial support from the child's father — or, lacking that, from the authorities in church and state.[16]

Consistory Cases

For all of Calvin's stern commentary on this impediment of lack or betrayal of presumed virginity and the explicit provision for annulment on this ground in the 1546 Marriage Ordinance, the Consistory produced little case law on point.

In a 1544 case, decided before the Marriage Ordinance was drafted, a man sought to annul an engagement both because of a dispute over dowry and because his fiancée had allegedly become impregnated by another man (**Doc. 8-7**). The Consistory and Council saw this case principally as a dowry dispute, which was not a sufficient ground for annulment.[17] They brushed aside the allegations of premarital adultery and pregnancy. They must have suspected the fiancé himself to be the father, though the record does not say.

Calvin and the Consistory were far less accommodating of a couple in a 1557 case of premarital adultery (**Doc. 8-8**). Claude Gra became engaged to Pierre Chavallier. Sometime thereafter, Pierre had sex with a woman in the Vaud region, yielding an illegitimate child. Claude complained of his conduct to the Consistory, and said further that she feared that Pierre may have become engaged to his lover as well. Pierre denied any new engagement, but admitted to

---

16. See illustrative cases in Spierling, pp. 170ff.; François Hotman, *De Spuriis et Legitimatione*, caps. II-IV, appended to Hotman, *De Sponsalibus*. On pre-Reformation Genevan cases, see Naef, 1:232ff.

17. See 1546 Marriage Ordinance, item 14, Doc. 1-2. See also Seeger, pp. 319-20.

fathering the illegitimate child. In fact, he testified that he had hired his lover to nurse the child and paid her a rather handsome settlement to raise the child without him. Pierre produced a notarized contract of settlement with the woman as well as an affidavit from the local vicar.

The Consistory must have thought that Pierre was trying to buy his way out of his trouble and to keep his philandering quiet from everyone, including his fiancée Claude. The Consistory came down hard on him, as well as on the notary who had notarized his settlement contract. They sent Calvin to the Council, where he successfully had both Pierre and his fiancée Claude banished from the city. Pierre's banishment is understandable: premarital adultery and duplicity were both serious offenses. Why Claude was banished is less clear, unless the Consistory judged that she was in on the scheme, or that her engagement to Pierre remained intact, and she was thus required to follow him.

In a few other cases, fiancés forgave their fiancée's premarital fornication instead of seeking annulment, and later accepted the illegitimate child and supported it.[18] A good example is the 1547 case of Pierre Butin and his fiancée Claude (**Doc. 8-9**). Claude's brother and cousins had helped to facilitate her engagement to Pierre. Either just before or just after her engagement, Claude had sex with Mammard de L'Horme, who was himself already engaged to another woman. Claude first sought to break up Mammard's engagement so that he would marry her and support their child. When that proved futile, Claude made her way back to Pierre, and sought to marry him quickly, encouraged by her brother and cousins. The couple forgot to post their banns, however, and the minister refused to marry them. In the course of the Consistory's investigation into her conduct, Pierre learned of Claude's adulterous liaison with Mammard and that she now carried his child. Pierre testified that he wanted to marry her anyway. Mammard's fiancée had since married him. After recommending that the Council punish Claude and Mammard for their fornication, the Consistory ordered that the marriage of Claude and Pierre could go forward.

We have found no cases (at least in our three sample years) where a man pled for annulment on grounds that his new fiancée or wife falsely held herself out as a virgin. This is not so surprising. In some cases, no doubt, the couple and their families dealt with these matters privately, and where necessary renegotiated the terms of the marital contract free from Consistory interference. In other cases, the presence of this impediment might well have driven one of the engaged parties to desert the other, leaving the other free to seek annulment for desertion.[19] Moreover, given the zealotry with which the authorities prosecuted

18. See, e.g., Case of Denis Potier et al. (1555-56), R. Conseil 50:10, 17, 20v, 21; R. Consist. X, 59v, 61, 63v, 73v, 80, 81, 85v; R. Consist. XI, 3 and discussion in Spierling, pp. 170-72.
19. See cases and discussion in Chapter 12.

fornication, and the publicity of the punishment for those convicted of the same, it would have been hard for a young woman to keep any such prior sexual history secret and to pretend to virginity only to be found out on her wedding night. Think of how reputations and rumors travel in a small town even today. Add the fact that it was the authorities who often lifted the privacy veil and forced public disclosures of sin, and it becomes hard to imagine that parties negotiating their marriages would not know what they were bargaining about. Only newcomers to Geneva would operate under a veil of ignorance. Even then town gossip was sure to emerge during the year that they were forced to wait before they were allowed to be married in Geneva.[20]

What is more surprising is that Calvin sought to punish men and women guilty of premarital adultery equally. The Bible and the tradition often treated a man's sexual crimes more leniently than a woman's, and Calvin perpetuated gender distinctions on other issues. But on the matter of premarital adultery, Calvin held men and women to the same standard, and would hear nothing of the traditional veneration of a woman's virginity or the traditional taboo of breaking it.

This was another example of Calvin's insistence on playing a new minor key on gender equality despite his traditional orchestrations on male headship.[21] Part of Calvin's reasoning in this case, no doubt, was that the consequences of premarital adultery were roughly the same to the later married couple. Either philandering party was just as likely to bring unwanted disease, such as syphilis, into the marital bed. Either party was just as likely to cause pregnancy with roughly comparable consequences. If an engaged woman became pregnant by another man, either her lover or her new husband would have to support the child. If an engaged man impregnated another woman, he would have to provide child support from afar, or he and his wife would have to assume custody and support of the child. The major difference was the risk of getting caught in the event of pregnancy. Unless she sought an abortion, which was very dangerous, the fiancée could not hide her sexual sin. Unless he was sued for child support, which was not common, the fiancé could hide his. The odds were disproportionately in favor of the man. Perhaps for this very reason, Calvin would punish him equally if caught.

---

20. 1546 Marriage Ordinance, item 19, Doc. 1-2.

21. See, e.g., the equality provisions on divorce in 1546 Marriage Ordinance, item 40, Doc. 1-2. See further Jane Dempsey Douglas, *Women, Freedom & Calvin* (Philadelphia, 1985); John Lee Thompson, *John Calvin and the Daughters of Sarah: Women in Regular and Exceptional Roles in the Exegesis of Calvin, His Predecessors and Contemporaries* (Geneva, 1992); David Blankenhorn, Don S. Browning, and Mary Stewart van Leeuwen, eds., *Does Christianity Teach Male Headship?* (Grand Rapids, 2004).

Contagion or Incurable Disease

The 1546 Marriage Ordinance stipulated that engagements could be broken "if one of the parties has a contagious and incurable bodily disease."[22] This was a common impediment of the medieval *ius commune*. It continued in Reformed Geneva, although the reformers forced annulment of these engagements much more readily than their medieval predecessors.

Theological Reflections

Calvin said little about contagion as an impediment to *engagement*. Beza commented on the subject at some length (**Doc. 8-10**). Beza distinguished (1) incurable contagious diseases, which were absolute impediments to engagement; (2) incurable non-contagious diseases or disfigurements that were permissible impediments; and (3) lesser ailments and deformities that were not impediments at all.

First, where either party contracted leprosy or a similar dangerous disease that was "clearly contagious and incurable," Beza wrote, the engagement must be annulled, even against the parties' wishes. Individuals could not be allowed to endanger their lives, or to produce diseased children who might well become wards of the state after the parents die of their contagion. It was no solution to allow a couple to live in a sexless "spiritual marriage," as the medieval canonists counseled. That would only expose them to inevitable temptations of adultery. It is as "if God himself, as the author" of marriage, "steps between promises of this sort," said Beza. To break up these engagements was "not separating what God has joined together but rather blocking [what] was wrongly joined together contrary to God's will." The diseased party was required to remain permanently single and, through pastoral counseling, to learn to live in continence. The healthy person was free to contract marriage with another.

Second, if one party had a serious and repulsive disease or condition that was not contagious the parties could marry. But either party had the right to seek an annulment of their engagement as well. Beza did not specify the kind of disease he had in mind. He was likely thinking of what the medieval *ius commune* had recognized by this impediment — cases of massive facial or bodily disfigurement caused by fighting, criminal assault, burning, or other accident, or cases of massive infections, bowel problems, or other conditions that produced repulsive bodily odor. Parties who could not abide these conditions could properly annul their engagements, though they need not. What made

22. 1546 Marriage Ordinance, item 13, Doc. 1-2.

these impediments permissible rather than absolute was that such diseases and conditions were not contagious and would not thereby endanger the health of the spouse or children.

These cases of permissible impediment had to be distinguished from a third type of case where one party to the engagement was inflicted with a less serious physical impairment (like blindness, deafness, or muteness) or had a longstanding but curable disease. Parties could not annul their engagements on these weaker grounds — though such conditions might justify delaying the wedding for a longer time than was normally indicated.[23]

While contagious disease was an impediment to engagements, it was not an impediment to existing marriages. If one of the parties contracted the contagious disease after their wedding, neither spouse could seek annulment or divorce.

Calvin touched on this issue in a 1546 letter to Pierre Viret.[24] Earlier that year, Calvin reported to Viret that one of the leaders of the "Children of Geneva" had died.[25] Calvin reported making a "tolerably long speech" before the Genevan Council, evidently to demonstrate once and for all that "this was a criminal and profligate man, a haunter of taverns, a drunkard, a brawler, much addicted to profane swearing, in a word, one of the most notorious despisers of God." Among his many sins was that this man had cavalierly "abandoned his wife" and children during the plague, despite the rebuke of another pastor. As his just reward, God had afflicted him with the plague as well, which had weakened him both in body and mind. When invited to repent of his sins, the man had sprung from his bed completely crazed, run off and leapt to his death in the river. When some locals begun murmuring pity for the man, Calvin proclaimed to the Consistory: "If you believe that there are any devils at all, here you clearly perceive the agency of the devil. Those who have no faith in God deserve to stumble in darkness in open day."

Calvin commented on this issue again in a 1561 *consilium* (**Doc. 8-11**). A husband contracted a form of leprosy, which was not only contagious but also apparently increased his sexual appetite. Could his wife seek to annul the marriage or divorce him, for fear of her own safety and that of her children? No, said Calvin. Couples were to remain married "in sickness and in health," as their vows stipulated, and this covered even cases of serious contagion. The couple could separate to reduce the risk of contagion. But their marriage was

---

23. See 1546 Marriage Ordinance, item 16, Doc. 1-2, stipulating that a wedding should normally follow formal engagements within six weeks.

24. (November 15, 1546), CO 12:413-16.

25. This was a group of anti-clerical dissidents who chafed under the Consistory's new discipline.

not, and could not be, broken by this new condition. Both the man and the woman had to remain chaste, however heavy a burden that imposed on them.

Consistory Cases

The Genevan Consistory addressed this impediment only rarely, despite the provision for annulment of engagements on this ground in the 1546 Marriage Ordinance. In a 1556 case, the Consistory and Council did annul the engagement of a woman to a man who had contracted syphilis after their engagement (**Doc. 8-12**). The woman's father had pressed the case for annulment, for he was concerned for his daughter's health. He also argued that his daughter's fiancé was now weakened by the disease and also impoverished. On the Consistory's recommendation, the Council annulled the engagement and banned the man from the city. Not only would his syphilis endanger the health of his future spouse, it also evinced his sexual misconduct. Either ground was enough to warrant annulment. Both grounds together made this a rather easy case.

Sexual Dysfunction

The 1546 Marriage Ordinance restricted marriage to "capable persons."[26] Among those "not capable" were parties who suffered from permanent sexual dysfunction because of castration, impotence, frigidity, injury to their sexual organs, or a physical condition that precluded sexual intercourse. The Marriage Ordinance called for annulment of marriages (and by implication of engagements) involving a party with such a condition. Calvin included a detailed provision in the Ordinance:

> [37.] If it happens that a woman complains that the one who has taken her in marriage is physically maimed and not able to have the company of a woman, and this is found true by confession or examination, let the marriage be declared void, the woman be declared free, and the man be forbidden to defraud any woman again.
>
> [38.] Likewise if the man complains of not being able to have the company of his wife because of some defect in her body and she does not want to allow it to be cured, after the truth of the fact is established let the marriage be declared void.[27]

26. 1546 Marriage Ordinance, item 13, Doc. 1-2.
27. Doc. 1-2. Calvin's 1545 draft added to item 37: "Nevertheless, in order to avoid any collusion or deceitful conspiracy, let diligent inquiry be made into all the circumstances until the case is duly verified." This sentence was dropped from the 1546 and 1561 versions.

Theological Reflections

Ten years after drafting his Marriage Ordinance, Calvin anchored this prohibition in the Bible. In Matthew 19:11-12, the disciples asked Christ whether all men should marry. Christ answered:

> Not all men can receive this saying, but only those to whom it is given. For there are eunuchs who have been so from birth, and there are eunuchs who have been made so by [other] men, and there are eunuchs who have made themselves eunuchs for the sake of the kingdom of heaven.

The import of this passage, said Calvin, is that eunuchs are really "not men"[28] and therefore cannot be husbands (**Doc. 8-13**). To be sure, Christ commends marriage to all "fit" adult men and women, save those rare individuals who are gifted with continence. But Christ also makes clear in this passage, said Calvin, that eunuchs are not "fit" for marriage, and thus they may not seek to contract it.

Calvin elaborated on this argument in an undated *consilium*, now including the frigid alongside eunuchs in his analysis (**Doc. 8-14**). The Bible provides that in marriage the man and the woman become "one flesh" (Gen. 2:24; Matt. 19:5; Mark 10:7-8; 1 Cor. 6:16).[29] A man who lacks the sexual capacity for true fleshly union, said Calvin, cannot live up to this literal biblical description of marriage. More importantly, he "completely obviates the nature and purpose of marriage. For what is marriage except the joining of a male and female, and why was it instituted except to produce children and to remedy sexual incontinence?" Calvin called for automatic annulment of any engagement or new marriage involving eunuchs or frigid parties, and the imposition of sanctions if either party had kept this condition secret prior to the wedding.

Beza was even harsher in his rebuke of eunuchs who tried to marry. He addressed the issue in two lengthy passages in his 1569 *Tract on Annulment and Divorce* (**Docs. 8-15 and 16**). Eunuchs betray the principal purposes of marriage — procreation, protection from sexual sin, and domestic sharing. Even if a cas-

---

28. Cf. Lect. Daniel 1:4ff. where Calvin argued that the repeated term "eunuchs" *(serisim)* means only "the boys who were nourished" and "held in honor and regard" "in the king's palace to become a seminary of nobles. This name is everywhere used in Scripture for the satraps of a king (Gen. 37:36; 40:2, 7), but since satraps also were chosen from noble boys, they were probably called eunuchs, though they were not made so." "They were youths, not so young as seven or eight years, but growing up, in whom there was no spot; that is, in whom there was no defect or unsoundness of body. They were also of beautiful aspect, meaning of ingenuous and open countenance, he adds also, skilled in all prudence, and understanding knowledge; and then, expressing their thoughts."

29. See Lect. and Comm. Gen. 2:22-24; Comm. and Serm. 1 Cor. 6:16.

trated eunuch is still capable of penetration and even emission, his act is in fact doubly perverse, for "he introduces his seed into a woman ineffectively." Indeed, said Beza with ample hyperbole, we "should consider such a man not only a fornicator but even a murderer." Rather than relieve sexual desire, eunuchs actually exacerbate lust in their wives — either because they cannot perform sexually at all, or because their wives will yearn for another man with whom to conceive children. While a eunuch and a wife might be able to help each other in a common household, they still live in a sexless marriage that is reserved to those with the rare gift of continence. "It justly follows that a marriage of this sort is void," Beza concluded. "Those who have been joined with such infamy and by such a monstrous crime" must have their relationship immediately and unilaterally annulled.

If the Bible prohibits marriage to eunuchs, Beza continued, marriage must also be foreclosed to others who are permanently impotent, frigid, injured, or otherwise physically incapable of sexual intercourse. Beza included those who were paralyzed and men who were born without sexual organs or had lost them in combat or accidents. He could also have included women with debilitating humps, tumors, or vaginal constrictions that precluded intercourse, as his younger colleague François Hotman did in his later tract on the subject.[30] Eunuchs, at least, are sometimes capable of sexual penetration, even if it is "fruitless" and "fraudulent." Those with permanent sexual dysfunctions cannot even do that; their attempted union makes an entire mockery of God's stated purposes for marriage. "With this natural impediment standing in the way," their engagement or marriage promises "are completely invalid." "It is as if God himself were so commanding, as if he were clearly showing by this permanent impediment being set in place that such promises to marry did not please him."

It was "pure papist trash," Beza later said, to allow parties to enter or to remain in new marriages despite their sexual dysfunction, as some medieval canonists open to "spiritual marriages" had counseled. We cannot expect people today to live chastely in a sexless marriage, as if they were "new Josephs and Marys." Even if they wish to go forward with their marriages, God and nature do not allow it.

Beza distinguished these cases of permanent sexual dysfunction from cases where the man was alleged to be sterile.[31] Sterility is not only harder to discern by physical examination; it may well be a temporary condition that is "curable." Sterility, therefore, was no impediment.

---

30. Hotman, cap. III, summarizing the *ius commune;* see medieval canon law antecedents summarized in Brundage, pp. 376-78.

31. It is worth noting that Beza himself, though married twice, produced no children, perhaps because of his own sterility.

Neither Beza nor Calvin dealt with the rather common question of whether elderly parties, with diminished or dissipated sexual drives or capacities, were similarly precluded from (re)marriage. Calvin frowned on marriages between the elderly and youths, as we shall see in the next section. But both Calvin and Beza countenanced the (re)marriage of the elderly, particularly if they were very lonely. Was sexual capacity essential to the validity of such elderly marriages? Did it make a difference if the woman was post-menopausal and no longer capable of procreation, thereby undercutting an essential part of the rationale for this impediment? In the absence of procreative potential, were other forms of intimacy, short of intercourse, a sufficient form of "one-flesh union" to call this a marriage? Calvin and Beza did not say.

Beza and Calvin did deal squarely with the issue of sexual dysfunction that commonly creeps into longstanding marriages. When either the husband or wife became incapable of sexual performance in later life, Calvin urged understanding and patience on the part of the other spouse. He would hear nothing of annulment, concubinage, separation, or divorce as a remedy or a result of this later sexual incapacitation. As he put in his Commentary on 1 Corinthians 7:

> [E]ven those who are not received by their husbands remain bound; they cannot take other husbands. But what if a wife is wanton, or otherwise incontinent? Would it not be inhuman to refuse her a remedy if she constantly burns with desire? I answer that when we are prompted by the infirmity of our flesh, we must have recourse to the remedy. After that, it is the Lord's part to bridle and restrain our affections by his Spirit, though matters should not succeed according to our desire. If a wife should fall into a lengthy illness, the husband would not be justified in looking for another wife. Similarly, if a husband should, after marriage, begin to labor under some distemper, his wife would not be allowed to change her condition of life.[32]

There was a rather blurry line between automatic annulment of a new marriage where one party proved sexually dysfunctional, and automatic perpetuation of a longstanding marriage where a spouse once capable of intercourse later became incapacitated. Calvin did little to clarify the line. Beza did, favoring perpetuation of any such marriage, and allowing for annulment only

---

32. Serm. and Comm. 1 Cor 7:11. See also Lect. Mal. 2:14, where Calvin writes: "The bond of marriage is indeed in all cases inviolable, even between the old, but it is a circumstance which increases the turpitude of the deed, when any one alienates himself from a wife whom he married when a girl and in the flower of her age: for youth conciliates love. We also see that when a husband and his wife have lived together for many years, mutual love prevails between them to extreme old age, because their hearts were united together in their youth."

if the sexually active party sought it within a few months of the wedding and (obviously) only if the couple lacked children.[33]

Consistory Cases

The Consistory and Council dealt with several cases of sexual dysfunction and dissolved both engagements and marriages when they found indisputable evidence of this impediment.

In a 1556 case, for example, the Consistory annulled the engagement of a fourteen-year-old young woman, Françoise Chastellain, who had a debilitating "hump" that would preclude pregnancy and perhaps even intercourse (**Doc. 8-17**). Françoise had consented to the union. Her father had approved the match, and executed a prenuptial contract with her fiancé and his family. Françoise's father now insisted that the Consistory allow the marriage to go forward. The Consistory decided not only that the woman was too young to be married now, but also that her "hump" was an impediment to marriage.

Issues of sexual dysfunction were more commonly raised in cases of adultery and divorce. It was a common defense in adultery cases for the philandering husband or wife to plead that a spouse's repeated sexual spurning had driven them to test another's bed. In a few cases, this defense to adultery was raised to a counterclaim that the spouses had never consummated their marriage, and that the sexually healthy spouse had been forced to resort to sex with a third party. This raised three nice legal questions: (1) whether the non-consummated union was, in fact, a marriage; (2) whether the party's philandering was simple fornication (which was less serious) or adultery (which was far more serious); and (3) whether the dispute should be resolved by annulment or divorce, which had dramatically different implications for the party's rights to marital property, child custody, and remarriage.

An excellent example of these legal niceties was raised in an intricate case involving Girard and Janon Favre (**Doc. 8-18**). Janon was a rather spirited soul who spent a good bit of time in the Consistory docket answering various charges of sin and crime. She was first summoned on charges that she had defamed a minister in Russin and also quarreled with her mother. During this hearing, Janon also came to be questioned whether she had been sexually intimate with her cousin-german, Pierre, who lived outside of Geneva. She denied any fornication with Pierre. Indeed, she claimed that she had enjoyed no sex whatsoever, including with her husband Girard.

This latter claim piqued the Consistory's interest. They called several wit-

33. Beza, TRD, 2:73-75.

nesses, including Girard's parents and servants, to investigate this charge. They sent several subpoenas to Girard. When he finally appeared, Girard protested that he and Janon had indeed had sex several times. Janon persisted in her claim that their marriage was never consummated, and testified further that Girard had told her that he would never have sex with her. Girard eventually conceded this. The Consistory ordered them to live "decently" as husband and wife. Calvin, the notary reports, "gave them strong remonstrances," no doubt about their respective marital duties.

A month later, the Consistory summoned the couple again to investigate whether they had had sexual intercourse in the interim. No, was the answer, though they testified that they still loved each other. They were banned from the Lord's Supper, and told to try again. Janon was further instructed to avoid Pierre, her cousin-german.

More than a year later, the Consistory summoned the couple again. They now charged Janon anew with sexual impropriety with Pierre as well as with beating her husband Girard. Girard protested that he and Janon had, in the interim, had sexual intercourse, and that there was no truth to the rumors of her fornication with Pierre. Janon denied the fornication, too, as well as the charge of beating Girard. An exasperated Consistory sent the case to the Council for appropriate criminal punishment.

Nine months later, the Consistory summoned Janon yet again, now charging that she had not only renewed her affair with her cousin Pierre but had produced an illegitimate child. When Janon again denied the affair, the Consistory sent the case to the Council for criminal investigation and punishment. The Council imprisoned Janon, and she and her husband were closely investigated, perhaps using torture which was not uncommon in such cases.[34] The Council found that Girard and Janon had never had "carnal company" with each other, but that Janon had enjoyed such company with her cousin-german Pierre, who had been married throughout the affair. The Council found further that Janon had given birth to Pierre's illegitimate child, but the child had since died.

In the Council's judgment, these facts easily supported a case for "divorce" — though it treated the situation more as an annulment than a divorce. The Council's stated grounds for the divorce was not Janon's betrayal of Girard but rather her "adultery with her cousin [Pierre] Jeute who is married." Noting that Girard and Janon "have been married for ten years without having each other's company," Janon was given permission to remarry after the divorce and after serving the criminal punishment for her adultery. She would have faced a far grimmer fate, perhaps execution, had this been a typical case of divorce on account of her repeated adultery and illegitimate pregnancy.

34. See Kingdon, AD, pp. 25-26, 84-88, 120-38.

What makes the case peculiar, however, is that Girard, too, was given permission to remarry. This was not consistent with a judgment that he had permanent sexual dysfunction. The Consistory and Council may have determined that Girard had sexual problems only with Janon, not in general.

Most cases were not nearly so complicated, nor so trying of the Consistory's patience.[35] In a more typical case in 1547, Martin Favre sought to divorce his wife Antoine for her adultery (**Doc. 8-19**). Antoine countered that she and Martin had never had sexual relations. Perhaps fearing a replay of the protracted Girard and Janon Favre case, the Consistory sent this case immediately to the Council. There Martin testified that his wife left him after a month and slept around. Antoine admitted her desertion and adultery, but insisted that Martin "lacked the powers of a man." The Council showed little sympathy. They granted Martin a divorce and the right to remarry. They barred Antoine from any sexual relations or remarriage on pain of whipping. While the divorce was still pending, Antoine was found in hot pursuit of another man with whom she had already had an affair. The authorities lost what little sympathy for her they had left. They now not only barred her from remarriage but banished her from the city altogether.

Disparities of Age

Though the Marriage Ordinance was silent on the subject, Calvin and the Consistory devoted a considerable amount of time and energy to discouraging, and sometimes annulling, engagements between parties with wide disparities in age. This was surprising. After all, Calvin and the Consistory did not consider differences of faith to be impediments to engagement or marriage — despite considerable biblical and traditional support for them.[36] Differences of age would seem to be even less of a concern — particularly since there was little biblical or traditional support for treating these as impediments. Yet, adducing "the order of nature," and "common decency," Calvin pressed for this impediment, and the Consistory sometimes annulled engagements between parties of widely disparate age, particularly if there were other aggravating circumstances.

Calvin's Views

Calvin revealed his concerns about age disparity in an early letter of 1540 (**Doc. 8-20**). Calvin was serving as pastor in a small church in Strasbourg at the time

35. See examples in Seeger, pp. 353-55.
36. See Chapter 10.

but visiting abroad. His deacon Nicolas Parent reported to Calvin that in his absence one of their younger congregants, Mathias, a former monk and evidently a formidable soul, had secretly married a seventy-year-old widow. The two were apparently now cavorting rather freely in public. In his reply letter to Parent, Calvin described this as a "scandal" that defied belief. It would be one thing for an elderly woman to court and marry an elderly man for mutual comfort and security.[37] It was quite another thing for her to marry a young man, apparently for physical pleasure. Ideally, the couple should be severely reprimanded, Calvin argued, though that might induce them to divorce as rashly as they got married, which would only compound the scandal. Calvin thus encouraged a strong pastoral word to the couple, which Parent found occasion to offer.

Not only should elderly women not marry young men, but elderly men should not marry young women. "If a decrepit old man falls in love with a young girl," Calvin wrote as late as 1563, "it is because of his base and shameless lust. He will defraud her if he marries her."[38] So firm was Calvin in this teaching that he risked his life-long friendship with Farel to oppose the elder Farel's marriage to a young woman.[39] Farel had helped Calvin find a wife twenty years before.[40] Farel, though not without ample opportunities for marriage, had seemed content to remain a bachelor for life. But in 1558, at the ripe old age of sixty-nine, Farel proudly announced his intention to marry a "respectable woman," Marie Turol, a refugee from Rouen who had moved to Neuchâtel, where Farel lived. Marie, however, was some four decades younger than Farel. To complicate things further, Farel had invited the destitute Marie and her son to lodge in his pastoral home right across the road from the church, until they could find a place of their own. When Farel told Calvin of his pending marriage to Marie, Calvin sought to dissuade him. But, if Farel insisted on getting married, he should at least publish the banns quickly to avoid compounding the seeming scandal. Farel, who was still traveling a great deal, took his time and began to plan a public wedding. This caused no small amount of rumor-mongering in the community and beyond as a local chronicler reported; this embittered Farel deeply (**Doc. 8-21**). Farel sent Calvin a formal invitation to his wedding. In a tart and dismissive letter to Farel of Sep-

---

37. The remarriage of widows and widowers is treated at length in a sequel volume. See also Lect. Joel 1:8, where Calvin writes: "The love of a young man towards a young woman, and so of a young woman towards a young man, is more tender than when a person in [his early] years marries an elderly woman."

38. Comm. Harm. Law Exod. 21:13.

39. David N. Wiley, "Calvin's Friendship with Guillaume Farel," in *Calvin Studies Society Papers 1995, 1997* (Grand Rapids, 1998), pp. 187-204, at pp. 202-4; *Guillaume Farel: Biographie nouvelle par un groupe d'historiens* (Paris, 1930), pp. 673ff.

40. See Chapter 3, Docs. 3-3 to 3-6.

tember, 1558 (**Doc. 8-22**), Calvin said he was too busy to attend. Even if he were available, he would not attend the wedding since he still strongly disapproved of the marriage, and since he feared that others would think he condoned Farel's scandalous conduct.

At the same time, a distressed Calvin wrote to the company of ministers in Neuchâtel urging them to see whether Farel's ill-advised engagement could be properly annulled (**Doc. 8-23**). The Neuchâtel Consistory was considering whether they could unilaterally annul Farel's engagement to end the scandal. Calvin advised against this. It was improper to dissolve engagements without cause, and to do so in this case would only encourage people to think that ministers were somehow above the new Protestant laws of marriage, indeed "a law unto themselves." A proper ground for annulment had to be found. Even great disparity of age, as in this case, was not a sufficient ground by itself to order the annulment against the wishes of the couple. Calvin urged his Neuchâtel colleagues to look harder for an impediment. Perhaps it could be viewed like other marriages that are "contrary to the order and seemliness of nature" and thus annulled? Perhaps this could be seen as a case involving a mentally unstable party? After all, six months ago, Farel never would have dreamed of such "silly" dalliance. Now, he seemed to have lost all sense. Perhaps that was reason enough to annul the engagement? The Neuchâtel pastors ultimately found no such grounds. The elderly Farel and the young Marie were married, much to Calvin's continued chagrin and at serious cost to Calvin and Farel's friendship.[41]

Consistory Cases

The Genevan Consistory treated these cases comparably. Disparity in age alone was not an impediment that could annul an engagement or marriage so long as both parties wished to go forward. Thus, when in 1557, Leonard Boulon sought permission to marry a woman less than half his age, the Consistory approved the match, assuming that she consented and there was no other impediment (**Doc. 8-24**).

If either party wanted out of such an engagement, however, the Consistory and Council showed no hesitation in ordering the annulment — and holding parties to it even if they later changed their minds and sought to be married after all. This was tantamount to making disparity in age an absolute impediment if invoked by either party. The general rule in Geneva was that a formal engagement could not be broken if one or both parties simply had a change of heart.

41. See Heiko A. Oberman, "Calvin and Farel: The Dynamics of Legitimation in Early Calvinism," *Journal of Early Modern History* 2 (1) (February, 1998): 32-60.

Now, a change of heart prompted by the disparity of age was enough to break the engagement permanently.[42]

Thus, for example, in a 1557 case the Consistory honored Thomas Lambert's request to annul his engagement to Jehanne-Marie, a widow nearly twice his age (**Doc. 8-25**). The couple had been properly engaged. They had twice had intercourse before the wedding. Sometime thereafter, Lambert had discovered that Jehanne was considerably older than he had thought. He had also learned that while married she had produced more than twenty children, who had been stillborn or died in their cribs before being baptized. When the Consistory confirmed that he was twenty-three and she around forty, Lambert asked if he could break off the engagement honorably. The Consistory recommended this to the Council. The Council annulled the engagement, though they also punished the couple for their fornication.

Lambert evidently rethought his position, for the couple appeared together before the Council the following month asking to have their engagement reinstated. The Council confirmed its decision, and now prevented the couple from getting re-engaged, let alone married.

The Consistory and Council overrode the wishes of engaged parties even more readily when they suspected foul play. This is evident in the case of the engagement of a seventy-year-old widow, Bartholomie, and her twenty-five-year-old servant, Ducreson (**Doc. 8-26**). The parties admitted to an earlier affair when Bartholomie had still been married. After her husband's death, the widow and her young servant became engaged. The Consistory suspected that he was after her money. They inquired closely into who had initiated the engagement. Ducreson said it was Bartholomie. She said it was the chambermaid. This same chambermaid had several times earlier encouraged Ducreson to marry a pretty girl in another household. She testified that Ducreson had responded that "there was no money" to be had from marrying the other woman.

That slip proved fatal to Ducreson's plans. The Consistory denounced this pending marriage as "against decency" and the "order of nature." They sent Calvin and two other ministers to the Council with a two-fold request: (1) to annul this engagement; and (2) to prepare a new statute that would prohibit marriages between parties who are not close in age, and between younger men and older women who are beyond child-bearing years.

The Council eventually annulled the engagement of Bartholomie and Ducreson, arguing that it had been contracted illicitly "for wealth" and not for "the chief objects of marriage, to have offspring or for generation, and other consolations." Such a marriage, the Council decreed, was "against God and should not be permitted." Bartholomie and Ducreson appealed this decision

---

42. See Seeger, pp. 329-31.

repeatedly, but the Council held firm and eventually threatened sanctions if the parties returned with another appeal. The couple then took their case to the Company of Pastors (the clerical bench of the Consistory). In a brief opinion, the Company confirmed that the union was permanently annulled.

The Council also ordered that a new statute be promulgated to prohibit all engagements and marriages between men and women with too great a disparity in age, particularly between younger men and older women who were beyond child-bearing age. No such law was forthcoming in Calvin's lifetime. The 1561 Marriage Ordinance was silent on the subject. When Beza summarized the prevailing marriage law of Geneva in 1569, he described engagements and marriages between parties with great disparities of age to be ill-advised but not illegal per se.[43] Age disparity eventually became an impediment in the 1576 version of the Genevan Marriage Ordinance.[44]

Summary and Conclusions

For Calvin and Beza, sexual intercourse was an essential part of marriage. Married couples were expected to retain a healthy sex life, even if they were not, or no longer, capable of having children. "Satan dazzles us . . . to imagine that we are polluted by intercourse," said Calvin.[45] But "when the marital bed is dedicated to the name of the Lord, that is, when parties are joined together in his name, and live honorably, it is something of a holy estate."[46] For "the mantle of marriage exists to sanctify what is defiled and profane; it serves to cleanse what used to be soiled and dirty in itself."[47] Husband and wife should not, therefore, "withhold sex from the other." Nor should they "neglect or reject" one another after intimacy or intercourse.[48] Couples may forgo their sexual obligations for a season, said Calvin echoing the traditional position on the "Pauline privilege." But such abstinence should occur only by mutual consent and only for a finite period — lest one party be tempted to adultery by too long a wait. The traditional option of voluntarily maintaining a sexless "spiritual marriage" was anathema to Calvin.

---

43. Beza, TRD, 2:125-126. But cf. Eugène Choisy, *L'État chrétien calviniste a Genève au temps de Théodore de Bèze* (Geneva, 1902), pp. 29-38, who describes the new legislation "sous l'influence de Calvin" including a provision on January 8, 1565 urged by Beza that stipulated the maximum disparity in age allowed between the parties. We have not been able to find this law of 1565, only a later amendment in the 1576 Ordinance.

44. The 1576 Ordinance included age disparity impediments. See SD, vol. 3, item no. 1183.

45. Serm. Deut. 5:18.

46. Serm. Deut. 22:13-19.

47. Serm. Deut. 5:18; Comm. 1 Cor. 7:6.

48. Serm. 22:13-19, 24:5-6.

This robust ethic of marital sex informed all four of the impediments of quality recognized in Reformation Geneva. This ethic was the obvious predicate for the impediments of sexual dysfunction and contagion. For both these conditions kept a couple from joining together in sexual intercourse. This ethic was also part of the rationale for the impediments of lack of virginity and age disparity. Lack of presumed virginity might well turn off a disappointed new husband; old age might well preclude a spouse from intercourse with a young new marital partner.

Each of these impediments of quality had further rationales as well. The real point of the impediment of lack of presumed virginity was not so much virginity as duplicity. There was nothing wrong for a man to seek a virgin for a wife, though, given his aversion to the medieval celebration of virginity, chastity, and celibacy, Calvin thought this quality unimportant. But it was scandalous for a woman to hold herself out falsely to her fiancé as a virgin. It was even worse for the woman to lose her virginity to another man after contracting her engagement — an offense Calvin found equally serious if committed by the engaged man. If the lack of presumed virginity was brought to the attention of the authorities shortly after the wedding day, the authorities would annul the new marriage. And if either engaged party was caught in "premarital adultery" with another, they were severely punished.

Concern for duplicity was also at work in the impediment of sexual dysfunction. Those who were eunuchs, frigid, or permanently unable to engage in sexual intercourse betrayed the fundamental nature and purpose of marriage. They were not capable of becoming "one flesh" in the expression of marital love and in the hope of having children. Beza went so far as to call a eunuch who married and sought to have intercourse with his wife "a fornicator," "even a murderer" in that he kept his wife from producing new life. If the healthy party brought the sexual dysfunction to the attention of the authorities either before or shortly after the wedding the Council would order an annulment. If the sexual dysfunction set in more than a few months after the wedding, however, the parties were required to live with this condition. The Consistory, however, was not above admonishing couples about their conjugal duties and calling them in occasionally to check on their love life.

The impediment of contagious disease was largely a health concern. Neither the healthy spouse nor the other members of the household should be exposed to the risk of mortal disease. Not only was this cruel, but it also risked making children wards of the state when their parents died. Those with known and permanent contagious disease, therefore, could not marry, and, if they tried, their putative marriages were involuntarily annulled. Those who were inflicted with contagious disease after the wedding could separate themselves from their spouse and children, though the marriage remained intact.

It is surprising that Calvin and the Consistory spent so much time and energy on disparity of age as an impediment. Age differences were of a different order of magnitude from issues of virginity, contagion, and sexual dysfunction, each of which raised serious inquiries about marital fitness. The Bible said very little about differences in age. Indeed, the Bible reports that Abraham, as a very elderly widower, took a young wife with whom he later produced six sons (Gen. 25:1-2). Having already made up his mind about this impediment, Calvin called Abraham's conduct "foolish" and "very absurd."[49] But why? Calvin indicated briefly his concerns about the younger spouse being "defrauded" and also adduced "natural order" and "common decency." But if Calvin's real concern was sexual dysfunction, there was already an impediment in hand to deal with that. If his concern was fraudulent exploitation of rich elderly widows or widowers (as in the case of Bartholomie and Ducreson in **Doc. 8-26**) why not deal with this instead with the impediment prohibiting "fraudulent inducement" to marriage, as the *ius commune* had done? Calvin did not say.

It is equally surprising that Calvin did not write this impediment into his 1546 Marriage Ordinance, especially since he had shown concern about the issue already six years earlier in his 1540 letter to Nicolas Parent in **Doc. 8-20**. Perhaps it slipped his mind. At the time, Calvin was writing statutes and theological tracts at a torrential pace. Or perhaps the thirteen parties who reviewed and revised Calvin's draft Marriage Ordinance objected to such an inclusion; after all, it was not uncommon for an elderly aristocrat in the day to marry a young maiden. The record leaves no clue, and Calvin left no reason.

---

49. See Comm. Gen. 25:2: "It seems very absurd that Abraham, who is said to have been dead in his own body thirty-eight years before the death of Sarah, should after her death marry another wife. . . . Abraham acted most foolishly, if after the loss of his wife he in the decrepitude of old age contracted another marriage."

8-1   Commentary on the Harmony of the Law
Leviticus 21:7-9, 13-15 (1563)[50]

[T]he priests' home must be chaste and free from all dishonor. At this time also God commands by the mouth of Paul that pastors should be chosen, who rule well their own houses, whose wives are chaste and modest, and their children well-behaved (1 Tim. 3:2; Titus 1:6). The same cause for this existed under the Law, lest those appointed for the government of the Church should be despised and looked down upon on account of their domestic vices. But God most especially had regard to the priesthood of Christ, that it should not be exposed to contempt. . . .

No law forbade private men from marrying a deflowered woman. What was permitted to the multitude, however, God condemned in the priests in order to withdraw them from every mark of infamy. And this reason is also expressed when he says that he would have the priests holy, because he has chosen them for himself. For, if the people had not respected them, all religion would have been contemptible. Therefore, in order to preserve their dignity, God commands them to take diligent heed not to expose themselves to ignominy. . . .

More is required in the high priest, namely, that he should not marry a widow. . . . [H]is wife, not having known another man, should manifest the modesty worthy of her station and quality of sacred honor. Some will object that the marriage of an old priest with a young girl was ridiculous and somewhat indecorous as well as liable to many inconveniences. I answer, that special regulations should be so expounded as not to interfere with general principles. If a decrepit old man falls in love with a young girl, it is a base and shameful lust; besides he will defraud her if he marries her. Jealousy and wretched anxiety will also arise. And, by foolishly and dotingly seeking to preserve his wife's love, he will cast away all regard for gravity.

When God forbade the high priest to marry any but a virgin, he did not wish to violate this rule about age, which is dictated by nature and reason. He desired that modesty and propriety should be maintained in the marriage, so that, if the priest were of advanced years, he should marry a virgin not too far from his own age. If he were failing and now but little fitted for marriage on account of his old age, the law that he should marry a virgin was rather an exhortation to celibacy than that he should expose himself to many troubles and to general ridicule.

50. CO 24:454-55 (OTC adapted).

8-2 Commentary on the Harmony of the Law
Deuteronomy 22:13-21 (1563)[51]

God provides against both cases: lest a husband should unjustly bring reproach upon a chaste and innocent young woman, and lest a young woman, having been defiled, should escape punishment by pretending to be a virgin. A third object is also to be noted, namely, that parents were thus admonished to be more careful in watching over their children. It is, indeed, an act of gross brutality that a husband should, wittingly and willingly, seek a false pretext for divorcing his wife by bringing reproach and infamy upon her. But it does not infrequently happen that the lustful become disgusted with their vices and then endeavor to rid themselves of them in every way.

It was thus necessary to correct this evil, and to prescribe a method whereby the integrity of the woman should be safe from the calumnies of an ungodly and cruel husband. It was equally just to give relief to an honest man, lest he should be compelled to cherish in his bosom a harlot by whom he had been deceived. It is a very bitter thing to ingenuous minds silently to endure so great an ignominy.

An admirable precaution is established here. If a woman was accused by her husband, it was in the power of her parents to produce the tokens of chastity which should acquit her. If they did not, the husband was not obliged against his will to keep her in his house after she had been defiled by another. It is plain from this passage that the tokens of virginity were taken on a cloth, on the first night of marriage, as future proofs of chastity. It is also probable that the cloth was laid up before witnesses as a pledge to be a sure defense for pure and modest young women. It would have been giving too much scope to the parents if it had been believed simply on their testimony. Moses speaks only briefly about this, for it was a well-known custom. . . .

[A husband's false charge against his wife] received a threefold punishment. First, he should be whipped for inventing the false accusation. Second, he should pay one hundred pieces of silver to the father of the girl. Third, he should never be allowed to put her away [by divorcing her per Deut. 24:1-4]. The reason given is "because he hath brought up an evil name upon a virgin of Israel." God here shows himself to be the protector of virgins, that young women may be the more encouraged to cultivate chastity.

---

51. CO 24:655-57 (OTC adapted).

8-3   Sermon on Deuteronomy 22:13-24 (1556)[52]

[I]f a girl has promised marriage, and she betrays the faith she has given, she not only pollutes her body and thus violates the temple of God, but she dishonors her husband, whose property she was. She steals the goods of another — goods that cannot be repaid either in gold or silver. She brings contempt upon a man for whom she should risk her life if there were need. Is it lawful therefore that this be tolerated? We note that when Our Lord wishes that girls who have promised marriage be stoned if they abandon themselves to a fornicator, it is because they have committed this outrage against their husbands and fiancés of not holding faith to them.

The male fornicator should be punished equally. Why? Because he has stolen the honor of another, and has acted against a holy and sacred promise. Forgers are punished. If anyone steals a public document or falsifies it he is severely punished; and is not marriage more important than a contract for a hundred écus, or a house, or a vineyard? It is a question of joining two human creatures for life and death. It is a question of a bond that God has established among us, so that utter confusion may be removed from this world and we may not be like brute beasts mingling together without discretion, but so a man may have his woman, and a wife her husband. If this is violated and abolished the whole order of nature is corrupted.

If we pretend to turn a blind eye and let all this go by, let us not deceive ourselves. For God will take a terrible vengeance for it. We see that it is not without cause that God punishes so severely fornication among women who have already promised or become engaged to a husband. If this is so, what will be done with a married woman? She was given to her husband to help him manage a household in the name of God. If she thus villainously gives herself to fornication, she not only steals her husband's honor and insults him, but she also steals the name of the family. She will have her lover, but his children will bear the name of her husband. In this manner, the goods and property of the legitimate children are stolen; behold the bastards who have what does not belong to them.

Do you not see that this is a much more vicious rebellion than if someone had broken open the door and the coffers, if someone had picked the lock and stolen everything, if someone had committed the most terrible robbery in the world? It is clear that this should be tolerated even less. The pagans knew this well. If we had only the Law of Moses we still ought to be greatly ashamed, when today adulterers are so pardoned and taken so little account of. But since the pagans teach us this lesson, and they followed a much better system than do

52. CO 28:45-53.

those who call themselves Christians today, I ask you, what testimony will this be against us on the last day? The blind have seen better than we do. . . .

But we always return to what we have said: that since this commandment concerning proper order is given to judges and magistrates, we should each be informed of our duty in order to labor carefully in our calling. If those who have the rod of justice in their hands permit fornication to persist and marriages to be corrupted, so that no faith or promise holds any longer, they will have to render an account for this before God.

8-4 Commentary on the Harmony of the Law Deuteronomy 22:23 (1563)[53]

[An] engaged woman is counted as a wife. And for very good reason, for she has plighted her troth. It is a sign of abandoned incontinency for the mind of a woman to be so alienated from the man to whom she is engaged, as to prostitute her virginity to another.

One who has been ravished, however, is not criminal. A woman is absolved if she is forced [to have sex] in a field. It is probable that she yielded unwillingly, since she was far from help. Although these terms were accommodated to the comprehension of a rude people, it was God's intention to distinguish [cases of] force from consent. Thus, if a girl was forced [to have intercourse] in a quiet part of a building, from where her cries could not be heard, God would undoubtedly have her acquitted, provided that she could prove her innocence by satisfactory testimony and conjecture.

8-5 Commentary on the Harmony of the Gospel Matthew 1:18-19 (1555)[54]

So far as respects marital fidelity, from the time that a young woman was engaged to a man, she was regarded by the Jews to be his lawful wife. When a "woman engaged to a husband" was convicted of being unchaste, the law condemned both of the guilty parties as adulterers: "the woman, because she did not cry out for help though she was in the city, and the man because he violated his neighbor's wife" (Deut. 22:23-24). . . .

"[Matt. 1:]19: "As he was a just man." Some commentators explain this to mean that Joseph, because he was a just man, determined to spare his wife.

53. CO 24:648-49 (OTC adapted).
54. CO 45:62-70 (NTC adapted).

They take "justice" as another word for humanity, or, a gentle and merciful disposition. But others more correctly read the two clauses in contrast with each other: that Joseph was a just man, but yet that he was anxious about the reputation of his wife. The justice that is here commended consisted in hatred and abhorrence of crime. Suspecting his wife of adultery, and even convinced that she was an adulterer, he was unwilling to hold out the encouragement of leniency to such a crime. . . . Joseph, therefore, moved by an ardent love of justice, condemned the crime of which he supposed his wife to have been guilty.

Yet, the gentleness of his disposition prevented him from going to the utmost rigor of law. It was a moderate and calmer method to depart privately, and move to a distant place. Hence we infer that he was not so soft and effeminate as to hide and promote uncleanness under the pretense of merciful dealing. He only mitigated stern justice, so as not to expose his wife to an evil reputation.

8-6   Theodore Beza on the Error of Virginity (1569)[55]

I accept error in quality if a woman through an error was promised in marriage as a virgin but turned out be defiled. Then I think the man cannot be forced to marry his fiancée. I know that the scholastics think differently, and the matter is also judged differently in many places. But in my judgment the contrary law we use in this Genevan church is based on very just reasons and the authority of God's Word. Doctor Philip Melanchthon also thinks the same.

First, God's Word is explicit and punishes this sort of defiled woman who puts herself forward as a virgin. She is subject to the same punishment of stoning as an adulteress. Thus [God's Word] already granted a divorce before sexual intercourse. The practice in Israel was that upright and honorable men were also bound to make public any deception that they had discovered, including copulation. This is made quite clear from those words which Matthew reports about Joseph: "Being a just man, he resolved to divorce her quietly" (Matt. 1:19), since otherwise he could get into a legal battle with her, not without shame and danger to her.

Then there is that explicit warning by the Emperor Leo, "for very serious reasons." I certainly think that here a similar argument may be put forward that Ulpian stated regarding a contract of purchase: "If I thought I was buying a young girl when she was already a woman, the sale is valid, but in a way that the seller is bound for the amount involved." I determined that the sale was valid in this case because the matter itself showed that the loss could be made good by the seller. What happens, then, when the loss cannot be added up or paid back,

---

55. Beza, TRD, 2:87-89.

as happens in the sort of cases we are dealing with? Who will ever add up the difference between sex with a chaste virgin and a prostitute? Thus it is very fair to claim that the contract is invalidated by a contrary reason and to punish most severely the person behind the trickery. Therefore the same Ulpian elsewhere openly claims that in the sale itself if anybody thought that he had bought himself a virgin, and after the woman showed up [he realized] the seller knowingly allowed him to err, the sale is not canceled for this reason, but the action to roll back the purchase depends upon the thing sold so that the woman is returned when the price is repaid. Hence if it is established that the husband was not deceived willingly or by crass negligence and that nothing showed up later about somebody from whom the spouse is rightly presumed to have later acquired knowledge of the matter and who could not have persuaded the husband to renounce his legal right, we in this church usually judge that the husband cannot be forced to consummate the marriage since his consent was restricted to a virgin.

But if the woman is also found to be pregnant from another man, we do not force the spouse to marry her since this seems shameful and intolerable in a Christian church for a pregnant woman to be married to somebody else.

8-7   Case of Jean Bolliet and Pernete (1544)[56]

(May 8, 1544). Jean Bolliet; Pernete, wife of Jean Bolliet; the mother of Jean Bolliet, miller.

Because son promised himself to a woman. Answers that this is not a possible thing because he was never told anything about her having misbehaved. And afterwards they did not tell him, and he asked eighty florins, and Durant wanted to give him forty. And indeed before day he swore faith, and they wanted to give him, as they said, eighty florins, and afterwards he was told she was pregnant and wanted to make an agreement with him. And at supper at Pierre Damour's house they spoke of the forty florins, and afterwards found that he did not want her thus and only stayed for the money. The mother answers that he may do what he wishes and that they tried to marry her to someone else. Jean answers that he does not want her and that he reconsidered since, and if they had been content to give him money he was content, and now he would rather abandon everything than take her, and he was content then for forty florins to have the woman and the child.

On these responses the Consistory advises that, since he was agreeable in

---

56. R. Consist. I, 195-96, translated in Robert M. Kingdon et al., eds., *Registers of the Consistory of Geneva in the Time of Calvin* (Grand Rapids, 2000), 1:392-93

the first place and afterwards consented, that he not be compelled. And as for the forty florins, if the marriage could be confirmed to avoid scandal, if he has not obtained a guarantee of the forty florins, unless he wants to come of his own good will.

Pernete, daughter of Francois Milliaud of Jussy, his promised wife, Durant's servant. Answers that she does not know how much she promised him, and it was at her master's at supper, and her master, and her brother and sister were present. She had spoken to her said master and no one had spoken to him. She told her master that this Bolliet would be good for her in order to hide her shame. And at this supper she swore faith to him and her brother gave him eighty florins. And if it pleases God and the Council she would like him well, and he would mistreat her afterwards and spend the money he would be given.

The advice of the Consistory is that Jean be recalled. If he intends to take her let him say so, and let her master and her and the husband, Bolliet, be summoned. Bolliet answers that it is not possible for her to be his and his heart is not in her, and even if he were given twice as much he would not want her. And if he were forced he would leave the place and would leave her to herself. And therefore it is ordered that he does not want it and that all four be summoned. Claude Durant, Bolliet, and Pernete. Their lordships of the Consistory advise that they be remanded to Monday to the Council. Claude Durant answers that he informed Jean Bolliet, and he wanted to give her at supper and Bolliet did not want her, and she was pregnant when he spoke to him, and Pernete urged him to swear faith to her. All three are remanded to Monday.[57]

8-8   Case of Pierre Chevallier and Claude Gra (1557)[58]

(Nov. 11, 1557). Pierre Chevallier of La Muraz and Claude, daughter of Jaquemo Gra of Lullier, living in the Grand Mézel, his fiancée, appeared. Asked about their case, Claude said that Chevallier, after becoming engaged to her, had the company of another woman, whom she thinks was his first fiancée. Chevallier answered that it is true that he had the company of another woman in the Vaud region, but he did not promise her marriage. It is also true that he had a son by her whom she nursed, and Chevallier left him with her. She promised to nurse

---

57. On May 12, 1544, Jean Bolliet asked the Council to annul his promise of marriage with Pernete Milliaud, denying at first having known that she was pregnant by Durant and then confessing he did not want to marry her because Durant could not give him the forty florins he had promised him. The Council acknowledged the validity of the marriage and named two arbiters to resolve "amiably" the question of the forty florins (R. Conseil 38:196v).

58. R. Consist. XII, 115, 119.

him provided [that she received] three gold écus, which he gave her. They then separated. He displayed a mutual and reciprocal letter of release to this effect recorded by [the notary] de Domo, dated the second of November, the present month, and contracted between him and the girl by whom he had this bastard. He also produced an affidavit signed by the vicar of La Muraz dated the first of November, the present month.

Decided: that he state the place where he had her company. Answered that it was in the house of [Nicolas] and [Françoise] Gentils in Beguin. Asked whether he has been registered as an *habitant*, he answered not yet.

Decided: that de Domo, who recorded such a release, be remanded here, also the witnesses who testified for him before the Council, that is Mermet Leconte and Humbert Carrier, to state the position to them and give them strict remonstrances for meddling in the affairs of Chevallier who has not been registered as an *habitant*. Also to remand the parties before the Council and ask them to purge their city of such people.

[On November 15, Calvin appeared before the Council and urged that they order Chevallier and Gra to leave the city and not to return without permission. Leconte, his wife, and Carrier were admonished for their involvement as witnesses. Furthermore, the Council ordered the notaries summoned so as to forbid them to record such releases from promises of marriage, in particular de Domo, who recorded this one.]

(Nov. 18, 1557). Egrege Martin de Domo, notary, appeared according to the remand. He was given strong remonstrances because of the mutual and reciprocal release he recorded, contracted between Pierre Chevallier of La Muraz and a woman by whom he had an illegitimate son. Henceforth he was to take care not to record such releases anymore, neither he nor the other notaries, since our Lords have prohibited them.

8-9 Case of Pierre Butin and His Fiancée Claude (1547)[59]

(Jan. 27, 1547). The minister of Jussy [Jean de Saint-André] said it is true that there is enough evidence of fornication committed by a widow named Claude Du Soys of Gy, who is at present pregnant. . . .

Remanded here for Thursday, and inform the castellan of Jussy of this; the syndic accepted this duty.

(Feb. 17, 1547). Claude, widow of François Guyon of Gy, was admonished to confess the truth about the rumor that she fornicated and wanted to oppose [the marriage of] someone who was married who had fornicated with her from

59. R. Consist. III, 10, 20, 27, 50, 83.

which she was now pregnant. She denied it in Consistory, and said the procurator fiscal or his servant and the clerk of the place, who is Delecta, incited and solicited her to say that she was pregnant by Mammard de L'Horme, as did Monsieur de Saint-André, the minister of Jussy. She was admonished that the thing will become obvious in time. She was asked again whether she did not say she was pregnant by Mammard. She still said no, and will submit to whatever [punishment] pleases the Council.

Decided: that considering that she [is to be] remarried, that the Council be informed tomorrow so that the information can be obtained about what she denies before she has her wedding.

(March 3, 1547). Claude, widow of François Guyon of Gy, was admonished to tell the truth about what she denied here last time, being pregnant by Mammard de L'Horme. Again, she denied it. She also denied having been in Collonges-sus-Bellerive to get married and that the minister of the place did not want to marry them because they did not bring her banns, pretending they had lost them on the road, and they were forbidden to have them because she was suspected of being pregnant, as she was admonished above. She answered concerning what she had said in seeking to oppose the marriage, that she was pregnant by Mammard de L'Horme; that one is often compelled to say things that are not so, of which one repents, and one does not think that it will become such a big issue. She also denied that she sleeps with her husband [that is, her fiancé].

(March 3, 1547). Pierre Butin of Collonges-sus-Bellerive, who is engaged to the aforesaid [Claude], was [questioned] about the above, why they have not married. He answered that there was an objection [raised to the marriage]. Asked whether he does not know she is pregnant, he answered that he knows nothing about it, but if she is, he still wants her as she is. He was asked about his confession, whether anything was promised to him if she was pregnant. He denied it, but did confess that he had indeed heard that she was pregnant.

She was called again so she might acknowledge her faults. She is still deceitful and does not want to confess the truth. She confessed that her brother, who is named Jean Du Soys, and her cousins are named Martin and Claude Du Soys, who wanted her to be engaged when she wanted to marry in Collonges. The aforesaid [Pierre Butin] was asked who promoted this marriage. He answered it was Gabriel Pasteur and Jean Moche, his neighbors.

Decided: that she be remanded before the Council with the evidence and confession.

[On March 7 the Council ordered the castellan of Saint-Victor to imprison Claude. The castellan remanded her to the Consistory after punishing her.]

(April 7, 1547). Claude, widow of François Guyon of Gy, has been remanded by the castellan after having been punished because she formerly denied that she was pregnant by Mammard de L'Horme and at present confesses it. She was admonished as to whether she repents.

Mammard de L'Horme has been remanded for the reasons as above. He confessed having had knowledge of the woman and did not show any sign of repentance.

Decided: considering that it is not clear that he repents for his faults, let Communion be forbidden him and let him present himself here in Consistory the week before Pentecost to learn whether he repents. And give her ample remonstrances, especially because she lied the last time she was here.

(May 26, 1547). Mammard de L'Horme of Gy was remanded to return here before receiving Communion; whether he would show better repentance for his faults, that he did not show repentance. He begged mercy of God.

8-10 Theodore Beza on Diseases Contracted Before Marriage (1569)[60]

What if either before or after the engagement, but without the marriage as yet being really consummated, some sickness is detected in one's partner which does not fully take away the use of the body but passes on an incurable contagious disease and is so vile that one partner rightly shrinks from any contact with the other partner? I respond that when it has been properly determined that the disease is clearly contagious and incurable, as is elephantiasis, then the promises to marry are to be invalidated, with the parties revoking them. God, as if he himself were the author, steps between promises of this sort. For, who in the end, would carry out a marriage that he cannot possibly enjoy, but rather would kill both himself and other citizens? Lastly he would beget children for lifelong misery and the country's detriment. Therefore this is not separating what God has joined together but rather blocking from going forward something which began by being wrongly joined together contrary to God's will.

But you will ask, "What should be done with them meanwhile?" Clearly, the healthy person should have the power of another marriage. But the magistrate will command the sick person to abstain from all marital union and at the same time provide a setting where he or she may live out agreeably whatever is left of life in isolation from other people. A caring pastor should console the same person and encourage him or her to pray for the gift of continence out of the faith because it is certain that the person from whom God has taken away the power of performing the marriage act in good conscience is called to a life of celibacy. . . .

60. Beza, TRD, 2:96-98 (translated by John P. Donnelly, S.J.).

But what if the disease will not have been contagious, although still incurable and so foul that the one person rightly abhors contact with the other? If this sort of problem should overtake the spouses, since it is hardly probable that if such a sickness was known previously, any one would be found who would want to use this condition, I should think here that both should be advised that they would prefer to voluntarily renounce their right rather than go forward to that union in which there is hardly any hope that they will live comfortably. If they agree to this advice, or at least one person demands his or her liberation, I would not doubt that the promises to marry should be annulled, as if God himself were the author [of the annulment], since it seems highly likely that God also makes void such a union. . . . But if both prefer to go ahead, then rightly, I think, they should in no way be impeded from also entering into the marriage itself as long as there is no suspicion of contagion.

Regarding sickness, even though long lasting but curable, or if some other trouble overtakes them such as one of them becoming lame, deaf, or mute, it does not seem that the promises to marry should be dissolved.

8-11 Calvin's *Consilium* on Contagious Disease in Marriage (1561)[61]

The subject you are asking about is very perplexing. Disease is not a proper cause for divorce, no matter what it is, and one party in a marriage remains bound to the other as long as the marriage remains firm. Paul urges both parties to give the good will that is owed by the husband to the wife and by the wife to the husband [1 Cor. 7:3].

We consider that the marriage bond is indissoluble, even if the wife is separated from the marriage bed. The question arises, however: If the husband contracts elephantiasis (which is commonly called leprosy), does this free the woman from her marital obligation? They say that men with elephantiasis may suffer from sexual craving and be unusually full of sexual desire, and the husband will use this as an excuse to say that he needs his wife.

If a man with elephantiasis has any sense of humanity, however, he will first refrain from injuring his wife and children and then take thought for the human race, to keep the contagion from creeping about more widely. He is caught in a situation where he cannot perform his duty as a husband or father and is even, in a certain way, an enemy to the public welfare. Unless he is overcome by a brutish sort of stupor, he should realize that he is loathsome to everyone and should hide himself away out of a sense of self-restraint.

We do not want to be cruel, and we do not venture to obligate the woman

---

61. CO 10/1:241-42, translated in *Calvin's Ecclesiastical Advice*, pp. 133-34.

to share a home and marriage bed with a husband who is forgetful of all the laws of nature. We feel that she must be allowed to live as a widow, after a legal investigation by judges has intervened. Meanwhile, she should continue to attend her husband and perform any duties she can, provided that he does not require of her anything virtually unnatural.

8-12   Case of Claude Fornier and Fiancée (1556)[62]

(Aug. 6, 1556). Toussant Aliet and his daughter and Claude Fornier, her fiancé [appeared]. Toussant presented a petition respectfully saying that he would like them [his daughter and her fiancé] to be divided and separated for the many reasons given in the petition, which is lengthy. Jaques [read: Claude], as described in the petition, has become very poor and is in a poor condition. He [Claude] excused himself [but said] he did not have the pox.

Decided: that considering that there is great physical damage and that he was only engaged, that he be remanded before the Council, and may it please them to have him examined, and if it is found that there is pox they may be separated.

[The Council found that Claude had developed *"verolle,"* a French word equivalent to English "pox" and usually meaning syphilis. They also found that Aliet was afraid his daughter would catch the disease if she married him. The Council decided that, since there was no evidence as to where Fornier was from or where he had been, and given his evident fornication, he should leave the city, his engagement being annulled.]

8-13   Commentary on the Harmony of the Gospel
Matthew 19:12 (1555)[63]

Christ distinguishes three kinds of eunuchs. Those who are so by nature or who have been castrated by men are debarred from marriage by this defect, for they are not men. He says that there are other eunuchs who have castrated themselves so that they may be more at liberty to serve God; these he exempts from the obligation to marry. It follows that all others who avoid marriage fight against God with sacrilegious hardihood, after the manner of the giants.

When papists urge the word "castrate" as if at their own pleasure men might lay themselves under obligation to continence, it is too frivolous. For Christ has

---

62. R. Consist. XI, 48v.
63. CO 45:532-34 (NTC adapted).

already declared that God gives continence to whom he chooses. A little later, he says that it is folly for any man to choose to live unmarried when he has not received this special gift [of continence]. This castration, therefore, is not left to free will. The plain meaning is that while some men are by nature fit to marry, though they abstain, they do not tempt God, because God grants them exemption.

8-14   Calvin's *Consilium* on Marriage of the Frigid and Eunuchs (n.d.)[64]

Christ clearly excludes from marriage those men who are frigid, and eunuchs to whom manhood has been denied. Being misled is thoroughly inconsistent with giving one's consent, and the marriage vow of a woman who thought she was marrying a [real] man cannot be regarded as binding. This deception completely overturns the nature and purpose of marriage. What is marriage except the joining of a husband and a woman, and why was it instituted except to produce children and to be a remedy for sexual incontinence? A woman who has been deceived should certainly obtain a divorce [technically, an annulment] when her case has been heard and well examined. There is no need to rescind the marriage, because it was null from the beginning. It is enough to state that a man who was not suited for marriage wrongfully and with wicked guile deceived a woman to whom he could not be a husband, and that therefore the contract which could not be kept by both parties was without effect and null.

8-15   Theodore Beza on Invalidity of Marriage for Eunuchs (1569)[65]

[N]one of those purposes for which God has ordained marriage applies in a union of this sort [involving eunuchs]. Procreation is the first reason why God established marriage. But not only are no persons conceived of such unions, but even in a certain terrible respect many persons are destroyed. For a eunuch introduces his seed to a woman ineffectively; so much so, that they should consider such a man not only a fornicator but even a murderer. Although there is great sin in fornication, yet it is not a sin directly against nature, but only a form of disorder. A second reason for marriage is that it is as a remedy for lust and incontinence. But violent desire, far from extinguished, is actually inflamed to the utmost [by such fruitless unions]. An additional reason [for marriage], which

---

64. CO 10/1:231-33, translated in *Calvin's Ecclesiastical Advice*, p. 122.

65. Theodore Beza, *Tractatio de repudiis & divortiis* (Geneva, 1569), pp. 254-56. We could not find this passage in the corrected 1610 edition from which we have drawn other excerpts.

some assert, is [the sharing of] domestic duties. While this reason appears to have some validity here, yet it is demonstrably vain and worthless. For how likely is it that such a man or woman will be able thus to cohabit together as one, just as if they had been granted the gift of continence? Therefore since these are the three legitimate reasons for marriage, none of which applies in these unions we are discussing, it justly follows that a marriage of this sort is void. Those who have been joined with such infamy and by such a monstrous crime of homicide clearly should rightly be judged intolerable.

One may object that in the case of sterility in one or both parties the first reason given above does not apply. I answer, first, that sterility is an inner defect and one detected not by the senses, but rather by trial and experience. I add, next, that sterility, although not always in fact curable, is nevertheless legitimately presumed to be curable. I say, further, that even though from the union of the sterile nothing is born, nevertheless it is to some extent a natural union, to which at least the second reason for marriage applies. These arguments show that the marriage of the sterile should be considered a very different matter from that of the castrated. . . .

8-16   Theodore Beza on Impediments of Sexual Disability (1569)[66]

What we have said . . . applies for a completely similar reason to all those impediments which render one person completely unable to fulfill a promise to marry, such as incurable paralysis and what utterly exhausts the body — incurable impotence or the absence of the genital organs or a very serious wound necessarily involves permanent inability to have coitus. Promises to marry contracted by persons already affected by any disease of this sort are completely invalid since those cannot be seen as having been called to marriage by God who are unable to fulfill the pledge made in their promise to marry with this natural impediment standing in the way.

But if the same trouble overtakes an engaged couple who still have not yet actually consummated their marriage, I think the same as about madness, namely that this sort of promise to marry is invalidated, as if God himself were so commanding, as if he were clearly showing by this permanent impediment being set in place that such promises to marry did not please him. . . .

[I]f perchance continence pleases them both, from where finally did the false image of marriage [come]? These fellows [the medieval canonists and scholastics] will give us new Josephs and new Marys, or other people more pure than the great Augustine. . . . This is pure papist trash.

66. Beza, TRD, 2:87-89, 93-95 (translated by John P. Donnelly, S.J.).

8-17   Case of François Chastellain (1556)[67]

(Jan. 2, 1556). François Chastellain and Françoise his daughter, from Cartigny, were admonished that there has been a scandal because he is engaged to a girl, who is very young, and has a friend who lives at François's house. He said that it is about fifteen months since the castellan promised to proclaim their banns and that the girl is fully fourteen and is hunchbacked [or has a tumor].[68] Admonished that this is difficult to believe, given the bodily development of the girl.

Decided: that on Thursday they return here and that he bring his friend and any witnesses he may have to [attest to] her age.

(Jan. 9, 1556). François Chastellain, his daughter, and Jaquemo Fontanne of Russin, her fiancé, Enard Chastellain, Mauris Chastellain, and Ami de La Fontanne, brother of fiancé, appeared. Following Thursday's decision, Jaquemo said that it is about a year or fifteen months since by the advice of his relatives he signed documents about a piece of land of his in Russin to give it to his [prospective] father-in-law, who will give him all his after his death, and he intends no deceit. This his brother Ami confirmed. Enard said he believes it is true, and he wanted to confirm that the [prospective] bride is about fourteen. Mauris [said] that his wife looked after her, she being . . . hunchbacked, and that the castellan approved such a marriage.

Decided: that considering that the castellan acted too casually, let the Council be informed about it. It seems right that it would be good to forbid them to associate, and meanwhile the promise should be declared void, and if a year from now they agree, the marriage may be carried out and such a distribution of goods be made, considering their ages.

8-18   Case of Girard and Janon Favre (1545-1547)[69]

(Nov. 5, 1545). Janon, daughter-in-law of [Pierre] Favre [and wife of Girard Favre was summoned]. She was asked whether once when people were throwing stones at Master Louis, the minister of Russin, she did not say to her husband: "It's God who sends him these stones," along with certain statements that it was for his sins of wanting to take away their games. She was admonished to take care from now on to live more decently and honorably.

She was asked about certain words she had with her mother and whether

---

67. R. Consist. X, 81, 83.

68. The word *"bossé"* had a variety of meanings; it might mean that she had the pox or had a tumor or any other sort of swelling, but "hunchbacked" is the most common meaning.

69. R. Consist. II, 7v, 10, 12v, 13, 21, 97v; R. Consist. III, 146, 157, 161, 175, 189.

her mother did not draw a knife on her. She was also asked whether she said to her mother, who admonished her, that she was not doing anything her mother had not done. [Janon] denied it. Asked whether a young man named Pierre Jeute was her lover, she denied having had his company. She said she has been seven years with her husband and has never had the company of a man, neither of her husband nor of other men. Said she wanted to be examined [to see] whether she has ever had the company of a man.

Decided: that the castellan of Russin be told to impose the fine [for offending] against the edicts, and as for Janon, that she return here with her husband next Thursday. Asked to recite the Lord's Prayer, she said it fairly well.

(Nov. 12, 1545). Janon de Russin was called. She had been remanded last Thursday with her husband because she stated it is seven years since she was married and said she had not had the company of any man whatsoever. She reaffirmed these words, saying it is true that when he married her he said he would never have a woman. François Servant [a Consistory elder] said in her presence that what she had stated was a lie, as he was told yesterday. He also stated that it is well known that she fornicates with Pierre Jeute. She was still resolute in her statement, and said that her husband did not want to come.

Decided: that the castellan of Saint-Victor be instructed to make the son of Pierre Favre of Russin come, because he must be heard to be better informed about the affair.

(Nov. 26, 1545). Richarde Favre, wife of Pierre Favre of Russin [and mother of Girard], appeared. She was asked why the son of her husband and her daughter[-in-law Janon] do not live together as was stated above last Thursday. She was also asked whether it is not rumored that Pierre Jeute has sexual relations with her daughter[-in-law]. She denied ever having heard it said. Asked whether she ever heard from her daughter[-in-law] that she did not have the company of her husband, she said no. She is very shifty. She also says that her husband cannot walk except around their house. She was told that on Sunday he went to gamble one or two leagues away from the village.

Decided: that the castellan of Saint-Victor be directed to investigate to learn whether the older Favre does not go out, as stated in the confession.

(Nov. 26, 1545). Girard Favre of Russin was called. He was asked . . . whether he had the company of his wife. . . and answered that he has many times had the company of his wife. The girl [Janon], the wife of Girard, was called, and admonished that her husband has had her company. She denied it. They were confronted with each other. The husband was asked to tell the truth about what he had already confessed. He took it back.

Decided: that the two parties, that is, the wife and her husband, be told to live together as a decent couple, and let them return here in two weeks to understand the affair better. And let her be forbidden to give occasion for talk about her and Pierre Jeute. Master Calvin gave them strong remonstrances.

(Dec. 24, 1545). Girard Favre of Russin and Janon of Russin, his wife, appeared. They were strongly admonished concerning the previous remand of last November 26 to learn whether they have had intercourse and had each other's company. They both said as above that they love each other as husband and wife. The wife was made to withdraw. Richard [i.e., Girard] was asked to say whether he has had the company of his wife. He denied having had the company of his wife. He is simple.

Decided: that she be spoken to; one can draw more from her than from Girard her husband who is simple. She was asked whether her husband has not had her company. She said yes. Richard [Girard] was brought in, who was asked to tell the truth. In front of her, Richard [Girard] again said no, and the woman was found to be a liar. They were also admonished as to why the father of Girard [Pierre Favre] has not appeared and come here. They said he is so old that it is not possible for him to come either on foot or on horseback. They were admonished that "the wedding lasts only three weeks" [a proverb meaning roughly, "the honeymoon is over"].

Decided: to instruct the castellan of Saint-Victor to try to get full information about the matters, also whether the father goes anywhere. And to forbid them both Holy Communion for this time and expressly to forbid her the company of Pierre Jeute.

(Dec. 16, 1546). Girard Favre of Russin was admonished as to whether after he was here he had the company of his wife. He said yes. Asked whether he did not say that he was not the master of his wife and that she fornicates with Pierre Jeute, he denied it, and [said] they are false reports. He does not want to tell the truth as he told it throughout the village.

His wife was admonished that her bad behavior and contemptuous treatment of her husband must continually be dealt with over again. She excused herself. She was admonished that she beats her husband but she denied it. . . .

Decided: that the affair be remanded to the Council, and to present the facts well in [a list of items of concern]. And that the Council command that they be made to behave well, and that they be informed about the matter.

[On December 23, 1546, the Council ordered the castellans of Peney and Saint-Victor to inquire into this affair, and if the accusations were verified, to imprison "the parties."]

(Sept. 22, 1547). Janon of Russin, maid of Jaquemo Jardy, was admonished because she has been here so many times and has always denied her fornication with Pierre Jeute, her cousin, until she was pregnant from it and convicted.

Decided: to inform the Council that the aforesaid [Pierre] is her relative, but it is not known in what degree. That the Council find out about it. Also to petition the Council concerning the punishment of fornicators.

[On September 26 the Council ordered the castellan of Peney to find out whether Janon was a relative of Pierre Jeute.]

(Oct. 13, 1547).[70] The castellan of Saint-Victor, Jean Lambert, [appeared] and stated that by command of the Council he obtained information about the fornication of a woman of Russin who has fornicated with her cousin-german who is named Pierre Jeute, who has been punished in Gex because he is a subject there.

Decided: that the Council be informed of the relationship.

[Janon Favre was imprisoned before October 24, when the Council ordered her husband summoned. On November 3 the Council register stated that she had been married nine years but had never had the "carnal company" of her husband and had instead fornicated with Pierre Jeute, by whom she had had a daughter who had died. On November 7 the Council decided a divorce could be declared between them and ordered the castellan of Saint-Victor to open a case against her.]

(Nov. 10, 1547). *Consistory decision:* Syndic Du Mollars stated that he is instructed by the Council to ask the advice of the Consistory as to how one should proceed in the punishment of a female prisoner who has had the company of a cousin of hers and never of her husband. [The questions are:] How one should proceed, whether and in what manner a divorce should be given, whether on behalf of the husband or the wife who has fornicated, and whether the fornicator may have her for a wife. . . .

The decision is that concerning the divorce, if the husband asks for it, there are grounds for its being granted to him, and also the ministers agreed to present and consult about it tomorrow in the congregation [that is, the Company of Pastors]. Afterwards they will inform the Council about it.

[On November 11, on the Consistory's advice, the Council ordered the couple separated and decided Janon should be "put in the collar," a type of pillory in Russin and banished from the lands of St. Victor.]

(Dec. 20, 1547). Girard Favre of Russin and Janon, his wife, was admonished as to whether he wants to take back his wife. He answered that, since she has committed such an act and has had a child by her cousin-german, he should not take her back. She shows great contrition, but states that her husband was the real cause of it, giving a certain reason and asking that consideration be given to her case.

Decided: that the matter is sufficiently clear to pronounce a divorce. Before the Council [with a recommendation] of divorce.

---

70. There are two entries with the same information; this is the second version, written in a different hand, which corrects the misstatements of names in the first.

[On December 27 the Council pronounced a divorce between Girard Favre and Janon "because she has had a child by Pierre Jeute, cousin-german of Girard, and committed adultery with Jeute who is married," for which she has been reproved and punished. Respecting Girard and Janon the Council found that "they have been ten years married without having each other's company." They were both given permission to remarry, but her case was ordered to be continued before the criminal courts.]

8-19   Case of Martin Favre and Antoine Favre Called Ponssonière (1547)[71]

(Dec. 15, 1547). Martin Favre, cutler, [has come] with a petition against his wife, asking for a divorce in the form of the petition. She answered that she was content with this, and that he is not a man for her. . . . [She also confessed] she never had his company.

Decided: that they be remanded before the Council. May it please them, with other fuller information they may [gain through] their confessions, that a divorce be declared.

[On January 5, 1548, Martin Favre requested a divorce of the Council by reason of his wife's adultery with "Claude La Suisse and others; and the thirty-fourth night after their marriage, she left him, and is nothing but a harlot." His wife admitted her guilt, saying that her husband lacked the "powers of a man." On January 9 the Council granted him a divorce with permission to remarry and commanded his wife Antoine "not to fornicate or marry in Geneva, under penalty of whipping."]

(Feb. 2, 1548). Claude La Suisse several times has rebelled and has not appeared when he was summoned. [We wish to hear] his repentance for fornication in the case of the Ponssonière [that is, Antoine]. He confessed it and acknowledged his fault, but said that since he came back from the wars she has kept after him. He begged that it may please the Council to forbid her to keep after him any more. . . .

Concerning the advice [previously given by the Consistory] the Council has asked of the Consistory after granting a divorce to the husband of the Ponssonière and to learn whether she may remarry in this place, the decision is that she should not remarry in this city, nor others in similar cases, but it would be good for the punishment also to include their banishment. She was admonished, having been remanded by the Council, in the presence of her husband, and remanded to to-morrow before the Council to announce the divorce to them.

71. R. Consist. III, 187, 206.

8-20 Letter to Nicolas Parent (December 14, 1540)[72]

What you say about the other man and the elderly woman was so extraordinary that I could not at first believe it. . . . There is not only the appearance of wantonness, which leads me to suspect that there is something wrong that has to be dealt with. But the man has also announced the marriage. I am utterly stupefied. It is certainly a scandal, which all the saints ought to hold in abomination. . . . [T]his silly woman is already seventy years old, and has a son old enough that she should be past the love-passage of married women. Had she only joined herself in marriage to some man of already declining years, she might have pretended that she sought something else than the delights of matrimony. [By marrying this young man,] she has now taken away not only every defense, but also every appearance of excuse. They thought that they laid their plans very cleverly when they took advantage of a secret marriage ceremony. But they have both learned, by experience, how dangerous a thing it is to trifle with God.

If you now ask me what your duty is in this matter, it is hard to know how to help you. I think that they ought to be severely reprimanded, unless we are willing to forego our duty. But this course is not without danger. We need to be extremely cautious, lest the couple, exasperated by us, take flight from each other with the same rashness by which they came together, and thus cause even greater scandal and more offensive profligacy. Therefore, unless you have some special occasion, I do not advise that you talk with the woman about this subject. But if you have a suitable occasion, you might tell her how displeased you are . . . and how very bitter and very sad this news is to me. . . .

P.S. When I was about to send away this letter, your other letter reached me in which you describe the wedding. You have certainly proved yourself a man of courage in having dared to approach Mathias, who does not easily suffer words of admonition, much less of rebuke. I rejoice, however, that he took it so well. Let us, therefore, be satisfied with this friendly counsel, without pursuing the interest of the Church any further. This example does admonish us to ensure that in the future nothing of a disorderly kind ought to be passed by.

8-21 Report on Farel's Marriage in *Annales Calviniani*[73]

This marriage was found very strange and unreasonable by most, and it seemed to them that since [Farel] had reached the age of sixty-nine without being

---

72. CO 11:130-32; Bonnet, Letter 58 (adapted).

73. Report by Christoph Fabri (or Libertet) in the Perrot mss. in Neuchâtel (copy in Bern), as reprinted in *Annales Calviniani*, CO 21:703, and translated in Cottret, pp. 253-54n.

bothered with marriage he could have dispensed with it, being on the brink of the grave. Farel was also much annoyed by the censures of his friends and the various rumors of the mob, who were ignorant of the causes that moved him. But having taken as a shield against all remarks the divine vocation that obliged him to do this now and the uprightness of his conscience, aiming at a good end and using legitimate means ordered by God, he made up his mind, considering these things and others, and all his friends later gave way to his arguments. And it has been the opinion of all ever since that in making such a marriage according as he was inspired by the Almighty (and it is very certain that people such as he have had extraordinary gifts and movements in their time) he proposed to himself to provide for his old age the proper and holy aid and solace, because of his weakness, by the means that God himself had ordered for man; and to make clear a formal disavowal of Roman celibacy, claimed to be necessary to salvation, since the grace of perpetual continence is not given to all or forever. And that not having a vocation to this or the requisite grace, [not to marry] is to oppose the ordinance of God and stubbornly displease and disobey him, and also to entrap one's soul in the toils of a perpetual torment and torture of the flesh, when this is not prevented by the power of a special grace.

8-22   Letter to Guillaume Farel (September, 1558)[74]

I told you to your face that I would not come either to your engagement or to your wedding, both because it was not possible to do, and because I judged it inexpedient. So I am surprised what your new invitation can mean. Even if I had the greatest desire to comply with your wishes, I am prevented by several causes. You know that [Pastor] Macaire is absent. Raymond [Chavet, Pastor] and another of my colleagues are still in their beds. The rest of us can scarcely meet the additional burden imposed on us. Certainly I cannot be absent without causing interruption to our meetings for public worship. In the current chaotic state of affairs, the Council would never permit me to withdraw any distance from the city. You see clearly then I [cannot] readily, and without serious losses, undertake a journey.

But, even if no obstacle stood in my way, my coming would afford an admirable handle for the ungodly and the badly disposed to vent their malice in speaking evil. You do not seem to have been prudent in inviting me, and I would not be acting with due consideration if I complied with your wishes. I wish you had rather followed the plan that you approved earlier, namely, to hasten your engagement, so that the marriage might have taken place at least im-

---

74. CO 17:335-36; Bonnet, Letter 516 (adapted).

mediately after your return. Now, by putting it off, I do not doubt that you have caused much secret talk, which will break out more freely afterwards. For you are much mistaken in thinking that the affair is quite a secret.

8-23 Letter to the Pastors of Neuchâtel (September 26, 1558)[75]

I am in such perplexity that I do not know how to begin my letter to you. It is certain that poor Master Guillaume has for once been so ill-advised that we cannot but blush for his weakness. But, as the matter stands, I do not see the possibility of applying to the evil such a remedy as, I hear, has been contemplated. For since there is no law which forbids such a marriage, to break it off when it is contracted is, I am afraid, beyond our power. We would thus certainly increase the scandal. Were this a case of a private person, I would be less at a loss about what to do. But in this case, what will the rumor-mongers say, and what will the simple think, but that the pastors want to have a law for themselves, that because of their profession they can violate the most indissoluble tie in the world? Although you intend something different, people will believe that the pastors are assuming a privilege above that of others, as if you were not subject to the law and the common rule.

Had people been informed in time of [Farel's intentions to get engaged], it would have been their duty to prevent this foolish enterprise as they would in a case of someone who has lost his mind. But to make matters worse, he acted so quickly that there are no easy means to undo the consequences of his fall.

Examine deliberately whether there is a suitable ground to annul an [engagement to] marriage which is already contracted. If it is alleged that such a promise, being contrary to the order and seemliness of nature, ought not to be kept, reflect whether this defect should not be tolerated like many others which cannot be remedied. Half a year ago our poor brother [Farel] would have declared that they should have bound like a madman the person who at so advanced an age desired to marry so young a woman. But since the deed is already accomplished, it is by no means so easy to annul it.

8-24 Case of Leonard Boulon and Wife (1557)[76]

(Nov. 25, 1557). Leonard Boulon, who is forty or fifty years old, stated that he would like very much to marry a girl, aged twenty, whom he presented. But he did not want to do it because of the difficulty that might result because of the

---

75. CO 17:351-53; Bonnet, Letter 515 (adapted).
76. R. Consist. XII, 121v.

difference in age. Boulon also said that he is from Saintonge and she from Norcier, and before doing this, he asks for permission.

Decided: that he be told that if there is no other impediment he may marry her.

8-25   Case of Thomas Lambert and Jehanne-Marie (1557)[77]

(April 22, 1557). Thomas Lambert was charged with having become engaged to a woman in this city and another in Brescia in Italy, and therefore there is fornication. He answered that he was, indeed, engaged to a woman in this city, but not to one in Brescia. It is true that, while staying in Brescia, he was a boarder in the house of a woman who lent him three écus.

Decided: that he and his fiancée must appear here on Thursday.

(April 29, 1557). Jehanne-Marie was charged that, when speaking of having children, she said that her body was entirely worn out. Asked to tell the truth about it and to state her age, she answered that she may well have said it. Concerning her age, she said that she does not know how old she is. To verify her honor and respectability, she produced as witnesses Guillaume Vignod and Huguette, his wife, and also Louis Febvre. Vignod said he has known her for twelve years; he does not know her to have a bad reputation. His wife and Febvre said likewise; they know nothing else.

Thomas Lambert and Jehanne-Marie, his fiancée, were called to learn from them the status of the marriage they have begun. Jehanne answered that they promised each other [that is, became engaged] in the presence of Lambert's mother and of her parents. Thomas Lambert, too, said they had promised to get married. He also said that, after the banns, he had twice had her company in bed in her house. Jehanne denied this, but when Lambert maintained it, she confessed it.

When questioned, Lambert said that after he became engaged to Jehanne, he heard she was a woman who was rather old, too old for him. He also heard that she has had twenty-two children who have not received baptism [that is, miscarried or died shortly after birth before baptism]. He thus asked for this [engagement] to be dissolved, if it could be done without dishonor.

Decided: in the first place, Communion be forbidden to them, then that they be remanded before the Council to Monday to be punished. As for the fornication and as for the claimed marriage, the Consistory is of the opinion that it should be dissolved, because Thomas is only twenty-three years old and Jehanne-Marie is forty.

---

77. R. Consist. XII, 35v, 38-38v.

[On May 3 the Council decided that the marriage should not be permitted because of the difference in age, as advised by the Consistory. Therefore it declared the engagement void and ordered that Lambert and Jehanne-Marie be punished for their fornication "according to our edicts and ordinances." Jehanne-Marie, with Lambert who had apparently changed his mind about the annulment, appeared before the Council on May 10 to petition that the marriage be permitted. But the Council confirmed its order of annulment, and the parties were forbidden to marry.]

8-26   Case of Bartholomie d'Orsières and Ducreson (1556-1557)[78]

(Dec. 31, 1556). Bartholomie and Ducreson were informed that a marriage between the two of them would be unequal. She could be at least [as old as] his grandmother, and Ducreson confessed that he was only about twenty-five years old. In this case, decency would not be preserved, since the order of nature that is preserved even among the pagans would be broken.

They answered that they intended to continue their marriage and live and die in that estate. Moreover, Bartholomie confessed that, during the lifetime of her late husband when he was in Lyon, she was once in Rigny with Ducreson. Ducreson also confessed that was true.

They were further asked which of the two had first spoken of their marriage. Ducreson answered separately that it was Bartholomie. She, when asked about this separately, answered that it was her chambermaid who spoke of it first, and made the agreement between the two of them. She further testified that when they became engaged Amy Verron and Ducreson's brother and de Courajau were present. [She also testified that] de Courajau had her solicit Ducreson three times about a pretty girl at Girardine's for him [to marry], but he did not want her, because there was no money.

By decision of the Consistory they were remanded before the Council, with an order that Calvin, Lullin, and Chiccant ask the Council in the name of the Consistory to command — to avoid the disorders that even the pagans would not endure, by which the order of nature would be overthrown — that women may not marry men who are not near their age, and also that those who are beyond an age for bearing children may not marry young men.

[On January 5 Calvin and company appeared before the Council, arguing that the marriage of a woman seventy years old with a man of twenty-six to twenty-seven was "a strange thing and against nature," and action should be

78. R. Consist. XI, 93, 96v. The last paragraph is the opinion from RCP (Hughes trans.), p. 321.

taken against it "both on this occasion and for the future." One of the castellans, who was related to Ducreson, appeared on his behalf to request that the marriage be permitted. The Council decided to put off the case for three days and meanwhile investigate how to proceed to prevent the marriage.]

(Jan. 7, 1557). Concerning what was stated to the Consistory by the syndic at the command of our most dread Lords concerning the proposed marriage between Bartholomie and Ducreson, it is ordered that the Consistory's decision be reduced to writing to be given to the Council.

[The Council took up this case again on January 8. On advice of the Consistory, the Council decided that such a marriage would be "against nature, and encourage fornication rather than the estate of marriage, which should be preserved in sanctity." Since it appeared that Ducreson sought marriage not for "the chief objects of marriage, to have offspring or for generation, and other consolations, but for wealth," the marriage was against God and should not be permitted. The couple appealed on January 11, but the Council confirmed its decision. On January 19 they requested that the case be brought before the Council of Two Hundred, but this was denied "because it is a matrimonial case" and not within that latter Council's jurisdiction. The couple appealed to the Council again on March 2, and the Council rejected them again, and threatened to put them in prison if they returned.]

[Bartholomie and Ducreson later took their case to the Company of Pastors who ruled briefly thus:] At about this time, by resolution of the Consistory and decree of the Council, the marriage contracted between the widow of Jean Achard, aged more than seventy, and a servant of hers, aged about twenty-seven or twenty-eight, was dissolved because of the too great inequality of age. The Consistory resolved further that [the Council] should be requested to make a ruling on this matter for the future.

CHAPTER 9

Thou Shalt Not Uncover
the Nakedness of a Relative

The Incest Impediments

While every person of the age of consent was free to choose a marital partner, we have seen that they were not free to choose just anyone. Parents and guardians set one limit. A valid marriage required their consent, at least in the case of minor children. Custom and culture set a second limit. The parties had to be of suitable piety and modesty, of comparable age and faith, of compatible social and economic status. The law of contracts set a third limit. Both parties had to have the freedom and capacity to enter contracts, and had to follow proper contractual forms and ceremonies.

God and nature set a fourth limit to the freedom of marital contract. Men and women could not marry those who were related to them by blood or by marriage — by bonds of consanguinity and affinity, as these relations were called. While the first three limitations on marriage — set by customs, contracts, and custodians — could sometimes be waived, this fourth limitation was absolute. To marry a blood or family relative in violation of the laws of God and nature was to commit incest, a mortal sin and a serious crime. Incestuous engagements and marriages were automatically annulled, and the parties were subject to severe criminal sanctions if they knew their union was incestuous.

The late medieval canon law that governed these incest impediments of consanguinity and affinity was exceedingly complex. Earlier canon laws had prohibited marriage to any parties related by blood or family up to seven degrees. This sweeping prohibition could impede marriage to thousands of potential partners — no small matter for someone seeking a spouse in a small insular community. The Fourth Lateran Council of 1215 had reduced this prohibition from seven to four degrees of blood or family relations. But local synods and canonists in the following centuries had slowly stretched the impediments of consanguinity back to five and six degrees of blood relatives. Others had extended the impediments of affinity to prohibit marriage to relatives not only of couples who were married, but also of couples who were guilty of fornication or adultery. Still others had added layers of spiritual impediments — barring engagement and marriage to godparents and godchildren and their relatives, to former monks and nuns and their relatives, to the illegitimate children of clergy and their relatives, and more. By the eve of the Reformation, these impediments of consanguinity, affinity, and spirituality took up several long chapters in canon law texts, confessional manuals, and pastoral handbooks.[1]

The first generation of Protestant reformers had issued long and withering attacks on this swollen medieval canon law of impediments. Major reformers like Martin Luther, Philip Melanchthon, Martin Bucer, Johannes Brenz, Johannes Bugenhagen, Ulrich Zwingli, and Heinrich Bullinger had all written at length on the impediments of consanguinity and affinity. And their views were reflected in scores of major new Protestant marriage ordinances that were circulating by the time Calvin sat down to work in 1536.[2]

Calvin built directly, but quietly, on these Protestant prototypes. He engaged in few polemics against the traditional laws of consanguinity and affinity. This was surprising. Calvin had added more than his share of vitriol to the Protestant critique of other traditional marital doctrines, such as celibacy, sacramentality, and divorce. Moreover, Protestant reformers of the day were still divided on precisely which impediments of consanguinity and affinity to accept. Indeed, some Anabaptists were pruning these traditional impediments so severely that they were courting charges of incest and polygamy by Catholic and Protestant opponents alike.[3] Calvin had little to do with all this infighting. He seemed content to accept the prevailing Protestant critique of the Catholic tradition. He spent his time and energy systematically rooting his preferred list of blood and family impediments in biblical and natural law, and institutionalizing them in Genevan law and practice. The theological and jurisprudential complexity of the topic engaged him deeply. Calvin wrote more on the impediments of consanguinity and affinity than on all the other impediments combined.

---

1. Brundage, pp. 355ff., 434ff.; Joyce, pp. 507ff.

2. Witte, LP, pp. 182-96, 241-45; Naef, 1:341ff., 2:433ff.

3. George Huntston Williams, *The Radical Reformation,* 3d ed. (Kirksville, MO, 1992), pp. 755-98; Paul Mikat, *Die Polygamiefrage in der frühen Neuzeit* (Düsseldorf, 1987).

Theological Teachings

Biblical Teachings

The Bible was his starting point. The core text was Leviticus 18:6-19. Here, Moses set out the blood and family ties that rendered sinful any sexual relations between parties. This text was a *locus classicus* for the crime of incest. It was also a *locus classicus* for the law of impediments. For, if mere sexual relations between these relatives was prohibited, marriage was prohibited as well since it presupposed ongoing sexual relations. A one-time act of incest was bad enough. A perpetual state of marital incest was worse.

It is worth quoting the relevant verses in Leviticus 18 in full, since Calvin and his colleagues adverted to them many times in their legal and theological writings:

> 6. None of you shall approach any one near of kin to him to uncover nakedness. I am the Lord.
>
> 7. You shall not uncover the nakedness of your father, which is the nakedness of your mother; she is your mother, you shall not uncover her nakedness.
>
> 8. You shall not uncover the nakedness of your father's wife; it is your father's nakedness.
>
> 9. You shall not uncover the nakedness of your sister, the daughter of your father or the daughter of your mother, whether born at home or born abroad.
>
> 10. You shall not uncover the nakedness of your son's daughter, or your daughter's daughter, for their nakedness is your own nakedness.
>
> 11. You shall not uncover the nakedness of your father's wife's daughter, begotten by your father, since she is your sister.
>
> 12. You shall not uncover the nakedness of your father's sister; she is your father's near kinswoman.
>
> 13. You shall not uncover the nakedness of your mother's sister, for she is your mother's near kinswoman.
>
> 14. You shall not uncover the nakedness of your father's brother, that is you shall not approach his wife; she is your aunt.
>
> 15. You shall not uncover the nakedness of your daughter-in-law; she is your son's wife, you shall not uncover her nakedness.
>
> 16. You shall not uncover the nakedness of your brother's wife; she is your brother's nakedness.
>
> 17. You shall not uncover the nakedness of a woman and of her daugh-

ter, and you shall not take her son's daughter or her daughter's daughter to uncover her nakedness; they are your near kinswomen; it is wickedness.

18. And you shall not take a woman as a rival wife to her sister, uncovering her nakedness while her sister is yet alive.

Other biblical passages underscored some of these impediments in Leviticus 18, but not all of them and not with equal force or obvious consistency.

Relations between a man and his mother, step-mother, or mother-in-law were thrice more condemned in the Mosaic law, once as a capital offense (Exod. 20:11, 14; Deut. 22:30; 27:20, 23). The gravity of this offense could be seen in the earlier biblical example of Reuben, Jacob's first-born son, who lay with Bilhah, his mother-in-law. Reuben was not executed for his incest, but he was condemned and disinherited despite his claims to primogeniture (Gen. 35:22; 49:2; 1 Chron. 5:1).[4] A similar example of incest between a son and mother-in-law recurred in the church of Corinth. St. Paul ordered the Corinthians to "deliver this man to Satan for the destruction of the flesh, that his spirit may be saved in the day of the Lord Jesus" (1 Cor. 5:1-5; cf. 2 Cor. 7:12).

Relations between a man and his daughter-in-law were once more condemned in the Mosaic law, also as a capital offense (Lev. 20:12). The clearest biblical example of this offense was Judah's one-time dalliance with Tamar, his widowed daughter-in-law (Gen. 38:12-30). But neither party was ultimately punished, let alone executed for their capital crime.

Relations between a brother and sister, and between a half-brother and half-sister, were twice more condemned in the Mosaic law, now with the punishment of banishment rather than execution (Exod. 20:17; Deut. 27:22). The most egregious biblical example of this offense was the incestuous relation between King David's two children Amnon and Tamar (2 Sam. 13:1-33).

The Mosaic law said nothing more about the two other impediments listed in Leviticus 18 — the relations between a grandfather and granddaughter, and between a man and his two sisters (Lev. 18:10, 18). And it said nothing at all about other kinds of relationships between close relatives that other ancient laws condemned — such as relations between a father and daughter, between a grandson and a grandmother, or between first and second cousins.[5]

Finally, the Mosaic law included four prohibitions on sexual relations that seemed to be condoned elsewhere in the Bible. First, it prohibited relations between a man and his paternal half-sister (Lev. 18:9; Deut. 27:22). But this was the very relationship that existed between Abraham and Sarah (Gen. 20:12). Second,

---

4. Calvin commented only briefly on this text. See Comm. Gen. 35:22.

5. These impediments might be imputed to the catchall admonition at the beginning of the classic passage in Leviticus 18: "None of you shall approach anyone near of kin to him to uncover nakedness" (Lev. 18:6).

it prohibited relations between a nephew and his aunts by blood or marriage, and the parties who chose to join contrary to this command were condemned to childlessness (Exod. 20:19-20). But this was precisely the relationship between the parents of Moses (Exod. 2:1-10; 6:14-27), who were obviously not rendered childless. Third, the Mosaic law prohibited relations between a man and two sisters (Lev. 18:18). But this was precisely what Jacob did in marrying two sisters, Leah and Rachel — an act of both bigamy and incest that nonetheless provided a critical early link in the genealogy of Christ (Gen. 29:1-30; Matt. 1:2). Fourth, relations between a brother and sister-in-law were prohibited in one part of the Mosaic law (Lev. 18:16; 20:21), again with the threat of childlessness to those who violated the command. But these very relations were commanded in another part of the Mosaic law precisely for the purpose of allowing the widow to have children (Deut. 25:5-10). The seriousness of this latter command was underscored by the story of Onan who failed to discharge his duties fully to his brother's widow Tamar. Onan did have sexual intercourse with Tamar. But he "spilled his semen upon the ground," the Bible reads, lest she become pregnant. For this breach of duties, "God slew him" (Gen. 38:1-10).

The New Testament did little to resolve the seeming tensions in these Old Testament laws and stories. Apart from the text in 1 Corinthians condemning son-mother incest (5:1-5), the New Testament touched lightly on the incest of King Herod and on Christ's discussion of the pharisees' hypothetical question about the eternal effects of marrying a dead brother's widow (Matt. 14:3-12; 22:23-33; Mark 6:17-29). All the other tangled impediments in the Old Testament remained without New Testament commentary, let alone resolution.

Biblical Law, Natural Law, Genevan Law

Calvin picked his way slowly and skillfully through this small avalanche of shifting biblical teachings on the impediments of consanguinity and affinity. As with several other complex issues of marriage and family life, Calvin began with a new law. He then gradually defended and amended this law in his commentaries, sermons, and *consilia*.

The 1546 Marriage Ordinance set out in some detail the new Genevan law of impediments of consanguinity and affinity. The Ordinance included the following impediments of consanguinity:

> [25.] In a direct line, that is of father with daughter or mother with son or all other descendants in order, no marriage may be contracted, since this contravenes natural decency and is forbidden both by the law of God and by the civil law.

[26.] Likewise of uncle with [niece] or great-[niece], of aunt with nephew or great-nephew and so on, because the uncle represents the father and the aunt is in the place of the mother.

[27.] Also between brother and sister, whether of [the same] father and mother or of one of these.

[28.] In the other degrees, although marriage is not forbidden either by the law of God or the Roman civil law, nevertheless to avoid scandal, because for a long time this has not been the custom, and from fear that the Word of God may be blasphemed by the ignorant, a cousin-german may not contract marriage with his cousin-german until, with the passing of time, it is otherwise decided by us. To the other degrees let there be no impediment.[6]

This list included all the impediments of consanguinity listed in Leviticus 18, to which Calvin added three more — prohibiting relations between father and daughter, between uncle and (great-) niece, and between first cousins.

The 1546 Marriage Ordinance listed the following impediments of affinity:

[29.] Let no man take to wife the widow of his son, or of the son of his son, and let no woman take the husband of her daughter or of the daughter of her daughter, nor of those following traced down in a direct line.

[30.] Let no one take the daughter of his wife or the daughter descending from her, and so on.

[31.] A woman also may not take the son of her husband or the son of his son, and so on.

[32.] Likewise let no one take the widow of his nephew or of his great-nephew, and also let no woman take the husband of her niece or great-niece.

[33.] Let no one take the widow of his brother, and no woman may take the one who was her sister's husband.

[34.] The one who has committed adultery with the wife of another, when it has come to be known, may not take her in marriage because of the scandal and dangers this entails.

This list included all the impediments of affinity listed in Leviticus, and added several more. The levitical prohibition on a man's relations with his son's widow was extended to include the widow of his grandson, nephew, and grand-nephew as well. A parallel prohibition was imposed on a woman's relations with her daughter's or granddaughter's widower, or the widower of her niece and grand-niece. The levitical prohibition on a man's relationship to his granddaughter was amended to include a parallel prohibition on a woman's relation-

6. Doc. 1-2.

ship with her grandson. Fathers and mothers were newly prohibited from relationships with their stepdaughters and stepsons. The Marriage Ordinance flatly prohibited marriage between a man and his brother's widow, and made it reciprocal by prohibiting marriage between a woman and her sister's widower. And the Marriage Ordinance prohibited marriage between parties who had earlier committed adultery with each other.

These impediments of consanguinity and affinity remained in place in Geneva during Calvin's lifetime. When, in 1569, Beza summarized the prevailing law of impediments in a series of convenient charts and tables (**Doc. 9-1**), very little had changed from what Calvin had set out in his 1546 Ordinance.[7]

In his 1546 Marriage Ordinance, Calvin cited natural law, Roman law, civil law, public custom, and common decency to defend his decisions to add to the biblical impediments of consanguinity and affinity.[8] He elaborated on his choices of extra-biblical impediments in his 1563 Commentary on Leviticus 18 (**Doc. 9-2**).[9] The levitical impediments were the core of God's law, Calvin insisted, and they could not be breached under any circumstances. But these levitical impediments were also specific illustrations of a more general principle of natural law. This natural law principle taught that direct and collateral relatives and their parents, their spouses, and their children could not marry. This created three vertical layers of direct relationship — among parties in the generations of grandparents, parents, and children. It also created three horizontal layers of collateral relationship within the same generation.

Leviticus 18 gave specific examples of each of the degrees of blood and family relationship that the natural law prohibited. It was easy enough to fill in the rest of the impediments of consanguinity and affinity that fit within this natural law scheme. It was also easy enough to make this exercise gender-neutral: biblical impediments that were binding on men's relationships with women should also be applied to women's relationships with men. "There is no reason that one party should be bound, and the other left in full liberty." "That would be unjust and against all reason."[10] And it was easy enough to confirm that this amended list of levitical impediments was consistent with the natural

7. Compared to Calvin's 1546 Marriage Ordinance, Beza extended the impediments of affinity to reach one more layer of step-relatives. But he excluded from the impediments of affinity the prohibition on marriage of former adulterous paramours.

8. Beza later cited ample canon law precedents as well. See Beza, TRD, 2:50-109, esp. 51-83.

9. CO 24:1–25:416. This late-life commentary, published in 1563, includes verbatim passages from several *consilia* excerpted below in Documents 9-3 to 9-5. They are undated, and they were not discovered until after Calvin's death. CO 10/1:233-44nn. It might be that these *consilia* were in fact excerpts from his 1563 Commentary on the Harmony of the Law and circulated separately.

10. Serm. Deut. 25:5-12.

law. For other ancient legal systems, particularly the pre-Christian Roman law, had adopted a similar set of impediments with only the natural law to guide them. If even the pagans commonly and consistently adopted this fuller list of impediments of consanguinity and affinity, then surely God's people in ancient Israel and in modern-day Geneva should do so as well.[11] This was Calvin's argument in a nutshell.

For Calvin, this argument was enough to explain most of the extra-biblical impediments of consanguinity and affinity included in the 1546 Marriage Ordinance. Both in his Commentary on Exodus 18 and in an undated *consilium* (**Doc. 9-3**), he added an argument from long-standing Christian custom to justify the impediment against marriages between first cousins. This impediment was not technically necessary under the natural law principle that Calvin had adopted, nor was it prohibited by Mosaic law. But marriage of first cousins had long been a subject of scandal and controversy within the church. The medieval canon law had prohibited such marriages formally, but had also quite easily granted dispensations from this prohibition. This led to ample confusion within the church, Calvin argued. To avoid further confusion, it would be better to prohibit such marriages altogether, and for individual parties to forgo this natural liberty to marry a first cousin, lest others be misled.

Calvin shifted from general principle to specific precept to resolve the seeming conflict between biblical laws about whether a man must or must not marry his deceased brother's widow. The legal issue, while hardly a common case in court, was pressing in Calvin's day for both political and theological reasons. This was the impediment at the heart of the dispute between King Henry VIII and the papacy that had triggered the English Reformation.[12] Protestant churches were being made and broken on getting this impediment right, and a new Protestant leader like Calvin would be wise to give it close attention. Moreover, if the Old Testament laws on these minute matters of marriage were so confusing, if not self-contradictory, why should modern-day Genevans adopt them — especially when the New Testament was virtually silent on the subject of impediments? Indeed on the particular impediment of marrying a late brother's widow, Christ himself seemed to be outright dismissive.[13] So, why were Calvin and his clerical colleagues imposing such arcane laws on Geneva?

---

11. This argument recurs in the Comm. 1 Cor. 5:1-2 discussed below and excerpted in Doc. 9-10 as well as in Calvin's Sermons on 1 Cor. 5:1-4.

12. Henry Ansgar Kelly, *The Matrimonial Trials of Henry VIII* (Stanford, CA, 1976).

13. Comm. Harm. Gosp. Matt. 22:23-33; Mark 12:18-27; Luke 20:27-40. In his brief commentary, Calvin was equally dismissive, not because the impediment was unimportant, but because this passage was about a silly pharisaic hypothetical that, in his view, deserved little attention.

No stranger to anti-clericalism,[14] Calvin saw this looming challenge and met it head on several times. He preached a lengthy sermon in 1555 on the law of impediments in Deuteronomy 25:5-12[15] and addressed the topic in two other undated *consilia* (**Docs. 9-4 and 9-5**). He repeated the arguments of these *consilia*, almost verbatim, in his 1563 Commentary on the Harmony of the [Mosaic] Law.[16]

Part of Calvin's argument in Documents 9-4 to 9-6 was linguistic. "It was impossible for God to contradict himself" in writing his law, he insisted.[17] Therefore, one needs to read these passages more carefully. The Hebrew word for "brother" in both passages does not mean "blood brother" alone. It can mean kinsman more generally, too. So, a "blood" brother, one within the prohibited degrees of consanguinity, may not marry his late blood brother's widow. That was the law of Leviticus 18. But a "non-blood" brother, a kinsman outside the prohibited degrees of consanguinity but still related, not only could but must marry his late kinsman's widow if she were left childless. Otherwise his deceased kinsman would have no successor or lineage. That was the law of Deuteronomy 25. Understood this way, the two laws were in perfect accord.

There was nothing new in these interlocking Mosaic laws, Calvin continued in his commentary on the story of Onan and Tamar in Genesis 38 (**Doc. 9-6**). Even before Moses, natural law imposed this obligation on a kinsman so that the family line and name could be preserved. That was what made so outrageous Onan's act of "spilling his semen on the ground" to avoid impregnating Tamar, his late brother's widow. Onan was just satisfying his sexual appetite without discharging his fraternal duty.

Calvin's argument to reconcile these two levitical laws was not only linguistic, but also contextual. The levitical prohibition on marriage to a brother's widow (Lev. 18:16) must be read together with the prohibition of a man's marriage to two sisters (Lev. 18:18). The common purpose of both prohibitions was to avoid envy and enmity between siblings, as was so sadly evident between the two sisters Rachel and Leah whom Jacob had married. God had put this prohibition in place to spare wives from worry about competition for their husband's affections from anyone — not least from their own sisters with whom

---

14. Robert M. Kingdon, "Anti-Clericalism in the Registers of the Geneva Consistory, 1542-1564," in *Anticlericalism in Late Medieval and Early Modern Europe,* ed. Peter A. Dykema and Heiko A. Oberman (Leiden, 1993), p. 617.

15. This sermon is excerpted above in Doc. 4-4, where we have analyzed it for its teachings on the requirement of consent to marriage.

16. Comm. Harm. Law Exod. 18:6; 20:11-21. I have excluded the section of this late-life commentary on the impediments of marrying two sisters, which repeat verbatim Calvin's *consilia* in Docs. 9-3 to 9-5.

17. Comm. Harm. Gosp. Matt. 22:24.

their husband would likely have more regular contact. And, since a man might similarly worry about competition for his wife's affections from his own brother, Calvin extended the prohibition to this case, too. Indeed, without this blanket prohibition on marrying a spouse's sibling, evil in-laws might be too tempted to seek the divorce of the couple or even the death of the unwanted spouse to enable themselves to get married thereafter. This impediment, together with the impediment against marriage between former adulterers, undercut those motives for interfamilial wrongdoing.

Biblical Stories of Incest

Calvin had an easier time reconciling the seeming tensions between the laws of impediments with the several biblical examples of early patriarchs who seemed to violate these laws with virtual impunity. The great patriarchs Abraham and Jacob had entered into incestuous marriages (Gen. 20:12; 29:1-30). Jacob's first son Reuben committed incest with Bilhah, his mother-in-law (Gen. 35:22). His other son Judah impregnated Tamar, his widowed daughter-in-law (Gen. 38:12-30). Moses was born of an incestuous marriage (Exod. 2:1-10; 6:14-27). Calvin had often pointed to the patriarchs as prototypes of Christian piety. What was a pious Christian reader to make of these biblical stories?

None of these stories was intended to be an example of sexual liberty for God's people to follow, Calvin argued. To the contrary, these stories were "remarkable instance[s] both of the infirmity of men and the grace of God."[18] They showed how weak a person could be when guided by the natural law alone, and how much we all need the fuller and firmer laws against incest set out in ancient Mosaic law and modern Christian law. "The imitation of the patriarchs is not safe when we think that we may indiscriminately adopt whatever they did."[19] Moreover, these stories showed how a gracious God could forgive these patriarchs their massive sins of incest and still preserve them as key actors in the drama of salvation.

Calvin offered variations on this argument in his 1554 Commentary on Genesis. Abraham compounded his sin of incest with the sin of duplicity, Calvin argued in his Commentary on Genesis 20.[20] The story records that Abraham and Sarah were guests in the household of the Philistine King Abimelech. Fearing that someone might kill him in order to take his beautiful wife Sarah, Abraham presented her as his sister, saying nothing about their marriage. This

18. Comm. Gen. 20:2.
19. Comm. Harm. Law Exod. 6:16.
20. Comm. Gen. 20:1-18.

was not an outright lie: She was a "sister" kinswoman of Abraham, said Calvin, in that they shared the same grandfather. But Abraham's half-truth nearly induced the king to seduce Sarah had not God intervened. Calvin largely brushed aside Abraham's incest. This is surprising, since Abraham had violated an impediment that Calvin had just imputed to the natural law and had added to the 1546 Marriage Ordinance. Calvin focused more on Abraham's lies and Abimelech's lust. And he used this story to drive home his familiar lesson that even the great patriarchs needed the firmer laws of God, beyond the laws of nature, to curb human sexual sins of all sorts. If this lesson was not clear enough from the story of Abraham, it became doubly clear in the story of Abraham's son Isaac. Isaac also was a guest in the household of the same King Abimelech, a few years later. And just like his father, Isaac held out his wife Rebekah as his sister, again tempting Abimelech to take her. God again had to intervene.[21]

Calvin treated the story of Jacob's bigamous incest with the sisters Leah and Rachel in similar terms. Jacob's bigamy was a graver sin than Abraham's duplicity. So Calvin dwelt at even greater length on Jacob's bigamy, though he had no patience with Jacob's incest either.[22] While God preserved Jacob's role in the drama of salvation, Calvin argued, God did punish him for his sins. Jacob had to endure the perennial bickering between his two sister-wives. Worse, he had to suffer the indignity and pain of watching his own children caught up in a massive tangle of rape, incest, adultery, and poverty.[23]

The most notorious such example was the incest of Jacob's first-born son Reuben and Bilhah, his mother-in-law (**Doc. 9-7**). This was a "sad and even tragic history," Calvin commented, for both parties knowingly acted in a manner "abhorrent to nature" itself. Yet, God's grace and mercy shines through even in the darkest of sinful places. Despite "this extreme act of iniquity" for which he was properly disinherited (Gen. 49:2), Reuben "retained his rank of a patriarch in the church." Lest any reader think that he, too, could sin like Reuben, confident that God's grace would abound, Calvin added:

> We must . . . remain under the custody of fear and watchfulness, lest temptation secretly seize upon us and the snares of Satan envelop us. For the Holy Spirit did not design to set before us an example of vile lust so that everyone

---

21. Comm. Gen. 26:1-11.

22. The passage is excerpted in Doc. 7-7 and analyzed in Chapter 7 for its discussion of polygamy. Calvin said nothing about the other incest evident in this story, namely, that Jacob had married his first cousins Rachel and Leah. Their father was Laban, the brother of Isaac's wife Rebekah (Gen. 28:2). Calvin's silence on this form of incest is a bit surprising, since he had just included this impediment in his 1546 Marriage Ordinance, and argued for it strongly in several writings.

23. Comm. Gen. 29:15–30:24; 34:1-31; 38:12-23.

would rush into incestuous relations. Rather, it exposed the infamous baseness of this crime in this honorable person, so that everyone might more vehemently abhor it.

Among Jacob's other children, even Judah, the lion of Israel, committed notorious incest compounded by adultery (**Doc. 9-8**). Judah was the father-in-law of the new widow Tamar whom we have just encountered above (Gen. 38:1-20). When Onan failed to discharge his duty toward her, Tamar should have been left free to leave Judah's household to marry into another family. But Judah unjustly kept her within his household. In revenge Tamar later tricked him. She veiled herself and pretended that she was a prostitute. A lustful Judah took her to bed, thinking he was merely consorting with a prostitute — an offense, which the law of the day tolerated for men, though not for women. When Judah later discovered that the widowed Tamar had become pregnant, he was ready to execute her for her adultery — following the custom of his day for a man to punish the adultery of a woman under his authority. When Tamar revealed that Judah in fact was the father, however, an ashamed Judah suspended the execution and faded from the story — albeit without being punished for his incest, adultery, and abuse of authority. Tamar gave birth to twin bastards, who would later be counted among the ancestors of Christ (Gen. 46:12; Num. 26:20; Matt. 1:3). For Calvin, this was a wonderful story to illustrate that, even though "the whole dignity of nature was subverted" by Judah, a gracious God forgave his sins and redeemed his acts for higher purposes.

Moses was born of the incestuous marriage between a nephew and his aunt (Exod. 2:1-10; 6:14-27). Moses' parents obviously did not suffer the fate of childlessness with which later levitical law would threaten such incestuous couples (Lev. 20:20). But in this story, wrote Calvin, "we see the terror that grips" such an incestuous couple. They exposed their child Moses "to the peril of wild beasts, of the weather, of the water, and more."[24] Moses would not have long survived floating in a basket in the Egyptian river had not God miraculously intervened, spared him, and brought him up to be the new leader of the Jews. What better person than Moses, then, to pronounce God's new law prohibiting the very incest by which he was conceived. "Moses was not hesitant to confess that he was born of an incestuous marriage. In this he not only fails to protect his own reputation, but also ingeniously proclaims the disgrace of his own parents, for the sake of illustrating solely the glory of God . . . and the need to prohibit [incest] in the express terms" of God's law.[25]

God's proclamation of a firmer and fuller law against incest did not, of

24. Comm. Harm. Law Exod. 2:1.
25. Comm. Harm. Law Exod. 6:14-30.

course, eliminate the sin of incestuous relationships and marriages. This could be seen clearly enough in the tragic story of incest within King David's household.[26] David's son Amnon lusted after his half-sister Tamar for a long time. She befriended and cared for him. But when she refused his sexual advances, Amnon raped Tamar to her great shame and grief. Tamar's full brother Absalom was outraged and had Amnon murdered. This set off a bitter feud within King David's household that eventually led to the infamous death of Absalom as well, which caused David great sorrow (2 Sam. 13:34–19:8).

Calvin preached at length on this passage in 1562 (**Doc. 9-9**). Though much of his homily turned on Amnon's deception and rape, Calvin also addressed the obvious sin of incest. He had little patience with earlier interpreters who regarded Tamar as an illegitimate child to whom Amnon was technically unrelated; that interpretation might have at least mitigated Amnon's crime of incest. Tamar was Amnon's half-sister plain and simple, said Calvin. His conduct toward Tamar was incest, and Tamar told him so — though Calvin thought she should have said more in protest. Amnon's incestuous rape was an outrage against God, nature, and his family. He deserved to be severely punished.

What punishment was appropriate for incest, however, Calvin did not so clearly say — in this passage or in others. Leviticus 20 ordered execution or banishment for more serious forms of incest, including incest between a (half-) brother and (half-)sister. It threatened childlessness on those guilty of less serious forms of incest between more distant relatives. Deuteronomy 27 proclaimed "curses" on those guilty of some of these same forms of incest, though not all. Some of the other biblical stories that we just saw described punishments of disinheritance and the violent death of the incestuous and their children.

Calvin largely repeated this range of biblical punishments for incest.[27] He did not create a hierarchy of degrees of incest based on the gravity of the biblical punishments assigned to them, as he had done in cases of fornication.[28] In his 1555 Sermon on Deuteronomy 27, he offered a brief spiritual interpretation. In "cursing" various types of incest, God was "evicting from his kingdom all

26. David himself was guilty of incest as well, in committing adultery with Bathsheba and then subsequently marrying her. This violated the impediment of affinity that precluded marriage between former adulterous paramours. David and Bathsheba's first son conceived in adultery died. But their second son, conceived after marriage, lived and later became the great King Solomon (2 Sam. 11:1–12:25). Though he preached at great length on these texts in 1562, Calvin treated David's sin as a scandalous form of adultery and homicide, that God ultimately redeemed for good.

27. Comm. Harm. Law Exod. 20:11-24; Serm. Deut. 27:16-23.

28. See, e.g., SD, vol. 3, items 1046, 1065.

who commit incest." This punishment made it unnecessary to differentiate among lesser forms of punishment. Banishment from the kingdom of God was the ultimate punishment, a fate worse than death. It made little difference that the banned might be variously subject to execution, childlessness, or disinheritance as well.

Calvin wrote in a similar and longer vein in his Commentary and Sermon on 1 Corinthians 5:1-4 (**Doc. 9-10**).[29] In this passage, St. Paul had instructed the church in Corinth that a son and mother-in-law caught in incest should be "turned over to Satan." The Christian tradition had long taken this passage to be a firm biblical warrant for severe punishment, sometimes execution, of parties convicted for serious incest. Calvin did not read the passage so expansively. He agreed that mother-son incest was "a shameful and abominable monstrosity," driven by "beastly lust." It destroyed even the most basic norms of "natural modesty" and was "deserving of the severest punishment." There was "no excuse" for a church to harbor such vile sinners.

But this passage does not teach bodily execution of the incestuous, Calvin argued. It teaches excommunication of his or her soul. "Delivering over to Satan is an appropriate expression for denoting excommunication. For, as Christ reigns *in* the Church, so Satan reigns *out of* the Church. . . . He who is cast out of the Church is in a manner delivered over to the power of Satan, for he becomes an alien, and is cast out of Christ's kingdom." This interpretation supported the power of the Genevan Consistory to excommunicate the incestuous. It provided little instruction, however, to the Genevan Council on what to do with the incestuous, whether or not excommunicated.

Consistory Cases on Incest

Incest was a serious crime in Geneva. When committed intentionally, it could lead to execution.[30] Most cases of flagrant and intentional incest went directly

---

29. Calvin wrote at even greater length, but to no different effect, in his later sermons on 1 Corinthians. The original text of Calvin's Sermon on 1 Cor. 5:1-4, which is not yet available in a modern edition, tracks much of the argument of his earlier Commentary on point.

30. A 1566 statute on fornication and adultery reflected this: "Fornication involving incest will be punished by death, in accordance with its severity and heinousness. We define incest as intercourse between persons whose marriage is flatly prohibited by the law of God and of nature." SD, vol. 3, item 1065. See scattered examples of incest cases in Naphy, Sex Crimes, pp. 139-56; E. William Monter, "Crime and Punishment in Calvin's Geneva, 1562," *Archiv für Reformationsgeschichte* 64 (1973): 281; Bernard Lescaze, "Crimes et Criminels à Genève en 1572," in *Pour une Histoire Qualitative. Etudes offertes à Sven Stelling-Michaud,* ed. Bernard Lescaze (Geneva, 1975), pp. 45-71.

to the Council for criminal investigation and prosecution. The Consistory, however, heard a number of cases where incest was suspected, or where it was discovered while investigating other conduct. When they came upon incest, the Consistory made findings of fact and issued spiritual sanctions and then removed the cases to the Council.

In a 1546 case, for example, the Consistory summoned Aime Rivilliod to answer charges that he had slept with his maid and impregnated her (**Doc. 9-11**). Rivilliod was quick to confess his crime, and testified that the child had now been born, that he made arrangements for its baptism, and that he was paying for its care and the care of the mother. Fair enough, but the Consistory's real concern was the rumor that Rivilliod and his maid were blood relatives. That would have aggravated the charges considerably. Rivilliod insisted that they were unrelated, and that, in fact, this rumor had been orchestrated by one of his rivals. The next week, he was back before the Consistory, with the rumor-monger in tow. The latter confessed that he had been paid to make inquiries whether Rivilliod and the maid were related, but he had found nothing. Without proof of incest, the Consistory fined and imprisoned Rivilliod for his fornication — though they released him temporarily to attend to a business affair, perhaps to mitigate the harm of the false charges of incest.

In a 1547 case, the Consistory wanted to know whether Claude Michallet had slept with his daughter-in-law rather than with his wife (**Doc. 9-12**). The Consistory questioned Claude, his wife, and a young girl who stayed in their house, about his whereabouts and intentions. Claude admitted that he and his wife had quarreled, and that he had left and slept at his daughter-in-law's house. But he swore that he stayed with her only because she was very ill at the time. The Consistory was satisfied with his explanation, and the parties were reconciled.

In a 1556 case, a widow named Antoine Chapuis was confronted with evidence that she slept with her nephew Michel, who had helped her a great deal after her husband had passed away (**Doc. 9-13**). Initially, Antoine claimed that Michel had slept at her house only while he was sick. When pressed, Antoine admitted that Michel did stay at her house regularly, along with other children, but she did not sleep with him or do anything wrong. The Consistory gave them stern admonitions about the scandal their conduct caused, and left the case at that.

In more serious cases of suspected incest, the Consistory removed cases to the Council. A good example is a 1547 case involving Girard Favre and his wife Janon.[31] Janon was indicted for committing incestuous adultery with her

---

31. The full record of this case is included in Doc. 8-18, where we have analyzed it for the issues of sexual dysfunction.

cousin-german who lived in a distant city which had yielded an illegitimate child, now dead. The Consistory pressed Girard to consider reconciliation. Janon showed great contrition for her sin, but she also argued that she was driven to it because her husband had never consummated their marriage. Girard refused to forgive her for her adulterous incest, and the Council divorced the couple on the Consistory's recommendation.

In a 1557 case, the Consistory charged André Duplot with incestuous fornication with his aunt, Jeanne Court, in the Catholic city of Avignon (**Doc. 9-14**). André was already under suspicion of being a papist and frequenting Mass; Jeanne was suspected of being a "whore." Jeanne admitted that André had stayed with her, but she denied having a sexual relationship with him. She did not help her cause, however, by then testifying that another man had tried to force her to have oral sex. That prompted the Consistory to ask André whether he had sought to have oral sex with her. André denied any such thought, let alone act. The Consistory was not so sure. They ordered the couple to stop sleeping together, and sent them to the Council who fined and imprisoned them.

The same year, the Consistory heard a troubling case involving Michel Pointeau's incestuous pursuit of his sister-in-law, Claudine (**Doc. 9-15**). Michel had begun soliciting Claudine already before his wedding to Claudine's sister. Claudine, then, was still a minor. The solicitation continued thereafter, even after Claudine had grown up and was married. One time, Michel had fondled her. Both Michel's wife and another sister-in-law testified both to Michel's philandering and to various blasphemies he had committed. Michel defended himself by saying that it was Claudine who was doing all the flirting. Nonsense, the Consistory judged. They banned Michel from communion, and recommended that the Council banish "such riff-raff" from the city, presumably after granting his wife a divorce.

Occasionally, parties on their own, or on orders by the Council, came to the Consistory for advice on whether an impediment of consanguinity or affinity barred them from marriage. In a 1552 case, for example, the Council sent Claude Michaud and Aima Manget to the Consistory to advise them on the propriety of their budding marriage (**Doc. 9-16**). Claude's brother was already married to Aima's sister. Did that create an impediment of affinity to the prospective marriage of Claude and Aima? No, said the Consistory. Nothing in the biblical law, or in the laws of Geneva or in the laws of surrounding Reformed polities like Bern, precluded such marriages. Such matters were addressed in detail in the draft 1546 Marriage Ordinance, the Consistory reminded the Council. It would be well for the Council to issue that law formally so that parties could be better instructed.

A more difficult question of incest for the Consistory turned on whether parties had committed adultery, rather than fornication, before their marriage. Sex between a single man and a single woman was fornication. The parties were free to marry after they had served their criminal sentences. Indeed, they could be compelled to get married, especially if the woman was now pregnant. Sex with a married man or woman, however, was adultery. The man and woman were not free to marry under any circumstances, even after their respective spouses had died or divorced them, and even if the woman was impregnated by her adulterous paramour. For the adulterous sex had created an impediment of affinity. Any further sex between them, let alone marriage, was a form of incest.

The nice evidentiary question for the Consistory to answer was precisely when the parties had their first sexual encounter. If one or both of them had a spouse at the time, their sexual dalliance not only exposed them to severe sanctions, but also led to the automatic annulment of their engagement or marriage.

The seriousness of this distinction can be seen in the 1546 case involving the remarriage of a former priest, Dom Legier Joli, and a woman, Jaqueme of Etaux (**Doc. 9-17**). Dom Legier's first wife died under suspicious circumstances. Scarcely two weeks later, Dom Legier and Jaqueme were engaged to be married. Jaqueme was reportedly pregnant. The Consistory wanted to know whether they had sexual intercourse before Dom Legier's wife had died. Despite ample testimony against them, the parties denied any sexual impropriety, and Jaqueme denied her pregnancy. A month later, the Council prosecuted the couple for adultery, but unsuccessfully.

The couple did not help their cause by moving in together shortly thereafter and drawing anew the attention of the authorities. Jaqueme was now obviously pregnant, and was far enough along in her pregnancy to make the timing of her conception newly suspicious. Having caught the couple in one lie, the Consistory wanted to know whether they had lied about the prior adultery as well. The couple still denied any impropriety. The Consistory court was not convinced. They sent the case to the Council with a recommendation that the parties' engagement be annulled. The Consistory was concerned that to do otherwise "would be a scandal and open the door for many to kill their wives" in order to marry their lovers. The Council ordered the annulment.

Jaqueme's father, no doubt distraught about the plight that faced his now pregnant daughter, pleaded with the Council to reconsider the annulment and allow the couple to marry. The Council stood by its order. Though adulterous incest had not been formally proved, the parties' conduct was simply too suspicious to allow their marriage to go forward.

Another case from 1546-1547 illustrates the lengths to which the Consistory went to discover the couple's exact sexual history and consequent relationship (**Doc. 9-18**). This case involved Claudine, a recent widow, and a young man

Amied de Leamon of Gy. The case was made more interesting because the leading interrogator on the clerical bench in this case, Pastor Henri de la Mare, was the brother-in-law of Amied de Leamon, one of the parties to the case. Rather than recuse himself out of conflict of interest, Henri stayed on. He seemed intent to break up the match by casting aspersions on the widow Claudine, evidently with an eye to giving pause to his brother-in-law Amied. In three separate hearings in 1546, Henri and the Consistory inquired closely about allegations of the couple's fornication with each other and Claudine's adultery and fornication with several others. Sundry witnesses were called to testify, including Pastor Henri himself who alleged that Claudine had committed adultery with several men during her husband's lifetime. The evidence, while voluminous, was insufficient to convict the parties. The Consistory ordered them to remain apart, and dismissed the case.

Six months later, Claudine was back before the Consistory now alleging that Amied had promised to marry her. She produced an engagement ring as evidence. Amied denied their engagement. The Consistory sent the troublesome couple to the Council for investigation. Under pressure, the couple confessed to their prior fornication. But they differed on the essential question of timing. Claudine admitted to their fornication after she had become a widow. Amied alleged that they had fornicated together much longer, even while she was still married. Amied may have been giving a true confession. But this new information was also a convenient means for him to escape marrying Claudine. If it found mere fornication, the Consistory might compel the parties to marry. If it found prior adultery between them, however, their engagement would be annulled, no matter what Claudine said. This was the dilemma that the Consistory tried to sort out. No final judgment on the propriety of their engagement survives. But the couple did not get married, as we shall see in a moment.

The more typical question put to the Consistory was not whether a pending marriage would be incestuous, but what to do with an existing marriage when one party committed incestuous adultery. This type of incest was at issue in a protracted 1551-1552 divorce case involving, inter alia, our familiar couple Claudine and Amied (**Doc. 9-19**). After her engagement to Amied had fallen through, Claudine had married one François Du Frêney. Sometime thereafter, she had resumed her affair with Amied. Their affair had produced at least one illegitimate child. Claudine was now again pregnant, apparently also by Amied. Both parties had been reprimanded repeatedly by the Consistory and the Council for their ongoing affair. Claudine and her husband François had separated.

Upon learning of this new pregnancy, François filed for divorce. The Consistory sought to reconcile the parties. Both parties objected, particularly François who regarded Claudine's habitual philandering as unforgivable. But when a demure Claudine promised to reform herself and submit to her husband's authority, the Consistory seemed to be moving toward an order of reconciliation — despite François's continued protests that he was entitled to a divorce. The Consistory's talk of reconciliation ended quickly, however, when Claudine charged François with incest. Two years before, she alleged, François had slept with his sister. She had witnesses to prove it. The Consistory called the witnesses, and they gave ample circumstantial evidence to corroborate her story. François vehemently denied the charges of incest as a slanderous plot by "this wicked woman." The Consistory was not so sure. They recommended that the Council grant François's petition for divorce. But they also recommended the Council to investigate the allegations of François's incest, and to punish him for causing such scandal.

The issue of post-marital incest again faced the Consistory in the 1556-1557 case of Jeanne and Jaques Marcellin (**Doc. 9-20**). Jeanne had committed adultery with her husband's brother, Claude. She was indicted before the Council for adultery and incest. On June 1, 1556, she confessed fully. The Council ordered her to kneel in the Council chamber to beg for God's mercy and justice. She obliged. Though her incest was a capital crime, the Council chose to banish her from Geneva and ordered her not to return, on pain of whipping.

Jeanne's husband, Jaques, forgave her the incest, and petitioned the Council to allow her to return to Geneva to live with him. On August 20, 1556, the Council submitted his petition to the Consistory. The Consistory rejected the petition for return, given the gravity of her offense of incest. While forgiveness of sins and reconciliation of estranged couples were high values, they could not overcome the scandal of allowing an incestuous party to return less than three months after conviction. If Jaques had so much pity on his wife, the Consistory concluded, he could go visit her, or join her in exile. Four days later, Calvin and a Consistory colleague appeared before the Council to urge this decision. The Council agreed.

Less than a year later, Jeanne petitioned the Consistory directly for the right to return. The Consistory directed her to the Council. She petitioned the Council the following week, accompanying her plea with another full confession of her fault. The Council rejected her "because of the enormity of the deed" of incest, and because she had already been granted great leniency in being merely banished instead of executed. She sent yet another petition to the Council. The Council now referred her case to the Consistory. Calvin and his colleagues on the Consistory had clearly had enough of these tiresome petitions. Jeanne had been spared execution. She lived in the nearby village of Cologny that had a Reformed church. Her husband was free to move there or to visit her. For the Consistory, that was the end of the matter. They asked the Council to instruct the parties that if the case came up again, the husband would be banished as well. No further petitions came forth.

Summary and Conclusions

Incest was an ancient taboo in the Western tradition. The Greeks and Romans had developed a complex latticework of rules prohibiting sexual and marital relations between various relatives. The Mosaic law was filled with detailed rules and procedures for stamping out the widespread practice of incest among the ancient Jews. The early Christian Church repeated many of these classical and Mosaic laws on incest, and the Church Fathers later anchored them in firm lines of biblical interpretation.

The medieval canon law of incest governed Geneva on the eve of the Reformation. From the twelfth to the sixteenth century, medieval canonists and theologians had worked out an intricate law of incest, rooted in part in Hebrew, Greek, Roman, and patristic precedents. Particularly important for our subject was the canon law of incest impediments that precluded engagement and marriage to at least four layers and generations of parties who were related by blood, family, or spiritual ties. This was an intensely complex jurisprudence that medieval canon law books, confessional writings, and household manuals alike spelled out in great detail.

For the early Protestant reformers, the complexity of this law of incest impediments was less of a concern than the casuistry by which it was sometimes applied. Incest was a complex issue. The biblical law of incest reflected this complexity, and there was nothing wrong for a modern legal system to have equally complex rules. But, to the reformers, there was something presumptively wrong about larding the biblical laws of incest with all manner of extra incest impediments, as the medieval canon law had done. And there was something even worse for the pope and other officials to grant dispensations for many of these incest impediments if the parties paid a high enough price. This was not only exploitative, but it also betrayed the artificiality of many of the incest impediments. The Protestant reformers thus issued blistering attacks on the swollen medieval canon laws of incest impediments in the 1520s and 1530s. "Back to the Bible" was the new Protestant mantra — back to the impediments of consanguinity and affinity that were laid out in Leviticus and Deuteronomy.

Calvin inherited these two traditions — a medieval canon law that had built an intricate system of incest impediments out of biblical, classical, and patristic sources, and an early Protestant civil law that insisted that the biblical law of incest was all a Christian commonwealth needed. Calvin created his own complex systematic theology and law of incest impediments, rooted in part in natural law. Like Catholic natural law theorists, Calvin filled in what he considered to be obvious omissions in the Mosaic law of incest impediments. Like Protestant biblical exegetes, he worked hard to reconcile a number of seeming tensions in the Old Testament passages on incest. Calvin's arguments were sometimes ingenious. Particularly impressive was his careful parsing of biblical terms to make sense of seemingly discordant biblical passages. Equally impressive was his creative discernment of the common purposes of a number of the biblical laws of impediments (such as the rules on Levirate marriage) that stood in seeming tension, and his ability thereby to harmonize these discordant laws.

But Calvin's arguments about the interrelations among the biblical law, natural law, and human law of impediments were not altogether cogent or altogether consistent with his usual style of legal argumentation. Calvin's usual argument was that the natural law, written on the hearts and consciences of all persons, had become too faded and weakened by sin to be understood fully. A gracious God had thus rewritten the natural law in the Bible to give a fuller and more forceful account of his will for humanity. Accordingly, natural law set a minimum standard of morality that was common to all persons. Biblical law set a higher standard of morality that was becoming of all believers. This familiar logic helped Calvin explain the incest of Abraham, Jacob, Judah, and others. The natural law was not strong enough to keep even these ancient Hebrew patriarchs from incestuous sin. They needed the fuller revelation of God's law in the Bible, which Moses would later record.

In discussing whether the Mosaic law of consanguinity and affinity was full enough, however, Calvin reversed his argument. Now the natural law of impediments was said to be the fuller revelation of God's law, and the biblical law in Leviticus was treated as a mere illustration of nature's more pressing commandments. But this argument presupposed a fully codified natural law of impediments that was nowhere in evidence — save, perhaps, in the ancient common law of pagan peoples. It was a risky business, however, to amend explicit biblical laws on the strength of pagan customs and common laws alone. Why give these non-biblical laws such a generous reading, while roundly denouncing so many others, such as those respecting adultery, polygamy, and infanticide? Calvin did not say.

It was lingering interpretive problems such as these that Beza took time to resolve more clearly and systematically in his *Tract on Annulment and Divorce* (1569). Beza showed that many of the extra-biblical impediments of consanguinity and affinity included in Protestant polities like Geneva were consistent not only with ancient pagan law but also more importantly with the teachings of the Church Fathers and the teachings of Christian moralists, theologians, and canonists ever since.[32] An even more expansive apologia for this new law of

---

32. Beza, TRD, and Tadataka Maruyama, *The Ecclesiology of Theodore Beza: The Reform of the True Church* (Geneva, 1978), pp. 68-79, which places this work in the context of Beza's broader work and methodology.

impediments, with attention to antecedents and parallels in classical and Christianized Roman law, was later offered by François Hotman.[33]

Calvin and Beza, of course, had other arguments to support their amendments to the biblical laws of impediments, namely the arguments from utility and expediency and the avoidance of scandal and confusion. They had used these pragmatic arguments several times, as we have seen in earlier chapters, to ground other impediments to engagement and marriage that were not so clearly prefigured in the Bible, and sometimes the subjects of biblical counter-example. They used these pragmatic arguments again on the issue of incest to support the prohibition of the marriages of father and daughters, of first cousins, and of former paramours, issues that occupied the Genevan Consistory at some length. Geneva was to be a new biblical commonwealth, Calvin and Beza insisted. But this did not mean that the Bible alone was its only valid source of law. God had moved in history to reveal other norms, habits, and procedures for his people to use to govern themselves, and some of these even the pagans could exemplify. The key was making use of these laws in a way that enhanced rather than eclipsed biblical norms of Christian discipline and discipleship.

---

33. See François Hotman, *De gradibus cognationis et affinitas libri duo* (Paris, 1547; Strasbourg, 1556) (a more conventional treatment of the *ius commune*); also *De castis incestisue nuptiis disputatio: In qua de sponsalibus et matrimonio ex iure civili, pontificio, et orientali differitur* (Louvain, 1594); and further *De jure connubiorum: hoc est, De sponsalibus et matrimoniis rite contrahendis ac dissoluendis, seu repudiis tam veterum Romanorum quam hominum nostri seculi* (Frankfurt an Oder, 1592; Leipzig, 1618). In 1549, Calvin described Hotman as one who has "resolved to dedicate his work to the Lord and to the Church. I especially approve of this resolution. For he has strong native talent, is of extensive erudition, and is possessed of other valuable qualities." Letter to Viret (May 7 or 9, 1549), CO 13:265-66.

9-1   Theodore Beza's Tables on Impediments (1569)[34]

A Table of Impediments of Affinity

Paternal great-uncle, aunt	Grandfather	Grandmother	Uncle, maternal great-aunt
Brother and sister of father-in-law's father	Father-in-law's father	Mother-in-law's mother	Brother and sister of mother-in-law's mother
Paternal uncle, aunt	Father	Mother	Uncle, maternal aunt
Brother and sister of father-in-law	Father-in-law	Mother-in-law	Brother and sister of mother-in-law
	Son, son-in-law	Daughter, daughter-in-law	
	Nephew, niece	Nephew, niece	
	Granddaughter's husband	Grandson's wife	
	Niece's husband	Nephew's wife	

Ways in Which These Affinities Can be Paired

Father, step-father	Mother, step-mother
Son and daughter	Son and daughter
Step-son and step-daughter	Step-son and step-daughter
Nephew and niece	Nephew and niece
Step-son's son	Step-son's daughter

Brother-in-law	Husband's brother	Husband, wife	Brother-in-law	Wife's brother
Sister-in-law	sister		Sister-in-law	sister

---

34. Beza, TRD, 2:61-62.

9-2   Commentary on the Harmony of the Law
Leviticus 18:6-18 (1563)[35]

6. *None of you shall approach any one near of kin to him.* This name does not include all female relations. For first cousins on the father's side or mother's side are permitted to intermarry. But it must be restricted to the degrees of relationship . . . that render marriages incestuous. We may, therefore, define these female blood relatives to be those which are referred to next: A son should not marry his mother, nor a son-in-law his mother-in-law, nor a paternal or maternal uncle his niece, nor a grandfather his granddaughter, nor a brother his sister, nor a nephew his paternal or maternal aunt, or his uncle's wife, nor a father-in-law his daughter-in-law, nor a brother-in-law his brother's wife, nor a step-father his step-daughter. The Roman laws accord with the rule prescribed by God, as if their authors had learned from Moses what was proper and agreeable to nature. . . .

It is true, indeed, that this was a part of the political constitution which God established for his ancient people [of Israel]. Still, it must be remembered that whatever is prescribed here is deduced from the very source of right law and from the natural feelings implanted in us by him. . . . The incest prohibitions set forth here are certainly not the kind of law that can be abrogated in accordance with time and place. For this law flows from the fountain of nature itself. It is founded on the general principle of all laws, which is perpetual and inviolable. Certainly God declares that the custom which had prevailed among the heathen was displeasing to him. And this is because nature itself repudiates and abhors filthiness, even though it might be suffered by men.

Thus when God would thereby separate his chosen people from heathen nations, we may assuredly conclude that the incests which he commands them to avoid are absolute pollutions. . . . If this discipline were founded on the utility of a single people, or on the custom of a particular time, or on present necessity, or on any other such circumstances, the laws deduced from it might be abrogated for new reasons, or their observance might be dispensed with in regard to particular persons, by special privilege. But since these laws were enacted only to protect the perpetual decency of nature, no dispensation of them would be permissible. . . . Just and reasonable men will acknowledge that, even among heathen nations, this law was accounted indissoluble, as if implanted and engraved on the hearts of men. On this ground, Paul, more severely to reprove the incest of a step-son with his father's wife, says, that such an occurrence "is not so much as named among the Gentiles" (1 Cor. 5:1).

Some object that such [incestuous] marriages are not prohibited to us in

35. CO 24:661-65 (OTC adapted).

the New Testament. I reply that the marriage of a father with his daughter is not forbidden, nor is a mother prohibited from marrying her son. Shall it therefore be lawful for those, who are near of kin, to form promiscuous unions? Although Paul expressly mentions only one kind of incest, yet he establishes its disgrace by adducing the example of the Gentiles, that at least we should be ashamed if more delicacy and chastity is seen among them. And, in fact, another admonition of the same Paul is enough for me. He writes to the Philippians: "whatever is true, whatever is honorable, whatever is just, whatever is pure, whatever is lovely, whatever is gracious, if there is any excellence, if there is anything worthy of praise, think about these things" (Phil. 4:8).

As to those who ascend or descend in a direct line, it sufficiently appears that there is a monstrous indecency in the connection of father and daughter, or mother and son. A licentious poet, being about to relate the frantic incest of Myrrha, says: "Daughters and fathers, from my song retire, I sing of horror."

In the collateral line, the uncles on both sides represent the father, and the aunts represent the mother. Thus relations with them are forbidden, for it would be something of a similar impropriety. The same rule affects affinity. For the step-mother or mother-in-law represents the mother. The step-daughter or daughter-in-law represents the daughter. The wife of the paternal or maternal uncle represents the mother. And, although these [relations] are not expressly prohibited, we must form our judgment by analogy. The uncle on the father's or mother's side is not forbidden to marry his niece. But, since the nephew is prohibited from marrying his paternal or maternal aunt, the mutual relation of the inferior to the superior degree must prevail. But if any should argue that there is a difference, the reason added by Moses refutes this objection, for it is said, "She is your father's or your mother's near kinswoman." Thus it follows that a niece is guilty of incest if she marries her uncle on either side.

As to brothers and sisters, God pronounces that marriage with a sister, or even with a step-sister, is unlawful; for he forbids uncovering the nakedness of a sister, who is either the daughter of your father or your mother.

9-3 *Consilium* on Consanguinity and Affinity (n.d.)[36]

We know the degrees of blood relationship within which God's law does not permit marriage: a sister may not marry her brother; a niece may not marry her paternal or maternal uncle, nor may a great-niece marry her great-uncle; an

---

36. CO 10:231-33, translated in Calvin, *Ecclesiastical Advice*, pp. 121-23.

aunt, whether on the mother's or father's side, may not marry her nephew or great-nephew. A first cousin, however, whether on the father's side or the mother's, is not forbidden to marry his cousin on the other side of the family.

It is not right to call into question anything in God's law as it applies to prohibitions, and marriages that are condemned by that law should be considered incestuous. It has become accepted by long usage, however, that first cousins should not marry, and the refusal to allow such marriages has become a cause for complaint among us. If anyone should ask for a final ruling on this, therefore, we will not simply reply that the man who marries his first cousin is committing a sin. This freedom exposes the Gospel of Christ to much abuse, however, and we must remember Paul's admonition that our freedom should not become a stumbling block for someone else [1 Cor. 10:23], and that we should refrain from even permitted acts unless they are free of harm to others. We need not fear this bondage which binds the faithful together in a mutual pledge of affection, for consciences remain free in God's presence.

9-4   *Consilium* on Whether a Man May Marry His Deceased Wife's Sister (n.d.)[37]

On the question that is debated today, whether it is appropriate for a man to take in marriage his deceased wife's sister, it has seemed to us that anyone who does so becomes, as St. Paul says, an example of those who delight in pleasing men but who will never make good servants of Jesus Christ.

In the first place, we would prefer that those who affirm this abstain from misinterpreting the two passages they often cite, for in truth they so distort and corrupt them as to produce a contrary meaning. Moreover, the problem could be solved if they would willingly acquiesce in the presence of truth and reason, rather than handing the bridle over to an unrestrained appetite that only interjects confusion in the world.

Without a doubt, when scripture forbade the taking of a brother's wife, God was declaring that a marriage contract of that sort was a truly repugnant act and, consequently, incestuous. As for the diverse reasons they offer, they are worthless, seeing one ought rather to hold to what God propounds. For if the brother's shame is uncovered, then so also is the sister's [see Lev. 18:16].

Nonetheless, we can judge for ourselves that, as in cases involving murder and poisoning, so also in this instance of cohabitation, what God condemns is not the consequence but the evil itself. They argue that the brother's wife is not the same vessel [as when he married her] but has become sordid, so as to lose

---

37. CO 10:233-35, translated in Calvin, *Ecclesiastical Advice*, pp. 123-25.

her chastity; they also insist on the same concerning mothers, daughters, aunts, and nieces.

But, let us affirm the way God has disposed of this matter. For Moses addressed this problem, not in any subtle way, but with a simplicity that ought to suffice. There can be no doubt about what he wrote, or any shadow of subtlety of meaning. "You shall not marry your wife's sister, as long as your wife lives" [Lev. 18:18].

If this were not the law — that a marriage with two sisters is illicit — then we could argue that such a marriage is acceptable. At least under the guise of this law we could argue that a marriage of this kind is prohibited only during the wife's lifetime, but that after her death it is permissible.

Now those who build their case on this exception miss the lawgiver's intention. For God is not concerned with turpitude or incest, but what he condemns is the cruelty of putting two sisters in contention with each other. Laws designed to protect humanity are abrogated when associated with laws defending incestuous marriages.

Certainly, God willed that the above exception be recognized in polygamous cases, so that if a Jew wronged his first wife by taking to bed a second, at least the fighting would be among sisters. For this reason the rabbis concluded that God specifically denied his ancient people the right to infer this caveat from Leah and Rachel, as if the patriarch Jacob's actions justified it.

In truth, this law must not be restricted to blood sisters; rather it pertains to cousins and the entire parentage, for to despise any of them is to fight among one's own kin. If our interpretation is not accepted, then let us, following St. Paul's practice, shake the dust off against them for ignoring what is so plain to their conscience.

9-5 *Consilium* on Whether a Man May Marry His Dead Brother's Widow (n.d.)[38]

It is clear what God has ordained about this in his law. Those interpreters are wrong who explain that a woman may not be taken from her former husband's marriage bed, or that if she has been divorced, she cannot make [a] valid marriage while her husband is still alive. It is improper to twist words into different meanings when they are stated in the same terms in a single passage. God forbids anyone to uncover the nakedness of his father's wife or his uncle's, or his son's, or his nephew's [Lev. 18:16], and it is absurd to make up a different meaning when he sets forth the same opinion about a brother's wife, in just so many

---

38. CO 10:235-38, translated in Calvin, *Ecclesiastical Advice*, pp. 125-29.

words. If it is wrong to marry the wife of one's father, son, uncle, or nephew, we should feel the same about a brother's wife, about whom an entirely similar law has been decreed, with the same substance and tenor. . . .

The law we are discussing now, therefore, concerning marrying the wife of a dead brother, is only directed toward those relatives who are not otherwise prohibited from such a marriage. God did not intend to allow incestuous marriages (which he elsewhere condemns) in order to keep a brother's name from coming to an end. These two things are entirely consistent: for a brother to be prohibited from marrying his brother's widow, and at the same time for kinsmen to be obligated by the law of relationship to raise up seed for the dead, when the marriage is otherwise free from the restriction imposed by the law.

Under this principle Boaz married Ruth, who had earlier been married to his kinsman. History makes clear that the law applied to all kinsmen, but if anyone argues that brothers are included in this number, then by the same reasoning a daughter-in-law would have to be allowed to marry her father-in-law, and a nephew's wife her uncle, and even a step-mother her step-son. Even speaking of this is shameful.

9-6 Commentary on Genesis 38:8-11 (1554)[39]

[At the time of this passage] no law had as yet been prescribed concerning brother's marriages, that the surviving brother should raise up seed to one who was dead. But is it not wonderful that, by the mere instinct of nature, men should have been inclined to this course? For since each man is born for the preservation of the whole race, if any one dies without children, there seems to be here some defect of nature. It was thus considered an act of humanity to acquire some name for the dead, which would provide evidence that he had lived. The only reason why the children born to the surviving brother should be treated as the children of him who had died was so that there might be no dead branch in the family. This was the way they took away the reproach of barrenness. Moreover, since a woman was given as a help to a man, when any woman married into a family, she was, in a certain sense, given to preserve the name of that family. Tamar was thus not altogether free, but was held under an obligation to the house of Judah to produce some offspring.

Now, although this does not proceed from any rule of piety, yet the Lord had impressed it upon the hearts of man as a duty of humanity. Thus he later commanded it to the Jews in their polity. From this, we can infer Onan's evil. He betrayed his brother's honor, and would not allow him, when dead, to ob-

---

39. CO 23:495-99 (OTC adapted).

tain the title of father. This cast dishonor on the whole family. We see that many grant their own sons to their friends for adoption. It was thus an outrageous act of barbarity [for Onan] to deny to his own brother what is given even to strangers. . . . Moreover he has not only shortchanged his brother concerning the right due to him, but he also spilled his semen on the ground rather than raise a son in his brother's name.

9-7 Commentary on Genesis 35:22 (1554)[40]

A sad and even tragic history is now related concerning the incestuous intercourse of Reuben with his mother-in-law. . . . How great and detestable was the dishonor that the mother of two tribes should not only contaminate herself with adultery, but even with incest. This crime is so abhorrent to nature that even the Gentiles have never tolerated it. . . .

Moses only relates that Jacob was informed of this crime. He conceals his grief, not because he was unfeeling (for he was not so stupid as to be insensible to sorrow) but because his grief was too great to be expressed. Moses here seems to have acted as the painter who, in representing the sacrifice of Iphigenia, put a veil over her father's face, because he could not sufficiently express the grief of his countenance. In addition to this eternal disgrace of the family, there were other causes of anxiety that transfixed the heart of the holy man. The sum of his happiness was in his offspring, from which the salvation of the whole world was to proceed. Already two of his sons had been perfidious and sanguinary robbers. Now his firstborn exceeds them both in wickedness.

Here the free election of God appears even more poignantly. God preferred the sons of Jacob over all others in the world — but not on account of their worthiness. Though they had fallen so basely, this election nevertheless remained firm and efficacious.

Warned by such examples, let us learn to fortify ourselves against those dreadful scandals by which Satan strives to disturb us. Let every one also privately apply this to the strengthening of his own faith. For sometimes even good men slide, as if they had fallen from grace. Desperation would necessarily be the consequence of such ruin, unless the Lord, on the other hand, held out the hope of pardon.

A remarkable example of this is set before us in Reuben. Despite this extreme act of iniquity, he retained his rank of a patriarch in the church. We must, however, remain under the custody of fear and watchfulness, lest temptation se-

---

40. CO 23:473-75 (OTC adapted). The CO version lists this as a commentary on Genesis 35:23, though the relevant passage is Genesis 35:22.

cretly seize upon us and the snares of Satan envelop us. For the Holy Spirit did not design to set before us an example of vile lust so that everyone would rush into incestuous relations. Rather, it exposed the infamous baseness of this crime in this honorable person, so that everyone might more vehemently abhor it.

9-8 Commentary on Genesis 38:12-30 (1554)[41]

[After recounting in detail Judah's incestuous adultery and Tamar's duplicitous seduction of him, Calvin wrote:] Tamar could have exposed the crime sooner. But she waited till she was subject to capital punishment, for then she would have a stronger ground to object. Judah was going to subject his daughter-in-law to severe punishment, for he thought that she was guilty of adultery. . . . Judah commanded Tamar to be brought forward in public so that, after the case was tried, she might be punished according to custom. . . .

Tamar's open reproach [of Judah] was motivated by her desire for revenge. She did not seek a hearing with her father-in-law in order to appease his mind. But she tried to make him a party to her death sentence. That Judah immediately acknowledged his fault is proof of his honesty. . . . Though no one was present who could extort a confession from him by force or threats, Judah voluntarily stooped to make one, and took the greater share of the blame on himself. . . . Such truth should likewise prevail among us. We should not be ashamed to confess before the whole world those sins with which God charges us. But we must avoid his partiality; lest, while we are harsh towards others, we should spare ourselves. This narrative also teaches us the importance of not condemning any one without a hearing — not only because it is better that the innocent should be absolved than that a guilty person should perish, but also, because a defense [in a hearing] brings many things to light which sometimes requires a different judgment. . . .

An atrocious and horrible crime had been committed. While Judah thought he was aggrieved, he pressed on with vehemence, and the door of judgment was opened. But now, after the accusation was withdrawn, both [Judah and Tamar] escaped punishment, even though it certainly was the duty of all to rise up against them. Moses, however, intimates that Judah was sincerely penitent: "he knew" his daughter-in-law "again no more." He also confirms what I have said before, that by nature men are imbued with a great horror of such a crime [as incest]. For how did it come about that he abstained from intercourse with Tamar unless he judged naturally that it was improper for a father-in-law to be connected with his daughter-in-law? Whoever attempts to destroy dis-

41. CO 23:497-501 (OTC adapted).

tinctions that nature dictates, between what is base and what is honorable, is like the giants who engage in open war with God.

9-9   Sermon on 2 Samuel 13:1-14 (1562)[42]

[H]ere is a case of incest: it was not legitimate for Amnon to cast an impure eye on his sister Tamar. He ought to have held her in honor, so that such a thought should never have entered his heart. When we see this, let us realize that even though God has favored us by declaring his will to us, since we know what his Law commands us, and what it forbids us, we must not consider ourselves to be exempt from every temptation. Rather, let us be vigilant and take heed to ourselves, for we see that our having knowledge to discern between good and evil does not amount to much after all. Our disposition dominates instead!

That is also how Amnon acted. He gave himself even greater license to do evil by using this pretext: "Tamar, sister of Absalom," so that the evil did not come directly before him to shame him into considering God. But in the end, when he wanted to cloak his fornication, then he "cut his throat" and no longer said: "Tamar, sister of Absalom," but: "Tamar, my sister." Although God constrained him to speak like this to wake him up, in fact it only resulted in hardening him, for the devil had such control of him that he did not know any more about kinship than a dumb animal. . . .

Now it says that Amnon wanted to force his sister, and that she resisted; but the situation was such that she was, in fact, violated by force. Wanting to avoid this, she pointed out: "My brother, you must not come to this, for this unworthy act ought not to be done in Israel, and you would be considered shameful in Israel" (2 Sam. 13:12-13). It is true that the word sometimes implies "folly"; but this translation would be entirely too mild. Hence, it is taken here to mean "unworthy act," as we have already seen. She said further that if he asked her in marriage from his father, "he would not refuse it." . . . She saw that incest was a wicked thing, and that it would be absolutely dreadful to do such a thing in her father's house against her will. She knew all these things. But then she referred the matter to the counsel of her father, as if her father were above the Law. Now that is where her counsel was only good in parts.

Be that as it may, let us carefully remember what is pointed out here and prepare ourselves so that the devil will not be able to surprise us. Let us also benefit from this chastisement given to David. He had given himself far too much liberty — that is, endlessly and unceasingly taking such a large number

---

42. Translated as John Calvin, *Sermons on 2 Samuel Chapters 1–13*, trans. Douglas Kelly (Carlisle, PA, 1992), pp. 613-28.

of wives. Thus, the appropriate salary and dividend was returned to him: God punished him.

9-10   Commentary on 1 Corinthians 5:1-5 (1546)[43]

[St. Paul] shows them what enormous wickedness it is to allow a man in their society to have an illicit connection with his mother-in-law. It is not certain whether the man had seduced her from his father as a prostitute, or whether he kept her under pretense of marriage. This does not much affect the subject in hand. The former case would have been an abominable and execrable whoredom. The latter would have involved an incestuous connection, abhorrent to all propriety and natural decency. . . .

[H]e affirms that [such incest] was "not named among the Gentiles." He does not mean that no such case had ever existed among them, or was ever recorded in their annals, for even tragedies have been written about it. Rather, he means that it was detested by the Gentiles as a shameful and abominable monstrosity. It is a beastly lust, which destroys even natural modesty.

Should any one ask, "Is it just to reproach all with the sin of one individual?" I answer, that the Corinthians are accused not because one of their number has sinned, but because, as is later stated, they encouraged by connivance a crime that was deserving of the severest punishment. . . .

Churches evidently are furnished with power so that, whatever fault there is within them, they can correct or remove it by strict discipline. There is no excuse for those churches that are not on the alert to have filth cleared away. For Paul here condemns the Corinthians. Why? Because they had been remiss in the punishment of one individual. Now he would have accused them unjustly had they not had this power. The power of excommunication is thus established from this passage. Churches have this mode of punishment put into their hands, and they commit sin, Paul shows here, if they do not use it when it is required. For otherwise he would act unfairly to the Corinthians in charging them with this fault.

Having condemned the Corinthians for negligently failing in their duty, he now shows what ought to be done. In order that this stain may be removed, they must cast out this incestuous person from the society of the faithful. He prescribes, then, as a remedy for the disease, excommunication, which they had sinfully delayed too long. . . .

"To deliver over to Satan," some think, only means the infliction of a severe punishment upon the body. But when I examine the whole context more

---

43. CO 49:377-81 (NTC adapted).

narrowly, and at the same time compare it with what is stated in the Second Epistle [2 Cor. 7:12], I give up that interpretation, as forced and at variance with Paul's meaning. I understand it simply as excommunication. For delivering over to Satan is an appropriate expression for denoting excommunication. For, as Christ reigns *in* the Church, so Satan reigns *out of* the Church — as Augustine has also remarked in his sixty-eighth sermon on the words of the Apostle, where he explains this passage. Since we are received into the communion of the Church and remain in it on the condition that we are under the protection and guardianship of Christ, I say that he who is cast out of the Church is in a manner delivered over to the power of Satan, for he becomes an alien, and is cast out of Christ's kingdom.

9-11   Case of Aime Rivilliod and His Maid (1546)[44]

(Nov. 11, 1546). Master Pierre Pillet was asked to tell the truth about what he knows about the rumor concerning Rivilliod's fornication. He answered that he knows nothing about it except by hearsay; nevertheless, it is said that the servant gave birth in Faucigny, and it was baptized in Ville-la-Grand.

(Nov. 25, 1546). Aime Rivilliod was admonished about a maid he had who was pregnant by him. He confessed it, and said that child was baptized in Ville-la-Grand. Asked whether he did not beg the minister of Ville to keep the thing secret, he confessed that the maid is from Ville and gave birth in Cluses last August.

Decided: that he be asked whether the girl is related to him. He denied it, and said it is true that there were those who wanted to persuade witnesses by gifts to confirm that the girl is related to him. He also answered that he would produce someone to whom someone promised a pair of hose if he would confirm the relationship. Let him return here Thursday to produce the witness.

(Dec. 2, 1546). Rivilliod brought his witness, who was asked to respond about its having come to notice that he was solicited by a present to testify against Aime Rivilliod to confirm that the girl he made pregnant was related to Rivilliod. Noble Claude, bastard of Grillier of Ville, called Monsieur Le Grand, answered that it is true that he undertook to execute the letter as the officer Claude Chatron, also known as Collette, asked him to and promised him a good pair of hose if it could be found that the girl was related to Rivilliod. And that the letter was at the instance of someone called Charvet. He denied that this is true, and said he knew the parents of the girl; she is related to his wife.

(Dec. 2, 1546). Rivilliod was asked to say who told him and who told the

---

44. R. Consist. II, 90, 92v, 93v, 94.

woman who nursed the child to nurse the child well, saying these words, "Look closely at me like this; I am wearing a gray cloak, but for the love of this child I would have a good black cape."

Decided: that between now and Saturday Rivilliod make the nurse speak to the syndic. Before the Council.

[Rivilliod was imprisoned for fornication with his servant. On December 6, the Council released him temporarily to attend the fair on business. On December 20, having "endured prison on bread and water according to the edicts," he was released after he begged mercy of God and justice and paid his expenses and a fine of sixty sous.]

9-12   Case of Claude Michallet and His Daughter-in-Law (1547)[45]

(Sept. 1, 1547). The son of Maria, watchman [that is, Claude Michallet] was asked to name a young girl who sleeps with his wife. Said he does not know, unless it is a little girl who turns the spit at Massona's.

A little girl named Andria confessed that it is true that she has slept with [Pernon,] the wife of the younger Maria, and that one night she told her she did not want anyone to sleep with her that night and that her husband had come. Asked how she knew that her husband had come, she said she knew nothing about it, but she kept changing her story. She said again that Pernon told her that she hoped that her husband would come that night.

The wife of Maria, watchman, called Michallet, was asked whether it is true that she sent the girl to sleep with her daughter-in-law. She said yes, when her son was not there. She was asked whether she did not say that her husband entered at night and went to sleep at her daughter-in-law's. She denied having said it, especially because she is disgusting her husband. The young woman [that is, the daughter-in-law] was admonished as to whether it is not true that her father-in-law went into their house through the window. She confessed he made the fire and slept with her, saying she was ill. The reason [the wife of Claude Michallet] mixed the girl up in this is because she told tales to bring them into conflict, and she slept that night with Donne Marie Goneri.

Claude Michallet was admonished because he slept with his daughter-in-law. He confessed it is true, but affirmed and submitted to be put in the fire in case he did it for fornication. He did it to assist her, she being then very ill. He was admonished. They were all reconciled; also that the old woman be tolerated.

45. R. Consist. III, 130-31.

9-13   Case of Antoine Chapuis and Her Nephew Michel (1556)[46]

(Oct. 22, 1556). Antoine, widow of the late Master Evrad Chapuis, was admonished that it has come to notice that she has a nephew who is already full-grown who has slept with her for three or four days. She said no, although he was ill with diarrhea in her late husband's bed, and denied the rest.

Decided: that for Thursday she return here, and summon her neighbor, the widow of the late Master Louis, formerly a preacher, named André, and Michel her nephew.

(Nov. 5, 1556). Andrée, widow of Master Reymond Faucheux, minister, [appeared] against the widow of Master Evrad Chapuis and Michel Castellio. She testified that it is true that she knew that they sleep together, but does not believe this was for any wrong. She heard that this has gone on for about two or three weeks, all in one bed, and that Michel has assisted them greatly in their need, also during the lifetime of Master Evrad.

Master Reymond [a minister] told her that she had raised a scandal. They were admonished for having denied having slept together, as was proven previously. They denied it even more strongly. They were confronted, and the aforesaid Andrée maintained it before them. They persisted in their denial that she had seen them in bed together, admittedly in the large bed, and there were other children there.

Decided: that they be admonished, since there is a strong suspicion.

9-14   Case of André Duplot and His Aunt Jeanne Court (1557)[47]

(June 24, 1557). André, son of Master Jehan Duplot, citizen, was summoned to learn whether he was not at mass in Avignon, where he lived a long time. And a short time ago he came to this city and settled with Jeanne, widow of Rollet Court, who is his aunt, who has had a bad reputation all her life of being a fornicator, with whom he has slept for the last three months. After being questioned, André answered that this is true. Jeanne his aunt, being called, confessed this to be true.

Concerning this it was decided that since André is of considerable age, having long lived in the papacy far from the fear of God, along with Jeanne, his aunt, who has the reputation of being a whore, that they be remanded before the Council to Monday, but that first they be examined further to learn whether they have had carnal relations with each other. Therefore Jeanne was ques-

46. R. Consist. XI, 70v, 75.
47. R. Consist. XII, 68-68v.

tioned first, who declared that they have not had an affair with each other. Moreover she said and declared that Girard Thomas, pin-maker, during the time when he lived in the house of Guillaume Perret, officer, and she served him, tried to perform a lascivious act with her, and he took her and put her head between his legs. Afterwards André was questioned, who said he never thought of committing a villainous act with her. Nevertheless they were remanded as above, and let them be forbidden to spend the night or sleep together any more.

[On June 28 the Council ordered both Duplot and his aunt imprisoned for three days on bread and water. The register also says that Duplot had attended mass in a papal territory. They were released on July 1, being further ordered not to sleep together anymore.]

9-15 Case of Michel Pointeau (1557)[48]

(Sept. 23, 1557). Claudine, wife of Remond Baldin, said that her brother-in-law, her sister's husband, solicited her to fornicate. He is named Michel Pointeau. He is present here and confesses it to be so, for which he repents; he did it while being led by the evil spirit. Concerning this Remond Baldin was heard. He said that, for himself, he pardons him [Michel], but he wishes the fault to be punished, especially because he kept [after] Claudine since she was a young girl, whom he solicited to fornicate. He does not know how [long] it was, after she was married, that he solicited her more closely.

After being reproved, he [Michel] said that whatever fault might exist, Our Lord is a greater pardoner than we ourselves are sinners. Pointeau's wife also said that her husband told her he had often been to Claudine, who often came to visit him in his room. Michelle, sister-in-law of Pointeau and wife of Jean Archevauld, also said she had heard Pointeau say that there is no sinner so great that God is not a greater pardoner. Pointeau was recalled, but he denied it. Michelle maintained it in his presence. Claudine maintained to him that he had solicited her to fornicate before and after she was married and that he put his hand under her apron.

Decided: that communion be forbidden to Pointeau, then he be remanded before the Council to Monday to purge their city of such riff-raff.

[Pointeau was summoned by the Council on September 27 but failed to appear. The Council ordered that he be found and required to answer the accusation. There is no further mention of this case in the Council register.]

---

48. R. Consist. XII, 99v.

9-16   Case of Claude Michaud and Aima Manget (1552)[49]

(Dec. 8, 1552). Claude Michaud, haberdasher, and Aima Manget presented a petition to get advice whether they may take each other in marriage. She said that the other wife was of the brother and she of the sister,[50] who were remanded here by the Council.

Decided: that they be remanded to the Council, that this lies in the discretion of the Council, that it is not forbidden by the law of God, the civil law, or the Council of Bern, and they may do it at their discretion. Also [we] ask them to enact edicts about it [i.e. the law of impediments], as they have so often been asked.

9-17   Case of Dom Legier Joli and Jaqueme of Etaux (1546)[51]

(Aug. 26, 1546). Dom Legier Joli and his fiancée, Jaqueme of Etaux, [were called]. The woman was admonished as to whether they have been engaged long. She said for two weeks, and it is only two weeks since the wife of Dom Legier died. Asked whether she has not said she is pregnant, she denied it. She confessed that three days after the death of the wife of Dom Legier she became engaged [to him]. She denied again having said that she was pregnant by Dom Legier. The aforesaid [Dom Legier] being asked how long his wife has been dead, answered that it is now two weeks, and that the following Sunday he became engaged to the woman [Jaqueme]. Asked whether her father knew anything about it in that short time, he said that on Friday he went to find the woman's father [to ask for his consent].

Decided: that Monsieur Mermet, their neighbor, should inquire of the neighbors between now and Tuesday and make a fuller report about it here.

(Aug. 31, 1546). Master Reymond spoke about the duty assigned to Mermet de Veyrier. [Mermet] could not come here, but he deputized him [Reymond] to report here. He said that it is true that the two watchmen of Saint-Gervais have heard several times that he [Dom Legier] said during his wife's lifetime that if she died he would take this woman, the wife [that is, the widow] of Master François Cousturier. He said that she told him she feared she was pregnant by Dom Legier and that the neighbors have a strong suspicion of it, and also that

---

49. R. Consist. VII, 108.

50. This wording is confusing, but it seems to mean that his brother had married her sister, and the question was whether he could still marry her. We found no mention of this case in the Council Register.

51. R. Consist. II, 77-78, 84v, 86v.

Uguette admonished her about it. She also said that the deceased had said, "I see well that I must give way to her."

Decided: that the Council inquire whether they fornicated beforehand and that the marriage should not take effect.

(Aug. 31, 1546). Dom Legier was admonished. He confessed having indeed said that, if his wife died, he would take this woman. Asked whether his late wife did not complain and did not fear the woman, he denied it. Also confessed having indeed been away while she drew near to death.

His fiancée was asked whether she did not say she feared she was pregnant, she denied it. Asked whether she said it to a neighbor only last Thursday, she denied it. Let her be strongly admonished that if it becomes known that they fornicated and then received communion they will be severely punished. They were remanded before the Council.

Decided: both were to be brought back to be informed that it is a scandal that they live together, and let her stay away until a decision about it is made.

[On September 6, 1546, the Council ordered that the case be investigated. Three days later the Council decided to prosecute both parties for adultery during the lifetime of Dom Legier's wife. The prosecution apparently failed.]

(Oct. 14, 1546). Dom Legier was asked where his fiancée lives. He said at his house. He was admonished because he denied that he had had her company, and it now appears that she is pregnant, and it was while his late wife was alive that they fornicated. Asked whether the Council had not forbidden them to spend time together, he denied it. They were remanded before the Council to be given the decision of the Council.

[On October 26, on the advice of the Consistory, the Council declared the engagement contract void and imprisoned Joli and his servant. They were released on October 28 and sent to the Consistory.]

(Oct. 28, 1546). Further decision concerning Dom Legier Joli, who has again been remanded before the Consistory to learn whether the marriage should go into effect. The decision is that it would be a scandal and open the door for many to kill their wives and provide the means, and that it will be shown that his late wife complained and died of distress. Before the Council.

[Pierre Gand, Jaqueme's father, asked the Council to permit the marriage. But in a declaration of January 25, 1547, the Council stood by its decision. What came of the couple is unclear, but by 1550 Dom Legier was married to a certain Guillauma, who was imprisoned that year for adultery.]

9-18   Case of Amied de Leamon and Claudine (1546-1547)[52]

(March 4, 1546). Amied de Leamon of Gy was admonished for having fornicated in the house of Françoise, so that his mother found him. He denied it. He
was again [admonished] as to why the woman about whom there is a rumor
against him went away and hid in the cow stable when his mother found him at
the house of the woman. He was artful and ill-willed, and still said he has done
nothing improper. Asked to give the name of the one who hid in the stable, he
named her Claudine. He does not want to confess. The minister Master Anry
[Henri de le Mare, brother-in-law of Amied] asked him whether it is not true
that under severe penalties he was forbidden the company of Claudine, a
whore. He denied it, and was shifty.

Decided: that the Council be asked to give orders to the castellan of Saint
Victor to inquire into the whole matter according to the law to obtain more certain information. Regarding the boy, to prohibit him from frequenting [her]
company any more and to obey his mother. She must return here in three weeks
to give a better account of her [recitation of the Lord's] prayer.

(March 11, 1546). Claudine, widow of François Mestra of Gy [appeared].
Master Anry of Jussy spoke of a woman who he said is a harlot, and especially
about a man who was here last Thursday, Amied de Leamon of Gy, as has already been stated, and others. She was admonished and asked whether it is not
true that once the mother of Amied de Leamon found her at the house of
Françoise, widow of the late Monet Mothu of Gy, and that she fled to the stable,
and Amied was there. She answered it is true, and it was to avoid having a quarrel with the mother of Amied. Asked whether she did not know Gonin Floutet,
she denied it. Asked whether Gonin did not desire her in marriage, she denied
it. Asked whether she has ever left her husband, she said no. Asked whether she
ever asked one named François Pytard, merchant, for red half-sleeves [as an engagement gift?], she denied it. Asked whether she knew Remond Favre, she said
yes respectfully. Asked whether she ever made his bed, she said yes, with his
niece. And asked whether he ever gave her anything, she denied it. Said that
Favre helped them with the threshing.

Master Anry said that he himself, with the Lieutenant, took great pains to
make her return to her husband, and that she is a liar. She could not deny it. She
was asked whether it is not true that in Cristini's time she was found alone with
Amied de Leamon. She could not deny it, because it was settled before Cristini,
who was then castellan. She confessed it. Asked whether she knows anything
about her sister, she said no and was deceitful.

Decided: a petition was read, and Master Anry was asked about a state-

52. R. Consist. II, 37, 38v, 91v; R. Consist. III, 56, 66, 70.

ment contained in the petition that he took action against her and her stepson. Master Anry gave a certain answer, that Bienvenustz had remanded her, and that this was known by the castellan. Also concerning those who have been injured or burned, said there are several, and the thing is sufficiently notorious.

Also decided: that Master Anry should send me, the secretary, the [names of the] fornicators in writing with the articles on the matter, and then they will be sent to the Council, and they will send them back to the castellan to make proper investigations. Before the Council.

Asked again to tell the truth, she said she did not know what to say, asking for justice against the minister.

[On March 23 the Council ordered the castellan of Saint-Victor to make an investigation of Claudine. We found no further reference to the matter in the Council register until September 7, when the Council ordered that "the whore from Gy" be imprisoned and questioned about the accusations.]

(Nov. 18, 1546). Antoine de Leamon of Gy was asked to say what he knows about Claudine and his brother [Amied]. Asked whether he knows that his brother associated with the aforesaid after he was forbidden to associate with her, he answered no, [they did not associate] except in the company of others. Confessed that on Sunday he went to a house where they drank, and that she brought wine there.

Martine, wife of Martin du Soyt of Gy, when asked about the aforesaid, said she knows them well. She said she has never seen them except in proper circumstances. Asked whether she knew that Claudine had burned anyone, she said she had heard that Claudine had burned Nicolas de la Planche, who is her relative. She also said that at the time when the vines were pruned she saw Claudine and Amied de Leamon in a vineyard alone, and that girl came to him. But she went off to fetch her cows and left them together and does not know anything else. She confessed that it is said that she [Claudine] is a fornicator and that he [Amied] entertains her. She confessed that Claudine gave her two quarterons of wine to keep and that she came to get them and took them to a banquet at the house of Richard Lanterme and that Amied was there.

(April 14, 1547). Amied de Leamon and Claudine, his fiancée, of Gy [were called]. She stated that the aforesaid promised her marriage and gave her drink and gave her a silver ring in the name of marriage. He denied it. She described the ring and said that he gave it to her in the presence of her brother about nine weeks ago. He still denied it. They were admonished for their rebelliousness and because they were forbidden to associate any more because of the suspicion of fornication.

She was taken away, and he was asked to tell the truth. Asked whether he did not give her the ring, he said no, he never saw it or had it or bought it, and does not want to confess it.

Decided: that they be remanded before the Council; that he be deposed under oath to acknowledge the ring.

[On April 18, 1547, the Council learned that the two "disagree about having fornicated together, François Mestra, the first husband of the aforesaid [Claudine], [still] being alive [at the time], Leamon confessing and the widow denying, although they agree about the promise of marriage and the fornication." The Council ordered the castellan of Saint-Victor to make them answer and punish them.]

(May 5, 1547). Consistorial decision: concerning the promise of marriage between Amied de Leamon of Gy and Claudine, widow of François Mestra, and since it is amply proven by the answers in a letter sent by order of the Council asking the advice of the Consistory concerning this, that it should be proven that they fornicated before her husband died, and make them come here Thursday to confront them so one can learn the truth about it better.

(May 12, 1547). Amied de Leamon and his fiancée who have again been remanded both by the Council and by the castellan of Saint-Victor to learn the truth better. Asked how long they have fornicated, he answered it has been for the space of fully three years. Asked how long her husband has been dead, she answered for a year and a half, and that the aforesaid [Amied de Leamon] lied wickedly, because previously and during the life of her husband he did not have her company. He affirmed everything stated above.

Decided: that the castellan obtain good information as to whether they had intercourse together beforehand, while her first husband was alive. If it is proven that they had intercourse before this the marriage should not go into effect. If it was afterwards, the marriage should take effect. Also to inquire into her reputation and whether he has a position as guardian.

9-19   Case of François Du Frêney and Claudine of Gy (1551-1552)[53]

(Dec. 31, 1551). Claudine, wife of François Du Frêney of Gy, was asked whether she lives with her husband. She said no: her husband lives in Jussy and she lives in Thoiry in the Gex district. She was admonished that she fornicates and is pregnant yet again, and has already had another [child]. She was obstinate and [uttered] many words of excuse.

Decided: that on Thursday she must return here. Let her not receive communion, and let a message be sent to the castellan of Jussy to make Amied de Leamon come to confront them, as well as her husband. For Thurs-

53. R. Consist. VI, 81-82, VII, 46, 51, 69, 78, 82, 86. Calvin was absent from the sessions on January 7 and September 8, 1552 (ibid., VI, 82; VII, 78).

day, and to Monsieur Bol(?), castellan, to make de Leamon and her husband come.

(Jan. 7, 1552). Monsieur Saint-André, minister of Jussy, stated that François Du Frêney of Jussy requests a divorce from Claudine, his wife, because of all the faults she has committed previously.

Decided: that both she and Amied de Leamon of Gy be remanded here for Thursday. The aforesaid [François] stated that his wife has deserted him and has offended as a fornicator. For Thursday to the castellan of Saint-Victor.

(June 9, 1552). Amied de Leamon of Gy was admonished that he does not reform from pursuing Claudine, his mistress. Whatever prohibitions the Council has laid on him, he denies having behaved otherwise than as instructed.

Decided: that he depart until he is summoned, and we will obtain more information. Decided: that the castellan be asked to get information. To the castellan of Saint-Victor.

(June 30, 1552). François Du Frêney of Gy and Claudine, his wife [appeared]. He stated that his wife is badly behaved, as we have already been sufficiently informed about her vicious life, and asked to be separated [that is, divorced] from her for the honor of God. She in a similar argument asked to be separated [that is, divorced].

Decided: that they be remanded before the Council, and may it please the Council to command the castellan to obtain more ample information before granting such a divorce, following so many prohibitions that have been laid on her to associate no more with her lover Amied de Leamon.

(Aug. 25, 1552). Amied de Leamon of Gy has been remanded here by the castellan after being punished for having fornicated with Claudine, for which he has been so many times admonished, and they have not improved.

Decided: that considering that they have still continued [fornicating], communion be forbidden him, and for the next one [that is, the next time communion is served] that he return here. He said that Master Henri, the minister, his brother-in-law, is the true cause, because he was the cause why he did not marry her.

(Sept. 8, 1552). Claudine of Gy was admonished why she does not live with her husband and why she has thus wandered through the country, and who remanded her here and why. Answered the castellan [brought her here], for having had a child. She begged for mercy.

Decided: that she and her husband come Thursday to try to reconcile them, and strict remonstrances.

(Sept. 29, 1552). François Du Frêney of Jussy, husband of Claudine of Gy, was admonished whether he does not want to be reconciled with his wife. He said it is not possible to take her back because of her great faults. She did not appear. Finally she appeared. She promised to reform and be obedient to him.

He said he would rather abandon the country and be drawn and quartered. He asked to be separated [that is, divorced]. She said he wanted to kill her before he married her.

They were admonished separately that there is a scandal that he sleeps with his sister. He denied it emphatically, and that a wicked woman should not be believed. She was admonished as to how she knows he sleeps with his sister. She said some people have told her so, such as Jean Gassant, officer, and the wife of his son-in-law Daniel, and Remond Favre, living in this city, and Louis Coster. Afterwards she named Monsieur Claude Deletra, whom she asked in Council whether she might not have him for a husband if her husband died.

Decided: that for Thursday we summon and send the castellan of Jussy a message to have him make the witnesses come.

(Oct. 13, 1552). Claudine, wife [of] François Du Frêney of Jussy, and her witnesses, the officer Gassand and Remond Favre [were asked] about the fact that she has said that they well know that Frêney has slept with his sister. The officer said that he indeed knew that he slept with her and had informed the castellan, who ordered him to check up on it, but he has not been able to observe anything. And Favre said that about two years ago he, being in the town of Jussy, entered their house one night, and he saw only one bed, and they slept together.

Decided: that if he [François Du Frêney] denies it, let him be confronted with Remond Favre. He [said] that while his wife was debauching herself he withdrew to his sister and slept there with her [i.e., he lodged at her house]. This was on Thursday the first of this month. He denied, on pain of having his head cut off, and there was only one bed.

Decided: that such a matter should be remanded before the Council, that it is a scandal, and also following his denial let it please the Council to take action. And as for the divorce he asks, it is reasonable, and he should be punished.

9-20   Case of Jeanne and Jaques Marcellin (1556-1557)[54]

(June 1, 1557). It was decided concerning the petition of Jeanne Cavette, wife of Jaques Marcellin, that she address the petition to the Council with other evidence that will be obtained in Thonon about her behavior, when she wishes, to obtain permission for her return.

(July 8, 1557). Concerning the petition sent to the Consistory by the Council, it was decided that since [Jeanne] Cavette, wife of Monsieur Jaques Marcellin, the petitioner, has committed incest, which would not deserve merely

---

54. R. Consist. XII, 55v, 72.

banishment or the whip but corporal [read: capital] punishment, that for the present the gate not be opened to her to return to this city, in order to avoid scandal. Since the Council has done her this grace of allowing her to live within their territories, and since she is in Cologny, where there is a church related to this [church], let her stay there until she has corrected herself further. And may it please the Council to bring and call before them Jaques Marcellin, her husband, who urges this business, and declare to him that if he importunes them further in this matter they will dismiss him . . . that he may go to live with her.

CHAPTER 10

Be Not Unequally Yoked with Unbelievers

The Theology and Law of Interreligious Marriage

Mixed marriages were the subjects of mixed messages in the Bible. The Old Testament often condemned the interreligious marriage of Jews and Gentiles.[1] Various passages pointed to interreligious marriage as a cause and consequence of moral decay among God's chosen people.[2] Those men who did intermarry were sometimes severely punished, and ordered to "cast out" and "separate" from their foreign wives and children.[3] Yet, the Mosaic law made provision for marriage between Jewish men and Gentile female captives.[4] And, several of the earlier patriarchs did marry foreigners, sometimes without evident reprisal. Esau married two Hittites. Joseph married an Egyptian, Judah a Canaanite, Moses a Midianite, Boaz a Moabitess, Samson a Philistine, Bathsheba a Hittite, and Solomon all manner of foreign women.[5] St. Paul commanded generically: "Be ye not unequally yoked together with unbelievers."[6] But he encouraged parties who found themselves in marriages with unbelievers not to seek divorce or separation in the hopes that the believer could help save the unbeliever.[7]

Based on these biblical texts, the medieval canonists had made differences in religion an impediment that allowed parties to annul engagements. Chris-

---

1. Deut. 7:3-4; Ezra 9–10; Neh. 13:3, 23-28; Mal. 2:11.

2. Exod. 34:16; Num. 25:1-18; Josh. 23:12; Judg. 3:5-6; 1 Kings 11:4; Isa. 2:6.

3. Num. 25:6-9; Neh. 13:25; Ezra 9:3, 10-11.

4. Deut. 21:10-14.

5. Gen. 26:34; 38:2; 41:45; Exod. 2:21; 12:1; Ruth 4:13; Judg. 14; 16:4-22; 2 Sam. 11:3; 1 Kings 11:4.

6. 2 Cor. 6:14 (KJV).

7. 1 Cor. 7:12-16.

tians engaged to Jews, Muslims, heretics, or "pagans" could and should have their engagements annulled, particularly if the non-belief occurred or was discovered after their engagement. It was a more controversial question whether difference of religion was an impediment that annulled marriages as well. A Christian and non-believing spouse were certainly bound by a natural bond and a civil contract; the question was whether an indissoluble sacramental bond had been formed when one or both parties remained unbaptized.[8] In the early thirteenth century, Pope Honorius III had declared famously that "the sacrament of marriage exists not only among the Latins [Catholics] and Greeks [Orthodox Christians], but also among the faithful and infidels."[9] But later medieval canonists continued to list differences in religion among the absolute impediments that would support cases of annulment of marriage as well as actions for formal separation. Such cases were particularly attractive if the parties had made religious compatibility a condition to their marriage, if the spouse had hidden his or her non-belief till after the marriage, or if the nonbeliever became an active enemy of the faith and a danger to the body and soul of the spouse.[10]

Calvin drew from these biblical passages a two-fold teaching about interreligious marriage.[11] First, Protestants should not marry Catholics, Orthodox, Jews, Muslims, or unbelievers. Those who sought to enter such mixed marriages should be strongly dissuaded, though they could not ultimately be prevented from marriage. Second, parties who were already in mixed marriages, or whose spouse lapsed from the faith after the wedding, should remain together. Those who sought to escape such mixed marriages should be strongly dissuaded, though they could not ultimately be prevented from separating from spouses whose abuse imperiled the body and soul of the believing spouse. Though none of this teaching on interreligious marriage found its way into Genevan statutes, the Consistory applied this law consistently throughout Calvin's lifetime.

---

8. See diverse opinions summarized in Sanchez, bk. 2, disp. 2-4; R. H. Helmholz, *The Spirit of the Classical Canon Law* (Athens, GA, 1996), pp. 240ff.

9. See c. 11, X, 1, xxxvi, using translation in Joyce, p. 211.

10. Weigand 1:139, 157ff., 207, 381ff.; Brundage, pp. 195ff., 238, 244, 573.

11. Calvin left no commentaries or sermons on Judges, Ruth, 1 Kings, Ezra, or Nehemiah. He did not regard Isaiah 2:6 as a commentary on interreligious marriage, though it had traditionally been interpreted as such. See Comm. Isa. 2:6. He regarded Miriam and Aaron's opposition to Moses in Num. 12:1-8 as a defiance of Moses' authority, not as an objection to his marriage to a Cushite (Midianite) woman. See Comm. Harm. Law Exod. 2:16-22; Num. 12:1-8.

Theological Teachings

Before Marriage

Calvin came to his position on interreligious marriage early, and he deviated little from it throughout his career. In a 1537 open letter on "Preserving the Purity of the Christian Religion," he wrote: "When contracting marriage, think about the fetters in which you get entangled if you take a wife differing from you in religion. . . . [H]ow can you expect a good wife from him whom you will not hear while strictly prohibiting you from being 'yoked with unbelievers' (2 Cor. 6:14)?"[12] "When a man is to marry," he later wrote, "he should (so far as possible) choose a wife who will help him in the worship of God . . . who knows God and his Word, and who is ready to give up all idolatry."[13]

For Calvin, several of the early Old Testament stories underscored the dangers of mixed or interreligious marriage. God set the laws against interreligious marriage already very early, Calvin argued — in the aftermath of Cain's murder of his brother Abel reported in Genesis (**Doc. 10-1**). This prohibition on interreligious marriage was designed to separate the children of God from evildoers, and to keep a remnant of the faithful pure for proper worship of God. But this law was honored in the breach from the start, for Seth's children married indiscriminately and did what was evil. Genesis reports that "the Lord was very sorry he had made man on the earth, and it grieved him to his heart" (Gen. 6:6). God resolved to purge the world through the Flood, sparing only Noah and his family.

After the Flood, however, interreligious marriage continued apace. Esau, the son of Isaac and brother of Jacob, took two Hittite women as wives when he came of age (Gen. 26:34-35). His polygamy was sinful enough, Calvin argued in his 1554 Commentary on Genesis, but no more sinful than that of his brother Jacob who took both Rachel and Leah as wives (**Doc. 10-2**).[14] What was more sinful was that Esau married foreign Hittite women contrary to God's commandment against interreligious marriage. These two daughters-in-law, Genesis 26:35 reports, "made life bitter for Isaac and Rebekah," Esau's parents. Therefore God cut Esau off from his inheritance — despite his claims as first-born son to primogeniture and despite his father Isaac's continued preference for him. Jacob,

---

12. CO 5:239, 275. See a comparable use of 2 Cor. 6:14 in his Serm. Deut. 21:10-14 (Doc. 10-4 below). In his 1548 Commentary on 2 Corinthians, however, Calvin argued that Paul's injunction "Do not be mismatched with unbelievers" was not about marriage but about associations more generally.

13. *Consilium* (April 28, 1556), CO 10:264-66; Lect. and Comm. 1 Cor. 7:12, 14; Serm. Deut. 21:10-14.

14. On polygamy, see Chapter 7.

Isaac's second born, inherited most of his father's fortune, albeit through duplicity, and came to stand in the line of the patriarchs (Gen. 27:5-30).

Similarly, Jacob's son Judah married a Canaanite woman, the daughter of Shua, "out of lust," and contrary to the commandment of God and the orders of his father (Gen. 38:2). Thus "God cursed the offspring" of this forbidden interreligious marriage, Calvin said (**Doc. 10-3**). Judah and his wife were the parents of three sons, all of whom died prematurely, including the ill-fated Onan, the one whom we saw God strike down for "spilling his seed upon the ground," rather than fulfilling his duty to impregnate his widowed sister-in-law Tamar.[15] This was the same Tamar whom Judah, her philandering father-in-law, later impregnated with the twin bastards Perez and Zerah, much to Judah's shame and that of the elder patriarch Jacob.[16] For Calvin, all these were the sad but necessary consequences of defying God's prohibition against interreligious marriage.

These sad stories were reason enough, said Calvin, for God to repeat the prohibition against interreligious marriage in the Mosaic law (Deut. 7:3-4), allowing it only if the foreign wife to be underwent a conversion and purification before marriage (Deut. 21:10-14). Calvin preached at length on these passages in the mid-1550s, perhaps troubled by the growing incidents of interreligious marriage between Protestants and Catholics in Geneva (**Doc. 10-4**).[17] To marry an unbeliever is to take "mortal poison" into your home, Calvin preached ominously. To be "yoked" permanently to an unbeliever through marriage is to risk being pulled off "the road to salvation. He therefore who couples himself consciously and of his own will with the unfaithful, such a one banishes himself from the kingdom of God as far as he is able."[18]

Calvin recognized that the Old Testament prohibitions against interreligious marriage were firmer than the laws that governed modern-day Christians. He addressed this squarely in his late-life Lectures on Malachi (**Doc. 10-5**). In the Old Testament, God had sought to erect an absolute "wall of separation" between Jews and Gentiles so that the Jews could remain a pure and holy people of God. The prohibition against interreligious marriage was part and product of that broader mandate.[19] In the New Testament, however, Christ

---

15. See Comm. Gen. 38:8-12, excerpted in Doc. 9-6 above.

16. See Comm. Gen. 38:12-30, excerpted in Doc. 9-8 above.

17. See also Serm. Deut. 7:1-4; Comm. Harm. Law Exod. 34:11-16; Comm. Harm. Law Num. 25:1. In his late-life Comm. Harm. Law Deut. 7:3-4, Calvin said nothing about the prohibition on interreligious marriage.

18. See also Comm. Harm. Law Num. 25:2, where Calvin described the Israelites' association with the Moabites as the first in a series of inevitable steps into deeper sin: first you marry a foreign wife, then you attend a worship service to idols to humor your wife, and soon you worship with full zeal.

19. Comm. Eph. 2:14.

broke down the "wall of separation" (Eph. 2:14) between "Jew and Greek," encouraging all to be united in Christ (Gal. 3:28; Col. 3:10-11). Does that change in relationship not encourage Christians to interact more freely with unbelievers, perhaps even to marry them in the hope of saving them?

Certainly not, said Calvin. Christ did not come into the world to "end the civil order . . . of the household" or to "sow confusion" about God's ancient commands.[20] While God does not now require Christians to be absolutely separated from nonbelievers, he commands them not to be "unequally yoked" with them (2 Cor. 6:14). Thus Christians need to "distinguish between the contracts which associate us" with the evil ways of unbelievers, "and those which do not all diminish our liberty." Marriages were clearly contracts of close association, for in the normal "civil order" of marriage spouses sacrifice their liberty to serve each other:

> As long as we live among unbelievers, we cannot escape those dealings with them which relate to the ordinary things of life. But if we get closer, so that a greater intimacy becomes necessary, we open the door as it were to Satan. Such are the alliances between kings and nations, and marriages between private persons. Thus Moses laid down rules about them for the ancient people. While our current condition [as Christians] is freer, we are still warned to avoid all temptations that might give occasion to this evil. It is well known that men are too apt to be led away by the blandishments of their wives; and also that men in their power compel their wives to obedience. So, those who mix with idolaters, knowingly and willingly devote themselves to idols.[21]

Calvin used this interpretation to counsel his followers to marry pious Protestants. On this issue, Calvin was less jealous about nice denominational distinctions among Protestants than he was on other theological issues. Calvin himself, as we saw, married an Anabaptist widow, even though he had long castigated Anabaptists for a number of disputed theological teachings — not least the teaching of adult baptism which would cause conflict if an Anabaptist-Calvinist couple had children.[22] The real test, for Calvin, was whether prospective spouses were of suitable Christian piety and modesty, not what precise Protestant denominational label attached to them.

Calvin elaborated on this advice in a pair of letters to Lelio Sozzini, an Ital-

---

20. Serm. Gal. 3:24-28.

21. Comm. Harm. Law Exod. 34:11-16. See also Comm. Harm. Law Num. 25:1.

22. See above Chapter 3 on Calvin's marriage to Idelette de Bure. We have found no evidence of any dispute between Calvin and Idelette on infant baptism, an issue that would have come up for resolution on the birth of their son.

ian refugee living in Zurich. Sozzini had asked Calvin whether it was proper for a Protestant to marry a Catholic or "other unbeliever" and how such mixed couples were to be received in the Protestant community.[23] "I have no doubt but that the marriage is sinful," Calvin replied (**Doc. 10-6**). But such marriages are not absolutely forbidden, and those who are intermarried should not be shunned.

In a return letter, Sozzini pressed for a fuller answer. Wasn't it better for a Protestant to marry a Catholic rather than a Muslim? Could the couple have their marriage consecrated in a Protestant church, or would they need to seek consecration in a Catholic church? Could they have their children baptized in a Protestant church?[24] Calvin was reluctant to "lay down a firm rule" or set a "firm limit" on how far a person could stray from the Protestant path in seeking a spouse (**Doc. 10-7**). Marriage to a Catholic, who believed in Christ, was better than marriage to a Muslim, who denied Christ. Even more so, if the former Catholic was now "divorced" from papal superstition. But Calvin was reluctant to define in the abstract which mixed marriages were altogether foreclosed to Reformed believers and which unions were precluded from blessing by a minister of the Reformed church. The children of such mixed marriages could, and indeed should, be baptized in the Reformed church.[25] Whether their parents' marriage could be equally well accepted and blessed, Calvin preferred to deal with on a case-by-case basis.

After Marriage

Once contracted, however, an interreligious marriage could not be broken. Parties who married in defiance of the biblical prohibition against interreligious marriage, or whose spouses later fell into disbelief after the wedding, had to cope with their condition. St. Paul had put this matter clearly in his first letter to the Corinthians:

> I say, not the Lord, that if any brother has a wife who is an unbeliever, and she consents to live with him, he should not divorce her. If any woman has a

23. CO 13:272-74.

24. CO 13:336-40.

25. Where both parents were Catholic, however, Reformed churches could refuse to baptize their child, even if the grandparents were Reformed. See Calvin's support of Guillaume Farel in this position as described in David N. Wiley, "Calvin's Friendship with Guillaume Farel," in *Calvin and His Contemporaries: Colleagues, Friends, and Conflicts*, ed. David Foxgrover (Grand Rapids, 1998), pp. 187, 196-97; *Guillaume Farel: Biographie nouvelle par un groupe d'historiens* (Neuchâtel/Paris, 1930), pp. 627-29.

husband who is an unbeliever, and he consents to live with her, she should not divorce him. For the unbelieving wife is consecrated through her husband. Otherwise, your children would be unclean, but as it is they are holy. But if the unbelieving partner desires to separate, let it be so; in such a case the brother or sister is not bound. For God has called us to peace. Wife, how do you know whether you will save your husband? Husband, how do you know whether you will save your wife? (1 Cor. 7:12-16)

In his 1546 Commentary on this passage, Calvin admitted that such a mixed marriage was not ideal (**Doc. 10-8**).[26] But if zealously pursued, the piety of the believer sanctifies the marriage more than the impiety of the nonbeliever pollutes it. And thus the believing spouse should not seek divorce, for that would break an oath before God, and deprive God of a means of saving the unbelieving spouse. But if the unbelieving spouse leaves, in breach of his or her oath to God, the marriage is broken, and the deserted spouse is free to seek marriage with another.

Calvin underscored this ethic many times in his letters to distressed wives who had converted to the Protestant cause, and now faced repression from their Catholic husbands. Could these women leave their homes and come to live among their new coreligionists in Geneva?[27] Calvin's repeated advice, following St. Paul's teaching, was that the wives should remain fervent in their faith in the hopes that their husbands would see the Protestant light. Only if their husbands left first or if the wives faced mortal peril by staying at home would Calvin condone their departure, and even then he was quite reluctant.

A good example of this advice came in Calvin's 1552 letter to a "certain noblewoman from Paris," as she anonymously identified herself (**Doc. 10-9**). She had sent a long letter to the Consistory complaining bitterly of her husband's "idolatry and persecution of Christians" and detailing six years of "grievous and severe assaults" on her "spirit and body." She asked whether "the law of marriage compels her to live with her husband, or whether the Gospel permits her to leave him and to seek liberty" in Geneva.

Calvin counseled her to stay home, even though he sympathized with her grim plight. "[W]hat God reveals to us in his Word" is that a marital couple's

---

26. Calvin's position on this passage did not change appreciably in his later Sermons on 1 Cor. 7:12-16.

27. See Charmarie J. Blaisdell, "Calvin's Letters to Women: The Courting of Ladies in High Places," *Sixteenth Century Journal* 13 (1982): 3; Nancy L. Roelker, "The Appeal of Calvinism to French Noblewomen in the Sixteenth Century," *Journal of Interdisciplinary Studies* 2 (1970-71): 405; Charmarie J. Blaisdell, "Calvin's and Loyola's Letters to Women: Politics and Spiritual Counsel in the Sixteenth Century," in Robert V. Schnucker, ed., *Calviniana: Ideas and Influence of John Calvin* (Ann Arbor, MI, 1988), pp. 235, 248-50.

differences in religion were no ground for separation or divorce. To the contrary, said Calvin, citing 1 Corinthians 7:13, "a believing party cannot, of his or her own free will, divorce the unbeliever," but should endure bravely and persevere with constancy and make every effort to "direct her husband toward the road of salvation." It would be an irony, said Calvin, "to abrogate the order of nature" in marriage for the sake of one form of Christianity over another. The parties must continue to live together, "and no matter how great his obstinacy might be, she must not let herself be diverted from the faith; rather must affirm it with constancy and steadfastness, whatever the dangers." She need not put soul and body in mortal jeopardy for the sake of the marriage; she may leave when faced with such a dire threat. But in this case, she has no excuse for leaving her husband, without having made a more adequate declaration of her faith to him. Calvin repeated this advice in several other letters, including a 1556 *consilium* that circulated widely in the Protestant world (**Doc. 10-10**).

Consistory Cases

The Genevan statutes drafted in Calvin's lifetime were silent on interreligious marriage. Differences in religion were not cited as impediments to engagement or to marriage. Nor were they included among the grounds for divorce. The Consistory, however, heard cases involving disputed engagements or marriages between Protestants and Catholics. Following Calvin's teachings, the Consistory worked hard to dissuade prospective couples from going forward with these mixed marriages, often sanctioning the couple and their parents severely, and sometimes banning them from the church and city if they persisted. But difference of religion alone was not a sufficient ground to annul an engagement, let alone a marriage.

A good example of the Consistory's pressure to end interreligious engagements was the 1547 case of a Genevan, Ami de la Rive, who had approved the engagement of his daughter Françoise to a Catholic man in Piedmont (**Doc. 10-11**). The fiancé was a business acquaintance and a friend of the family, and Françoise resigned to marry him. Unconvinced that this was a licit engagement, the Consistory declared the engagement to be altogether "against God, reason, and the Bible" and that Françoise was going "into idolatry." They banned the whole family from communion, and urged the Council to bar the wedding if they could find another impediment to the marriage. The Council ultimately did allow the wedding to go forward, so long as the couple stayed away in Piedmont.

Similarly, in a 1556 case, François Danel of Jussy had approved the engagement of his sister to a Catholic in a distant town (**Doc. 10-12**). François had the

Genevan syndic authorize her banns, presumably as the first step to having her marriage approved in Geneva. But he did not tell the authorities that this was to be an interreligious marriage. Upon discovery, the Consistory requested the Council to reprimand François and rescind the banns, arguing that they had been delivered under false pretenses. The Council obliged, and ordered the mixed couple to stay where they were, and not to come to Geneva.

The Consistory and Council took a firmer stand in a case the following year involving Jaquemoz Conte, a church warden and member of the local court (**Doc. 10-13**). He and his wife had consented to the marriage of their daughter into a wealthy Catholic family in another town. The daughter apparently did not protest the match, but testified that her uncle had promised to increase his wedding present to her if she married a Catholic. The Genevan Consistory was outraged. They recommended that Conte be stripped of his offices, and barred him and his wife from communion for consenting to this union. They also banned from communion two other parties who had facilitated the match and had the Council imprison the principal matchmaker.

On the Consistory's recommendation, the Council also annulled the marriage. The grounds for the annulment, however, were not clearly stated. Marriage with a Catholic was woefully imprudent, but not of itself illegal. The record does suggest the possibility of bribery (through the promised increase of the wedding gift). The Consistory also indicated (contradicting its earlier findings) that the father had not consented to the marriage. These grounds, particularly the lack of parental consent, would have been grounds to annul the marriage.

The Consistory normally would not annul a marriage on grounds of differences in religion alone. This was made clear in the 1556 case of Jean Mercier (**Doc. 10-14**). Mercier was apparently a recent immigrant to Geneva, and had become a communicant member of the Reformed church. Shortly after he had taken his communion, however, he traveled to the French city of Avignon, and married a Catholic woman in a Catholic wedding service, and then returned to Geneva with her. The Consistory admonished him sternly and banned him from communion. But when a penitent Mercier returned a few months later for permission to rejoin the communion, they granted it to him with no further reprisal, and with no talk at all of annulling his marriage.

A related issue that the Consistory faced was how to deal with the marriages of former Catholics, particularly former Catholic priests and monks, to Protestant women.[28] The Company of Pastors addressed this issue in a 1547 case involving a former French monk, Pierre Boucheron, and a Protestant woman,

---

28. See Chapter 13 below on the issue of what to do in the case of marriages consecrated by the Catholic church, for which the couple now sought blessing in a Protestant church.

Marguerite des Bordes (**Doc. 10-15**). While in France, the couple had courted and married properly. But Pierre had not told Marguerite of his prior monastic life and vows until after they were married. Marguerite was concerned that the marriage was improper, since Pierre had broken his vows. The couple sought the Genevan pastors' counsel. The Company of Pastors ruled that Pierre's former monastic life and his breach of monastic vows were not impediments. Pierre's failure of full disclosure of his background to Marguerite was more troubling, but if Marguerite still accepted him the marriage could continue, so long as the couple produced sufficient documentation of their marriage.

These kinds of cases became more frequent in the 1550s as ex-monks and ex-priests renounced their vows of celibacy, joined the Reformed Protestant cause, and began to move to Geneva, often with new Protestant wives. The Genevan Consistory generally approved these marriages, provided the man had clearly abandoned his Catholicism, and the couple had properly courted and married. A 1557 case involving ex-priest Bernard and his wife Pavicte was quite typical (**Doc. 10-16**). The couple had been properly engaged and married in the town of Cahors. Pavicte had moved to Geneva first, already pregnant, and supported herself while awaiting Bernard. He came later. The couple now wanted the Consistory to bless their union and remove any hint of scandal surrounding their marriage and Pavicte's pregnancy. They produced several witnesses to corroborate their story. Ensured of the couple's Protestant piety and marital propriety, the Consistory and Council approved the marriage, though not without reprimanding Bernard for leaving his pregnant wife to travel and live on her own.

These legal and theological teachings on interreligious marriage remained consistent in Geneva throughout Calvin's lifetime and beyond. Writing in 1569, Beza summarized the prevailing teaching, and defended it against the medieval canonists and the new laws issued by the Council of Trent in 1563 (**Doc. 10-17**). "Marriage promises of a believer with an unbeliever are to be strongly discouraged and even forbidden by civil law and severely punished," Beza wrote, particularly if the unbeliever is an aggressive heretic, or a dangerous Jew or Muslim. But marriages, once contracted, cannot be broken by believers, even if the nonbelieving spouse is an enemy of the faith. "But if the unbeliever deserts the believer, then the brother or sister is completely free of the obligation in the promise to marry." And, if the nonbeliever imperils the body or soul of the believing spouse, voluntary separation is not only licit but commended.

Summary and Conclusions

Søren Kierkegaard once said, tongue-in-cheek, that for every one hundred married men who reached heaven, ninety-nine would get there because of the faithfulness of their wives. Something of this same sentiment informed the theology and law of interreligious marriage in Reformation Geneva. To contemplate marriage to someone outside the Protestant faith was notoriously ill-advised, but it was permitted. To be married to someone who lapsed from the faith was not a license for marital dissolution but an opportunity for Christian evangelism. As Calvin put it, "the piety of the believer sanctifies the marriage more than the impiety of the nonbeliever pollutes it."

This was a marked departure from Catholic teachings. The Catholic Church taught that marriage is a sacrament, a channel of divine grace whose proper celebration and performance sanctifies the couple, their children, and the church. An interreligious marriage, particularly a marriage to someone who had not been baptized at all, was, by definition, an adulteration of the sacrament, the creation of a defective channel of grace. Such a mixed marriage could not symbolize properly the sublime relationship between Christ and his church. It could not bring spiritual edification to the couple, their children, or the church. As the great Catholic moralist Thomas Sanchez put it: the channel of grace would "leak" on the non-believer's side. While God could certainly move in mysterious and miraculous ways his grace to perform, it was not for the couple to deprive God of a regular channel of grace in the sacrament of marriage.

Calvin and his colleagues rejected this sacramental theology of marriage.[29] Calvin certainly stressed the sacred and sanctifying qualities of marriage, but without ascribing to it sacramental functions. In his later years he described marriage in sweeping spiritual terms as "a sacred bond," "a holy fellowship," a "divine partnership," "a loving association," "a heavenly calling," "the fountain-head of life," "the holiest kind of company in all the world," "the principal and most sacred . . . of all the offices pertaining to human society."[30] Conjugal love is "holy" when "husband and wife are joined in one body and one soul."[31] Calvin also believed that marriage could symbolize the relationship of God and humanity. He analyzed the Old Testament image of Yahweh's covenant of marriage with Israel, and Israel's proclivity for "playing the harlot" — worshipping false gods and allying with gentile neighbors, much as delinquent spouses abandon

29. See Institutes (1536) excerpted in Doc. 1-1 above.
30. Comm. Gen. 2:21; 2:24; 6:2; Serm. Deut. 21:10-14; Lect. Mal. 2:14, 16; Comm. Matt. 19:11; Comm. 1 Cor. 7:14; 9:11; "Contra la Secte des Libertines," in CO 7:212ff.
31. Comm. Gen. 2:18.

faith in God and faithfulness to each other.[32] He returned repeatedly to the New Testament image of Christ's marriage to the church — holding up Christ's faith and sacrificial love toward us as a model to which spouses and parents should aspire.[33] But none of this proved that marriage was sacramental or that faith was a prerequisite to legitimate marriage.

This new theological teaching on marriage led Calvin and his Consistory colleagues to tolerate interreligious marriage, and to reject difference of religion as a formal impediment to engagement or marriage. Reformed Protestants could marry Lutherans, Anabaptists, and other Protestants. They should not marry Catholics, Orthodox, Jews, Muslims, or unbelievers. Those who sought to enter such mixed marriages should be strongly dissuaded through the use of spiritual sanctions, Calvin insisted, though they could not ultimately be prevented from engagement or marriage. Parties who were already in mixed marriages, or whose spouses lapsed from the Reformed faith after the wedding, should remain together unless the unbelieving spouse became notoriously abusive. Those who sought to desert their non-believing spouses should be strongly encouraged to remain at home. But if the non-believing spouse deserted the home, there was no obligation to chase after or encourage that spouse to return.

---

32. Lect. 44-47 on Ezekiel 16; Lect. Mal. 2:14-15; Lect. Hosea 2:2; Serm. Deut. 21:10-14.
33. Serm. Eph. 5:28-30, 31-33; Comm. Eph. 5:30-32.

10-1 Commentary on Genesis 6:1-2 (1554)[34]

Although all mankind had been formed for the worship of God, and sincere religion should have prevailed everywhere, most men had prostituted themselves either to complete contempt of God, or to depraved superstitions. It was thus fitting that the small portion which God had specially adopted to himself, should remain separate from others.

But the ungrateful children of Seth mixed with the children of Cain, and with other profane races, voluntarily depriving themselves of the inestimable grace of God. It was intolerable so to pervert and to confound the order appointed by God. It might at first sight seem silly that the sons of God should be so severely condemned for having chosen for themselves beautiful wives from the daughters of men. But we must know: (1) that it is not a light crime to violate a distinction established by the Lord; (2) that for the worshippers of God to be separated from profane nations was a sacred appointment which ought reverently to have been observed, in order that a Church of God might exist upon earth; and (3) that the disease was desperate, seeing that men rejected the remedy divinely prescribed for them. In short, Moses describes this as the most extreme disorder, when the sons of the pious, whom God had separated to himself from others, as a peculiar and hidden treasure, became degenerate.

10-2 Commentary on Genesis 26:34 (1554)[35]

For many reasons Moses relates the story of the marriages of Esau. He mixed himself with the inhabitants of the land, from whom the holy race of Abraham was separated, and contracted into various entangled relationships. This was a kind of prelude of his rejection. It happened also, by the wonderful counsel of God, that these daughters-in-law were grievous and troublesome to the holy patriarch and his wife. This precluded them from gradually becoming more favorably disposed to this reprobate people. If their manners had been pleasing, and they had had good and obedient daughters, perhaps also, with their consent, Isaac might have taken a wife from among them. But it was not lawful for those to be bound together in marriage, whom God designed to be perpetual enemies. For how would the inheritance of the land be secured to the posterity

34. CO 23:111 (OTC adapted).
35. CO 23:369-70 (OTC adapted).

of Abraham, but by the destruction of those among whom he sojourned for a time? Therefore God cut off all inducements to these improper marriages.

10-3   Commentary on Genesis 38:2 (1554)[36]

Moses charges Judah with perverse lust, because he took a wife out of that nation with which the children of Abraham were divinely commanded to be at perpetual strife. Neither he nor his other brothers were ignorant that they sojourned in the land of Canaan. They knew the commandment that their enemies were to be cut off and destroyed, in order that they might possess the promised dominion of the land. Moses, therefore, justly regards it as a sin for Judah to entangle himself in a forbidden alliance. The Lord eventually cursed Judah's offspring so that the prince and head of the tribe of Judah might not be born, nor Christ himself descend, from this connection.

10-4   Sermon on Deuteronomy 21:10-14 (1555)[37]

Now we must discuss, concerning marriage, why Our Lord so strictly wished and commanded that the Jews not take wives from among the pagans or infidels. Not without cause does St. Paul compare our associations to yokes [1 Cor. 6:14]. When one couples two oxen together, if one advances, the other must follow; if one pulls to one side, the other must conform as well. So it is when one is on familiar terms with someone.

It is true that we may converse with the pagans without being joined to them; for we would have to depart from this world, as St. Paul says, if we wanted to communicate only with the good and with the children of God. But there are methods of doing business, and it must be carried on as if in passing. Someone who buys from a man will not inquire about his respectability, except insofar as he fears being swindled; but otherwise he buys, then goes his way, and he is not linked to the one with whom he has dealt.

But if there is domestic communication, as in eating and drinking, if there is such an alliance that men as it were lead a common life, this is a yoke, says St. Paul. Now we know that marriage is the most holy association there can be in this world; a man shall leave his father and mother and shall be joined unto his wife. Therefore it is impossible for a man to contract marriage without being coupled to his wife, to communicate in counsel, in will, and in all respects.

---

36. CO 23:493-95 (OTC adapted).
37. CO 27:654-57.

For we see what has happened, how those who have so abandoned themselves have finally become corrupted, and God has as it were cut them off from his people, of whom they have become rotten members. This was the advice of Balaam [Num. 22–24]. For he saw that God did not open his mouth to curse his people, and rather than having conspired to deliver curses, he was forced to speak exactly the opposite. When he saw this, as his last refuge he said that the Jews should be allowed to take pagan women, and these would deceive their hearts and corrupt them to idolatry, provoking the vengeance of God against them, and this would redound to their confusion.

The case of Solomon alone is enough to make the hair of anyone who considers well how he stumbled stand on end. Here was a man who was excellent; God wished to set him as a mirror or a pearl among the rest. His wisdom was so great that everyone was amazed at it. He was also a prophet of God. But the pagan women [he married into his harem] deceived his heart, and he permitted idolatry to be in fashion and reign in the country that God had reserved and dedicated to himself. He also had temples built to idols. When we see that such a man, who was like an angel from heaven, fell into hell, and that God held him in reproof, that he was so brutalized that he perverted the service of God and religion, how will it be with those who are still far from having profited as he did?

Thus we see that it was not without cause that God strictly forbade the Jews to take foreign women, and above all those from this country of Canaan. But in general he did not wish them to be yoked with idolaters. Why? Because this is an opening, a breach made for Satan, so that he can reduce everything to desolation and pervert and confound everything. God therefore wished to provide against this.

Today, of course, since the Gospel has been published throughout the whole world, it is true that there is no longer either Greek or Jew, that we no longer have such a distinction as there was under the Law. For the wall [of separation interposed by the Law], St. Paul says [Eph. 2:14], is broken. We should all be joined in fraternal concord, because God wishes to be invoked by all nations. Just as we call him Abba, Father, we must therefore be united together.

This is true. But we do not need to unite with those who separate themselves by infidelity, and who do not wish to be part of the body of the church, and who renounce that God who declared himself to us through Jesus Christ, and who do not wish to be participants in that adoption he offers to all, both great and small. We do not need to unite or adhere to them if we do not wish to be alienated from our God and from the road to salvation. He therefore who couples himself consciously and of his own will with the unfaithful, such a one banishes himself from the kingdom of God as far as he is able. . . .

And why is it that there are so many marriages today that do not come to a good result, unless because there is no regard for God, because some think of their pleasure or their concupiscence, while others seek for gain? Thus God does not come into the matter, and he must avenge himself for such scorn, and does so, as experience shows. All the more therefore should we note what is said in this passage, that if a man wants to take a foreign wife, that is, an infidel wife, who has not been brought up in the fear of God, who has not had instruction from his Word, let him see that she is totally changed before he ever approaches her. For this would be like a mortal poison, unless the woman had previously renounced her past life and promised henceforward to live according to God, to adhere purely to his truth, and to forget all her past upbringing, and even as it were to strip off her skin, as it is said.

10-5 Lecture on Malachi 2:11 (ca. 1560)[38]

Judah has polluted the holiness of Jehovah because the men indulged their lusts, and procured for themselves wives from heathen nations. . . . [T]he Jews rendered themselves vile, though God had consecrated them to himself. They polluted holiness, even when they had been separated from the world. . . .

[T]he Jews were ungrateful to God, because they mingled with heathen nations, and knowingly and willfully cast aside that glory by which God had adorned them by choosing them, as Moses says, to be to him a royal priesthood (Exod. 19:6). We know that holiness was strongly commended to the Jews, so that they would not abandon themselves to any of the pollutions of the heathens. Thus God had forbidden them under the law to take foreign wives, except they were first purified, as we find in Deuteronomy 21:11-12. If anyone wished to marry a captive, she was to have her head shaved and her nails pared; this intimates that such women were impure, and that their husbands would be contaminated unless the women were first purified. Even observing this law respecting marriage of a captive was not altogether blameless, for God finds it abominable that they were not content with their own nation, but lusted for strange women. . . .

The Prophet underscores their profanation by saying that they had married the daughters "of another god." He calls them the daughters of a strange god as a form of reproach. He might have simply said foreign daughters. But he intended here to imply a comparison between the God of Israel and idols. It was as though he had said: "Where did your wives come from? From idols. You should have hated them, as if they were monsters. If you had any faith in your heart, anything that came from idols should have been detestable to you. But your hearts have become attached to the daughters of false gods."

38. CO 44:446-49 (OTC adapted).

10-6   Letter to Lelio Sozzini (June, 1549)[39]

Since a Christian man must marry a woman under no other rubric than that she prove herself to him in respect to all the requirements of a pious life a help-meet and companion, when there is even the slightest variance from this purpose, I have no doubt but that the marriage is sinful. Further, whoever takes in marriage a woman who is still involved in the impious superstitions of the papacy, what else does he take into his home than profanation? For if the wife is the body of the man, there can be no apology for the man who unites himself to a woman daily prostituting herself to perverse cults so that he becomes defiled in half of himself. I will not go so far as to say that, if anyone takes unto himself such a wife, he will be forced to consecrate his marriage under magic auspices. Besides, I should not certainly venture to compare with an enemy of religion a girl of otherwise right opinion who nevertheless by fear of the flesh is detained by the sham of idolatry. For the farther a person is from Christ, the more it behooves us to shrink from that person's company. But the sort of woman you describe to me is certainly quite far from belonging to the class of professed enemies.

10-7   Letter to Lelio Sozzini (December 7, 1549)[40]

If anyone asks for my judgment concerning marriage, I shall not persuade him to do otherwise than to marry a wife who is prepared to follow Christ with her husband. And let her not only profess this with her mouth, but demonstrate it in practice. For whoever marries a woman who otherwise thinks rightly but nevertheless does not wish to depart from the profession of impiety puts on the worst of halters. Too often have I observed in many how much they draw back from Christ when they entangle themselves in such marriages.

But to answer you in detail. You ask whether a papist marriage should be no less avoided than a Turkish one. I would not dare to place those who inwardly retain the papal superstitions in which they were educated in the same class with the Turks. For they [the Catholics] approach [marriage questions] somewhat nearer to us. But the comparison aside, I deny that it is proper for a Christian man to join himself to a wife who is alien to Christ. Yet we know that all papists are among that number. Whoever holds it to be proper for him to receive one who is still held entangled by many errors seeks his own justification only in Christ, but does not reflect how many things there will be strife

39. CO 13:307-8.
40. CO 13:484-87.

about with her in the future. No one therefore shall incur that danger by my authority.

Rather this is my judgment: a person does not contract matrimony piously or with the Lord if he takes to himself any other partner than one who has previously been divorced from the Pope. I know that a free choice is not always given. But difficulty does not remove guilt. If there is a complete rejection of papal rites this should indeed be praised. But I do not dare to require this as if it were necessary, any more than to set a definite limit as to how far a woman ought to have progressed in the doctrine of piety to be taken as a wife. I wish only this: that a man abandon the enemies of Christ and bid farewell to manifest impiety, and dedicate his name to Christ.

Regarding your question whether the church should hold such [inter-religious] marriages valid or invalid, I do not sufficiently grasp how far it extends. For just as mutual consent of both parties is required for the nuptials to be consecrated under the rites, name, and protection of God, so if one deviates from his duty, the marriage bond does not cease to be legitimate by which each is bound to the other. His inconstancy is indeed rightly condemned, but nevertheless the [pledge of marital] faith given is not dissolved. If of two evils the lesser should be chosen, I judge that those living under the papacy cannot do otherwise than to offer their children for baptism, however corrupted. If they detest the corruptions that conflict with the command of God, they act piously and according to the duty of Christians. There is indeed mortal danger present; but that constancy more greatly deserves praise that is not shaken by fear, however great, from making a confession worthy of its piety. Whoever deprives his children of baptism commits more than a double offense. Therefore I have not advised this.

10-8   Commentary on 1 Corinthians 7:12-16 (1546)[41]

The relationship of marriage is singularly close. The wife is one half of the man as the two are one flesh (1 Cor. 6:16). The husband is the *head of the wife* (Eph. 5:23). She is her husband's partner in everything. Thus it seems impossible that a believing husband should live with an ungodly wife, or vice-versa, without being polluted by so close a connection. Paul, however, declares here, that the marriage is still sacred and pure. We must not worry that the wife would contaminate her husband as if she were contagious.

Let us, however, bear in mind, that [Paul] speaks here not of contracting marriages, but of maintaining marriages that have already been contracted. For where the matter under consideration is, whether one should marry an unbe-

---

41. CO 49:411-15 (NTC adapted).

lieving wife, or whether one should marry an unbelieving husband, then that exhortation is on point: "Be not yoked with unbelievers, for there is no agreement between Christ and Belial" (2 Cor. 6:14). But one who is already bound [in marriage] no longer has a choice; hence the advice given is different.

While this *sanctification* [that the believing spouse brings to the non-believer] is taken in various senses, I refer it simply to marriage in this sense. . . . [T]he piety of the one has more effect in sanctifying marriage than the impiety of the other in polluting it. Hence a believer may, with a pure conscience, live with an unbeliever, for in respect of the use and intercourse of the marriage bed, and of life generally, he is sanctified, so as not to infect the believing party with his impurity. Meanwhile this sanctification is of no benefit to the unbelieving party; it only serves thus far, that the believing party is not contaminated by intercourse with him, and marriage itself is not profaned.

But if the faith of a husband or wife who is a Christian sanctifies marriage, should it not follow that all marriages of ungodly persons are impure and no differerent from fornication? I answer, that to the ungodly all things are impure (Titus 1:15) because they pollute by their impurity even the best and choicest of God's creatures. Hence it is that they pollute marriage itself, because they do not acknowledge God as its Author, and therefore they are not capable of true sanctification, and by an evil conscience abuse marriage.

It is a mistake, however, to conclude from this that their marriage is no different from fornication. For, however impure their marriage is to them, it is still pure in itself, inasmuch as it is appointed by God, serves to maintain decency among men, and restrains irregular desires. For these purposes, marriage was approved by God, like other parts of the civil order. We must always, therefore, distinguish between the nature of a thing and the abuse of it. . . .

In the second part of his statement, Paul sets at liberty a believing husband, who is prepared to dwell with an unbelieving wife, but is rejected by her, and in like manner a woman who is, without any fault on her part, repudiated by her husband. In this sad case, the unbelieving party makes a divorce with God rather than with his or her partner. There is, therefore, in this case a special reason [to separate], for the first and chief bond [of marriage] is not merely loosened, but completely broken. . . . We must not, therefore, rashly separate from unbelievers, unless they first make a divorce. . . .

For unbelievers are not in so hopeless a condition, that they cannot be brought to believe. They are dead, it is true, but God can even raise the dead. So long, therefore, as there remains any hope of doing good, and the pious wife knows not but that she may by her holy conversation (1 Peter 3:1) bring her husband back into the way, she ought to try every means before leaving him; for so long as a man's salvation is doubtful, it becomes us to be prepared rather to hope the best.

10-9 Letter to Anonymous Woman (July 22, 1552)[42]

At issue is a request from a pious woman who, because of her desire to follow the truth and pure religion, has been treated badly by her husband and subjected to cruel and harsh servitude. Thus she wishes to know if it is permissible to leave her husband and to come here or withdraw to another church where she might rest her conscience in peace. Accordingly, we offer the following advice.

First of all, with respect to her perplexity and agony, we are filled with pity and compassion for her and are drawn to pray that it will please God to give her such a sense of relief that she will be able to find the wherewithal to rejoice in him. Nevertheless, since she has asked for our counsel regarding what is permissible, our duty is to respond, purely and simply, on the basis of what God reveals to us in his Word, closing our eyes to all else. For this reason, we beg her not to take offense if our advice does not correspond with her hope. For it is necessary that she and we follow what the Master has ordained, without mingling our desires with it.

Now, with regard to the bond of marriage, one must remember that a believing party cannot, of his or her free will, divorce the unbeliever, as St. Paul makes clear in 1 Corinthians 7:13. Without a doubt St. Paul emphasizes this, fully knowing the suffering each party may be experiencing. For at that time the pagans and the Jews were no less poisoned against the Christian religion than the papists are today. But St. Paul commands the believing partner, who continues to persevere in the truth of God, not to leave the partner who resists God.

In brief, we ought so to prefer God and Jesus Christ to the whole world that fathers, children, husbands, and wives cease to constitute something we value. So much is this so, that if we cannot adhere to him and renounce all else, we ought to make ourselves do so. This does not mean that Christianity ought to abrogate the order of nature. Where the two parties consent, it is especially fitting for the Christian wife to double her efforts to be submissive to her husband — here regarded as an enemy of truth — in order to win him if at all possible, as St. Peter advises in 1 Peter 3:1.

Nevertheless, as matters stand today in the papal church, a believing wife ought not to relinquish her hope without striving and trying to direct her husband toward the road of salvation. No matter how great his obstinacy might be, she must not let herself be diverted from the faith; rather she must affirm it with constancy and steadfastness — whatever the dangers might be.

However, if the above party should be persecuted to the extent that she is in danger of denying her hope, then she is justified in fleeing. When a wife (or

---

42. CO 10:239-41, translated in *Ecclesiastical Advice*, pp. 131-33.

husband, as the case may be) has made her confession of faith and demonstrated how necessary it is not to consent to the abominations of the papacy, and if persecution arises against her for having done so and she is in grave peril, she may justly flee when God grants her an occasion to escape. For that does not constitute a willful divorce but occurs because of persecution.

Hence it is appropriate that the good lady who has sought our counsel endure until the above occurs. For according to her letters, she currently only holds her peace and quietly goes along; being required to taint herself before idols, she bows before them in condescension. For this reason she may not justify leaving her husband until she has amply declared her faith and resisted greater pressure than presently encountered. Therefore she needs to pray for God to strengthen her, then she needs to fight more valiantly than she has, drawing upon the power of the Holy Spirit, to show her husband her faith, doing so in gentleness and humility, explaining to him that she must not offend God for the sake of pleasing him.

We have also taken into consideration her husband's rudeness and cruelty, of which she has advised us. But that ought not to prevent her from taking heart to commend the matter to God. For whenever we are so preoccupied with fear that we are afraid to do what we ought, then we are guilty of infidelity. That is the foundation on which we should build.

If, after having attempted what we have advised, she should come into imminent peril, or her husband should persecute her to the point of death, then she is free to exercise that liberty which our Lord grants to all his own, i.e., to flee ravenous wolves.

10-10   *Consilium* (April 28, 1556)[43]

The case of the married woman is more difficult. I cannot approve of her leaving her husband unless she is driven to it by some extreme violence, or if her husband, on the pretext of religion or some other excuse, is treating her in an intolerable manner. I will not define that intolerable manner, either, since she may be treated even more harshly at home. She ought to show every degree of tolerance before resorting to that remedy.

If she cannot be safe from idolatry except by clearly endangering her life, and if her husband presses her to such an extent that he actually persecutes her himself, then she will be permitted to take thought for herself and flee. Her intent should not be to turn away from her husband and desert him, however harsh and intolerable he may have shown himself to be, but only to avoid obvi-

---

43. CO 10:264-66, translated in *Ecclesiastical Advice*, pp. 162-63.

ous danger, and only until the Lord causes her husband's savage heart to grow mild and calm. It is wrong to sin against God to please any mortal.

10-11 Case of Ami Andrion de la Rive and Daughter Françoise (1547)[44]

(May 24, 1547). This is a Consistory decision concerning Lord Ami Andrion de la Rive, apothecary, who has engaged his daughter to someone from Piedmont, which is against the Gospel. It is decided that one of the elders should go to one of the Lords on the Council on behalf of the Consistory to forbid de la Rive to send his daughter out of the city and the country of the Reformation under [pain of] the indignation of the Council, and to make the [fiancé] come here.

(May 26, 1547). Ami Andrion [de la Rive] and his daughter Françoise were admonished because he has engaged his daughter to someone from Piedmont, which is papist. This is against God and reason and against the commandment of God. Although the daughter consented [to the marriage] in order to obey her father and mother, it was against her conscience. The father answered that he had gone to Piedmont to sell his goods, and found a good dealer there to whom he delivered goods. He was admonished that it is against God and his commandments [to marry papists]. He was further admonished that it is said that either he or his wife said that St. Paul talked too much. He denied it.

The father was made to withdraw and the daughter was questioned separately to learn her feelings. She answered that the engagement cannot be undone because it is done; and if they have free will over there, then they have the Word of God just as [we do] here. She was admonished as to whether she is going into idolatry without regret. She answered yes and denied having complained about it. And since she has him [her fiancé] she does not want anyone else.

(May 26, 1547). The mother was admonished in the same way, and she answered like the others. She said that her other son-in-law wanted the girl to be near him. Moreover, the husband [fiancé] has done them many services, including lending them money. She was admonished with ample remonstrances, that this is selling their daughter.

Decided: that they be forbidden communion and remanded before the Council, admonishing them that this would be an open door to their bourgeois and citizens and a bad example against God and the law. They were then asked who was present at the [swearing of the engagement] oath; they answered no one except Aime du Pan. They were admonished under [pain of] the indignation of the Council also to present their daughter.

44. R. Consist. III, 77, 83.

[On May 28 the Council decided that since this marriage violated the edicts it should not take place. On June 3, however, a French official sent a letter to the Council supporting the marriage. Although it continued to assert that the marriage was "against religion," the Council decided "that they should do as they please."]

10-12 Case of François Danel of Jussy (1556)[45]

(Nov. 12, 1556). François Danel of Jussy has been remanded to us because he has engaged his sister Claude in the town of Fillinges in the papacy and wanted to force the minister to publish the banns. The minister refused because the banns were not signed by the castellan. François presented a request written by the curial [the castellan's secretary Jean Delestra] to permit and command him to sign and seal the banns and have them proclaimed.

Decided: considering that . . . he wanted to compel the minister to commit a fraud by publishing their banns without their being signed, that the Council be informed of it and he be re[pri]manded.

(Nov. 15, 1556). Egrege Jean Delestra was admonished that he wrote a request contrary to his duty to have banns signed for the sister of François Danel who married in the papacy.

[On November 16 the Council ordered that François Danel be strictly admonished for having brought banns to be signed by the minister under false pretenses, which he had confessed. It also ordered that the banns not be signed and that the woman in question "remain where she is."]

10-13 Case of Bernard and Rolette Vel (1557)[46]

(Sept. 23, 1557). Jean Voysin, called Pastorez, from Vandoeuvres, stated that he helped to contract the marriage of the daughter of Jaquemoz Conte with Thyven Vel of Lucinge, a papist, with the consent of Conte, the father of the girl.

Decided: since Conte did not appear, that he be remanded with his wife, his daughter, and Voysin to Thursday.

(Sept. 23, 1557). Jaquemoz Conte, [church] warden and member of the court of Vandoeuvres, was examined. He confessed having married his daughter [Rolette Conte] to someone from Lucinge [Bernard Vel] of the house of Ve[l]. He had done so at the instigation of Jean Voysin, called Pastorez, and de-

45. R. Consist. XI, 76v, 80.
46. R. Consist. XII, 99v-100, 103, 108-108v.

clared that his intention was and is to send his daughter to Lucinge in the papacy, for he is poor and the house of Vel is rather wealthy.

Decided: first, that communion be forbidden him on this occasion, and he should not receive it until he has first appeared here to be permitted to receive it. Then let him be remanded before the Council for the purpose of being removed from his two offices, because while a [church] warden he sets a bad example to others of not coming to the communion sermon until the end. Then let the Council be told that such a marriage should not hold.

[On September 27 the Council decided, as advised here, to deprive Conte of his two offices, to pronounce the marriage void, and to forbid him communion.]

(Sept. 30, 1557). Jean Voysin of Vandoeuvres, his wife, and Rolette, daughter of Jaquemoz Conte, were summoned. They were admonished for the marriage they contracted in the town of Lucinge between Rolette and Bernard Vel. She said that she has an uncle in Annecy who promised her the sum of forty florins or thereabouts to increase her marriage [portion], provided she was married to a papist.

Decided: since the girl contracted marriage without her father's knowledge with people in the papacy, where she was ready to go to live, let her and Voysin be remanded to Monday. And let communion be forbidden to them.

[On October 4 the Council ordered the castellan to imprison Voysin for three days on bread and water and also to inform the girl that the marriage was void.]

(Dec. 16, 1557). Jaquemoz Conte of Vandoeuvres and his wife appeared according to the remand issued formerly on their prohibition from communion. They were forbidden communion for having married their daughter to a Catholic. After hearing them, and seeing that there is malice in them, it was decided to permit communion to Conte, but before receiving it he should find one of the ministers before Christmas to give him an account of his faith. As for his wife, [prohibition of] communion is continued until Easter.

(Dec. 16, 1557). Amied Doctet, called Burnet, of Vandoeuvres appeared to ask that communion be permitted him. After stating his case, he was asked whether it is not true that he helped the daughter of Jaquemoz Conte to marry a Catholic. He answered that he did not take her, though it is true that he attended the banquet. It was further reported by Master Baduel, minister of Vandoeuvres, that he heard that Jean Chappelle, speaking to Doctet, said that Messieurs Calvin, Colladon, and the other ministers were wicked men.

Decided: since no sign of repentance is seen he cannot be granted communion; the prohibition of it continues.

10-14   Case of Jean Mercier (1556)[47]

(April 2, 1556). Jean Mercier, velvet-maker, was admonished that he was in this city, and after having received communion here he withdrew to the city of Avignon where he took a wife whom he brought here, and married in the papacy in the manner [followed there], and afterwards received communion here.

The decision: that since he received communion and afterwards profaned it, that before receiving communion he return here to learn how he will behave.

(Sept. 3, 1556). Jean Mercier asks that it may please [the Consistory] to admit him to communion, which was forbidden him for the fault he committed; after having lived in this city he returned to the papacy and married a wife there. Mr. Coppus stated that he keeps a manservant and a maid who sleep together at his and his wife's feet. [Mercier] said that he has taken care of it, and that it was in a wagon. He was admitted to communion on his conscience.

10-15   Case of Pierre Boucheron and Marguerite des Bordes (1547)[48]

On Tuesday the first day of November in the same year a man named Pierre Boucheron declared before the ministerial brethren of the city that, having left the habit of a Jacobin, he had contracted a marriage with a woman named Marguerite des Bordes, a native of Paris, with the consent of her father whose name was Pierre des Bordes, a boatman and fishmonger living in the Rue Saint Honoré in Paris; that the marriage was solemnized in the parish of Saint-Germain de L'Auxerrois at the mass at about ten or eleven o'clock in the morning towards the end of the month of July last; but that he had not revealed to Marguerite that he had previously been a Jacobin until several days later when they were traveling from Paris to this city, and that Marguerite whom he had taken and married as his wife felt some scruples about this in her conscience. It was his desire that she should be reassured and consoled, and also that their marriage should be accorded approval so that there should remain no scandal to the Church of our Lord. Thereupon Pierre was questioned concerning his association with Marguerite and the means by which he had entered into this marriage. He replied that in order to be far away from the university, where there are Jacobins by whom he would be recognized, he went to live in the house of Marguerite, and there fell ill; that after having been carefully nursed by her and restored to health he made a proposal of marriage, to which she consented, and also her father; and that it was solemnized as has been described.

47. R. Consist. XI, 15, 57.
48. RCP (Hughes trans.), pp. 68-70.

Pierre was then caused to withdraw and Marguerite was called in and questioned regarding this same matter. She was found to be in agreement concerning the fact of the marriage, but alleged that at the time she was unaware that Pierre had been a Jacobin and that on learning of it she had been troubled in her conscience, but that after she had learnt the reasons she was happier about it than had previously been the case. It was explained to her that the vows in question were monastic vows, and that it was the commandment of God that all who cannot contain themselves should marry, but that for her part it was necessary that she should declare whether she felt able to live with Pierre as her husband with a clear conscience. She replied in the affirmative that such was her resolve. She was then asked to withdraw.

While they were outside the brethren conferred together. Then by common consent both of them were recalled and told that the beginning of this marriage had not been good, since what is not done in faith is not done with a clear conscience and is contrary to God, and that it was not right to proceed in this way, but since they intended to live together and had been united they should agree to do so in good conscience and to live together in seemly union. It was decided that the brethren who knew them in Paris should try to obtain attestation of their marriage in order to avoid all scandal and to meet their request. In the meantime they were to take care to live in such a manner that the Church might be edified.

And because Pierre had mentioned to some of the brethren that he had undertaken to make a journey to Lyons he was admonished to make suitable provision for his wife, so that she might not be exposed to danger.

10-16 Case of Bernard and Pavicte Martin (1557)[49]

(March 11, 1557). Bernard Martin and Pavicte his wife appeared for the purpose of declaring that they are married. Evidently, [they were married] a long time ago in the papacy, but without the required solemnization. For this reason, they ask that their marriage be avouched and accepted in the congregation of the faithful.

To verify their marriage Mr. Fabri, a doctor, and Martin Taschard, Pierre Schuz, and Jean Blanc appeared as witnesses to verify that, to their knowledge, the two are married. After having taken the customary oath, Fabri said that he knew that Martin was a [former] priest, holding some cure or benefice, but that Martin was a respectable man. He had heard that Martin had long planned to come here [to Geneva], having acted honorably toward many respectable peo-

49. R. Consist. XII, 12v-13.

ple. As for Pavicte, he has heard that she came to this city pregnant. He said further that she had worked for her living in this city after she had arrived and before Martin had arrived.

Martin Taschard said that when Pavicte came to this city, he took her into his home, but not just because she was pregnant. Schuz said he had known her in Cahors to be a respectable woman, and that she had [converted to] the true religion already in Cahors. He also knew that she had been engaged and later married to Martin, and he himself was present at their engagement. He further said that they had a firm intention of coming to live here according to the true reformation of the Gospel.

Decided: since Martin waited so long to come to this city after his wife, that he be admonished for it by the Council, before whom he is remanded. As for the rest, because there has been good evidence of his good will and respectability, let him be received into the marriage previously alleged and it be sworn to and confirmed.

[On March 15 the Council decided that since the Consistory had obtained good evidence of the Martins' respectability, their marriage should be ratified, and it so ordered.]

10-17   Theodore Beza on Marriage with Unbelievers (1569)[50]

Now for a long time there have been discussions about whether promises to marry by a believer to a non-believer are legitimate. This can become controversial in two ways. First, when both parties were unbelievers at the time when the marriage promise was made but one of them afterwards converted to the true religion. Second, when promises to marry are made at a time both are professing the true religion and one then falls into heresy or manifest impiety. I answer that if this inequality should come about either before or after the promises to marry it is not right to tear apart the promises to marry (if no other reason stands in the way) as long as the unbeliever agrees to cohabit with the believer. . . .

The marriage promises among unbelievers which we are discussing are true ones, that is, they were entered into by words understood as applying to the present time. If they are true [promises] it follows that they cannot be torn apart because of the unbelief of the other partner and hence should be valid and firm.

This is clear also from the Word of God. If this were prostitution or defilement, as Tertullian hyperbolically calls it, Paul would never have urged a be-

---

50. Beza, TRD, 2:99-103, 122 (translated by John P. Donnelly, S.J.).

liever to remain on with an unbeliever even for a moment [1 Cor. 7:12-16]. But, they say, Paul is speaking there about marriages that had already been contracted which it was not good to tear apart. This I do indeed concede, but who can show that the Apostle is dealing only with those marriages that were initially contracted between two unbelievers and not also with those marriages that somebody who was already a believer entered into with an unbeliever? But if they also think these marriages are so firm that a believer cannot dissolve them, this certainly also makes valid promises to marry from which that binding link gets its start.

Still I do not deny that some already consummated marriages are valid, whose initial stages were otherwise invalid. But I say this obtains at the time when, because true and full consent was lacking, it is cleaned up by subsequent copulation, as for instance if somebody contracts promises to marry before puberty, under force, or through a mistake then on reaching puberty or after knowing the mistake later freely knows his woman he espoused. This is certainly something that does pertain to the sort of case we are dealing with. But if somebody interprets Paul as prohibiting any one from taking on a bond with unbelievers — I grant that also, and I strongly approve the scattered attacks that the Fathers launch here and there against marriages of this sort, but provided that their hyperbolic expressions are softened. For I deny that this makes promises to marry invalid, even if they were contracted imprudently or with an insufficiently right conscience, if indeed many things urge on very good grounds that once they have been made they cannot be dissolved.

Therefore in general our opinion is clearly consistent, in my view, with the Word of God. But I add this exception, "unless the non-believer will have departed," since an obligation remains, whether the obedience of a brother or sister, without the marriage having been consummated; as the Apostle says, it is clear that this is to be upheld much more when only promises to marry are involved. But I still think that here there is a place for a many-sided distinction.

First, we must lay down a greater distinction between a person who becomes only a heretic, that is one who claims that he is of Christ's Church but disagrees with the true Church on some dogmas, and a person who explicitly opposes the Christian religion, as do the Jews and Muslims of today. Second, since not all sects are of the same importance a distinction has to be made among those who do not just go astray (for who is without all danger of error?) but who also tenaciously defend their error and drag others into their sect or attach themselves to others of the same sect (such people are called heretics) in order that we do not put them all in the same place since not all heresies are of the same importance. Third, this too should be maintained: they do not expose themselves to as much danger as young maidens who seek in-laws for themselves, since wives in the end transfer themselves to the family and power of their husbands and hence these are rightly seen as having gone astray more than the others. Lastly, I think it should also be noted that a person should not be regarded as an unbeliever who promised to go over to the true religion in such a way that it seemed that she or he rightly deserved to be believed.

Given these considerations, I conclude that we should follow the teaching of the Apostle [Paul]. Those seem worthy of ecclesiastical punishment (but to be moderated by considering the circumstances) who seek out marriages with other partners than with those whose status in the true religion was above all quite clear. But magistrates are acting prudently and in a wholly Christian way who restrain the taking of such promises to marry. I also add that they seem to be rightly punished by the death penalty as clear apostates who (after the truth of the Gospel has been made more than sufficiently clear) contract marriages with its [the Gospel's] open enemies such as with Muslims and Jews. If those magistrates are doing their duty, the question of a bond of such promises to marry or marriages seems superfluous. But lest I simply dare to pronounce such marriage promises are to be dissolved, the Apostle [Paul] clearly advises a believer not to separate from an unbeliever as long as he or she agrees to the duty of matrimony (which he calls cohabitation). . . .

This is the main point of all these things. Marriage promises of a believer with an unbeliever are to be strongly discouraged and even forbidden by civil law and severely punished. But if perchance they have been contracted, whether both were unbelievers at the outset or only one of them, or both were unbelievers and one became a believer, or when both were believers and one later became an unbeliever, for instance a Jew or a Muslim or one of the sort of heretics who deny the foundation of godliness — such promises to marry, I say, if nothing else stands in the way, remain completely firm and immutable as long as the unbeliever consents to the duties of his or her spouse. But if the unbeliever deserts the believer, then the brother or sister is completely free of the obligation in the promise to marry.

CHAPTER 11

For Richer or Poorer

The Economics of Engagement and Marriage

The Tradition

In sixteenth-century Geneva, as much as today, marriage was not only a union of persons. It was also a merger of properties — land, money, jewelry, clothing, household commodities, social titles, property rents, business interests, and sundry other "real" and "personal" property.[1] When the parties were members of the aristocracy or of the ruling class, a marriage could be the occasion for a massive exchange of power, property, and prerogatives that was distilled into lengthy written contracts. But even paupers who intended marriage generally made at least token exchanges of property and oral agreements about future transactions.

While these marital property contracts were often joined with marriage contracts, they were actually independent agreements with different legal implications. For the marriage to be valid, a marriage contract, an oral or written agreement by the couple to marry, was essential; a marital property contract, an agreement to exchange property in anticipation or in consideration of marriage, was not essential. Indeed, a marital property contract could be negotiated and executed by other parties besides the couple, such as their relatives, with or without confirmation or even mention of the engagement or marriage. To conjoin the marriage contract and marital property contract in

---

1. The terms "real property" or "immovables" refer to land and the houses, barns, and other permanent improvements thereon. The terms "personal property," "personalty," or "movables" refer to all other property.

one instrument was both prudent and efficient. But it was not legally necessary.[2]

Three types of marital property exchanges were distinguished in pre-Reformation Geneva and in the surrounding polities governed by the *ius commune*.[3]

First, it was customary for a man to accompany his marriage proposal with some form of gift to the woman, and sometimes to her family. At minimum, the man offered the woman a token gift to signify his affection and to seal his engagement promise — a ring, hat, flower, feather, kerchief, pin, or bottle of wine, or some form of "earnest money." A man of ample means could be more elaborate, offering expensive jewelry or clothing to his fiancée, or a horse and carriage to her or to her family. These gifts of engagement to the prospective bride (and her family) were a carryover of the Frankish and Germanic custom that a man paid a purchase price to the woman's family for the right to marry her, often a rather hefty price. By the sixteenth century, this once lucrative windfall to the bride's family had become largely ceremonial.[4] To be sure, a few women (and their families) could still insist on a more elaborate engagement gift, particularly if the woman was highly coveted or if a marital tie to her family was highly prized. But an elaborate engagement gift was neither required nor customary by the sixteenth century.

2. Philip L. Reynolds and John Witte, Jr., eds., *Marrying in the Middle Ages* (forthcoming); R. H. Helmholz, *Marriage Litigation in Medieval England* (Cambridge, 1974), pp. 25-73.

3. The sources at our disposal contain no special Genevan statutes on marital property, leading us to assume that the subject was governed by the canon law and civil law that prevailed in Geneva and in the Savoy, much of it comparable to prevailing French law in the neighboring regions. For detailed sources on this *ius commune* of marital property in this period, see Coing, II/1, pp. 345-48. For particular local studies, see Antoine Flammer, *Le droit civil de Genève, ses principes et son histoire* (Geneva, 1875), pp. 6-8, 13-16. For studies of early modern marital property law, see Martha C. Howell, *The Marriage Exchange: Property, Social Place, and Gender in Cities of the Low Countries, 1300-1500* (Chicago, 1998); Alfred Havenkamp, *Haus und Familie in der spätmittelalterlichen Stadt* (Cologne/Vienna, 1984); Marion A. Kaplan, ed., *The Marriage Bargain: Women and Dowries in European History* (Haworth, 1985); Paul Ourliac and J. de Malafosse, *Histoire du droit privé* (Paris, 1968), vol. 3; Jack Goody et al., eds., *Family and Inheritance: Rural Society in Western Europe, 1200-1800* (New York, 1976); Jean Brissaud, *A History of French Private Law*, trans. R. Howell, repr. ed. (Boston, 1968). See also local case studies, cited below note 7.

4. Diane Owen Hughes, "From Brideprice to Dowry in Mediterranean Europe," in Kaplan, ed., *The Marriage Bargain*, pp. 13-59. The engagement or marriage gift, traditionally called the *pretium*, was now sometimes called the dowry *(dot, dos)*, not to be confused with the notion of dowry discussed below. In medieval Frankish and Germanic law this gift was large and usually held by the family. In later medieval civil law, the gift grew smaller but was often held by the woman. See samples in *De Dot, tractatus ex variis iuris civilis interpretivis decerpti* (Louvain, 1569).

If the engagement ripened into marriage, the engagement gift vested. It was now the woman's property (or her family's property, if they received the gift) to be used or disposed of without interference from the donor man, even after the marriage. If the engagement fell apart, however, it was customary for the woman (or her family) to return these gifts. Failure to return these gifts could lead to litigation in the secular courts for their recovery — particularly if the engagement gift was an expensive piece of jewelry or clothing.

Second, it was common for the woman, and her family, to bring property to the marriage. This was called her dowry *(dos, dot)*. The dowry consisted, at minimum, in the woman's clothing and personal effects. But the dowry usually involved a good deal more. Frequently, it included other personal property such as household furnishings and decorations, cooking utensils and linens, poultry and cattle, standing orders for newly harvested fruit and grain, and more. Sometimes, especially with an aristocratic marriage, the dowry was a form of real property, whether land, a home, a rental property, or a place of business. The type and value of the dowry was open to negotiation between the couple and their families (or representatives). But dowry was often a very expensive proposition for the woman and her family, and an ample source of tension for the couple and their families during the marital property negotiations. It was not uncommon for the bride's family to give the woman (a portion of) her inheritance in advance to meet the high costs of dowry.

Once delivered, the woman's dowry did not pass entirely beyond her control or that of her family. The civil law provided that a portion of the dowry remained reserved to the woman and her family after the wedding. This was called the "marriage portion." The type and the amount of dowry property included in the marriage portion were open to negotiation between the couple and their families, but some portion was generally reserved.[5] The wife could retain custody of this marriage portion, but usually the husband controlled all the marital property, including the marriage portion. The property in the marriage portion, however, could not be sold, mortgaged, given away, or destroyed. The wife and/or her family had the right to retrieve the marriage portion when the marriage ended by annulment or death. They could also request the Council to assign a *tuteur* over wastrel husbands who were suspected of squandering or damaging the wife's marriage portion. If the marriage portion had been invested, they could seek a portion of the profits as well. If it had been damaged or destroyed, they could seek restitution of its value from the husband's own property. Once retrieved, the marriage portion was redistributed within the wife's family, with the wife herself (if she survived) and her children given priority.

---

5. The engagement gifts to the woman were usually included in the marriage portion as well.

Third, not only did the wife reserve rights over a portion of her own property through the law of the marriage portion. Upon marriage, she also gained rights over a portion of her husband's property through the law of dower *(douaire)*. Dower was a form of built-in insurance designed to provide for the wife upon her husband's death. If the wife became a widow, she would be entitled to one-third to one-half of all the personal property (that is, the movables, not the land) owned by her husband during the marriage. This was not just the personal property that the husband brought into the marriage or left at his death. Dower rights attached as well to any personal property that the husband acquired during the marriage — including, importantly, the personal property in his inheritance from his own family. The cumulative value of all that personal property was calculated on the husband's death, and the widow assigned her dower. Typically the widow received a life estate or usufruct in this property — the right to use and possess the dower property for her lifetime, but with no right to sell or dispose of the property. This dower property would revert to the couple's children upon her death, or, in the absence of children, to her late husband's family. If the widow sold or gave away her dower property to third parties or damaged or destroyed it during her life estate, her children or her late husband's family could bring suits for its restitution when their reversionary interests vested.

Dower rights imposed an ample restriction on the husband's rights to dispose of his own personal property during the course of his married life. He could not simply sell, encumber, or give away his personal property without consideration of his wife's dower interests. Nor could he craft his last will and testament without taking these dower interests into account. For, after his death, his wife and the children could claim their dower rights against third parties who had acquired interests in the late husband's property without the wife's consent or without advance payment to her. Moreover, in cases where a husband had squandered or misused all his personal property, or where he sought to give his entire estate to others, the wife could make priority claims on the balance of her husband's estate to have her dower interests made whole.

While engaged parties could negotiate about the types and amounts of property subject to dower, they could not renounce dower altogether. "To allow a woman to contract herself out of her [dower] rights would put her rights at the mercy of the unscrupulous."[6] The canon law, in particular, made

---

6. W. S. Holdsworth, *A History of English Law* (London, 1922-66), 3:194-95, quoted and discussed in Eileen Spring, *Law, Land, and Family: Aristocratic Inheritance in England, 1300 to 1800* (Chapel Hill/London, 1993), pp. 41ff. Contrary to the *ius commune* on the Continent, English common law dower attached to real property (land), not to personal property, and attached to one-third rather than to one-half of the husband's property.

dower mandatory, and punished severely unscrupulous husbands who sought to avoid its effects through fancy property schemes. Only if the wife was convicted for adultery or malicious desertion of her husband would she forfeit her dower.

This was the basic law of marital property that prevailed in Geneva on the eve of the Reformation. In practice, this law was doubtless a good deal more complex and nuanced. A systematic study of the relevant late medieval Genevan case law remains a desideratum. It would doubtless reveal endless variations on and exceptions to these general rules — if studies of the case law in neighboring late medieval cities are any indication.[7] But this was the basic law of marital property on the books.

A good illustration of this law can be seen in a 1536 contract between the distinguished Genevan jurist Germain Colladon and a woman named Claude Bigot. Germain Colladon was a well-heeled soul, son of an attorney and nephew of a judge in the nearby French city of Bourges. Bigot had lost her parents while still a youth, but she had inherited a good deal of money and property that was being held in trust by her grandmother. The grandmother was also Claude's guardian. She was, evidently, a skilled negotiator, given the quite generous marital property agreement she struck for Claude.

Document 11-1 is the marital property contract that the parties executed after their formal engagement to marry. The agreement confirms that Germain and Claude promise to be married in the future (art. 2). Both their families give their consent to the pending union (art. 3) and become parties to the marital property agreement.

The economics of the marriage are the principal concern of the instrument. Claude, the future wife, and her guardian grandmother promise to bring to the marriage an ample dowry of land, movables, and a yearly income, drawn from Claude's inheritance. As a way of protecting themselves, they agree to make the dowry payments in installments over two years, future payments pre-

---

7. Dominique Favarger, *Le régime matrimonial dans le Comté de Neuchatel du XVe au XIX siècle* (Neuchâtel, 1970); Gerda Lamprecht, *Das eheliche Güterrecht des Kantons Luzern in seiner rechtshistorischen Entwicklung* (Diss. Jur., University of Zurich, 1940); Jean Hilaire, *Le régime de biens entre époux das la region de Montepellier de début du XIIIe siècle à la fin du XVI siècle* (Montpellier, 1957); Pierre-André Pidoux, *Histoire du mariage et du droit des gens mariés en Franche-Comté depuis la redaction des coutumes en 1459 jusqu'à la conquête de la province par Louis XIV en 1674* (Thesis, Paris, 1902). See also scattered discussion in Auguste Dumas, *La condition des gens mariés dans la famille périgourdine aux XVe et XVIe siècles* (Diss., Paris, 1908); Francis Michon, *La condition des gens mariés dans la famille vaudoise au XVIe siècle (1536-1618)* (Thesis, Lausanne, 1960); Hans Steiner, *Das eheliche Güterrecht des Kantons Schwzy mit vergleichenden Hinweisen auf das eheliche Güterrecht des schweizlichen Zivilgesetzbuches* (Aarau, 1909).

sumably to be withheld if the marriage goes amiss or is annulled after the wedding. They also promise to furnish Claude's own clothing and ornaments (arts. 4, 5). They even promise substitute dowry payments if the projected yearly income from one of the dowry properties falls short (art. 11). One-third of this dowry is stipulated to become marital property, for the common use of husband and wife, which either party takes upon the death of the other. Two-thirds of this dowry is reserved as Claude's marriage portion (arts. 5, 6).

Germain, the future husband, in turn, promises to return the marriage portion, along with Claude's rings, clothing, and personal effects, to Claude's heirs if she predeceases him (art. 8). If he predeceases her, Germain promises Claude a dower of one-half of his personal property of her choice, plus a stipulated monetary inheritance beyond this standard dower (arts. 7, 9). Germain's father also makes a gift of land to his son, in consideration of the marriage (art. 10). The *ius commune* would give Claude no rights over her husband's real property, and nothing in what survives of the contract changes that presumption.

The Reformation

Much of this tradition of marital property remained unchanged in the course of the Reformation in Geneva. John Calvin did offer some theological reflections on issues of marital property. But he proposed little new legislation on the topic and mostly followed legal conventions in his pastoral work as matchmaker and in his adjudication of marital property cases on the Consistory bench. Calvin left it to the same Germain Colladon, whom we just encountered, to craft a new Genevan statute on marital property. That statute, passed in 1568, mostly codified the relevant *ius commune*, with a few significant changes.

Pastoral Writings

Calvin knew well the value of having a couple and their families settle their marital property affairs in advance: "Domestic affairs never go well without a private mutual understanding and a settlement of the conditions required on both sides," he warned in a pastoral letter of 1546.[8] Calvin had learned this lesson a few years before. In his own search for a bride in 1540, he had been pressed to take a "certain young girl of noble rank . . . with a fortune above my condi-

8. (October 4, 1546), CO 12:392-94, excerpted in Doc. 3-12 above.

tion," as he put it in a letter to Farel.[9] The woman's brother, acting as her representative, had apparently made Calvin a rather extravagant offer, "blinded by his affection" for Calvin and acting "against his own interest." Calvin hesitated, perhaps worried in part about whether the woman would remain too beholden to her family, and no doubt to her family's wealth. Calvin was more attracted to a woman his own brother Antoine had just recommended who would "bring a dowry large enough, [but] without any money at all." Though this match did not work out either, the promise of a more modest dowry, commensurate with his own modest property holdings at the time, was more to Calvin's liking.

Two years later, Calvin saw first-hand the dangers of failing to reach agreement over marital property. In a 1542 letter, he reported with dismay his attempts to quell a bitter family feud over dowry payments and household property that had caused scandal in Geneva (**Doc. 11-2**). In his subsequent role as matchmaker, Calvin thus sometimes took pains to ensure that his suitors found a "suitable party" of comparable social and economic status.[10] In a 1558 letter, he included the dowry capacity of a woman and her family as an important criterion to consider in determining whether there was a suitable match (**Doc. 11-3**).[11] In another letter, Calvin endorsed a proposed engagement contract where a man both stipulated what the widow's inheritance would be if he predeceased her, and required her not to pick favorites among the children in distributing her inheritance, particularly not children from a subsequent marriage (**Doc. 11-4**). This latter provision, which had biblical analogues that Calvin noted, eventually found a place in the 1568 Civil Code of Geneva.[12]

Theological Writings

Calvin had little biblical reason to reform much of the tradition of marital property that prevailed in Geneva before the Reformation. The Bible did not speak to technical issues of a widow's dower rights, and Calvin did not either. The Old Testament touched obliquely on the dowry *(zebed)* a woman brought to the marriage, but Calvin said little about this.[13] The Old Testament did dis-

---

9. This letter is reproduced in Doc. 3-5 above, where we have analyzed it as an illustration of courtship and matchmaking.

10. See Chapter 3 above.

11. See also Letter to de Falais (Nov. 16, 1546), Doc. 3-13 above.

12. Cf. Harm. Law Deut. 21:15-17 (a man must treat equally the inheritance rights of children of a first and second marriage). See below, Doc. 11-13, arts. 10-11.

13. See Gen. 30:20; Josh. 15:18-19; 1 Kings 9:16. Calvin said nothing about the dowry issue in Gen. 30, and dealt with Josh. 15 under marriage gifts. He left no commentaries or sermons on 1 Kings.

cuss the marriage price a few times.[14] But the marriage price *(mohar)* of the Old Testament was not the (largely ceremonial) engagement gift of Calvin's day. It was, instead, the man's payment to the father of money, goods, services, or valorous deeds for the right to marry his daughter[15] — or the penalty he paid him for seducing, raping, or damaging his daughter.[16] While these biblical passages were not quite on point, Calvin did draw from them some important lessons for the law and custom of marital property in his own day.

The most convenient biblical case on point was the story of Jacob's protracted courtship of his beloved Rachel. Rachel's father Laban had put Jacob to work for seven years to pay his marriage gift for her. But he tricked Jacob into marrying his elder daughter Leah instead, and put Jacob to work for seven more years to pay his dowry for Rachel's hand (Gen. 29:9-30). Calvin drew three lessons from this story relevant to the law of marital property (**Doc. 11-5**). First, the natural law commended parties to reach clear agreements about marriage and marital property in advance, and to stick to them, lest they be tempted by their own greed. Second, it was appropriate for a suitor like Jacob to have to make a marriage gift, whether of property or labor, to his prospective bride's father, although seven years of labor was clearly excessive. Here was at least tacit biblical approval of the modern-day practice of the engagement gift. But, third, it was scandalous for the father to sell his daughter as a piece of expensive merchandise and to withhold from her any portion of this dowry payment or marriage gift. Calvin drew this latter lesson against the crass commodification of daughters from other biblical passages as well.[17]

Calvin did draw modern-day instruction about engagement gifts from the biblical story of the courtship of Jacob's parents, Rebekah and Isaac.[18] Isaac's father Abraham had sent out his chief servant to search for a bride for Isaac from among his kin. The servant had found Rebekah. He gave her an expensive gold ring and two gold bracelets and asked to see her parents. He asked Rebekah's mother and uncle to approve her engagement to Isaac. They approved. The jubilant servant, the Bible reads, piled on "jewelry of silver and gold, and raiment, and gave them to Rebekah; he also gave to her brother and to her mother costly ornaments."[19]

---

14. See texts in Joseph Blenkinsopp, "The Family in First Temple Israel," in Leo G. Perdue et al., *Families in Ancient Israel* (Louisville, KY, 1996), pp. 48-103, at 60ff., and more generally Boaz Cohen, *Dowry in Jewish and Roman Law* (Brussels, 1955).

15. 1 Sam. 18:25; Hos. 3:2.

16. Gen. 34:12; Exod. 22:16-17; Deut. 22:28-29. See also Doc. 4-2 and 4-3 above.

17. Comm. Harm. Law Exod. 21:7-11; Lev. 19:29. But cf. Comm. Josh. 15:16-19; Serm. 1 Sam. 18:22-30; 2 Sam. 3:14-16 (where Calvin does not criticize fathers for offering their daughters as prizes for valor).

18. Gen. 24:1-67.

19. Gen. 24:22, 53.

Opposed as he was to material excess, Calvin had trouble commenting on this passage (**Doc. 11-6**). He admitted that engagement gifts are "not ill-bestowed" or "given for a dishonorable purpose." But he immediately warned his readers that to follow this one biblical example in giving extravagant engagement gifts was "not only dangerous, but even foolish." For the Bible elsewhere condemned luxury, and even wealthy suitors like Abraham and Isaac should have known better than to flaunt their riches to impress a woman. Some modest engagement gift, Calvin believed, was appropriate "to facilitate the marriage contract." But extravagant gifts would simply not do.[20] Having made his point, Calvin simply ignored the later verse reporting the servant's delivery of even more extravagant gifts to Rebekah and her family when they approved the marriage. He echoed his concern for modesty in dress and jewelry in his sumptuary legislation, making only a single exception that parties may wear a bit of extra jewelry on their wedding day. But, even on this great day of celebration, the bride and groom had to be modest, as we shall see.[21]

Calvin put aside his concerns about the size of the engagement and marriage gift in cases of fornication and rape. Glossing a text in Exodus 22, Calvin argued that if a man had sex with a woman, particularly a virgin, he was required to marry her and to pay the full marriage gift that her father demanded. If her father refused to consent to the marriage, the man had to pay the gift nonetheless as a penalty for his sexual misconduct and a recompense for despoiling the woman.[22] These rules were doubly imperative in cases where a man (or a member of his family) had sex with his own fiancée or with his bonded servant or slave, or where he had raped a woman. To spurn any such woman after seducing or raping her was an outrage that Jewish law condemned, and Calvin condemned even more loudly.[23] At minimum, in these cases of seduction and rape, the woman and her family deserved the full marriage gift, as Exodus 22 enjoined.[24] More properly in such cases, Calvin argued glossing a parallel text in Deuteronomy 22, the parties should be compelled to marry, and the man deprived of any right to divorce her.[25] The man's loss of a right to divorce was a small price for him to pay for his sin of seduction, fornication, or rape. Properly,

20. See also Comm. Josh. 15:16-19 excerpted in Doc. 5-4.

21. See SD, vol. 3, items 1050, 1052 and discussion in Chapter 13.

22. See Doc. 4-2 above, where we have analyzed this passage for its understanding of individual consent to marriage. See also Gen. 34:1-12, where Shechem and his father Hamor offered to pay Jacob the dowry payment for Shechem's rape of Jacob's daughter Dinah. Calvin did not comment on this part of the passage.

23. Comm. Harm. Law Exod. 21:7-11.

24. But see Lect. Hos. 3:2 where Calvin approves a lower marriage gift for a woman who has had illicit sex, but still is taken in marriage.

25. Doc. 4-3 above.

he should be executed, but that would leave the woman ravaged and without ongoing support. So the man had to marry the woman, to pay the full gift, to live peaceably with his wife, and never bring an action for divorce.

Legal and Consistory Materials

While Calvin wrote a good deal about the theology of marital property, he seems to have written less about the law in question. He certainly would have had some training in the relevant civil law and canon law of marital property. Lectures on the subject were standard fare for a licentiate in law at the universities at Bourges and Orleans where Calvin had trained. His law professors, L'Estoile, Alciatus, and Budé, were all noted experts on the law of marriage and marital property.[26] Indeed, all three of these great jurists, together with Lorenzo Valla, were embroiled in a celebrated debate over the interpretation of Roman law texts, just at the time Calvin was studying law, and Calvin followed this debate with interest. The debate turned in part on interpretation of certain classic legal texts and their medieval glosses on the subject of (marital) property and inheritance.[27]

Calvin may have written, or at least intended to write, more on the subject of marital property than has survived. The outline of his proposed Code of Criminal Law and Civil Law for Geneva does include titles for separate entries on dower, dowry, and usufruct, as well as detailed titles on testamentary succession, which also would have dealt with the dower rights of widows.[28] It is unclear whether Calvin wrote these provisions in his proposed code; if he did, they have not survived. What has survived is a fragment of Calvin's proposed statute on the division of marital property in the event of a couple's formal separation (**Doc. 11-7**). But this fragment does not address the thorny question of dowry and marriage portion rights that a separation case would raise.

Calvin did include two brief provisions on marital property in his 1546 Marriage Ordinance:

26. See relevant sources in Coing, 1:41-60, 155-65, 276-91; II/1:171-213, 341-49; Paul Emile Viard, *André Alciat 1492-1550* (Paris, 1926), pp. 12-17, 71-76; Ernst von Moeller, *Andreas Alciat (1492-1550): Ein Beitrag zur Entstehungsgeschichte der modernen Jurisprudenz* (Breslau, 1907), pp. 57ff.; Josef Bohatec, *Budé und Calvin: Studien zur Gedankwelt des französischen Frühumanismus* (Graz, 1950).

27. See Michael L. Monheit, *Passion and Order in the Formation of Calvin's Sense of Religious Authority* (Ph.D. Diss., Princeton, 1988), pp. 130-210; Basil Hall, "John Calvin, the Jurisconsults and the *Ius Civile*," in C. J. Cuming, ed., *Studies in Church History* (Leiden, 1966), 3:202-16; Donald R. Kelley, *Foundations of Modern Historical Scholarship: Language, Law, and History in the French Renaissance* (New York, 1970).

28. CO 10/1:130-31.

7. Where children marry without their father's or mother's permission at the age permitted above and it is established by the court that they have done this lawfully because of the negligence or excessive strictness of their fathers, let the fathers be required to grant them a dowry or provide them such a share or position as [they would have given] if they had consented to it....

[14.] Failure to pay a dowry or money or provide an outfit shall not prevent the marriage from coming into full effect, since these are only accessory.[29]

We have not found any cases (at least in our three sample years) where the Consistory compelled parents to pay a dowry to a daughter from whom they had unreasonably withheld their consent to marry, though most such cases would have gone to the Lieutenant's Court for disposition. The Consistory did occasionally override parents if they unreasonably withheld their consent to a child's marriage, allowing the marriage to proceed.[30] But the implications of these cases for dowry payments were evidently for the "ordinary authority" of the Council, not the Consistory, to resolve.[31]

From the start, the Consistory enforced the second provision of the Marriage Ordinance — that engagements should not be dissolved for mere failure to deliver engagement gifts or dowry. Already in a 1545 case, for example, the Consistory summoned Louis Piaget and his fiancée to inquire why they had not married (**Doc. 11-8**). It turned out that Louis was awaiting payment of a rather handsome dowry by his fiancée's master, and his fiancée had meanwhile returned to her father, a Catholic no less. The Consistory inquired closely whether the only issue was over money. When that proved to be the only obstacle, the Consistory ordered the couple to get married, and sent the fiancée's master to the Council who ordered him to pay the promised dowry.

The Consistory ruled similarly in two cases the following year. Jean de Landécy and Mia had become properly engaged before witnesses (**Doc. 11-9**). Mia had promised Jean a dowry of money to be paid in installments. But, because she had not been able to collect money owed to her, she had substituted various household items and tools for her first dowry installment. Jean had accepted the goods, but evidently wanted his dowry money as well and threatened

---

29. Doc. 1-2.

30. See examples in Chapters 3 and 4 above.

31. See Seeger, pp. 315-17. In his commentary on the Adultero-German Interim, chap. 21.11, Calvin wrote: "Whether parents ought to be permitted in this case [of a marriage entered without parental consent] to punish the disobedience of children by withholding, or at least diminishing the dowry, or by any other means, is a matter which we think ought to be left to ordinary authority." Translated in John Calvin, *Tracts and Treatises in Defense of the Reformed Faith*, trans. Henry Beveridge (Grand Rapids, 1958), 3:301-2. See further discussion in Chapter 5.

to break off the engagement. Mia promised to try to fulfill her dowry demands. That was good enough for the Consistory to remand the case to the Council, with a recommendation that marriage be required. The Council ordered the couple to marry.

Similarly Nicolas Adduard and Jehanne had been properly engaged before witnesses.[32] Jehanne and her uncle had made an unconditional promise of a dowry of money, cattle, and all their household goods. Jehanne now argued that she had been swindled, and wished neither to marry nor to furnish the dowry. Nicolas wanted to marry only if he could get his hands on the promised dowry. The Consistory would hear nothing of breaking the engagement over a dowry dispute. They sent the parties to the Council. The Council ordered them to marry, notwithstanding Jehanne's continued protests. This became the standard procedure and result in later years, as the brief 1552 case of Robert Moreau and Jeanne illustrates (**Doc. 11-10**).

The 1552 case of Philibert Berthelier reports Calvin's action in a disputed engagement case that included dowry issues (**Doc. 11-11**). Berthelier had earlier been engaged to a woman, whose brother-in-law had promised to pay an ample dowry of money and clothing. Berthelier had broken off the relationship. He then appeared before the Council to explain why, and to request the Council's approval for him to proceed with a new marriage. Calvin, a bitter enemy of Berthelier, represented the Consistory at the Council hearing. The Council decided that witnesses should be heard, and the new marriage be allowed only if and after Berthelier was granted a formal divorce from his prior engagement or marriage. The Council has no further record of the case. But ten days later, Calvin hailed Berthelier before the Consistory. Calvin ordered him to confess his faults and to explain why he had broken off his prior relationship, which one witness declared to be an actual marriage for which an ample dowry had been paid. The Consistory decided to send Calvin back to the Council to testify about the illegality of Berthelier's breakup, and its serious implications for restitution of the dowry. While nothing survives of Calvin's testimony, a week later, the Council sent a tart order to the Consistory to stop interfering with Berthelier's plans for new marriage. A chastened Consistory sent another minister to apologize to the Council. Calvin could not have been happy.

The 1552-1553 case of Thomas Bonna illustrates that a man could not condition his consent to marriage upon full and exact satisfaction of the dowry promise (**Doc. 11-12**). The engagement promise and the dowry promise were separate agreements, the Consistory insisted. Breach of the dowry promise could not serve as a ground for dissolving the engagement, particularly if a man

---

32. The case record is reproduced in Doc. 4-8 where we have analyzed it for the issues of conditional consent.

tendered an engagement gift. The case, which bounced back and forth between the Consistory and Council for more than a year, was an important precedent. Had Bonna prevailed, it would have been easy enough for a man, or his father, to demand perfect tender of a dowry before giving his consent to the marriage. This would defeat the principle on which Calvin had insisted — that questions of marital property were to remain ancillary to questions of the validity of the engagement and marriage contract itself.

The Consistory case law did not depart far from the *ius commune* that prevailed in Geneva on the eve of the Reformation. What was new was the division of jurisdiction over marriage property disputes between the Consistory and the Council (or Lieutenant's Court). Most such questions would have been fully resolved in the bishop's court before the Reformation. What was also new — and surprising — was the Consistory's insistence on compelling couples to marry, even in the face of earnest disputes over marital property arrangements that had alienated their affections from each other and their families. To be sure, this principle was of a piece with Calvin and Beza's insistence that neither engagement nor marriage contracts should be made lightly or dissolved easily. But this principle stood in tension with the *ius commune* that gave parties some chance to dissolve engagements that fell apart over property, particularly if they both wanted out.

This principle that property disputes cannot break engagements also stood in tension with Calvin's opening admonition that: "Domestic affairs never go well without a private mutual understanding and a settlement of the conditions required on both sides." Calvin, the pastor, had complained about the damage that family fights over property could inflict, as we saw in **Doc. 11-2**. One would think that if these problems were exposed in advance he would hesitate to set marriages and families upon such a collision course. Calvin, the lawyer, however, stuck to his principle. He and the Consistory forced into marriage a good number of parties that were still squabbling over property on the eve of their wedding. Predictably, several of these parties returned repeatedly to the Consistory because of family quarrels.

Not only case law, but also statutory law on marital property largely followed the traditional *ius commune*. No new statute was forged in Calvin's own day. But, in 1568, four years after Calvin's death, Germain Colladon prepared a lengthy new title for the new Civil Code of Geneva (**Doc. 11-13**). This new marital property law largely repeated the traditional law of dowry. It made one change that was potentially advantageous to women. The full amount of the dowry that the woman brought to the marriage was now presumptively her marriage portion, unless the parties stipulated otherwise. Her husband could use that property during their married life, but she was entitled to full recovery of all of it (arts. 3, 4, 6, 13) upon his death. Traditionally, a wife's marriage portion had been on the order of a third or a half of the dowry.

The new marital property law also repeated the traditional law of dower. But it made two changes, both potentially harmful to widows. First, in many cases widows received no priority over other creditors in securing their dower interests from their late husband's estate (art. 17). This could leave a widow with nothing, if her husband had been incompetent in managing his property or died heavily in debt. Second, a husband could order his heirs to support his widow upon his death. If she accepted their support, the widow would forfeit her dower interest and its accrued value. This provision could expose widows to the designs of unscrupulous heirs. It was a notable departure from the canon law rule that a woman's dower rights could not be renounced under any condition, save her conviction for adultery or malicious desertion.

Not every marriage contract required the kind of detail that was set out in the 1568 statute. But the statute did seem to encourage Genevan parties to get their marital affairs in written order. Perhaps this reality dawned on a Genevan couple, Michel Guichon and Pernette Cuvat. For, in 1569, the year after the statute came into effect, the parties executed a simple marital contract to formalize a marriage they had already celebrated and consummated (**Doc. 11-14**). This was, evidently, a couple of modest means, and they agreed simply to merge their respective properties with full mutual rights of survivorship. In the event of children, however, Pernette would receive her stipulated marriage portion and then serve as trustee of the balance of the marital property, using it to support the children. All this was in perfect accord with the 1568 law.

Summary and Conclusions

Both before and after the Reformation in Geneva, marriage triggered a series of important property transactions. On engagement, the man gave a betrothal gift or earnest money to his fiancée and/or her family. On the wedding day, the woman brought her dowry property into the new marital household. When the husband died, his widow would take dower interests in one-half of his personal property, with the property reverting to her late husband's family and the couple's children upon her later death. When the wife died, her family would take ownership in the marriage portion of the dowry that she had brought into the marriage. While the types and amounts of property were subject to some negotiation between the parties and their families, these basic property transactions followed automatically upon each fateful step.

Calvin, Colladon, and their Consistory colleagues made few changes in the prevailing laws of marital property. Both encouraged engaged parties to get their property affairs in order before the wedding to avoid disputes thereafter. Both were firm proponents of clear marital property contracts that stipulated each party's property rights and duties in advance and that made ample provision for the rights of widows and dependent children. Calvin discouraged excessive engagement gifts, thinking these a form of sumptuousness. Colladon relaxed dower rules, thinking them too restrictive on the heirs. But these were only equitable adjustments to traditional customs and rules.

Calvin and his colleagues did depart from the late medieval tradition in two important respects. First, contrary to tradition, they insisted that marital property disputes be left to the Council, not to the Consistory, to resolve finally. Before the Reformation, most such questions were resolved in the bishop's court. This was in part an exercise of the Church's jurisdiction over the sacrament of marriage. It was also an extension of the Church's jurisdiction over last rites (or extreme unction), whose rules and procedures had important implications for the inheritance and disposition of marital property. The reformers did not regard marriage and last rites as sacraments, and thus did not recognize the Church's jurisdiction over these affairs. These were all matters for the "ordinary authority" of the magistrate.

Second, contrary to tradition, Calvin and his colleagues insisted that marital property disputes could not break engagement contracts, even if the parties and their families had become bitter enemies. Marital property matters were ancillary to marriage itself, the reformers insisted. Marriages could not be conditioned on delivery of property.[33] And marriages could not be broken if the promise to deliver property was broken. This lesson was consistent with the reformers' principle that both engagement and marriage contracts should not be lightly made or lightly broken.

This was a firmer extension of this principle than seemed necessary. After all, marital property transactions and negotiations could not begin in earnest until the parties had become engaged. Money and property disputes, as Calvin himself experienced, could drive apart the fastest of friends and the most loving of couples. It seemed imprudent, if not cruel, to drive couples to the altar while they and their families remained locked in bitter dispute over property. Surely, the one brief consensual step of becoming engaged could not trigger such devastating consequences, particularly when the parties had become so obviously estranged. Surely, this could be seen to violate the most elementary marriage rule that Calvin championed: that marriage depended in its essence on the mutual consent of the man and the woman.

Calvin and his Consistory colleagues, however, held firmly to this principle. They dragged many couples still bickering over property to the altar to get married within six weeks of their engagement. It was no surprise that many of these same couples later appeared before the Consistory with all manner of

---

33. See Chapter 4.

family quarrels to resolve. It was also no surprise that subsequent generations of Calvinists amended these marital property rules to allow bitter property disputes to delay weddings for a time, if not cancel them altogether.[34]

34. See sources in FSC, pp. 126ff., 165ff.

11-1 Marriage Contract of Germain Colladon and Claude Bigot (1536)[35]

1. Master Germain Colladon[36] the younger, attorney at law, of the one part, and the respectable Claude Bigot, daughter of the late honorable, respectable, and august Master Nicolas Bigot, during his lifetime counselor of our lord the king and lieutenant-general of the bailiff of Berry, and of the respectable Cathérine Charrier his wife . . . by the respectable Guymon Thévenin, widow of the late Ythier Charrier, her maternal grandmother, for her of the other part.

2. Which parties have stated that a marriage by words *de futuro* has been agreed to between the said Master Germain Colladon and the said Claude Bigot according to the agreements, articles, and decisions which follow, by which the said Colladon, by the advice, counsel, and judgment of the honorable, respectable, and august Masters Germain Colladon, judge and warden of La Chastre, his father, Léon Colladon, attorney, counselor, and barrister of Bourges, his brother, [and] Urbain Chauveton, his brother-in-law . . . has promised to take the said Claude Bigot as wife and spouse.

3. Likewise Claude Bigot by the will . . . and counsel of the said Guymon Thévenin, her said grandmother, and by the advice of the prudent and respectable Robert Bigot, paternal uncle of the said Claude, and of the honorable, respectable, and august Master Léon Colladon, Jean Artuys, [and] Jean Deschamps, brothers-in-law of the said Claude, has promised to take the said Master Germain Colladon as husband and spouse, if God, etc.

4. And in favor and expectation of the said marriage the said Guymon Thévenin, the aforesaid grandmother, having the administration of the bodies and goods of Masters Nicolas and Pierre Bigot . . . , of Etienne and Magdelaine Bigot, and of the said Claude, all minor children of the said late Master Nicolas Bigot and the late Cathérine Charrier, has promised and promises to pay and give to the said future spouses from the goods fallen in by succession from the said deceased and which are common to the said minor children the sum of 1500 livres tournois, and this to cover all rights falling and payable to the said Claude by the said succession from the said deceased, that is:

---

35. Original in Bourges, Arch. dép. E4453 (Minutes of the notary Jean Ragueau), ancien: 4453, reprinted in Erich-Hans Kaden, *Le Jurisconsulte Germain Colladon ami de Jean Calvin et de Théodore de Bèze* (Geneva, 1974), pp. 141-43. The ellipses and fragments are per the reprinted text.

36. "Colladon" is rendered variously in the contract as "Collaidon" and "Coilhaidon."

(a) For the sum of 300 livres tournois, a house as it stands, situated in this city of Bourges on the rue d'Oron next to. . . .

(b) Also for the sum of 200 livres, the sum of 13 livres tournois of rents. . . .

(c) Also for the sum of 260 livres tournois, a body of land in several parcels situated near this city of Bourges, acquired by the said late Master Nycolas Bigot from the widow of the late Bélin.

(d) Also the sum of 140 livres tournois in movables.

(e) Also the sum of 600 livres tournois in cash, the sum of 400 livres on the day of the nuptial blessing by the said Guymon Thévenin, the aforesaid grandmother, and the sum of 200 livres tournois within two years, counting from the day and date of the present act.

(f) And the said widow shall clothe . . . the said Claude with wedding clothes and garments well and properly according to her estate, by the judgment and decision of herself and of the other relatives and friends of the said Claude.

5. And it was stated and agreed that of the said sum of 1500 livres tournois, the sum of 1000 shall be accounted a personal inheritance for the said future wife . . . and the sum of 500 livres tournois shall be accounted movables. And this . . . the goods, movables, and acquisitions . . . that they gain and acquire during the said marriage are and shall remain common to the said future spouses.

6. Also it was agreed between the said parties that if the said future wife should happen to pass from life to death before the said future husband without legitimate descendants of the said marriage, the said future husband shall be required to render to the heirs of the said future wife the said sum of 1000 livres tournois accounted as an inheritance, or the inheritance which shall have been acquired with the said sum, and the common goods of . . . and the said sum of 500 livres accounted as movables or that which . . . shall have been . . . without the said heirs of the said Claude being able to claim any common right in the goods and joint estate of the said future husband.

7. Also if it happens that the said future husband passes from life to death before the said future wife without or with legitimate descendants of the said marriage, she shall have a right of choice and election of her common property from the goods, movables, and acquisitions of the said future husband along with the heirs of the said future husband, and in so choosing the said common goods, she shall take and have the sum of 500 livres only for her said inheritance and half of the movables and acquisitions, and in case she makes a choice and promise of marriage and does not wish to take her said community property, she shall have for an inheritance the said sum of 1000 livres tournois, and if . . . and the said 500 livres accounted as movables and the said. . . .

8. And whatever goods she chooses, she shall have in addition her jewelry and her . . . in whatever amount they may be and the dower . . . as a stipulated

addition, and shall have time and space for making the said choice of three months, counted from . . . of the said husband, during which time she shall live off the community goods without . . . of her said choice.

9. And whichever choice she makes, the said future husband . . . one or the other,[37] in case there are children of the said marriage, of the sum of 30 livres tournois of rents only for the life of the said Claude, or the sum of 300 livres paid all at once, and in case there are no children of the said marriage, one or other of the said sum of 30 livres tournois of rents during her life or the sum of . . . 400 livres tournois paid all at once, at the choice and election of the said Claude Bigot.

10. And also the said Master Germain Colladon . . . in favor of the said marriage both gives and gives by act . . . by pure and simple and irrevocable gift . . . solemnly *inter vivos* to the said Master Germain Colladon, his said son, . . . and he accepts a meadow . . . located and situated in . . . [the] outskirts of La Chastre next to the road . . . going from . . . from the said town to Nevers . . . next to the meadow of Germain B . . . next to the vineyard of Simon and . . . and this as a marriage gift,[38] and also . . . to the said Master Germain Colladon and to his future . . . of the said Master Germain . . . of the said meadow. . . .

11. Also it was further stated and agreed that in case it is found that the rent of the said Orron house and for the said . . . and the said body of land in La Chastre do not come to the sums aforesaid at which they have been rated, in the said case the said widow . . . pay to the said future husband the sums and . . . at which they have been estimated and rated within three years, or the lowest value . . . the said Claude shall promise to return in dividing with her said brothers and sisters . . . the aforesaid goods or that which . . . shall be.

12. . . . pledged . . . of the august Senate and given at Bourges the twenty-fifth day of the month of June of the year 1536 before the respectable Jean Ragueau . . . merchant residing in Bourges and the prudent and respectable François Deschamps, residing . . . to the witnesses summoned.

Ragueau

11-2   Letter to Viret (August 19, 1542)[39]

As soon as you were gone, strange bickerings broke out between Sebastian and his brothers-in-law, which have sorely exercised me in trying to settle them by a

---

37. The French phrase is *"douche et douche."*

38. The French word is *"préciput,"* meaning in this case a sum given at marriage, without prejudicing his right to an equal inheritance with his siblings on his father's death.

39. CO 11:427-30; Bonnet, Letter 90 (adapted).

little friendly involvement. My motive for taking part in these disputes was so that the quarrel might not go too far, and that the scandal of it would not reach abroad to the disgrace of the school. For all my care and efforts, however, I could not even get the one party to stop abusing the other; they are thus everywhere the talk of the town for most people. As soon as the common dispute about the dowry payment was somewhat resolved, new disputes broke out between Sebastian and Peter, partly about the management of household expenses, and partly about their dwelling. I have never seen a more complicated affair. After much wrangling with each other they came at length to a sort of compromise, but this eventually occasioned another new dispute. Tempers on both sides were so high that one can scarcely hope for any solid friendship between them, such as ought to exist among brethren.

11-3   Letter to Farel (July 1, 1558)[40]

I could mention some young ladies of honorable parents who have been modestly brought up. But since they are rather poor, I do not venture to propose them; indeed, there does not occur to me any young woman who is both beautiful and virtuous and, at the same time, possessed of a good dowry. I mentioned three only in my letter. Time will, perhaps, suggest others to me. There are two young neighbors of ours, of great personal beauty and liberally educated, the one a daughter of Dommartin, the other of Saint-Laurent, who, though their dowry is not very ample, will, nevertheless have something. If I should hear of anything else, I will let you know.

11-4   Letter to de Falais (July 17, 1548)[41]

I believe that it will be best as it is. If it had been possible to speak together about the contract, I would have much desired to do so; but I do not know whether you will be able to come this week. However, the man offers, in case he should leave his wife a widow without children that she shall have a thousand crowns. In the event of his leaving children, she shall have the half [of his property], but on condition that, if she marry afterwards, and have also children by the second marriage, she must not have the power of preferring them to those of the first. The present assignment will be founded upon the instrument of Paris, to be implemented, when he shall have made good his money and ex-

40. CO 17:227-28; Bonnet, Letter 500 (adapted).
41. CO 13:7-9; Bonnet, Letter 225 (adapted).

penses. I am of opinion that his offer is very liberal; for it is quite right that the husband retain some control in his own hand.

11-5   Commentary on Genesis 29:14-25 (1554)[42]

[A] great principle of equity is set before us in the example of Laban; inasmuch as this sentiment is common to almost all minds, that justice ought to be mutually cultivated, lest blind greed draw them away in another direction. God has engraven in man's nature a law of equity, so that whoever declines from that rule, through an immoderate desire of private advantage, is utterly without excuse. But a little while after, when it came to a matter of practice, Laban forgets about this equity and thinks only of what may be profitable to him. Such an example is certainly worthy of notice. For men seldom err in general principles. They can thus say out of one side of their mouth that every man ought to receive what is his due. But as soon as they come down to their own affairs, perverse self-love blinds them, or at least envelops them in such clouds that they are carried in an opposite direction.

Let us, therefore, learn to restrain ourselves so that a desire of our own advantage may not prevail to the sacrifice of justice. . . . Laban, in wishing to enter into a contract [with Jacob], does what tends to avoid contentions and complaints. . . . [F]or the purpose of preserving the peace, firm agreements are necessary, which may prevent injustice on one side or the other.

But Laban's iniquity betrays itself in a moment. For it is a shameful act of barbarism to hold out his daughter as a reward for Jacob's services, making her the subject of a kind of barter. He should not only have given a portion [of this dowry] to his daughter, but also acted more liberally towards his future son-in-law. . . . Moses does not here relate something rare or unusual, but most common. For though men do not put their daughters for sale, yet their greed hurries most of them so much that they prostitute their honor and sell their souls. . . .

11-6   Commentary on Genesis 24:22 (1554)[43]

[The servant's] adorning the young woman with precious ornaments is a token of his confidence. For since it is evident by many proofs that he was an honest and careful servant, he would not throw away without discretion the treasures

42. CO 23:401-3 (OTC adapted).
43. CO 23:335-37 (OTC adapted).

of his master. He knows, therefore, that these gifts will not be ill-bestowed; or, at least, relying on the goodness of God, he gives them, in faith, as an earnest of future marriage.

But it may be asked whether God approves ornaments of this kind, which pertain not so much to neatness as to pomp? I answer that the things related in Scripture are not always proper to be imitated. Whatever the Lord commands in general terms is to be accounted as an inflexible rule of conduct; but to rely on particular examples is not only dangerous, but even foolish and absurd. Now we know how highly displeasing to God is not only pomp and ambition in adorning the body, but all kind of luxury. In order to free the heart from inward greed, he condemns that immoderate and superfluous splendor, which contains within itself many allurements to vice. . . .

With respect to the earrings and bracelets of Rebekah, I do not doubt that they were those in use among the rich, so the uprightness of the age allowed them to be sparingly and frugally used. Yet I do not excuse the fault. This example, however, neither helps us, nor alleviates our guilt, if, by such means, we excite and continually inflame those depraved lusts which, even when all incentives are removed, it is excessively difficult to restrain. The women who desire to shine in gold, seek in Rebekah a pretext for their corruption. . . .

11-7 Fragment of Calvin's Draft Ordinance on Matrimonial Property (n.d.)[44]

Moreover, because otherwise we could not bring them to an agreement, we have ordered and order that beforehand and ahead of everything they must make an inventory both of their merchandise and of the business they do, debts, bonds, and everything else depending on it, and of their movables, utensils, common possessions, and purchased property. Let them settle and close their accounts and so arrange between them that there is a definite resolution, to put an end to all previous quarrels, and so that from this time on each may know what is his, so that there may be no retraction.

And we desire this to be done as soon as possible, at the latest within a year, without formal proceedings, but peaceably and with goodwill. If it happens that one of the parties does not want to consent to this — that is, to making such an inventory and settling their accounts without a suit or going to court — the other shall have the option and liberty of renouncing the present agreement and returning to his first course [of legal action?].

This being done, it shall be our desire that the two parties live together,

44. CO 10/1:143-44.

keeping a common household as they have done until now, both for their own contentment and repose and to avoid the gossip of the world and the scandal that might result from their separation.

Nevertheless, since we cannot get them to agree to this, we order[45] that the separation be carried out when the accounts are finished, that is within a year. So that they must separate and each withdraw himself peaceably,[46] under penalty of returning to their previous condition, that is that each respectively should continue in the rights and actions he had taken as though this present agreement had never been made.

Nevertheless, if it happens afterwards that for the ease and convenience of the two parties or of one of them it seems proper to them to arrange and carry out a separation, we leave them at liberty to do this.

11-8   Case of Louis Piaget and Fiancée (1545)[47]

(Oct. 15, 1545). Louis Piaget and the Bordons' maid were called to learn about their quarrel, because they are engaged, and how it happens that they have broken their promise and why they do not want to have the wedding. Levet's widow spoke certain verbose words about the girl, also about the Bordons. Also that Donne Claudine provided for him fully 200 florins p.p. [petit poids], and it was pledged by Monsieur Julian Bordon, or otherwise he did not make the promise, urging the need he has to provide in his business for what he owes and endures.

The girl was asked whether she agrees to marriage and whether the difference is only over money because he [Piaget] says that her father agreed to hand over 200 florins to Bordon, which Bordon had promised to [her prospective] husband Piaget.

Decided: [the prospective] husband was made to withdraw, and the fiancée was admonished for having gone back to her father and for having followed their papist practice.

Decided: Monsieur Claude du Pan took on the duty of making Monsieur Julian Bordon get the father to come here by Thursday, and then a good agreement can be reached.

[A week later Bordon was remanded before the Council for October 26.

---

45. Calvin first wrote: "Nevertheless, if it cannot be done otherwise and both the parties prefer to live separately, or one of the two desires this, we order. . . ."

46. Original text: ". . . they are mutually obligated to separate, each at the other's request. . . ."

47. R. Consist. II, 2.

On that date the Council ordered that the marriage should go into effect and that Bordon should pay the "marriage" (that is, the dowry) within three weeks afterwards.]

11-9   Case of Jean de Landécy and Mia (1546)[48]

(March 4, 1546). [The parties] were admonished to give the reason why they have come. Jean said that the woman promised him in marriage about 200 or 300 florins, and there were present at the house of Bernard Cloye, tailor, . . . Bernard and Claude Roch, baker, and Pierre Pricqua. Mia said she had given him various household goods and carpenter's tools, as is stated in a list she has presented to us that has been read.

Decided: he confessed having almost all the contents [on the list]. Nevertheless, he said he will not marry her if she does not give him what she promised. They were remanded here to Thursday to bring the witnesses.

(March 11, 1546). Claude Roch, baker, was admonished and asked to tell the truth about what he knows and that he was present at the promise of marriage of Jean de Landécy. He answered that it is true that his fiancée promised to provide him about two hundred florins in one way or another — eighty florins cash on the announcement, the rest afterwards or at the wedding. Asked whether a promise of marriage was made, he said yes, and that they both swore on the bread.

Pierre Pricqua was also asked about the above. He said it is true that Master Claude [Roch] asked the fiancée, that is Mia, whether she wanted Jean. Then she said yes, and the promise was made on the bread, and they drank together. Asked whether it was stated that if he did not have the [dowry] money he would not marry her, he said he did not hear anything said about that.

Decided: that they be remanded before the Council and that the promise appears to be valid, and that the Council should order the woman to give what she promised to her husband.

The fiancée was called, and was admonished that she was to keep the promise that she promised. She said she wanted to do it. Asked whether she did not say that she would give twenty-four florins immediately to her husband, she said she will certainly do it, and that it [the promise] is secured by a piece of land at Cruseilles. She said further that Guillaume Coustel owes her a certain sum that he denies, and that Coustel asks her for documentation [of his debt], and that it is on his conscience.

Jean, the fiancé, was summoned, and was admonished that the marriage and

48. R. Consist. II, 38, 40.

promise were made and that he should carry them out and that the woman will give him all she can; if not, they are remanded to Monday before the Council.

[On March 23 the Council summoned them for the following Monday, but the resulting decision is not reported. In January, 1547, Jean de Landécy, grave-digger, had still not married Mia. He was then suspected of theft, and was released on condition that he marry Mia, which he did.]

11-10 Case of Robert Moreau and Jeanne (1552)[49]

(March 10, 1552). Robert Moreau, velvet-maker, and Jeanne his [prospective] wife, were admonished as to why they do not proceed to marry as they promised on Thursday, January 21, of this year. Answered that it is because her parents do not want to give him the money they have promised him.

Decided: that if he does not agree to marry between now and Sunday, let them be remanded before the Council for Monday to require and compel it, and let them hand over the banns.

11-11 Case of Philibert Berthelier (1552)[50]

(June 30, 1552). Philibert Berthelier stated that Monsieur Calvin told him last time that he had to come here to the Consistory. He [Calvin] answered that this is true, because Communion has been forbidden him for a long time, and before marrying it is proper to come here to show evidence of repentance. . . .

(July 7, 1552). Monsieur Calvin stated that he has heard that the secretary Berthelier had previously made a promise to the sister of Monsieur de Rogemont's wife and that it would be good to hear them, both Rogemont and Berthelier, to learn the manner in which such a marriage was broken off. So decided.

Berthelier appeared promptly and answered that he does not know what this is about. He asked us to proclaim his banns [for his new marriage] and to do him this honor. [He testified that] it is true that some proposals were made to him about the bastard daughter of L'Argentier, brother-in-law of the said Monsieur de Rogemont, but there was no promise [of marriage].

Decided: that since this is not the last time, that it not be suspended, and that for Thursday Rogemont, the syndic Vandel, and Monsieur Jean Lambert be summoned.

49. R. Consist. VII, 7. Calvin did not sit on this case.
50. R. Consist. VII, 51-58.

(July 14, 1552). Noble Jean Lambert testified against the secretary Berthelier that a year and more ago . . . Monsieur Rogemont told him on the road that Berthelier had become engaged to the illegitimate daughter of his brother-in-law L'Argentier and that Monsieur Vandel had carried out the marriage in La Roche with the appropriate ceremonies, and that she . . . had promised [to bring] a dowry of two hundred écus with her clothes. But, afterwards, she had remarried.

Decided: that the Council be informed tomorrow, that Monsieur Calvin should be consulted, that the majority vote [sentence unfinished]

(July 21, 1552). The secretary Berthelier stated that the Council has remanded him here with their order that it pleases them not to obstruct him further from proclaiming his banns, signed by Noble Beguin on the date above.

Decided: that the Consistory go tomorrow to remonstrate with the Council for the exoneration of the Consistory, that is, Master Abel with some elders.

11-12   Case of Thomas Bonna and Claudine de Loelmoz (1552-1553)[51]

(Aug. 30, 1552).[52] Thomas Bonna was admonished why he does not proceed to marry his fiancée. He answered that when he made such a promise she had not reached her [age of] majority, and he told them [her family] that he did not want goods but money, and did not want land or lawsuits. He would otherwise not marry her until they gave him what they promised, and meanwhile he would serve his uncle Bienvenu until they gave him the money.

Decided: that for Thursday he be remanded before the Council, and despite all his excuses it is found that he should proceed with the banns. And let him bring his witnesses before the Council and everything he may use to assist him. . . .

(Sept. 21, 1553). Thomas Bonna and Claudine de Loelmoz [appeared]. Claudine produced the [Council's] orders given previously, asking that action be taken on it so the matter may be properly concluded. Thomas still alleges that he did what he did under the condition that he get cash. Afterwards he was read a bill stating how this same Bonna gave [Claudine] golden rings, and that he made her sell stored wine and chests, when she was brought to his house. Bonna said indeed he gave her rings, and as for the chests, he did not receive them, but it was done without his command.

---

51. R. Consist., VII, 71; VIII, 54v, 55. We have omitted intervening Consistory discussions of Council procedure on Dec. 1 and 8, 1552, and Jan. 12 and Sept. 13, 1553, reported in R. Consist. VII, 103, 106, 127; VIII, 54v.

52. Calvin was absent from this hearing.

Considering all the procedures and examinations and orders given in Council, including the last, [the marriage promise is valid]. Thomas confesses the promise of marriage, but maintains that the condition [to marriage has not been met]. But considering the gift of rings, [and] that he made her mistress and governor of his goods and house, he broke his claimed condition, not holding to it. And it is evident that he promised [marriage], as he confesses.

It was decided unanimously by the Consistory that it does not appear to them at all that this [engagement] may be dissolved. There is a marriage here which cannot be broken off according to God for the reasons given by Thomas. Also considering that he gave her a procuration as from a fiancé to a fiancée, as the procurator Gallatin, who received this procuration, has stated here. And therefore he is remanded to Monday before the Council with the decision aforesaid.

11-13   Civil Edicts (January 29, 1568)

Title XIV
Marriages, Dowries, Dowers, and Accrual[53]

1. The age, authority, and consent required for marriage are stated in the Ecclesiastical Ordinances [of 1561].

2. Guardians or trustees may not establish contracts or promises to marry between themselves or their relatives and those under their authority during the period of their authority and until they have surrendered their accounts and the residue of their trust; after having done so, they may not contract or make promises [of marriage] without the relatives' consent.

3. If there is no express provision of a dowry, conveyed and granted at the marriage, all of the wife's property will be deemed assigned and constituted as the dowry, and the husband will have its use and usufruct during the marriage to defray costs. And the husband must make an inventory of the property and give his wife proper acknowledgment of it, to serve her and hers in case of restitution.

4. The dowry provided, of whatever it consists and from whomever it derives, is assigned to the wife as her property to dispose of and devise to her

---

53. SD, vol. 3, item 1081. The French word for dower is *douaire*, meaning a wife's (and widow's) life interest in a portion of her (late) husband's property. The French word for dowry is *dot*, meaning the property that a woman brings into a marriage or sometimes receives at the time of marriage from her family. While the statute's title makes this linguistic distinction, the text throughout uses only the term *dot/dottes*. Where it is obvious that the text is referring to "dower," rather than "dowry," we have translated *dot* as dower.

heirs, unless there is a contrary agreement and exception in the contract establishing it.

5. The law of increase and accrual is that, unless it is otherwise agreed, half of the value of the dower[54] will be given to the wife from her husband's assets as a life estate, she giving warranty that after her death the capital will be returned to be preserved for the children of the marriage, if there are any; otherwise it will belong entirely to her.

6. And if the dowry does not consist of money but of real property or other goods rather than money, the value of the goods will be appraised by knowledgeable people to establish and assess the said accrual at the rate of one-third of the value of the goods which the husband will have had the use of because of his wife.

7. If a daughter married by her father has some property from her mother's side, and when providing the dowry her father does not state from whose property it is derived, the dowry will be presumed to come from the father's property, and her maternal property will be preserved to her.

8. And if a mother or grandmother, having authority over her daughter, provides a dowry on her marriage without declaring from whose property it derives, the said provision will be imputed to her paternal property; and if this does not suffice, the remainder of the dowry will be taken from the property of the mother or grandmother.

9. Those joined in marriage may not convey to each other during their lifetimes, at death, or by will more than half of their property derived from their parents to the prejudice of their parents in direct line or their brothers and sisters in collateral line. But they may dispose at will of the property they have acquired [during the marriage].

10. And if they have children they may not convey or devise to each other's benefit more than the usufruct of a third of their property. But the husband may leave to his wife the entire usufruct of all his property for the purpose of supporting his children, and this usufruct will last until the children reach the age of majority or marry.

11. Someone who marries a second time, having children by a previous marriage, may not convey property to his or her spouse for the said marriage or during it in excess of the portion of that one of his or her said other children to whom the least has been given.

12. What has been conveyed from one of those joined in marriage to the other whether by contract, will, or other disposition will revert to the children

---

54. Here is a clear instance where *dot* means dower, not dowry. Item 4 had just indicated that the dowry (*dot*) is the wife's property to be disposed of at her will. Item 5 says that the dower (*dot*), however, is only a life estate interest, with remainder interest in the children.

of the said marriage after the donee's death, even if the donation included the power to dispose of it at the donee's wish.

13. If a wife survives her husband she will have and retain the dresses, rings, and jewelry that she brought to her husband [at the marriage], to dispose of at her pleasure. As for dresses, rings, and jewelry that she received from her husband before or during the marriage, these, like her accrual, will be subject to restitution to the children, unless it has been stated otherwise in the marriage contract or the will.

14. But if the wife dies before her husband her heirs may demand of her husband only the dresses, rings, and jewelry found to be those that she brought to him on contracting or during the marriage, unless she has disposed of them differently.

15. A wife convicted of adultery will lose her dowry,[55] and the said dowry will be given to her husband unless she has children by a previous marriage, in which case these children will receive only their own reserved portions.[56]

16. A widow, if she is unfaithful to her deceased husband, will lose and render the accrued value of her dower to her husband's heirs. And if she was one of his heirs she will lose her inheritance to the designated substitute, or in default of such, to her husband's closest relatives.

17. Women owed dowers will not be preferred to creditors who hold previous bonds or mortgages, except for property that was expressly acquired using the dower money and without fraud.

18. If a wife, after the death of her husband, carries away or hides any goods belonging to her said husband, on being duly convicted of this she will be required to make restitution of three times the value of the goods taken, with deprivation of her accrual and of other goods given to her by her husband.

19. If a husband, by will or otherwise, has ordered that his wife be supported by his heirs during her widowhood, if she wishes to accept this provision, then during that time she may not recover either her dower or its accrued value.

20. If a husband sells some of his wife's real property, even with her consent, she will be recompensed with the price set on it from her husband's property, unless the said amount has been used for her or for other purchases for her benefit.

---

55. It is a closer question whether *dot* here means dower or dowry. It was commonplace of the *ius commune* that a wife sacrifices her dower interest if convicted of adultery. But normally only the children of the present marriage, not her prior marriage, would inherit her dower interests. Thus it could well be that the statute is referring to her dowry (which all her legitimate children, by whatever marriage) would inherit.

56. The reserved portion (*légitime* in French) was the amount of an estate required to be left to a child or other natural heir, regardless of the amount willed elsewhere.

21. If a husband has purchased property in his wife's name during their marriage she may not retain the said property unless she pays over its price or proves that it was purchased with her money.

11-14 Marriage Contract of Michel Guichon and Pernette Cuvat (1569)[57]

Let it be known and manifest to all that a marriage was recently contracted and duly solemnized and carried out in the Christian church of this city between the Honorable Michel, son of the late François Guichon, of Mésigny, boatman, resident of Geneva, on one part, and Pernette, daughter of the late Egrege Claude Cuvat of Geneva on the other part, without anything concerning the said marriage having been reduced to writing, as the parties state.

Now today, the fourth of the month of April, 1569, before me, the undersigned notary public, and the witnesses named below, there appeared personally the aforesaid Michel Guichon and Pernette Cuvat, his wife. The parties, in consideration of this marriage and following the agreement made when it was contracted, of their own free will, for themselves and all their heirs, have taken and take each other, for whatever goods they have at present or may have afterwards, whether movable, immovable, gold, silver, deeds, titles, or claims of any sort, so that the survivor will be and remain the sole and exclusive heir of the first decedent.

If, however, it pleases God to give them children by the present marriage, the wife after the death of her husband will take and receive from all the property of Guichon her husband the sum of fifty florins in all, together with the furnished bed she has brought to Guichon and all clothing, rings, and jewels and all movables she has brought to him, which are here taken to be specified. Guichon consents and is content that Pernette his wife will then act with a good and healthy conscience to manage and dispose of the whole [marital property] at her good pleasure and will.

So the said parties have promised and sworn by an oath taken before me, the undersigned notary, having agreed to keep good, firm, and valid the present act and to preserve, observe, and inviolably accomplish all its contents without ever contradicting or contravening it in any way or manner whatever. For this purpose, they have pledged and expressly hypothecated all their goods whatever, movable and immovable, present and future, which, for the complete observation of the present contract, they have submitted and submit to all the

57. A.E.G., Notaires, Aimé Santeur, v. 2, folios 128v-129v. Paragraph breaks added to the original.

course and rigor of the law where they are found, renouncing all rules, laws, statutes, edicts, and privileges by which they might aid and serve themselves to contradict what is written above, notably the rule that says that a general renunciation is not valid if a specific one does not precede it. For which purpose the said parties have indeed asked that each of them be provided a contract made publicly according to the advice and correction of knowledgeable people, without changing its substance.

Concluded and enacted in Geneva in the house of the couple Claude Tissot and Jean Bonnex, boatmen, citizens of Geneva, Jean Samoen, cobbler, and Jaques Marquis, also a cobbler, both residents of Geneva, being present as the required witnesses, and I, Aimé Santeur, the undersigned notary.

Santeur

CHAPTER 12

"The Perilous Interval"

Premarital Delay, Sex, and Desertion

George Bernard Shaw once called the period between a couple's engagement and wedding "the perilous interval." This was a time when couples faced both heightened temptation and heightened anxiety. Loving couples who could not contain themselves succumbed to premature sexual intimacy. Anxious parties who could not commit themselves resorted to desertion of the other. Bickering parties who could not agree on their future resigned to postponement of their wedding. This was as true in sixteenth-century Geneva as it is today.

The Genevan authorities regulated this perilous interval in some detail in their statutes and cases. Genevan couples had six weeks to wed after the announcement of their engagement. If the couple procrastinated in their wedding plans, the Consistory would reprimand them. If they persisted in their delay, the Council would compel them to marry. If they consorted too closely or cohabited before the wedding, they faced prison and various shame penalties. If the prospective groom disappeared without cause, the woman was bound to her engagement for a year. If the prospective bride disappeared, the man could break off the engagement after posting notices — unless there was evidence that she had been kidnapped or involuntarily detained.

Delayed Weddings, Premarital Sex, and Cohabitation

Theological Reflections

Calvin distinguished four types of fornication. These involved sexual relations: (1) between two unrelated parties; (2) between an engaged party and a third party; (3) between a married party and a third party; and (4) between two parties who were engaged.[1]

The first three types of fornication were increasingly serious violations of the seventh commandment: "Thou shalt not commit adultery."[2] The Bible, particularly the Old Testament, included numerous examples of all three types of fornication. Calvin took pains to gloss many of these biblical texts to press his campaign against the rampant sexual promiscuity that he found in Geneva. He showed how all three types of fornication offended God and the community's covenant to uphold God's law. He also showed how each type, at least by women, further harmed specific parties. The first offense (sex between two unrelated parties) harmed the father's interest in protecting his daughter's virginity. The second offense (sex between an engaged woman and a third party) violated the interests of her fiancé who had tendered his marriage gift. The third offense (sex between a married party and a third party) violated the interest of the innocent spouse. The Bible prescribed severe punishments for fornication — divorce,[3] mutilation,[4] public stripping,[5] and execution.[6]

The fourth type of fornication (sex between two engaged parties) did not fit easily into this biblical catalogue and calculus. The Bible had no clear commandments against premarital sex or examples of fiancés being punished for such behavior. The Bible did address several other aspects of the engagement. For example, the Mosaic law set out the legal consequences of rape or bondage of an engaged woman by her fiancé or a third party.[7] The Mosaic law also set

1. See further Kingdon, AD, pp. 116-19; see statutes on point in SD, items 826, 841, 965, 971, 992, 1046, 1065. Calvin addressed the issue of adultery and fornication frequently in his writings; we shall analyze them in detail in a sequel volume. See, e.g., Comm. Harm. Law Exod. 20:14, 17, 21; Lev. 18:20; Num. 5:11-31; Deut. 5:18, 21; 25:11-12; Serm. Deut. 5:18, 21; Serm. Deut. 21:15-17, Deut. 22:13-30; Serm. 2 Sam. 11:1-27; Lect. Comm. Hos. 3:2; Lect. Ezek. 16, 18:5-9; Comm. Harm. Gospel Matt. 5:27-28; Comm. John 8:1-5, 11; Comm. 1 Cor. 6:13-19; Serm. and Comm. Eph. 5:3-7; 6:19-20; Comm. 1 Thess. 4:4-5.

2. Exod. 20:14; Deut. 5:18.

3. Deut. 24:1-4; Jer. 3:8; Hos. 2:4.

4. Ezek. 23:25.

5. Hos. 2:5, 12; Jer. 13:22-26; Ezek. 16:37, 39.

6. Lev. 20:10; Deut. 22:22.

7. Exod. 22:16-17; Lev. 20:23; Deut. 22:23-29. See Docs. 4-2 and 4-3 and related discussion in Chapters 4 and 11 on the consent and property issues raised by these cases.

elaborate legal procedures for a man to charge his fiancée with fornication or to dismiss a fiancée who no longer pleased him.[8] Both the Prophets and the Gospels provided examples and admonitions concerning a man's acceptance and forgiveness of his fiancée despite her faults and shortcomings.[9] For all its attention to the conduct of engaged parties, however, the Bible was silent on the issue of consensual premarital sex between fiancés.

Furthermore, Calvin's and Beza's emphasis on the gravity of engagement contracts almost seemed to promote premarital sexual relations. As we have seen, engagement contracts could not be lightly made in Calvin's Geneva. They required parental consent, two witnesses, "sober" and "simple" promises by the man and the woman, public banns and registration, and more. Once properly made, these engagement contracts could not be easily trespassed or broken. If either fiancé had sex with a third party, they were guilty of adultery. If they became engaged or married to that third party, they were guilty of polygamy. Even if the parties mutually agreed to separate or became utterly antagonistic to each other, they could not dissolve the engagement contract unless they could prove the existence of an impediment.

If engagement was so much like marriage in all these restrictions, why could engagement not be like marriage in all of its liberties, including the liberty to enjoy sex and to live together? How could Calvin insist that engaged parties abstain from all third parties because that would breach faith to their fiancés, but not let the couple express their faith to each other through sexual intercourse?

Calvin said little to solve this puzzle. He did explicitly reject the solution of the medieval canonists who declared that a proper engagement contract, followed by voluntary sexual intercourse, constituted a valid marriage. For Calvin, this rule only encouraged the secret marriages that he and the Genevan authorities were working so hard to stamp out. Without the involvement of parents, peers, and pastors, there could be no proper marriage. Calvin also had trouble with the solution of the Jewish rabbis of his day, which Martin Luther had condoned, that the engagement period should be shortened to a day or two, so that the couple would not have much opportunity to commence sexual relations.[10] Calvin insisted that engagement periods in Geneva be shortened to six weeks, in part to reduce the temptation to premarital sex. But to make the engagement period any shorter, he argued, would again deprive the community from participating in the public scrutiny and rituals that properly become marriage.

---

8. Deut. 22:13-21; 24:1-4. See Docs. 8-2 to 8-4 and related discussion on the consequences of premarital adultery by either the fiancé or fiancée.

9. Hos. 2:19-20; 3:2; Matt. 1:18-19. See Doc. 8-5 on Joseph's treatment of Mary on first discovering her premarital pregnancy.

10. See Witte, FSC, pp. 56ff.

Calvin's main argument against sexual intimacy during the engagement period was a simple syllogism. All sexual contact by non-married parties is adultery. Engaged couples are, by definition, not yet married. Sex between engaged couples, therefore, is adultery. But this bracketed the hard question of why engagement should be treated like marriage in so many other ways but could not be so treated like it with respect to sexual conduct.

Statutes

While Calvin was vague on his rationale for the prohibition on premarital sex, he and the Genevan authorities were clear that such conduct was forbidden during the brief engagement period. A series of statutes, drafted or inspired by Calvin and other ministers, set increasingly stern penalties for premarital cohabitation, fornication, and pregnancy. The 1546 Marriage Ordinance provided:

> [16.] After the [engagement] promise is made, let the marriage not be delayed for more than six weeks; otherwise let the parties be called to the Consistory to be admonished. If they do not obey, let them be remanded before the Council to be compelled to celebrate it. . . .

> [21.] During the engagement the parties shall not live together as man and wife until the marriage has been blessed in the church after the custom of Christians. If any are found who have done the contrary, let them be punished by prison for three days on bread and water and be called to the Consistory to be admonished for their fault.[11]

A 1547 statute, inspired by the ministers, required that single women who became pregnant, including brides to be, do public confession of their sin of fornication:

> The ministers stated that many secret fornications are committed in Geneva that cannot become manifest until the women are pregnant. While they are pregnant they are not kept in prison, and still less after their delivery, because they are nursing. Thus they remain unpunished. [The ministers] ask in the name and on behalf of the Consistory that ordinances concerning this

11. Doc. 1-2. This language was largely repeated in the Ordinances for the Country Churches (May 16, 1547): "Let those who have promised each other marriage not cohabit together as man and wife until the marriage is celebrated in the church; otherwise they shall be punished as fornicators." SD, vol. 2, item 841; reprinted with slight variations in CO 10/1:53-58 (listing item as proposed on February 3, 1547, and accepted on May 17, 1547).

be drafted, so that they may feel ashamed of falling into such fornication and the church of God may be honored and served in all holiness.

Resolved that ordinances concerning this be drafted, namely, that all women found pregnant through fornication should come to the chief sermon on Sunday to beg for mercy publicly of God and the law, so that they may repent of their sin. And let the aforesaid ministers be consulted.[12]

A 1549 statute, advocated by Calvin, singled out new brides-to-be who were guilty of fornication. On their wedding days, they could not wear the traditional wreath of flowers that symbolized their purity:

Minister John Calvin reported that he has heard that among respectable girls there is a rumor that there are girls who have misbehaved with their bodies, who nevertheless do not refrain for this reason from wearing wreaths of flowers when they present themselves to be married in the church, just as if they had carried themselves with honor. And therefore resolved that the ministers should announce that such silly girls should not present themselves in church with wreaths and that this will not be permitted.[13]

Evidently, this symbolic reprimand was not sufficient deterrence. For, in 1563, Calvin and Beza urged the Council to pass a new statute that required ministers to announce the couple's premarital sins during their wedding service:

This concerns what Monsieurs Calvin and Beza have stated on behalf of the Consistory: that under pretext of marriage many fornicate together before carrying out such a marriage. To remedy this, it seemed to them it would be desirable, when such people marry in the church, that the minister make a public declaration of their fault, which they should also acknowledge to repair the scandal. Ordered that this be done and observed hereafter.[14]

These early prohibitions and penalties were brought together in the 1566 statute.

A man and woman who, being engaged and having promised each other marriage, fornicate before being solemnly married in the church according to the customary procedure, will go to prison for three days on bread and water and will acknowledge their offense when they are married in the church, because of the profanation of holy matrimony.[15]

12. SD, vol. 2, item 845.
13. SD, vol. 2, item 862.
14. SD, vol. 3, item 1042.
15. SD, vol. 3, item 1065.

Consistory Cases

This law on the books determined much of the law in action. Each year, the Consistory heard a number of cases with engaged couples who delayed their weddings, often while cohabitating and/or enjoying sexual relations as well. In several cases, this premarital experimentation led to pregnancy and childbirth. Engaged couples who delayed their wedding beyond the six-week statutory window were generally reprimanded and ordered to marry immediately if no impediment stood in the way. Those who spent too much time together were ordered firmly to separate till their wedding day. Those found guilty of sexual misconduct faced spiritual and criminal punishment, doubly so if this resulted in pregnancy.

Shortly after the 1546 Marriage Ordinance, the Consistory summoned a Monsieur Pernodi on charges that he had delayed his wedding by some four months for no evident reason (**Doc. 12-1**). This was a "scandal" that "mocked God." The Consistory sent Pernodi to the Council for punishment for his contempt, and ordered him to marry his fiancée within a week.

The following year, the Consistory charged François Chapuis and his fiancée for delaying their wedding for two months — an infraction made worse by their intermittent cohabitation (**Doc. 12-2**). The couple was publicly admonished for their sin "so that others may be warned not to behave so." Thereafter, the Consistory declared, "we will marry them."

The Consistory applied this short engagement rule even for engagements contracted outside of Geneva. Jehanne Belletta and Guillaume Douq found this out in 1547 when they moved to Geneva (**Doc. 12-3**). Shortly after their arrival, the Consistory discovered that the couple had been engaged for about ten years, but had never married. When confronted, they confessed to a single lapse into sexual intimacy and admitted that their lengthy engagement was wrong. They agreed to get married. The Consistory gave them three weeks to plan their wedding and ordered them back the following week to report on their wedding plans as well as to face charges for their confessed fornication.

The Consistory sometimes relaxed this six-week engagement rule if a legitimate condition caused the delay. In a 1546 case, for example, they charged the widow Simon and her fiancé with delaying their wedding for months, even while they slept together when he was in town (**Doc. 12-4**). The widow confessed immediately, but justified their protracted engagement on grounds that her fiancé was trying to get his property in order so that he could move to Geneva and settle down with her properly. The Consistory accepted this testimony without further investigation. They ordered her and her fiancé to desist from further sexual relations, but neither punished the couple for their sin nor ordered them to get married quickly.

The Consistory was normally not nearly so tolerant. Perhaps they took pity on Simon because she was a widow, and was so contrite and candid. In most cases, even the appearance of impropriety by fiancés triggered close scrutiny and, at minimum, a reprimand. Bertrand Guignon and Annette de Bellevaux, a newly engaged couple, found this out in 1556 (**Doc. 12-5**). Between attending Sunday services, they had spent several hours together in a closed room. The Consistory wanted to know what they were doing. The couple insisted that they had just fallen asleep together. With no proof of fornication, the Consistory dismissed the parties with a reprimand and ordered them to remain separate until their wedding day.

Another engaged couple, Toussaint de La Mare and Catherine Senarti, faced sterner punishment for their suspected fornication (**Doc. 12-6**). The couple was accused of sleeping together several times. Both the couple and their witnesses insisted that they were honorable souls, who did not and would not have sexual relations before their wedding, even though they occasionally shared the same bed. The Consistory found their habits "scandalous," and sent them to the Council who punished them for presumed fornication.

The Consistory had no patience with couples who defended their premarital sex on grounds of ignorance or of contrary local custom. Pierre Deveaux tried this defense in a 1550 case (**Doc. 12-7**). Pierre had just moved to Geneva and become engaged to Guigonne with the blessing of Simon Du Terte who ran the inn where Deveaux was staying. Du Terte told Pierre that, in Geneva, "when one had become engaged to a girl, he could sleep with her." Pierre and Guigonne evidently took this advice, at least so far that they slept together in the same room. This earned them a hearing before the Consistory on charges of premarital fornication and suspicion that Guigonne was pregnant. Pierre confidently asserted his defense that the couple was in fact engaged to be married and that made their conduct licit. The Consistory would hear none of it. Pierre began "wavering." He did not help his cause when it was discovered that he might have been engaged or married to another woman before he moved to Geneva. Pierre ultimately produced a signed release from his prior relationship, which relieved him and his fiancée of charges of polygamy and adultery. Nonetheless, he and Guigonne were separated for "a year and a day," evidently to determine whether Guigonne was pregnant. They were also sent to the Council to be punished for their premarital fornication.

Monsieur Simon Du Terte was fortunate not to have been prosecuted as well. Accessories to premarital fornication could face stern punishment, as Jean Pascart discovered (**Doc. 12-8**). His daughter Claudine had been properly engaged to Jean Pillet. The couple was getting ready for their wedding. Claudine lived in another town with her parents. For three nights Jean stayed at Claudine's home, and they slept in the same room, evidently with father

Pascart's permission. When confronted, the couple denied having any sexual relations, intimating that this was just a convenient way to accommodate Jean's visit. The Consistory was not so sure. They sent the couple and Pascart to the Council. There was no record that the young couple was punished. Pascart, however, did not fare so well. He at first denied giving the couple his permission to sleep together, but eventually admitted doing so. His perjury cost him dearly. The Consistory banned him from communion; the Council fired him from his job as church warden.

The Consistory was particularly impatient with long engagements when they resulted in premarital pregnacy or illegitimate birth. This can be seen in a series of Consistory cases involving new immigrants in Geneva. One such couple, Mia de Grilliez and Bernard du Pan, had been engaged for some two years (**Doc. 12-9**). They already had an illegitimate child. Mia was summoned before the Consistory on suspicion that she was pregnant again. She testified that she and Bernard had delayed their wedding until he could get money from her parents — perhaps her dowry or some support money for their first illegitimate child. Bernard was now away on business. The Consistory ordered Mia to alert them immediately when Bernard returned from his trip, intimating that it would not go well with him when he appeared. Bernard evidently did not return.

The Consistory came down even harder on Jean Millet and his fiancée (**Doc. 12-10**). The couple had been engaged some time before in the Catholic city of Fribourg where they had attended Catholic masses. They had recently moved to Geneva, and slept together regularly as had been their habit in Fribourg. They now wanted to get married in Geneva. The Consistory sent them instead to the Council for punishment. Their prison sentence of six days on bread and water was double the normal punishment prescribed for engaged couples guilty of fornication; perhaps their cohabitation was treated as an aggravating condition. Only after they served their sentences were they permitted to prepare for their wedding and marriage, and only on condition that they live separately till the wedding day.

The Consistory dealt similarly with George Tardi and his very pregnant fiancée Renée (**Doc. 12-11**). The couple submitted a petition and produced character witnesses in support of their request that the Consistory "confirm" their marriage immediately, perhaps in an effort to legitimate their imminent child. It is unclear from the cryptic record whether George and Renée were already married elsewhere and just wanted to have their marriage confirmed by the Reformed authorities. They may have been married in a Catholic ceremony or been married without a guardian's consent (the record mentions she was a bastard without a guardian). Whatever their motivation, the couple was eager to have the authorities recognize them as married. The Consistory first admonished them for their fornication and sent them to the Council for punishment. The Council ordered that both their wedding and their imprisonment for fornication be delayed until after the birth of the child. Delaying the imprisonment may well have simply been a prudent step to ensure that the child and new mother would be properly cared for. It also suggests that the authorities had determined that the couple was already married, albeit defectively. Normally, it would have been better to rush even a fully pregnant bride to the altar to ensure the legitimacy of the child.[16]

Later that same year of 1556, the Consistory heard yet another case of this sort, this time involving Aubigny Gardet and his fiancée Madeleine (**Doc. 12-12**). The couple had been engaged for some three years. They had already produced two illegitimate children, and were living together as a family. They had recently converted to the Reformed faith, had moved to Geneva, and now seemed eager to get their lives in Christian order. They sought the Consistory's permission to marry properly. The Consistory sent them to the Council with instructions to register first as *habitants*. The Council sent them back to the Consistory because they had neither character witnesses nor proper documentation. The Consistory sent them back to the Council again, with a recommendation that the couple first be punished for their repeated fornication. When the couple failed to appear, the Council ordered them banished from the city.

Perhaps exasperated by this rash of cases, Calvin, on his own initiative, petitioned the Council on November 16, 1556, to pass a firmer new statute against foreigners who came to Geneva to marry "lightly" to cover their prior sins of fornication.[17] This was of a piece with Calvin's repeated emphasis in the mid-1550s that Geneva was not a place to divorce "lightly" either. Calvin was all for parties' desire to convert to the Gospel, to confess their sins, and to start their lives afresh. But forgiveness for sin was not the same as exoneration for crime. Parties would have to bear criminal punishment for their fornication before they could marry, just as they would have to prove their own innocence and the fault of their spouse before they could divorce. The Council passed no new statute along these lines. But the Consistory continued to punish premarital sex — even after couples were married. If a newly married couple had a child less than nine months after their wedding, they were invariably brought before the Consistory on suspicion of premarital fornication.[18]

Antoine and Aima Tornier discovered that the statute of limitations on

16. See summary of recent literature on the *ius commune* of illegitimacy in Thomas Kuehn, *Illegitimacy in Renaissance Florence* (Ann Arbor, MI, 2002), pp. 16-69 and the relevant Genevan law in Spierling, pp. 158-92.

17. *Annales Calviniani*, CO 21:654-55.

18. Spierling, pp. 176ff.

prosecution for premarital fornication did not end with their wedding (**Doc. 12-13**). Shortly after the birth of their first child, the Torniers faced charges that their child was conceived before the wedding, perhaps even while Antoine was still married to his first wife. Had the couple, in fact, committed adultery while Antoine was still married to his first wife, their marriage would have been annulled involuntarily, and their child illegitimated.[19] As it turns out, their affair had taken place in the time between Antoine's marriages. They were publicly admonished, and imprisoned briefly, and at different times so that the child was not left without care.

These cases and the many others on the books show how resolute the authorities remained to stamp out illicit sexual conduct in Geneva, including that of newly engaged couples. But they also show how resigned they were to the reality that premarital sex occurred and had to be dealt with justly and prudentially, without destroying the couple or forcing them to abandon the children born of their sexual experimentation.

The spiritual and civil authorities in Geneva worked hard to deter premarital sex — and not only through Calvin and Beza's relentless preaching and lecturing on the topic. One deterrent was the brevity of the engagement period — a mere six weeks. Too long an engagement, the reformers believed, would only encourage sexual intimacy. But too short an engagement would deprive the community of the opportunity to participate in the formation of the marriage. Hence the abridged and very public engagement period, and the Consistory's ready orders for couples to remain separate until their wedding day if they were caught consorting too closely.

A second deterrent to premarital sex was the publicity of the punishments of those who were convicted — public admonition, public announcement of the sin on the day of the wedding, a public record of their imprisonment. And, if the couple produced illegitimate children, the public baptismal registry would list the children as bastards, signaling various restrictions on the child's later property and inheritance rights.

The punishments inflicted for premarital sex, however, were not crippling. They were certainly not on the order of severity that Calvin related in some of his sermons and commentaries on biblical texts that called for the execution, mutilation, or public stripping of adulterers and adulteresses. Public admonition and brief bans from communion were the normal spiritual sanctions — and even these punishments were softened if the parties confessed their sins candidly and contritely. Prison for three days was the normal criminal sanction — though this punishment could be increased if parties were found guilty of

---

19. See above Chapter 9 for discussion of the impediment against marriage of former adulterous paramours.

contempt or perjury, or if they compounded their fornication with cohabitation or illegitimate birth. We have found no cases, however (at least in our three sample years), where couples were prevented from marriage, or deprived of children conceived before marriage, just because of their premarital fornication. Nor have we have found any cases where premarital conception illegitimated a child born after marriage. To the contrary, the more typical order was for them to get married quickly to avoid further premarital sex or illegitimation of their forthcoming children.

Premarital Desertion

The opposite problem of premarital sex was that of premarital desertion. Some engaged parties got "cold feet" in anticipation of their marriage and took flight from Geneva, with or without notice or explanation. Others had to be away during their engagement for business, to answer a court summons, to visit family or friends, or to serve in the military, and then were detained, imprisoned, sick, or died. Still other engaged parties were whisked away by parents or occasionally by former lovers or spouses who did not want them to marry their new beloved. This was a day of relatively poor communications and public record-keeping in a city with a transient population. Was desertion an impediment that could break the engagement contract? How long was a deserted party to wait before being free to pursue another? What procedures should be followed to inoculate an innocent party against polygamy charges if the deserter later returned and challenged a second engagement or marriage contract?

Calvin dealt with this issue squarely and at length in the 1546 Marriage Ordinance.

> [46.] If a man, after having sworn faith [that is, become engaged] to a girl or woman, goes to another country, and the girl or woman comes to make a complaint about this, asking to be delivered from her promise because of the other's disloyalty, let inquiry be made whether he did this for an honorable reason and with the knowledge of his fiancée, or instead through debauchery and because he does not wish to complete the marriage. If it is found that he has no apparent reason [for his departure] and that he has done it from bad motives, let one inquire to what place he has gone, and if possible let him be notified that he must return by a certain day to carry out the duty he has promised.
>
> [47.] If he does not appear, having been warned, let it be proclaimed for three Sundays in the church that he must appear, such that there is a gap of [two weeks] between two proclamations and thus that the whole term is

six weeks. If he does not appear within the term, let the girl or woman be declared free and the man banished for disloyalty. If he appears, let him be compelled to celebrate the marriage the first day it can be done. If it is not known to what country he has gone and the girl or woman, along with his closest friends, swear they do not know [his whereabouts], let the same proclamations be made as if he had been notified, with the object of freeing her [from the engagement].

[48.] If he had some good reason and also informed his fiancée, let the girl or woman wait for the space of a year before proceeding against him in his absence, and meanwhile let the girl herself and her friends make diligent efforts to induce him to return. If after a year has passed he does not return, then let the proclamations be made in the manner described above.

[49.] Let the same course be observed against a girl or woman, except that the [prospective] husband shall not be required to wait a year even if she departed with his knowledge and consent, unless he gave her permission to make a journey that requires such a long absence.

[50.] If a girl duly bound by a promise is fraudulently transported outside the territory [of Geneva] in order not to complete the marriage, let one inquire whether there is anyone in the city who has aided in this so he may be compelled to make her return, under whatever penalty may be decided: or if she has guardians or trustees, let them likewise be enjoined to make her come back if they can.[20]

Beyond drafting these detailed provisions for the 1546 Ordinance, Calvin said little about desertion of fiancé(e)s. In both his Commentary and Sermons on 1 Corinthians 7:12-16, as well as his later correspondence, Calvin did say that a Christian believer who had been deserted by an unbelieving spouse had no duty to pursue him or her — the so-called "Pauline privilege" that Calvin would doubtless have applied even more readily to engaged parties.[21] Calvin did allow wives to desert chronically abusive husbands who posed grave threats to their bodies and souls, provided that these women gave adequate notice of their intentions. If Calvin allowed wives to desert in these cases, he doubtless would have condoned it even more readily for fiancées.[22] But Calvin had little

20. Doc. 1-2. This desertion section of the 1546 Marriage Ordinance was a greatly expanded version of the brief sentence on desertion included in Calvin's original 1545 draft. Calvin might well have developed this section in response to the Council's remand of the case of Jehanne Besson, alias Fontanna, discussed below Doc. 12-15.

21. Comm. and Serm. 1 Cor. 7:15; Kingdon, AD, pp. 150-55.

22. See also Chapter 10 above; and the case of wife abuse and desertion discussed in Letter to Pierre Viret (November 15, 1546), CO 12:413-16. Note, however, that Calvin did not preserve the traditional impediment to engagement of "excessive cruelty" by either fiancé.

formal to say about premarital desertion beyond what he wrote into the 1546 Marriage Ordinance.

Beza said a good deal more. In his 1569 *Tract on Annulment and Divorce,* he defended the law of Geneva as the "most fair" among available civil laws and canon laws on desertion (**Doc. 12-14**). Genevan law properly distinguished three types of cases of premarital desertion, Beza argued. First, if the engaged party left maliciously, the deserted party had to post three notices over the course of six weeks for him or her to return, before they could seek annulment of the engagement. Second, if the engaged party disappeared inexplicably, without evident malice, the deserted party had to make earnest efforts to find him or her, before they could post the notices and seek annulment. Third, if the engaged party left with full knowledge and consent of the other but then did not return, the rules were different for engaged men and women. Engaged men could post notices immediately, except where their fiancées were involuntarily detained or had received their fiancé's permission to extend their time away. Engaged women had to wait for a year before they could post such notices, and even then would first have to make earnest inquiry of their fiancé's whereabouts.

Beza did not explain the disparity in treatment of men and women in these latter cases. He sharpened this disparity, beyond what the 1546 Marriage Ordinance required, by insisting that if a deserted woman had since married another, and her first fiancé reappeared after involuntary delay, she was obliged to return to him. A deserted man had no such obligation to return to his first fiancée if she reappeared after involuntary delay.

Later Protestant writers would explain that a deserted woman needed to wait for a year to be sure that she was not pregnant. This would put beyond dispute the paternity of a child born of any new relationship. Other writers added that young women could exercise better sexual discipline than young men. Young men, who were ready for the cooling balm of marriage, would be too tempted to sexual sin if they were forced to wait for a year. Those rationales might well have been Beza and Calvin's as well, given their acute concerns in other cases to establish paternity and to deter fornication.

These rationales do not, however, explain Beza's rule that a once-deserted woman, now married to another man, had to return to her first fiancé if he reappeared after being involuntarily detained. This seems, instead, to be a rather harsh application of Beza and Calvin's rule that engagement contracts were permanent, unless properly dissolved by proof of an impediment. A woman's subsequent marriage, and even her production of children with her new husband, did not dissolve her first engagement contract. While her mistake about her fiancé's desertion might excuse her from punishment for polygamy, her first engagement contract remained intact. To be consistent, Beza should have applied this same return rule to cases where a once-deserted man, who had married another woman, had his first fiancée return to him after her involuntary delay. But this Beza did not do — perhaps because of a second rule he introduced that also went beyond the Genevan Marriage Ordinance.

Beza's second novel rule was that parties must not use desertion as a way to dissolve unwanted engagements for which there was no other impediment to plead. He called for punishment of parties who conspired together to stage a desertion to escape their engagements. In Calvin's Geneva, engagement contracts were presumptively indissoluble unless an impediment could be proved. A staged desertion could provide both parties with a ready escape, even while allowing them both eventually to live in Geneva.

Beza's no-staged-desertion rule might well have been designed to close the loophole left in his one-sided return rule. Beza's return rule, as formulated, still allowed a couple to stage a desertion by the woman: The fiancée would temporarily depart. Her fiancé would declare her a deserter and post notices. Within six weeks, he would be freed from his engagement to her so he could marry someone else. When the first fiancée returned, the man had no obligation to take her back. After modest punishment for her desertion, this former first fiancée, too, would be free to marry someone else. Shrewd parties could have exploited this loophole, especially if instructed by legal counsel. Beza's no-staged-desertion rule made this charade vulnerable to censure by the Consistory.

Consistory Cases

The Consistory from the start followed the detailed rules for desertion set out in the 1546 Marriage Ordinance. Indeed, Calvin had a chance to apply these rules even as he was drafting them. One month after he had completed his first draft in 1545, the Council remanded the case of Jehanne Besson, alias Fontanna, to the Consistory (**Doc. 12-15**). Some three years before, Jehanne had become engaged to one Jaquemin Malbuisson. Jaquemin had then deserted her without a word and was presumed dead. Jehanne had petitioned the Consistory of Ternier to annul her engagement. They sent her to Geneva. Jehanne petitioned the Council of Geneva directly to annul her engagement on grounds of desertion. Lacking any statute on the subject, the Council remanded the case to the Consistory for advice. The Consistory asked Calvin to report to the Council on his provisional statute. Evidently the Council followed his provisional draft, for they granted Jehanne the right to dissolve the engagement, after she issued the three public notices that the 1546 Marriage Ordinance later prescribed.

Proof of the deserter's marriage to another was prima facie evidence of malicious desertion, and was sufficient to warrant an annulment of the first engagement. Jeanne Verney, for example, presented the Consistory with a petition and affidavits testifying that her former fiancé had married another woman in France (**Doc. 12-16**). The Consistory was satisfied, and recommended to the Council that her engagement be annulled, and she be declared free to pursue another.

Similarly, Gervaise Bochue requested the Consistory to dissolve her engagement to Claude Bonadventura (**Doc. 12-17**). Shortly after their engagement, Claude had moved away, and now lived in Geogne. A witness testified that Claude had told him he was now engaged to another woman. Gervaise testified further that she did not want to move to Geogne, evidently a Catholic region, a fear that she had apparently already communicated in a private letter to Calvin.[23] The Consistory ordered her to get an affidavit to prove that Claude had since married the other woman. Six months later, Gervaise returned to the Consistory, with several affidavits in hand. The Consistory sent her to the Council with a recommendation that she be freed from her engagement. The Council told her to be patient a little while longer, probably to provide time to post the three notices.

While proof of a deserting fiancé's marriage to another created a relatively easy case for annulment by malicious desertion, proof of the deserting fiancé's fornication did not. Françoise Collonbeyre, for example, had not seen or heard from her fiancé[24] for some three years (**Doc. 12-18**). A year after his departure, she requested the Consistory to dissolve her engagement and grant her permission to remarry. Apparently, she had not followed proper "formalities," and her request was denied. Two years later, she petitioned the Consistory again, and now produced witnesses who testified that, during his last visit to Geneva, her fiancé had consorted with one or more women, even while ignoring Françoise altogether. One witness, however, testified that it was Françoise who had refused to see her fiancé when he was in Geneva, not the other way around. The Consistory was still not convinced that Françoise had made out her case of desertion. Since Françoise knew her fiancé now lived in Romans, which was relatively close to Geneva, they ruled that she should first go there to confront him and tell him "he could not live with her if he did not stay here." The case does not appear in the record again.

The Consistory proved a bit more solicitous when the deserted woman

---

23. The letter does not appear in CO, but is referred to in the case record.

24. It is not clear from the record whether the man was a fiancé or husband of Françoise, though it is quite clear he had deserted her without cause or explanation. It is likely that this was an engaged, rather than married couple, else the man's conduct would have raised a case of divorce for adultery.

was left pregnant or with a new child. In a 1547 case, for example, the Consistory summoned an unmarried maid named Aima Portier to explain her pregnancy.[25] She testified that her master's brother, Roland Vuarrier, had promised to marry her and that she wanted to marry him. The couple had been sexually intimate rather freely since their engagement. The Consistory admonished her for her fornication, and sent her to the Council for punishment. But their real interest was to find Roland to corroborate Aima's testimony, and to compel him to marry her if it proved true that they were engaged. Roland was not to be found. He had evidently moved to the region under Bernese control and told Aima that he was subject to Bern's authority, not Geneva's. The Consistory sent the case to the Council. The Council ordered that Roland be "properly punished" should he return.

The 1556 case of Jeanne Nepveur and Louis Blanchet illustrated the wisdom of Beza's warning that the desertion rules could be abused.[26] Jeanne and Louis and her parents had executed a written engagement contract, without stipulating any conditions. Later, the couple had decided to break their engagement by "mutual consent." Louis had indicated the need to move back to his hometown of Orléans for a time. Jeanne had not wanted to accompany him or to delay the wedding until he returned. Moreover, Louis had not delivered his promised dowry payment to Jeanne's parents. They had thus withdrawn their parental consent. By the time of the case, Louis was living in Orléans on his own. Jeanne and her parents thus submitted a petition to the Genevan Consistory setting all this out and requesting permission for Jeanne to be free to marry another.

The Consistory granted nothing of the kind. An unconditional engagement contract, they ruled, could not be broken either by the mutual consent of the couple or by the subsequent withdrawal of parental consent. Moreover, failure of a dowry payment was never a sufficient ground for annulment, as the 1546 Marriage Ordinance made clear. Jeanne was still bound by her promise, unless her father could prove that Louis had actually deserted her.

On the Consistory's instruction, Jeanne's father wrote to Louis, politely requesting him to return to Geneva to marry Jeanne. Louis did not reply. Jeanne's father produced evidence that Louis had received the letter but had ignored it. To prove doubly sure, the Consistory instructed Louis's brother-in-law to write a further letter. Louis ignored that letter as well. The Consistory declared him guilty of both desertion and contempt. They recommended that the Council annul the engagement contract and free Jeanne to post banns to marry another.

25. The record of the case is in Doc. 4-11, where we have analyzed it for the issue of consent in a case of premarital pregnancy.

26. The record of the case is in Doc. 5-10, where we have analyzed it for the issue of post-engagement withdrawal of parental consent.

Another case of protracted betrothal raised more sinister facts. Jaques Regnau petitioned the Consistory to dissolve the engagement contract between his minor daughter Anne and one Jean Philippe (**Doc. 12-19**). Jaques had approved the engagement some two years before. Jean had then deserted Anne inexplicably, and had stolen money and several items of his master's property. The Consistory ordered Jaques to make diligent inquiry where Jean had gone, and to ask him to return. Three months later, Jaques was back before the Consistory with a lengthy petition documenting his efforts to find Jean. He also produced several witnesses. They testified to Jean's continued acts of crime and transience. Even worse, they testified that Jean was fraudulently exploiting the one-year period that deserted fiancées in Geneva had to wait before being freed from their engagements. The young man, they said, "did not want to take her for his wife, but he would return here every year to prevent the girl from getting married, and he would oppose any man who would like to marry her." This was proof enough for the Consistory and the Council. They ordered Jaques the father to post the requisite notices, and if Jean did not appear, they annulled the engagement and freed Anne to post banns for her marriage to another.[27]

Virtually all the premarital desertion cases that came to the Consistory in Calvin's day involved men who had deserted their fiancées.[28] Where the deserted fiancée had a strong father or guardian to press her case, as did Jeanne Nepveur and Anne Regnau, the Consistory would eventually annul the first engagement contract and allow the woman to marry another. Where the deserted fiancée was on her own, however, as in the cases of Aima Portier and Françoise Collonbeyre, the authorities were not particularly solicitous. Though the maid Aima was promised marriage, became pregnant, and was then deserted by her master's brother, Roland, the Consistory's only firm action was to have Aima punished for her fornication. They made no effort to get her master involved in finding his brother, or to alert the authorities in nearby Bern to compel Roland to return to assume his responsibilities. The matter was left that Roland would be "properly punished" if he returned to Geneva, which he evidently never did.

Likewise, Françoise Collonbeyre was deserted for more than three years by her fiancé, who did have time to return to Geneva secretly to consort with other women. Françoise's first attempt to claim desertion, a year after his departure, was rebuffed because of her failure to satisfy the "formalities" of the statute. Her second attempt to claim desertion, three years after his departure, was defeated by a single witness who speculated that Françoise may not have sought her

---

27. This corrects Witte, FSC, p. 118, which was based on a confusion of notes both of the Regnau case and another case.

28. Seeger, pp. 398-403.

fiancé out when he was in Geneva. The Consistory's remedy was that she should go to him and put him on notice that he should return. They did nothing to prosecute him for his evident fornication, nor advise her on pursuing a separate action for annulment for premarital adultery.

Summary and Conclusions

"Stay close, but not too close" was the proper ethic for engaged couples in Reformation Geneva. Engagement was a six-week window in which couples were expected to prepare themselves, their families, and their properties for their life together. Delayed weddings earned the couple firm spiritual sanctions. Repeated delays invited fines and imprisonment as well. Engaged parties were permitted to spend time together, provided they did not have sexual relations with each other. They were permitted to spend time apart, provided they did not desert the other. If engaged couples were proven to have been sexually intimate, they faced the shame of public confession and brief prison sentences. If their premarital experimentation led to pregnancy, they faced bans from communion, short stays in prison, and the shame of doing public confession and forgoing wedding flowers. If a fiancé deserted his bride to be, she could annul the engagement after a one-year delay. If a fiancée deserted her husband to be, he could annul the engagement more quickly, provided the desertion was not staged.

12-1 Case of Pernodi (1546)[29]

(Aug. 19, 1546). Pernodi was admonished that about four months ago he became engaged to a woman and keeps her with him without ever having married her, which is a scandal, and not according to God. He promised to do his duty, and will marry her a week from Sunday.

(Oct. 28, 1546). Pernodi [must] be remanded before the Council tomorrow, and that the Consistory is not content that he has mocked God in this way.

12-2 Case of François Chapuis (1547)[30]

(Aug. 18, 1547). Master François Chapuis and his fiancée were admonished and confessed they have lived together about two months and are not yet married.

Decided: that they be admonished so others may be warned not to behave so. We will return them their banns and marry them.

12-3 Case of Jehanne Belletta and Guillaume Douq (1547)[31]

(Dec. 8, 1547). Jehanne Belletta confessed she has been engaged for about ten years to one named Guillaume who is from Thorens, and at present they are both inhabitants of Geneva. She denied ever having had his company.

Decided: that they both return here next Thursday. Asked again whether she has not had his company, does not want to confess, except once.

(Dec. 29, 1547). Guillaume Douq of Thorens and Jehanne Belletta, his fiancée, were admonished that they have been engaged for about ten years and have not yet married. Confessed having done wrong; nevertheless they wish to accomplish it shortly and do as respectable people should.

Decided: that they be made to carry out and complete the marriage and be given three weeks as a term, and that the following Thursday they return here, and they will then be remanded before the Council. Note: to return here in three weeks.

29. R. Consist. II, 75, 87.
30. R. Consist. III, 121.
31. R. Consist. III, 185, 194.

12-4   Case of the Widow Simon (1546)[32]

(Oct. 28, 1546). The widow of Simon, miller, was admonished that she has been engaged to a man for a long time and her fiancé has slept there, and why they do not marry. She said that her [prospective] husband intended to separate his property and settle down like a respectable man. She confessed having had the company of her [prospective] husband after they were engaged. She was forbidden to have her [prospective] husband stay there any more until they have had their wedding.

12-5   Case of Bertrand Guignon and Annette de Bellevaux (1556)[33]

(July 2, 1556). Bertrand Guignon, weaver, and Annette de Bellevaux, his fiancée, [were] admonished that it has come to notice that he has sworn faith to a girl named Henriette, and one Sunday during the catechism and until the next sermon they shut themselves up together. She confessed being engaged to the aforesaid and that it is true that they fell asleep and remained so about three hours, and it was to discuss how they could conduct themselves.

The decision: that they be given strong admonitions, and that it is indeed to be presumed that they fornicated, and to forbid them [each other's company] until they are married.

12-6   Case of Toussaint de La Mare and Catherine Senarti (1556)[34]

(Oct. 28, 1556). Toussaint de La Mare and Catherine Senarti, his neighbor, [were] admonished that before becoming engaged they created a scandal and slept together, both in this country and abroad. Confessed, and denied the company [that they had sex]. She said her husband died in Rouen and they came here together.

Decided: that for Thursday they bring here evidence of their life and respectability.

(Nov. 5, 1556). Mammad Panisseaud, Pierre Burdigny, and Guillame de La Fontane for Toussaint and Catherine Senarti, his fiancée. The first said that he has only known them for the last two months, that they lodge at his house and he has seen him visit her, she being ill. He knows nothing more. The next said

32. R. Consist. II, 87.
33. R. Consist. XI, 37v.
34. R. Consist. XI, 73, 76.

that he came from Rouen with them and has seen them sleeping together and not alone, in the fields, in complete honesty. The other has known the woman only in this city, and as for him, he knew him in Rouen, working satisfactorily as a journeyman cap-maker. Also, that they have no license to inhabit [Geneva]. Let the Council be informed of this.

[On November 9 the Council ordered Toussaint and Catherine imprisoned three days on bread and water.]

12-7   Case of Pierre Deveaux and Guigonne (1550)[35]

(Feb. 20, 1550). Master Claude Royer and Anthoine Vassier, witnesses, were asked to testify concerning someone named Jean [read Pierre] Deveaux from Thiers in Auvergne, diocese of Clermont, who has become engaged to a woman named Guigonne. Did they know whether Jean had been engaged to another woman. The servant said that he is from the same country as [Pierre] and knows that he had another wife in his own country and that he had been separated from her, though only between themselves. Master [Claude] said he had only heard it said. They both said that they had heard both from Guigonne and Deveaux, her fiancé, that the fiancé has had Guigonne's company. He also said that they had heard from the fiancé that Master Simon Du Terte had said that the practice and custom in this city is that as soon as one has become engaged to a woman one may go to bed with her.

The decision: to summon Master Simon, and that their testimony be remembered for the future.

(March 6, 1550). Master Simon Du Terte was asked what he knows about the marriage [engagement] of the aforesaid. He said that it was done at his house [which is an inn] and that the aforesaid came to lodge at his house the day he came to this city and that when the promise was made the aforesaid [Pierre] had been in this city only three days.

Decided: that she be remanded before the Council informing them that their decision should be to stay [the wedding for] a year and a day, and there was good testimony, and that such a marriage and banns were very casually signed. Also assemble the preceding evidence.

(March 20, 1550). Pierre Deveaux from Thiers in Auvergne, husband [fiancé] of Guigonne, stated that it had been said that someone said that he had slept with his wife [fiancée]. He confessed that three days after arriving in this city he had become engaged to Guigonne by the agency of Master Simon, his host. Asked about the statements Master Simon made to him, answered that it

---

35. R. Consist. V, 2, 7-7v, 11v.

is true that Simon told him that he had found him a good partner and that he made him the statements in the evidence. Confessed that he slept in his wife's [fiancée's] bed in her room. He also confessed that Master Simon made statements to him, but that he did not follow his advice. Moreover, he said that Master Simon told him that when one had become engaged to a girl, one could sleep with her. He also said that a friend of his had advised him that he [the friend] had said that he [Deveaux] had slept with his wife [fiancée] and that it is not true that he had slept with her.

He constantly wavered, denying having slept with her, and said moreover that it was not his fault that she had not slept with him. Asked whether he had not been engaged to another woman, he said yes, in his own country. He presented certain affidavits from his country on parchment, or a release, signed by a notary named [blank], dated March 3, 1549. Also an affidavit signed by Grasset, vicar of Thiers, on May 1, 1549.

Decided: that they be remanded before the Council both for the frivolity of the marriage and because they have fornicated together, with the assembled evidence, declaring that a discharge does not follow to proceed with such a marriage for three reasons, and forbidden to live together. Also she was admonished about certain statements she made against the Consistory to M. François Servand in going to the sermon. She excused herself, denying the charge.

[We have found no record of the case in the Council.]

12-8   Case of Jean Pillet and Claudine Pascart (1557)[36]

(April 13, 1557). Claudine, daughter of Jean Pascart of Céligny, said she is engaged to one named Jean, son of Claude Pillet [of] Divonne, with whom she slept after the engagement. But she denied having had his company. Aymé, widow of Jaquemo Pascart, aunt of Claudine, was called and questioned to learn whether Jean slept with Claudine, her niece. She answered that he went to bed with her in her presence three nights, without her knowing for sure that he had her company. She also said that her father and mother knew it well.

The decision is that, since they were forbidden to associate with each other until they were married and despite this they have slept with each other, although they did not fornicate, that they be remanded before the Council to be punished on Monday.

(April 15, 1557). Jean Pascart of Céligny was summoned to learn what secret marriage was made between his daughter and one from Divonne named Jean. He answered that a month ago he promised her to him in marriage, and

---

36. R. Consist. XII, 29, 32, 92v.

he understood that before the banns were published they slept with each other in his house in Céligny. It was decided that because he contradicts himself, in the first place communion be forbidden him, then he be remanded before the Council to Monday, who will be asked that it may please them to see that such people are not made churchwardens.

[The Council took up this case on April 19. Since Pascart and his daughter had failed to appear, the Council ordered the castellan of Céligny to punish them according to law, and also that Pascart be dismissed from his office of warden.]

(Sept. 2, 1557). Jean Pascart of Céligny appeared, asking that he be permitted to receive communion, which was forbidden him for having lied in the Consistory when he had his daughter sleep with her fiancée before marrying him, confessing having done wrong.

Decided: that he be received with strong admonitions.

12-9   Case of Mia de Grilliez (1547)[37]

(July 21, 1547). Mia de Grilliez, fiancée of Bernard du Pan, servant of Domaine Franc, was asked whether she is pregnant. She said she does not know for sure, and it was about two years ago that she swore faith to a servant who lives at Domaine Franc's and is named Bernard. She is from Annemasse; she has already had a child by him which is at present with its father, and he does not want to marry her until he has money from her parents, and at present he has gone to Aosta for his master.

Decided: that she be forbidden to have his company any more until the matter has been decided, and that she make it known at once if her fiancé comes secretly.

12-10   Case of Jean Millet (1556)[38]

(April 30, 1556). Jean Millet, armorer, and his fiancée [were] admonished that they have been promised to each other for a long time, and meanwhile have slept and fornicated together, and now they publish their banns. They confessed that he promised himself to her in Fribourg, and that is the custom there. And she confessed that she went to Mass there during the time when she lived there. She is also of this city.

37. R. Consist. III, 106.
38. R. Consist. XI, 22.

The decision: that they be remanded before the Council.

[On May 11 the Council ordered them both imprisoned six days on bread and water.]

12-11   Case of George and Renée Tardi (1556)[39]

(Sept. 17, 1556). George Tardi and Renée his wife presented a petition to confirm their marriage and declaring having before the wedding and solemnization of their marriage conversed together, [as is explained] more fully in the contents of [their] petition. [They also] said that she came [here] a week ago, being a prisoner in Bar-le-Duc, and he seven weeks ago, who went to fetch her.

Decided: that since he has presented himself here he should bring his witnesses. [Remanded till next] Thursday.

(Sept. 24, 1556). Jaques Ribaut and Jaqueme [struck: his wife and Etienne] the mason for George Tardi, Catherine, daughter of the Sieur de la Bonaye of Angers [all appeared]. Ribaut testified that in Paris he heard that Guillaume de Sellon of Angers had promised his daughter Renee, a bastard, and he heard that he was of good reputation, and she had served him two years. Jaqueme said she had also heard such statements, and Catherine did not know him except by hearsay.

Decided: that he deserves strong remonstrances for having fornicated before marriage, and as for the marriage, let them be remanded before the Council, and he may be permitted to marry her after she has recovered [from childbirth].

[On September 28 the Council ordered that they be punished with imprisonment "according to the edicts," after which they could proceed with the marriage.]

12-12   Case of Aubigny Gardet and Madeleine (1556)[40]

(Sept. 17, 1556). Aubigny Gardet and his wife [fiancée] presented a petition, according to which they have lived together three years without marrying, asking that they be permitted to marry according to the order of the Gospel.

Decided: that in the first place they separate and abstain from communion, and that they first present themselves to the Council to become *habitants,* and then if they are received as such they should produce witnesses. They confessed that they have acknowledged the Gospel about two years, and [have lived] in this city only a short time.

39. R. Consist. XI, 59, 60v.
40. R. Consist. XI, 58v, 76, 82.

[Gardet applied to the Council on October 26 to be received as a *habitant*. The Council ordered that he be received if he furnished proper evidence of identity. On October 30 the Council decided that Gardet, who had asked pardon for his offense, should be remanded to the Consistory again to obtain their advice.]

(Nov. 5, 1556). Aubigny Gardet and Madeleine have been remanded by the Council to learn the opinion here about their proposing to ratify their marriage.

Decided: that for Thursday they bring witnesses to their respectability.

(Nov. 26, 1556). Aubigny Gardet and his wife [that is, fiancée, appeared, saying] that witnesses to their respectability have not been found, and they are not married, and she has had two children by him. [Remanded to] the Council.

[Since they did not appear, on November 30 the Council ordered that Gardet and his fiancée be banished from the city.]

12-13   Case of Antoine and Aima Tornier (1552)[41]

(July 25, 1552). Antoine Tornier and Aima, his wife, were admonished that it has come to notice that in the wake of having liberty to remarry he fornicated with his present wife for the space of six months, and after their wedding had a child by her. He said that he became engaged to her six weeks before having had her company.

Decided: that for next Thursday he bring his letter of divorce, if things are as he has stated, saying he will make it evident.

(Aug. 4, 1552). Antoine Tornier of Bourdigny was remanded Thursday to bring evidence of his liberation by the Council, since before having leave he already fornicated with the wife he has now, about the fact that he said his wife gave birth about midsummer's day.

Decided: that he make confession of his fault, and notify the castellan to punish him.

12-14   Theodore Beza on Desertion of Fiancés (1569)[42]

What if the absence of one [party] impedes the marriage from being able to be completed? I reply that a question should be asked about the absence since someone is absent either unwillingly or willingly. If he is absent willingly, again

---

41. R. Consist. VII, 60, 62.
42. Beza, TRD, 2:123-25 (translated by John P. Donnelly, S.J.)

it must be asked why he left, how long was he gone, and if he has reasons for not returning.

In this church [in Geneva] we use this law which seems most fair to me: If the engaged man goes abroad with his fiancée's knowledge and for a good reason before consummation and is willingly absent for a whole year even though he was warned about his duty, if the fiancée petitions three times in six week intervals, with a public previous denunciation both in a church gathering and before the ordinary magistrate, she has a right to accept a different husband, with the promises to marry dissolved [that is, her engagement contract with her first fiancé is annulled]. But, in the case where he has reappeared and then is heard, then (unless she will have proved that there was a just cause for the repudiation) she is compelled to fulfill her pledge by the authority of the magistrate.

If it is the fiancée who with the knowledge of her partner goes abroad, the same law applies with this one exception, that the man is not forced to wait a full year unless perchance she undertakes to be gone for a longer time with his permission or by agreement.

If the engaged man or woman is found to have moved away because of bad will or for a deceitful reason, however, every effort should be made so that the person be warned about his or her duty. When this is done right or at least when it will be determined that it has been attempted (in so far as it was possible) and he or she who is involved does not reappear, then after three denunciations, just as before, the same person can be recognized in absentia as a deserter.

Care must still be taken that if by his or her trickery one of them is found to have arranged that his or her engaged partner has been sent away elsewhere, the person after being severely punished in other ways is bound to seek the absent partner and appear in court. This burden is also imposed on the teacher and guardian in whose power they were.

But what if the other person was missing involuntarily and not through any trickery? For instance, he was a captive or kept elsewhere by force or sickness or was being punished by exile or deportation or was terrified by a rightful fear? Then, of course, the person who wants the promise to marry to be fulfilled is bound to go to that place, as far as it is possible — or at least await his or her return, however long the delay, or patiently wait for certain information about his or her death.

A person also cannot be thought to be a deserter who is absent against his will. Thus it was rightly declared in the past that even if a woman thought that her husband had died in captivity, and she married another man, she must be returned to her husband after he returns.

12-15 Case of Jehanne Besson, alias Fontanna (1545)[43]

[Jehanne Besson, called Fontanna, had already appeared before the Consistory of Ternier to ask that she be freed from her engagement to Jaquemin Malbuisson. The Consistory of Ternier sent her to Geneva. On November 20, 1545, the Genevan Council had ruled: "Jeanne, daughter of Andrier Besson, alias Fontanna, versus Jaquemin Malbuisson, who asked that she be permitted to marry, considering that it is not known where he [her promised husband] is, thinking he has been dead since the year 1542, and that her case be provided for. Ordered that she go to the Consistory to get their advice."]

(Nov. 26, 1545). Remanded is a girl named Jehanne Fontanna of Landecy, who referred to a certain suit prosecuted at Ternier against Jaquemin Malbuisson, asking for a divorce [i.e., dissolution of her engagement]. Our Lords Superior have remanded them here to obtain an opinion.

Decided: that one follow the edicts that might exist concerning this, although they are not yet enacted, and inquire of those of this city who were present at the release that was signed of marriage. To ask Monsieur Calvin before Monday.

[The following Monday Jehanne Fontanna testified to the Council she did not know Malbuisson's whereabouts, and again requested freedom from her engagement. The Council granted her the annulment, provided her fiancé did not appear after notices were proclaimed for three Sundays.]

12-16 Case of Jeanne Verney (1557)[44]

(Sept. 16, 1557). Jeanne Verney appeared, producing a petition aimed at being set at liberty to find another partner than Claude de La Grange, who a short time ago remarried in the town of Sise near Nevers after having abandoned the petitioner in this city. It was ordered and decided to set her at liberty and make the customary proclamations, and for this purpose she was remanded before the Council.

[On September 20 the Council decided, as the Consistory had advised, that since her husband had taken another wife, as she had shown by reliable affidavits, she should be freed, and the proclamations would be made in the customary fashion.]

43. R. Consist. II, 13v.
44. R. Consist. XII, 98v.

12-17   Case of Gervaise Bochue and Claude Bonadventura (1547)[45]

(April 14, 1547). Gervaise Bochue submitted a petition asking for a divorce [that is, annulment]. She was remanded to Thursday for verification.

(April 21, 1547). Pierre Chatronet of Geneva said it is true that in the city of Lyon he was spoken to by a companion asking him if he knew Gervaise in Geneva. He answered yes, and he is named Claude Bonadventura. He told him he had been engaged to her but that he had refrained from marrying her because a servant of [Laurent Meigret] the Magnificent had become engaged to her, and he knew well that he had been engaged to someone else near Carpentras. He [knows] nothing else.

(April 21, 1547). Gervaise was asked what letter she once sent to Monsieur Calvin from Yverdon. She answered that she left it at his house. She also said that she did not want to marry because she did not want to go to Geogne, which is in the papistry.

Decided: that she see that she gets an affidavit from Morges that the aforesaid [Claude] has married another woman in Morges.

(Dec. 1, 1547). Decision concerning Gervaise, who again presented herself before the Consistory to obtain the decision of the Consistory, asking for a divorce and producing several affidavits. The decision is that the matter be remanded before the Council with affidavits, and if they seem sufficient to them let them free her, considering his disloyalty.

[On December 9 the Council ordered the latter to continue to be patient for a little while.]

12-18   Case of Françoise Collonbeyre (1556)[46]

(June 25, 1556). Françoise Collonbeyre presented a petition to be at liberty to remarry, as she proposed previously about two years ago. Admonished that there are many formalities required in such a case, and other things can be found in the register.

Decided: that she prove the contents of her petition; and it was about three [years] ago that she was here with her [prospective] husband.

Decided: that she bring her witnesses on Thursday.

(July 2, 1556). Nicolas Bisat, Pierre Arnaux, and Jeanne, wife of Louis Tavennay, for Françoise Collonbeyre. The first testified that three years ago the [prospective] husband of Françoise was in this city, and as a neighbor of hers he

45. R. Consist. III, 56, 61, 184.
46. R. Consist. XI, 36v, 38, 39v.

does not know whether they slept together, but he does not believe so. Pierre said that he is from his country and he carried a letter, asking for an answer. He answered him that he did not want to send anything; and he saw a maid there. In truth he does not know whether he entertained her. The aforesaid woman said that she saw that he took a girl, and she does not know about their behavior except by hearsay.

Decided: that this testimony is not sufficient to free her [Françoise from the engagement]. Let her bring more [evidence] that she went before her husband [to say] he could not live with her if he did not stay here.

(July 9, 1556). Marguerite, widow of Jean Langroys, testified, for Françoise Collonbeyre, that the husband of the aforesaid was in her room while he was in this city and confessed that he entertained another woman because she did not want to return to him.

Decided: that she bring still further affidavits as she was told Thursday, and that it is not too far from here to Romans to send there before proceeding further.

12-19   Case of Jean Philippe and Anne Regnau (1556-1557)[47]

(Nov. 5, 1556). Jaques Regnau presented a petition against one named Jean Philippe who had promised [to marry] a daughter of his, asking that he be provided for according to the petition, aiming at setting his daughter free [from the engagement].

Decided: that for the next two months he still strive diligently to prove his case and that he address himself to me [the secretary] to search the register.

(Nov. 26, 1556). Jaques Renau was remanded here three weeks ago, that meanwhile the register be searched according to his petition. . . .

(Nov. 26, 1556). Claude Pilletet and his wife testified having known Jean Philippe, that at the time when he went away he was his servant, and he left without permission; that he brought him shoes, sword, food(?), and money, about two years ago. They heard he went to Paris, at least the rumor said so.

Decided: that considering the matters in the petition, that the girl could be set free [from the engagement], but to proceed better let him use greater diligence in the case for the next three months.

(March 4, 1557). Jaques Regnau produced a petition aiming at making provision for him concerning the marriage made between Jean Philippe and his daughter two years and four months ago, and he left her and returned, and it is said he passed through Dijon with some soldiers. And because he has shown

47. R. Consist. XI, 76, 82v, XII, 12, 14v, 18v, 42v.

the required diligence for the three months allotted to him, and he has heard Philippe returned to his own country and enlisted as a soldier, he asks [us] to provide for it as above.

The decision is that he is remanded to Thursday to bring Blaise, a mason, whom he has proposed as a witness, also those who have heard Philippe say that he would return here, not to marry the girl, but to contend against and restrain anyone who would marry her and to oppose it. Also to prove the diligence he has claimed.

(March 11, 1557). Jaques Regnau produced Cermie, wife of Claude Pilletet, to prove his intentions concerning the diligence he claims in the marriage of his daughter and Jean Philippe. She said that Philippe lived some time in this city in her house, from whom she heard when he went away that he would not return for a long time, and in going he robbed her husband of a sword and certain small items. Joyseau said he knew him well and also brought him letters. Blaise de Marque, a mason from Dijon, said he found Philippe in Dijon, who said nothing to him except in passing, and he had never seen him before except once in this city, and he has not seen him since. Regnau and the husband of a woman and she were remanded to Thursday, with other witnesses.

(March 18, 1557). Claude Pilletet, mason, and Jaques Pilletet his son produced as witnesses by Jaques Regnau concerning the marriage of his daughter and Jean Philippe, who said, that is, Claude, that he knew that Philippe had promised to take to wife the daughter of Regnau. Nevertheless, because they did not want to hurry the marriage he went away, and as he was about to go he said he would never take the girl to [be his] wife, but he would return here every year to keep the girl from marrying, and he would oppose the banns between her and the first husband she got. Jaques Pilletet said as much, adding that Philippe stole a sword from him and some other small items.

It was decided that since Philippe went away after committing larceny and boasted he would prevent the girl from marrying, saying he would come here every year to oppose the banns published for the girl and any husband she might get, that the girl may not and should not for these reasons remain unprovided for; let the case be remanded before the Council to Monday to provide for the girl.

[On March 22 the Council ordered that proclamations be made "as is customary under our edicts," and if Philippe did not appear to carry out his marriage the girl would be released from her promise and be free to marry elsewhere.]

(May 6, 1557). Jaques Regnau appeared, presenting the order given by our Lords concerning the remand made to them by the Consistory concerning the marriage or promise of marriage between Anne, his daughter, and Jean Philippe, who has left this city, the order being aimed at permitting publication of the banns newly drawn up of the girl and another; and if following the proclamation of these banns and their publication Philippe did not appear, that the girl be set at liberty. And because in carrying out and obeying the order the proclamation of the newly-drawn-up banns was made from Sunday, March 28, of the present year until April 25 following, and Jean Philippe was proclaimed, who did not appear, therefore he asked the liberation of his said daughter to be avouched in Consistory. This was done.

CHAPTER 13

I Now Take Thee

Of Banns and Weddings

M arriages without weddings were invalid in Calvin's Geneva. Weddings were essential confirmations not only that the couple privately consented but also that the church and the state publicly consented to the marriage. All weddings had to be announced in advance by the publication of banns. These banns were signed by a local magistrate and declared by a local minister for three successive Sundays before the wedding. Weddings took place in the church where the banns were pronounced — in Sunday services or on a weekday when a public Bible lecture was scheduled. The local minister presided over the wedding following a liturgy that Calvin drafted. Marriages that had been secretly contracted or improperly celebrated elsewhere had to be announced and celebrated anew in a church wedding in Geneva. Public wedding ceremonies could be followed by private wedding parties, provided the parties were modest in size and moderate in decorum. Wedding hosts and guests found guilty of excessive dancing, drinking, and debauchery faced firm spiritual and civil sanctions.

Wedding Laws, Liturgies, and Feasts

Calvin wrote little on the theology of weddings. His focus from the start was on wedding laws and liturgies, in which the theology lay implicit. Building on a generation of Protestant liturgical reforms, Calvin simply took it for granted that "the public and solemn" wedding ceremony was "essential" for a marriage to be "true and lawful," as he put it in 1542.[1] He repeated this position in 1554: "No marriages are lawful, except those that are rightly consecrated."[2] Calvin did develop a bit of a biblical ethic for marriage feasts, but this came only after he had put his wedding laws and liturgies in place.

Wedding Laws

In Calvin's Geneva, weddings were to take place in the local church — announced in advance, attended by the congregation, and presided over by the minister. The couple's public and solemn declaration of their vows encouraged them to treat their marriage with "greater honor, reverence, and esteem" and deterred them from committing "fraud or deceit" in forming their marriage. The church's participation allowed the pastor "to duly admonish" the couple of God's will for their marriage and enlisted the whole congregation "to pray for their salvation."[3]

The 1541 Ecclesiastical Ordinances, which Calvin drafted shortly after his return to Geneva, included a brief provision on weddings:

> After the calling of the customary banns the weddings shall be performed when the parties request it, whether on Sundays or on workdays, provided that it be done only at the beginning of the public worship. On a day when the [Lord's] supper is celebrated it will be desirable to abstain for honor of the sacrament.[4]

Calvin's 1546 Marriage Ordinance provided more detailed instruction:

> [16.] After the promise [of engagement] is made, let the marriage [wedding] not be delayed for more than six weeks; otherwise let the parties be called to the Consistory to be admonished. If they do not obey, let them be remanded before the Council to be compelled to celebrate it. . . .

> [20.] Let the banns be published for three Sundays in the church before the wedding is held, the signature of the first syndic being obtained beforehand to attest that the parties are known; nevertheless the wedding may be held on the third publication. And if one of the parties is from another parish, let there also be an affidavit from that place. . . .

1. CO 6:203-4 (see Doc. 13-2 below).
2. Comm. Gen. 24:59.
3. CO 6:203-4.
4. CO 10/1:26.

[22.] When it is time for the parties to be married, let them come modestly to the church without drummers or fiddlers, preserving the order and gravity proper to Christians, and do this before the end of the tolling of the bell, so that the blessing of the marriage may take place before the sermon. If they are negligent and come too late, let the marriage be postponed.

[23.] It is permissible to celebrate marriages every day, that is on working days at the sermon [that is, the day of lectures on the Bible] that seems best to the parties, on Sunday at the sermon at dawn or at three in the afternoon, except on the days when communion is celebrated, so that then there may be no distractions and everyone may be better disposed to receive the sacrament.[5]

The "banns" referenced in these laws were written announcements of a pending wedding. The minister usually read these banns from the pulpit during the Sunday worship service. This "publication" of banns was an ancient practice of the church. What was new in Geneva, compared to late medieval Catholic practice, was that the publication of banns was mandatory for every wedding. Marriages were not valid without weddings, and weddings could not proceed without banns. What was also new in Geneva, compared to some other Protestant communities, was that banns were to be announced in the church, not in the public square or in city hall.[6] A political official had to sign the banns after the parties registered their engagement. But the minister had to pronounce these signed banns in the church where the parties intended to be married. This underscored a central point of Calvin's marriage theology — that marriages were at once public and private, spiritual and temporal, ecclesiastical and political in nature.

The permission to celebrate weddings on any day, save on a Sunday when the Eucharist was celebrated, was a marked departure from the late medieval Catholic tradition. Medieval canon law prohibited weddings on any of the sixty odd holy days on the religious calendar, as well as throughout the period of Lent. Several local synods also prohibited weddings on Sundays and discouraged them on Fridays.[7] But when church weddings were celebrated, the Eucharist had to be included in the liturgy. Calvin and his colleagues eliminated most holy days, and softened considerably the Lenten restrictions, freeing up days for weddings.[8]

---

5. Doc. 1-2.

6. See samples of late medieval and early Protestant marriage liturgies in Searle and Stevenson.

7. See examples in J.-B. Molin and P. Mutembe, *Le Rituel du mariage en France du XIIe au XVIe siècle* (Paris, 1994); Kenneth W. Stevenson, *Worship: Wonderful and Sacred Mystery* (Washington, DC, 1992).

8. Benedict, pp. 495ff.

But, more to the point, they allowed weddings on any days that the congregation gathered to hear biblical exposition — whether the Sunday sermon or the week-day lecture. This underscored an accent of Calvin's liturgy, that weddings were congregational events that featured exposition of the Bible not celebration of a sacrament.

Two other legal provisions governed Genevan weddings in Calvin's day. A 1536 statute required that virgins be veiled during the wedding service[9] — a provision that Calvin later condoned.[10] A 1549 statute upheld the tradition whereby first-time brides wore wreaths of flowers, unless they had been found guilty of premarital fornication.[11]

We get a "remarkably vivid picture" of this Genevan wedding law in action from a 1556 traveler's diary, called *The Parisian Passwind* (**Doc. 13-1**).[12] According-ing to this account, the groom and his party, all carrying flowers, collect the bride at her home. She is dressed in a wedding gown, her hair down and veiled, and wreathed in flowers. Her bridesmaids carry bouquets. The bridal party marches two-by-two from her home to the church: the groomsmen first, then the couple holding hands, then the bridesmaids. The wedding party waits at the church door until the congregation is assembled and the preacher is ready.[13] The groom then takes the bride's hand, and the wedding party processes in pairs to the front of the church to participate in the marriage liturgy. The min-ister or a deacon presides at the wedding, head uncovered, facing the congrega-tion. After the liturgy — and presumably after the sermon and the rest of the

---

9. SD, vol. 2, item 699 (April 28, 1536): "Master Cristoffle [Fabri or Libertet], the preacher, stated that presently there are many weddings to be performed and that many women of this city refuse to cover the heads of virgins. Therefore there should be a decision about it, since he does not intend to marry anyone except as the Holy Scriptures direct. Concerning which it was decided that the parents of the said brides should be told not to bring them with their heads un-covered." This Christoph Fabri is the same man to whom Calvin wrote in 1553. See Doc. 13-3 be-low.

10. See Comm. Genesis 29:22: "For this was the occasion of Jacob's deception that out of regard for the modesty of brides, they were led veiled into the chamber. Today, however, with that ancient discipline rejected, men have become almost brutal."

11. SD, vol. 2, item 862. See further Chapter 12 on the effects of premarital fornication.

12. Benedict, p. 493. Benedict attributes this tract to the French Franciscan Antoine Cathelan who had spent some seven months observing Reformed life in Lausanne. The book is in part a fictitious, and sometimes salacious, traveler's diary about daily life in Reformation cit-ies like Geneva. But it includes striking accounts of Reformed liturgical life in Geneva, including a crisp account of the marriage liturgy.

13. Contrary to what the 1545 and 1546 Genevan law and liturgy provide, this diary says that the wedding liturgy took place after the sermon, not before. Perhaps by 1556, when the diary was drafted, the Genevan churches had transposed the wedding liturgy and sermon. But it is more likely that the diary was reading Lausanne patterns onto Geneva. In Lausanne, after 1551, the wedding liturgy came after, not before, the sermon. Vuilleumier, 1:346; Benedict, pp. 491-92.

regular worship service — the wedding party marches out of the church, and then marches in the same order to the groom's house for a celebration.

Wedding Liturgy

Calvin prepared a wedding liturgy in 1542, the year after his return to Geneva. He issued another liturgy, with a preamble and instructions, in 1545 (**Doc. 13-2**). This 1545 text remained the basic wedding liturgy for churches in Geneva and surrounding villages throughout Calvin's tenure — with a few cosmetic changes made in editions of 1547, 1558, 1559, 1562, 1563, and 1566.

Calvin's wedding liturgy moved in three phases: (1) biblical exhortation on marriage and its duties; (2) the consent of the couple and congregation and exchange of vows; and (3) blessing, prayer, and further exhortation.

In the first phase, the minister offered the couple a mosaic of biblical teachings on marriage, citing a dozen Old and New Testament passages. Man and woman were created for each other. The two shall become one flesh. Their voluntary union shall be permanent. The wife shall subject herself to her husband. Both husband and wife shall surrender their bodies to each other. Marriage protects both parties from lust. Their bodies are temples of the Lord to be maintained in purity.

After this lengthy opening exhortation, the minister moved to the second phase, asking the man and the woman separately whether they each consented to the marriage as so described. Part of the concern was to ensure that both the man and the woman fully and freely consented to the marriage — and were not pursuing this marriage frivolously, fraudulently, or under any false illusions. Part of the concern was to ensure that each party had a detailed understanding of the nature and responsibility of marriage. The minister also asked the congregation whether they consented to the union, or knew of any impediment.

With all consenting to go forward, the minister then administered the vows. Some of the phraseology of the vows will be familiar to Protestants today. But note that these vows were taken before God and his congregation, and that the parties were bound by God's word. Note, too, the disparities in the duties the husband and wife owe each other.

> Do you, N., confess here before God and his holy congregation that you have taken and take for your wife and spouse N. here present, whom you promise to protect, loving and maintaining her faithfully, as is the duty of a true and faithful husband to his wife, living piously with her, keeping faith and loyalty to her in all things, according to the holy Word of God and his holy Gospel?

Do you, N., confess here before God and his holy assembly that you have taken and take N. for your lawful husband, whom you promise to obey, serving and being subject to him, living piously, keeping faith and loyalty to him in all things, as a faithful and loyal wife should to her husband, according to the Word of God and the holy Gospel?

The third phase of the liturgy combined blessing, prayer, and further biblical exhortation. The minister called on God to bless the new couple in the "holy estate" and "noble estate" to which "God the Father had called" them "for the love of Jesus Christ his Son." The minister quoted the familiar passage of Matthew 19:3-9, with its solemn warning: "what God has joined together, let no man put asunder" (v. 6) He enjoined the couple to live together in "loving kindness, peace, and union, preserving true charity, faith, and loyalty to each other according to the Word of God." The minister then led the couple and the congregation in a prayer. The prayer repeated much of the language of the opening biblical exhortation. It also called upon God to help the couple live together in holiness, purity, and uprightness, and to set good examples of Christian piety for each other and the broader community. The parties and congregation were then blessed with the final peace.

Compared to other Catholic and Protestant liturgies of the day, Calvin's wedding liturgy was long on instruction and short on ceremony. The liturgy was amply peppered throughout with choice biblical references, quotations, and paraphrases. The liturgy began and ended with lengthy biblical teachings on the respective duties of husband and wife. More biblical instruction followed in the regular sermon for the day. The vows again confirmed each party's godly duties in marriage as did the concluding prayer. There was evidently no Eucharist, no kneeling at the altar, no ritualistic clasping of hands, no lifting of the veil, no kissing of the bride, no exchange of rings, no delivery of coins, no music or singing — all of which were featured in other liturgies of the day.[14] The Genevan wedding liturgy was to proceed, the preamble insisted, "respectably, religiously, and properly in good and decent order," so that the couple can "hear and listen to the holy Word of God that will be administered to them."

Calvin's wedding liturgy was a "beautiful collection of biblical texts," writes a leading historian of liturgy.[15] It was also a surprising collection — and not just because of its length and the number of biblical passages adduced. First, only two of the three traditional goods of marriage were referenced in the liturgy — mutual love and companionship and mutual protection from sexual

---

14. See samples in Searle and Stevenson; Molin and P. Mutembe, *Le Rituel du mariage*.

15. Kenneth Stevenson, *Nuptial Blessing: A Study of Christian Marriage Rites* (London, 1982), p. 131.

sin. Nothing was said anywhere in the liturgy about the blessing and procreation of children. Though the liturgy referred to Genesis 1, it did not, like many other wedding liturgies, quote the familiar biblical instruction: "Be fruitful and multiply" (Gen. 1:28). Second, the natural qualities and duties of marriage were emphasized more than the spiritual. The opening exhortation did speak of "honorable holy matrimony instituted by God" and the "sacred" obedience that a wife owed her husband. The final blessing did speak of the "holy estate" and "noble estate" of marriage. But much of the biblical material was focused on the natural qualities of marriage — its origins in creation, the mandate of fleshly union, the need for mutual bodily sacrifice, the command of continence, the analogy of the body as the temple of God, the need for bodily purity. Not even the familiar analogies between marriage and the covenant between Yahweh and his elect or Christ and his Church were referenced. These emphases — together with the express prohibition of any eucharistic celebration during the wedding, or even on the day of the wedding — underscored Calvin's fervent belief that marriage was both a natural and spiritual estate, but it was not a sacrament.

Calvin's marriage liturgy made clear that the formation of marriage was a fundamental concern of the church community.[16] For three Sundays before the wedding, the church proclaimed the banns, which served as a general invitation not only for anyone to raise impediments, but also for everyone to attend the wedding service. The wedding liturgy took place during the worship service. The wedding took place *in* the church — not at the church door, as was customary in some late medieval liturgies, and certainly not in a private home, as was also customary in some Protestant and Catholic communities.[17] The minister's duty, according to the preamble to the Marriage Liturgy, was "to approve and confirm this marriage before the whole assembly." The congregation consented to the marriage. Both the husband and wife confirmed their consent and swore their vows "before God and his holy assembly." The congregation prayed for the blessing of the couple. While the minister presided at the wedding, he stood with the couple on the same level, not in the pulpit. His head was uncovered. He faced the couple and congregation throughout the ceremony; he made no turn to the altar as had been customary in medieval liturgies. And the entire liturgy was in the vernacular, so that all could understand the service in which they were participating. All this underscores that in Calvin's Geneva a wedding

16. Bryan D. Spinks, "The Liturgical Origins and Theology of Calvin's Marriage Rite," *Ecclesia Orans* 3 (1986): 195, 208-10.

17. See examples in Steven Ozment, *When Fathers Ruled: Family Life in Reformation Europe* (Cambridge, MA, 1983); also his *The Bürgermeister's Daughter: Scandal in a Sixteenth-Century German Town* (New York, 1996); and *Ancestors: The Loving Family in Old Europe* (Cambridge, MA, 2001).

liturgy was very much a church affair, a public congregational event. Even the couple's parents and relatives had no special place in the wedding liturgy.

Calvin did not create his wedding liturgy from whole cloth. A good bit of it came from the "radical revision" introduced by Farel in 1533.[18] Farel's wedding liturgy was in turn built, in part, on liturgical reforms introduced in the 1520s in Bern, Strasbourg, Zurich, and other Protestant cities.[19] Calvin actually downplayed the novelty of his liturgy. When the Council of Bern later charged him with liturgical iconoclasm, Calvin insisted: "The form of marriage has always remained in its original state, and I follow the order which I found established like one who takes no pleasure in making innovations."[20] Calvin was being forgetful or perhaps too modest, for he had made a number of changes to Farel's 1533 liturgy.[21] It is evident, though, that he was not preoccupied with the exact form of the liturgy. Wedding liturgies, he wrote, concerned "things indifferent [adiaphora], wherein the churches have a certain latitude of diversity." "[W]hen one has weighed the matter carefully, it may be sometimes considered useful not to have too rigid a uniformity respecting them, in order to show that faith and Christianity do not consist in that."[22]

While Calvin considered the form of the wedding liturgy to be a matter of discretion, he considered the wedding event to be of cardinal importance. Calvin presided over at least 275 weddings in Geneva — almost all of them in the 1550s, when he was at the height of his power. According to the *Annales Calviniani*, he presided over only one wedding in 1547, and none in the next two years. In 1552, he conducted 30 weddings. In 1557, the number reached 51, sometimes 3 or 4 in a day. In 1562, the oft-bedridden Calvin had time and energy for only 4 weddings. Almost all these ceremonies took place at the churches of Saint-Gervais or Saint-Pierre, and most were celebrated in the late spring and summer, at the Sunday afternoon service.[23]

18. Searle and Stevenson, p. 227; Vuilleumier, 1:310-14, 345-48; Köhler, pp. 523-24.

19. See also the influence of Bucer's reforms of marriage law, lore, and liturgy discussed in Elfriede Jacobs, *Die Sakramentlehre Wilhelm Farels* (Zurich, 1978); Herman J. Selderhuis, "Das Eherecht Martin Bucers," in *Martin Bucer und das Recht*, ed. Christoph Strohm (Geneva, 2002), pp. 185-99.

20. (April, 1555), CO 15:537-42. See also Letter to Ministers of Bern (February, 1537), CO 10/2:82-84: "We have compared your directory of liturgies, which Maurus translated at our request, with ours, and find no difference except that it is more concise. I brought it with me lately to Lausanne, as there was some prospect that I might also visit Bern."

21. See analysis in Spinks, "The Liturgical Origins."

22. CO 15:537-42. On the meaning of adiaphora in Calvin's thought, see John L. Thompson, *John Calvin and the Daughters of Sarah* (Geneva, 1992), pp. 227ff.

23. See entries in *Annales Calviniani*, CO 21, where Calvin is reported to have "blessed the marriage" or "married" the following numbers of couples: 1547:1; 1550:9; 1551:14; 1552:30; 1553:35; 1554:30; 1555:28; 1556:34; 1557:51; 1558:22; 1559:4; 1560:7; 1561:4; 1562:4. There are no weddings listed

Calvin also attended the weddings of several friends, and sent wedding presents.[24] He sent notes of commendation to couples whose wedding he had to miss, and occasionally offered advice to friends who were planning weddings. In a 1553 letter to Christoph Fabri (Libertet), Calvin apologized for having to miss the wedding of his old friend who had been an early reformer in Geneva (**Doc. 13-3**). Calvin warmly commended this marriage not only because it served Fabri's "private good, but also because the brethren have considered it to be for the good of the whole Church." Calvin would have gladly undertaken the three-day winter journey. But Geneva was beset by political strife at the time, and he could not risk being away, much as he wanted to be there for Fabri.

In a 1548 letter, he offered his patron Monsieur de Falais some advice on the forthcoming wedding of his niece, a ceremony which Calvin planned to attend. Calvin urged an ethic of modesty and moderation even though de Falais was fully capable of financing a grand affair:

> The wedding, I hope, will go off well. There needs to be some company, but no great multitude. And besides, we must not be too hard on you, for it will be necessary to find lodgings for them. I think ten persons will be a reasonable number, including myself.[25]

This counsel of modesty was in keeping with the provisions of Calvin's 1545 Marriage Liturgy (echoed in the 1546 Marriage Ordinance): "When it is time for the parties to be married, let them come modestly to the church without drummers or fiddlers, preserving the order and gravity proper to Christians. . . ."

Wedding Feasts

Modesty and moderation were Calvin's watchwords not only at wedding services but also at the wedding feasts to follow. Some wedding feast was appropriate, given the importance of the new marriage and the many examples of wed-

---

before 1547 or after 1562. The 1557 annals lists the following dates for weddings over which Calvin presided: January 10 and 24 (2 weddings), February 14 (2) and 21, March 8 and 21, April 4 and 25 (4), May 2 (3), 9 (3), and 30, June 7 (2), 13, and 27 (3), July 4 (2), 18 (3), and 25, August 1, 8 (3), 15 (3), and 22, September 6 and 12, October 17 and 24, November 7 (2), 21 (2), and 28 (2), and December 5 and 19. These Annales, prepared by the editors of CO, are valuable sources, but they sometimes do not reflect a comprehensive reading of the Genevan Registers. The number of weddings where Calvin presided is likely a bit higher. See further study and charts in Lambert, pp. 291ff.

24. See, e.g., Chapter 3 regarding the wedding of Pierre Viret.

25. Letter to Monsieur de Falais (July 17, 1548), CO 13:7-9. See further Chapter 3 on Calvin's involvement in the earlier courtship of Falais's niece, Mademoiselle de Wilergy.

ding feasts in the Bible.[26] "I am not so austere as to condemn the . . . rejoicings of those who celebrate their nuptials," Calvin insisted.[27] "[T]here is nothing in itself wrong with putting on a banquet," even an expensive banquet.[28] But the wedding host should avoid the "dazzling pomp, vanities, and excesses" that inevitably lead his guests into "a gulf of ruin."[29] "The human mind is so inclined to licentiousness, that when the reins are loosened, people quickly go astray." "[T]here is scarcely a single entertainment, whatever its cost, that is free from wicked debauchery. First, men drink more freely. Second, the door is opened to filthy and immodest conversation. Third, no moderation is observed."[30]

Knowing people's proclivities to excess, Calvin helped draft strict legal guidelines for weddings and other feasts. A 1539 ordinance, drafted already before Calvin's return to Geneva, set limits on dancing, songs, and plays:

> Also let no one dance any dance, except at weddings, or sing indecent songs, or disguise himself or present a mask or play, and this under penalty of sixty sous and of being put in prison three days on bread and water for everyone doing the contrary.[31]

This provision was repeated, and then glossed, in several laws on sumptuousness and public morality issued in the 1540s and 1550s. Included was a 1549 law on public morals that prohibited dancing altogether, even at weddings.[32] Included as well was a 1558 law that provided "that at banquets there be no more than three courses, and in each course no more than four dishes."[33] In 1560, Calvin and his colleagues distilled these sundry laws into a comprehensive new edict on public morality, with several pointed restrictions on diet, dress, and drunkenness at wedding feasts:

> 22. Also it is forbidden to all and everyone, of whatever estate, quality, or condition they may be, to commit any excess in food, either at weddings,

---

26. Comm. Harm. Gospel Matt. 22:1-4; Luke 14:15-24; Comm. John 2:1-12.

27. Letter to Duke de Longueville (May 26, 1559), CO 17:532-33 (referring to the excesses of a duke's wedding).

28. Comm. Harm. Gospel Matt. 14:3-12; Mark 6:17-29 (referring to the grand celebration of King Herod's birthday).

29. CO 17:532-33.

30. Comm. Harm. Gospel Matt. 14:3-12; Mark 6:17-29.

31. SD, vol. 2, item 756.

32. SD, vol. 2, item 866: "Let it be known on behalf of our most dread Lords Syndics and Council of this city that no one, of whatever estate or condition he may be, should be so daring or bold henceforth as to sing indecent songs or dance in any manner whatever, under penalty of being put in prison for three days on bread and water and of sixty sous for every occasion."

33. SD, vol. 3, item 974.

banquets, feasts, or otherwise, or in clothing and apparel. But everyone in such circumstances should contain himself and behave modestly and dress decently and simply, according to his estate, under penalty of sixty sous for each occasion when he is known to have done the contrary. And moreover those persisting and rebelling [shall be] punished according to the needs of the case.

23. Also let no one wear slashed hose or doublets, under penalty of sixty sous for each occasion.

24. Also let no one, of whatever estate, quality, or condition they may be, men or women, wear chains of gold or of silver, but those who have been accustomed to wear them should set them aside after this proclamation, under penalty of sixty sous for each occasion.

25. Also let no women, of whatever quality or condition they may be, wear farthingales, gilding on their heads, gold caps, or embroidery on half-sleeves or other clothing, under the said penalty for each occasion.

26. Also let no one, of whatever estate, quality, or condition they may be, men or women, wear more than two rings on their fingers (except that it shall be permitted for those being married, on the day of the wedding and the next day, to wear more), under penalty of sixty sous for each occasion.

27. Also let no one, of whatever estate, quality, or condition he may be, holding weddings, banquets, or feasts, provide more than three courses or servings at the banquets, or in each course more than four dishes, dignified and not excessive, besides fruit, under penalty of sixty sous for each occasion.[34]

A 1564 statute on banquets was even more austere:

Let it be known on behalf of the most honorable Lords Syndics and Council of this city: As we see that the scourge of our God has descended on various neighboring nations and peoples, and also that it approaches nearer to us, let everyone be more diligent than ever in prayers and supplications, both in their houses and privately and in public, and especially to assemble on the day of prayer, that is Wednesday, more carefully than is usual, to obtain the grace and mercy of God. And also, in order to be better prepared to appeal to God, let everyone refrain on that day from banquets and superfluities, humbling themselves before God in sobriety and fasting, so that it may please him to turn aside his anger from us and to continue his grace and blessings to this poor republic, showing himself its protector, as he has done heretofore.[35]

34. SD, vol. 3, item 992.
35. SD, vol. 3, item 1052.

All this talk of moderation and modesty at wedding feasts seemed hard to square with the Gospel's generous commendation of weddings. After all, one of Christ's most famous parables featured a king who threw a great wedding feast for his son, and even "compelled" his guests to come in so that the wedding hall was filled (Matt. 22:1-14; Luke 14:15-24). And Christ's first miracle took place at the wedding feast in Cana, where he turned many pots of water into vast quantities of excellent new wine (John 2:1-12). How could Calvin be so churlish about wedding feasts when even the Lord himself ensured that fine wine flowed there so freely?

In his 1553 Commentary on John 2, Calvin insisted that traditional inter-preters had missed the main points of this passage (**Doc. 13-4**). One point was that clergy were as welcome to attend weddings as laity. "There are some an-cient canons that forbid clergy" to attend wedding parties, lest "by being the spectators of the wickedness usually practiced on such occasions, they might in some measure be regarded as approving of it." For Calvin, this restriction made no sense, given Christ's presence at the wedding feast of Cana. Ministers were as welcome at wedding parties as anyone else — indeed more so, for they could deter immoral conduct through their word and example.

A second point of this story was that it was precisely because the host of the wedding at Cana lacked modesty that he risked running out of wine. The host was a man of humble means. He should have sent fewer invitations. By in-viting too many guests, he risked the shame of running out of food and drink. Only Christ's miracle spared the host from embarrassment.

Finally, Christ did not turn so many pots of water into wine to condone excessive drinking at weddings. Rather it was "to prove the truth of the miracle" and to test the faith of the people. Had Christ changed only enough wine to drink for the rest of the evening, people would have doubted that he had per-formed a miracle; they may well have thought that a servant had belatedly found the host's remaining stock. With so much new wine of such high quality suddenly at hand, the miracle was put beyond doubt. People would be induced to faith by the miracle. But then came the test:

> It is wonderful that a large quantity of wine, and of the very best wine, was supplied by Christ, who is a teacher of sobriety. I reply, when God daily gives us a large supply of wine, it is our own fault if his kindness is an excitement to luxury. On the other hand, it is an undoubted trial of our sobriety, if we are sparing and moderate in the midst of abundance.

This clever exegesis of the Cana wedding story might have been convinc-ing in theory, but not always in practice. The same 1556 traveler's diary that we sampled above notes that Genevan wedding guests sometimes defied Calvin's call for moderation:

Those who don't care too much for Calvin and his fellows . . . go to and return from the church with a Swiss tambourine or another instrument, and after dinner they dance or play in their chambers in great secrecy on pain of being called before the Consistory.[36]

Consistory Cases

The Consistory heard several cases involving weddings. One cluster of cases involved disputes over the publication of banns. These the Consistory disposed of quickly by either ordering the banns or canceling the wedding. A second cluster of cases raised questions of the validity of weddings that had been contracted and/or celebrated elsewhere. The Consistory dealt with these more carefully with widely varying results. A third cluster of cases involved dancing and drinking at wedding parties. These usually earned the perpetrators severe spiritual and criminal sanctions.

Disputes over Banns

As we have seen many times in the prior chapters, when the Consistory or Council wanted the parties to marry, they ordered them to publish their banns and then celebrate their wedding. Weddings without banns were invalid in Geneva, and the authorities would delay weddings beyond the maximum six-week period of engagement allowed by the 1546 Marriage Ordinance to ensure that the banns had been announced on three successive Sundays.

The banns served as a screen against improper marriages. Not only did they invite the community to raise impediments but also allowed the authorities to second guess whether they wished to marry the couple. The 1556 case of François Danel of Jussy was a good illustration.[37] François had consented to the engagement of his sister, who lived in a distant town but was moving to Geneva. He had the Genevan syndic sign her banns, as the first step to having her marriage approved and celebrated once she moved to Geneva. But François did not tell the Genevan authorities that his sister was marrying a Catholic. Upon discovering this, the Consistory requested the Council to reprimand François and rescind the banns, arguing that they had been delivered under false pretenses. The Council obliged, and ordered the mixed couple not to come to Geneva.

---

36. Quoted by Benedict, p. 494.

37. The record of this case is in Doc. 10-12 above, where we have analyzed it for issues of interreligious marriage.

Interreligious marriages were not formally prohibited in Geneva, but the practice was strongly discouraged.[38] The Consistory was not about to be drawn into condoning such a marriage through a fraudulent posting of banns.

Similarly, in a 1548 case Jean Leccot appeared before the Consistory, complaining that the local syndic would not sign his banns (**Doc. 13-5**). The syndic said he had refused because he suspected Jean of already being engaged to another woman in Bourges. Had the marriage gone forward, Jean would have been guilty of polygamy, and the syndic could have been charged as an accessory. Bring me an affidavit proving that the Bourges engagement is over, the syndic told Jean, and I shall sign your banns for this new marriage. The Consistory concurred in this.

Foreign Marriages

The corollary to the concern over polygamy was the concern over marriages contracted and/or celebrated elsewhere, particularly in Catholic polities. Should Geneva recognize these foreign marriages, or did the parties need to re-celebrate their wedding in Geneva to validate their marriage? The Consistory heard a number of these cases, particularly as French immigrants and refugees poured into Geneva in the 1550s and 1560s.

The Consistory generally recognized the marriages of new immigrants who produced valid marriage certificates or affidavits from their hometown, whether Protestant or Catholic. In a 1557 case, for example, Etienne de Faye and Marie Salmon petitioned the Consistory to ratify their marriage that had been celebrated in a Reformed church in France (**Doc. 13-6**). They produced a notarized certificate of marriage, signed by four parties whose names were known in Geneva. Their marriage was deemed fully valid. The Consistory likewise approved the marriage of Arnauld Casaubon and Mengine Rousseau, even though they had been married in the Catholic city of Bordeaux (**Doc. 13-7**). The couple produced a notarized marriage certificate. They also produced two witnesses who authenticated the certificate and its signatures and testified that the couple had been married in a church ceremony. This was proof enough of the validity of their marriage.

The Consistory would look beyond the documents, however, when they suspected foul play. Antoine Maurin, a former priest and a son of a distinguished barrister of Paris, found this out in 1556 (**Doc. 13-8**). He petitioned the Consistory to recognize his marriage, and introduced a marriage certificate and notarized affidavit. The Consistory summoned Antoine and his wife for rou-

38. See above Chapter 10.

tine questioning. When the parties ducked the subpoena, the Consistory became suspicious — doubly so when they heard that Antoine had a reputation as a "swindler." On review, they judged the marriage certificate to be a forgery and sent the case to the Council. The Council imprisoned Antoine and his wife, and then banished them permanently from Geneva.

Those who petitioned for marriage ratification faced a heavier burden of proof when they appeared before the Consistory without a marriage certificate. Claude de Boyssiere and Antoine Lenarde could not meet this burden when they requested the Consistory to ratify their marriage (**Doc. 13-9**). The couple and five other witnesses testified that they had been married in their home country of Dauphiné. The witnesses also testified that Claude was a good religious man, and that Antoine's parents had consented. This was not proof enough for the Consistory. They sent the couple to the Council, who ordered them to contract and celebrate their marriage anew in Geneva.

A similar fate faced Jean and Catherine Bret, a former monk and nun, who had been married some eight years before in a part of Catholic France (**Doc. 13-10**). They had recently moved to Geneva, and asked the Consistory to confirm their marriage. They could not have had certification of their marriage, for ex-monastics were forbidden from marriage in Catholic Europe. The Consistory ordered them to start their marriage anew. They were to remain separate, until they had posted their banns and celebrated their wedding before the congregation.

In an unusual 1547 case, however, the Company of Pastors did ratify a marriage without a certificate and without ordering a new ceremony (**Doc. 13-11**). The case involved a noble couple named Adam Fumée and Michelle de Millone. Before moving to Geneva, they had contracted a private marriage before witnesses. They had neither celebrated a church wedding nor publicized their new marriage. They wanted the Genevan authorities to ratify their marriage, but they feared any publicity of a wedding ceremony, lest their relatives at home be endangered. They asked the Company to put their case quietly to the Council. The record says nothing about the nature of the danger to the relatives, but the Company was sympathetic. They sent Calvin and a colleague to represent the couple at the Council, who later ratified their marriage without requiring any further steps.

Dancing Cases

The Consistory heard a number of cases of dancing, drunkenness, and debauchery at wedding feasts. They sometimes investigated these cases at great length to ensure that they had found all guilty parties and crafted punishments to fit their crimes.

A striking early example is the lengthy 1546 case against Antoine Letz and his wedding party (**Doc. 13-12**). Letz was charged with hosting a Sunday wedding party for his daughter that featured dancing and drunkenness. The party involved many members of the Genevan aristocracy, including a syndic, Amblard Corne, and another political leader, Ami Perrin, captain of Geneva, who would later become prominent in the opposition to Calvin. Some of the guests were suspected of dancing in a nearby village as well. The Consistory ultimately accused and examined twenty-five wedding guests, confronting each with the escalating body of evidence of dancing and, in a few cases, of drunkenness. Husbands were forced to testify against wives, wives against husbands, a servant against his master, friends against each other. Most of the parties failed to cooperate. Several were suspected of perjury. One witness was contemptuous of the Consistory, saying that such matters should be adjudicated by the Council. Another said that biblical admonition for sin should be done privately, not in such a public hearing. Another took on Calvin by accusing him of improperly equating dancing with debauchery, contrary to Scripture; Calvin corrected him in his exegesis.

Exasperated with what it judged to be a campaign of orchestrated perjury, the Consistory sent this whole company to the Council to be examined under oath, including Syndic Corne and Captain Perrin. The Council apparently found them less than cooperative as well, for they imprisoned the whole group, and then remanded each separately to the Consistory to do confession. Most parties admitted to their dancing and their participation in the attempted cover-up. They were admonished for their sin and readmitted to communion. Those that were more defiant were denied communion and faced further admonition until they cooperated.

The Consistory also reprimanded Syndic Corne and Captain Perrin. They upbraided Corne for "tolerating offenses" by "the great" of society that would have been punished if committed by "the small." Corne accepted this admonition and castigated himself severely.

Calvin reprimanded Perrin similarly in a private letter (**Doc. 13-13**). While the case was still pending, Perrin had traveled to Lyon, apparently in the hopes that the case would blow over. He did not bother to appear before the Consistory with the others after his release from prison. This only exacerbated his offense in Calvin's view. "We cannot enjoy weight for weight with an unequal balance," Calvin wrote to Perrin. "[I]f impartiality must be observed in the administration of human law, any departure from it cannot be tolerated in the Church of God." Then, perhaps fearing that Perrin might think him too wooden in his judgment and too contemptuous of political authority, Calvin threw down the gauntlet: "I am one to whom the law of my heavenly Master is so dear, that the cause of no man on earth will induce me to flinch from maintaining it with a pure conscience. I cannot believe that you yourself have any other end in view, but I observe that no one has his eyes wide enough open when the case is his own." Calvin let Perrin know that he had caught wind of Perrin's complaints that he, Calvin, was "stirring up a slumbering fire" and would get burned if he continued. Calvin pounced on this challenge: "I desire . . . to serve not only for the edification of the church and your salvation, but also for your convenience, name, and leisure. For how odious would be the imputation which is likely to fall upon you, that you seemed to be free from and unrestrained by the common law to which every one is subject?" Then Calvin moved to a more general vindication of his efforts to reform Geneva: "I did not return to Geneva either for the sake of leisure or of gain. . . . The convenience and safety of church and state made me willing to return. If measures are now being taken against me alone, I want to say, once and for all, to all who think me troublesome: 'What you do, do quickly.'"

Calvin was considerably exercised by this case. In a private letter to Farel and Viret, he admitted that he was "incensed" by the parties' "shameless lies," and their "contempt of God" and of the Consistory (**Doc. 13-14**). He saved his bitterest vitriol again for Ami Perrin and his wife, whose contemptuous words and conduct he considered "perfidious mockery." I resolved to "unbar the truth, even though it might be at the cost of my own life," Calvin wrote dramatically, "lest they should imagine that any profit was to come of lying."

It was obvious that Calvin saw much more at stake than a bit of raucous dancing among the local aristocracy. This was the first year in which Calvin's new Marriage Ordinance and Marriage Liturgy were being implemented. Calvin was still relatively young in his tenure in Geneva, and the Consistory's authority was still being challenged. Calvin must have seen this as an ideal case to test his mettle against the political authorities and to test their devotion to the Reformation cause and to his leadership of it.

What is surprising is that a case was brought against Antoine Letz in the first place. The 1539 statute that we quoted above allowed for dancing at weddings, though not on any other occasion. It was not until 1549, three years after this case, that dancing was prohibited altogether even at weddings. Perhaps Antoine's daughter had only become engaged, not married, making this dancing party technically illegal. The record says at one point that Antoine only "promised his daughter to Claude Philippe," though it later refers to this feast as a "wedding party." As the case unfolded, it was the perjury, the discovery of drunkenness and gaming, and the procedural contempt that got the parties into trouble more than the dancing. But the initial case against dancing seems suspect.

Any doubt about such cases was removed when the 1549 statute abolished dancing altogether in Geneva, and attached heavy fines for those found guilty.

This statute did seem to deter misconduct at wedding feasts. The number of cases of abuse reported to the Consistory fell off sharply thereafter, though the Consistory continued to hear occasional cases of dancing, drunkenness, gaming, and sexual improprieties at wedding feasts.[39] They continued to punish the parties severely. And when magistrates failed to police these weddings properly or report improprieties promptly, they faced severe reprimand from the Consistory as well.[40]

Summary and Conclusions

The wedding liturgy was the final step in the validation of marriage in Calvin's Geneva. Mutual consent of the couple was absolutely essential. Parental consent was required, at least for youngsters, as was the validation by peers. The community's consent was absolutely essential, too, and the wedding was the occasion for its communication. Both magistrates and ministers helped to voice the community's consent. Magistrates voiced their consent through the signing and validation of the banns and the registration of the new couple's marriage contract and marital property. Ministers voiced their consent through the announcement of the banns and the celebration of the wedding liturgy and, after 1548, by recording and registering the marriage.

Calvin took banns and weddings as seriously as he had taken the earlier stages of marriage formation. Wedding preparations and celebrations were solemn steps in the final divine confirmation and validation of a marriage. These final steps of marriage could not be rushed. Parties would have to start over if they failed to announce their banns or celebrate their weddings properly. These final steps of marriage were also to be free from drunkenness, dancing, or debauchery at the wedding party. Such behavior insulted the marital vows that the couple had just taken to be moral exemplars to each other and the community.

Calvin also took seriously the need for a delay between engagements and weddings. The point of a public engagement and waiting period was to invite others to weigh in on the maturity and compatibility of the couple, to offer them counsel and commodities, and to prepare for the celebration of their union and their life together thereafter. And it was to prepare their families and congregations to give their solemn consent to this budding new union. Too long an engagement would encourage the couple to engage in premarital intimacy. But too short an engagement would discourage them from introspection. Too secret a wedding would deprive couples of the essential counsel and com-

---

39. See, e.g., the protracted 1557 case reported in R. Consist. XII, 5v, 36, 37, 39-39v, 44.
40. See, e.g., R. Consist. XII, 102v.

modities of their families and friends. But too open a wedding would deprive couples of the consent and confirmation of the community that counted. Too solemn a wedding ceremony would smother the joy that a new marital love should bring. But too raucous a wedding party would trespass the duties that the new marriage had just brought. Calvin thus strove to strike a judicious balance between engagement and wedding, publicity and privacy, waiting and consummating, celebration and moderation.

13-1 The Parisian Passwind, Observations of Genevan Weddings (1556)[41]

Those who want to do the will of Calvin, the great Satrap of Geneva, do as follows. The groom and his party, all carrying bouquets or rosemary branches, go to find the bride and her party who are waiting at her lodging. She is dressed as they do there, that is to say with her head covered if she is a widow and with her hair down if she is a maiden, and is wearing a hat of flowers whether she is a widow or a maiden, while the women in her party each have a bouquet in their hand or on their breast. Then they all go to the sermon, the men in front two by two, then the groom leading his bride by the hand for fear of losing her, then the women behind two by two, and in this formation they go as far as the door of the church (which they call the temple), and there they all take their places and wait for the preacher to start. After the sermon, the groom takes the bride by her hand again and they proceed to the door of the choir or the steps where the high altar used to be, and there the deacon or the minister in his absence joins them by a ceremony as long or longer than ours, his head uncovered and facing the people, emphasizing that he only does so to ratify in the presence of the church the promise they had already [made] among themselves. Then they all return to the groom's house in the same order, and after dinner everyone retires so that the married couple can chat about their private matters. . . .

13-2 The Manner of Celebrating Holy Matrimony (1545)[42]

The public and solemn ceremony of confirmation of marriage was instituted by Christians so that true and lawful marriage might be held in greater honor, reverence, and esteem and so that no fraud or deceit might be committed between the parties, but all might be done in good faith and loyalty, and so the church might pray for the salvation of the married couple. Therefore it is the duty of the ministers of the church to proclaim publicly from the pulpit those who wish to be joined together in marriage, to approve and confirm this mar-

---

41. *Passevent parisien, Respondant à Pasquin Romain: De la vie de ceux qui sont allez demourer à Genève, et se dissent vivre selon la reformation de l'Evangile* (1556; Paris, 1875, translated in Benedict, pp. 493-94).

42. CO 6:203-8. The editions of 1542, 1545, 1547, 1558, 1559, 1562, 1563, and 1566 are the same, except for small variations of wording. The preamble appears first in the 1545 edition.

riage before the whole assembly, and to show them the dignity and excellence of the estate of matrimony from Holy Scripture. And afterwards [it is the duty of ministers] to tell them what is the duty of married people, that is, how the husband should treat his wife and likewise the wife her husband so that they may be one. This is to be done according to the institution of God contained in Genesis 2, Matthew 19, 1 Corinthians 7, Colossians 3, 1 Timothy, Titus 2, and 1 Peter 3. And it would not be irrelevant or useless for the minister to assemble the exhortations and consolations found in these places dealing with this subject and matter. And so that everything may be done respectably, religiously, and properly in good and decent order, the whole wedding company should enter the church without drum or other musical instrument to hear and listen to the holy Word of God that will be administered to them.

It must be noted that before it is celebrated, the marriage is to be announced in the church for three Sundays, so that if anyone knows of an impediment to it he may come report it in good time, or if anyone has a claim he may oppose it.

This done, the parties come to present themselves at the beginning of the sermon. Then the minister says:

Let our help be from the name of God, who made the heavens and the earth. Amen.

God our Father, after having made the heavens and the earth and all that is in them, created and formed man in his image and likeness, who had dominion and sovereignty over the beasts of the field, the fishes of the sea, and the birds of the air. After creating man, God said: "It is not good that the man should be alone; let us make him a helpmate similar to him." And Our Lord made a deep sleep fall on Adam, and while Adam slept God took one of his ribs and of it made Eve, making it clear that man and woman are one body, one flesh, and one blood. Wherefore a man leaves his father and mother and cleaves to his wife, whom he should love as Jesus loves his Church, that is the true believers and Christians for whom he died. And also a wife should serve and obey her husband in all sanctity and honor, for she is subject and under the power of her husband, since she lives with him (Gen. 1 and 2; Matt. 19:5; Eph. 5:28ff.; Col. 3:18; 1 Tim. 2:12). And this honorable holy matrimony, instituted by God (Heb. 13:4), is of this virtue, that through it the husband does not have the power of his own body, but the wife; also the wife does not have the power of her own body, but the husband (1 Cor. 7:1ff.). Wherefore those joined by God cannot be separated, except for a time, by the consent of both, to attend to fasts and prayers, being careful not to be tempted by Satan through incontinence. And nevertheless they should return to each other. For to avoid fornication every man should have his wife and every woman her husband, so that all those who cannot control themselves and do not have the gift of continence are obliged by the commandment of God to marry, so that the holy temple of God, that is our body, may not be violated or corrupted. For since our bodies are members of Jesus Christ, it would be too great an outrage to make them members of a harlot (1 Cor. 6:15). Therefore one should preserve them in all sanctity. For if anyone violates the temple of God, God will destroy him (1 Cor. 3:17).

You therefore *(naming the husband and wife),* N. and N., knowing that God has so ordained it, do you wish to live in this holy estate of matrimony that God has so greatly honored? Do you have such an intention, as you testify here before this holy assembly, asking that it be approved?

They answer: Yes.

The minister: I take all of you who are present here to witness, asking you to remember this. Nevertheless, if there is anyone who knows of any impediment, or that either of them is bound in marriage with another, let him say so.

If no one objects, the minister says the following: Since there is no one who objects and there is no impediment, Our Lord God confirms the holy desire he has given you; and let your beginning be in the name of God, who made the heavens and the earth. Amen.

Speaking to the husband, the minister says the following:

Do you, N., confess here before God and his holy congregation that you have taken and take for your wife and spouse N. here present, whom you promise to protect, loving and maintaining her faithfully, as is the duty of a true and faithful husband to his wife, living piously with her, keeping faith and loyalty to her in all things, according to the holy Word of God and his holy Gospel?

He answers: Yes.

Then speaking to the wife, he says: Do you, N., confess here before God and his holy assembly that you have taken and take N. for your lawful husband, whom you promise to obey, serving and being subject to him, living piously, keeping faith and loyalty to him in all things, as a faithful and loyal wife should to her husband, according to the Word of God and the holy Gospel?

She answers: Yes.

Then the minister says: May the Father of all mercy, who by his grace has called you to this holy estate of matrimony, for the love of Jesus Christ his Son — who by his holy presence sanctified marriage (John 2:1ff.), working there his first miracle before his apostles — give you his Holy Spirit to serve and honor him in this noble estate. Amen.

Hear the Gospel, how Our Lord wishes holy matrimony to be preserved, and how it is firm and indissoluble, as it is written in Saint Matthew in the nineteenth chapter:

> The Pharisees also came unto him, tempting him, and saying unto him, "Is it lawful for a man to put away his wife for every cause?" And he answered

and said unto them, "Have ye not read, that he which made them at the beginning made them male and female, and said, 'For this cause shall a man leave father and mother, and shall cleave to his wife, and the two shall be one flesh? Wherefore they are no more two, but one flesh. What therefore God hath joined together, let not man put asunder.'"

Believe in these holy words that Our Lord Jesus spoke, as the evangelist repeats them, and be certain that Our Lord God has joined you in this holy estate of matrimony. Therefore live piously together in loving-kindness, peace, and union, preserving true charity, faith, and loyalty to each other according to the Word of God.

Therefore let us all pray to Our Father with one heart: Almighty God, beneficent and omniscient, who from the beginning foresaw that it was not good for the man to be alone, for which reason you created for him a helpmate similar to him and commanded that two should be one: we pray and humbly ask you, since it has pleased you to call these before us to the holy estate of matrimony, that of your grace and bounty you may wish to give and provide them with your Holy Spirit: so that in true and firm faith, according to your will, they may live in holiness, overcoming all evil thoughts and living purely, edifying others in all honor and chastity: giving them your blessing as you did to your faithful servants Abraham, Isaac, and Jacob, that being of holy lineage they may praise and serve you, comprehending this and strengthening it for your praise and glory and for the benefit of their neighbors, in the advancement and exaltation of your holy Gospel. Hear us, Father of mercy, through Our Lord Jesus Christ your beloved Son. Amen.

May Our Lord fill you with every grace and cause you to live in all happiness together long and piously. Amen.

13-3 Letter to Christoph Fabri (1553)[43]

I am exceedingly glad that you are about to get married, not only because it will be for your own private good, but also because the brethren have considered it to be for the good of the whole church. And while I do not know enough about the lady, yet I confidently trust, from various guesses, that each of you will turn out according to our wishes. We have good reason, therefore, to congratulate you, and we feel thankful to God in no ordinary degree.

I would have gladly been present at your marriage, had I not been detained at home by the wickedness of those whose madness does not cease to

---

43. (January 13, 1553), CO 14:455-56; Bonnet, Letter 308 (adapted).

bring destruction upon themselves and the community. I have good reason to call it madness, for they have never exhibited more unbridled licentiousness. I shall say nothing of their mischievous plots for the destruction of the faith, of their gross contempt of God, of their impious conspiracies for the scattering of the Church, of the foul Epicurianism of their whole life — not because these are light evils but because they are not unknown to you. The entire republic is at present in disorder, and they are striving to root up the established order of things.

Had your marriage been a month later, I would have had more leisure. I cannot move a foot at the moment. I have not been through the city gates for the past month, even for recreation. I wish I had less of a reason to be excused. Certainly, the winter season would not have stood in my way.

But we shall pray that your marriage comes off well, the effects of which will be felt even here. I would not have thought it lost effort to endure the expense of the cold and trouble of a three days' journey to have a conversation with our beloved Farel and your chief magistrate. But one consideration was sufficient for me, that you wished me to discharge a duty which I was as willing to fulfill, as you were earnest in desiring it. I hope to find it more convenient to visit my friends on another occasion. Adieu, very dear brother in the Lord.

13-4   Commentary on the Gospel of John 2:1-11 (1553)[44]

It was probably one of Christ's near relations who married a wife, for Jesus is mentioned as having accompanied his mother. From the fact that the disciples also are invited, we may infer how plainly and frugally he lived, for he lived in common with them. It may be thought strange, however, that a man who has no great wealth or abundance (as will be made evident from the scarcity of the wine) invites four or five other persons, on Christ's account. But the poor more readily and easily send invitations. They are not, like the rich, afraid of being disgraced if they do not treat their guests with great costliness and splendor. The poor adhere more zealously to the ancient custom of having an extended company.

Again, it may seem that the bridegroom allowed his guests, in the middle of the party, to be in need of wine. He seems less than thoughtful not to have enough wine for his guests. I say that nothing is said here that does not often happen, especially when people are not accustomed to the daily use of wine. Besides, the context shows that the wine fell short towards the end of the party, which was when it was apparently customary that people had already drunk

44. CO 47:37-42 (NTC adapted).

enough. For the master of the party says: "Other men place worse wine before those who have drunk enough, but you have kept the best till now." . . .

Christ supplied them with a great abundance of wine — enough for a banquet of a hundred and fifty men. Both the number and the size of the water-pots serve to prove the truth of the miracle. If there had been only two or three jars, many might have suspected that they had been brought from some other place. If only the water of one vessel had been changed into wine, the certainty of the miracle would not have been so obvious, or so well ascertained. It is not, therefore, without a good reason that the Evangelist mentions the number of water-pots, and states how much they contained. . . .

For the same reason, Christ wanted the flavor of the wine to be tested by the master of the feast, before it had been tasted by himself, or by any other of the guests. The readiness with which the servants obey him in all things shows us the great reverence and respect in which he was held by them. The Evangelist gives the name of the master of the feast to him who was in charge of preparing the banquet and arranging the tables. Not that the banquet was costly and magnificent, but because the honorable appellations borrowed from the luxury and splendor of the rich are applied even to the marriages of the poor.

It is wonderful that such a large quantity of wine, and of the very best wine, was supplied by Christ, who is a teacher of sobriety. I reply, when God daily gives us a large supply of wine, it is our own fault if his kindness is an excitement to luxury. On the other hand, it is an undoubted trial of our sobriety, if we are sparing and moderate in the midst of abundance. . . .

It is a high honor given to marriage, that Christ not only deigned to be present at a wedding banquet, but honored it with his first miracle. There are some ancient canons that forbid the clergy to attend a wedding. The reason of the prohibition was, that by being the spectators of the wickedness which was usually practiced on such occasions, they might in some measure be regarded as approving of it. But it would have been far better to carry to such places so much gravity as to restrain the licentiousness in which unprincipled and abandoned men indulge, when they are withdrawn from the eyes of others. Let us, on the contrary, take Christ's example for our rule; and let us not suppose that any thing else than what we read that he did can be profitable to us.

13-5 Case of Jean Leccot (1548)[45]

(Feb. 2, 1548). Master Jean Leccot, bookseller, stated it is true that he wanted his banns signed by Syndic Girardin [de La Rive], who refused, saying he should

---

45. R. Consist. III, 207.

bring an affidavit of his divorce from the woman he had already been engaged to in the city of Bourges. Note: the Consistory stands by this.

13-6   Case of Etienne de Faye and Marie Salmon (1557)[46]

(May 6, 1557). Etienne de Faye, Sieur de La Tour, appeared, alleging and stating that after having [lived] a long time in this city he withdrew to France, where he married a woman named Marie Salmon, here present and appearing with him. Concerning their marriage, they produced a certificate dated April 10 last signed by Master François Pane, Gaucherie, De Cuillir, and one other. He said that their marriage had been solemnized in the congregation of the faithful and in the Christian church that by the grace of God has been begun in France. He asked that such a marriage be avouched and confirmed in the church of this city.

It was decided, since the signature on the certificate was recognized and it was clearly known that it was not produced by fraud but proceeded according to the commandments of God, that such a marriage should be approved and avouched in this city in the church of God.

The contents of the certificate: "The undersigned François Pane by these presents attests that Etienne Faye, Esquire, Sieur de La Tour, and Marie Salmon, gentlewoman, are joined together in a good, true, and legitimate marriage, which has been made and celebrated in the church of God by a faithful minister of the word of Our Lord and of his sacraments. In proof and testimony of this I have asked the principals who were present at the celebration of this holy marriage to be witnesses to it and to sign these presents, and I have signed here beneath. The year of grace 1557, the tenth of April. François Pane, Gaucherie, De Poyrier, De Cuillir." On the front of the certificate is written: "Salvation, grace, peace, and mercy in Our Lord Jesus Christ."

13-7   Case of Arnauld Casaubon and Mengine Rousseau (1557)[47]

(Sept. 9, 1557). Arnauld Casaubon and Mengine Rousseau, spouses, appeared asking that the marriage between them celebrated in Bordeaux be confirmed and approved. They produced for this purpose Roland Byas and Guillaume Manget to testify to the validity of the signature of the certificate of this marriage produced by the aforesaid. Manget said that he was present when the mar-

---

46. R. Consist. XII, 41.
47. R. Consist. XII, 96.

riage was celebrated and himself helped to sign the certificate. Byas said that he recognized the signature of Lermet who also signed the certificate. The parties having been heard in their petition, also considering the deposition of witnesses, it was decided to approve and ratify their marriage according to their said certificate, signed Pagen (Manget, M. Lermet, M. de la Marque), dated November 22, 1556.

13-8   Case of Antoine Maurin and Wife (1556)[48]

(Feb. 6, 1556). Antoine Morin of Paris presented a petition aimed at ratifying his marriage, with an affidavit that he has been a curate, canon, and priest and that they became engaged in the country of Normandy, signed Lanbert and sealed.

The decision: that if he is questioned about it, he will be found . . . to be a swindler and that the affidavit is false. That for the first Thursday we hold [a session], he and his said wife be summoned. Thursday in two weeks.

(Feb. 20, 1556). Antoine Maurin of Paris still did not appear although he was remanded here by the Council to get the advice of the Consistory about a petition and certificate presented by him before our Lords asking them to ratify his marriage.

Decision: Since he did not appear, and since on review the certificate is written on paper with the watermark of a serpent, in which are contained several statements that a notary would not dare to make in the country of France without great danger; also [since] they [notaries] are accustomed to inscribe them on parchment with the seal of fleurs-de-lis, but this is a common and private seal, the decision is that tomorrow the syndic inform the Council about it.

[Maurin and his wife were imprisoned on February 21. He confessed having forged the document, and on February 25 the Council banished him in perpetuity under pain of public whipping and ordered his wife to follow him.]

13-9   Case of Claude de Boyssiere and Antoine Lenarde (1557)[49]

(April 13, 1557). Claude de Boyssiere and Antoine Lenarde presented themselves with a petition to permit them to be received in marriage and [have] it be confirmed. [The marriage] was begun in their own country which is in Dauphiné. They produced for the recognition of the two of them Master Piernis, Spanish *correcteur,* Pierre Faugeasse, Jaques Rapetu, and Nycolas Pavin, who said they

48. R. Consist. X, 90, XI, 2.
49. R. Consist. XII, 30v.

knew well and know that De Boyssiere is a good religious man. As for the woman, none of them knew her except one, who said that this marriage was made with the consent of the girl's father. It was decided, since it is not proven that this marriage was contracted between the two of them, that this marriage be begun [contracted and celebrated again] in this city and that for this purpose they be remanded before the Council to Monday.

[The Council decided on April 19, in accord with the advice of the Consistory, that their previous marriage was invalid but that they would be permitted to marry again.]

13-10   Case of Jean-Antoine and Catherine Bret (1557)[50]

(Sept. 23, 1557). Jean-Antoine Bret and Catherine, his wife, from Evordes in the county of Fosse, state that they have been married for eight years, and they married in the papacy. Because they knew they were living wretchedly, they left the place of their birth and came to this city, where they hope to live in the fear of God. They ask, therefore, that their marriage be confirmed in this city in the church of the faithful.

Decided: that they be remanded before the Council and that they be informed that the two are forbidden to associate at all until they have first been received as *habitants;* then let the banns of marriage begin again and let them proceed with it after the beginning of the marriage.

[The Council register states that they had been a priest and nun. The Council decided on September 27 to abide by the advice of the Consistory. On September 28 the Council accepted their affidavits and received them as *habitants.* There is no further mention of them, but presumably their marriage was carried out.]

13-11   Petition of Adam Fumée and Michelle de Millone (1547)[51]

On 20 October 1547 the ministerial brethren of the city were assembled at the request of a nobleman, Adam Fumée, and Mlle Michelle de Millone, who revealed that a marriage had been contracted between them in the presence of honest persons, but that they had no certificate or testimonial of it, and that it had not been performed in public. They declared that it was their earnest desire that it should now be publicly contracted and approved in the Church of God,

---

50. R. Consist. XII, 101v.
51. RCP (Hughes trans.), p. 68.

but that there were certain very weighty reasons against making it known, and that if it were known their friends and close relations might be in great danger. He therefore requested the brethren to stand witness for him before the Seigneurs of this city that Michelle de Millone had been kept by him as his wife, as he still wished to keep her, and that she should be acknowledged as such. He also asked that the Seigneury should give him a certificate and testimonial which he could use in case of necessity, until such time as the matter could be made public with greater freedom. In consenting to this the brethren resolved that Monsieur Calvin and Monsieur Abel should approach the Council to make this request and declaration, as agreed by the brethren.

13-12 Case of Dancing, Drinking, and Debauchery at Wedding (1546)[52]

(March 25, 1546). Consistory decision that we send immediately for Monsieur Antoine Letz, of whom it is said that there has been a dance at his house.

(April 1, 1546). Monsieur Antoine Letz was admonished and questioned because it is said that there was a dance in his house a week ago last Sunday. He answered that it is true that on the previous Saturday he promised his daughter to Claude Philippe. The following Sunday, when Claude Philippe and Monsieur de Crans were at his house with Tabusset who played [the drum], Monsieur de Crans said that the custom in Bernese territory is to dance. He excused himself and said it is true that there was a dance, and named certain people, both women and men, who were [there:] his wife for one, Guido Mallet's wife, Syndic Amblard Corne, and Captain Perrin.

Decided: he was told that the Council wants to be informed more clearly about the affair, and he shall send his wife here. He said he will send her.

The wife of Monsieur Antoine Letz, Donne Rolette, was admonished and asked about the above because of the dance that was held at their house, as was asked above by her husband. She said what she knows about it and denounced the men who were there. She said it is true that they were coming from Bellerive very late, about seven o'clock at night, and that after their supper Tabusset was at their house. He came with Monsieur de Crans and someone from Thonon. She did not want to confess having danced, but de Crans did so with the bride. Asked whether some stranger did not come there, she said it is true that Syndic Amblard Corne and Perrin [did], and said they had ceased to dance. Asked to tell the truth whether there was not dancing after the arrival of the syndic and captain, she denied knowing anything about it. Asked whether there was not a

52. R. Consist. II, 175, 179, 189-92, 195, 198, 202, 208, 209, 210, 211, 213, 221, 225.

dance in Bellerive, she denied knowing anything about it. Asked to tell the truth, she said it is true that she thinks someone danced; she denied it and did not want to confess.

Decided: that they be summoned here for Thursday, their confession having been seen and heard, and for this they will be remanded before the Council to deal with this.

(April 8, 1546). Jean-Battista Sept was admonished whether he did not dance, both in Bellerive and at Monsieur Antoine Letz's house at the engagement of Letz's daughter. He denied it. Asked whether there was not a dance, he said he did not know and that it may be there was dancing. He was given strict remonstrances to tell the truth. He denied being at a dance in Bellerive. Asked about [whether there was a dance in] this city, he said it is true that Monsieur de Crans danced and someone from Thonon with the young sister of the Philippes. He said it is true that he saw others dance but does not know their names. Asked about those who were present, he said Monsieur Amblard Corne, Monsieur Perrin, Gruet, Bergeron, and Mallard. Asked whether the bride did not dance, he said he knew nothing about it and did not want to say any more.

Mia, sister of the Philippes, was admonished as to when she danced. She said it was at Monsieur Antoine Letz's house on returning from Bellerive. Asked to name those who danced, with remonstrances, she did not want to confess any except the four named already. Asked whether Captain Perrin's wife did not dance, she said she knew nothing about it, and that when Syndic Corne and Perrin arrived the dancing ceased. She did not want to say any more.

The wife of Claude Baudichon was admonished about the above-mentioned because she was at the dance. She said as above that she did not dance. She was admonished to tell the truth and that they remembered. She was told and the elders named those who danced. She named only the afore-said two.

The wife of Monsieur Ami Perrin [Françoise Favre] was admonished about the above. She denied as above having danced, but did not deny having seen dancing. She also said about that [when] the syndic [Corne] and Perrin entered the dancing ceased. She got upset, saying that we have stained them, her father and brother and brother-in-law [François Favre, his son Gaspard, and Pierre Goujon]. She was admonished about her father who is an adulterer and subsequently about the others and given strong remonstrances whether we must be subject to the house of Favres, that they should be so privileged above others. She was given strong remonstrances that her father has confessed and that the fornication is proven. [She said] that she wants to maintain her father's cause and that her father should be warned in private and not in public. She was admonished that it is no more for him than for the least of the city. Asked again to name those who danced, she answered as above and [named] no others. She said twice that she would rather go before the Council and be dragged before all the judges than go to the Consistory.[53]

The wife of Monsieur Donzel [Françoise] was admonished about the above. She answered that she did not dance first in Bellerive, denied having seen it, and did not want to name others. Asked about [whether there was dancing after supper], she answered as above.

The wife of Guido Mallet was admonished about the above. She did not want to confess any more than was said by the others above. We named and asked her to name those who danced. She did not want to confess any but the four above.

Jaques Gruet was admonished about the above. He said it is true that he [was] in the company both in Bellerive and in this city, and said nothing except as above. He was given strict remonstrances to tell the truth, and said he never saw any dancing except that mentioned above. Asked about a statement he made here that false reports are the cause of scandals. He was admonished that admonitions from the Gospel and concerning vice are not scandals.

[Jean] Bergeron was admonished about the above. He answered that he never saw dancing or danced [himself]. He said he did not meddle in anything but served at the request of his master, who was formerly Monsieur Claude Philippe, and said as above, and denied having heard that there was dancing.

Decision: Let them all be remanded before the Council, both men and women, and let them be put under oath whether they danced or saw dancing elsewhere and masking at any time. Note: the wife of Monsieur Ami Perrin said that she was very willing to go before the Council and was angry at being dragged to the Consistory.

[On April 12 the Council ordered the imprisonment of everyone involved in both dances, including all those named here "and many others, men and women." On April 15 they released Amblard Corne, Guido Mallet's wife, and Mia Philippe and sent them to the Consistory (see below). On April 16 the Council ordered Jean Bergeron, Jean-Baptiste Sept, Rolette Buisson, Mia Letz, the wife of Claude Baudichon, and Françoise Donzel released "on begging mercy of God and justice" and remanded them to the Consistory. Françoise Favre and Jaques Gruet, being more guilty than the others (because of their defiance of the Consistory), were to be kept in prison another three days. On April 16 the Council ordered again that the rest of those involved be imprisoned. Jaques Mallet was released on April 17; on April 19 Ami Perrin, Louis Franc, Denis Hugues, Claude Philippe, Balthasar Sept, Françoise Favre, Jeanton Desbois, Jaques Gruet, Claude de La Palle, and Pierre Moche were released.

---

53. An original "than to return and go to the Consistory" is lined out and replaced by "and be dragged, etc." In the margin it is stated that this is *correctione M. Calvini.*

Finally, on April 22 the Council ordered the release of the wives of Amblard Corne, Denis Hugues, and Mathieu Canard.]

(April 15, 1546). Syndic Corne was admonished concerning the dance he was at and having been in prison, which was held at Monsieur Antoine Letz's [house]. He was admonished not to tolerate [offenses by] the great more than by the small and that the main point is that those who were here last Thursday lied, and that if he had been here at first the others would not have lied this way. The syndic answered with thanks for the admonitions, both according to God and according to the edicts of the Council; nevertheless he excused himself from sitting in his place which he did [sic]. He was admonished.

(April 15, 1546). The wife of Guido Mallet and the sister of the Philippes were admonished because last Thursday they were here and did not want to confess having danced, which they had done. Guido answered that they promised each other not to reveal it. And they were admonished both for the lies and for the dancing, the syndic excusing himself that although he was present himself he did not order them to tell the lies. There was a discussion of the tale that certain dissolute acts were performed concerning the prisoners, Syndic Corne and the others. The syndic excused himself, saying that although they had abundance of food, they used it with reverence and honestly, and that he acknowledged having done wrong.

(April 20, 1546). Jaques Gruet and Pierre Moche [were called]. Gruet was given remonstrances that he was here because of the dance, that he denied it and lied to the Consistory, and Moche was at the dance. And they were in prison and later sent here for remonstrances. Gruet excused himself, saying he did wrong to lie, notwithstanding that this might not have been such a scandal, with other [statements].

He [Gruet] also slandered Monsieur Calvin who said in his sermon that dancers were debauchees. Monsieur Calvin answered him that he had said that debauchery results from dancing, and not as he stated. He was admonished because they made *fleurets* [a kind of dance step], which demonstrates venial sin. Monsieur Calvin admonished him that one must not liken the ministers to *fleurets* and love games. [He was further admonished] because in the evening he was drunk, and it was a scandal. He said that Our Lord said that one should admonish his brother in secret. He was admonished that this was a scandal.

Moche, when asked whether he did not dance after his remonstrances, said no.

Decision about Jaques Gruet: that he be remanded here for Thursday to see whether he shows better repentance. Also he was admonished and asked what was done in the evening. He said that he had supper at the Bouchet [Inn], and that having gone to bed and when sleeping, a cord was attached to his toe, and he cried out. He excused himself to go to Chambéry, and might it please us to consider him excused.

Further decision: considering that he is so sharp-tongued and badly inclined, let him again be admonished to come here before receiving communion, or to beg mercy of God on his knees, stating out loud that he spoke wrongly. He was remanded here for Thursday with strict remonstrances.

(April 22, 1546). Dame Françoise Perrin, Donzel's wife, and the wife of Claude Baudichon were given strict remonstrances after having been in prison, both for their lies and for having danced at Monsieur Antoine Letz's house, that our said lords remanded them here to be admonished, and especially for their lies. Dame Donzelle begged mercy, and Dame Françoise answered, might God pardon her, that she did not offend except against the edicts and against God. And she said, without anything being said to her, that she would not beg mercy of men and that if she sinned in lying it was against God, and was still arrogant. All three confessed having done wrong and begged mercy of God.

Decision concerning the Captain [Ami Perrin]. A decision was made concerning the fact that Captain Perrin has not obeyed by coming here. He was sent for. The officer said he had gone abroad.

The wives of Syndic Corne, Denis Hugues, and Mathieu Canard were admonished as above because of the dance, who were in prison and remanded here by our said lords. They showed true repentance.

Jaques Gruet, Claude Philippe, Denis Hugues, Louis Franc, de La Palle, Jeanton de La Coppe, Balthasar Sept, [and Claude] Bergeron were admonished after having been in prison because of the dance, and some of them for having lied here, and remanded here by our magnificent lords to be given remonstrances. They all showed good will and repentance. Louis Franc remained alone speaking to Monsieur Calvin about a charge against him because of fornication. Monsieur Calvin gave him strict remonstrances. Remonstrances were also given separately to Jaques Gruet concerning his last remission for what he said in the city. He excused himself that he was badly informed.

Bergeron was admonished separately because he was among those who lied here. Bergeron answered that concerning the lies, he did it to show honor to his princes, and was sharp-tongued and obstinate and bad-hearted, and said he had confessed before the Council. Asked whether our superiors did not establish the Consistory, he said yes. Asked whether he fears more to offend men than God, he answered that he thinks that one who maintains the honor of the lords of justice maintains God, and still showed a bad will. He was admonished to beg mercy of God. He said that he begs mercy of God morning and evening and that he has begged mercy enough, and what he said was said and he thinks he spoke well.

Decided: he was forbidden communion, and let him return here Thursday.

Donne Rolette and Mia, daughter of Monsieur Antoine Letz, were admonished as above, and that Donne Rolette also told lies here. They showed good will and repentance.

Decision about Jean-Baptiste Sept who did not appear here and had leave to go to Lausanne. The decision is that we tell his household that as soon as he returns he must go to Syndic Corne, and the syndic will send to Monsieur Calvin to admonish him before communion and to remand him here for Thursday.

(May 13, 1546). Captain Perrin was admonished following the previous remand about the dance, as he was already in prison with the others, and they were afterwards all remanded to the Consistory. Asked whether there is any obstacle in his conscience to receiving communion, because he did not receive it last time. He humbly gave thanks for our strong admonitions, and as for his not receiving communion last time, answered that this was because of some slanderers who had unjustly attacked him. Nevertheless he pardons everyone, although they entered into communion as wretched traitors and wicked men, and such he wishes to maintain them to be.

Decided: considering that he did not wish to name the persons against whom he has hatred and rancor, let him be pursued like another, and if action is not taken there may be a great scandal from this. Further decision: that we ask the Council and tell them to take strong action to avoid the evils that may result.

Jean-Baptiste Sept was admonished like the others who denied the truth, that they had danced.

13-13   Letter to Ami Perrin (1546)[54]

I should willingly have met you, Lord Captain, had it not appeared to me that a different course was expedient. You will have an opportunity to hear the reason from me at a proper place and time. I would have wished, however, that you had appeared at the Consistory, by way of example to others. As in that respect you did not do your duty, because you had perhaps not been warned, I wanted you to be present at least at the close of the meeting today, so that Syndic Corne and I might discuss the matter with you. What there was to prevent you I do not see.

But I wish you to consider this: we cannot enjoy weight for weight with an unequal balance, and if impartiality must be observed in the administration of human law, any departure from it cannot be tolerated in the church of God. You yourself either know, or at least ought to know, what I am. I am, at all events, one

---

54. April, 1546, CO 12:338-39; Bonnet, Letter 164 (adapted).

to whom the law of my heavenly Master is so dear that the cause of no man on earth will induce me to flinch from maintaining it with a pure conscience. I cannot believe that you yourself have any other end in view, but I observe that no one has his eyes wide enough open when the case is his own. As far as I am concerned, I desire, in this very matter, to serve not only for the edification of the church and your salvation, but also for your convenience, name, and leisure. For how odious would be the imputation which is likely to fall upon you, that you seemed to be free from and unrestrained by the common law to which every one is subject? It is certainly better, and in accordance with my zeal for your welfare, to anticipate the danger than that you should be so branded.

I have heard what has come from your house, namely, that I should take care lest I stir up a slumbering fire, lest what occurred before should again take place, in the course of the seventh year. But this talk carries no weight with me. I did not return to Geneva either for the sake of leisure or of gain, nor will it again grieve me to be constrained to leave it. The convenience and safety of the church and state made me willing to return. If measures are now being taken against me alone, I want to say, once and for all, to all who think me troublesome: "What you do, do quickly."

The unworthy treatment and ingratitude of some parties, however, will not cause me to fail in my duty. I shall lay aside my devoted attachment to this place only with my last breath, of which I take God as my witness. Nor will I ever yield to the humors of any other person, as hereafter to dispense with his personal attendance. These observations do not refer to you, but to the member of your family that is nearest to you. Nor do I write them with the view of spreading quarrels, but only to make clear how firmly I am about to proceed, whatever may happen.

I am especially eager to impress upon you the necessity of speaking earnestly to acquire the primary virtue of obedience to God, and respect for the common order and polity of the church. May the Lord protect you by his own defense, and show you how greatly even the stripes of a sincere friend are to be preferred to the treacherous blandishments of others!

13-14 Letter to Guillaume Farel and Pierre Viret (1546)[55]

After your departure the dances caused us more trouble than I had supposed. All those who were summoned to the Consistory, with the two exceptions of Corne and Perrin, shamelessly lied to God and us. I was incensed, as the vile-

---

55. (April 21, 1546), CO 12:333-37; Bonnet, Letter 163 (adapted). Bonnet, however, lists the addressee as Farel only.

ness of the thing demanded, and I strongly inveighed against the contempt of God, in that they thought nothing of making a mockery of the sacred investigations we had used. They persisted in their contumacy.

When I was fully informed of the state of the case, I could do nothing but call God as a witness that they would pay the penalty of such perfidy. At the same time, however, I announced my resolve to unbar the truth, even though it might be at the cost of my own life, lest they should imagine that any profit was to come of lying. . . .

[Ami Perrin] had meanwhile gone to Lyon, hoping that the matter would be silently buried. I thought that they should be forced to a confession of the truth under oath. [Syndic] Corne warned them that he would by no means suffer them to perjure themselves. They not only confessed what we wished, namely, that on that day they danced at the house of the widow of Balthazar. They were all cast into prison. The syndic was an illustrious example of moderation. He spoke against himself and the whole herd so severely that it was unnecessary to say much to him. He was, however, severely admonished in the Consistory, being deposed from his office until he gave proof of repentance. They say that Perrin has returned from Lyon; whatever he may do, he will not escape punishment.

CHAPTER 14

Concluding Reflections

The Emerging Covenantal Model
of Engagement and Marriage

Courtship. Individual Consent. Parental Consent. Infancy. Mental Inability. Polygamy. Virginity. Contagion. Sexual Capacity. Age Disparity. Incest. Religious Differences. Marital Property. Premarital Sex. Desertion. Banns. The Wedding. These were the main topics of the law and theology of courtship, engagement, and marriage in John Calvin's Geneva. These were the main issues that triggered the scrutiny and activity of the Consistory and the Council. These were the main grounds on which engagements and marriages were made and broken.

Calvin treated all these topics, some of them in close and exacting detail. He addressed many of them for the first time in his 1541 Ecclesiastical Ordinances, 1542/5 Marriage Liturgy, 1545/6 Marriage Ordinance, and several more discrete statutes passed in the 1540s. But these early (largely legal) documents left many hard questions unanswered or under-analyzed. Calvin often had to refine his early teachings as he came upon new problems in his correspondence or in his work on the Consistory bench. He also had to rethink some of his early teachings as he moved verse-by-verse through the Bible in his sermons, lectures, and commentaries and came upon new insights and interpretations. Calvin was all for consistent and insistent application of the new Reformed norms of courtship, engagement, and marriage that governed Geneva. But he rarely clung stubbornly to early formulations that faded in the light of new biblical insights or that failed in their application by the Consistory or the Council. He changed his mind when he needed to; think of the changes in his doctrine of parental consent. He abandoned practices that proved counterproductive; think of his retreat from his early efforts at matchmaking. And he delegated tasks that were beyond his ken or interest; think of the many technical legal issues that he left for Theodore Beza, Germain Colladon, and François Hotman to resolve.

Calvin did not live long enough to write a full systematic theology and jurisprudence of courtship, engagement, and marriage. What he left were hundreds of thin strands of argument strewn all over his commentaries, sermons, letters, *consilia,* Consistory opinions, and legal fragments — many of which we have sampled and analyzed herein. Calvin did not have time and energy in his later years to sew all of these strands of argument together. His health was deteriorating rapidly. He faced escalating demands for his pastoral and political counsel. He was consumed by burning controversies triggered by Servetus, the Children of Geneva, and others. And he had many other subjects of reform to attend to that had nothing to do with marriage and family life.

Even so, Calvin in his last decade did move toward a synthesis of some of his theological and legal thinking on courtship, engagement, and marriage. The thread that ran with increasing boldness through his later-life formulations was the doctrine of covenant, which he began to use to stitch together several of his early strands of argument. More of this stitching was done by Calvin's successors, Theodore Beza and François Hotman. And a generation after them, Puritans, Presbyterians, and Pietists alike developed these early insights into a robust covenantal model of marriage.[1]

The idea of a divine covenant or agreement between God and humanity had long been taught in the Western church. Theologians, at least since the time of Irenaeus in the second century, had discussed the interlocking biblical covenants: (1) the covenant of works whereby the chosen people of Israel, through obedience to God's law, are promised eternal salvation and blessing; and (2) the covenant of grace whereby the elect, through faith in Christ's incarnation and atonement, are promised eternal salvation and beatitude. The covenant of works was created in Abraham, confirmed in Moses, and consummated with

---

1. See, e.g., William and Malleville Haller, "The Puritan Art of Love," *Huntington Library Quarterly* 5 (1941-42): 235; James T. Johnson, *A Society Ordained by God: English Puritan Marriage Doctrine in the First Half of the Seventeenth Century* (Nashville, TN, 1970); Edmund Leites, *The Puritan Conscience and Modern Sexuality* (New Haven, 1986); Max L. Stackhouse, *Covenant and Commitments: Faith, Family, and Economic Life* (Louisville, 1997). Another important source of the later covenant model of marriage was Heinrich Bullinger's *Der christlich Eestand* (Zurich, 1540). Though Calvin and Bullinger corresponded regularly, we have found no evidence that they shared their views of covenant marriage. They both did know Zwingli's early brief discussion of a covenantal theology of marriage in his *De vera et falsa religione commentarius* (1525), in *Huldreich Zwinglis Sämtliche Werke* (Zurich, 1982), 3:590, 762-63. See further discussion in Charles S. McCoy and J. Wayne Baker, *Foundation of Federalism: Heinrich Bullinger and the Covenantal Tradition* (Louisville, 1991); Kenneth Hagen, "From Testament to Covenant in the Early Sixteenth Century," *Sixteenth Century Journal* 3 (1972): 1.

the promulgation and acceptance of the Torah. The covenant of grace was created in Christ, confirmed in the Gospel, and consummated with the confession and conversion of the Christian. These traditional teachings on the covenant were well known to the early reformers, and Calvin used them to fortify his doctrines of sin and salvation, law and Gospel, man and God.[2]

In his later years, Calvin began to note with increasing regularity how often the Bible uses the term "covenant" to describe marriage. In the Old Testament, Yahweh's covenantal relationship with Israel is analogized to the special relationship between husband and wife. Israel's disobedience to Yahweh, in turn, is frequently described as a form of "playing the harlot." Idolatry, like adultery, can lead to divorce, and Yahweh threatens this many times, even while calling his chosen to reconciliation. This set of images about marriage and divorce comes through repeatedly in the writings of the Prophets: Hosea (2:2-23), Isaiah (1:21-22; 54:5-8; 57:3-10; 61:10-11; 62:4-5), Jeremiah (2:2-3; 3:1-5, 6-25; 13:27; 23:10; 31:32), and Ezekiel (16:1-63; 23:1-49).[3] Between 1551 and 1564, Calvin preached, commented, or lectured on every one of these texts (except Ezekiel 23), and took increasing note of their lessons for modern-day understandings of marriage and divorce.[4]

The Bible also speaks about marriage as a covenant in its own right (Prov. 2:17; Mal. 2:14-16).[5] The Prophet Malachi's formulation is the fullest:

> You cover the Lord's altar with tears, with weeping and groaning because he no longer regards the offering and accepts it with favor at your hand. You ask, "Why does he not?" Because the Lord was witness to the covenant between you and the wife of your youth, to whom you have been faithless, though she is your companion and your wife by covenant. Has not the one God made and sustained for us the spirit of life? And what does he desire? Godly offspring. So take heed to yourselves, and let none be faithless to the wife of his youth. "For I hate divorce, says the Lord the God of Israel, and covering one's garments with violence, says the Lord, the God of hosts. So take heed to yourselves and do not be faithless" (Mal. 2:13-16).

2. See sources and discussion in Daniel J. Elazar, *Covenant and Commonwealth: From Christian Separation through the Protestant Reformation* (New Brunswick, NJ, 1996).

3. Gordon P. Hugenberger, *Marriage as Covenant: A Study of Biblical Law and Ethics Governing Marriage Developed From the Perspective of Malachi* (Leiden, 1994); John Witte, Jr., and Eliza Ellison, eds., *Covenant Marriage in Comparative Perspective* (Grand Rapids, 2005).

4. In the order of their appearance, see Comm. Isaiah 1:21-22; 54:5-8; 57:3-10; 61:10-11; 62:4-5 (1551); Serm. Deut. 5:18; 22:22 (1555); Comm. Harm. Gospel Luke 1:34-38 (1555); Comm. Ps. 16:4; 45:8-12; 82:1 (1557); Lect. Hosea 1:1-4; 2:19-20; 3:1-2; 4:13-14; 7:3, 9-10 (1557); Lect. Zech. 2:11; 8:1-2 (ca. 1560); Lect. Mal. 2:13-16 (ca. 1560); Lect. Jer. 2:2-3, 25; 3:1-5, 6-25; 13:27; 23:10; 31:32; 51:4 (1563); Comm. Harm. Law Deut. 11:26-32 (1563); and Lect. Ezek. 6:9; 16:1-63 (1564).

5. Calvin did not preach or comment on Proverbs.

Using this passage, Calvin began to use the doctrine of covenant to describe not only the vertical relationships between God and man but also the horizontal relationships between husband and wife. Just as God draws the elect believer into a covenant relationship with him, Calvin argued, so God draws husband and wife into a covenant relationship with each other. Just as God expects constant faith and good works in our relationship with him, so God expects connubial faithfulness and sacrificial works in our relationship with our spouses. "God is the founder of marriage," Calvin wrote in his 1558 Sermons on Ephesians:

> When a marriage takes place between a man and a woman, God presides and requires a mutual pledge from both. Hence Solomon in Proverbs 2:17 calls marriage the covenant of God, for it is superior to all human contracts. So also Malachi [2:14] declares that God is as it were the stipulator [of marriage] who by his authority joins the man to the woman, and sanctions the alliance. . . .
>
> Marriage is not a thing ordained by men. We know that God is the author of it, and that it is solemnized in his name. The Scripture says that it is a holy covenant, and therefore calls it divine.[6]

God participates in the formation of the covenant of marriage through his chosen agents on earth, Calvin believed. The couple's parents, as God's "lieutenants" for children, instruct the young couple in the mores and morals of Christian marriage and give their consent to the union.[7] Two witnesses, as "God's priests to their peers," testify to the sincerity and solemnity of the couple's promises and attest to the marriage event.[8] The minister, holding "God's spiritual power of the Word," blesses the union and admonishes the couple and the community of their respective biblical duties and rights.[9] The magistrate, holding "God's temporal power of the sword," registers the parties, ensures the legality of their union, and protects them in their conjoined persons and properties. This involvement of parents, peers, ministers, and magistrates in the formation of the marriage covenant was not an idle or dispensable ceremony. These four parties represented different dimensions of God's involvement in the marriage covenant. They were essential to the legitimacy of the marriage itself. To omit any such party in the formation of the marriage was, in effect, to omit God from the marriage covenant.

---

6. Serm. Eph. 5:22-26, 31-33; see also Serm. Deut. 5:18: "[M]arriage is called a covenant with God, . . . meaning that God presides over marriages."

7. Comm. Harm. Law Lev. 19:29; Serm. Deut. 5:16; Comm. 1 Cor. 7:36, 38; Serm. 1 Cor. 7:36-38; Serm. and Comm. Eph. 6:1-3.

8. Comm. 1 Thess. 4:3; Comm. 1 Peter 2:9; Institutes (1559), 4.18.16-17.

9. Serm. Eph. 5:31-33.

The doctrine of covenant thus helped Calvin integrate what became universal requirements of valid marriage formation in the West after the mid-sixteenth century — mutual consent of the couple, parental consent, two witnesses, civil registration, and church consecration. It also provided a standing response to the centuries-long problem of secret marriage. Marriage was, by its covenantal nature, a public institution, involving a variety of parties in the community. To marry secretly or privately was to defy the very nature of marriage.

God participates in the maintenance of the covenant of marriage not only through the one-time actions of his human agents, but also through the continuous revelation of his natural or moral law. The covenant of marriage, Calvin argued, is grounded "in the order of creation," "in the order and law of nature."[10] By nature, the man and the woman enjoy a "common dignity before God" and a common function of "completing" the life and love of the other.[11] Before marriage, they stand at arm's length, each entitled to give, withhold, or condition their consent to move forward, each expected to bring property and purpose to the budding union, each responsible for the costs and consequences of their premarital experimentation. Through marriage, husband and wife are "joined together in one body and one soul," but then assigned "distinct duties" and "different authorities."[12] God has appointed the husband as the head of the wife. God has appointed the wife, "who is derived from and comes after the man," as his associate and companion — literally his "helpmeet."[13] "The divine mandate" of creation, said Calvin, "was that the husband would look up in reverence to God, the woman would be a faithful assistant to him, and both with one consent would cultivate a holy, friendly, and peaceful intercourse."[14]

Calvin grounded various biblical rules against illicit sexual unions in this created structure of marriage. Marriage was created as a heterosexual monogamous union — a joining of two opposites, "male and female," who have the physical capacity and natural inclination to come together in love. Citing Moses and St. Paul, Calvin condemned as "monstrous vices" sodomy, buggery, bestiality, homosexuality, and other "unnatural" acts and alliances — arguing cryptically that to "lust for our own kind" or "for brutes" was "repugnant to the modesty of nature itself."[15] He condemned incestuous engagements and marriages

---

10. Letter, CO 10/2:258; Comm. and Lect. Gen. 2:18; Comm. and Serm. Deut. 24:1-4; Lect. Mal. 2:14-15; Comm. Harm. Gosp. Matt. 19:3-9; *Consilium,* CO 10/1:239-41.

11. Comm. and Lect. Gen. 1:27-28.

12. Comm. and Lect. Gen. 2:18, 22.

13. Comm. Gen. 2:18; Comm. and Lect. 1 Cor. 9:8; 11:4-10.

14. Comm. Gen. 2:18.

15. Comm. Gen. 19:4-9; Comm. Harm. Law Exod. 22:19; Lev. 18:22; 20:13-16; Deut. 27:16; Serm. Deut. 22:13-24.

between various blood and family relatives — arguing that God had prohibited such unions to avoid discord, abuse, rivalry, and exploitation among those who were "too close." He condemned, at greater length, the ancient practice of polygamy, which a few Protestant groups were again experimenting with. To allow polygamy, Calvin argued, is to ignore the creation story of "the one man and the one woman" whom God had created and joined together in Paradise. "God could have created two wives for Adam if he wanted to," Calvin preached. "But God was content with one."[16] "Since this mutual union was consecrated by the Lord, the mixture of three or four persons is false and wicked" and "contrary to the order and law of nature."[17]

Calvin saved his greatest thunder for the sin of adultery as the most fundamental violation of the created structure of the marital covenant. He read the commandment "Thou shalt not commit adultery" expansively to outlaw various illicit alliances and actions, within and without the marital estate. Within marriage, the obvious case of adultery was sexual intercourse or any other form of lewd sexual act with a party other than one's spouse. Calvin regarded this form of adultery as "the worst abomination," for in one act the adulterer violates his or her covenant bonds with spouse, God, and broader community.[18] "It is not without cause that marriage is called a covenant with God," Calvin thundered from his Geneva pulpit. "[W]henever a husband breaks his promise which he has made to his wife, he has not only perjured himself with respect to her, but also with respect to God. The same is true of the wife. She not only wrongs her husband, but the living God."[19] "She sets herself against his majesty."[20]

For Calvin, the commandment against adultery was equally binding on the unmarried, and equally applicable to both illicit sexual activities per se, and various acts leading to the same. Calvin condemned with particular vehemence the sin of fornication — sexual intercourse or other illicit acts of sexual touching by non-married parties, including those who were engaged. He decried at length the widespread practice of casual sex, prostitution, concubinage, premarital sex and cohabitation and other forms of bed-hopping that he encountered in modern-day Geneva, as well as in ancient Bible stories. All these actions openly defied God's commandment against adultery and God's commendation of chaste and holy marriage.

Calvin stretched the reach of the commandment against adultery far beyond the sin of actual fornication. In his more exuberant moments, he tended

16. Serm. Deut. 21:15-17; Comm. and Lect. Gen. 2:18; Lect. Mal. 2:15.
17. Comm. Gen. 2:24.
18. Comm. Harm. Law Lev. 20:10; 22:22-27.
19. Serm. Deut. 5:18.
20. Serm. Eph. 5:22-26.

to treat all manner of mildly sexual activities — lewdness, dancing, bawdy gaming, sexual innuendo, coarse humor, provocative primping, suggestive plays and literature, and much more — as forms of adultery, punishable by the state. He was especially eager to stamp out such sexually-charged conduct at wedding feasts, which was the last place they belonged. Calvin would not tie the dapper dancer and the habitual whoremonger to the same stake for flogging or execution. He viewed these more attenuated forms of adultery as violations of milder criminal laws against sumptuousness, punishable by admonition and fines. But he was insistent that even such attenuated sexual conduct was a form of adultery that deserved both spiritual reproof and criminal sanctions.

When properly structured, the marriage covenant serves three main purposes, Calvin argued. First, it fosters the mutual love and support of husband and wife. Second, it protects both parties from sexual sin and temptation. Third, it enables the licit procreation and nurture of children.[21] Given these three purposes Calvin and his colleagues regarded sexual dysfunction as a serious impediment to engagement and marriage, for it vitiated all three purposes of marriage. Thus putative engagements and marriages of young children, not yet capable of sexual function let alone marital love, were void, at least until the child reached maturity. Similarly, engagements or marriages of eunuchs and others with permanent sexual injuries and disabilities were void, for such unions "completely obviate the nature and purpose of marriage."[22] Marriage with those suffering from permanent contagious diseases were also void, for such conditions precluded safe sexual contact and endangered any children born of the same.

Calvin also grounded a number of prudential norms for the unmarried in the three created purposes of marriage. Citing Moses' account of the evil world on the eve of the Flood — "the sons of men saw that the daughters of men were fair and took to wife such of them as they chose" — Calvin counseled against entering marriage with undue levity or lust. "Marriage is a thing too sacred to allow that men should be induced to it by the lust of their eyes," he wrote. "Elegance of form" may certainly have a place in the calculus of marriage. But we "profane the covenant of marriage" when "our appetite becomes brutal, when we are so ravished with the charms of beauty, that those things which are chief are not taken into account."[23] Calvin laid out "those things which are chief" in his account of what he sought in his own wife: a woman of piety, modesty, and virtue, of comparable age, status and education. Physical beauty and virginity

---

21. Comm. and Lect. Gen. 1:27-28; 2:18, 21-22; Comm. and Serm. 1 Cor. 9:11; Comm. and Serm. Eph. 5:22-31.

22. *Consilium,* CO 10/1:231.

23. Comm. Gen. 6:2.

could certainly enter the calculus of courtship and marriage, Calvin allowed, but these attributes were not for him the most important.

Citing both Moses and St. Paul, he counseled Christians against marrying unbelievers. For such unions would invariably jeopardize all three created functions of marriage. The unbeliever could not know the true meaning of love reflected in Christ, would not know how to raise children in the love of God, and might not resist the temptations to lust which marriage was supposed to remedy. Calvin did not regard differences in religion as an absolute bar to the contracting of engagement or marriage — let alone a ground for annulment or divorce. They were notably imprudent, though not legally prohibited.

Calvin's covenantal understanding of marriage mediated both the sacramental and the contractual models of marriage that pressed for recognition in his day. On the one hand, this covenant model confirmed the sacred and sanctifying qualities of marriage — without ascribing to it sacramental functions. Calvin now held a far more exalted spiritual view of marriage than he had espoused when he had first arrived in Geneva in 1536. He described marriage in sweeping spiritual terms as "a sacred bond," "a holy fellowship," a "divine partnership," "a loving association," "a heavenly calling," "the fountainhead of life," "the holiest kind of company in all the world," "the principal and most sacred . . . of all the offices pertaining to human society."[24] Conjugal love is "holy" when "husband and wife are joined in one body and one soul."[25] "God reigns in a little household, even one in dire poverty, when the husband and the wife dedicate themselves to their duties to each other. Here there is a holiness greater and nearer the kingdom of God than there is even in a cloister."[26] Calvin had come a long way from the glum description of marriage in his 1536 *Institutes:* "a good ordinance, just like farming, building, cobbling, and barbering."

With this more exalted spiritual view of marriage, Calvin also described more fully the biblical uses of marriage to symbolize the relationship of God and humanity. He analyzed at length the Old Testament image of Yahweh's covenant of marriage with Israel, and Israel's proclivity for "playing the harlot" — worshipping false gods and allying with gentile neighbors, much as delinquent spouses abandon faith in God and faithfulness to each other. He returned repeatedly to the New Testament image of Christ's marriage to the church — holding up Christ's faithfulness and sacrificial love toward us as a model to which spouses and parents should aspire. He went so far as to say that "marriage

24. Comm. and Lect. Gen. 2:21; 2:24; 6:2; Serm. Deut. 21:10-14; Lect. Mal. 2:14, 16; Comm. Harm. Gosp. Matt. 19:11; Serm. and Comm. 1 Cor. 7:14; 9:11; *Contra la Secte des Libertines,* CO 7:212ff.

25. Comm. Gen. 2:18.

26. Serm. 1 Tim. 5.

is the holiest bond that God has set among us," for it is "a figure of the Son of God and all the faithful," "a symbol of our divine covenant with our Father."[27] But then, almost in self-chiding, Calvin reiterated his earlier position that marriage, though symbolic of God's relationship with persons, is not a sacrament for it does not confirm a divine promise. "Anyone who would classify such similitudes with the sacraments ought to be sent to a mental hospital."[28]

On the other hand, Calvin's covenant model confirmed the contractual and consensual qualities of marriage — without simply subjecting it to the personal preferences of the parties. "It is the mutual consent of the man and the woman that . . . constitutes marriage," Calvin insisted, echoing traditional views.[29] Lack of true consent — by reason of immaturity, drunkenness, insincerity, conditionality, mistake, fraud, coercion, or similar impairment — perforce breaks the marriage contract, just as it breaks any other contract.

But marriage is more than a contract, and turns on more than the voluntary consent of the parties. God is a third party to every marriage, Calvin believed, and has set its basic terms in the order and law of creation. "Other contracts depend on the mere inclination of men, and can be entered into and dissolved by that same inclination."[30] Not so the covenant of marriage. Our "freedom of contract" in marriage is effectively limited to choosing which party to marry — from among the mature, unrelated, virile members of the opposite sex available to us. We have no freedom to forgo marriage — unless we have the rare gift of natural continence — for else we "spurn God's remedy for lust" and "tempt our nature" to sexual perversity.[31] We also have no freedom to abandon marriage, "for otherwise the whole order of nature would be overthrown."[32] "Consider what will be left of safety in the world — of order, of loyalty, of honesty, of assurance — if marriage, which is the most sacred union, and ought to be most faithfully guarded, can thus be violated," Calvin thundered.[33] "In truth, all contracts and all promises that we make ought to be faithfully upheld. But if we should make a comparison, it is not without cause that marriage is called a covenant with God," for it cannot be broken.[34]

Calvin's covenantal model of marriage not only mediated the sacramental and contractual models of marriage which he encountered in Geneva. It also

---

27. Serm. Eph. 5:28-30; Lect. Ezek. 16:9, 17; Lect. Hosea 2:2; Serm. Deut. 21:10-14.

28. Institutes (1559), 4.19.34. This repeats verbatim what Calvin had written in Institutes (1536), chap. 5.69 (Doc. 1-1).

29. Comm. Gen. 29:27.

30. Comm. 1 Cor. 7:11.

31. Institutes (1559), 2.8.42.

32. Serm. Deut. 22:25-30.

33. CO 7:212ff.

34. Serm. Deut. 5:18.

modified the social model of marriage which he inherited from Wittenberg. Using the two kingdoms theory, Martin Luther and his colleagues had treated marriage as a social estate of the earthly kingdom.[35] Calvin echoed and endorsed these evangelical Lutheran teachings on marriage. But he also superimposed on this two kingdoms framework a doctrine of marriage as covenant. The effect of this was to add a spiritual dimension to marriage life in the earthly kingdom, a marital obligation to spiritual life in the heavenly kingdom, and complementary marital roles for both church and state in the governance of both kingdoms.

Marriage was an earthly order and obligation for all persons, said Calvin. But it also had vital spiritual sources and sanctions for Christians. Marriage required the coercive power of the state to preserve its integrity. But it also required the spiritual counsel of the church to demonstrate its necessity. Marriage was grounded in the will and consent of the parties. But it was also founded in the creation and commandments of God. Marriage deterred sinful persons from the lust and incontinence of this earthly life. But it also symbolized for them the love and sacrifice of the heavenly life. Marriage served the social purpose of procreation and protection from sin. But it also served the divine purpose of sanctification and edification by grace. None of these sentiments was altogether original with Calvin. But, using the doctrine of covenant, Calvin was able to cast these traditional teachings into a new ensemble, with new theological emphases and new legal applications.

35. See quotations above Chapter 1.

General Index

Most of the numbered documents appear below in the lists of cases, commentaries, *consilia*, lectures, letters, sermons, and statutes, as well as documents of Beza.

Index to Biblical Sources